FEDERALISM AND DECENTRALIZATION IN THE CONTEMPORARY MIDDLE EAST AND NORTH AFRICA

This volume, the first of its kind in the English language, examines the law and politics of federalism and decentralization in the Middle East and North Africa. Comprised of eleven case studies examining the experience across the region, together with essays by leading scholars providing comparative and theoretical perspectives and a synthetic conclusion by the co-editors, the volume offers a textured portrait of the dilemmas of decentralization during a period of sweeping transition in the region. The collection addresses an important gap in the comparative decentralization literature, which has largely neglected the MENA region. Both retrospective and forward-looking in orientation, the book is a valuable resource not only for scholars of comparative politics, constitutional design, and Middle East studies, but also for policymakers evaluating the feasibility and efficacy of decentralization as a vehicle for improving governance and responding to identity conflict in any part of the world.

Aslı Ü. Bâli is Professor of Law at Yale Law School. Previously she served as a professor of law and Director of the Center for Near Eastern Studies at UCLA. She is president-elect of the Middle East Studies Association and she also co-chairs the Advisory Council for the Middle East Division of Human Rights Watch. She is co-editor of *Constitution Writing, Religion and Democracy* (Cambridge, 2017).

Omar M. Dajani is Professor of Law at McGeorge School of Law, University of the Pacific where he is co-director of the Global Center for Business and Development. Previously, he served as legal adviser to the Palestinian negotiating team in peace talks with Israel. He contributes to peacebuilding and legal infrastructure development projects for think tanks, governments and international organizations.

ASCL Studies in Comparative Law

ASCL Studies in Comparative Law publishes monographs and collections that broaden theoretical and practical knowledge of the world's many legal systems. Published under the direction of the American Society of Comparative Law, the *ASCL Studies* examines legal problems in a comparative light to advance legal science, develop technical insights, and promote greater cooperation across jurisdictional and cultural boundaries. This book series serves legal practitioners and those seeking to improve law and justice by publishing in-depth comparative studies of specific legal problems in every area of law.

The series has two general editors. David Gerber is Distinguished Professor of Law and Co-Director of the Program in International and Comparative Law at Chicago-Kent College of Law, Illinois Institute of Technology. He is past President of the American Society of Comparative Law. Mortimer Sellers is Regents Professor of the University System of Maryland and Director of the Baltimore Center for International and Comparative Law. He is past President of the Internationale Vereinigung für Rechts-und Sozialphilosophie.

Federalism and Decentralization in the Contemporary Middle East and North Africa

Edited by

ASLI Ü. BÂLI

Yale Law School

OMAR M. DAJANI

University of the Pacific, California

CAMBRIDGE
UNIVERSITY PRESS

CAMBRIDGE
UNIVERSITY PRESS

University Printing House, Cambridge CB2 8BS, United Kingdom

One Liberty Plaza, 20th Floor, New York, NY 10006, USA

477 Williamstown Road, Port Melbourne, VIC 3207, Australia

314–321, 3rd Floor, Plot 3, Splendor Forum, Jasola District Centre, New Delhi – 110025, India

103 Penang Road, #05–06/07, Visioncrest Commercial, Singapore 238467

Cambridge University Press is part of the University of Cambridge.

It furthers the University's mission by disseminating knowledge in the pursuit of education, learning, and research at the highest international levels of excellence.

www.cambridge.org
Information on this title: www.cambridge.org/9781108831239
DOI: 10.1017/9781108923682

First published 2023

A catalogue record for this publication is available from the British Library

A Cataloging-in-Publication data record for this book is available from the Library of Congress

ISBN 978-1-108-83123-9 Hardback

Contents

Contributors

George R. M. Anderson currently advises the United Nations, the World Bank, International Institute for Democracy and Electoral Assistance, Humanitarian Dialogue and nongovernmental organizations on constitutional transitions, notably relating to political devolution and to natural resources.

Samer Araabi currently works as the research director at Accountability Counsel. Previously he worked as a government relations manager for the Arab American Institute in Washington, DC, a project manager for the Syrian Assistance Coordination Unit, and a Syria specialist at the Italian Ministry of Foreign Affairs.

Sami Atallah is an economist and political scientist who is the founding director of the Policy Initiative, a Beirut based think-tank. He was previously the director of the Lebanese Center for Policy Studies for ten years, where he led research on decentralization, local governance, and municipal finance, among others. He co-drafted the decentralization law for Lebanon and served on the related parliamentary committee.

Aslı Ü. Bâli is Professor of Law at the Yale Law School. Previously, she was Professor of Law at the University of California, Los Angeles (UCLA) School of Law, where she was also the founding faculty director of the Promise Institute for Human Rights and the director of the UCLA Center for Near Eastern Studies.

Peter Bartu teaches at the University of California, Berkeley, on political transitions in the Middle East, the Gulf States, and international organizations and global governance. In fall 2016 he spent three months conducting ethnographic research in Iraqi Kurdistan during the battle of Mosul.

Sari Bashi is a human rights lawyer, writer, analyst, and lecturer in law. Ms. Bashi co-founded the Israeli human rights group Gisha and served as its executive director of Gisha from its foundation in 2005 until 2014. She also served as the Israel–Palestine Advocacy Director at Human Rights Watch.

Benoît Challand is Associate Professor of Sociology at the New School for Social Research, New York. His research focuses on civil society and foreign assistance in the Middle East and he has conducted extensive fieldwork on the Yemeni constitution drafting process.

Sujit Choudhry is an internationally recognized authority on comparative constitutional law and has been an advisor to governance, constitution building, rule of law, and peacebuilding processes for over twenty years, including in Egypt, Jordan, Libya, Nepal, South Africa, Sri Lanka, Tunisia, Ukraine, and Yemen.

Omar M. Dajani is Professor of Law at the University of the Pacific, McGeorge School of Law, where he also serves as co-director of the Global Center for Business and Development. He previously served as legal adviser to the Palestinian negotiating team in peace talks with Israel.

Tom Ginsburg is the Leo Spitz Professor of International Law at the University of Chicago School of Law; he also holds an appointment in the Political Science Department at the University of Chicago.

Mona Harb is Professor of Urban Studies and Politics and co-founder of the Beirut Urban Lab at the American University of Beirut. She is working on governance and configurations of activism, collective life, and solidarities in contexts of limited statehood, crises, and disasters.

Leila Hilal is a senior fellow for the International Security Program and the former director of the Middle East Task Force at the New America Foundation, Washington, DC. She focuses on Syria, the Israeli-Palestinian conflict and issues related to US foreign policy, constitution-making, and transitional justice in the broader Middle East and North Africa.

Joost Jongerden is an associate professor of rural sociology at Wageningen University in the Netherlands and project professor at the Asian Platform for Global Sustainability and Transcultural Studies at Kyoto University, Japan.

Intissar Kherigi is Programme Director of the Jasmine Foundation (Tunisia), a qualified solicitor in the UK, where she worked in the House of Lords, and is completing her doctoral dissertation at the Institut d'etudes politiques (Sciences Po) Paris in comparative political sociology.

Will Kymlicka is the Canada Research Chair in Political Philosophy at Queen's University in Kingston, Canada.

Aidan MacEachern completed her master's in global studies with an area concentration on the Middle East at the University of California, Berkeley, and focuses her research on Kurdish political movements.

Ali Al-Mawlawi is head of research at the Al-Bayan Center, an independent Iraqi think-tank based in Baghdad, where he specializes in foreign affairs and institutional reform.

Karim Mezran is a senior fellow at the Atlantic Council's Rafik Hariri Center for the Middle East, Washington, DC, whose research focuses on processes of political change in North Africa, with a concentration on Libya.

Elissa Miller is completing a policy degree at the Fletcher School of Law and Diplomacy at Tufts University. Previously, she served as a nonresident fellow with the Atlantic Council's Rafik Hariri Center for the Middle East, where she focused on political and security developments in Libya, Tunisia, and Egypt.

Philip G. Roeder is a professor in the Department of Political Science at the University of California, San Diego.

Dahlia Scheindlin is a political scientist, public opinion expert, and political strategist. She has advised on eight national campaigns in Israel and in fifteen other countries. She conducts extensive public opinion and policy research on the Israeli-Palestinian conflict for local and international NGOs and she is a policy fellow at the Century Foundation.

Omar Yousef Shehabi is a legal officer with the United Nations Office of Administration of Justice and a JSD candidate at Yale Law School where he also received his LLM degree. His research focuses on international dispute settlement, the law of international state responsibility, international labor law, and the law of international organizations.

Kian Tajbakhsh is Visiting Professor of Urban Planning at the Graduate School of Architecture, Planning and Preservation at Columbia University. He is an international expert in the areas of local government reform and civil society capacity building whose research focuses on the Middle East with a concentration on Iran.

Acknowledgments

This book grew out of a series of conversations during the 2016 convening of the Yale Law School's Middle East Legal Studies Seminar, which has long provided a wonderful forum for us to come together annually to join discussions with leading experts from the Middle East and North Africa. We are grateful to the McGeorge School of Law, University of the Pacific, for hosting the workshop that formally initiated this project in May 2017. That workshop brought together a group of scholars and interlocutors, some of whom are authors of chapters in this volume, to debate the degree to which decentralization might serve as a framework for addressing the challenges faced in the region in the aftermath of the Arab uprisings. In June 2018, we convened a second workshop where early drafts of most of the chapters included in this volume were first presented at the University of California, Los Angeles (UCLA) School of Law, with generous support from the UCLA Center for Near Eastern Studies and the Promise Institute of Human Rights at UCLA Law. The participants in both workshops provided constructive suggestions for particular papers and invaluable feedback for the conceptual organization of this volume. We would particularly like to thank Zaid al-Ali, Stephanie Koury, Andrew March, John McGarry, Haila al-Mekaimi, and Balakrishnan Menon for their input at an early point in this project. In addition, we would like to thank the participants of the UCLA Law School Faculty Workshop for constructive comments on an early draft of the theoretical framework for the volume, and audience members at several panels where we presented draft chapters at the Middle East Studies Association annual conferences of 2018 and 2019, for their helpful questions; and the participants of the Northern California International Law Scholars workshop in 2020 for their generous feedback on our concluding chapter. We are grateful to Abdallah Ali, Ahmed Ali, Jordan Hutchings, Melis Kilic, Matthew McDonald, Daniel Michaelsen, and Brittany Newell for their excellent research assistance; to Sherry Yuan at UCLA and Stevey Clement and Casandra Fernandez at McGeorge for administrative assistance with the workshops; and especially to Tom Randall at Cambridge University Press, with whom it has been a pleasure to work on this volume. Finally, we thank Jean Marie, Tal, and Ayla for their patience, encouragement, and love, without which we could not have completed this project.

Acknowledgements

1

Introduction

From Revolution to Devolution?

Aslı Ü. Bâli and Omar M. Dajani

The Arab uprisings gave voice to long, simmering demands to end corruption, hold government officials accountable, and improve service delivery. The chants of protesters that echoed from Tunisia to Egypt and from Syria to Yemen revealed widely shared frustration with a style of governance so ubiquitous in the Middle East and North Africa (MENA) region that it had come to distinguish the region: authoritarian, deeply centralized regimes holding together divided polities through patronage and coercion, rather than through democratic engagement.[1] Like the Green Movement in Iran in 2009, the uprisings failed in most instances to deliver meaningful political, fiscal, or administrative reform, in some cases resulting in even more acute governance failures and stirring identity conflicts along ethnic, sectarian, and regional lines.[2] The Gezi protests of 2013, likewise, failed to mount an effective challenge to deepening authoritarianism in Turkey.[3] But these waves of protests did enliven debates about the structure of the state in the countries of the region that continue today even as revolutionary fervor – and optimism – have subsided. Across them all, a recurring controversy has been the extent to which overly centralized authority is a source of the region's conflicts and governance problems – and, conversely, whether federalism and decentralization in their myriad forms offer a way forward.

This book examines the law and politics of decentralization in the MENA states. Unless otherwise indicated, we use the terms "decentralization" and "decentralizing reforms" in a generic sense to refer to a variety of arrangements involving the shift of responsibility and/or authority from central governments to other levels (such as provincial, state, or municipal governments). This broad category includes a range of models sometimes labeled "territorial pluralism" or "territorially based autonomy,"

[1] See generally, J. L. Gelvin, *The Arab Uprisings* (New York: Oxford University Press, 2012).

[2] See generally, M. Lynch, *The New Arab Wars: Uprisings and Anarchy in the Middle East* (Philadelphia: Perseus Books, 2016).

[3] See generally, K. Genç, *Under the Shadow: Rage and Revolution in Modern Turkey* (London: I.B. Tauris, 2016).

including federal and confederal systems, as well as arrangements involving less robust shifts of political, administrative, and fiscal authority away from the central government, such as devolution, delegation, and deconcentration.

Widely advocated by donor agencies, intergovernmental institutions, and scholars of comparative politics and law, decentralization has been urged as a means of advancing two distinct but related goals. First, as a framework for self-determination, it may enable identity groups – typically, ethnic, linguistic, or religious minorities – to exercise a measure of autonomy without challenging the territorial integrity of the state.[4] Second, as a vehicle for improving governance, it may bolster accountability by bringing government closer to the people it serves.[5] Decentralization may also improve the efficiency of service delivery by enabling local authorities to tailor services to the specific needs and conditions of their constituents and multiply opportunities for experimentation and innovation in generating policy solutions to persistent problems on the ground.[6]

While these two sets of goals are distinct, the line separating them is often unclear in practice. On the one hand, demands for self-determination are sometimes driven in part by poor governance at the center. On the other, decentralizing reforms often face resistance precisely because they are understood to be motivated by a group's desire for greater self-determination, opponents fearing that even modest devolutionary steps may strengthen secessionist or irredentist tendencies. Indeed, while most studies focus on one or the other of these two goals, it tends to be the link between them that makes decentralization an incendiary item on states' reform agendas.

The benefits of decentralization continue, moreover, to be hotly contested.[7] Experts disagree about the extent to which it contributes to the political stability

4 See, e.g., K. M. Bakke, *Decentralization and Intrastate Struggles: Chechnya, Punjab and Québec* (Cambridge: Cambridge University Press, 2015); D. Brancati, *Peace by Design: Managing Intrastate Conflict through Decentralization* (New York: Oxford University Press, 2009); L. Anderson, "Ethnofederalism and the Management of Ethnic Conflict: Assessing the Alternatives," *Publius*, 46(1) (2016), 1–24; N. Bermeo, "A New Look at Federalism: The Import of Institutions," *Journal of Democracy*, 13(2) (2002), 96–110; J. McGarry and B. O'Leary, "Federation as a Method of Ethnic Conflict Regulation," in Sid Noel (ed.), *From Power Sharing to Democracy: Post-conflict Institutions in Ethnically Divided Societies* (Kingston, ON: McGill-Queen's University Press, 2005), 263–96; and S. Choudhury and N. Hume, "Federalism, Devolution and Secession: From Classical to Post-Conflict Federalism," in T. Ginsburg and R. Dixon (eds.), *Research Handbook on Comparative Constitutional Law* (Cheltenham: Edward Elgar, 2010), 356–85.

5 See, e.g., J. Faguet and C. Pöschl (eds.), *Is Decentralization Good for Development? Perspectives from Academia and Policy-Makers* (Oxford: Oxford University Press, 2015); R. C. Schragger, "Decentralization and Development," *Virginia Law Review*, 96(8) (2010), 1837–1910.

6 E. Ahmad and G. Brosio, eds., *Does Decentralization Enhance Service Delivery and Poverty Reduction?* (Cheltenham: Edward Elgar, 2009).

7 For an overview of the debate, see D. Treisman, *The Architecture of Government: Rethinking Political Decentralization* (New York: Cambridge University Press, 2008), 11–15; P. Smoke, "Rethinking Decentralization: Assessing Challenges to a Popular Public Sector Reform," *Public Administration and Development*, 35 (2015), 97–112; R. Prud'homme, "The Dangers of Decentralization," *The World Bank Research Observer*, 10(2) (August 1995), 201–20.

and territorial integrity of states.[8] Skeptics cite evidence that decentralization also tends to exacerbate inequality between regions and produce increased opportunities for corruption.[9] In addition, they raise concerns about its feasibility in the diverse settings where it has been urged, pointing out that devolving power to provincial and local governments is an expensive undertaking that requires greater macroeconomic stability and local capacity than many developing countries possess. Despite these continuing controversies, decentralization has been a major global trend for several decades.[10]

Until recently, however, the states of the MENA region seemed largely immune to decentralization. In a 2007 report, the World Bank highlighted what it characterized as "a different pattern of decentralization" in the MENA region – one in which authority (political and fiscal) remained largely concentrated in central governments, even as limited responsibility for policy implementation had begun to be devolved to municipal and/or provincial governments.[11] At the time, two notable exceptions to this regional pattern were Iraqi Kurdistan and the West Bank and Gaza Strip, where more far-reaching (if in many ways problematic) autonomy arrangements had been in place, de facto or de jure, for more than a decade. Since the start of the Arab uprisings in 2010, however, decentralization in one form or another has emerged as a focus of discourse and debate in virtually every part of the region.

Decentralization is the framework within which the self-determination claims of identity groups – ethnic, religious, linguistic, tribal, and/or regional – are being conceptualized, contested, and negotiated.[12] That remains the case in Iraqi Kurdistan, where, following an abortive 2017 referendum on independence, Erbil now finds itself obliged to renegotiate its federal compact with Baghdad through which the region had secured more sweeping autonomy than any other subnational unit on the planet. At the same time, Kurdish leaders in Turkey and Syria have begun to rethink nationalist separatism altogether, instead embracing (and, in Rojava, experimenting with) self-determination through a form of radically decentralized governance they call democratic confederalism. In Israel-Palestine, the failure of the Oslo process to deliver independence to Palestinians has produced a search for alternatives – not only to the oppressive quasi-decentralized governance introduced by the arrangements defined in the Israeli-Palestinian Interim Agreement for a so-called "transitional" period, but also to the vision of partition based on ethnic separation that

8 For contrasting views, see P. G. Roeder, "Ethnofederalism and the Mismanagement of Conflicting Nationalisms," *Regional & Federal Studies*, 19(2) (2009), 203–19; and J. McGarry and B. O'Leary, "Must Pluri-national Federations Fail?" *Ethnopolitics*, 8(1) (2009), 5–25.

9 D. Horowitz, "The Many Uses of Federalism," *Drake Law Review*, 55 (2007), 953–69, at 963.

10 Regarding the phases of global engagement with decentralization, see G. S. Cheema and D. A. Rondinelli, *Decentralizing Governance: Emerging Concepts and Practices* (Washington, DC: Brookings, 2007), 7–8.

11 World Bank, *Decentralization and Local Governance in MENA: A Survey of Policies, Institutions and Practices* (Washington, DC: World Bank, 2007).

12 See P. G. Roeder, "Decentralization to Manage Identity Conflicts," Chapter 2 in this volume.

dominated peace talks for two decades. Among these alternatives, confederal models are garnering increasing attention, if not yet political traction. Confederalism is also being contemplated in Yemen as a framework for reimagining the country's battered political system in a post-conflict future, the federal arrangements defined in the 2015 draft constitution having failed to mollify secessionist movements in southern Yemen. In Libya, by contrast, concern about secessionist ambitions in Benghazi has pushed debates about the future structure of the state in the opposite direction, undermining support for federalism in favor of a limited program of administrative decentralization. Similarly, in Morocco, the regime has seized upon administrative decentralization and regionalization as a formula for restricting Western Sahara's longstanding claim to self-determination to the confines of Moroccan sovereignty.

Decentralization has also served as a framework for addressing – and, in some cases, containing – a broader governance agenda. In a few contexts – Tunisia, Yemen, Iraq, and initially Egypt – reformers urged decentralization as a democratizing measure; a means of shifting authority away from an overbearing central government toward peripheral regions and/or a long-disempowered citizenry. Just as often, however, initiatives styled as decentralizing reforms have originated within central governments themselves as a means of consolidating their authority over the periphery. An early example in this vein is the local government law passed by Iran's parliament in the mid-1990s following riots by slum dwellers in a number of cities. A generation later, the governments of Jordan, Syria, and Morocco adopted a similar strategy in the shadow of Arab Spring protests, launching decentralization initiatives with considerable fanfare but ultimately relinquishing minimal authority.

This diversity is explored in rich detail in this volume, which presents a series of twelve case studies examining the experience across the region, along with a collection of chapters placing that experience in comparative and theoretical perspective and a synthetic conclusion by the co-editors. The case studies, which focus respectively on Iran, Kurdistan (as a whole), Iraq, Iraqi Kurdistan, Libya, Morocco and Western Sahara, Palestine/Israel, Syria, Tunisia, Turkey, and Yemen, offer a textured portrait of the law and politics of decentralization during a period of sweeping transition in a region the comparative decentralization literature has largely neglected. With a view toward facilitating comparative analysis, each case study examines a common set of variables: the aims that have animated support for decentralization as they have evolved over time; the processes and institutions through which it has been pursued; the forms it has taken; the obstacles it has encountered; the controversies it has engendered; and its likely future trajectory. In addition, the case studies illuminate dynamics and questions distinctive to each context. Both retrospective and forward-looking in orientation, the book promises to be a valuable resource not only for scholars of comparative politics, constitutional design, and Middle East studies, but also for policymakers evaluating the feasibility and efficacy of decentralization as a vehicle for improving governance and responding to identity conflict in any part of the world.

DEFINING DECENTRALIZATION

We began by noting that the broad category of decentralization encompasses a wide array of strategies ranging from the least ambitious – deconcentration – to the most robust approaches – like federalism – that transfer substantial power over resources, decision-making, and implementation to local actors.[13] Defining the range of policies encompassed under the catch-all of decentralization is an important first step to understanding the relationship between various approaches to the design of decentralizing reforms and objectives ranging from good governance to conflict resolution.

At the most general level, decentralization refers to the transfer of legal and political authority from the central government and its agencies to lower levels of government. The authority in question may include policy formulation, resource allocation, and management of public functions.[14] The lower levels of government to which such powers are delegated may be subordinate units of central government, appointed regional or municipal authorities, or semi-autonomous elected local officials governing over territory- or identity-based communities. The definition also encompasses broad variation in the degree of restructuring of authority required by decentralization, the degree of shared responsibility over transferred authorities among different levels of government, and the relationship among various subnational units of government (i.e., how regional and local/municipal branches interact).

In defining the spectrum of decentralization policies, the comparative law and comparative politics literatures typically distinguish at least three approaches – deconcentration, delegation, and devolution – the last of which may include forms of federalism and confederalism if sufficiently robust.[15]

Deconcentration is the most modest form of decentralization, essentially shifting authority between offices or units of the central government.[16] To the extent that one purpose of decentralizing reforms is to bring the implementation of policies to

13 In addition, there are several subsets of federalism that have been explored in the academic literature including asymmetric federalism and multiethnic or pluri-national federalism. On the former, see Horowitz, "The Many Uses of Federalism"; Bakke, *Decentralization and Intrastate Struggles*, 193, 209–10, 239 (discussing the case of Québec); and Brancati, *Peace by Design*, 95–96 (discussing asymmetry in the Spanish model of decentralization). On multiethnic or pluri-national federalism, see L. D. Anderson, *Federal Solutions to Ethnic Problems: Accommodating Diversity* (London: Routledge 2013) (see especially ch. 3).

14 For discussions of the different authorities that may be decentralized, see J. M. Cohen and S. B. Peterson, *Administrative Decentralization: Strategies for Developing Countries* (West Hartford, CT: Kumarian Press, 1999).

15 International IDEA, *Decentralization in Unitary States: Constitutional Frameworks for the Middle East and North Africa* (n.p.: Center for Constitutional Transitions, International Idea, & UNDP, 2014).

16 See, e.g., J. Regulska, "Decentralization or Deconcentration: Struggle for Political Power in Poland," *International Journal of Public Administration*, 20(3) (1997), 643–80.

the most local level to adapt them to the exigencies of local communities, this goal may be served by deconcentration where authority is transferred from offices in the capital to regional and local subordinate offices of the central government. But such lower-level units are typically staffed with officials who are appointed by and accountable to the central government rather than the local constituencies with which they interact. Thus deconcentration does not directly serve goals of local empowerment, capacity-building, subsidiarity, or improving transparency. The dispersal of authority from the capital to more peripheral parts of the country generally shifts the territorial locus of implementation with few other decentralizing entailments.

An intermediate form of decentralization is delegation, which involves the transfer of authorities and resources for the implementation of central government–defined policies to subunits of the government. Delegation may also transfer to the local-level powers of decision-making concerning clearly specified functions.[17] This is distinct from deconcentration because the officials, offices, or units to which authority is transferred are either locally/regionally controlled or at least semi-autonomous from the central government. Thus, while policies themselves continue to be set at the central government level, the power to implement, administer, and manage such policies – and make decisions concerning some functions related to them – is delegated to regional and/or local subunits that are not under the direct control of the government. Here the lower levels of government receiving the transfer of power may be either appointed or elected, but in either case they are at least partly accountable to the local constituencies to which they are more proximate. Such decentralization serves a number of goals beyond ensuring local adaptation of policies at the implementation level, which may also occur with deconcentration. Specifically, delegation is expected to produce greater transparency about central government policies (which have to be clearly defined in the course of delegation), enhanced accountability to local actors for the ways such policies are implemented (with administration under the control of locally selected officials), and even some resource transfers (and efforts at capacity-building to enable relevant subunits to execute policies) that enhance local empowerment.

In the tripartite scheme of decentralization, devolution entails the most extensive and robust transfer of authorities from the central government to local and regional levels.[18] With devolution, in contrast to delegation, the local and/or regional subunits

[17] See, e.g., United Nations Development Program, *Decentralization: A Sampling of Definitions* (October 1999), http://web.undp.org/evaluation/documents/decentralization_working_report.pdf.

[18] Devolution also encompasses or overlaps with the categories of federalism and confederalism. For discussions of these various forms of devolution, see N. Aroney, "Types of Federalism," in *Max Planck Encyclopedia of Comparative Constitutional Law* (Oxford: Oxford University Press, 2016), https://oxcon.ouplaw.com/view/10.1093/law-mpeccol/law-mpeccol-e294?prd=MPECCOL; McGarry and O'Leary, "Federation as a Method of Ethnic Conflict Regulation"; and D. Halberstam, "Federalism: Theory, Policy, Law," in M. Rosenfeld and A. Sajo (eds.), *The Oxford Handbook of Comparative Constitutional Law* (Oxford: Oxford University Press, 2012), 576–608.

of government are separate from the central government and autonomous, which means that they are typically composed of elected officials whose legal authority derives from the provincial or local elections through which they gained office. By devolving certain authorities to these autonomous subunits of government, the central government formally relinquishes its direct control over policy-making, implementation, and accountability in those domains. Often, devolution will also entail the transfer of certain fiscal authorities to lower levels of government, which will be tasked with raising revenues to be allocated for the provincial or local-level policies that they design and implement. The extent of the transfer of authority to the provincial or local level generally requires the existence of a parallel structure of government at these lower levels, a characteristic commonly identified with federal or confederal arrangements. Devolution will require a legal definition of the cooperative relationship to be established between the formally autonomous levels of government, setting forth which authorities reside exclusively with the central government and which are transferred to local government as well as arrangements for areas of concurrent jurisdiction.[19] As with the constitutional system of the United States, a federal system will typically have territorially defined subunits with legally recognized boundaries endowed with the authority to perform public functions, secure fiscal resources, and exercise local control over policies relating to an array of domains such as education, culture, public order, and municipal services ranging from utilities to sanitation. There will also remain domains – such as those having to do with national security – that are exclusively within the authority of the central government.

Beyond variation in the extent of authorities transferred under different forms of decentralization, there is also considerable variation in the functional domains that may be the subject of decentralizing reforms. Here, too, the scholarly and policy literatures have identified a tripartite typology, with the principal domains defined as administrative, policy, and fiscal decentralization.[20] These categories, familiar from constitutional law, define the range of responsibilities and powers that may be subject to transfer through decentralizing reforms. Administrative decentralization involves the transfer of responsibility for the planning and implementation of policies from central government to subordinate levels and is the most common domain in which decentralization – from deconcentration to devolution – occurs. Policy (or political) decentralization involves transferring authority for decision-making to local-level authorities, which may happen through delegation or devolution. For policy decentralization to be deemed legitimate as a governance reform, there is an expectation

19 On the need for formal allocation of authorities, see W. H. Riker, *Federalism: Origin, Operation, Significance* (New York: Little Brown, 1964); see also J. McGarry and B. O'Leary, "Territorial Pluralism: Taxonomizing Its Forms, Virtues, and Flaws," in K. Basta, J. McGarry, and R. Simeon (eds.), *Territorial Pluralism: Managing Difference in Multinational States* (Vancouver: University of British Columbia Press, 2015), 13–53.

20 See, e.g., International IDEA, *Decentralization in Unitary States*, 12–13.

that the lower level of government exercising policy authority be accountable to its local constituency, typically through elections. Finally, fiscal decentralization refers to the transfer of responsibility for collecting taxes and allocating resources. Like policy decentralization, transfers of authority for taxation entail accountability and are only likely in contexts with extensive delegation or, more likely, devolution of powers. A government can be decentralized to varying degrees along each of these dimensions, and recent scholarship has suggested that underlying societal traits are essential to understanding the optimal design of decentralization for each axis.[21]

The design of decentralization policies will, of course, be a function of the objectives being pursued. This volume engages with a wide spectrum of theoretical perspectives from which the advantages and disadvantages of decentralization are addressed for multiple and sometimes overlapping objectives, from conflict resolution to minority rights protections to improved economic service provision and hopes for greater accountability. If the goal is improving governance performance, then the emphasis will be on those reforms that enhance government accountability and transparency, improve service delivery by building local government capacity, and permit greater local input and participation. If, on the other hand, the goal of decentralization is to address self-determination demands while maintaining territorial integrity, the emphasis will be on reforms that enhance local autonomy, particularly over those policy domains that are implicated in identity conflicts, such as education and cultural policies. In the Middle East, there is tremendous overlap between these objectives because a record of poor governance has generated calls for political liberalization and anti-corruption reforms while also amplifying minority groups' demands for self-determination. The interlinkages and entanglements of demands for self-determination on the one hand and improved governance on the other are evident across many of the cases engaged in this volume, including Kurdistan, Libya, Morocco, Palestine, and Yemen.

LIMITATIONS OF DECENTRALIZATION

The definitions of the forms of decentralization in the abstract are, of course, quite detached from the actual practice of decentralizing reforms. The neat divisions between deconcentration, delegation, and devolution, as well as the discrete policy domains to which these modalities might be applied, bleed together on the ground, mitigating the degree to which they may be tied back to expectations modeled by the literature. Policies that appear to contemplate robust devolutionary transfers of power on paper are often realized through modest deconcentration measures in practice. Functions are transferred without the necessary resources being made available to local officials, or overlapping authorities are multiplied in ways that obscure accountability instead of enhancing transparency. In short, beyond

[21] Bakke, *Decentralization and Intrastate Struggles*, ch. 6.

the formal spectrum of policies and practices described in the literature there is enormous variation in implementation that means that decentralization rarely achieves the ambitious goals in terms of governance or self-determination set out by policymakers.

Beyond these general observations, it is also worth noting that the MENA governments may be especially inhospitable to decentralizing reforms.[22] Almost all the country cases surveyed in this volume, with the possible exceptions of Tunisia Turkey, are nondemocratic regimes where efforts at political liberalization have largely foundered. In many instances, from the Arab world to Iran to Turkey, decentralizing reforms are being debated against a backdrop of recent mass protest movements pursuing radical reforms that they were unable to secure. As a consequence, in many instances frustrated reformists may invest hopes in devolution to accomplish the goals of incomplete revolutions across the region, raising unrealistic expectations and setting the groundwork for popular disaffection with the incrementalism of experiments in decentralization. The region is also characterized by a number of cases of ongoing conflict or immediate post-conflict reconstruction, contexts that pose particularly daunting challenges for any reform efforts. Moreover, in countries where long-term denial of self-determination claims has been one of the sources of conflict – as in the Palestinian, Kurdish, and Yemeni cases – decentralization will be fraught with anxieties over territorial integrity and secessionist demands that are more acute than in other settings. Finally, while many regimes in the region have publicly embraced some measure of decentralization, there is little concomitant commitment to political liberalization. In such cases, decentralization may be a necessary but insufficient condition for improving governance, service delivery, and the performance of public functions. In short, experiments in decentralization across the region often take place under challenging circumstances, to put it mildly.

Because decentralization has in the past been treated in the region as a backdoor to territorial partition, there has been reluctance to pursue decentralizing reforms. Yet at present there is widespread interest in policy experimentation with decentralization across the region. The bottom line is that these efforts offer the modest promise of incremental improvements in governance, participation, and local accountability at a time when most other reform initiatives have failed. The transfer of power to subordinate levels of government has the potential to generate virtuous cycles or positive feedback loops, with local experiences of improved services or increased participation generating opportunities to chip away at the impasse of civil strife and authoritarian governance at the national level

This volume explores this potential through context-specific, realistic, and empirically grounded studies of experiences with and prospects for decentralization in the twelve country cases presented herein. The trajectories of decentralizing reforms

22 M. S. Tosun and S. Yilmaz, "Centralization, Decentralization and Conflict in the Middle East and North Africa," *World Bank Policy Research Paper* 4774 (Washington, DC: World Bank, 2008).

are a consequence of many factors, to be sure, but exploring whether and to what extent decentralization might yield such (perhaps modest) benefits in the Middle East is a question worth engaging with. Beginning from the premise that decentralization is neither a scourge nor a panacea for the governance and conflict resolution challenges in the region, the case studies provide both thick description and normative and policy insights that form the basis for the generalizable lessons we discuss in our synthetic conclusion.

STRUCTURE OF THE VOLUME

We believe an edited volume is the best (and perhaps the only) way to address the region's diverse and complex recent experience at this juncture. No single author would have a command of both the range of cases explored here and the theoretical and comparative dimensions of current debates about decentralization necessary to provide the seminal contribution that we believe our collection offers.

The book builds upon discussions during a pair of symposia at McGeorge School of Law, University of the Pacific, in May 2017, and at the University of California, Los Angeles, in June 2018. These meetings were designed to take stock of the scholarly literature in the fields of comparative law and comparative politics on decentralization and to address the lacunae of studies on this topic in the Middle East. We set out to bring academic and policy experts on decentralization into conversation with regional experts studying the law and politics of the countries of the region that have experimented with decentralizing reforms. The first of our meetings enabled regional experts to engage with literature review presentations that covered the main debates in the study of decentralization and theoretical contributions about the goals served by decentralization and the lessons of policy experimentation in other regional contexts. We then asked invited authors to undertake studies of decentralization in the countries of their expertise, selected on the basis of their recent experiences, with strategies ranging from limited deconcentration to federal and confederal arrangements. We met again one year later for the presentation of the case studies.

The volume is structured to tease out themes running across these cases, as well as their broader comparative and theoretical implications. Following our Introduction, the book begins with Part I: a collection of essays by leading scholars framing the region's recent experience in light of insights from the theoretical literature and experience elsewhere. Philip G. Roeder considers the challenges presented by designing decentralized institutions for the different kinds of plural societies in the MENA region. Tom Ginsburg explores issues of constitutional design in circumstances where states grapple with territorial cleavages. Will Kymlicka considers whether decentralization presents a credible alternative to group rights as a framework for minority protection. Mona Harb and Sami Atallah examine the dominant practice in the Middle East of deconcentration and examine the ways in which such measures serve to strengthen central control rather than devolving authority to local government despite claims that deconcentration is part of a broader decentralization agenda.

The case studies that follow are organized into three parts. Part II explores three cases – Iran (by Kian Tajbakhsh), Iraq (by Ali Al-Mawlawi), and Tunisia (by Intissar Kherigi) – in which decentralization initiatives have been undertaken primarily as a vehicle for governance reform, albeit in sharply differing political contexts. Part III focuses on contexts where decentralization is being pursued or contemplated as a framework for self-determination, addressing Kurdistan in general (Joost Jongerden), Iraqi Kurdistan (Peter Bartu and Aidan MacEachern), Turkey/Turkish Kurdistan (by Aslı Ü. Bâli), Palestine/Israel (by Sari Bashi – on Oslo as decentralization under occupation – and Omar M. Dajani and Dahlia Scheindlin – on confederal models for resolving the conflict), and Morocco/Western Sahara (by Omar Yousef Shehabi). The final set of case studies in Part IV examines decentralization initiatives pursued in the shadow of territorial fragmentation and identity conflict (Sujit Choudhry and George R. M. Anderson), addressing the cases of Libya (by Karim Mezran and Elissa Miller), Syria (by Samer Araabi and Leila Hilal), and Yemen (by Benoît Challand).

Finally, in a synthetic conclusion, we draw out and reflect upon the themes running across the volume and the lessons that may be learned from it, offering a new typology of the drivers of decentralization and plotting its trajectory in the countries of the region.

CONTRIBUTION

The scope of this volume makes it innovative in several distinct ways.

First and foremost, this volume is the first scholarly work entirely in the English language to address decentralization in the greater Middle East. Other than in individual country studies, scholars of Middle East law and politics have given decentralization little systematic attention, and the region has been largely absent from comparative scholarship about decentralization.[23] Filling this gap provides an important corrective to two bodies of literature. While decentralization, federalism, and their variants have long been topics of study in comparative politics and comparative constitutional law, scholarship in those fields has focused on a set of standard cases in developed democracies and parts of Latin America, South and Southeast Asia,

[23] Quite nearly the sole significant exception to this trend is a volume (with a mix of contributions in English and French) edited by Mona Harb and Sami Atallah and published by the Lebanese Center for Policy Studies addressing decentralization policy initiatives in five Arab countries. M. Harb and S. Atallah (eds.), *Local Governments and Public Goods: Assessing Decentralization in the Arab World* (Beirut: Lebanese Center for Policy Studies, 2015). Our volume adds to this important contribution by covering an additional six country cases, expanding the lens beyond decentralized service delivery to address decentralization in the state-building and post-conflict contexts, and including contributions that draw on relevant experiences in other regions by leading comparative politics and comparative law theorists in the English-language literatures on decentralization.

and Africa. Extrapolating from these cases, it has elaborated a series of lessons to be applied and risks to be avoided that form the basis for subsequent comparative analysis of the potential for decentralizing reforms to effect governance improvements or address identity-based conflicts in other parts of the world. Because many of the presumptive characteristics of successful decentralization based on these models are absent in the MENA region, the literature tends to treat it as either pathological or exceptional, or simply fails to address it at all.

We fill this gap by providing in-depth empirical studies of the principal experiences with decentralization in the region and a set of theoretical engagements that situate these cases in the broader literature. We seek to identify some alternative lessons to those offered by the standard set of cases from which the literature currently draws. We are explicitly interested in depathologizing the region and situating the experiences with decentralization in the MENA region within the broader context of worldwide trends in decentralization. In certain cases – such as that of Kurdistan and Israel-Palestine – we believe that creative ideas currently being engaged by civil society actors may offer new ways of thinking about the potential of decentralizing reforms to address longstanding identity-based conflicts. Elsewhere, we believe a region much in need of redistribution of executive power but loathe to embrace standard decentralizing prescriptions may be innovating alternative pathways to a measure of decentralization, as in Tunisia. The potential for new directions in decentralizing reforms that we see percolating in the MENA region – from service delivery experiments in contexts of de facto decentralization to theories of non-territorial self-determination through democratic confederalism – are all the more interesting for emerging from what has long been treated as inhospitable terrain.

Second, the volume bridges two bodies of literature that are too infrequently in conversation with each other: studies that examine federalism and other forms of territorial pluralism as a framework for managing diversity in divided societies and those focused on decentralization as a device for improving public sector performance. As the region's recent experience makes clear, citizens and governments modulate nimbly between these models and agendas in debates about the structure of the state – a demand for political autonomy met with an offer of administrative decentralization, a proposal for limited devolution arousing controversy because it appears to benefit a particular identity group. Addressing them in a single volume enables the development of a fuller account of the politics of decentralization and of transitions – and a richer menu of options for policymakers. Moreover, the volume provides an important contribution in addressing the interaction effects between the different goals of governance reform, self-determination, and conflict management. In some cases, efforts to improve service delivery through decentralization are undermined because of the imputed territorial anxieties triggered by such measures notwithstanding the governance goals of proponents. In other cases, de facto decentralization as a consequence of conflict-driven territorial partition creates a context in which experimentation with forms of previously foreclosed decentralized service delivery suddenly becomes possible. Because the MENA region is characterized by societies that oscillate between the two registers of decentralization, such interaction effects are evident in several of the case studies, inviting comparative reflection on how frustrated demands for self-determination and governance reform may be mutually reinforcing, requiring a more integrated approach to designing strategies of decentralization. Theorizing about the implications of such interaction effects through the study of cases in the MENA region, our synthetic conclusion provides an original and agenda-setting contribution to the literature.

Third, the volume's territorial scope not only breaks new ground by addressing a region infrequently studied in this context, it also reaches cases like Iran, Israel, and Turkey that tend to be excluded from studies focused on the Arab world. This territorial scope allows for deeper comparative analysis – permitting, for example, an examination of how three different states have responded to Kurdish demands for self-determination and how their responses relate to broader debates about democracy, governance, and identity within their polities. It also facilitates analysis of the region as a unit. Despite its lack of political cohesion and supranational organization, MENA in many ways has operated as a region over the last decade, waves of revolution and counter-revolution spreading rapidly across borders despite efforts to limit contagion. The scope of the volume permits the excavation of common strands of political history that continue to shape attitudes across the region and identification of patterns that distinguish MENA from other parts of the world.

Another distinctive feature of the volume is the interdisciplinarity of the contributors, including scholars and policy analysts with expertise in a diverse array of fields – constitutional law, conflict resolution, comparative politics, comparative law, political theory, sociology, and urban planning – and diverse perspectives regarding the merits and risks of decentralization. The breadth of the background of those we have invited to contribute to our study reflects the nature of the audience we hope will find this volume to be of interest. The volume targets not only academic social scientists and legal scholars, but also policy circles, legal practitioners, and civil society actors interested in thinking carefully about the potential of decentralizing reforms to meet goals ranging from service delivery to self-determination and from economic development to political liberalization. The empirical case studies contained herein map the potential for decentralization in the MENA region in ways designed to be of interest to specialists on the comparative law and politics of the Middle East as well as to those studying the broader question of decentralization and governance reform in authoritarian settings on the one hand, and those studying the potential for territorial pluralism to regulate identity-based conflict on the other. Because the volume draws on comparative lessons from experiences with decentralization in other regions, scholars who focus on similar challenges in the African, Asian, and South American contexts should also find much of interest in our study. With generalizable empirical findings, the case studies collected here offer insights into process design questions concerning the form and framing of decentralizing reforms that are relevant in a wide array of regional contexts. The volume makes an important contribution to the comparative study of territorial pluralism and comparative research on decentralization and governance that engages head-on with the growing backlash against policy prescriptions tied to models of decentralization and the relative resilience of authoritarianism and identity-based conflict in the MENA. These are issues of increasing concern for advocates of rule of law and governance as well as those involved in conflict resolution. The lessons in this volume offer insights into how these challenges might be met by advocates and policy analysts, including those at international financial institutions, intergovernmental organizations, and agencies involved in development assistance where targets of programs include goals tied to governance improvement or conflict resolution.

PART I

Theoretical and Comparative Context

2

Decentralization to Manage Identity Conflicts

Philip G. Roeder[*]

Institutions to decentralize government have been proposed as remedies to mitigate the four key political challenges of statehood, self-government, peace, and prosperity. That is, institutional decentralization purportedly can keep states whole against the threat of secession, promote or preserve democracy and civil liberties, secure peace against escalating civil violence, and create the political foundations for economic growth and equity. Yet, around the world these institutional remedies are severely tested in societies torn by what have come to be called identity conflicts involving deep cultural divides along such lines as language or religion.

Any project to apply these remedies to deeply divided societies in the Middle East and North Africa (MENA) confronts a daunting task due to the complexities of the societies in the region. Despite a shared history and some real present-day similarities, the MENA societies vary substantially in their patterns of sociocultural diversity that could give rise to threats to statehood, self-government, peace, or prosperity. Thus, there probably is no single optimal institutional solution that is appropriate for all MENA polities. As in many other regions, there are also powerful political actors in governments and in oppositions with agendas that lead them to resist decentralization or to use decentralization to destabilize existing political orders. Any effort to ensure the longer-term stability of institutional arrangements will require very careful matching of institutional design to the specific political challenges in each country. Despite these reasons for caution, institutional innovations in other parts of the world suggest a variety of potential solutions that may be appropriate to specific plural societies of the MENA region.

WHAT TYPES OF MENA IDENTITIES MIGHT BE ADDRESSED BY DECENTRALIZATION?

There is no typical MENA society and the design of political institutions for each country will need to take into account its distinct patterns of potential and realized

* I have benefited enormously from the constructive and informative comments from the editors, Aslı Ü. Bâli and Omar M. Dajani, from fellow participants in the conferences they organized, and from Konstantin Ash and Matthew Nanes. I sincerely thank them all.

sociocultural identity conflicts.[1] To begin, as Table 2.1 shows, based on sociocultural criteria, the eighteen states of the MENA region fall into as many as twelve distinct patterns based on four considerations. First is whether the titular nationality (the ethnic group for which the state is named, such as Libyan Arabs in Libya) is divided by subtitular (ST) ethnolinguistic divisions (such as Cyrenaicans and Tripolitanians). Second is whether there are substantial Indigenous (IN) ethnolinguistic minorities (such as the Bedouins and Berbers) that do not belong to the titular nationality. Third is whether there are substantial expatriate (EX) ethnolinguistic minorities (such as the Egyptian Arabs in Libya). And fourth is whether there are substantial religious (RE) minorities belonging to either a different denomination within the same religion or a different religion.[2] This last distinction, of course, does not include the acute divides inside religious communities concerning religiosity or what is often labeled as fundamentalism. These sociocultural distinctions do not necessarily shape the political orientations of the populations; these define potential platform populations that may be targeted for discrimination or mobilization, but their members and their governments may not always and everywhere attribute political significance to them.

The term "platform population" underscores political construction rather than demographic givens. That is, the sociocultural divisions in Table 2.1 define potential platforms on which enthusiasts may (or may not) build a political campaign for a cause such as group rights, secession, or control of the central government. As well, each of the platform populations may become the target of discrimination, exclusion, or oppression by central governments. Yet, none is deterministic: enthusiasts and activists must decide that there is enough realized or potential popular support within the platform population to sustain a challenge to the status quo. Central governments must see the minorities as potential or realized threats to the key projects of the state before undertaking costly acts of oppression. The realized identity conflicts that actually emerged within the different MENA societies reflect (but only imperfectly) the variety of sociocultural divisions identified in Table 2.1. Standard lists compiled by social scientists identify, on the one hand, minorities at risk of political discrimination, exclusion from government, or oppression (including genocide) by their governments and, on the other hand, minorities that have become platforms for protest and violence in demonstrations, terrorism, or civil wars.[3] As Table 2.2

[1] In this analysis I omit Israel, the West Bank, and Gaza, because this would complicate the analysis with cases that may be unique and would necessitate an overly long chapter.

[2] The classifications of ethnic groups are from G. F. Simons and C. D. Fennig (eds.), *Ethnologue: Languages of the World*, 21st ed. (Dallas, TX: SIL International, 2018), which identifies languages and classifies these as "indigenous" and "non-indigenous." The population of each group is based on the Joshua Project (2018) database, joshuaproject.net. The classifications and numbers for religious groups are from United States Central Intelligence Agency, *The World Factbook* (2018), cia.gov.

[3] I rely on the standard lists so as to minimize the likelihood that my codings are biased by my analysis here. The datasets used are L.-E. Cederman, B. Min, and A. Wimmer, *Ethnic Power Relations*

TABLE 2.1 *Patterns of sociocultural diversity*

Diversity Pattern[a]	Countries	Substantial sociocultural community type[a]: ST: Subtitular	IN: Indigenous	EX: Expatriate	RE: Religious
No dimensions of substantial sociocultural diversity					
1 None	Tunisia	—	—	—	—
One dimension of substantial sociocultural diversity					
2 IN	Algeria	—	X	—	—
	Turkey	—	X	—	—
Two dimensions of substantial sociocultural diversity					
3 ST, EX	Jordan	X	—	X	—
4 ST, RE	Egypt	X	—	—	X
	Saudi Arabia	X	—	—	X
	Yemen	X	—	—	X
5 IN, EX	Morocco	—	X	X	—
6 IN, RE	Iran	—	X	—	X
7 EX, RE	Bahrain	—	—	X	X
	Kuwait	—	—	X	X
	Lebanon	—	—	X	X
	Qatar	—	—	X	X
Three dimensions of substantial sociocultural diversity					
8 ST, IN, EX	Libya	X	X	X	—
9 ST, IN, RE	Syria	X	X	—	X
10 ST, EX, RE	Oman	X	—	X	X
11 IN, EX, RE	UAE	—	X	X	X
Four dimensions of substantial sociocultural diversity					
12 ST, IN, EX, RE	Iraq	X	X	X	X

Sources: This summary table is based on the information in Appendix Table 1.

[a] Diversity pattern and substantial sociocultural community type are defined as:

ST: At least one subtitular ethnolinguistic minority constitutes at least 5 percent of total population;

IN: At least one Indigenous ethnolinguistic minority constitutes at least 5 percent of total population;

EX: At least one expatriate ethnolinguistic minority constitutes at least 5 percent of total population;

RE: At least one religious minority constitutes at least 5 percent of total population.

Dataset (2018), icr.ethz.ch/data/epr; M. Marshall, T. R. Gurr, and B. Harff, *State Failures Problem Set: State Failures and Failures of Governance, 1955–2016* (2018), systemicpeace.org; Minorities at Risk, *Minorities at Risk Dataset* (2018), cidcm.umd.edu/mar; National Consortium for the Study of Terrorism and Responses to Terrorism, *Global Terrorism Database* (2018), start.umd.edu/gtd; Nonviolent and Violent Campaigns and Outcomes, *NAVCO Data Project* (2018), du.edu/korbel/sie/research/chenow_navco_data.html; and Uppsala Conflict Data Program, *UCDP/PRIO Armed Conflict Dataset* (2018), pcr.uu.se/research/ucdp.

TABLE 2.2 *Patterns of platform targeting for discrimination or mobilization*

	Targeted platform type[a]				
Diversity pattern[a]	None	ST: Subtitular	IN: Indigenous	EX: Expatriate	RE: Religious
1	Tunisia				
2 IN			Algeria		
			Turkey		
3 ST, EX		—		Jordan	
4 ST, RE		—	[Egypt][b]		Egypt
		—			Saudi Arabia
		Yemen			Yemen
5 IN, EX			Morocco	—	
6 IN, RE			Iran	[Iran][b]	Iran
7 EX, RE				—	Bahrain
				—	Kuwait
	Qatar			Lebanon	Lebanon
				—	—
8 ST, IN, EX		Libya	Libya	—	
9 ST, IN, RE		—	Syria		Syria
10 ST, EX, RE		Oman		—	—
11 IN, EX, RE	UAE		—	—	—
12 ST, IN, EX, RE		—	Iraq	—	Iraq
Percentage of major sociocultural communities becoming political platforms[b]		37.5	87.5	20.0	75.0

Sources: Cederman, Min, and Wimmer, Ethnic Power Relations Dataset, covering years of independence from 1946 to 2017; Marshall, Gurr, and Harff, State Failures Problem Set, covering years of independence from 1955 to 2017; Minorities at Risk, Minorities at Risk Dataset, covering years of independence from 1950 to 2006; National Consortium for the Study of Terrorism and Responses to Terrorism, Global Terrorism Database, covering years of independence from 1970 to 2018; Nonviolent and Violent Campaigns and Outcomes, NAVCO Data Project, covering years of independence from 1946 to 2013; and Uppsala Conflict Data Program, UCDP/PRIO Armed Conflict Dataset, covering years of independence from 1946 to 2018.

[a] Diversity pattern and targeted platform type are defined as:
ST: At least one subtitular ethnolinguistic minority constituting at least 5 percent of total population;
IN: At least one Indigenous ethnolinguistic minority constituting at least 5 percent of total population;
EX: At least one expatriate ethnolinguistic minority constituting at least 5 percent of total population;
RE: At least one religious minority constituting at least 5 percent of total population.

[b] Bracketed countries indicate a targeted platform population that did not constitute at least 5 percent of the total population and so does not appear in the diversity pattern. These countries are omitted from the percentages for each column.

shows, subtitular (ST) divisions created platforms for discrimination or mobilization in Libya, Oman, and Yemen. Divisions between the titular nation and Indigenous ethnolinguistic minorities (IN) created these platforms in Algeria, Egypt, Iran, Iraq, Libya, Morocco, Syria, and Turkey. Divisions between religious communities (RE) created such platforms in Bahrain, Egypt, Iran, Iraq, Lebanon, Saudi Arabia, Syria, and Yemen. The only expatriate ethnolinguistic groups (EX) that became platforms for realized conflict were the Palestinians in Jordan and Lebanon.

Table 2.2 shows that only three of eighteen MENA states escaped any major identity conflicts – Tunisia (the most homogeneous society) and the Gulf states of Qatar and the United Arab Emirates (with large expatriate and religious minorities). Alternatively, Egypt, Iran, Iraq, Lebanon, Libya, Syria, and Yemen suffered multi-dimensional challenges from more than one platform type. Indigenous (IN) ethnic minorities and religious (RE) groups were substantially more likely than subtitular (ST) or expatriate (EX) groups to become platforms for politicized discrimination or mobilization. (Compare the percentages at the bottom of each column in Table 2.2.) Seven of eight states with substantial Indigenous minorities (87.5 percent) plus one state without a substantial (that is, over 5 percent) Indigenous minority experienced such conflicts involving these platform populations. Nine of twelve states with substantial religious minorities (75 percent) experienced identity conflicts involving these. Conversely, only 37.5 percent of states with substantial subtitular (ST) ethnolinguistic groups and 20 percent with substantial expatriate (EX) ethnolinguistic groups reported political conflicts involving these groups.

As Table 2.3 shows, the standard lists identify twenty-eight different sociocultural communities as the targets of political discrimination or exclusion from power by central governments and these are almost equally divided between thirteen ethnolinguistic and fifteen religious platform populations. Three groups, the Baha'is in Iran and the Kurds in both Iran and Iraq, are identified as targets of governmental genocides. Nineteen communities (specifically, thirteen ethnolinguistic and six religious groups) were platforms for rebellions, which involved extensive violence and required large-scale mobilization of personnel and support networks. Thirteen platforms were associated with more limited or individualized violence in the form of terrorism; seven of these were religious platforms and six were ethnolinguistic platforms. The standard lists give less attention to the goals of these groups, but a cursory accounting would include secession, regional autonomy, communal autonomy, equal civil rights, inclusion in governance, and control of the central government. These simple cross-sectional comparisons do not reflect the substantial variation over time in each of these groups.

The lack of determinism leading from sociocultural diversity in MENA societies to the realization of political conflicts is reason for some optimism. This suggests an important role for human agency, including the possibility (but not the guarantee) that political institutions might be designed for MENA states so as to keep any disputes associated with these divides from escalating to jeopardize statehood, self-government, peace, and prosperity.

TABLE 2.3 *Types of conflicts associated with different platform populations*

Country	Platform	*Targeted with:* Discrimination	Genocide	*Platform of Mobilization for:* Protest	Terrorism	Rebellion
Algeria	Berbers	X			X	
Bahrain	Shi'is	X			X	
Egypt	Bedouins				X	
	Copts	X		X		
Iran	Arabs	X				X
	Armenians	X			X	
	Assyrians	X				
	Azeris					X
	Baha'is	X	X	X		
	Bakhtiaris	X		X		
	Baluchis	X				X
	Kurds	X	X			X
	Turkmen	X				X
Iraq	Kurds	X	X			X
	Shi'is	X				X
	Sunnis	X				X
Jordan	Palestinians	X				X
Kuwait	Shi'is	X			X	
Lebanon	Armenians	X			X	
	Druze	X				X
	Kurds	X				
	Maronites	X				X
	Palestinians	X				X
	Shi'is	X				X
	Sunnis	X				X
Libya	Bedouins				X	
	Cyrenaicans				X	
	Toubous				X	
	Tripolitanians				X	
Morocco	Berbers	X		X		
	Saharawis	X				X
Oman	Dhofaris					X
Saudi Arabia	Shi'is	X			X	
Syria	Alawis	X			X	
	Kurds					X
Turkey	Kurds	X				X
Yemen	Shi'is				X	
	Ta'issi-Adenis					X

Sources: See Table 2.2.
This table only includes platform populations if they constituted at least 1 percent of the country's population or comprised 100,000 members. Excluded are Iran's Jewish and Zoroastrian and Turkey's Armenian and Roma communities.

DO MENA POLITICAL FORCES SUPPORT DECENTRALIZATION?

Around the world the challenge in designing institutional decentralization is not only overcoming resistance to its introduction, but also ensuring its longer-term survival in the face of competing political forces attempting to recentralize authority and to decentralize further. The element of a stable equilibrium that balances centripetal and centrifugal pressures and keeps each side in check is often the critical missing piece of decentralization arrangements, and so many decentralization institutions have ended in failure.

The MENA states are no exception to this global challenge. Central governments have tended to favor centralization whenever they have the means to implement it. Holders of decentralized power have often used it to paralyze the central government and sometimes even pressed for the breakup of the state. Leaders of many MENA states have seen unitary government with tight centralization of decision-making authority as the best constitutional arrangement to defend the state's sovereignty against security threats, to create new national identities and unity among peoples divided by tribal or ethnic groupings, or to reinforce the vanguard role of the central government in modernizing traditional societies. Of course, in the MENA region, the Ottoman heritage included an imperial organization that granted vassal states substantial autonomy, which varied with the strength of the central government, and instituted the millet system, offering nonterritorial decentralization to religious communities.[4] Yet, few of the independent states that emerged since World War I have sustained territorial or nonterritorial decentralization except when central governments were too weak to extend their rule up to the borders of their formally sovereign states.

The only two federal systems in the MENA states emerged from alliances of traditional rulers forged under the patronage of colonial powers.[5] The federations were cobbled together in the rush by European powers to exit a military administration of the former Italian colonies of North Africa and a protectorate over the Trucial States. Neither was designed to address either ethnolinguistic or religious differences. The federal government in the United Kingdom of Libya between 1951 and 1963 bracketed the three colonies of Cyrenaica, Tripolitania, and Fezzan. Libyan federalism was challenged by both centrifugal and centripetal pressures: it was at first deadlocked by strong regional governments and then overwhelmed by a suddenly much more powerful central government. Despite the provision whereby the king appointed the governors in each province, the provincial administrations initially exercised broad de jure authority and possessed greater de facto administrative

4 D. Géza, "Administration, Provincial," in G. Ágoston and B. Masters (eds.), *Encyclopedia of the Ottoman Empire* (New York: Facts On File, 2009), 13–17; B. Masters, "Millet," in ibid., 383–4.

5 As discussed later in this chapter, Iraq's plans for a federation had not been implemented at the time this chapter was written.

capacity than the king's government. The resistance of Tripolitania and Fezzan to Cyrenaica's domination resulted in deadlock in the center, during which the regional authorities attempted to wrest more authority from the government of King Idris I.[6] This was a system, according to Dirk Vandewalle, that was "increasingly incapable of coming to terms with its growing internal difficulties." It ended following the confirmation of petroleum deposits in June 1959, which gave the central government financial resources that tipped the balance of power toward the center. Within four years the Libyan prime minister secured adoption of a statute replacing federalism with a unitary state.[7]

Alternatively, the United Arab Emirates became a remarkably resilient federation of emirs. A half century later, despite the initially temporary nature of the 1971 constitutional order, the league of emirs continued to resist institutional change. The emirs defeated proposals in the 1970s to check their powers in the Supreme Council of Rulers and to democratize government at the federal and individual-emirate levels.[8] Decisions within the Supreme Council continued to be reached by supermajorities of five out of seven emirs that could be vetoed by either Abu Dhabi or Dubai.[9] The United Arab Emirates (UAE)–wide Federal National Council remained a consultative body rather than a true legislature; only half of its members were elected (after heavy vetting), while the remainder were appointed by the emirs.[10] In Christopher Davidson's assessment, power in many decisions remained in the hands of the emirs' separate *diwans* (courts) and he describes the UAE as "a hybrid neopatrimonial government of seemingly modern institutions grafted onto powerful traditional authorities."[11] This might have contained lessons for preserving a stable decentralization arrangement in MENA states, except that the balance between centripetal and centrifugal pressures in the UAE has been maintained by the emirs, who fear that movement in either direction will erode their rule. Pressure for centralization has tended to be associated with the forces for democratization and expanded powers for the Federal National Council, while decentralization might leave some of the weaker emirs separately vulnerable to the same pressures. The emirs must hang together or possibly hang separately.

6 R. Owen, *Libya: A Brief Political and Economic Survey* (Oxford: Oxford University Press, 1961), 5, 8, 9; D. Vandewalle, *A History of Modern Libya* (New York: Cambridge University Press, 2012), 47–8.

7 Ibid., 45, 49, 61–4; United States Library of Congress, Federal Research Division, *Libya: A Country Study* (Washington, DC: Federal Research Division, 1989).

8 F. Heard-Bey, "The United Arab Emirates: A Quarter Century of Federation," in M. C. Hudson (ed.), *Middle East Dilemma: The Politics and Economics of Arab Integration* (New York: Columbia University Press, 1999), 128–49.

9 A. O. Taryam, *The Establishment of the United Arab Emirates, 1950–85* (New York: Croom, 1987), 203–4.

10 K. Ulrichsen, *The United Arab Emirates: Power, Politics, and Policymaking* (New York: Routledge, 2017), 56–8.

11 C. M. Davidson, *The United Arab Emirates: A Study in Survival* (Boulder: Lynne Rienner, 2005), 188–89, 192–208, 238.

The precarious balance in autonomy arrangements to address potential or realized identity conflicts is underscored by the only autonomous region established in the MENA states – the Kurdistan Regional Government (KRG) in Iraq. This was resisted by central governments in Baghdad. Kurds had won promises of cultural protections from the Qasim, Arif, and Baathist regimes, but regional autonomy was never actually implemented.[12] Instead, the autonomous region emerged under the no-fly zone imposed by the United States in October 1991 under Operation Provide Comfort. The 2005 Iraqi Constitution negotiated under American occupation promised a federal arrangement for all of Iraq, but only the KRG had been formed fifteen years later.[13] The relationship between the KRG and central government in Baghdad has been buffeted by competing centripetal and centrifugal pressures, reflecting the changing balance of consolidation inside each government. On July 1, 2014, Masoud Barzani, leader of the KRG, announced that an official referendum on independence would be called, and in February 2016 he repeated this call. This produced a growing crisis with Baghdad, the United States, and potentially Turkey as preparations for the September 25, 2017 referendum went forward. The vote demonstrated how the Barzani leadership could use the KRG institutions to produce a crisis with the central government in Baghdad: with a reported turnout of 72.16 percent, the officially reported vote for independence showed 93.2 percent in favor. Within twenty days, the Baghdad government forces launched an attack on Kurdish positions in northern Iraq. With its armed victory in the north, the Baghdad government began to rake back some of the powers taken by the KRG during the period of central government paralysis.[14]

The vulnerability of decentralization to centripetal pressures in MENA states is suggested in the failure to preserve the separate institutions of Syria within the United Arab Republic (UAR) between 1958 and 1961 and of South Yemen within the Republic of Yemen after 1990. In the UAR, even though Egypt and Syria already possessed their own governing institutions, the newly unified common-state, according to Mustapha Kamil Al-Sayyid, moved toward "a single president, a central government, a single national assembly, a uniform political system based on the single mass organization and uniform economic policies with the extension of economic planning, agrarian reform, and nationalization of big private firms to

[12] B. O'Leary and K. Salih, "The Denial, Resurrection, and Affirmation of Kurdistan," in B. O'Leary, J. McGarry, and K. Salih (eds.), *The Future of Kurdistan in Iraq* (Philadelphia: University of Pennsylvania Press, 2005), 21.

[13] P. W. Galbraith, "Kurdistan in a Federal Iraq," in O'Leary, McGarry, and Salih, *The Future of Kurdistan in Iraq*, 268–81; O. Bengio, *The Kurds of Iraq: Building a State Within a State* (Boulder, CO: Lynne Rienner, 2012), 301–3.

[14] D. Zucchino, "Deadly Violence Erupts between Kurds and Iraqi Soldiers," *New York Times* (October 25, 2017); D. Zucchino, "Iraqi Forces Overpower Kurds, but a War of Words Still Rages," *New York Times* (October 23, 2017); A. Rafaat, *Kurdistan in Iraq: The Evolution of a Quasi-State* (New York: Routledge, 2018), 197–212.

the Syrian region."[15] Despite the original design of the UAR, as James Jankowski notes, the government reorganization on October 7, 1958, just seven months later, "reduced the status of the regional cabinets to administrative rather than policy-making bodies, centralized authority in Cairo and increased the central government's responsibility for policy-making in both regions of the UAR." Exactly a year after that, "Nasser placed overall authority for the supervision of the Syrian region of the UAR in the hands of Marshal 'Abd al-Hakim 'Amir." And then within the next year, Nasser's minister of interior in Syria, 'Abd al-Hamid Sarraj, came to exercise "primacy in the governance of the Syrian region."[16] Devolution was not considered seriously by Nasser; instead, in the words of Al-Sayyid, Nasser "treated anyone who expressed preference for the federal framework as a traitor."[17] Similarly, in the unification of North and South Yemen, "the old states constituted the nuclei for collective identity, based on unifying historical and cultural experiences," and they represented separate political traditions, ideologies, and institutions. Many of the institutions for regional autonomy within a federal arrangement were already in place. Nevertheless, the leaders of the united Republic of Yemen opted for a unitary state rather than either a federal union or regional autonomy for the South.[18]

The resistance to decentralization in the MENA states is reflected in Table 2.4, with comparative numbers on decentralization of decision-making authority to provincial ("first-order") and local governments. These show the percentage of governments that empowered provincial or local jurisdictions to select local leaders (as opposed to central appointment) and to set policy over spending, taxation, and human resources. The first three columns of numbers are the averages of annual averages for 2000 to 2015. The last five columns show snapshots for 2005 indicating the percentage of states in that year with particular forms of decentralization. The pattern is consistent: like many countries outside the Organisation for Economic Co-operation and Development countries, the constitutional orders in the Middle East and North Africa region tend to be centralized on most dimensions. Executive authority at both the provincial and local levels tends to form a hierarchical chain of command from central capital to locality. The decision-making authority of provincial governments over spending, taxing, and legislation is limited.[19] The authority

15 M. K. al-Sayyid, "The Rise and Fall of the United Arab Republic," in M. C. Hudson (ed.), *Middle East Dilemma: The Politics and Economics of Arab Integration* (New York: Columbia University Press, 1999), 118.

16 J. Jankowski, *Nasser's Egypt, Arab Nationalism, and the United Arab Republic* (Boulder, CO: Lynne Rienner, 2002), 119, 124, 128.

17 Al-Sayyid, "The Rise and Fall of the United Arab Republic," 123.

18 J. Kostiner, *Yemen: The Tortuous Quest for Unity, 1990–94* (London: The Royal Institute of International Affairs, 1996), 43. See also R. D. Burrowes, "The Republic of Yemen: The Politics of Unification and Civil War, 1989–1995," in Michael C. Hudson (ed.), *Middle East Dilemma: The Politics and Economics of Arab Integration* (New York: Columbia University Press, 1999), 187–213.

19 Based on Database of Political Institutions 2015 variables for STATE, MUNI, and AUTHOR; see C. Cruz, P. Keefer, and C. Scartascini, *Database of Political Institutions 2015* (2016).

TABLE 2.4 *Decentralization by global region, 2000–2015*

Region	Powers of First-Order Jurisdictions, 2000–2015 (percent)			Powers of Local Jurisdictions, 2005 (percent)				
	Elected legislature	Elected executive	Policy authority	Elected legislative	Elected executive	Spending authority	Taxation authority	HR authority
MENA	31	6	6	60	17	8	14	14
Adjacent regions								
Sahara	8	0	14	14	14	4	21	7
South Asia	32	11	22	43	22	5	31	31
Central Asia	50	0	0	60	0	38	0	25
Transcaucasus	67	0	0	67	33	11	33	100
Balkans	69	14	12	77	77	14	42	65
Non-adjacent regions								
Developing	38	17	13	45	30	15	28	26
OECD	84	51	39	79	64	23	77	79

Sources: Cruz, Keefer, and Scartascini, Database of Political Institutions 2015; Ivanyna and Shah, 'How Close is Your Government to the People?'. The figures are the percentages of countries in each region of the world. The figures under First-Order Jurisdictions show the regional averages of each country's annual average from 2000 to 2015. The figures under Local Governments show the percentages of countries in 2005 only.

of local governments to determine tax bases and set rates, and their discretion in hiring, firing, and setting terms of employment are more limited than in most other parts of the world.[20]

In sum, the histories of the independent states suggest that the usual challenges from center and periphery to the stability of decentralization arrangements are likely to be at least as strong in the MENA states as elsewhere. Decentralization will be a difficult path to initiate and will need special effort to sustain. There is little indication that many central governments will adopt or implement such arrangements on their own. And so far, decentralization has not led to stable institutional arrangements in the MENA region. The past is only cautionary, however, and should not preclude a serious consideration of the ways in which decentralization might be made more acceptable to central governments and more resistant to termination.

CAN DECENTRALIZATION BE DESIGNED FOR MENA CONTEXTS?

Containment of these centripetal and centrifugal pressures so as to preserve a constitutional order is addressed most directly through careful institutional design. Proponents of different institutional remedies have suggested that these can balance potentially competing identities, interests, and capabilities. In this logic, properly designed institutions create a political environment that accommodates both a common-state identity and separate community identities.[21] They enable responses to both shared and community-specific interests (such as both a common defense and community-specific education programs). They distribute powers so that both the common-state nation and its specific communities possess the capacity (powers and revenues) to govern in their respective policy domains.

If identity divides such as ethnicity or religion are institutionalized through decentralization, one potential danger is that they will they become the defining frame for all subsequent politics. If decentralization creates jurisdictions that deepen and strengthen community identities and loyalties at the expense of countrywide identities and loyalties, then citizens and politicians may find that they must choose between their common-state or their community. If this divide comes to define the alternatives in more and more policy domains, decision-making in the common-state can deadlock and more issues are postponed.

A parallel danger concerns fights over the allocation of powers. Can political institutions be designed so as to encourage the balanced development of both

[20] Based on Worldwide Indicators on Localization and Centralization variables for lgexpdec, lg_taxaut, and lg_hrpol; see M. Ivanyna and A. Shah, "How Close Is Your Government to the People? Worldwide Indicators on Localization and Decentralization" World Bank Policy Research Working Paper 6138 (Washington, DC: World Bank, 2012).

[21] The term "common-state" refers to the state that is "in common" to the majority and minority and subsumes any autonomous jurisdictions ("segment-states") that may exist within it.

common-state and community rather than escalating conflict between them? The institutions must empower both the common-state and communities to achieve their objectives, but those objectives often pull in opposite directions. On one side, governments of the common-state that are preoccupied by threats to national security and unity or committed to implementing a transformational agenda, such as Islamism, socialism, or pan-Arabism, often demand more centralization of powers. On the other side, members of communities concerned with identity issues in the narrowest sense often demand greater regional or local autonomy in cultural issues. More pragmatic members of the communities may demand greater regional authority to deliver jobs and funds to community members. And for those members who have developed nationalist programs, statehood for the homelands and self-rule may be the essential demand. Leaders seeking to build or retain their positions within the jurisdictions created by decentralization will typically demand more decentralization of those powers and revenues that enable them to deliver the results demanded by their communities' culturalists, pragmatists, and nationalists.[22] If the powers assigned the center and jurisdictions become weaponized and used to induce the other to concede, political disagreements over the allocation of decision-making are more likely to escalate in intensity and even undermine statehood, democracy, peace, and prosperity.[23]

Thus, the two most important design questions concern what types of jurisdictions to create and which powers to assign these jurisdictions. For central governments, each choice affects the ability to achieve its common-state goals. For communities, each choice impacts the development of community identities, response to local interests, and capabilities controlled by community leaders.

What Types of Jurisdictions?

Jurisdictions can be drawn along nonterritorial, homeland, subdivision, or multicultural lines.

Nonterritorial decentralization. Where a minority is not geographically concentrated in an identifiable homeland, but dispersed among other communities (for example, in heterogeneous urban centers) or across broad stretches of territory, nonterritorial autonomy can permit these communities to govern themselves in some policy domains. For example, separate court systems may enforce separate family law traditions within each community or separate education administrations may maintain minority language schools with curricula that preserve each community's cultural traditions. These

22 P. G. Roeder, *National Secession: Persuasion and Violence in Independence Campaigns* (Ithaca, NY: Cornell University Press, 2018), 71–73.

23 D. Rothchild and P. G. Roeder, "Power Sharing as an Impediment to Peace and Democracy," in P. G. Roeder and D. Rothchild (eds.), *Sustainable Peace: Power and Democracy after Civil Wars* (Ithaca, NY: Cornell University Press, 2005), 36–41; P. G. Roeder, *Where Nation-States Come from: Institutional Change in the Age of Nationalism* (Princeton: Princeton University Press, 2007).

parallel institutional hierarchies can coexist in the same cities and regions, where there are heterogeneous populations. The millet system in the Ottoman Empire is often cited as an early example of nonterritorial autonomy. The provisions for autonomous self-government within Lebanon's religious communities is sometimes portrayed as a modern extension of the millet system.[24] In some European states, corporatism has been extended to religious and ethnic minorities, so that, for example, the Netherlands' Calvinists and Catholics maintained parallel education systems. Nonterritorial institutions may complement territorial arrangements as in Belgium: communities for Flemish, German, and Walloon (French) populations were created alongside the ethnofederal arrangement for the Flemish, Walloon, and bilingual-capital regions. Although the Flemish regional authority was later united with the Flemish cultural community institutions, the Belgian Walloon experience suggests that where the community is not contained within an autonomous territory (for example, the French speakers living in the federal capital region), the ethnocorporatist institutions serve a specific need that the territorial governments may not provide so well.[25]

In the MENA region, nonterritorial autonomous jurisdictions might be appropriate for religious communities that do not have identifiable homelands or compact settlement patterns within their states, such as some Shi'a or Coptic communities. Similarly, ethnolinguistic minorities could govern themselves through nonterritorial jurisdictions where territorial boundaries are difficult to draw because ethnolinguistic minorities live in multiethnic urban centers, in homogeneous towns interspersed among settlements of other ethnic groups, or in remote locations dispersed across vast stretches, such as the Assyrians and Turkmen of Iraq, Bedouins in North Africa, and Berbers of the Oases in Algeria.

On the positive side of the ledger that suggests this could lead to a stable institutional arrangement, nonterritorial jurisdictions are compatible with strong central governments pressing to maintain national unity and less likely to isolate their communities or cultivate a particularistic identity that challenges the common-state nation. Nonterritorial administrations are better able than territorial administrations to enfranchise all members of a dispersed community while limiting their jurisdiction to just community members. They are typically limited to fewer policy domains than territorial administrations, because so many government services, such as water or police, are territorially based, and so leaders of community jurisdictions have fewer opportunities to create obstacles to countrywide policies. Nonterritorial administrations tend to command fewer capabilities, such as legislative powers or coercive agencies, and so they are much less likely to have the capabilities to escalate disputes with the central government to a point that threatens state failure.

24 A. Lijphart, *Democracy in Plural Societies: A Comparative Exploration* (New Haven: Yale University Press, 1977), 155.

25 K. Deschouwer, *The Politics of Belgium: Governing a Divided Society* (New York: Palgrave Macmillan, 2009), 61.

On the other side of the ledger that suggests an unstable arrangement, nonterritorial administrations are not as strong as territorial administrations in protecting their communities from assimilationist pressures and defending the cultural markers that identify a group. The more limited powers and policy domains of nonterritorial jurisdictions may leave them relatively defenseless against a predatory central government that seeks to end community autonomy. The limited powers of communities may not satisfy pragmatists within the community demanding a greater share of government services or the jobs that come with running those services. The nonterritorial jurisdiction is unlikely to satisfy nationalists who demand that their platform population have a state of its own.

Homeland autonomies. The autonomies may be territorial and with borders drawn to correspond to regions that cultural communities consider their homelands. In the MENA region, the Kurdish Regional Government is the clearest example of this, although the three states of Cyrenaica, Tripolitania, and Fezzan within the United Kingdom of Libya may have an element of this to the extent that these constituted sociocultural homelands.

Proposals for homeland autonomy are most commonly associated with regionally concentrated minorities such as the Kurds of Turkey, Iran, Iraq, and Syria; some Berber communities in Morocco and Algeria; and Sahrawis in Morocco. Iran could reasonably create ten segment states for Arabs, Azeris, Balochis, Gilakis, Luris, Mazanderanis, Qashqais, Talyshes, and Turkmen as well as the Kurds. Homeland autonomy might also be granted to substantial subtitular groupings in Egypt (Upper and Lower Egypt), Libya (Cyrenaica and Tripolitania), Oman (Dhofar and Central Oman), Saudi Arabia (Hejaz and Nejd), and Yemen (Aden, Hadhramaut, and North Yemen). Ronald Watts stresses the importance of this correspondence with homelands so as to achieve ethnic homogeneity within individual jurisdictions.[26]

On the positive side of the ledger, homeland administrations most fully express the aspiration of nationalists within each community for statehood without dissolving the common-state. These administrations possess the full powers of a territorial administration and so may be best equipped to preserve sociocultural identities and traditions within the part of the community residing within its borders.

On the other side of the ledger, compared to nonterritorial jurisdictions, homeland administrations may be less able to meet the needs of the parts of their community residing outside the officially sanctioned homeland. Homeland administrations may pose a greater threat to common-state unity. They may strengthen community identities inside the homelands at the expense of the common-state identity. They create opportunities for minority nationalists to secure positions of power from which to press their agendas to tear apart the common-state.[27] The enhanced

26 R. L. Watts, *Multicultural Societies and Federalism* (Ottawa: Information Canada, 1970), 86.

27 D. Lublin, *Minority Rules: Electoral Systems, Decentralization, and Ethnoregional Party Success* (New York: Oxford University Press, 2014), 237–8.

capabilities of the homeland administration create more opportunities for these nationalists to escalate conflicts with the common-state government. Some powers (such as representation in the common-state executive or legislature) may even be used to produce deadlock at the national level and so weaken the central government's response.

Subdivided homelands. The jurisdictions in territorial decentralization can, instead, be drawn so as to divide community homelands and grant autonomy to ethnically homogeneous subdivisions. This "cantonization," as it is sometimes called, permits members of the identity groups to foster cultural policies at the canton level, such as instruction in the local language in local schools, but creates obstacles to any common front by a united sociocultural community that may challenge the unity of the common-state.[28] Granting federal standing to the provinces of Dohuk, Erbil, and Sulaymaniyah and dissolving the KRG would be an application of this logic to the MENA region. The Swiss Confederation has divided the major linguistic and religious communities among multiple cantons: seventeen of Switzerland's twenty-six cantons are officially German-speaking, four French speaking, three bilingual (French and German), one Italian, and one tri-lingual (German, Italian, and Romansch).[29] After the failed secession of Biafra, Nigeria divided its three original segment states into smaller units and has continued to divide states as subethnic groups and smaller minorities have demanded states of their own. Thus, the Eastern State that became Biafra was divided into three states at the end of the war, and then into four states by 1976, five by 1989, seven by 1996, and nine by 2018.[30] Prior to the adoption of the homeland autonomy arrangement in Bosnia, the Carrington–Cutileiro plan proposed devolving central decision-making powers to the municipalities or cantons, each of which would be designated as a Bosniak, Croat, or Serb jurisdiction. This was rejected by the Bosnian Serbs who demanded a unified Bosnian Serb state to implement their community's agenda.[31]

On the positive side of the ledger, as these recent experiments suggest, these subdivided homelands can give expression to ever more localized sociocultural subdivisions. Cantonization creates obstacles to the consolidation of community-wide identity and its mobilization into politics in ways that might challenge the unity of the common-state. In Nigeria, for example, although the Biafra independence campaign continues, it no longer commands the resources of a Biafra-wide

[28] Ibid., 225–26, 271–91.

[29] T. Stauffer, N. Töpperwien, and U. Thalmann-Torres, "Switzerland (Swiss Confederation)," in A. L. Griffiths (ed.), *Handbook of Federal Countries* (Montreal: McGill-Queen's University Press, 2005), 342–56; A. Vatter, *Swiss Federalism: The Transformation of a Federal Model* (New York: Routledge, 2018).

[30] R. T. Suberu, *Federalism and Ethnic Conflict in Nigeria* (Washington, DC: United States Institute of Peace, 2001), 19–46.

[31] S. Woodward, *Balkan Tragedy: Chaos and Dissolution after the Cold War* (Washington, DC: The Brookings Institutions, 1995), 280–2.

administration to propagate this goal, and the boundaries of its proposed republic have become much less clear to its platform population and more contested by others.[32] Most importantly, the Biafra campaign does not now command the resources to hold a community-wide referendum, issue a declaration of independence implementing this, and mobilize an army within its claimed homeland. Cantonization encourages the expression of local interests that create political debates inside sociocultural communities. Subdivisions within one sociocultural community may unite with subdivisions from other communities to form policy coalitions in countrywide policy-making. The openness of a central government to creating new states can keep sociocultural divisions from becoming fixed political divisions.

On the other side of the ledger, typically leaders committed to the project of community solidarity resist the division of their homelands and platform populations. The smaller administrative units may not command the resources necessary to maintain cultural traditions and resist centralizing assimilation pressures. The smaller size and more limited capabilities may leave cantons more vulnerable to predation from a central government seeking to rake back powers.

Multicultural jurisdictions. Different sociocultural communities or parts of these can be combined to create multicultural jurisdictions. Where individual communities are too small to serve as the bases of an autonomous government, jurisdictions can be based on several communities. For example, Ethiopia's Southern Nations', Nationalities', and Peoples' Region includes over forty-five Indigenous communities, including seven that constitute over 5 percent of the region's population but none that tops 20 percent; this combination puts their shared jurisdiction on a par with the other ethnically based regions within the federation. Among dispersed minorities, subdivided homelands may be combined with subdivisions of other homelands to create multicultural jurisdictions with compact territories and contiguous populations of sufficient size to sustain a regional government. For example, the proposal to unite the parts of Iraq's Assyrian, Turkmen, and Yazidi communities living north of the KRG region into an Al-Rafidain Autonomous Region represents such a plan. The dispersed and small populations of the Assyrians, Turkmen, and Yazidis make subdivision and cross-ethnic unification a practical solution.

On the positive side of the ledger, the purported benefit of such multicultural jurisdictions is increased incentives to reach local compromises and to keep conflicts localized. Even where local intergroup conflicts resist compromise, the stakes are lower so that any negative impact on countrywide stability is limited. In countrywide politics, the pressures to work together against other regions in the competition for resources can create cross-community coalitions. Seymour Martin Lipset stressed the stabilizing effect of such crosscutting pressures created by multiethnic

[32] I. Johnson and A. Olaniyan, "The Politics of Renewed Quest for a Biafra Republic in Nigeria," *Defense and Security Analysis*, 33(4) (2017), 320–32 at 330.

jurisdictions.[33] In addition, multicultural leadership in these jurisdictions may block nationalists in the separate communities from using the powers of the jurisdiction against the common-state government. For example, the Soviet Union sought to limit the challenge from nationalists among the Circassians by dividing them among subgroups – Adygeis, Cherkesses, and Kabards. It also sought to contain the challenge from the Karachai-Balkar tribes by dividing them into separate Balkar and Karachai peoples. And then to check each of these, it united the subdivisions across linguistic lines into the multicultural jurisdictions of Karachai-Cherkessia and Karbadino-Balkaria – jurisdictions that united communities that had often been in competition with one another.

On the other side of the ledger, multicultural jurisdictions are unlikely to satisfy community leaders who seek a jurisdiction or independent state of their own. These jurisdictions are likely to be less effective at preserving and developing community cultures unless decision-making in the jurisdiction is further decentralized to the separate communities. And, as critics of the Soviet examples argued, multicultural jurisdictions are vulnerable to the divide-and-rule tactics of a common-state government that seeks to assimilate each community.[34]

What Powers to Regional Institutions?

Major institutional design choices affecting the powers of regional jurisdictions concern the selection and removal of regional leadership, the policy-making powers of regional governments, and the emergency powers of the central government to reverse regional decisions or even suspend regional decision-making processes. Agreement on the allocation of powers between the common-state and jurisdictions and the stability of any allocation will depend on how these powers impact the capacity of the common-state government and of culturalists, pragmatists, and nationalists within each community to achieve their goals.

Regional and local political accountability. Decentralization arrangements differ substantially in the extent to which they make regional and local office holders accountable to the local population or the central government. Although this is often thought of in terms of who elects the legislature and executive, it may be equally and perhaps more important to ask who can remove an incumbent: the performance of regional and local officials will be heavily influenced by the expectation that they will lose their office, if they fail to satisfy this principal who can remove them. The most extensive autonomy comes with local nomination and election of both the executive and legislative authorities plus local hiring of administrators, who are

[33] S. M. Lipset, *Political Man: The Social Bases of Politics* (Garden City: Doubleday, 1960), 91–92.

[34] D. L. Horowitz, *Ethnic Groups in Conflict* (Berkeley: University of California Press, 1985), 602, 619, 620, dismisses many of the arguments for and against multiethnic jurisdictions as dogma without sound empirical evidence based on comparison of multiple cases.

protected by limits on the central government's powers of removal except in extreme cases after judicial proceedings. For example, the Walloon Parliament in Belgium is elected by the citizens of the five provinces of the Walloon Region and its minister-president is elected by this parliament; there is no centrally appointed governor as even a symbolic representative of the center in the region. A more limited form of semi-autonomous governments provides for local election of the legislative council plus administrative devolution, but central appointment and termination of the executive authority (a prefect in many systems). For example, in India the centrally appointed governor in each state exercises a suspensive veto over (can "withhold assent" to) legislation by the state parliament, requiring the parliament to pass the legislation a second time.[35] In one-party states, such as China (and, formerly, the USSR), the party's first or second secretaries provide this central check on regional state officials that keeps them responsive to the central government's preferences.[36] Centralization just short of no local administrative apparatus at all is represented by what Lisbet Hooghe, Gary Marks, and Arjan Schakel identify with the Napoleonic label *déconcentration* – a thoroughly subordinate regional administration that has "the paraphernalia of self-governance … but is a central government outpost."[37]

Central governments often require regional and local executives and administrators to respond to a central chain of command. Yet, culturalists in the sociocultural communities often expect that only lawmakers chosen from and accountable to the identity group will adopt the appropriate policies to protect and foster local cultural traditions and institutions. Pragmatists who want expanded powers to allocate jobs and funds often demand that the legislature and executive that allocate these resources be responsible to local interests. For nationalists, locally constituted executive and legislative authority is a sine qua non of statehood. Reading the current sentiment within the platform population (and the balance among culturalists, pragmatists, and nationalists) may be essential to the long-term stability of institutions.

As Table 2.4 shows, many MENA states have a tradition of locally elected legislative bodies, but not at the level of first-order jurisdictions (provinces). And at both local and provincial levels MENA executives are much more likely to be centrally appointed. Any proposal for accountability of legislatures and executives to homelands will require building institutions de novo. A notable exception is the provision in the KRG for direct popular election of the Iraqi Kurdistan Parliament (IKP) and president and the selection of the Kurdistan prime minister by the IKP.

Policy-making powers. The policy domains controlled by regional and local administrations are typically distinguished into such categories as culture, education,

35 Constitution of India, Article 200.

36 S. Bialer, *Stalin's Successors: Leadership, Stability and Change in the Soviet Union* (New York: Cambridge University Press, 1980), 214–15; J. Miller, "Cadres Policy in Nationalities Areas" (1977) 29 *Soviet Studies* 1, 3–36.

37 L. Hooghe, G. Marks, and A. H. Schakel, *The Rise of Regional Authority: A Comparative Study of 42 Democracies* (New York: Routledge, 2010), 14.

social welfare, economics, and law and order. For many members of sociocultural communities, and particularly the culturalists, control of culture, education, and family policy often comes to play a prominent role in identity politics and the design of institutions must give them confidence that jurisdiction governments will be empowered to protect the community against majority assimilation.[38] For example, Belgium's Communities were originally assigned responsibility for language-related issues such as education, language usage, and media, but extended this to include youth, family, social welfare, and health policies. Yet, the pragmatists in the community may demand control over economic policy and the nationalists may demand control over law and order within their state. Thus, Belgium's regions expanded their reach so as to exercise an impressive array of powers, including economic regulation and development, employment, agriculture, housing, public works, energy, transport, environmental protection, and foreign trade.[39]

Community power in any specific policy domain may vary to the extent that the regional authorities can legislate, can only regulate, or must implement policies adopted at a higher level. Legislative authority, which may extend to one or many policy domains, is the ability to establish fundamental principles such as establishing a homeland educational system on the basis of the platform population's distinctive cultural traditions. Regulatory authority may be limited to amending or adding to policies adopted by the central government, such as deciding whether to add a required language course in homeland schools to a curriculum that is otherwise identical throughout the country. Administrative authority guarantees only that the implementers of centrally determined policies are drawn from the region's population, speak the same language as the local citizens, and perhaps observe some cultural sensitivities in the application of the centrally determined rules.[40]

As Table 2.4 shows, compared to most other regions of the world, the MENA states have given less policy authority to first-order jurisdictions (provinces). Local governments of a still lower order in the MENA region also have less fiscal independence in setting taxes or spending priorities. In short, decentralization to autonomous governments for the purposes of addressing identity conflicts will represent a break with MENA practices. The KRG once again offers an innovation toward much greater decentralization, but it also offers a cautionary note: the undefined allocation of responsibility for oil and national security has produced sharp clashes

38 R. L. Watts, "Multinational Federations in Comparative Perspective," in M. Burgess and J. Pinder (eds.), *Multinational Federations* (New York: Routledge, 2007), 235.

39 Deschouwer, *Politics of Belgium*, 54–7. Pragmatists in poorer homelands may object to decentralization without provision for greater local resources through subventions, particularly when any reduced role for the central government includes reduced inter-regional transfers. Thus, K. M. Bakke and E. Wibbels, "Diversity, Disparity, and Civil Conflict in Federal States" *World Politics*, 59 (2006), 1–50 at 3, find that, where ethnic groups are concentrated in regions, fiscal decentralization in the presence of interregional inequality increases the likelihood of ethnic rebellion and protest.

40 R. L. Watts, *Comparing Federal Systems*, 3rd ed. (Montreal: McGill-Queen's University Press, 2008), 83–93; Hooghe, Marks, and Schakel, *Rise of Regional Authority*, 14–22.

with the central government in Baghdad that could threaten the decentralization arrangement.[41] Around the world, such ambiguities in the allocation of powers often become the focus of conflict.

Central intervention. A critical institutional design choice is whether the central government may suspend regional government legislation and regulations without resort to an extraordinary procedure that entails approval by an independent agency such as a constitutional court. Central intervention limits regional autonomy and gives central governments leverage to deter regional governments from policies disfavored by the center. The power of central governments to suspend the regional government itself and rule directly is a still more powerful deterrent. For example, Article 356 of the Indian Constitution provides for President's Rule whereby "the center assumes the functions of the government of that state and can declare that the powers of the state legislature be exercised by the central parliament."[42] President's Rule must be approved and renewed every six months by both houses of the India Parliament, but has been invoked extensively: from 1951 to March 2016 it was invoked 115 times and as many as ten times in the troublesome minority region of Manipur alone.[43]

For culturalists and pragmatists in the sociocultural communities the central power to suspend self-rule and so to deter or reverse some policies may be seen as an obstacle to achieving their most important policy goals. For nationalists within these communities, this supremacy of the common-state government over the community goes to the heart of their claims to sovereignty and so may inspire strong resistance. For example, negotiations over the frozen conflicts of Abkhazia and Transdniestria have become deadlocked because the representatives of the breakaway regional governments have refused to concede that the Georgian and Moldovan governments will exercise such sovereign authority over them.[44]

The allocation of powers between central and regional governments can present a delicate balancing problem. A checks-and-balances arrangement seeks to empower both the center and regions to defend against predation by the other. Yet, the powers configured in this way can be weaponized to pressure the other side to submit to centripetal or centrifugal pressures. And an allocation whereby both sides block the other can result in policy deadlock, even in the face of mounting pressing problems. Certainly, Iraq's constitutional crisis of 2018 following the deadlock with Kurdistan is a cautionary tale. The solution to this dilemma may be finding a balance where essential government decision-making can proceed even during center–region deadlocks and where the defenders of the decentralization arrangement

[41] Rafaat, *Kurdistan in Iraq*, 197–212.

[42] K. Adeney, *Federalism and Ethnic Conflict Regulation in India and Pakistan* (New York: Palgrave Macmillan, 2007), 115.

[43] India Ministry of Home Affairs, "All You Need to Know about President's Rule," *The New Indian Express* (September 7, 2018).

[44] Roeder, *National Secession*, 139–40.

can always block centrifugal or centripetal challenges. This requires very careful constitutional design.

Finally, it should be noted that these discussions of institutional design limit their consideration of options to decentralization within the state, but this overlooks opportunities to decentralize many decision-making powers to individual citizens in civil society. The oldest democratic answer to decentralization in response to identity conflicts was the Anglo-American liberal solution that decentralized important decisions about culture (notably religion) from the governmental to the private sector.[45] The reliance on civil society has the virtue that it leaves to groups themselves to self-organize and permits them to evolve. In comparing this type of decentralization with alternative forms of power-sharing, Scott Gates and his collaborators find that only this type of "constraining power-sharing," as they label it, has "a pacific effect" that avoids civil wars by limiting the incentives for mass mobilization.[46]

HOW TO MAKE DECENTRALIZATION STABLE IN MENA STATES?

The balancing and checking of centripetal and centrifugal pressures to improve the odds that decentralization will survive is in part addressed by the proper selection and design of the institutions described in the previous section. For example, two-unit or binational federations may be particularly fragile. The examples of Belgium, Cameroon (until 1972), Czechoslovakia (until 1993), Pakistan (until 1971), and Serbia-Montenegro (until 2006) have been cited by authors as evidence of this.[47] The relative sizes of the units may be particularly important. John Pinder argues that no single state should be so large as to become a "hegemon" within the federation: "Either it will dominate the other states, which they are not likely to accept for any length of time, particularly if they include nations; or it will defer to them to an extent that its citizens are not likely to tolerate."[48] The failures of the West Indies Federation (dominated by Jamaica), Nigeria (dominated by Northern Nigeria

45 P. G. Roeder, "Power Dividing: The Multiple-Majorities Approach," in S. Wolff and C. Yakinthou (eds.), *Conflict Management in Divided Societies: Theories and Practice* (New York: Routledge, 2012), 66–83.

46 S. Gates, B. A. T. Graham, Y. Lupu, H. Strand, and K. W. Strom, "Power Sharing, Protection, and Peace," *Journal of Politics*, 78(2) (2016), 512–26 at 512; K. W. Strøm, S. Gates, B. A. T. Graham, and H. Strand, "Inclusion, Dispersion, and Constraint: Powersharing in the World's States, 1975–2010," *British Journal of Political Science*, 74(1) (2017), 165–85 at 173, define "constraining power sharing" as "a variety of institutions designed to protect the rights of individuals and social groups from encroachments and predation by, for example, politicians or armed forces."

47 J. McGarry and B. O'Leary, "Territorial Pluralism: Taxonomizing Its Forms, Virtues, and Flaws," in K. Basta, J. McGarry, and R. Simeon (eds.), *Territorial Pluralism: Managing Difference in Multinational States* (Vancouver: UBC Press, 2015), 13–53.

48 J. Pinder, "Multinational Federations: Introduction," in M. Burgess and J. Pinder (eds.), *Multinational Federations* (New York: Routledge, 2007), 8.

initially), and the USSR (dominated by the Russian Soviet Federative Socialist Republic) seem to confirm this claim. Alternatively, the states cannot be so small and underpowered that they cannot resist encroachment by the central government, and they cannot be so numerous that coordination among them to resist centripetal pressures becomes an intractable problem.[49]

The balancing of powers between center and periphery so that each can check predation by the other may create a knife-edge equilibrium that will unravel under the slightest exogenous shock. And so, it may require additional constitutional arrangements to reinforce the equilibrium.[50] Most common are provisions that make amendment of the decentralization arrangement difficult. Other proposals suggest embedding decentralization jurisdictions within a larger constitutional structure with either shared rule in the center, asymmetrical jurisdictions around the country, or power-dividing that limits the replication of the same sociocultural divides in every policy domain. Rarer are proposals for a third-party guarantor of the decentralization arrangement. Given the shocks that originate both outside the region and from within the region, these reinforcements of the equilibrium in any arrangement may be particularly important when decentralizing in the MENA states.

Limits on amendment. Unilateral power to rescind any allocation of decision rights and to reallocate powers is a potential threat to the long-term stability of decentralization. If the central legislature, executive, or judiciary can change the allocation of decision rights between center and periphery or can admit new jurisdictions and change the existing jurisdictions without the consent of existing jurisdictions, decentralization may give way to central hegemony. John McGarry and Brendan O'Leary warn that without provisions that require concurrent approval of such amendments by both the central and autonomous governments, the center may be able to take away rights and even abolish the autonomous jurisdictions.[51] The Northern Ireland Constitution Act of 1973 by which London terminated home rule in that region provided evidence that this threat is not simply imaginary. The 1998 Scotland Act and Northern Ireland Agreement both stipulate that London may change and even suspend institutions. In India, by the Jammu and Kashmir Reorganisation Act that went into effect October 31, 2019, the central legislature in Delhi unilaterally repealed the state's special autonomy status under Article 370 of India's Constitution, divided the state in two by creation of the jurisdiction of Ladakh, and reduced the constitutional status of both from state to union territory with more direct rule from the central government.[52]

49 Pinder, "Multinational Federations," 8; Watts, "Multinational Federations," 233.

50 P. G. Roeder, "Power Dividing as an Alternative to Ethnic Power Sharing," in P. G. Roeder and D. Rothchild, *Sustainable Peace*, 5861.

51 McGarry and O'Leary, "Territorial Pluralism," 16–20.

52 "The Jammu and Kashmir Reorganisation Act," *The Gazette of India* (August 9, 2019).

Stronger constitutional constraints on such unilateral amendments of decentralization institutions and on changes to the members of the federation reinforce the stability of the status quo.

Yet, in countries with limited traditions of constitutionalism, such as many MENA states, such constitutional provisions alone may be insufficient to protect decentralization arrangements. And inviolable barriers to amendment can become means to preserve privileged positions in the political order that block adaptations to changing conditions, such as the emergence of new identity communities demanding a voice in decision-making. Given the rapidly changing societies of the MENA region, high barriers to amendment may render specific decentralization arrangements quickly outdated.

Shared rule at the center. To limit the power of the central government to recentralize power, representatives of the regions may be included in central decision-making organs. Hooghe, Marks, and Schakel define this "shared rule" as "the capacity to co-determine the exercise of authority for the country as a whole."[53] This checks predation by the central government through the common action of regional representatives within the central organs. In addition, Watts argues that this participation in common federal decision-making may be essential to foster national unity among regions: "effective autonomous 'self-rule' by itself is insufficient. Institutions and processes for effective 'shared rule' have been equally essential in order to provide the glue to hold the different national groups within a federation together."[54]

Shared rule co-opts into central decision-making organs representatives of non-territorial communities, homeland populations, or jurisdiction governments. These provisions may assign seats within the central legislature, executive, judiciary, or administration to specific sociocultural communities. Thus, Lebanon's National Pact of 1943 allocated key leadership positions, including president (Maronite), prime minister (Sunni), legislative speaker (Shi'a), deputy prime minister (Eastern Orthodox), deputy speaker (Eastern Orthodox), and cabinet posts (proportionately among these). Or provisions may co-opt representatives of the governments of autonomous jurisdictions into a legislative chamber, a cabinet, or a supreme court that includes ex officio members of (or delegations appointed by) the corresponding organs of the communities' governments. Direct popular election from the homelands is a more common remedy: the upper house of the national legislature can be designated as a senate, federal council, or chamber of nationalities that gives proportionate or even equal representation to each autonomous jurisdiction. For example, the 2005 Iraqi Constitution provides for a federation council as the upper chamber of its parliament, but this has yet to be implemented. If this is

53 Hooghe, Marks, and Schakel, *Rise of Regional Authority*, 6.

54 Watts, "Multinational Federations," 231; also see Watts, *Multicultural Societies and Federalism*, 87.

in fact implemented, the Iraqi Federation Council will be a bold innovation in the MENA region. Compared to other regions, MENA states are much less likely to grant representation of first-order jurisdictions in an upper chamber. Indeed, between 2000 and 2015 only Tunisia maintained such a chamber. The Chamber of Advisors included representatives of the governorates alongside representatives of professional organizations and prominent national leaders, until the 2011 Revolution dissolved this chamber.

The literature on institutional decentralization in deeply divided societies began with claims that a key to democratic unity among communities is a grand coalition of leaders from all major communities. Under the label "consociationalism," Arend Lijphart argued that the guiding rule in institutional design should be that on all matters of common concern to all communities they should be included in decision-making proportionately at the center, but on all other matters they should be left to decide for themselves locally.[55] In subsequent writings, Lijphart substituted the term "power-sharing democracy" for consociationalism, but the essential elements of his model remained the same – grand coalitions of all communities in the central government, mutual vetoes at the center, proportionality in the allocation of central government offices and resources, and segmental autonomy or federalism.[56] Like Eric Nordlinger, Lijphart saw this grand coalition as the key element for balancing and keeping in check the competing centripetal and centrifugal pressures.[57]

Yet, to the extent that these councils dominate policy-making, they may tend to turn every policy issue at the center into another dimension of the overarching conflict among sociocultural communities. And the empowerment of community representatives in the central government can lead to deadlocked decision-making and the weaponization of deadlock (including threats of deadlock) to induce the other side to concede. To avoid the knife-edge equilibrium where central powers and periphery powers check one another, Roeder proposes a constitutional arrangement that he labeled power-dividing or the multiple-majorities constitution. In this arrangement, decision-making is divided among separate independent institutions at the common-state, regional, and local levels; policy-making at the regional level is parceled among different overlapping jurisdictions limited to specific policy domains; and the rules of representation increase the likelihood of different (often

55 Lijphart, *Democracy in Plural Societies*, 41.

56 A. Lijphart, "Multiethnic Democracy," in S. M. Lipset (ed.), *The Encyclopedia of Democracy* (Washington, DC: Congressional Quarterly, 1995), vol. 3, 853–65; A. Lijphart, "The Wave of Power-Sharing Democracy," in A. Reynolds (ed.), *The Architecture of Democracy: Institutional Design, Conflict Management, and Democracy in the Late Twentieth Century* (New York: Oxford University Press, 2002), 37–54.

57 E. A. Nordlinger, *Conflict Regulation in Divided Societies.* (Cambridge, MA: Harvard University Center for International Affairs, 1972), 21–33.

noncultural) divisions emerging in each institution. Thus, members of each sociocultural community, who may be unified in one body where sociocultural policy is decided, are likely to ally in other bodies with members of other sociocultural communities based on some noncultural shared interest.[58]

Asymmetry among jurisdictions. To contain the centrifugal pressures of ethnofederalism, some analysts propose embedding autonomy for sociocultural communities within a larger pattern of territorial jurisdictions that vary between majority- and minority-dominated areas. The term ethnofederalism has come to refer to constitutional orders like the Soviet Union and Yugoslavia that divide the entire expanse of their territories into constitutionally equal jurisdictions such as Ukraine and Croatia and with one of these reserved for the majority population – Russia and Serbia respectively. Valerie Bunce, Carol Skalnik Leff, and Roeder have each stressed the fragile nature of such arrangements.[59]

Henry Hale amends the ethnofederalism argument to suggest that the most dangerous feature in these constitutions was a single core ethnic region, such as Russia or Serbia, with "dramatic superiority in population." This arrangement is likely to bring collapse following conflict between this region and the federal government.[60] Hale proposes that ethnofederalism can be made more stable by dividing the majority's homeland into multiple units but assigning these the same rights as the minority homelands. Thus, under the 1993 Russian Constitution, the oblasts with Russian majorities are subjects of the federation equal in standing to the republics based on ethnic minorities.[61] Eight countries have attempted this, in addition to Iraq, where the 2005 Constitution promises this arrangement when fully implemented. They have, indeed, avoided challenges from hegemonic majority-based regional governments. Thus, partial ethnofederalism is more likely to endure than full ethnofederalism, but this has not protected partial ethnofederations from other challenges, including secessionist violence.

An alternative form of asymmetry is to create autonomous jurisdictions not for the majority but only the minorities. McGarry and O'Leary assign the label "federacy" to states in which only parts of the state territory are recognized as autonomous

58 Roeder, "Power Dividing as an Alternative"; Roeder, "Power Dividing Multiple-Majorities Approach."

59 V. Bunce, *Subversive Institutions: The Design and the Destruction of Socialism and the State* (Cambridge: Cambridge University Press, 1999); C. Skalnik Leff, "Democratization and Disintegration: Federalism and the Break-up of the Communist Federal States," *World Politics*, 51(2) (1999), 205–35; P. G. Roeder, "Soviet Federalism and Ethnic Mobilization," *World Politics*, 43(2) (1991), 196–232; P. G. Roeder, "Peoples and States after 1989: The Political Costs of Incomplete National Revolutions," *Slavic Review*, 58(4) (1999), 854–82; G. Roeder, "Ethnofederalism and the Mismanagement of Conflicting Nationalisms," *Regional and Federal Studies*, 19(2) (2009), 203–19.

60 H. E. Hale, "Divided We Stand: Institutional Sources of Ethnofederal State Survival and Collapse," *World Politics*, 56(2) (2004), 165–93 at 166.

61 Hale, "Divided We Stand," 166–67.

regions.[62] The Aland Islands in Finland, home to a Swedish population, constitute the classic example, but such arrangements have existed in some twenty-four countries since 1945. The current de facto arrangement with the Kurdish Regional Government in Iraq is a MENA example, but this is supposed to become part of a de jure partial ethnofederal arrangement once the 2005 Iraq Constitution is fully implemented. O'Leary identifies federacy as the best arrangement, but Watts warns that experiments with giving some provinces more powers than others have exacerbated rather than reduced tensions: "Consequently, in these federations there has usually followed either an attempt to reduce differences among provinces in their degree of autonomy, or the eventual secession of the more autonomous units."[63] This danger seems to have been confirmed in the past decade by support for independence by over 98 percent of voters in both the 2011 South Sudan and the 2019 Bougainville referenda.

Watts suggests that there is no clear relationship between asymmetry and federal stability: asymmetry can both accommodate and exacerbate tensions and so getting the institutional design just right for the particular country is key.[64] Thomas Christin and Simon Hug cut through these debates about symmetry and argue that all forms of autonomy "where regional borders follow as closely as possible settlement patterns of minorities" are "particularly conflict-prone." Stability, they find, depends on the portion of the subnational jurisdictions controlled by ethnic minorities: the likelihood of violence is lower where there are fewer jurisdictions controlled by minorities.[65]

International guarantors. Where centripetal and centrifugal pressures pushing a decentralization arrangement in opposite directions are particularly strong, some external power may be necessary to keep these in check. The arrangements in Bosnia and Iraq may confirm this. Under the Dayton Accords, the high representative for Bosnia and Herzegovina, selected by the international Peace Implementation Council, is empowered to remove Bosnian officials who violate legal norms, to vet candidates for ministerial posts, and to decree policy when Bosnian officials are unable to reach agreement. This prevents the jurisdictional entities from seceding and the central government from collapsing under perpetual deadlock.[66] Similarly, the role of the United States in keeping the KRG

62 McGarry and O'Leary, "Territorial Pluralism," 26–27.

63 Watts, *Multicultural Societies and Federalism*, 86. Also see Roeder, *Where Nation-States Come from*, 192.

64 Watts, *Multicultural Societies and Federalism*, 236.

65 T. Christin and S. Hug, "Federalism, the Geographic Location of Groups, and Conflict," *Conflict Management and Peace Science*, 29(1) (2012), 93–122 at 93, 96, 117.

66 S. Bose, *Bosnia after Dayton: Nationalist Partition and International Intervention* (New York: Oxford University Press, 2002), 275–77; C. Bennett, *Bosnia's Paralyzed Peace* (New York: Oxford University Press, 2016).

from seceding from Iraq and keeping the Baghdad Government from pressing its military advantage to crush the KRG has been essential to the balance between centrifugal and centripetal forces.[67]

In designing institutional arrangements for collapsing or failed states, Stephen Krasner has suggested that the options should include both "de facto trusteeship" that places central governments under international supervision and "shared sovereignty" that engages foreign powers in making decisions in key policy domains.[68] This may be particularly important for the MENA states that face strong pressures – originating both from outside and inside the region – that can overburden any decentralization arrangements. In the MENA region, the United States has played this role in Iraq. Who, if anyone, could play this role in identity conflicts in Iran, Syria, Turkey, and elsewhere remains to be seen. To avoid the stigma of great power neocolonialism, the role of external guarantor might be played by interim administration missions of the United Nations or regional organizations such as the Arab League or the Organization of Islamic Cooperation. Yet, even this international constraint on the sovereignty of MENA common-states might encounter strong resistance throughout the region.

A CAUTIOUS CONCLUSION

Institutional decentralization that brings government closer to the citizens can be a powerful tool for furthering democracy and unleashing local innovations that express the manifold diversities within a country's population. Few raised in the liberal democratic tradition would dispute that these are goals worth pursuing. This has led to broad hope that governmental decentralization to sociocultural communities might be the best remedy to the many challenges associated with potential or realized identity conflicts. The evidence from real-world experiments that have gone before show that designing sustainable decentralization institutions to resolve identity conflicts is a complex undertaking. The few exemplary successes may well suggest that, while decentralization to accommodate sociocultural diversity in MENA countries is an undertaking with high risk of failure, the benefits of success are worth the risk. At the same time, the failures alongside the successes underscore that there is no simple road map that can be imported from other regions to guide institution builders throughout the MENA region. The devil may truly be in the details of institutional design and their ability to accommodate the specific patterns of diversity in each country's population.

67 Zucchino, "Iraqi Forces Retake all Oil Fields"; *Rafaat, Kurdistan in Iraq*, 197–212.

68 S. D. Krasner, "Sharing Sovereignty: New Institutions for Collapsed and Failing States," *International Security*, 29(2) (2004), 85–120 at 105–8.

APPENDIX TABLE 1 *Sociocultural divisions by country*

COUNTRY Titular Ethnolinguistic Group (percent)	Subtitular Ethnolinguistic Groups (percent)	Indigenous Ethnolinguistic Groups (percent)	Expatriate Ethnolinguistic Groups (percent)	Religious Groups (percent)
Algeria Algerian Arabs (68.0)		30.9 Bedouins (6.3) Berbers (24.4)	1.1	Sunnis (99.0)
Bahrain Bahraini Arabs (54.5)		0.0	45.5 South Asians (14.7) Persians (13.1) Other Arabs (9.8) Kurds (3.5) Filipinos (2.0) British (1.5)	Shi'is (38.3) Sunni (32.0) Christians (14.5) Hindus (9.8) Buddhists (2.5)
Egypt Egyptian Arabs (83.7)	Lower Egyptians (60.1) Saidis (23.6)	2.8 Bedouins (2.2)	13.5 Sudanese (4.7) Roma (2.1) Algerians (1.7) Moroccans (1.7) Gulf Arabs (1.6)	Sunnis (88.0) Copts (9.0) Shi'is (2.0)
Iran Persians (45.1)		51.0 Azeris (19.8) Kurds (8.7) Luris (3.5) Gilakis (3.5) Mazanderani (2.9) Iranian Arabs (1.7) Bakhtiaris (1.5) Balochi (1.5)	3.9	Shi'is (91.9) Sunnis (7.5)

Continued

Appendix Table 1 Continued

COUNTRY Titular Ethnolinguistic Group (percent)	Subtitular Ethnolinguistic Groups (percent)	Indigenous Ethnolinguistic Groups (percent)	Expatriate Ethnolinguistic Groups (percent)	Religious Groups (percent)
IRAQ		24.4 Kurds (21.6)	9.9	Shi'is (64.1)
Iraqi Arabs (65.7)	Baghdadis (39.6)		Azerbaijanis (6.0)	Sunnis (31.5)
	Northerners (21.7)		Turkmen (1.2)	Yazidis (2.4)
	Najdis (4.3)		Egyptians (1.2)	Christians (1.0)
			Persians (1.2)	
JORDAN		0.4	43.6	Sunnis (97.0)
Jordanian Arabs (57.0)	Levantine (42.2)		Palestinians (28.4)	Eastern Orthodox (2.0)
	Bedouins (13.8)		Syrians (6.3)	
	Najdis (1.0)		Iraqis (4.1)	
			Kabardinians (1.5)	
KUWAIT		0.0	67.9	Sunnis (43.7)
Kuwaiti Arabs (32.1)			South Asians (31.8)	Shi'is (26.2)
			Egyptians (9.6)	Christians (16.7)
			Saudis (6.1)	Hindus (8.4)
			Filipinos (4.3)	Buddhists (2.8)
			Syrians (3.9)	
			Ethiopians (2.2)	
			Arabized Blacks (1.6)	
			Lebanese (1.3)	
			Persians (1.3)	
LEBANON		0.0	28.7	Sunnis (27.0)
Lebanese Arabs (71.3)			Palestinians (9.5)	Shi'is (27.0)
			Syrians (5.3)	Maronites (21.0)
			Kurds (4.8)	Greek Orthodox (8.0)
			Armenians (3.2)	Druze (6.5)

			Egyptians (1.5) Bedouins (1.0)	Greek Catholics (5.0) Armenians (3.0)
Libya Libyan Arabs (54.3)	Cyrenaicans (25.4) Tripolitanians (28.9)	19.7 Bedouins (14.3) Berbers (5.3)	26.0 Egyptians (8.0) Algerians (4.4) Sudanese (3.6) Tunisians (3.0) Punjabi (1.0)	Sunnis (94.1) Christians (2.7) Shi'is (2.5)
Morocco and Western Sahara Moroccan Arabs (52.0)		33.8 Berbers (27.2) Jebala (3.4) Saharawis (1.1)	14.2 Algerians (12.7) Lebanese (1.5)	Sunnis (99.0)
Oman Omani Arabs (45.5)	Omanis (43.1) Dhofaris (2.4)	4.9 Mahris (1.8) Shaharis (1.1)	49.4 Gulf Arabs (15.5) South Asians (13.9) Balochis (13.7) Persians (1.3) Swahilis (1.0)	Sunnis (38.7) Ibadhis (38.7) Christians (6.5) Hindus (5.5) Shi'is (4.3)
Qatar Qatari Arabs (18.4)		0.0	81.6 Palestinians (13.5) South Asians (12.3) Lebanese (10.5) Persians (10.1) Arabized Blacks (9.6) Syrians (9.5) Filipinos (4.5) Saudis (3.0) Egyptians (2.0) Sudanese (2.0) Balochis (2.0)	Sunnis (60.7) Christians (13.8) Hindus (13.8) Shi'is (7.0) Buddhists (3.1)

Continued

Appendix Table 1 Continued

COUNTRY Titular Ethnolinguistic Group (percent)	Subtitular Ethnolinguistic Groups (percent)	Indigenous Ethnolinguistic Groups (percent)	Expatriate Ethnolinguistic Groups (percent)	Religious Groups (percent)
Saudi Arabia		3.9	21.7	Sunnis (87.0)
Saudi Arabs (74.4)	Hijazis (31.0)	Bedouins (3.9)	South Asians (7.4)	Shi'is (12.0)
	Najdis (40.5)		Filipinos (2.8)	
	Gulf Arabic (2.9)		Egyptians (1.8)	
			Yemenis (1.5)	
			Palestinians (1.2)	
			Swahilis (1.2)	
			Lebanese (1.0)	
Syria		11.8	6.8	Sunnis (74.0)
Syrian Arabs (81.4)	Levantine (73.4)	Kurds (8.4)	Palestinians (2.6)	Shi'is (13.0)
	Najdi (7.4)			Eastern Orthodox (4.6)
				Druze (3.0)
				Oriental Orthodox (2.2)
				Catholics (1.6)
				Armenians (1.1)
Tunisia		0.04	7.86	Sunnis (99.0)
Tunisian Arabs (92.1)			Algerians (2.4)	
			Libyans (4.4)	
Turkey		26.7	4.3	Sunnis (99.0)
Turks (69.0)		Kurds (20.4)	Kabardinians (1.4)	
		Arabs (3.5)		

UAE		8.5	68.8	Sunnis (64.6)
Emirati Arabs (22.7)		Bedouins (8.3)	South Asians (31.8)	Shi'is (11.4)
			Pashtuns (7.7)	Christians (9.0)
			Balochis (5.2)	Hindus (7.0)
			Egyptians (4.3)	Buddhists (5.0)
			Persians (3.8)	
			Omanis (3.5)	
			Nepali (1.7)	
			Saudis (1.5)	
			Somalis (1.4)	
			Jordanians (1.0)	
			Hazara (1.0)	
Yemen		0.9	14.2	Sunnis (65.0)
Yemeni Arabs (84.9)	Sanaani (42.5)		Arabized Blacks (5.1)	Shi'is (35.0)
	Ta'issi-Adeni (22.2)		Somalis (4.0)	
	Tihami (14.8)		Sudanese (1.8)	
	Hadrami (5.3)		South Asians (1.1)	

Sources: Joshua Project; Simons and Fennig, Ethnologue; U.S. Central Intelligence Agency, World Factbook.
The listed groups are from the sources and report conventionalizations that emerge through social practice within each country. Grouping and labelling practices vary among countries. Only sociocultural communities that constitute 1 percent or more of the country's population are listed.

3

Devolution and the Promotion (or Evasion) of Minority Rights

Will Kymlicka

In the Middle East, as in the rest of the world, a wide range of ethnonational groups have struggled for various forms of autonomy or self-government. As Walker Connor notes, this is a ubiquitous phenomenon, affecting certain countries:

> [I]n Africa (for example, Ethiopia), Asia (Sri Lanka), Eastern Europe (Romania), Western Europe (France), North America (Guatemala), South America (Guyana) and Oceania (New Zealand). The list includes countries that are old (United Kingdom) as well as new (Bangladesh), large (Indonesia) as well as small (Fiji), rich (Canada) as well as poor (Pakistan), authoritarian (Sudan) as well as democratic (Belgium), Marxist-Leninist (China) as well as militantly anti-Marxist (Turkey). The list also includes countries which are Buddhist (Burma), Christian (Spain), Moslem (Iran), Hindu (India) and Judaic (Israel).[1]

Given their ubiquity, minority aspirations for self-government could well be seen as a normal and predictable feature of contemporary politics. Unfortunately, these aspirations are instead widely seen as abnormal, and indeed as an existential threat to normal politics. They are seen at best as regrettable and outmoded forms of "tribalism," and at worst as destabilizing sources of disloyalty and conflict. Nation-states have therefore been very reluctant to accept minority demands for autonomy. Indeed, in many countries the very idea of "group rights," "ethnic autonomies," or "ethnic federalism" is considered toxic and taboo, and states actively inhibit any attempt to discuss these issues freely, or to mobilize politically for such demands.

Yet these demands are not disappearing and attempts to suppress these aspirations often simply worsen the problem, exacerbating distrust and conflict between the state and minorities. Attempts to "solve" the minority problem by coercive assimilation, expulsion, or demographic engineering are neither legitimate nor effective. As a result, an increasing number of commentators around the world

[1] W. Connor, "National Self-determination and Tomorrow's Political Map," in A. Cairns (ed.), *Citizenship, Diversity and Pluralism* (Montreal: McGill-Queen's University Press, 1999), 163–4.

are accepting, grudgingly, that there may be no alternative but to accommodate minority aspirations for autonomy.[2]

So we are in the somewhat paradoxical situation where minority autonomy seems both impossible and inevitable. In many countries it cannot be openly discussed, but there may be no credible alternative to it. Under these circumstances, I would argue that the first step must be to create more space for the public discussion of these claims, to enable members of minority groups to explain publicly their aspirations for autonomy and the hopes and fears that underpin them. We need to make these claims legible to the larger society, so that they can be discussed reasonably, in the hope of developing an overlapping consensus in society on appropriate forms of, and limits on, autonomy. We need, in short, to remove minority autonomy from the "taboo" category, as a first step toward a sustainable response to state–minority conflicts.[3]

Some commentators, however, have argued that the question of minority autonomy is too toxic to address directly, and that we need therefore to find a more indirect way of addressing minority aspirations. These commentators would like to find a way of reforming the state that de facto will make greater room for a plurality of cultures and identities but that avoids any explicit mention of, or tie to, ethnonational autonomy.

One popular proposal in this regard is the idea of decentralization or devolution, understood as a countrywide process that shifts power from the central state to lower levels of government, such as regions, provinces, cantons, or even municipalities. For many proponents, this provides a neat way of finessing claims to minority autonomy. Rather than creating a special or exceptional ethnic autonomy for the Kurds in the north of Syria, for example, we might instead promote a general process of decentralization or devolution across the country as a whole. Insofar as Kurds are a small minority in the country as a whole but a majority or plurality in parts of the north, they will de facto benefit from having power moved from the center to regions or municipalities. But the framework of devolution need not make any explicit mention of Kurds, or any other ethnic group. Devolution would be framed as a desirable policy for all Syrian citizens and would be applied in a consistent way across the country. This model thereby tacitly and indirectly enables some degree of minority autonomy without having to officially endorse any idea of group rights, and without having to institutionalize ethnic differences.

We see versions of this idea surfacing around the world, often championed by international organizations. Generalized decentralization or devolution is seen as

[2] On the global trends toward autonomy, see W. Kymlicka, *Multicultural Odysseys: Navigating the New International Politics of Diversity* (Oxford: Oxford University Press, 2007).

[3] I develop this argument in reference to postcommunist eastern Europe in W. Kymlicka, "Justice and Security in the Accommodation of Minority Nationalism: Comparing East and West," in A. Dieckhoff (ed.), *The Politics of Belonging: Nationalism, Liberalism and Pluralism* (New York: Lexington, 2004), 127–54.

a way of deescalating state–minority conflicts. It gives territorially concentrated minorities some genuine power to protect their languages, cultures, and habitats, and so assuages their fears of being the targets of state oppression or majoritarian tyranny. But it does so in a way that avoids appeal to controversial ideas of ethnic group rights or ethnic autonomy, and thereby helps assuage the fears of the state. Creating a one-off ethnic autonomy for the Kurds in the north of Syria could be seen as implying that this territory does not fully belong to Syria, and that Kurds have rights over themselves and their territory that are different from those of other Syrian citizens. It is therefore seen as a potential stepping stone to secession. By contrast, generalized devolution does not recognize rights of ethnic self-government of the sort that can lead to secession. Generalized devolution provides the substance of minority protection without the overheated rhetoric of minority group rights. Or put another way, generalized devolution indirectly provides a level of minority protection without directly challenging the toxic and taboo character of minority rights claims.

Despite the popularity of this approach, I am skeptical that it can succeed. The basic problem is quite simple: decentralization as such is not inherently empowering of minorities. Whether decentralization empowers minorities depends on the details, in particular details about where the boundaries of the decentralized units are drawn and how powers are allocated between different levels of government. It is entirely possible – indeed, all too common – for these decisions to be made in a way that in fact is deliberately *disempowering* of minorities. I discuss some examples in this chapter.

To be sure, there are ways of drawing internal boundaries and dividing powers so as to empower minorities. But this requires conscious attention to the needs of minorities in the process of decentralization, and this is precisely what is precluded when the very discussion of minority aspirations is toxic and taboo. As a result, I am skeptical that we can finesse claims to minority self-government through generalized decentralization. Minority rights claims need to be examined on their own terms, as a response to the distinctive needs and aspirations of ethnonational groups who find themselves as minorities within a larger nation-state, rather than trying to finesse them as an indirect by-product of generalized decentralization. And this requires overcoming the taboo on discussing minority rights.

If this is right, then we are left with a difficult challenge: how do we overcome the taboo nature of minority rights claims? I cannot offer a complete answer here, but I conclude with some reflections on the crucial role that national identities play in this regard.

THE "MINORITY PROBLEM"

In order to understand the limits of generalized decentralization as a strategy for addressing minority claims, we need to step back and consider why minorities and minority claims are so often seen as a "problem." As many scholars have noted, this is a distinctly modern perception, tied to the rise of the nation-state. Indeed, the rise of the nation-state has often been catastrophic for ethnic and religious minorities. Consider the Balkans and the Middle East. For some 1,500 years, a panoply of ethnic, linguistic, and religious communities lived side by side under both the Byzantine and Ottoman empires. Yet ever since these empires were replaced with nation-states, we have witnessed a terrible "unmixing of peoples," due to civil wars, ethnic cleansing, genocide, and forced assimilation. Intercommunal relations of tolerance and conviviality that had survived for centuries were torn apart in a few short decades under the nation-state.[4]

These conflicts are often described as evidence of "ancient ethnic hatreds," but in fact they are the result of the rise of the modern nation-state, whose very logic turns "minorities" into a "problem." It is worth noting that none of the ethnic or religious groups in the Byzantine and Ottoman empires were considered "minorities," in part because there was no "majority." These empires did not rule in the name of a particular majority nation, but rather ruled as a dynasty over all their diverse subjects. These multiethnic dynastic empires have now been swept away by the rise of nation-states, each of which claims to rule in the name of a particular people or nation. (What was once the territory of the Ottoman Empire now comprises forty-three such nation-states.) Romania, for example, gained independence in the name of the self-determination of the Romanian nation. The Romanian people were seen as having a legitimate right to govern themselves and their national territory, and the Romanian state is the means through which the Romanian people exercise those legitimate aspirations. And the creation of a Romanian nation-state meant, inevitably, the creation of minorities – namely, all those living on the territory of the Romanian state at the time of independence who were not seen as members of the Romanian nation, such as the ethnic Hungarians and Ukrainians.[5]

This new status – being a minority within someone else's nation-state – has proven to be precarious. Minorities pose a persistent existential threat to state legitimacy. Each nation-state's claim to sovereignty flows from the claim that it represents "the people" in whose name it governs. It is therefore destabilizing of a state's legitimacy to have a group within the boundaries of the state who think of themselves as

4 On the unmixing of peoples in the transition from empires to nation-states see R. Brubaker, "Aftermaths of Empire and the Unmixing of Peoples," *Ethnic and Racial Studies*, 18(2) (1995), 189–218.

5 It is common in the international law literature to distinguish "minorities" present at the time of independence, from "migrants" who enter a country after its independence. Migrants are assumed to understand that they are entering a state as foreigners. Minorities, by contrast, wake up one day to find themselves within someone else's state due to the way international boundaries are drawn at the time of independence. Whether this distinction between minorities and migrants is morally significant is a source of debate, see R. Medda-Windischer, *Old and New Minorities: Reconciling Diversity and Cohesion* (Baden-Baden: Nomos, 2009). However, I focus on minorities in the traditional sense of groups present on the territory of the state when it gains independence.

forming or belonging to a distinct people. If the boundaries of Romania incorporate territory that is traditionally settled by Hungarians or Ukrainians, and is part of the historic homeland of the Hungarian and Ukrainian people, what gives Romania the right to rule those inhabitants and those territories?

Minorities, therefore, are a "problem" in a world of nation-states: they pose a challenge to a nation-state's legitimacy. Virtually all countries around the world face some version of this challenge – the state governs in the name of a particular people but includes communities and territory that could be seen as belonging to another people or nation.[6] As a result, minorities are "marked" citizens: they don't fully belong to the nation, and may be deemed presumptively disloyal.[7] This is particularly true where minorities share an ethnic identity with a neighboring state, such as the Arabs in Israel, or where they have historic ties to imperial powers, such as the Copts in Egypt. They are often assumed to be a fifth column whose true loyalty lies elsewhere.[8]

From the beginning of the era of nation-states, therefore, the minority question has been a concern, primarily for realpolitik reasons. And until quite recently, states granted each other wide latitude in how they dealt with this problem. Since minorities were a stain on state legitimacy, and a potential threat to interstate peace, the obvious solution was to eliminate, or at least to weaken, these minorities. And if necessary, coercive means could be employed to achieve this, including expulsions, population exchanges, other forms of demographic engineering (e.g., encouraging large numbers of the majority group to settle in the minority's homeland), or forced assimilation.[9]

6 Consider New World states in the Americas. These states are the products of settler colonialism, built on the lands of Indigenous peoples. What gives settler states the right to rule over Indigenous peoples and their historic homelands?

7 On minorities as "marked citizens" in the Middle East, see J. Klein, "The Minority Question: A View from History and the Kurdish Periphery," in W. Kymlicka and E. Pföstl (eds.), *Multiculturalism and Minority Rights in the Arab World* (Oxford: Oxford University Press, 2014), 27–52. Historians and anthropologists of the region rightly emphasize that this should be seen not as the product of ancient animosities, or as something intrinsic to Arab culture or Islamic religion, but rather as a product of the imperatives of colonial administration and postcolonial nation-building (e.g., G. B. Büyüksaraç and J. Glasser, "Introduction to the Special Issue: Inhabiting the Margins: Middle Eastern Minorities Revisited," *Anthropological Quarterly*, 90(1) (2017), 5–16; J. Gorgas and B. White, "Introduction to Special Issue: The Fragments Imagine the Nation? Minorities in the Modern Middle East and North Africa," *British Journal of Middle Eastern Studies*, 43(2) (2016), 135–39.

8 As Picard puts it, speaking of the Middle East, "[i]n the past, communal groups opposed to the government were suspected of collusion with European powers; now they are accused of being 'agents' of Israel and the United States. Instead of being part of the legitimate political game, protestation by minorities became stigmatized as manipulation by the West and Israel, and repressed through land confiscation, restriction of public expression, and heavy security rules." (E. Picard, "Nation-Building and Minority Rights in the Middle East," in A. N. Longva and A. S. Roald (eds.), *Religious Minorities in the Middle East: Domination, Self-empowerment, Accommodation* (Leiden: Brill, 2012), 339.

9 On demographic engineering to disempower minorities, see J. McGarry, "Demographic Engineering: The State-Directed Movement of Ethnic Groups as a Technique of Conflict Regulation," *Ethnic and Racial Studies*, 21(4) (1998), 613–38; and P. Morland, *Demographic Engineering: Population Strategies in Ethnic Conflict* (London: Routledge, 2016).

Some of these measures were acknowledged to be harsh, even inhumane. The population exchange between Greece and Turkey after World War I, or the expulsion of ethnic Germans from Czechoslovakia and Poland after World War II, involved uprooting centuries-old communities. Few denied that this involved injustice to minorities, who were sacrificed in the name of stabilizing the international order. However, it was widely felt that the needs of minorities must be subordinated to the larger interest in "making the national state secure, and its institutions stable, even at the cost of obliterating minority cultures and imposing homogeneity upon the population."[10] It was seen as essential to weaken the capacity of minorities to challenge state power, either domestically or internationally.[11] And so the international community generally condoned coercive measures to weaken minorities, on the ground that there was no other way to stabilize nation-states. And since virtually every state faced some version of this challenge, states accorded each other wide latitude in deciding how to address their "minority problem."[12]

The result, in the Middle East and elsewhere, was the development of "unanimist" political cultures, in which states made claims to "national unanimity" that could only be sustained by suppressing minority voices.[13] This process is often labeled "nation-building," but as Connor famously argued, it is more aptly described as "nation-destroying" – that is, the goal was to destroy any potentially competing national identities and national projects.[14] Wherever minority groups were seen as potential carriers of a competing national project, they had to be suppressed, whether through coercive assimilation, expulsions, or demographic engineering.

This anxiety and hostility regarding minorities remains a powerful factor domestically and internationally. Recently, however, it has been supplemented by a more minority-friendly approach. This is partly due to broader changes in international norms, including the human rights revolution and the decolonization movement. Treating minorities as marked citizens to be contained and suppressed contradicts

10 I. Claude, *National Minorities: An International Problem* (Cambridge, MA: Harvard University Press, 1955), 80–81.

11 J. Jackson-Preece, *National Minorities and the European Nation-States System* (Oxford: Oxford University Press, 1998), 43.

12 Some minorities were too large – or had sufficiently powerful protectors – that states were unable to impose these anti-minority strategies. In these cases, the international community helped negotiate bilateral treaties in which a particular state would agree to respect the rights of those minorities with powerful international friends. Several of these "minority protection" treaties were negotiated in the interwar period (see Jackson-Preece, *National Minorities and the European Nation-States System*). But they did little to change the anti-minority tenor of international relations. Indeed, by connecting minority rights with foreign protectors, they confirmed the suspicion that minorities are presumptively disloyal, with greater loyalty to some kin-state or imperial power than to their own country. And they offered no generalized principle of respect for minorities: those minorities which lacked foreign protectors, such as the Roma, were ignored.

13 On Arab states as "unanimist," see Picard, "Nation-Building and Minority Rights," 332.

14 W. Connor, "Nation-Building or Nation-Destroying?" *World Politics*, 24(3) (1972), 319–55.

evolving ideas about the rights of individuals and communities. Many anti-minority policies violated basic individual civil and political rights (e.g., expulsions, bans on the use of minority languages). These policies also conflicted with evolving international ideas about the equality of races and peoples, tied to decolonization struggles, the African American struggle for desegregation, and the struggle against apartheid in South Africa. What all of these struggles had in common was the repudiation of ideologies of ethnic and racial hierarchy. A legitimate state cannot espouse supremacist ideologies about the superiority of some people over others. The coercive suppression of minorities was often intimately tied up with such supremacist ideologies. This is clearest in the way settler states justified their rule over Indigenous peoples, which rested on claims about the superiority of "civilized" whites over "backward" Indigenous peoples. But this is hardly unique: dominant groups around the world have claimed some form of civilizational superiority over minorities, in part to justify their right to rule over them.[15]

In short, older models of minority suppression have been increasingly delegitimized and at odds with emerging ideas of individual human rights and the equality of races and peoples. And so, the 1960s and 1970s witnessed efforts to formulate new approaches to minorities, both at the domestic and international level. Domestically, various countries started to experiment with models of multiculturalism, which granted official recognition to minorities and accepted that they are a permanent and valued part of the political community.[16] Internationally, proposals were made to formulate new international standards of minority and Indigenous rights. By the early 1990s, a wide range of international organizations came to believe that the tendency of states to try to secure their legitimacy by suppressing minorities was counterproductive, generating cycles of instability and violence. To preserve international peace and security, new approaches were needed, in which minorities would be accepted, and could feel a sense of belonging, rather than being marked as disloyal outsiders. And this in turn required formulating new models of "nation-building" that do not depend on "nation-destroying."

Indeed, we can say that these pro-minority and pro-diversity ideas are now part of "world culture," in the sense popularized by John Meyer. According to Meyer, the postwar period has witnessed the "rise of global models of nationally organized progress and justice" which articulate the appropriate goals of state action, such as economic development and individual rights, while delegitimizing older goals, such

15 These ideologies of hierarchy often involve a dense web of interlocking beliefs about religious orthodoxy, cultural contribution, political loyalty, and personal virtues. For how these interact to justify the oppression of the Akhdam minority in Yemen, see L. Nevola, "On Colour and Origin: The Case of the Akhdam in Yemen," *Open Democracy* (February 13, 2018).

16 For an overview of such experiments in multiculturalism, see the "Multiculturalism Policy Index," www.queensu.ca/mcp, and discussed in K. Banting and W. Kymlicka, "Is There Really a Retreat from Multiculturalism Policies? New Evidence from the Multiculturalism Policy Index," *Comparative European Politics*, 11(5) (2013), 577–98.

as the pursuit of divine missions or racial and religious purity.[17] While Meyer did not include respect for diversity in his original account of the core values of world culture, others have shown that it has indeed become equally pervasive – as measured, for example, by the spread of ideas of multiculturalism and minority rights in school textbooks around the world which expose students "to a depiction of their own societies as ones filled with validated diversity along many dimensions."[18] And these normative expectations are increasingly applied to Middle Eastern states. Indeed, some commentators have argued that "for every state of the Middle East, respect for minority rights has become – together with women's rights – the barometer of its successful transition to democracy."[19]

What we see, therefore, is a complex and contradictory terrain regarding the minority question. Older ideas about minorities as a problem to be contained or weakened remain powerful, but they coexist with newer ideas about minorities as the legitimate bearers of minority rights. Some commentators argue that the older ideas remain dominant, and that newer ideas of legitimate diversity and pluralism remain largely rhetorical and ineffective.[20] When push comes to shove, international organizations continue to prioritize respect for the sovereignty and territorial integrity of existing states over any minority claims that could be interpreted as threats to nation-states. Yet respect for pluralism and diversity is now often seen as one of the requirements of a decent and modern state. Unanimist ideas of national homogeneity are discredited, and states are expected to present "a depiction of their own societies as ones filled with validated diversity along many dimensions."[21]

In short, we live in an era where pluralism is increasingly valorized as both desirable and inevitable, but where autonomy-seeking minorities remain marked as a presumptively disloyal problem to be contained. This then is the background to current debates about decentralization. For many commentators, decentralization provides a way of protecting pluralism and diversity without triggering the fraught

17 J. Meyer et al., "World Society and the Nation-State" *American Journal of Sociology*, 103(1) (1997), 144–81.

18 F. Ramirez, P. Bromley, and S. Russell, "The Valorization of Humanity and Diversity," *Multicultural Education Review*, 1(1) (2009), 29–54. See also L. Terra and P. Bromley, "The Globalization of Multicultural Education in Social Science Textbooks," *Multicultural Perspectives*, 14(3) (2012), 136–43; and P. Bromley, "Comparing Minority and Human Rights Discourse in Social Science Textbooks: Cross-national Patterns, 1970–2008," *Canadian Journal of Sociology*, 39(1) (2014), 1–44.

19 Picard, "Nation-Building and Minority Rights," 67.

20 For the view that international organizations still instinctively privilege state unity over minority accommodation, see J. McGarry, B. O'Leary, and R. Simeon, "Integration or Accommodation? the Enduring Debate in Conflict Regulation," in S. Choudhry (ed.), *Constitutional Design for Divided Societies: Integration or Accommodation?* (Oxford: Oxford University Press, 2008). In reality, there are deep disagreements within and between international organizations on this issue. Human rights organizations, for example, have a different perspective than development-oriented institutions or security-oriented institutions. For a preliminary attempt to map these differences, see J. Boulden and W. Kymlicka (eds.), *International Approaches to Governing Ethnic Diversity* (Oxford: Oxford University Press, 2015).

21 Ramirez, Bromley, and Russell, "The Valorization of Humanity and Diversity."

politics of minority rights. Decentralization, we might say, is an attempt to protect minorities while defanging or declawing minority politics.

THE LIMITS OF DECENTRALIZATION

The problem, however, is that decentralization is not inherently empowering of minorities: it can instead be used as a tool to disempower minorities. Consider regional autonomy. The European Union has been promoting ideas of regionalization and subsidiarity. But how have the boundaries of regions been drawn? In some Western democracies, these boundaries have been drawn to enable regionally concentrated minorities to form a local majority, and thereby benefit from processes of state decentralization – for example, Catalonia in Spain, or South Tyrol in Italy (which has an ethnic German majority). In Slovakia, by contrast, the boundaries of regions were drawn explicitly to prevent the Hungarian minority from forming a local majority in any subunit, even though they are regionally concentrated in the south.

This different approach to regionalization reflects the fact that minority autonomy is taboo in Slovakia but not in Spain or Italy. And this in turn is related to different conceptions of nationhood. Most members of the Slovak majority firmly reject the legitimacy of minority self-government. They think it would be illegitimate to create a Hungarian-dominated subunit, an injustice to the Slovak majority and a violation of national sovereignty. This is the official position of the Slovak government, and of all the mainstream Slovak political parties. Their conception of Slovak nation-building requires undermining any competing Hungarian national project, and so regional autonomy was deliberately designed in a way to disempower Hungarians.

Spanish and Italian nation-building, by contrast, no longer seeks to destroy the sense of nationhood among Catalans or German-speakers. The Catalans and German-speakers are widely recognized as "nations within" or as "nested nationalities" – that is, as national groups who are nested within, and a constituent part of, the larger Spanish or Italian nation – and as such, as having legitimate interests in governing themselves and their historic territory.[22] Where this idea of nested nationalities is accepted, regional autonomy is likely to be designed in ways that are minority-empowering.

In both Spain and Italy, this acceptance of the legitimacy of the nations within is a relatively recent development. In the original phase of regionalization in Italy in 1948, the German-speaking region of South Tyrol was submerged into the much larger Italian-speaking region of Trentino. This reflected the legacy of an older policy, dating back to Mussolini's dictatorship, of seeking to "Italianize" the German-speaking

[22] On the idea of nested nationalities, see D. Miller, *Citizenship and National Identity* (Cambridge: Polity Press, 2000) ; W. Kymlicka, "Multicultural Citizenship within Multination States," *Ethnicities*, 11(3) (2011), 281–302. On the idea of "nations within," see Augie Fleras and Jean Leonard Elliott, *The "Nations Within": Aboriginal–State Relations in Canada, the United States, and New Zealand* (Toronto: Oxford University Press, 1992). I return to these ideas in the final section of the chapter.

areas, both by restricting language rights for the German minority, and by settling large numbers of Italian-speakers in the area. But this nation-destroying policy was gradually abandoned, the legitimacy of South Tyrol's ethnonational aspirations was accepted, and so in 1972, the regional autonomy scheme was redrawn to enable South Tyrol to be self-governing. The resulting framework for securing minority autonomy is now widely seen as a model.[23]

Similarly, during the Franco dictatorship, Spanish nation-building was seen as requiring the destruction of Catalan and Basque nationalism. But one of the defining features of the transition to democracy in Spain in the 1970s was the renunciation of this unitarist conception of Spanish nationhood in favor of a more nested nationalities model. And as a result, in Spain today, there is broad (though not unanimous) acceptance that regional autonomy should naturally and appropriately involve creating minority-dominated subunits. Regional autonomy today, therefore, in both Italy and Spain fits hand-in-glove with ideas of minority empowerment. But in both cases, this only take place *after* the state had abandoned its commitment to nation-building through nation-destroying. Where that commitment remains in place, as in Slovakia, regional autonomy becomes a vehicle for minority disempowerment.

We can see the same dynamics at work in the case of federalism. Whether federalism serves as vehicle for empowering or disempowering minorities depends on whether it is tied to a vision of "nation-building through nation-destroying" or to a vision which acknowledges the nations within. In Canada and Belgium, federalism is tied to a recognition of the nations within, and so provincial boundaries have been drawn in a way that enables the Quebecois and the Flemish to exercise self-government. By contrast, consider the United States. As the USA engaged in territorial expansion to the west and overseas, it incorporated the territories of Indigenous peoples and other ethnonational groups (e.g., Hispanics in Puerto Rico or the southwest). In principle, one could have imagined federalism being used as a tool to protect the self-government rights of these groups, through the establishment of Hispanic-dominated or Indian-dominated states. In reality, however, the national aspirations of these groups were seen as a threat to the Manifest Destiny of the American nation, and so they needed to be contained and weakened. And federalism was part and parcel of this nation-destroying process. Admission to statehood was conditional on the state being controlled by Anglo settlers, whether by drawing boundaries so that Indian tribes or Hispanic groups were outnumbered, or by delaying statehood until anglophone settlers swamped the older inhabitants.[24]

23 See J. Woelk, J. Marko, and F. Palermo (eds.), *Tolerance through Law: Self-Governance and Group Rights in South Tyrol* (Leiden: Brill, 2007).

24 S. O'Brien, "Cultural Rights in the United States: A Conflict of Values," *Law and Inequality Journal*, 5(2) (1987), 267–358. For an alternate view about whether American federalism was the "archenemy of peripheral nationalism," see J. Kincaid, "Territorial Neutrality and Cultural Pluralism in American Federalism: Is the United States the Archenemy of Peripheral Nationalism?" *Swiss Political Science Review*, 22(4) (2016), 565–84.

As a result, none of the fifty states can be seen as ensuring self-government for a national minority, the way that Quebec ensures self-government for the Quebecois or Flanders ensures self-government for the Flemish.

Indeed, far from helping national minorities, there is reason to believe that American federalism has made them worse off. Throughout most of American history, Hispanics, American Indian tribes, and native Hawaiians have received better treatment from the federal government than from state governments. State governments, controlled by colonizing settlers, have often seen national minorities as an obstacle to greater settlement and resource development, and so have pushed to strip minorities of their traditional political institutions, undermine their treaty rights, and dispossess them of their historic homelands. While the federal government has been complicit in much of the mistreatment, it has often at least attempted to prevent the most severe abuses. Even today, "states' rights" is the cry of those who wish to undermine the rights of Indian tribes. We can see the same dynamic in Brazil, where the federal government has often fought to protect the rights of Indians in Amazonia against the predations of local state governments.[25] The same is true in Australia, where the federal government had to take away jurisdiction over Aborigines from state governments because of the level of abuses.[26]

These cases – where local governments are more hostile to minorities than central governments – are often intimately tied to demographic engineering. States and empires have long encouraged loyal groups to move into frontier zones, dating back to medieval practices of encouraging settler-soldier groups to settle into the "marches." These settler groups tend to view themselves as loyalists, and as having the political function of defending the regime against the potentially disloyal natives of the region. Where these settler groups come into control of local or regional authorities, they tend to be particularly hostile to minorities.

These examples caution us against the optimistic idea that members of majority groups are likely to become more understanding and tolerant of minorities if they live alongside them in areas of traditional minority settlement, and hence have more personal interaction with them. This "contact hypothesis" – that personal contact leads to greater respect and acceptance – is indeed true as a generalization in various apolitical contexts. But if we bring politics back in – and in particular, if this contact is structured by larger state imperatives of nation-building through nation-destroying – then local settler groups may in fact be unusually hostile to minorities. The interaction of federalism with demographic engineering is likely to be particularly devastating to minorities.

[25] This is changing under President Jair Bolsonaro, who seeks to remove federal protection of Indigenous rights. Human Rights Watch, "Bolsonaro's Plan to Legalize Crimes against Indigenous Peoples," March 1, 2020.

[26] N. Peterson and W. Sanders, *Citizenship and Indigenous Australians* (Cambridge: Cambridge University Press, 1998), 11–19.

So here again, federalism, like regionalization, is not inherently good for minorities. It depends on whether federalism is tied to projects of nation-building through nation-destroying or to projects of accommodating the nations within. If the former, then federalism is likely to disempower minorities; if the latter, it is likely to empower minorities.

In exploring the limits of decentralization for minorities, I have focused so far on cases where boundaries are drawn so that minorities are outnumbered even within the decentralized unit – that is, where a minority group and its territory is submerged into a larger unit. But I should also note that decentralization can sometimes have the opposite problem – namely, of fragmenting a minority into many smaller units in a way that is designed to prevent any sort of collective action. A classic example of this is the way the Canadian government dealt with Indigenous peoples up until the 1970s. Europeans encountered a number of Indigenous nations or peoples or tribes as they colonized what is now Canada, many of them quite large and capable of effective collective action. The Canadian state, however, until quite recently, was committed to disempowering Indigenous peoples, and so it broke up these larger nations or peoples into hundreds of smaller "bands" – essentially, villages – most of which are under 1,000 people. The Cree nation, for example, was seen as a potential competitor to Canadian nation-building, and so it was broken up into dozens of small villages, which then became the unit of Indigenous autonomy. This was a deliberate policy of denationalization, eroding any capacity for Indigenous nationhood. And when Cree bands sought to federate together to reassert their nationhood, they were legally prevented from doing so.[27]

This is a familiar pattern which we can still observe in much of the world: local self-government at the village level is used as a tool to subvert effective collective action by an ethnonational group, and indeed to denationalize the group. Consider the ethnic Serbs in Kosovo. They have consistently mobilized to secure a form of minority autonomy, but Kosovo has instead offered only local self-government. When the leaders of the Serbian villages sought to federate, as a route to minority autonomy, this was rejected by the state and criticized as a threat to Kosovo's national sovereignty.[28] Serbs are allowed to act politically qua distinct villages, but not as a collective group.

So too with local self-government in Romania. The main political parties representing the ethnic Hungarians in Romania have called for various forms of

[27] As Canada shifted from a policy of nation-destroying to recognizing Indigenous "nations within," this policy was abandoned, and there are now several efforts to reestablish Indigenous nationhood through the federating of bands, although the damage done by the older policy of fragmenting nations endures. On this shift, and the challenges it faces, see B. Thom, "The Anathema of Aggregation: Toward 21st-Century Self-government in the Coast Salish World," *Anthropologica*, 52(1) (2010), 33–48.

[28] There was an EU-brokered agreement in 2013 to create a federation of Serbian municipalities in Kosovo, but it remains unimplemented due to political opposition amongst Albanian nationalists.

minority self-government, including territorial autonomy in their traditional homeland (Szeklerland). Romania has instead introduced a generalized scheme of local self-government at the village level. When the mayors of villages with ethnic Hungarian populations sought to federate, as a step toward minority autonomy, the Romanian state rejected this.

In these cases, the problem is not that minorities are outnumbered at the village level. In many cases, the ethnic Serbs or ethnic Hungarians form a clear majority at the village level. The problem is that village-level self-government does not match the needs and aspirations of the nations within, which include some form of collective agency. As many commentators have noted, this is a defining feature of nationhood, and what distinguishes it from other forms of ethnic, class, or regional identities. To think of oneself as a nation is, in part, to think of oneself as belonging together, acting together, and thereby sharing a common fate. This requires some mechanism of self-government.[29] Village self-government does not enable this sort of national collective agency. Indeed, as we've seen, village self-government has often been introduced precisely in order to denationalize the group: to block and dissolve aspirations to collective agency. Where village self-government is proposed in place of minority autonomy, it is often precisely with this nation-destroying goal.

In short, whether we look at regionalization, federalism, or municipalization, the same pattern emerges. All of these forms of decentralization are as likely to disempower minorities as to empower them. They are as likely to be tools for nation-destroying as to be tools for accommodating national aspirations. Decentralization is only a reliable vehicle for minorities if states disavow ideas of nation-building through nation-destroying, and more specifically, if they disavow (1) demographic engineering; and (2) drawing internal boundaries in ways that submerge or fragment minorities so that they are unable to act effectively.

This is indeed recognized in some of the most important international legal instruments relating to local self-government and minority rights. For example, the European Charter for Regional or Minority Languages requires states to ensure that "existing or new administrative divisions do not constitute an obstacle" to minority language groups (Article 7, para. 1b), and "condemns practices which fragment a language community among a number of administrative or territorial units"[30] – that is, it forbids submerging or fragmenting minority communities in the process of decentralization. Similarly, the Framework Convention for the Protection of National Minorities requires states to "refrain from measures which alter the proportions of the population in areas inhabited by persons belonging to national minorities and are aimed at restricting the rights and freedoms flowing from the

[29] For an account of nationhood that stresses these ideas of collective agency and shared fate, see D. Miller, *On Nationality* (Oxford: Oxford University Press, 1995).

[30] Council of Europe, *Explanatory Report to the European Charter for Regional or Minority Languages* (1992), paragraph 60.

principles enshrined in the present framework Convention" (Article 16) – that is, it forbids demographic engineering. These are all indications that any proposed decentralization must be evaluated with a clear prior commitment to minority rights. International organizations have learned, from bitter experience, that without these explicit safeguards for minority rights, decentralization can be a tool for undermining minorities.

NORMALIZING MINORITY RIGHTS

If the analysis so far is correct, the prospects that decentralization will be an effective way of protecting minorities in the current circumstances of the Middle East are relatively poor.[31] Minorities are marked citizens in many Middle Eastern states, and remain so even after the Arab Spring,[32] in part because states remain committed to conceptions of nation-building that rest on suppressing the national aspirations of minorities. As a result, there is no credible prospect that decentralization proposals will be judged by reference to standards of minority rights. Indeed, it is taboo to even raise that question. There is nothing to prevent the adoption of minority-disempowering forms of decentralization.

If we cannot finesse minority claims through generalized decentralization, the question then is whether we can directly challenge the perception that minorities are a "problem"? How can we overcome the marked nature of minorities, the taboo nature of minority rights, and the conception of nation-building through nation-destroying?

The experience of other countries – including the examples of Italy and Spain discussed earlier – show that this is possible. Countries that once sought to denationalize their minorities have embraced a model of nested nationalities, and hence adopted minority-empowering forms of decentralization. However, the experience of

[31] There are cases where minorities have simply seized territory through the force of arms in rebellion against the state, including the Kurds in Syria or the Houthis in Yemen. Whether these will prove durable is an open question. My focus in this chapter, however, is on state-sponsored processes of decentralization, as part of broader democratic and/or constitutional transformations.

[32] Indeed, the very term "Arab Spring" is sometimes viewed as evidence of the invisibility of minorities. Some commentators argue it could equally be called an "Amazigh spring," given the central role they played in the process. C. Jay, "A Berber Spring: The Breakthrough of Amazigh Minorities in the Uprisings' Aftermath," in F. A. Gerges (ed.), *Contentious Politics in the Middle East* (New York: Palgrave, 2015). For surveys of the parlous status of minorities in the region after the Arab Spring, see P. Rowe (ed.), *Routledge Handbook of Minorities in the Middle East* (London: Routledge, 2018); I. Zabad, *Middle Eastern Minorities: The Impact of the Arab Spring* (London: Routledge, 2016); J. Castellino and K. Cavanaugh, *Minority Rights in the Middle East* (Oxford: Oxford University Press, 2013); W. Kymlicka, and E. Pföstl (eds.), *Multiculturalism and Minority Rights in the Arab World* (Oxford: Oxford University Press, 2014); L. Robson (ed.), *Minorities and the Modern Arab World: New Perspectives* (New York: Syracuse University Press, 2016); and S. Aslan, *Nation-Building in Turkey and Morocco: Governing Kurdish and Berber Dissent* (Cambridge: Cambridge University Press, 2014).

other countries also suggests that this process is difficult, and depends on a number of propitious conditions, not all of which are within the control of domestic actors.

For example, if we return to the case of South Tyrol, one key condition that enabled the normalization of minority autonomy in Italy was the role of the EU and NATO in providing regional security. Once Italy and Austria became firm allies within the umbrella of the EU and NATO, Italy no longer had any reason to fear that Austria would use the German-speaking minority in South Tyrol as a means of destabilizing Italy. Where all the neighboring countries are allies, the treatment of minorities can move out of the "security" box into the "normal democratic politics" box, free from anxieties about minorities being used as a tool of intervention or manipulation by rival or enemy states.[33]

Regrettably, we are very far from this situation in the Middle East today. There is nothing comparable to the EU or NATO to provide regional security.[34] On the contrary, the region remains the site of competing geopolitical strategies, with the USA, Russia, Iran, Israel, Saudi Arabia, and others all looking to exploit weaknesses in their perceived rivals or enemies, including by recruiting and arming disaffected minorities.

Indeed, the long history of external actors using minorities as a tool to weaken rival states is arguably one of the central factors in explaining the taboo status of minority rights. In order to avoid accusations of disloyalty and collaboration, minorities have not only to vocally and visibly swear their loyalty, but they may even have to renounce appeal to the very idea of minority rights. As Saba Mahmood puts it in the case of the Copts, "because the principle of minority rights was the vehicle for the subjugation of national sovereignty to foreign rule it cannot now serve as the instrument for Coptic salvation. Any embrace of this principle necessarily entails the inscription of Copts in this longstanding colonialist project." Indeed, she describes this as "the impossible paradox that haunts the discourse of minority rights in the Middle East."[35]

CONCLUSION: REIMAGINING NATIONHOOD

Unless and until there is change in the larger geopolitical context discussed in this chapter, it will be difficult to normalize minority politics in the Middle East. But these geopolitical constraints do not entirely predetermine how domestic actors

33 On how European integration facilitated the desecuritization of minority politics in Western Europe, see Kymlicka, *Multicultural Odysseys*.

34 For competing views about whether the Arab League might provide a vehicle for normalizing minority politics in the region, compare O. Dajani, "Responding to Ethnic and Religious Conflict in the Emerging Arab Order: the Promise and Limits of Rights," *UCLA Journal of International Law and Foreign Affairs*, 17(1) (2013), 29 (who is pessimistic); with J. Yacoub, "How Does the Arab World Perceive Multiculturalism and Treat Its Minorities?" in W. Kymlicka and E. Pfostl (eds.), *Multiculturalism and Minority Rights in the Arab World* (Oxford: Oxford University Press, 2014), 250–78 (who is more optimistic).

35 S. Mahmood, "Religious Freedom, the Minority Question, and Geopolitics in the Middle East," *Comparative Studies in Society and History*, 54(2) (2012), 418–46, 440.

deal with the challenges of diversity, and the experience of other countries suggests that another key factor here is the conception of national identity and narratives of nationhood that citizens and state officials operate with.

As Rogers Smith puts it, every state contains various "stories of peoplehood," about how its citizens came to be a self-governing people, about why they belong together in a single polity, and about what are the ties that bind them together.[36] As I noted earlier, in many countries, in both the East and West, these stories of peoplehood have historically been tied to narrow, exclusionary, unanimist, and supremacist conceptions of nationhood that require undermining any competing national identities among minorities. The normalizing of minority politics often requires a dramatic revision to these stories of peoplehood, and a willingness to accept what I've been calling nested nationalities or nations within.

The process of revising these stories of peoplehood is, in the first instance, "culture work." It requires academics, intellectuals, artists, journalists, and others to engage in new forms of political imagination and to tell new stories about how and why we belong together. Building new cultural norms and cultural narratives around nationhood is as important as the building of new legal or political institutions. Sustainable practices of minority rights require new narratives that enable citizens to see the exercise of these rights as legitimate forms of belonging and contribution. Even the best-designed institutions will fail if citizens enter these institutional spaces with fearful or exclusionary attitudes about who belongs or who contributes or who can be trusted.

This intellectual work of telling new stories of peoplehood is an ongoing and contested process, even in the "successful" cases that are often pointed to as models, such as South Tyrol or Catalonia. Recent developments in Catalonia make clear how much the apparent consensus on regional autonomy hides deep disagreements on how Catalonia should be nested within Spain. Indeed, I have argued elsewhere that it is a defining feature of these multination states that they will always contain diverse and competing "stories of peoplehood."[37] But the persistence of these disagreements just confirms the importance of the culture work of articulating and comparing and translating these narratives, of making the aspirations of co-citizens intelligible to each other, and of designing institutions and procedures that make sense from the perspective of these different narratives. Part of the explanation for the current crisis in Catalonia, arguably, is that the stories of peoplehood in Catalonia and the rest of Spain started to diverge in ways that were not sufficiently recognized, in part because the ongoing culture work of knitting these stories together was not maintained. The initial success of the post-Franco regionalization process led to a complacency about the need to continually update our stories of peoplehood.

36 R. Smith, *Stories of Peoplehood: The Politics and Morals of Political Membership* (Cambridge: Cambridge University Press, 2003).

37 Kymlicka, "Multicultural Citizenship Within Multination States."

In thinking about the prospects for minority rights in the Middle East, therefore, I would argue that we need to pay attention, not only to the hard realities of geopolitics and interstate rivalries, but also to the intellectual work of reimagining nationhood. And so we might ask, as we read through the various case studies in this volume, who is doing the work of reimagining Arab nationalism? Who is trying to imagine a new conception of nested nationhood that makes room for Kurds or Amazigh or Houthis (or Palestinians in Israel), not as disloyal marked citizens, but as constituent peoples of a multination state? The evidence to date suggests that democratic reformers in the region have not made this a priority, and few intellectuals have tried to make the case for the potential transformative effects of minority rights for broader processes of democratization, human rights, and tolerance.[38]

The result, I believe, is that opportunities for normalizing minority politics in the region have often been lost. These opportunities may be few and far between, given the hard constraints of geopolitics, but that makes it all the more important to recognize these opportunities when they do arise, and to take advantage of them. And we can only do this if we set ourselves the task of directly engaging with the minority question on its own terms, rather than succumbing to the mirage that generalized decentralization can do the work for us. As various international organizations have recognized, we need clear standards and commitments regarding minority rights as a basis for evaluating models of decentralization. For too long, reformers in the region have evaded the question of minority rights. It would be regrettable if discussions of decentralization become simply one more evasion.

[38] The idea that minority rights can have a positive transformative effect for politics more generally is familiar in international debates but is absent from most debates on the Middle East. On this puzzle, see E. Pföstl and W. Kymlicka, "Minority Politics in the Middle East and North Africa: The Prospects for Transformative Change," *Ethnic and Racial Studies*, 38(14) (2015), 2489–98. See also J. Mundy, "The Failure of Transformative Minority Politics in Algthe: The Kabyli Citizens' Movement and the State," in M. Mbanaso and C. Korieh (eds.), *Minorities and the State in Africa* (Amherst, NY: Cambria Press, 2010).

4

Constitutional Design Options for Territorial Cleavages in the Middle East

Tom Ginsburg

The question of how to design constitutions for divided societies is a central one for international policy-making and is becoming more so. The territorial nation-state remains the central organizing unit for international society, and yet no nation-state is internally homogenous. This means that in practice all constitutional systems have to deal with internal diversity.

Managing diversity is a general problem for political and legal systems, but it is particularly acute when political conflict and mobilization is organized around territory. Such "territorial cleavages," as they are known in the literature, may sometimes overlap with ethnic ones, but they present special problems and have their own distinct character.[1] Territorially organized divisions facilitate political mobilization, in part because communication and organization of interests is easier on a smaller geographical scale. Conflicts over valuable resources and fiscal arrangements can spill over into the broader political system, and mutual vetoes of different regions can create gridlock. Threats of secession can provoke violent counter-reactions. In short, managing territorial divisions is an enduring and real problem for countries all over the world, and the Middle East is no exception.

Indeed, as other chapters in the volume discuss, the current turmoil in the Middle East has produced a set of new demands for territorial accommodation. There is a sense of kaleidoscopic displacement in some parts of the region. Populations are moving, political regimes are crumbling, and violent civil war is currently the state of affairs in at least three countries (Libya, Yemen, and Syria). While the international community continues to resist formal partition of states, there have been regions in each of these three countries that have de facto autonomy. When – and if – conflict subsides, these states may develop more segregated spatial organization, with Iraq serving as a harbinger of things to come. As Iraq has developed into

[1] U. M. Amoretti and N. G. Bermeo (eds.), *Federalism and Territorial Cleavages* (Baltimore: Johns Hopkins University Press, 2004); G. Anderson and S. Choudhry (eds.), *Territory and Power in Constitutional Transitions* (Oxford: Oxford University Press, 2019). Note that this chapter draws from my chapter in the latter volume.

a formally federal state, it has also become one in which Sunni, Shia, and Kurds increasingly do not live in the same physical space, and myriad other smaller groups have been totally marginalized or exiled.

Whatever the political configuration that emerges from the current round of conflicts, I expect that it will require some memorialization in formal constitutional law. This chapter surveys the various options, including federal arrangements, decentralization, and special autonomy, rights to secession, and various central government institutions that can provide rights and representation at the central state level. It surveys what we know about the consequences of these design choices and their implications for the Middle East and North Africa (MENA) region.

FEDERALISM

Constitutional federalism is, of course, the standard mechanism for dealing with territorial difference. In a federal system, there is a constitutional division of authority between a central government and one or more subunits, the distinguishing feature of which is that there are some topics on which the subunit's ability to create rules will stand in the face of central opposition.[2] Roughly 11 percent of all countries are nominally federal in the sense that the Constitution uses the term explicitly; roughly 18 percent are actually so, in the sense that one or more regions has designated policy areas in which it has a veto or final authority.[3]

One of the distinctive features of the MENA region is how infrequently federalism has been tried. Northeast Asia with its fairly homogenous nation-states may be the only world region without a major country that is formally federal, but MENA comes close. Other than the United Arab Emirates, and Iraq since 2005, there has been no sustained federal system. The supranational United Arab Republic, which merged Egypt and Syria from 1958 to 1961, was not particularly stable. Libya's federal flirtation in the 1950s did not work well, and Sudan's federal structure hobbles along but failed to prevent the secession of the South. One reason for the failure of federalism to gain traction may be that elites who fought colonial powers have a negative association with federalism, viewing it as a legacy of "divide-and-conquer" strategies to weaken national actors. Al-Ali notes that "federali" is an unpopular word in the region.[4] Yet there have been enduring territorially based demands for

[2] This is my working definition from the Comparative Constitutions Project. Note the slight distinction from Will Kymlicka's definition of federalism as a system "which includes a constitutionally entrenched division of powers between a central government and *two* or more subunits, defined on a territorial basis, such that each level of government has sovereign authority over some issues" (emphasis added). W. Kymlicka, "Is Federalism a Viable Option for Secession?" in Percy Lehning (ed.), *Theories of Secession* (London: Routledge, 1998), 119.

[3] Data from the Comparative Constitutions Project on file with author.

[4] Z. Al-Ali, "Deconcentrating Power in Arab-Majority Countries," *Lawfare Blog* (August 17, 2018).

more autonomy, in the Hijaz in Saudi Arabia, Cyrenaica in Libya, and Kabylie in Algeria, to take just a few examples. What elements of federalism might make it an effective solution to MENA territorial cleavages?

The literature on federalism is vast, and its advantages extend well beyond resolving territorial cleavages. The founding fathers of the United States argued that multiple governments can reduce the risk of tyranny, as having power divided into two different levels of government would serve to limit domination by either one.[5] Madison saw the danger of tyranny arising not just from the government, but also from the society over which it governed. Federalism would ensure that no single region would be permanently dominated, but also that minority interests within any particular territory would be better respected, as minority groups could leave for another jurisdiction (or to obtain help from the central state or federal government, as eventually occurred later with African American constituents). This benefit of federalism implies the need for subnational autonomy within a broader national framework, as distinguished from having a large number of independent countries or confederate states. (Note that Will Kymlicka, in his broader work and in his contribution in Chapter 3, contests this view of US federalism as enhancing minority representation.)[6]

Beyond the promotion of liberty and the protection of rights, several other crucial rationales are often employed in support of federalism. First, federalism allows public goods to be produced on a smaller scale than that of an entire country, presumably allowing for better overall alignment between preferences and policies for certain types of goods.[7] Only if there are externalities that impose costs across regions should an issue area be allocated to a higher-level government. This is basically the principle of subsidiarity as it has been articulated in European Union law, which is a powerful motive for the global shift toward devolution, even in unitary states. Of course, the theory does not mean that actual allocations of powers match the ideal, since they are subject to political negotiation.

A second, related point is that jurisdictions that compete with each other for citizens will be encouraged to produce optimal sets of policies for a diverse society. The basic idea is that citizens will "vote with their feet" and move to different jurisdictions that better reflect their particular preferences.[8] This will lead to more responsive government. This rationale, however, assumes that territorial lines do not reflect deep cultural divisions that can inhibit movement. Many peoples in the MENA

5 J. Madison, Federalist No. 51.

6 W. Kymlicka, "Federalism, Nationalism, and Multiculturalism," in D. Karmis and W. Norman (eds.) *Theories of Federalism: A Reader* (London: Palgrave Macmillan, 2005).

7 D. C. Mueller, *Public Choice III* (Cambridge: Cambridge University Press, 2003) 287; M. Filippov, P. C. Ordeshook, and O. Shvestova, *Designing Federalism: A Theory of Self-Sustainable Federal Institutions* (Cambridge: Cambridge University Press, 2004), 2.

8 C. M. Tiebout, "A Pure Theory of Local Expenditures," *The Journal of Political Economy*, 64(5) (1956), 416.

region would be reluctant to leave traditional homelands for other regions in which different groups are dominant. Mobility assumes economic opportunity and tends to lead to greater urbanization, rather than a true market for policies in which all regions of a country can compete on equal footing.

A third advantage of federalism is that it allows for experimentation in policies. In the United States, it is often said that the states are policy laboratories for democracy.[9] If policies work in one state, that might provide the basis for the adoption of a policy elsewhere, either in the central government or through horizontal, peer-to-peer processes such as imitation or learning. Fourth, it is sometimes argued that federalism has systemic advantages in providing "minor league" environments for the training of political leadership. This refers to the idea that politicians can gain executive experience at a lower level of government, which might make them more attractive as national leaders.

All of these rationales are general and may have little purchase on the problems of territorial cleavages, in which issues of identity are at the fore. As Sujit Choudhry and Nathan Hume note, federalism in post-conflict settings is qualitatively different from "old" or traditional federalism.[10] They argue that the principal goals in such contexts "are not to combat majority tyranny or to provide incentives for states to adopt policies that match their citizens' preferences, but rather to avoid civil war or secession."[11] In the context of territorial cleavages, the need to hold the country together, and to defuse or resolve conflict, is primary.

In this regard, it is important to remember that constitutional federalism need not treat all the subunits equally. In Iraq, for example, Kurdistan was largely self-governing after the First Gulf War. When the Constitution was being negotiated after the second Gulf War, Kurdistan secured explicit recognition as a "region," and it remains the only such entity in the country.[12] Regions have a good deal of power in the Iraqi constitutional scheme. Kurdistan also received constitutional protection for its prior laws and contracts.[13] In other parts of the world, there are many examples of so-called asymmetric federalism, from Quebec to Zanzibar, which gives special concessions to territorially concentrated groups, and this might merit consideration.

[9] The phrase comes from Justice L. Brandeis in *New State Ice Co.* v *Liebmann*, 285 US 262 (1932), 311 ("It is one of the happy incidents of the federal system that a single courageous State may, if its citizens choose, serve as a laboratory; and try novel social and economic experiments without risk to the rest of the country"); J. A Gardner, "The 'States-as-Laboratories' Metaphor in State Constitutional Law," *Valparaiso University Law Review*, 30(2) (1996), 475.

[10] S. Choudhry and N. Hume, "Federalism, Devolution and Secession: From Classical to Post-conflict Federalism," in T. Ginsburg and R. Dixon (eds.), *Comparative Constitutional Law* (Cheltenham: Edward Elgar 2013).

[11] Ibid.

[12] P. Bartu and A. MacEachern, "The Devil Is in the Details: Iraqi Kurdistan's Evolving Autonomy," Chapter 10 in this volume.

[13] Iraq Constitution 2005, Art. 141.

If federalism indeed enhances the power of territorially concentrated minorities, it might be a useful goal for particular minorities in the MENA region. A federal Syria, for example, might include discrete Alawite and Kurdish areas, among others; however, the viability of such substates may depend on the particular size and concentration of the group. The Yazidis in Iraq are geographically concentrated but perhaps too small to successfully have negotiated for a province in which they are the majority. Other minorities, such as the Copts in Egypt, are spread throughout the country but a majority nowhere (even if they are more densely concentrated along the Upper Nile).[14] For such a group a territorial "solution" is unlikely to resolve problems of minority protection or to generate a greater sense of inclusion in the polity.

Beyond minority accommodation, the other general advantages of federalism – jurisdictional competition, policy laboratory, and minor league for political leadership – may not have any purchase in the context of enduring territorial cleavages, and indeed these advantages may be undermined by the particular arrangements adopted.

To develop this point, we need to recall that constitutions are often political bargains concluded by a small set of decision-makers. Political bargains are subject to the threat of renegotiation. This is consistent with one theme in the literature on federalism, namely that it is less a one-time allocation of duties and powers than an ongoing and dynamic set of negotiations.[15] When working well, this iterated quality of constitutional federalism allows multiple levels of government to adjust their responsibilities over time to better serve citizens. But ongoing or repeated iterations of renegotiation can also be a source of tension, and in some cases, they may even allow the development of secessionist movements.

Dividing authority over crucial issues can help reduce the stakes of the overall constitutional bargain and thus facilitate agreement. For example, if a territorial cleavage overlaps with a distinct religious or ethnic identity, allowing language or religion to be determined locally might make an overall constitutional bargain possible. Language, in particular, does not allow for neutrality, as official business must be conducted in some language. Federalism reduces the zero-sum nature of having an official language, reducing alienation and increasing efficacy. This parallels the public goods argument for federalism.

However, the particular bargain that is concluded will not necessarily overlap with the overall optimal scheme for producing public goods. It may be the case that, for example, granting special fiscal benefits to a particular subunit leads to high overall rates of taxation, as both the center and subunit impose duplicative taxes. This is a different form of jurisdictional competition – not a positive-sum competition to attract citizens through the adoption of good policies, but a negative-sum exercise in what is called rent-seeking, reducing the pie for other states.

14 M. Purcell, "A Place for the Copts: Imagined Territory and Spatial Conflict in Egypt," *Ecumene*, 5(4) (1998), 432–51.

15 C. J. Friedrich, *Trends of Federalism in Theory and in Practice* (London: Pall Mall, 1968).

The federal solution also risks institutionalizing interests and creating the capacity for renegotiating the bargain later on, perhaps even leading to pressures for secession. Indeed, one study shows that mechanisms for integrating minorities may succeed in resolving some problems, but ultimately reduce attachment to the national state.[16] Philip Roeder has argued that a key element in the probability of successful secessionist movements is what he calls the segment state. Substates with administrative infrastructure and other indicia of statehood, such as regional institutions of government, had a much easier time seceding than those that do not.[17] Having a subunit in place that is already capable of producing some public goods, and allowing for the formation of a collective voice, might lead local elites to promote secession and give them some credibility in reopening negotiations down the road.[18] This dynamic was particularly apparent in the breakups of the socialist federalisms of Yugoslavia and the Soviet Union, in which each subunit had a dominant ethnicity for whom it was named.

The point about reducing attachment to the national unit is particularly important in the MENA region. Central authorities have, at times, struggled to build national identities among the disparate groups in the region, be they the Bedouin of the Sinai, the Touareg of the Maghreb, or the Kurds of Syria. It is hard to see why authorities would be attracted to enshrining these centrifugal pressures into law. Federalism is also sometimes proposed as a solution to the Israel-Palestine problem, but the notion that these two peoples with their history of bitter conflict would ever become attached to a supranational federation seems far-fetched. (Note that Dajani and Scheindlin are somewhat more optimistic about confederalism in Israel-Palestine in their contribution to this volume.)[19] Federalism may work best when there are multiple different groups involved as opposed to two: the binational federalism that is Belgium has not succeeded in creating much national identity, even in the midst of wealthy Europe.

The track record of federalism on political mobilization has been decidedly mixed.[20] Dawn Brancati notes that a corollary to decentralization is that regional parties can thrive, creating pressure for secessionist movements. She observes that certain variables will be more likely to exacerbate regional tensions: the presence of regional legislatures, for example, can lead to a locally dominant party with an interest in pushing the regional identity. It would be going too far to say that federalism in

16 Z. Elkins and J. Sides, "Can Institutions Build Unity in Multiethnic States?" *American Political Science Review*, 101(4) (2007), 693.

17 P. G. Roeder, *Where Nation States Come from: Institutional Change in an Age of Nationalism* (Princeton: Princeton University Press, 2007).

18 Elkins, Ginsburg, and Melton, *The Endurance of National Constitutions*, 133.

19 O. M. Dajani and D. Scheindlin, "'Stuck Together': Can a Two-State Confederation End the Israeli-Palestinian Conflict?" Chapter 13 in this volume.

20 D. Brancati, *Peace by Design: Managing Intrastate Conflict through Decentralization* (Oxford: Oxford University Press, 2009).

Sudan, for example, created the tensions between the northern and southern parts of the country, but it certainly provided a basis for mobilization. The victory of the Southern Sudan Federal Party for the southern parliamentary seats in the country's first election in 1958 may have helped to consolidate southern demands. Eventually, the federal structure did help to secure the secession of South Sudan in 2011.

Thus, federalism may undermine national integration in some cases. This is particularly true in cases in which a territorial cleavage maps directly onto an ethnic one. In Iraq, the disadvantaged status of Kurds in the country's history culminated in the establishment of de facto autonomy after 1991 and a fully recognized Kurdish Autonomous Region in the 2005 Constitution, a de facto mini-state with its own military, revenues, and other attributes of statehood. This did not end the pressure for secession, however, as discussed by Bartu and MacEachern in this volume.[21] A 2017 referendum in which voters overwhelmingly chose secession seems to have led to precisely the opposite result, as Iraqi government forces retook the crucial city of Kirkuk and the Kurdish region lost a measure of its autonomy.

To be sure, there are some recent counterexamples to the idea that segment states are an *essential* prerequisite of secession: in South Sudan, and arguably Kosovo, secessionist movements succeeded without much prior administrative infrastructure.[22] Secessionist pressures have also arisen in unitary states such as Egypt, Morocco, and Yemen. Still, the point that federalism can be centrifugal is an important one in the context of enduring cleavages and helps explains why federalism is not always the best solution. For example, in Libya, the initial commitment to move from a unitary to a federal system did not survive long in the convoluted constitutional drafting process, and as Mezran and Miller note in this volume, it remains unpopular.[23] In Yemen, a constitution-making process that had initially envisioned a federal state failed to prevent a vicious civil war from erupting, as discussed by Challand in this volume.[24]

Part of the problem is psychological. Many of the MENA governments greatly fear that federalism will lead to the disintegration of weak states. But in other regions of the world, the evidence is clear that federalism need not lead to disintegration and can, instead, be a valuable tool of integration. Consider the case of India, where debates over the national language have been a major issue, exacerbating linguistic cleavages that also had a territorial component. The 1956 States Reorganization Act and its successor statutes created several states with one dominant language, but

21 Bartu and MacEachern, Chapter 10.

22 In these two cases, the international context was crucial to the successful secession bids, as the international community supported both efforts. To some degree this support was punitive in nature, responding to international frustration with Slobodan Milošević and Omar al-Bashir. This illustrates again that national constitutions have an international context.

23 K. Mezran and E. Miller, " The Promise – and Limits – of Stabilization through Local Governance in Libya," Chapter 16 in this volume.

24 B. Challand, "Decentralization in Yemen: The Case of the Federalist Draft Constitution of 2015," Chapter 18 in this volume.

also took into account the cultural boundaries and economic viability of each new region.[25] The states, which generally have equal powers, have relative autonomy within the federation. The reorganization has been successful in lessening conflict and securing stability. In some sense, the cases show that federalism may play a role in "extending the Republic," as Madison imagined. By creating linguistically and ethnically defined states in a larger diverse entity, the Indian state reduced the stakes of politics at the center while ensuring that no one entity or group could dominate the country as a whole.

To summarize, federalism – with its myriad variations – is an important part of the toolkit to ameliorate tensions that have led to conflict in the first place. On the other hand, federalism may create new sources of identity formation and tension. In this regard, facilitating subunit representation at the center is paramount in working out shared governance. Issues of timing, with relation to the particular history of grievance and conflict, may be critical in determining whether federalism reduces the cleavage, stabilizes it, or provides a mere way station toward disintegration. One recent study finds that the existence of prior conflict is crucial for determining when, and whether, autonomy helps to ameliorate or exacerbate tensions.[26]

MENA is a region where federalism has been rarely attempted or sustained, even though comparative evidence suggests it might have some benefits. In the short term, the resistance to the federal idea means that a more practical and achievable set of tools lies elsewhere. As we shall see, some of the advantages of federalism may be achieved even without invoking the "F-word" as a formal matter.

DECENTRALIZATION AND SPECIAL AUTONOMY

The global trend toward decentralized government through statutory or nonconstitutional schemes seeks to leverage some of the general advantages of federalism even within unitary states. Decentralization is argued to advance the efficient and responsive production of public goods, and to facilitate policy competition and experimentation. Decentralization also reduces the stakes of controlling the central government, and so can ameliorate latent territorial tensions. Decentralization schemes tend to be fairly uniform throughout a country, but there is also the possibility of providing differentiated schemes for particular geographic areas. Special autonomy is a strong version of this. This section discusses decentralization and special autonomy in turn.

[25] S. Choudhry, "Managing Linguistic Nationalism through Constitutional Design: Lessons from South Asia," *International Journal of Constitutional Law*, 7(4) (2009), 577.

[26] L.-E. Cederman, S. Huq, A. Schadel, and J. Wucher, "Territorial Autonomy in the Shadow of Conflict: Too Little, Too Late?" *American Political Science Review*, 109(2) (2015), 354. When divisions are not preceded by conflict, territorial decentralization decreases the probability of future conflict, but there is no such effect in post-conflict settings. This suggests that in such contexts, only representation at the central government is likely to be effective.

Decentralization

A general program of decentralization is likely to reduce the emergence of territorial cleavages in the first place. This trend is born from a simple notion – people who have a say in their own government are less likely to feel that policies are imposed on them by a distant center. As noted in the discussion of federalism, giving localities control over local policies reduces the stakes of controlling the center, and so can lower the temperature of political conflict.

Once a territorial cleavage arises, decentralization is surely part of the toolkit for responding to it. Yet again, decentralization, by increasing local capacity, may also create the building blocks for future territorial demands, including for more formal federal schemes. The 1994 decentralization law in Bolivia, for example, created new political units and guaranteed each a share of the national budget. This created the basis for a broader mobilization in both the east and west of the country once an economic shock hit. The two sides had very different demands, with politicians in the resource-rich eastern lowlands demanding a strengthening of local autonomy at the departmental level, while those in the western highlands advanced a more centralized but plurinational vision in which revenues were broadly shared. But both utilized the local capacities that had been developed for a very different purpose a decade earlier. When conflict in the constitution-making process led to violence, departments passed their own autonomy statutes.[27]

One could imagine similar dynamics in the MENA region. Libya's traditional provinces have remained a basis for political organization in the post-Qaddafi era. Equal representation among the three in the constitution-making process seemed a natural way to accommodate the regional differences but led to stalemate at particular junctures. Given the functional separation of east and west in the current civil war, decentralization has been a fact of life; this de facto reality may, however, make putting the country back together again as difficult as the proverbial problem of Humpty Dumpty.

Devolution can also function to devolve corruption and rent-seeking. Much of the commentary on devolution in Kenya following the 2010 Constitution has made note of this feature. Instead of providing local public goods, counties are providing local private goods, replicating the venality of the national politicians. There is some evidence of enhanced local public goods provision, and perhaps a devolution of ethnic tensions, as losers in one county may be winners in a neighboring one.[28] Furthermore, the requirement of minority representation at county government level ensures that groups may cooperate, even if only to carve up the pork.

27 D. Landau, "Constitution-Making Gone Wrong," *Alabama Law Review*, 64(5) (2013), 923.

28 Y. Ghai and J. Cottrell, "Constitutional Transitions and Territorial Cleavages," in G. Anderson and S. Choudhry (eds.), *Territory and Power in Constitutional Transitions* (Oxford: Oxford University Press, 2019).

Iraq is an interesting model in that it deploys both federalism, as between the center and the "regions" of the country (of which there is only one in existence), and decentralization, as among its provinces not incorporated into a region. Decentralization has been an evolving story, as recounted by Ali Al-Mawlawi in this volume, but certainly in the first few years under the 2005 Constitution it has not led to better service delivery.[29] The ongoing problem of party-based corruption and poor services resulted in serious protests in several provinces in southern and central Iraq beginning in 2018. Continuing evolution of the institutional scheme is likely there and the significance of decentralization to that trajectory remains in question.

As decentralization has become a development trend, several MENA countries have adopted decentralization laws, but many of these have been ineffective. Arguably the one country to seriously grapple with decentralization has been Tunisia. Not coincidentally, it is the only country to emerge as a democracy after the Arab Spring. In 2018, it passed a decentralization law that allows for local referenda on development plans and significant power for local councils, as detailed in Intissar Kherigi's chapter in this volume.[30] While there are some ambiguities in the law, it is surely a serious attempt to leverage decentralization in a difficult environment. A critical step for achieving meaningful decentralization in the MENA region will be the development of a measure of genuine fiscal autonomy at the local level. Al-Mawlawi's discussion of Iraq suggests that, whatever the formal powers allocated to subnational governments in the region, the jealous guarding of prerogatives by ministries of finance is a serious barrier to meaningful reform.[31]

Special Autonomy

Another design option is special autonomy arrangements, a kind of asymmetric devolution in which one (or more) regions is given authority over certain subjects.[32] As compared with federalism, special autonomy arrangements are relatively flexible in terms of institutional design and can be tailored to the particular needs of the territorial cleavage. Such arrangements have had varying degrees of success around the world. Crimea had special autonomy within the Ukraine for several years before its eventual annexation by Russia.[33] In Indonesia, special autonomy laws were drawn up for both Aceh and Papua in 2001, and again for Aceh in 2006. The 2001 Law on Aceh failed to placate the secessionist movement, partly because of the

[29] A. Al-Mawlawi, "Salvaging State Legitimacy in Iraq through Decentralization," Chapter 7 in this volume.

[30] I. Kherigi, "Decentralization Reforms in Post-Revolution Tunisia: The Struggle between Political and Bureaucratic Elites," Chapter 8 in this volume.

[31] Al-Mawlawi, Chapter 7.

[32] See Y. Ghai, "Introduction: The Nature and Origins of Autonomy," in Y. Ghai and S. Woodman (eds.), *Practicing Self-government: A Comparative Study of Autonomous Regions* (Cambridge: Cambridge University Press, 2013).

[33] G. Sasse, "The 'New' Ukraine: A State of Regions," *Regional & Federal Studies*, 11(3) (2001), 69, 82.

government's refusal to negotiate or consult popular opinion.[34] In 2006, a new agreement, produced with the help of external mediation from the former president of Finland, led to the passage of a new law. (The external shock of the 2004 tsunami's devastation of Aceh also led to cooperation in the rebuilding effort, which spilled over into the broader political debate.)

Special autonomy may be particularly useful when the population of the unit in question is quite small. Larger autonomous units are likely to create larger spillovers into the rest of the polity, and thus be more politically sensitive, as evidenced by the debate in the UK over whether MPs from the devolved regions should vote on laws that do not affect their constituents. Another crucial variable is the presence of minorities within the prospective autonomous regions, which was a major obstacle in the creation of Bangsamoro in the Philippines; it was resolved by permitting small areas to opt in or out of the arrangement by referendum. That said, where the root of the cleavage is about local self-determination over cultural issues, autonomy may be a viable and indeed attractive option.

One of the general conjectures in the literature is that asymmetric grants of benefits will have knock-on effects, as other units will seek similar treatment. This has surely been the case in Spain, where the expression "coffee for one, coffee for all" captures the spread of devolved powers initially contemplated only for a small number of units.[35] A similar dynamic has been apparent with Scottish devolution, which has led to complex discussions about the other regions of the United Kingdom, and the role of dominant England in the Constitution. The secession of East Timor led to increased demands in Aceh and West Papua. But in other countries, there is not much evidence of the knock-on effect. When the beneficiaries of special arrangements are relatively small in number, or when they are the result of distinctive histories, as in Jammu and Kashmir in India, the center and other regions may simply not care very much.[36] In short, asymmetry might be a tool that can be wielded more frequently in confronting territorial cleavages.

The implications of this discussion for the MENA region are significant. Several of the areas and communities that have demanded autonomy are relatively small. The entire population of Western Sahara, for example, is about a half million out of some forty million in Morocco, and the kingdom has made (unaccepted) offers of special autonomy to the Polisario Front.[37] The North Sinai Peninsula in Egypt,

34 J. Bertrand, "Indonesia: 'Special Autonomy' for Aceh and Papua," in G. Anderson and S. Choudhry (eds.), *Territory and Power in Constitutional Transitions* (Oxford: Oxford University Press, 2019), 12–13.

35 The one exception is the Basque country, which has longstanding special fiscal arrangements not available to any other autonomous community.

36 Note though that the current Indian government has raised the issue of Kashmir's special status, embodied in Article 370 of the Constitution.

37 O. Y. Shehabi, "'*Dans ses Frontiers Authentiques*'? Morocco's Advanced Regionalization and the Question of Western Sahara," Chapter 14 in this volume; J. A. Clark, *Local Politics in Jordan and Morocco: Strategies of Centralization and Decentralization* (New York: Columbia University Press, 2018).

where Bedouins have engaged in an insurgency since 2011, has only a few hundred thousand people. The Berbers who have sought their own state in Algeria are also a small minority. MENA governments have been reluctant to offer genuine autonomy, but in most countries, it would be unlikely to lead to the "coffee for one, coffee for all" dynamic. Special autonomy should thus be actively considered as a possible solution for these conflicts.

In other places in which populations are diverse, special autonomy might lead to knock-on effects. Syrian Kurdistan might, in theory, be given special autonomy, but the centrifugal nature of the ethnically diverse Syrian polity might lead to other groups asking for the same. And where cleavages involve larger groups, such as those in North and South Yemen, special autonomy might not be feasible. In Israel-Palestine, neither group at present would be willing to accept special autonomy under a system in which the other was sovereign. But in practice, the current situation is de facto one of special "autonomy" for Palestinians, in which they have no rights in the central government but can control their own internal affairs in the so-called "A" Areas set up under the Oslo Accords.

RIGHTS, REDISTRIBUTION, AND REPRESENTATION AT THE CENTER

Another set of institutional arrangements to deal with territorial cleavages concerns the center and can be divided into three subcategories: rights, redistribution, and representation.[38] These are not mutually exclusive, but rather, different tools that can be deployed in different combinations.

Rights refers to the idea that protecting the interests of greatest importance to people will reduce their desire to leave the political system. Protecting the ability of people to practice their religion, speak their language, and engage in communal life means that they will fear government less even if this does not produce greater attachment to the center or to the country as a whole, and it will reduce the felt need to take drastic action with regard to the structure of the state.

Rights, both group and individual, are often a major component of constitutional settlements.[39] Guarantees of communal rights were an important component of the Indian constitutional story, and the South African constitutional bargain put rights at the very center. Yet rights alone are unlikely to be able to resolve territorial cleavages without representation or devolution. In the MENA region, we sometimes observe governments reframing territorial disputes into ones about identity, in the hope that they can be more easily resolved. Shehabi's chapter in this volume argues that this has been a strategy of the Moroccan government in the Western Sahara.[40]

38 D. J. Levinson, "Rights and Votes," *Yale Law Journal*, 121(6) (2012), 1286–1363.

39 On group rights see S. Choudhry, "Group Rights," in M. Rosenfeld and A. Sajo (eds.), *Oxford Handbook of Comparative Constitutional Law* (Oxford: Oxford University Press, 2012), 1100–23.

40 Shehabi, Chapter 14.

By reframing the territorial cleavage as being essentially about Sahrawi minority rights, the government can maintain the powerful appeal of national unity. Similarly, the new Tunisian Constitution recognizes the Berber language. Cultural rights, if effectively implemented, can redirect demands for external self-determination toward internal self-determination over matters that are of most importance to the people concerned.

Redistribution from rich areas to poor is also a central feature of territorial settlements, though not always guaranteed explicitly in a constitution. Redistribution concerns the allocation of revenues throughout a territory. Sometimes territorial cleavages are exacerbated by virtue of the presence of valuable resources in one part of the country or another. Providing for mechanisms of fiscal equalization can help to ameliorate some tensions, particularly if the region in question is poorer than the rest of the country.[41] On the other hand, if a region is rich with natural resources, it might seek to minimize the flow of wealth to other regions. Bargaining over redistribution is a central political issue implicating territorial cleavages.

Another institutional mechanism is special representation at the center. Representation in central institutions binds the region to the rest of the polity, ideally giving it a stake in maximizing overall welfare. It thus is a useful tool for managing territorial cleavages. At the same time, representation can generate resentment to the extent that it dilutes the power of the rest of the country.

Representation takes various forms, but one important one is giving the units a special role in constitutional amendment, either in general or just for specific provisions.[42] More than 5 percent of constitutions in force give at least one territorial unit some role – this accounts for nearly half of countries that are nominally federal or confederal – and such rules can prevent unilateral modification of the founding bargain.[43] Providing a dual consent requirement for constitutional amendments with regard to territorial arrangements is a way of rendering the territorial arrangements self-enforcing. Another common means of providing voice to states at the center is through representation in an upper chamber of the legislature. In the United States, each territorial state has equal representation in the Senate, meaning that small states have more political weight relative to their population than do large states. Members of the upper house may be directly elected at the level of the subunit or selected by constituent unit executives or legislatures. The jurisdiction of the upper house might focus primarily on legislation that affects federal

[41] See P. Beramendi, *The Political Geography of Inequality: Regions and Redistribution* (Cambridge: Cambridge University Press, 2012).

[42] J. Marshfield, "Decentralizing the Amendment Power," *Lewis and Clark Law Review*, 19(4) (2015), 963–1030.

[43] As of 2014, the list of countries included Brazil, Canada, Colombia, Comoros, Ethiopia, Mexico, Nigeria, Russia, Switzerland, Uganda, and the United States. In Australia, a dual majority is required and several proposed constitutional amendments that won a majority in national referendums nevertheless failed because they were unable to secure the required ratification by a majority of voters in a majority of states. Australia Constitution, section 218. See Ibid., 984, note 122.

arrangements. Ethiopia's upper house, elected by the state legislatures, has a role in resolving disputes over federal jurisdiction as well as the budget. Kenya and South Africa have upper houses, but with very limited powers restricted for the most part to issues related to provinces or counties. Spain's upper house was also designed to represent provinces and autonomous communities, but because most of its members are elected by popular vote it does not play a major role in this regard.

Regions can also get designated representation in executive, military, or judicial institutions. In Canada, for example, the culturally distinct province of Quebec is guaranteed three seats on the Supreme Court. Informal arrangements may also be effective in this regard, such as in Nigeria's principle of rotation of the presidency between north and south, or Ukraine's "Faustian bargain" of de facto regional decentralization which was stable until 2015.[44] Another important form of representation concerns state institutions. While classical thinking about representation focuses on electoral institutions, appointments in the state bureaucracy, military, judiciary, and regulatory institutions are perhaps more important in contemporary government.[45]

In short, representation at the center is an important policy lever to be considered in trying to manage territorial cleavages, particularly for areas with large populations. In the MENA region, one example is the transitional regime in Iraq (2004–2005), with its joint presidency, which gave Kurdistan a de facto veto for a time. (Representation and veto may be less important for discrete small units that can be dealt with through asymmetric arrangements.) Conversely, the lack of representation and rights at the center was one of the factors that contributed to the failure of Nigeria's first republic. Interestingly, the military in Nigeria drew from all ethnicities and regions, providing a channel for national integration.[46]

There is no guarantee that these mechanisms will be effective, as they can be undermined by political factors. A national political party, for example, can undermine the effectiveness of subnational inclusion at the center. Studies in some countries have shown that upper-house legislators tend to vote based on national party rather than regional interests in constitutional amendment proposals, and this seems to be how the Iraqi political system has developed.[47] In South Africa too, territorial differences have largely been attenuated over time, through special accommodations at the outset and the presence of a dominant political party that integrated various interests. Ethiopia has accommodated tremendous diversity in a federal scheme through a dominant (and not particularly democratic) party regime. In such environments, though, there may be a corollary benefit that subunit leaders can end up rising through party ranks to become national leaders – the "minor league" rationale for federalism.

44 L. Way, "Dealing with Territorial Cleavages: The Rise and Fall of Ukraine's Faustian Bargain," in G. Anderson and S. Choudhry (eds.), *Territory and Power in Constitutional Transitions* (Oxford: Oxford University Press, 2019), 297.

45 H. Gerken, "Exit, Voice, and Disloyalty," *Duke Law Journal*, 62(7) (2013), 1349–86.

46 S. Huntington, *Political Order in Divided Societies* (New Haven: Yale University Press, 1968).

47 Marshfield, "Decentralizing the Amendment Power," 1006.

SECESSION AND GUARANTORS

Two final questions with regard to institutional arrangements are worth considering. The first question is whether to include specific provisions governing secession in decentralized constitutional arrangements. The second issue is determining what mechanisms should be put in place for monitoring and enforcing the terms of constitutional arrangements, and more specifically whether the Constitution establishes clear guarantors for its provisions on decentralization. These questions are considered in turn in this section.

A few constitutions include a right to secession for certain subunits, or all of them. The wisdom of this approach has been the subject of a central debate within political theory.[48] Some scholars, such as Cass Sunstein, believe that a right to constitutional secession will encourage subunits to exercise it.[49] Others believe that such clauses will form a kind of precommitment on the part of a majority to deal fairly with the subunit population, and will thus encourage deliberation.[50] Both sides recognize that secession clauses will give relevant groups substantial bargaining power in everyday politics: if the larger units' actions are unfavorable, they can simply threaten to exercise the right to secession.

In a recent empirical exploration, Mila Versteeg and I illustrate the benefits of clarity with regard to the secession provisions.[51] We find that where secession is explicitly allowed, breakups tend to be smoother; where it is prohibited, either explicitly or implicitly, it tends not to occur. In situations where the Constitution is somewhat ambiguous, such as Iraqi Kurdistan, politicians may be tempted to try to mobilize around secession to get support, and this can lead to violence, as that example shows.

While the inclusion of secession provisions may be exceptional, all decentralization agreements must incorporate mechanisms for monitoring and enforcement. In the case of territorial cleavages, these roles may fall to a constitutional court. Indeed, disputes over territorial authority have played a major role in the jurisprudence of the German Constitutional Court, the United States Supreme Court, and others. South Africa's Constitutional Court had to certify the constitutions of provinces for conformity with the Constitution, and it rejected the proposed constitution of KwaZulu Natal.[52]

48 D. Haljan, *Constitutionalizing Secession* (Oxford: Hart Publishing, 2014); D. Weinstock, "Constitutionalizing the Right to Secede," *Journal of Political Philosophy* 9(2) (2002), 182–203; K. Scott, *Federalism: A Normative Theory and Its Political Relevance* (New York: Continuum, 2011), 134–69.

49 C. Sunstein, "Constitutionalism and Secession," *University of Chicago Law Review*, 58(2) (1991), 633–70.

50 Scott, *Federalism: A Normative Theory.*

51 T. Ginsburg and M. Versteeg, "From Catalonia to California: Secession in Constitutional Law," *Alabama Law Review*, 70(4) (2019).

52 South Africa Constitution 1997, Art. 144.

Courts are also players in the process of resolving territorial cleavages, and they sometimes serve as voices for national integration, even blocking agreements when necessary. In this sense, external monitors can exacerbate rather than resolve cleavages. In the Philippines, the Supreme Court ruled unconstitutional an initial agreement to establish an independent juridical authority in the putative Bangsamoro region. In Sri Lanka in 2004, the government and the Liberation Tigers of Tamil Eelam (LTTE) came to an agreement recognizing the latter as a self-governing entity for post-tsunami reconstruction. Opponents of the deal then brought a case to the Supreme Court, which ruled the arrangements unconstitutional on the grounds that they undermined Parliament's role in spending public funds. This decision led many to think that no deal with the LTTE would ever pass constitutional muster.[53]

On the other hand, the presence of the electoral and constitutional courts became crucial in a situation of deep political division in Bolivia, as both institutions helped to channel political attention to Congress on the question of how to institute departmental autonomy and constitutional reform. The Constitutional Court of Bosnia-Herzegovina has sought to ensure that the entities in the country did not themselves discriminate against their own minorities, which led to a replication of quota-based governance within each entity. In these cases, neutral institutions were able to refine and advance the values of the territorial settlement. Endowments of prior institutions, such as the presence of a relatively autonomous judiciary in South Africa, may help to make bargains possible that would not otherwise be.[54]

In the MENA region, the Supreme Federal Court of Iraq has issued a number of decisions about the relationship between national and local government. This allows various claimants to argue about institutional powers and responsibilities within a legal framework, as opposed to through a more violent means. Turkey's Constitutional Court has generally been reluctant to push back too hard against the Erdoğan regime, but one does see occasional decisions that uphold Kurdish rights, including the ability to discuss issues of territorial governance.[55]

Outside of courts and independent institutions, political mechanisms seem to prevail. For example, in Iraq, the Transitional Administrative Law provided for the collective presidency to appoint arbitrators for interregional disputes, with the backstop of the UN secretary-general if the presidency could not agree. The question of external guarantors raised by this example is one that might be fruitful to pursue in a number of MENA contexts where internal institutions associated with the central state – including the judiciary – might not be deemed trustworthy guarantors for new decentralized arrangements.

53 Choudhry, "Federalism, Devolution and Secession."

54 J. Meierhenrich, *The Legacies of Law: Long-Run Consequences of Legal Development in South Africa, 1652–2000* (Cambridge: Cambridge University Press, 2008).

55 A. Kucukgocmen, "Turkish Court Rules Academics Rights Violated in Kurdish Letter Case," *Reuters* (July 26, 2019).

CONCLUSION

The institutional options for managing territorial cleavages are ample. This chapter has considered the role of territorial assignments of power; rights, redistribution, and representation at the center, as well as veto; and the role of courts and international actors in establishing and guaranteeing bargains. In any particular situation, the precise allocation of institutional options will, of course, be the subject of intense bargaining and may be highly contextual.

Three themes emerge from this review. First, a combination of representation and decentralization may be sufficient to stabilize territorial cleavages. The rights component is actually rather underdeveloped in many of these cases, and even in theory, it is insufficient on its own to guarantee success. Only a small set of countries with deep territorial cleavages are fully consolidated democracies, but representation seems to be a necessary condition for resolving conflicts. So in some sense, the evidence suggests that voice precedes rights, at least when it comes to territorial cleavages.

Second, asymmetry is a useful tool. Special autonomy has been useful in many these divided countries, especially when the territory in question is small relative to the whole. Knock-on effects in other units have not usually led to an unraveling of the overall territorial bargain; yet as the Crimean example shows, special autonomy will not be enough in the face of a large outside power intent on exploiting territorial cleavages.

Despite its prominence in the theoretical literature, rights to secession do not seem to be a frequent solution to problems of territorial division. While secession clauses facilitated the breakup of the large plurinational federations of Yugoslavia and the Soviet Union, rights to exit create too many incentives for secessionist behavior to recommend themselves as a design tool. Voice, it seems, trumps exit. Furthermore, constitutional clarity prohibiting secession may be advisable; the failed Kurdish referendum is a central example in this regard.

Finally, the traditional rationales for federalism fit uneasily with the resolution of territorial cleavages. Resolution of a cleavage may reflect concerns about public goods, jurisdictional competition, training of officials, or even tyranny, but the primary driving force is often distribution of political and material goods, and fights over voice and identity. This means that while resolution of a territorial cleavage may involve resolving a Hobbesian dilemma, and may serve to end conflict, it need not present an optimum set of policies and institutions for the country as a whole. Poor governance may sometimes be the price for peace.

The MENA region is one in which these general considerations take on special importance because of the relative paucity of experience with federalism and the apparent reluctance to pursue special autonomy as a serious matter. Meaningful decentralization would help to reduce the salience of territorial cleavages and would have corollary benefits for good governance as well. As the other chapters in this volume make clear, demands for decentralization are unlikely to go away, even as their implementation remains a tough challenge.

5

How Decentralization Efforts Have Recentralized Authority in the Arab Region

Mona Harb and Sami Atallah

Has decentralization contributed to democratic accountability, civic engagement, transparency, and efforts to combat corruption in the contemporary Arab region? In this chapter, we present key findings from a two-year study assessing decentralization policies and initiatives in five countries – Jordan, Lebanon, Morocco, Tunisia, and Yemen.[1] We begin with a review of the literature, highlighting the costs and benefits of decentralization, and identifying some considerations that should inform the design of decentralized institutions. We then present key findings yielded by our fieldwork.

In all of the cases we examined, colonial experiences have left an enduring imprint on the structure of states following independence. One prominent feature of this legacy is the continuing prevalence of deconcentration, through which responsibility has been shifted to local actors accountable primarily to central governments, rather than to the communities they are presumed to serve. Indeed, we found that this simultaneous promotion and subversion of decentralization was not only practiced by governments across the region, but was also often subsidized by international assistance. We also found that the effectiveness of local governments in the region is constrained by the opaque regulatory environments within which they are expected to operate and the limited human and financial resources at their disposal. These weaknesses have been exacerbated by resistance on the part of central governments to delegate taxing authority to local counterparts and by the failure of some municipalities to fully act on the authority they have been granted. Against this backdrop, however, our study also points to instances of success and innovation, where capable leadership, engaged civil society, and other factors have paved the way toward palpable improvements in service delivery and urban management.

[1] This chapter is drawn from our earlier edited volume, M. Harb and S. Atallah (eds.), *Local Governments and Public Goods: Assessing Decentralization in the Arab World* (Beirut: Lebanese Center for Policy Studies, 2015).

COSTS AND BENEFITS OF DECENTRALIZATION: A REVIEW OF THE LITERATURE

Decentralization is considered desirable as part of a democratization effort for two reasons: one, it enhances participation and accountability in managing local affairs; two, it is expected to lead to better developmental outcomes. The underlying assumption is that delegating authority to lower echelons will make service provision more effective, as it will be more responsive to the actual needs of beneficiaries, while political representation will also be enhanced through better participatory practices.[2] Moreover, decentralization is believed to increase representation for religious and ethnic minorities and to empower local communities. Another claimed advantage is that decentralization encourages flexibility, creativeness, and innovation. Finally, to the extent that local governance makes local politicians responsible for outcomes, there is an expected increase in direct accountability.

There are many limitations to decentralization reforms and not all of them lead systematically to better outcomes in terms of service delivery and democratic representation. Indeed, local policies vary across local governments, depending on levels of local knowledge and the availability of financial and other resources, as well as the "free riding" of smaller and less wealthy municipalities. Often, decentralization does not benefit disadvantaged communities and territories that are unable to address complex local development issues. Decision-makers may seek to capture decentralized service provision for their narrow political and economic interests, and thus decentralization could enhance clientelism and corruption.[3] This scenario is plausible in the context of less democratic political systems where checks and balances are not strongly institutionalized and operative, such as countries in the Arab region.[4] The literature suggests, however, that effective decentralization can be achieved when a central government transfers enough responsibilities to the local level and when local opposition parties have limited ability to block decentralization efforts and influence citizen participation.[5]

2 The following discussion of the pros and cons of decentralization is partly based on P. Bardhan, "Decentralization of Governance and Development," *Journal of Economic Perspectives*, 16(4) (2002), 185–205; and M. S. De Vries, "The Rise and Fall of Decentralization: A Comparative Analysis of Arguments and Practices in European Countries," *European Journal of Political Research*, 38(2) (2000), 193–224.

3 S. P. J. Batterbury and J. L. Fernando, "Rescaling Governance and the Impacts of Political and Environmental Decentralization: An Introduction," *World Development*, 34(11) (2006), 1851–63; and S. I. Bergh, "Introduction: Researching the Effects of Neoliberal Reforms on Local Governance in the Southern Mediterranean," *Mediterranean Politics*, 17(3) (2012), 303–21.

4 Harb and Atallah, *Local Governments and Public Goods*.

5 B. Goldfrank, "The Politics of Deepening Local Democracy: Decentralization, Party Institutionalization, and Participation," *Comparative Politics*, 39(2) (2007), 147–68; and Bergh, "Introduction: Researching the Effects of Neoliberal Reforms on Local Governance in the Southern Mediterranean."

Political reformists attempt to address these challenges and propose legal, institutional, and fiscal models that can improve the practice of decentralization. The key questions that occupy them relate to governance administration and tiers, fiscal responsibilities, and geography. In other words: how many tiers of government should a country have in a post-authoritarian era? How should the competences and responsibilities be assigned between the different tiers of government, that is, central, regional, and local? How should these local and regionally elected governments ensure their fiscal autonomy, which is a key component of decentralization? How large should these regional and local governments be?

Another set of considerations relates to the fact that different levels of government have different levels of administrative and technical capacity. Most of the time, central administrations attract more qualified and talented people than regional and local administrations.[6] The type of service also determines the level of governance: services that require minimum expertise such as street cleaning and garbage collection work well at the local level while services requiring technical know-how such as power generation or urban planning are better delivered via regional and central echelons.[7] Decentralized control is also more successful when human services are important and when the provided service can be variable, such as education or health.[8] The administrative scale should thus depend on the type of service delivered or the policy sector.

The discussion about the "right" scales of decentralization regularly fluctuates between giving primacy to the local level (localism) or regional level (regionalism), or advocating recentralization.[9] In fact, reasons for devolving certain responsibilities and certain levels of government are used at different times to argue for different positions, and are often embedded within political conflicts.[10] Hence, one must recall that decentralization is not a neutral policy-making process but an inherently political tool that reshuffles the distribution of power among decision-makers and leaderships, and therefore is the object of resistance and contestation. Understanding the historical specificity of the studied context is of primary importance: decentralization is closely associated with the social and political history of a place. Accordingly, generalizing about the "right" governance scale is misguided.

The debate on centralization or decentralization and its relationship to better democratization and service delivery is especially complex when it comes to administrative and fiscal decentralization, as there is no clear and generic correlation

6 P. Bardhan, "Decentralization of Governance and Development," *Journal of Economic Perspectives*, 16(4) (2012), 185–205.

7 Ibid.

8 De Vries, "The Rise and Fall of Decentralization."

9 Ibid.

10 N. Brenner, "Globalisation As Reterritorialisation: The Re-scaling of Urban Governance in the European Union," *Urban Studies*, 36(3) (1999), 431–51.

between all elements. The policy shift from conventional administrative structures, where roles are monopolized and centralized, to new structures, where roles are shared through devolution and delegation, is not straightforward. Many issues need to be taken into account, namely accountability, efficiency, effectiveness, and their impact on resource mobilization.[11] Policymakers and scholars still struggle with devising context-specific strategies for administrative systems to change from being monopolistic to pluralistic in their composition and control. Who should have the authority to distribute the public good and whether financing should be centrally or locally designed – or a combination of both scales – is an open-ended question closely related to the degree of the public service spillover and to the heterogeneity of districts.[12]

DECENTRALIZATION IN THE MENA REGION

In the context of the Middle East and North Africa (MENA) region, decentralization was partially put in place by colonial authorities to control the power of strong local leaderships. After the establishment of independent nation-states, governments favored social welfare policies to gain support and legitimacy, often in conjunction with establishing authoritarian rule. During the 1980s and 1990s, socioeconomic challenges made these policy choices more difficult to sustain. Progressively, structural adjustment policies and neoliberal reforms drastically altered the sociopolitical system in place in favor of the governing authorities and their associated elites, and at the expense of the low- and middle-income categories. Poverty levels increased drastically. Governments in the MENA region continued advocating decentralization, frequently under the auspices of foreign donors, but very little effective decentralization of authority was being implemented.[13] "Deconcentration" was the actual dominant practice, which served to strengthen rather than redistribute central government powers.[14] This often led to a major crisis of accountability between different levels of government as well as vis-à-vis citizens. Simultaneously, on the ground, local governments were gaining more and more strength and demanding more loudly their rights to manage their own affairs. The Arab uprisings clearly gave voice to some of these frustrations and demonstrated the growing significance of the local and territorial scale of politics.

11 J. M. Cohen and S. B. Peterson *Administrative Decentralization: Strategies for Developing Countries* (West Hartford, CT: Kumarian Press, 1999).

12 T. Besley and S. Coate, "Centralized versus Decentralized Provision of Local Public Goods: A Political Economy Approach," *Journal of Public Economics*, 87 (2003), 2611–37.

13 Bergh, "Introduction: Researching the Effects of Neoliberal Reforms."

14 M. Jari, "Local Governance in the MENA Region: Space for (Incremental and Controlled) Change? Yes, Promoting Decentralized Governance? Tough Question," *Journal of Economic and Social Research*, 12(1) (2010), 9–32.

Many MENA countries depend on international aid, which is tied to demands to put in place decentralization policies.[15] Foreign donors operate in the context of multilevel governance and globalization,[16] and are generally disconnected from the specifics of the local.[17] This gap leads to inequalities in the elaboration and implementation of decentralization policies that benefit the already powerful groups (and local governments) at the expense of more marginalized communities who do not master the jargon of international development. Thus, these decentralized policies change the responsibilities and capabilities of political actors in ways that are frequently in opposition to their aims of better governance, as they are not associated with administrative accountability and protective legal mechanisms.[18] Additionally, local opposition groups can become more radicalized in reaction to decentralization policies that threaten their power, and strongly contest and prevent decentralization reform.[19]

In summary, decentralization produces a new complex landscape of powers that may impede development aims. Central actors obstruct the transfer of power to the local level, or they partially transfer authority to the parties they have control over, resorting to the selective implementation of laws, threats of violence, and claims that local actors are unable to meet their responsibilities. Nongovernmental organizations (NGOs), experts, and entrepreneurs strategically position themselves as intermediaries between the central government and the local administration, but they are accountable to neither.

It is at the level of service delivery that studies clearly show how decentralization is not being effectively implemented in MENA countries. Since the 1950s, Arab countries, especially the oil-rich countries, were able to significantly expand their service provision policies. Yet, this only benefited selected regions and groups, thus

[15] Bergh, "Introduction: Researching the Effects of Neoliberal Reforms." Bergh notes that decentralization and neoliberalism are part of New Institutional Economics, which is geared toward efficient transactions and accountability, and rooted in three key ideas: information (and how it leads to better choices); laws, contracts, and their enforcement; and competition.

[16] Multilevel governance includes relationships at different scales between different institutions, national or transnational. Peters and Pierre argue that multilevel governance in Western countries is an outcome of the shift in the role of state from a "command and control" type to an "enabling" type. It responds to the globalization of the world as well as to the increasing need for local autonomy and subnational networks. Here, it is important to remember, with Brenner, that globalization is a process in which the accelerated movement of commodities and capital under capitalism occurs, enabled by the framework of fixed territorial configurations. Thus, deterritorialization and reterritorialization are both part of the globalization process. Before globalization, in the 1970s, the state was the most important spatial scale. Now, no one scale is more important than another. See: B. G. Peters and J. Pierre, "Developments in Intergovernmental Relations: Towards Multi-level Governance," *Policy & Politics*, 29(2) (2001), 131–35; and Brenner, "Globalisation as Reterritorialization."

[17] Jari, "Local Governance in the MENA Region."

[18] Batterbury and Fernando, "*Rescaling Governance and the Impacts of Political and Environmental Decentralization.*"

[19] A. R. Poteete and J. C. Ribot, "Repertoires of Domination: Decentralization as Process in Botswana and Senegal," *World Development*, 39(3) (2011), 439–49.

furthering inequality. In the following decades, the economic crises largely limited this welfare strategy. Today, public goods provision in the Arab region is plagued by poor performance, coverage gaps, insufficient funding, and ineffective administration.[20] Political and administrative reforms have been promoting decentralization as it could significantly improve public goods provision. However, despite introducing some decentralization policies, most governments in the Arab region still retain power and authority over local and regional governments through fiscal control.[21] Central public sector institutions still deliver services that are usually the responsibility of local councils elsewhere.

FACTORS IMPACTING DECENTRALIZATION IN THE ARAB REGION

Our study explored two hypotheses developed based on our literature review and initial overview of the state of decentralization in the region. The first is that central governments in the Arab region are not fully engaged in the process of decentralization. While they commit to some decentralization regulations, they simultaneously contain their implementation so as to maintain their domination over political and economic life. As such, decentralization policies may be furthering centralization. Our second hypothesis is that, despite this constraining context, regional and local-level governments and actors are resisting this domination, and some are developing creative ways through which they are able to exercise their authority. Through the examination of service delivery, we identified and documented some examples of power struggles at the regional and local levels and analyzed the features that explain varying successes and failures.

Drawing on fieldwork conducted in Jordan, Lebanon, Morocco, Tunisia, and Yemen,[22] we underscored five crosscutting themes concerning the course of decentralization in the Arab region: (1) the impact of colonial legacies and regional histories on contemporary decentralization debates and practices; (2) the paradoxical role of the state in simultaneously promoting and subverting decentralizing initiatives; (3) the inadequate provision for civil society participation and public–private partnerships in local urban management and service delivery; (4) the reluctance of municipalities to collect local taxes; and (5) instances of municipal and regional government innovation that managed to achieve effective decentralized practices

[20] S. Belghazi, "Local Governance, Development and Service Delivery," unpublished paper delivered at the Arab States Local Governance Forum, Sana'a, Yemen (December 6–9, 2003).

[21] Ibid.

[22] This analysis draws on the country chapters published in our co-edited volume: S. Y. Turki and E. Verdeil, "Tunisie: La constitution (du Printemps) ouvre le débat sur la décentralisation"; A. Bouabid and A. Iraki, "Maroc: Tensions centralisatrices"; Omar Abdulaziz Hallaj, "Yemen: Between Tides of Unity and Tribal Approval"; M. Ababsa, "Jordanie: La décentralisation par décision centralisée et la démocratie par volonté royale"; and Mona Harb and Sami Atallah "Lebanon: a Fragmented and Incomplete Decentralization," in Harb and Atallah, *Local Governments and Public Goods*, 11–228.

despite national-level constraints. In the following section, we discuss our findings, with select examples drawn from our cases.

Colonial Legacies and Regional Histories

Interactions and hierarchies between groups living in the Arab region prior to colonial rule were very much regulated according to a decentralized power structure. Colonial regimes deeply reconfigured these relationships by drawing new territorial and administrative boundaries that cut across regions and hinterlands. They used the technical and administrative dimensions of decentralization to justify their reforms with a primary goal of controlling territories and opposition groups. Thus, decentralization was foremost about deconcentrating administrative, financial, security, and other services from the central state to regional and local scales, rather than providing political representation to localities and regions. The aim was to have a firm grip on the newly formed nation-state's territories, especially on areas that presented threats. Thus, the geographic basis upon which districts were drawn was often a function of the territorial belonging of opposition groups: administrative boundaries were used to cut their hinterland and constrain their ability to communicate, gather, and potentially mobilize – applying the classic "divide to rule" adage.

With the establishment of independent nation-states, this approach was further pursued and consolidated, using the narrative of the need to build a strong modern state. Deconcentration reforms continued with the same objective of extending the eyes and ears of the central state to regions and localities. However, municipal elections started to be held, and democratic representation slowly began to emerge at the local level, which changed the rules of the game as more lobbying at the local and regional scales, and from within the state, was being exercised to further the implementation of decentralization reforms toward more democratization.

This colonial legacy of decentralization is not the same across Arab states. While in Morocco, Tunisia, Lebanon, and Jordan, the building of postcolonial nation-states used centralization to consolidate state power, in Yemen, decentralization was preferred as a tool to balance the power of regions. In either case, centralization and decentralization narratives were used to consolidate the interests of the ruling elites and their networks. These narratives were frequently accompanied by a modernization rhetoric that praised the values of the strong state needing to control service delivery and secure its authority over the national territory against enemies' threats of secession. In Jordan, the king advocates decentralization to further secure the power of original Jordanian families, create jobs, and maintain social peace, while controlling the emergence of Islamist groups within municipalities. In Lebanon, municipalities are also taken up by sectarian ruling powers to further their authority over territories and access economic development rents, as well as distribute services to their clientele.

The social and territorial organizational system of Tunisian tribes provided services to constituencies according to a decentralization hierarchy that was replaced under colonial rule with a new administrative geography aiming to control their power. The independent Tunisian nation-state consolidated further this territorial subdivision and positioned its representatives to supervise regions and localities and administer service delivery. It also differentiated between urban and rural municipalities, providing less leverage to rural localities where the fear of opposition was more acute than in Tunisian cities. In Morocco, the deconcentration of state services similarly enables "eyes on the street" over the most remote tribal regions, via an administrative system led by rural circle chiefs (named *super caïd*) and urban district chiefs (named *pacha*), who supervise *sheikhs* and *moqaddems* whose role is to directly administer streets and neighborhoods. This policing system parallels and intersects with the electoral system of regional and local councils. Such an ambivalent system that both centralizes and decentralizes authority illustrates well the policy tensions and contradictions that characterize decentralization issues in Morocco, opposing the monarchy to nationalist parties. The duality is also found in how the state removes certain cities and regions from the rest of the decentralization architecture, depending on their strategic stake. In Lebanon, Beirut's municipality is the only one which does not have executive authority and depends on the governor for implementing its decisions – thus leading to major bottlenecks in terms of service provision and local development in the capital city. Conversely, Amman and Aqaba in Jordan have extraordinary powers as "special economic zones" directly associated with the prime minister's office, outside any control or accountability mechanisms.

States that Promote and Subvert Decentralization

National actors in Arab countries quickly understood the importance of promoting decentralization as a reform tool, given the large amount of financial resources that could be made available to them via international donors' agendas that were loudly promoting decentralization programs. Surely, several public officials who are believers in a modern welfare state genuinely advocate for decentralization and local democracy. However, many were wary of relinquishing power and resources, and paid lip service to decentralization. Still, both forces pushed toward adopting decentralization policies while simultaneously finding ways to circumvent their full implementation.

Such dual positioning leads to paradoxical situations where governments elaborate decentralization policies that are undermined by other policies, often financial, restricting their applicability. The ambiguity is put to good use as well through requesting additional aid from donors, as public actors show partial achievements in the journey toward decentralization and find enough reasons to justify delays and gaps. Thus, our findings show how international donors are indirectly contributing to the increased centralization of state power and services, not to mention furthering corruption and inefficiency, through programs that seek to promote the opposite agenda. The overlapping programs of central agencies involved in decentralization, which generate gaps and ambiguities that can be easily instrumentalized to serve the interests of public agents, further enable this contradiction.

Prior to its revolution and civil war, Yemen was a case in point where decentralization was strongly encouraged by the central state in terms of policy-making. Thanks to extensive donor aid, reforms were leading to the relatively effective deconcentration of technical and administrative services. However, with regard to political decentralization, legal, fiscal, and territorial tools were used to restrict the effective empowerment of local authorities.

In Morocco, the monarchy exercises stringent controls over elected local authorities via financial and administrative mechanisms that keeps their actions under scrutiny. In addition, international aid (namely of the French-funded program advocating decentralization, referred to as "decentralized cooperation") is used to strengthen central state services and appointed regional authorities rather than empowering locally elected governments. Ironically, rhetoric advocating the need to modernize the Ministry of Interior with the aim of consolidating decentralization and deconcentration accompanies the process. The Lebanese Ministry of Interior is another case in point, as it benefits from multiple sources of funds to study decentralization reforms, train its employees, and establish in-house service structures, ultimately consolidating its own constituents and networks at the expense of enhancing local and regional governance. A major tool the central state uses to manage the works of local and regional governments is financial controls. Indeed, municipalities can enjoy many prerogatives on paper, but their ability to operate and execute is impeded by withholding payments, like in Lebanon, or by requesting additional financial contributions for unexpected expenses, like in Tunisia. Financial controls also serve to operate unequal payments (sometimes against the law), favoring partners and hurting enemies – a strategy encountered in Jordan, Lebanon, and Yemen.

In all the cases we examined, except for Lebanon and Yemen, regional governments are not elected and operate as deconcentrated authorities representing the central state. However, since the Arab uprisings of 2011, debates about regionalism are gaining ground as possible means to tame opposition forces. In Morocco, discussions about political and institutional reforms involve the reorganization of territories and the endowment of regions with additional authorities. In Tunisia, a new committee on regional and local governments was created as part of the Constituent Assembly, which developed a new decentralization law to expand regional autonomy and empower local authorities. In Jordan, the king has repeatedly supported decentralization agendas in his speeches, although he has also postponed local elections. In Lebanon, where regional councils have a relatively large margin of maneuver, the state sponsored the study of a decentralization law that seeks to give them more leverage and independence, but it is yet to appear on the Parliament's voting agenda.

Issues of Urban Management and Public–Private Partnerships

Urban management and service delivery incorporate, in most cases, relatively centralized services operated by national-scale public agencies. But, increasingly, infrastructural and technical services (such as water services and garbage collection) are being decentralized to local levels, without sufficient human and financial resources to operate, manage, and maintain their provision. Such delegation is often coordinated via public–private partnerships according to complicated legal and institutional setups that do not always guarantee the quality of service provided, equitable distribution to beneficiaries, or efficiency costs for operators. Such opaque setups lead to management and provision problems, which local governments are directly bearing because issues of accountability have not been clearly defined.

Finance systems are also unhelpful to efficient service delivery. Mostly, urban municipalities are the ones able to have relative fiscal autonomy, while smaller and rural municipalities are dependent on the central state's transfers. Even so, large and urban municipalities still depend on the central state in defining their revenues and securing their budgets. In addition, while it could be useful to pool resources and improve service delivery, legislation does not encourage intermunicipal coordination in most cases, and is also impeded by parochial competition among mayors who are not keen on teamwork.

In Morocco, local governments are in a situation where they constantly need to negotiate with the central state access to urban services and financial resources to manage them, generating tensions and crises, especially in situations where internal conflicts within local governments prevent bargaining. Central agents become directly implicated in such crises, taking sides and supporting interests against others – impeding the effective decentralization of authority and sound service delivery. In cases where local governments are directly in charge of the service (like garbage collection in Morocco), the constraints of the regulatory systems ruling public–private partnerships and limited financial funds at the local government level hinder efficient operation and management of the service. For example, a municipal federation in Lebanon (Baakline) managed to get funding to build a waste management plant in its district but failed at securing a steady flow of financing to maintain the plant, and hence ended up relinquishing its operation to the central state agency.

In Tunisia, local governments are unable to control and regulate urban management and planning because of their limited resources, the lack of legal tools, and the pressure of private economic interests. This has led to the multiplication of illegalities and to poor levels of infrastructure and services. People are also not engaged in municipal affairs (though this is changing) and do not comply with paying taxes. Local governments thus become delegitimized, which reinforces the role of central state agencies in service provision, and further limits the possibility of innovation in terms of policy-making. Sometimes, major hurdles in service provision have to be addressed, like in the case of garbage collection.

In Jordan, the amalgamation reform of municipalities in 2001 did not succeed in improving service delivery. On the contrary, it increased clientelism and inequality in accessing services. Jordanian municipalities are thus mostly unable to effectively provide services to their dwellers, and have been encouraged by the government to operate through public–private partnerships. However, the lack of technical and financial know-how to negotiate contracts and fees with private operators entailed added burdens with expenses they were not able to meet, and with service costs that were beyond the capacities of beneficiaries. Thus, municipalities reverted to the ministry to cover their costs, and ended up with an increased dependency on the central government.

In some instances, local and regional governments successfully partner with civil society groups and are able to effectively manage projects. In Tunisia, a dynamic mayor worked closely with NGOs concerned with public transportation and coordinated a free school transportation system for the town's children. In Lebanon, another charismatic mayor facilitated the work of civil society groups eager to promote sustainable development in the town and helped them establish a successful ecotourism project.

Resistance to Municipal Tax Collection

The fourth theme relates to the reluctance of municipalities to collect local taxes. In all of the cases we studied, municipalities suffered from low revenues. This is largely attributable to how central governments have provided local administrations with little tax authority: few taxes to collect, a low tax base to collect from, and/or narrow or no margins to set the rate of the tax or fee. Central governments have also stalled in distributing funds to local authorities from the intergovernmental grant system. They have reduced the amount to be distributed, delayed its disbursement, or paid in installments. In some instances, like in Jordan and Yemen, fiscal allocations to local governments followed a political logic, favoring towns from which ministers and parliamentarians originated.

Moreover, some local governments have failed to optimize on the tax authority they were granted. For some, it was a matter of weak human resources and a poor system of identifying taxpayers. For others, they chose not to collect taxes or fees from their constituencies, especially around election times. Municipalities thus unofficially exempted some taxpayers from paying local taxes in return for (the hope of) gaining political loyalty. Another possible reason for dodging tax collection could be attempting to appease the population from additional costs, and thus preventing potential social upheavals. In 2003, in Jordan, up to 40 percent of municipal revenues were not collected. Jordanian mayors seemed to prefer negotiating grant transfers from the central state rather than antagonizing their immediate constituency through tax payments. In Morocco too, the fear of losing the electoral base, clientelism, and mistrust of public finance led mayors to be reluctant in imposing tax collection. Similarly in Yemen, local councils did not want to upset the popular base they needed to appease. Yemeni communities responded with great strife against the introduction of local taxes and fees, as they became accustomed to national subsidies. Matters are certainly not improving with the increasing economic crisis, forced displacement, and violent conflicts that characterize many Arab countries today.

Effective Decentralization and Innovations against the Odds

Our research also revealed innovations undertaken by local and regional governments' leaders and their teams against administrative, financial, and political odds. We explored the features that explain the noteworthy performance of some local and regional governments, and their ability to negotiate hurdles to deliver better services, think holistically about development projects, and establish various partnerships for spatial planning ends. Such features include leadership, networks, civil society dynamics, political competition, governance, and territoriality. Innovative experiences are not to be romanticized and do not exclude contestations, inefficiencies, and inequalities. They demonstrate, however, that when particular conditions converge (i.e., strong leadership, active networks, vibrant civil society dynamics, healthy political competition, good governance, and territoriality attributes), decentralization policies can open up avenues for improved service delivery and urban management, and for potential social and political change, even if such change is timid and contained. Still, major challenges persist, namely specifying the operational terms of intermunicipal cooperation (currently ill-defined in all case studies), the legal terms of public–private partnerships, and the scales of decentralization of infrastructural services in ways to ensure flexibility and diversity according to the type of service and to geographical specificities. Also, efficient systems of management and a high level of technical expertise are required within local and regional governments, which are currently sorely lacking.

In prewar Yemen, limited opportunities were available that allowed some innovations in terms of local development. Indeed, some local leaders with strong abilities to negotiate with national authorities managed to advance solutions that met their constituencies' needs, often using both legal and extrajudicial networks. For instance, one local councilor managed to establish cultural activities in his town, despite partial funding, while another brought water and sanitation services to their constituency, despite technical and geographic hurdles. Some regional governments in Lebanon succeeded at negotiating grant packages and mobilizing local partnerships in ways to enable strategic planning for their region and initiate economic development through ecotourism strategies (e.g., Jezzine, Sour, and Dinniye). Service delivery at the regional level was also successful in Tunisia where experiences of public transportation in the district of Sidi Bouzid generated positive outcomes. Indeed, the partnership between the governorate and private bus owners led to establishing an effective and affordable system for collecting school children. Another partnership with a local NGO also yielded encouraging results. In Morocco, some municipalities led by charismatic figures have succeeded in establishing institutional setups and capturing international grants, although they were not intended for their localities. For instance, in Agadir, the mayor, with the support of a local committee including representatives of civil society groups, implemented an avant-gardist transportation system despite constraints imposed on him by the Ministry of Interior. Matters were more complex in Jordan, where strong centralization and direct interventionism by the king prevented opportunities for maneuvering autonomously at the local or regional levels.

CONCLUSION

Based on our research, we conclude that despite many constraints, decentralization policies in the Arab region may occasionally present significant policy windows that could form opportunities for social, political, and economic changes, if mobilized adequately. In a study we conducted on the performance of municipal federations in Lebanon, we identified three sets of conditions required to capitalize on those windows: effective leadership, strong multi-scalar networks, and political competition. It remains to be seen whether these conditions are also valid for other political contexts in the Arab region. Thus, future research on decentralization, regional and local governments, urban management, and service delivery is essential to pursue. Our study is designed in part to identify a critical research agenda that calls for closer examination of issues such as ethnographies of municipal institutions, sociological profiles of municipal councilors, local stakeholder analysis, detailed analysis of local projects, and tracing of policies, to name but a few. More studies along these dimensions would better inform policy-making across the Arab region and gage the historical and political context for furthering (or not) decentralization. Indeed, we should be careful in advocating for the devolution of power when it can be instrumentalized or co-opted by undemocratic ruling authorities, at the expense of people's livelihoods and rights, and in ways that aggravate extraction, corruption, inequality, and autocracy.

PART II

Decentralization and Governance Reform

6

Decentralization, Ideology, and Law in the Islamic Republic of Iran

Kian Tajbakhsh

Generally, nation-state–building combines established territorial boundaries, a settled population, and an authoritative political and legal system that governs and ensures internal and external security – in short, a country, a people, and a regime.[1] Historians of modern Iran agree that the concentration of state power in a group, person, or branch of government has shaped state–society relations and the character of nation-state–building. Centralized state power, they argue, has typically crowded out the independent power of civil society actors, private sector interests, and minority social identities, thereby hindering the growth of democratic pluralism. Democratization of the country is thus unlikely.[2]

And yet at the turn of the twenty-first century, the Islamic Republic of Iran (IRI) embarked on an ambitious decentralization of the state system by establishing elected local governments in cities and villages throughout the entire country. In February 1999, millions of Iranians went to the polls in elections for over 200,000 local government posts in over 600 cities and 37,000 villages across the country (*shuray-e eslami shahr va roosta*). This stunning change came about peacefully and with a high degree of consensus at the national level.

How should we explain political decentralization in an authoritarian, nondemocratic regime? To answer this question, this chapter analyzes the political decentralization of the IRI with an understanding both of the concentration of power in the country and of a factor historians' accounts typically underplay: the modern bureaucratically organized state is a uniquely *territorial* organizational form, and this sets it apart from other forms of social power such as markets, social classes, and local or regional groupings. Weber famously noted that the modern state "claims binding

1 C. Offe, "Political Liberalism, Group Rights, and the Politics of Fear and Trust," *Studies in East European Thought*, 53(3) (2001), 167–82.

2 E. Abrahamian, *A History of Modern Iran* (Cambridge: Cambridge University Press, 2008); S. A. Arjomand, *After Khomeini: Iran under His Successors* (Oxford: Oxford University Press, 2012); S. A. Arjomand, *Sociology of Shi'ite Islam: Collected Essays* (Leiden and Boston: Brill, 2016), 440; A. Amanat, *Iran: A Modern History* (London: Yale University Press, 2017).

authority, not only over the members of the state, the citizens ... but also to a very large extent over all action taking place in the area of its jurisdiction. It is thus a compulsory organization with a territorial basis."[3] In this chapter I offer an overview of two distinct forms of state power, the different accountability relationships they entail, and the definition of local democracy relevant to the case of decentralization in Iran, before turning to a case study of decentralization in Iran.

LOCAL GOVERNMENT AND AUTHORITARIAN STATE-BUILDING IN MODERN IRAN: THEORETICAL CONTEXT

To explain the function of political decentralization in state-building in Iran I draw on the distinction between two types of state power which, following Michael Mann, I call despotic and infrastructural forms of power.[4] These capture two different ways a state can be strong in relation to society (meaning nonstate social interests and actors within the state's territory). This distinction is directly related to the two vectors making up the power of the modern state: power *over* and power *to*.[5] Power *over* is the ability of the state to rule without routine negotiation with citizens, civil society groups, and nonstate social forces. I use *despotic* power to capture the ability of a state to dominate society in the absence of broad consent or legitimacy; a state with strong despotic power rules over a society with which it is in conflict. Thus, despotic power is a measure of the state's autonomy from its citizens; its ability to exercise arbitrary authority and to subjugate or repress social forces with violence and force. By contrast, power *to* is a measure of a state's ability to implement legitimately designed policies to achieve collectively desired goals developed through consensus (articulated clearly by thinkers such as Talcott Parsons and Hannah Arendt[6]). Here the state rules through and in cooperation with society; there are institutional channels for flows between citizens and state policy which is executed on behalf of society. Thus, *infrastructural* power depends on legitimacy and collective agreement and also points to the geographic and spatial reach of state authority highlighted by writers such as Charles Tilly and Guillermo O'Donnell.[7] While the two vectors – power to and power over – may function together, they are independent in that strength in one area does not imply strength in the other.

3 M. Weber, *Economy and Society: An Outline of Interpretive Sociology* (Berkeley: University of California Press, 2013), 56.

4 M. Mann, *The Sources of Social Power*, 2nd ed., 4 vols. (Cambridge: Cambridge University Press, 2012), vol. 2.

5 Steven Lukes, *Power: A Radical View*, 2nd ed. (New York: Palgrave Macmillan, 2004), 34.

6 T. Parsons, *Sociological Theory and Modern Society* (New York: Free Press, 1967); H. Arendt, *On Violence* (New York: Harcourt, Brace & World, 1970).

7 C. Tilly, *Coercion, Capital, and European States, AD 990–1992* (Cambridge, MA: Blackwell, 1992); G. O'Donnell, "On the State, Democratization and Some Conceptual Problems: A Latin American View with Glances at Some Postcommunist Countries," *World Development*, 21(8) (1993), 1355–69.

The ideal liberal democratic state, for example, is despotically weak but strives to achieve high levels of administrative competence across the entire territory of the nation-state. Failed states may have a high degree of despotic power but they lack infrastructural power, which leads to an inability to administer services to meet the basic needs of the society. An effectively managed authoritarian state such as the IRI seeks high levels of both despotic and infrastructural power. In Iran, the reformists promoted political decentralization in the hope that it would weaken despotic power, but the regime killed that hope, increasing infrastructural power without interfering with despotic power.

The defeat of the reformists' vision reflects the persistence of authoritarianism in the IRI. Most accounts highlight the centralization of power in the ruling regime as the key variable in explaining the regime's success in dominating societal forces.[8] Yet these studies typically fail to distinguish between infrastructural and despotic power. While they come to the correct conclusion about the unlikelihood of democratization of Iran under the current regime, they cannot explain the genesis or impact of the far-reaching decentralization reforms in the late 1990s. By establishing elected local government throughout the country's cities and villages, these reforms significantly expanded the number of electoral institutions without leading to democratization.

Researchers have wondered why the decentralization of this period has not led to democratization – why reformists did not achieve what they hoped for. I argue that one clue lies in the distinction between the two types of power. Competing actors championed political decentralization to achieve incompatible political and ideological objectives. Some sought democratization, but in the end, the goals of Islamization and technocratic efficiency won out. The ruling regime initially supported political decentralization primarily as a means of increasing the state's infrastructural power as a way to gain legitimacy and stability through assuaging local grievances without ceding the regime's monopoly of power. In contrast, the Islamic reformists' chief hope was that political decentralization would attenuate the regime's despotic power through the dispersion of the power concentrated in the capital city and in the ruling elite by expanding electoral competition to cities and towns and to new social groups. While the reformists also saw increased administrative capacity as an important outcome of decentralization, their greatest hope was for political liberalization. Ultimately the regime's priorities won out and political decentralization failed to enhance local democracy. For convenience I refer to these competing projects as local electoral authoritarianism and local democracy. The former prioritized the administrative dimensions of decentralization, and the latter emphasized the political dimensions.

8 M. Parsa, *Democracy in Iran: Why It Failed and How It Might Succeed* (Cambridge, MA: Harvard University Press, 2016); A. Gheissari and S. V. R. Nasr, *Democracy in Iran: History and the Quest for Liberty* (Oxford: Oxford University Press, 2006).

Our understanding of these two distinct projects can be deepened if we pay attention to the distinct forms of accountability they embody. Scholarship on decentralization, including the literature on fiscal federalism, advances three types of *accountability relationships* to distinguish the incentive structures characterizing the institutions of local administration and local democracy.[9] First, the democratic project of political decentralization aims to institutionalize the government's *downward accountability* to its citizens through local elections, whose criteria I elucidate further below. The second type of accountability is *social*. This occurs when citizens demand accountability from local government through civic engagement and civil society associations. Of course, absent the preconditions required for effective local collective action, civil society fails, leading either to no collective action or to such action as ultimately leads to welfare reduction, such as clientelistic distortion of the benefits of decentralization.[10] Finally, local government's supply of public services through top-down administrative decentralization (or as it is sometimes called, deconcentration[11]) operates primarily through strengthening the *upward accountability* of local governments to higher levels of government. The major threats to upward accountability are principal–agency problems between tiers of bureaucracy. As I argue, Iran's decentralization has created upward accountability but not downward and social accountability.

In general, the motivation to decentralize government derives from two distinct pressures: one for more efficient public administration, the other arising from demands by a variety of social interests for a greater power of self-government, be they nonterritorial, such as ethnic or religious minorities, or territorial, such as regions or cities. To preserve its legitimacy the state has an incentive to cede to the first pressure, at least to some degree – to fashion a bureaucracy capable of supplying a minimal level of public goods (such as ensuring domestic security as well as managing land and civil works) throughout the nation's territory and at every tier of subnational public administration (regions, cities, villages, and so forth). Through administrative decentralization the state can expand its infrastructural power. At the same time, the state may be forced to decentralize or delegate decision-making power to respond to demands for local self-government from social interests that may come from varying subnational levels. In such cases political decentralization constrains and weakens the state's despotic power insofar as it must share power with subnational social forces. In Iran, the primary motivation to decentralize emerged (top down) from the regime's desire for greater administrative efficiency and less so

9 World Bank Social Development Department, "Local Government Discretion and Accountability: A Local Governance Framework" (June 2007), 4.

10 G. Mansuri and V. Rao, *Localizing Development: Does Participation Work?* (Washington, DC: World Bank Publications, 2012), 54; R. Prud'homme, "On the Dangers of Decentralization," *The World Bank Research Observer*, 10(2) (August 1995), 201–20.

11 World Bank Social Development Department, "Local Government Discretion and Accountability," Annex 1.

from (bottom-up) demands for a measure of local self-government. The pressure to augment administrative efficiency has led the state to decentralize its internal administrative architecture to smaller and lower jurisdictional scales; it has thereby increased its penetration and domination of the national territory.

I examine the Iranian case as well as the justifications for decentralization that democratic reformists in Iran advanced in the second half of the 1990s according to the following definition of local democracy. Democratic government is based on majority rule articulated through free and fair elections. Local government can be called (liberal) democratic when local decisions (such as those related to land-use regulations, development of physical infrastructure, and the budget) satisfy three basic features of democratic politics. These features are that voters (1) express their sovereignty by authorizing representatives to rule on their behalf; (2) choose a preferred bundle of policies offered by a political platform through prospective voting (i.e., representatives have a mandate); and (3) endorse or punish past performance of representatives through retrospective voting. In the ideal democratic scenario, then, the people demonstrate their sovereignty because only they select their rulers, they get the policies they want, and they get the politicians they want. Extending this to decentralized local government implies the following additional criteria: all those affected by local government decisions have an opportunity to influence decisions by voting for a policy platform put forward by candidates in contested local elections; information about costs and benefits of local government policy are transparent and readily available to the relevant voting public to inform retrospective voting in subsequent elections where politicians are evaluated and then endorsed or voted out; and citizens can legally protest and appeal government decisions that impact their livelihoods and private property through an impartial judicial system and by means of civil society institutions such as uncensored media and voluntary associations.

Of course, the mere existence of local elections cannot guarantee that they are democratic, and an important strand of literature has identified the myriad ways political decentralization can lead to undesired negative outcomes, vitiating its democratic potential. These include political capture, elite capture,[12] and the extension of electoral authoritarianism from the national to the local level.[13] Elite capture excludes the poor and disadvantaged from the institutions and the benefits of decentralization. Political capture integrates the local population through electoral mechanisms, which politicians manipulate through clientelistic or patronage politics to secure reelection and maintain their grip on power while delivering benefits to only a narrow segment of the population. Electoral authoritarianism undermines

12 D. Mookherjee, "Political Decentralization," *Annual Review of Economics*, 7(1) (2015), 231–49; S. Khemani, "Political Capture of Decentralization" in J.-P. Faguet and C. Pöschl (eds.), *Is Decentralization Good for Development?* (Oxford: Oxford University Press, 2015), 196–223.

13 A. Schedler (ed.), *Electoral Authoritarianism: The Dynamics of Unfree Competition* (Boulder, CO: Lynne Rienner, 2006).

downward accountability because it involves the central state and national politicians effectively deploying local politics to enhance their dominance rather than permitting the dispersion of power among local social interests and localities. Gridlock is another negative outcome of political decentralization that undermines the positive potentials of local politics.

Bringing these various and complex strands together, we can say that at the heart of a realistic project of local democracy lies the challenge of balancing several elements: popular rights to representation, rights to contest government decisions (typically over land use), and individual private property rights (to land and housing particularly), together with the need to complete civil works within a reasonable time frame. Achieving such a balance was part of the Islamic reformists' project of local democracy, which involved maximizing the infrastructural power of the state while minimizing, if not eliminating, its despotic power. This was a political program we (for I had the honor and misfortune of working closely with them) understood to be a continuation of ideals first expressed in the Constitutional Revolution at the start of the twentieth century. A brief look at that earlier period provides important historical context for understanding the ideological dimensions of the struggle over political decentralization decades later.

THE HISTORICAL ORIGINS OF MODERN LOCAL GOVERNMENT IN IRAN

Elite republicans first established modern local government in Iran in the Constitution of 1907. The new laws required towns to assume a range of responsibilities including ensuring order, supervising local sanitation and public health, maintaining the streets and thoroughfares, and advising the central government on priorities for the expenditure of local revenues. Through these laws the central state sought to accommodate and co-opt a wide range of local voluntary associations (*anjumans*), which had played a prominent role in the revolutionary battle to impose constitutional limitations on the absolute power of the monarchy. European, particularly Belgian and French, models of center–local relations were incorporated into the new Constitution. However, from the outset the central government elites envisioned locally elected councils as mere instruments of state administration. The demand of some local governments for greater autonomy and political authority soon led to conflict with the central government, whose authority ultimately collapsed in the face of internal fissures, civil war, and external aggression, particularly from the Russian invasions of some northern cities in 1911–12. Ultimately, local government fell into abeyance for decades as the Pahlavi dynasty, starting in the 1920s, pursued a robust project of modernization directed by the central state. An aborted attempt to revive it in the first year of the 1979 revolution left local government as an appendage to the central government. In the first two decades of the new revolutionary regime, four groups contended over the fate of local government and struggled against and with each other to define what political decentralization could and should be within the framework of the Islamic Republic. The four groups pursued three different projects.

FOUR ACTORS, THREE COMPETING PROJECTS: ISLAMICIZATION, ADMINISTRATIVE MODERNIZATION, AND DEMOCRATIZATION

Three societal projects have shaped the evolution of local government and central–local relations in Iran since 1979: Islamization, technocratic modernization, and democratization. Four key social and political actors have championed these three projects: the *velayi* Islamists who make up the regime's leadership and core supporters, government bureaucrats, moderate technocratic Islamists, and democratically minded Islamist reformists. The adherence of these groups to the three projects in each case reflects a set of ideological assumptions about the value of local political institutions. The *velayi* Islamists, who espouse a maximalist interpretation of the *velayat faqih* principle of clerical dictatorship, viewed the councils as a religiously sanctioned institution for organizing populist forms of participation within Islamist bounds. They pursued Islamization. Government bureaucrats, members of the administrative bureaucracy and state planning agencies, and moderate technocratic Islamists formed an alliance in favor of technocratic modernization. These groups viewed decentralization of bureaucracy to subnational jurisdictions as necessary for local management that would deliver greater public goods (notably land-use regulation, some urban services, and physical infrastructure), as well as economic modernization. (Law and order has never been a responsibility of Iranian local government.) While not openly opposed to the democratization championed by the fourth group, they were largely indifferent to it. For example, the technocratic Executives of Construction of Iran Party (*Hezb-e kargozaran-e sazandegi*) described economic development as the best path to long-term political stability, rather than a path to the liberalization of government. This contrasts with the Islamic reformists' political agenda to fill the new institutional vessels of elected local government with democratic content with the objective of deepening political participation at local levels. They hoped in this way to democratize state–society relations, that is to say, to shift the polity's center of gravity from central state institutions dominated by the clerical elite and their lay allies to empowered plural electoral and civil society institutions. In other words, the reformists hoped decentralization would augment infrastructural power while diminishing despotic power. The apolitical technocrats and the bureaucrats concurred about infrastructural power and had little interest in despotic power. The *velayi* Islamists, in contrast, believed decentralization could increase infrastructural power without interfering with despotic power.

Democratization was and remains very controversial in the Iranian context. The regime's official discourse never invokes the word "democracy," so the ruling Islamists' accusation that the reformists' aims would undermine the ideological foundations of the regime – effectively representing a policy of regime change – has, on its face, some logical justification. The three projects for local government and their four categories of supporters would shape how political decentralization evolved over three decades.

ADMINISTRATION NOT DEMOCRATIZATION: THE ORIGINS OF THE 1996 LOCAL COUNCIL LAW

In the reconstruction phase of the early 1990s after the Iran–Iraq war, unemployment and underemployment were rampant in urban centers throughout Iran, with poverty rates climbing to 40 percent.[14] As a consequence, accelerating urbanization led to the growth of large, informal urban settlements. The state response, including brutal slum clearance, ignited major urban riots over the first half of the 1990s. The fourth Islamic Majlis (1992–96) reacted by turning to the provisions in the 1979 Constitution concerning the place of local councils in the national administrative framework, seeking a solution to social unrest and improvement in local administration. Neither the government nor the parliament had any direct interest in democratization or in enhancing civil society development per se. The majority of deputies in the fourth Majlis were from the conservative[15] "traditionalist right-wing" (*rast sonati*) Combatant Clergy Association (*Jame'e-ye Rowhaniyyat-e Mobarez*), whose slogan was "obedience to the Supreme Leader and support to President Rafsanjani"; in other words, they believed economic development need not pose a risk of political liberalization. In fact, it was a cleric and member of the Combatant Clergy Association, a stalwart of the revolution and former chief of the "ideological correctness" office (*aghidati*) of the army, who drafted and introduced a decentralization bill in 1993. He and his supporters saw decentralization only as a means to meet public service needs in order to assuage mounting grievances in cities throughout the country and affirm order. Contrary to the conventional understanding, which associates local councils with the agenda pursued by Islamic reformists several years later, it was in fact the conservative fourth Majlis (parliament) that passed the first local council law in 1996.

THE EMERGENCE OF DEMOCRATIC AMBITIONS FOR LOCAL GOVERNMENT

The reformist Khatami administration (1997–2004) implemented a vast program of political decentralization by establishing elected local councils in all cities and villages throughout the country in 1999.[16] The new administration raised

[14] D. Salehi-Isfahani, "Poverty, Inequality, and Populist Politics in Iran," *The Journal of Economic Inequality*, 7(1) (2009), 5–28, at 13.

[15] "Conservative" is an inexact but commonly used label. I use it to refer to core regime supporters who support the principle of *velayat faqih*. I refer to them elsewhere as *velayi* Islamists.

[16] K. Tajbakhsh, "Political Decentralization and the Creation of Local Government in Iran: Consolidation or Transformation of the Theocratic State?" *Social Research*, 67(2) (2000), 377–404.

the promise of elected local councils to a central plank of their reform program, framing them as expressions of a democratic civil society, and supported countrywide local elections. However, passing this agenda required the approval of the supreme leader,[17] the endorsement of the Guardian Council, and the support of the technocratic elites, both in the central government planning agencies such as the Management and Planning Organization and the new moderate political faction in parliament headed by the technocratic mayor of Tehran. The dynamic deputy minister of interior, a leader of the radical democratic wing of the Islamic reformists, oversaw local elections throughout the entire country in February 1999, which took place peacefully. Despite this critical role, the democratizing agenda of the reformists did not originate local council law or implement it alone, and at no time did the reformists' challenge to the regime's concentration of power solely drive decentralization.

The reform radically changed the organization of local government in cities and villages. Whereas the central state had previously appointed and supervised mayors, now the popularly elected city or village council (*shura*) appointed them and held them accountable. Although the central government oversees them, councils nonetheless retain substantive legal autonomy to hire and fire mayors. Further, local governments' functions did not change substantially.[18] The most significant change is that councils now have legal responsibility for overseeing the municipality's entire operations and the budget, which they approve and supervise (although in practice not always consistently or regularly).[19] In 2017, the fifth round of local elections took place throughout the country, marking two decades of successful institutionalization of local government. It was remarkable after a century of anemic local government under three regimes.

The reformists' ideal of democratic Islamism stood in sharp contrast to the regime's model of Islamic populist participatory governance under the *velayat faqih* (*mardom salari deeni velayi*). Said Hajjarian,[20] one of President Khatami's key advisors, openly criticized the clerical monopoly of power, for instance rejecting "any

[17] In a 2017 oral history interview, the deputy minister in charge of local government in the Khatami administration said that the country's leadership's main hesitation about establishing elected local government was managerial, not political. He does not explain his decision to proceed with the council reforms despite the supreme leader's concerns. M. Tajzadeh "Mostafa Tajzadeh: Oral History Interview," *Tarikh Online* (January 20, 2017).

[18] These include providing public services such as fire services, waste disposal, and street cleaning, maintaining and upgrading the city's roads, local taxi and buses service, parks and green space, property registration, and collection of local taxes. Municipalities are not responsible for major utilities, education, or policing.

[19] K. Tajbakhsh, "Decentralization, Municipal Management and Local Economic Development in Iran," unpublished draft, World Bank, Finance, Private Sector Development and Infrastructure Group Middle East and North Africa Region (May 2006).

[20] جمهوریت، افسون‌زدایی از قدرت *Jumhuriat: Afzunzadegi az ghodrat* [Republicanism: Disenchantment of Power] (Tehran: Tarhe No, 2001), 270.

meta-social norms (*eraadeye foq eradeye umumi*) capable of reversing legitimately produced laws expressing the popular will" – echoing prominent formulations in Western democratic theory.[21] Hajjarian compared local councils to a "trench" (*sangar*) from which to consolidate power for reformists and to advance to higher political office, legally and electorally "going from trench to trench" (*sangar be sangar*).[22] Mostafa Tajzadeh, chair of the main reformist political party and the deputy minister of interior overseeing the first and second local council elections, explicitly justified the reformists' aspirations for the elected local councils in terms of their broader political project of democratizing both power relations *within* the state system and *between* state and society.[23] Tajzadeh recalls that, when the reformists lost in the second round of local elections in Tehran, he immediately congratulated his conservative opponent to emphasize his faith in competitive elections, demonstrating that preserving a system of fair elections was more important to his party than winning.

The reformists' understanding of the role of elections was considerably at odds with the dominant perspective held by the regime. *Velayi* Islamism circumscribes the institutions and issues subject to popular voting to a limited set of policy arenas. It also has an ambiguous relationship to the majority rule principle, endorsing it when elections affirm illiberal Islamic rule (as in the 1979 referendum) but rejecting it if it contradicts their interpretation of Islamic principles. By contrast, many reformists had come to accept two things. First, elections should be based on informed consent arrived at individually rather than the emulation of religious elites (*taqlid*). Second, electoral outcomes should not violate minority and human rights – two assumptions they recognized to be integral to liberal constitutionalism.[24] Although they rarely acknowledged it publicly, the reformists were, in effect, advancing a dualistic understanding of the state–civil society relationship, which they contrasted to the organic or monist political theology of *velayat faqih*.[25] The reformists hoped to bolster and expand reformist political party power by winning local council seats throughout the country and, with the help of allies in the media, to influence public opinion by exposing them to ideas of tolerance, pluralism, and

21 Compare the influential statement by Habermas in W. Rehg (trans.), *Between Facts and Norms: Contributions to a Discourse Theory of Law and Democracy* (Cambridge, MA: MIT Press, 2001), 26. He describes "the modern situation of a predominantly secular society in which normative orders must be maintained without metasocial guarantees."

22 "Bayad be fekr fath-e sangar be sangar bud" [We Must Think about Civil Society, from Trench to Trench] “باید به فکر «فتح سنگر به سنگ“ بود,” (Nov. 21, 2016), namehnews.ir/fa/news/374146/حجاریان-باید-به-فکر-فتح-سنگر-به-سنگر-بود.

23 "Tajzadeh on Local Councils, Democracy and Political Parties (Interview)," Isna.Ir. (May 6, 2006).

24 M. Kadivar, "Human Rights and Religious Intellectuals Part 1," *Aftab*, 27 (1382 Tir 2003), 54–59. It is worth pointing out that many reformists are skeptical of several other features underlying classical liberal models of secularism, particularly the privatization of religious convictions. I discuss the reformists' ideal of nonliberal, nontyrannical democracy in Kian Tajbakhsh, "What Are Iranians Dreaming about Today? Reflections on the Islamic Revolution at 40," *Social Research: An International Quarterly*, 86(1) (2019), 305–35.

25 My use of "dualism" follows Jean L. Cohen and Andrew Arato, *Civil Society and Political Theory* (Cambridge, MA: MIT Press, 1992).

democracy. They hoped that expanded participatory electoral politics would be able to constrain and balance the theocratic political elites and democratize the central government bureaucracy.[26]

The reformists' support for decentralization also encouraged several local governments to experiment with their own participatory approaches. Municipalities large and small, including both Tehran and Kashan, initiated projects encouraging local or neighborhood voluntary associations to cooperate with local government in supplying urban services and, in some cases, economic development. Tehran led the country's municipalities in introducing new participatory approaches to urban policy and planning, pushing the decentralization logic further down the territorial hierarchy to embrace city districts and neighborhoods as potential partners with municipal governments and introducing the idea of a people's city charter.[27] These initiatives were motivated in part by the search for alternatives to unpopular forms of urban management. Large-scale urban renewal projects of the mid-1990s, for example, had bulldozed large swaths of Tehran to construct a highway, destroying some twenty neighborhoods and displacing over a quarter of a million residents, leading to widespread condemnation by the nation's urban planning professionals.[28] The ensuing controversy prompted the Tehran municipality to adopt models of local participation.

Thus, decentralization did succeed in creating new local electoral institutions and encouraging participation. Yet, after more than twenty years in operation, the reformists' substantive goals of empowering local democracy remain unachieved. The widespread institutionalization of forms of popular participation in neighborhood and local councils demonstrates, instead, the greater success of the Islamic form of participatory governance in channeling political participation in directions acceptable to the regime. The next section illustrates how contention over two dimensions critical to the institutionalization of political democracy – the scope of political participation in local elections and the degree of legislative authority afforded local government – has limited democratization in the Islamic Republic.

POLITICAL PARTICIPATION AND DISQUALIFICATION OF CANDIDATES

One recent study makes the controversial claim that elections under the IRI are "on balance, basically fair but not free."[29] "Fair" would imply that the qualification

26 For the democratic discourse of the reformists during this period, see Kadivar, "Human Rights and Religious Intellectuals Part 1," and M. Kamrava, *Iran's Intellectual Revolution* (Cambridge: Cambridge University Press, 2008). C. Kurzman, *Liberal Islam: A Source Book* (New York: Oxford University Press, 1998), presents earlier examples of democratic and liberal Islamic discourse in Iran and elsewhere.

27 A. Khatam, "کنگره منشور تهران: اولین تجربه تدوین یک میثاق شهری Tehran Citizen's Charter," *Gofte-Gu*, 30 (1379 2000), 184–87.

28 H. Bahrainy and B. Aminzadeh, "Evaluation of Navab Regeneration Project in Central Tehran, Iran," *International Journal of Environmental Research*, 1(2) (2007), 114–27.

29 N. Hashemi, "Renegotiating Iran's Post-revolutionary Social Contract," in M. Kamrava (ed.), *Beyond the Arab Spring* (Oxford: Oxford University Press, 2014), 198.

process does not reflect partisan bias and that results of voting are not marred by outright fraud. One might indeed find little evidence of fraud in the five past election cycles. But elections are not free because the regime has barred candidates from some political groups based on political ideology. These include secular, monarchical, or communist parties as well as quasi-banned political parties and factions such as religious nationalists (*melli mazhabi*). The most notable banned parties are the two main reformists political parties, the Participation Front for Islamic Iran (*Hezb-e jebheh-ye mosharekat-e Iran-e eslami*) and the Organization of the Mojahedin of the Islamic Revolution of Iran (*Sazman-e Mojahedin-e Enqelab-e Islami-ye Iran*), which after the "Green movement" uprising in 2009 and subsequent crackdown have ceased to operate. Thus, the IRI has unfair elections in that they allow the regime to subvert the democratic potential of local government.

Given the role of disqualification of candidates, it may be possible to argue that candidates not subject to specific exclusions do face a fair qualifying process. In favor of this argument, reformists point to the distinctions between the process that applies to candidates for local government and the approach the clerical-dominated Guardian Council employs for elections to all other offices, including the presidency and the parliament, which requires candidates to "prove" that they are good Islamic citizens.[30] At the local level, the parliamentary electoral supervisory committee (*hayat markazi nezarat*) and the parliament's provincial-level executive electoral oversight committee (*hayat ostan*) only ensures candidates meet minimal criteria such as age, literacy, and education. Optimists indicate that, when a body reflective of the different factions represented in the parliament oversees the process, the qualification process will necessarily be fairer. However, this contrast is overstated because candidates for local office are also required to pass a religious test and a national loyalty test. Article 30 of the Local Council Law stipulates that candidates must "believe in and have practical commitment to Islam and the *velayat faqih* and must express their loyalty to the Constitution of the Islamic Republic of Iran."[31] This is substantially the same as the Guardian Council's requirement.

At the same time, evidence that the decisions of the provincial or central parliamentary supervisory committee (*hayat markazi nezarat*) systematically reflects partisan bias and a pattern of systematic political disqualification is not apparent for elections prior to 2013. In 1999, the chair of the central parliamentary committee, who had sponsored the legislation for establishing elected local councils in 1994, openly implied that well-known reformists who sought to stand for the Tehran City

30 S. A. Arjomand, *After Khomeini: Iran under His Successors* (New York: Oxford University Press, 2012), 43.

31 Persian text is: ج -اعتقاد و التزام عملی به اسلام و ولایت مطلقه فقیه. د- ابراز وفاداري به قانون اساسی جمهوري اسلامی ایران. Majlis Laws, "Qanun tashkilat, vazaef va entekhab shura-haye eslami [1996 (2017) Local Council and Mayors Elections Law plus amendments] قانون تشکیلات، وظایف و انتخاب شوراهای اسلامی – قانون اصلاح موادی از قانون تشکیلات، وظایف و انتخابات شوراهای اسلامی کشور و انتخاب شهرداران مصوب ۱۳۷۵/۳/۱ و اصلاحات بعدی," July 23, 2017, rc.majlis.ir/fa/law/show/1030043.

Council elections were disqualified on grounds of religious ideology,[32] yet reformists went on to dominate the first Tehran City Council. Likewise, in 2003, the reformist government approved members of two quasi-banned political parties to run for local office, belying in this case the narrative of *direct* political control of the political process by the *regime*. (None of the controversial candidates were elected, so they might have been ultimately blocked from office.) Then in 2006, at the height of the Ahmadinejad hardline presidency, four prominent reformists won seats to the Tehran City Council.

However, the pall of the 2009 sedition (as the regime calls the Green movement protests) still hung heavily over all candidates in 2013. The central parliamentary supervisory committee disqualified two well-known reformist incumbents who had publicly supported the Greens and publicly criticized regime policy. The partisan mood persisted into the 2017 elections, exemplified by a senior member of the judiciary who asserted that it was his duty to intervene and override any candidates whom the parliamentary committee had "mistakenly" approved by disregarding their support for the Green movement of 2009.[33] The outcome was that moderate reformists (as they called themselves) swept the fifth round of local elections in Tehran, in some cases likely taking the seats of more radical reformists who had been convicted or sidelined after the 2009 protests. The fact that the marginalized radical reformists endorsed the moderates in the fifth council suggests that partisan bias played little role. However, regime-aligned forces in the central government forced the widely respected reformist mayor selected by the fifth council to resign after only a few months in office, which likely does indicate partisan bias.

Thus, despite hopes to the contrary, control over the scope of participation in local as in national politics remains an important arena of contestation. Disqualification of candidates remains a tool of political control, even if the regime doesn't always wield it openly. In fact, the robust institutionalization of mechanisms for blocking opposition forces from participating in elections means that, as a general rule, the regime's objectives for the selection process have been effectively achieved prior to the stage at which explicit candidate evaluation takes place by parliamentary oversight or even by the Guardian Council.

Likewise, civic associations have not ensured fair elections, notwithstanding some outward appearances to the contrary. From their inception, elected local governments in Iran have supported a range of associations in what, in a sociological but not juridical sense, can be called civil society. In the early 2000s, when the reformists dominated the local councils, the parliament, and key central government ministries, they encouraged a wide range of associations which they saw as

32 Tarikhirani, "The Dissolution of the Tehran City Council Was a Big Mistake (Interview with Mohammad Atrianfar)," Tarikhirani.Ir (February 26, 1996).

33 Gholam Hossein Esmaili, "Head of Tehran Judiciary Complains about the Approval of Political Dissidents to Stand in Local Elections," Mizan Online (May 10, 2017).

necessary for the development of an independent civil society and of course a potential future source of votes. In Tehran, independent voluntary associations, nongovernmental organizations (NGOs), and social institutions, such as cultural centers (*farhang-sara*) without any overt religious programs, proliferated, often with the help of municipal resources. Even associations with opposing political views such as *velayi* Islamic students' associations could receive support. Another innovation by the Tehran municipality was the creation of neighborhood councils (*shurayari*) with the goal of extending participation in urban governance as a means of enhancing cooperation between the local government and civil society. This led soon to a conflict between the elected local council and the Ministry of Interior over which should have primary control over the advisory neighborhood councils. This no doubt reflected a worry on the part of central government that the neighborhood councils could mobilize grassroots support for the reformist democratization agenda outside the control of the central government.

In light of the definition of local democracy I set out above, we must conclude that civil society actors have been unsuccessful in holding local government accountable to criteria such as transparency or equity or social justice more broadly. There are, in theory and in law, some areas where citizens and social forces can try to engage with urban policy and, to a very limited extent, contest these policies. For instance, proceedings of elected councils tend to be relatively transparent, and can on occasion be open to public input. Most significantly, the elected local council has legal responsibility for overseeing the budget and the municipality's performance. Tehran municipality's budget is larger than several government ministries, which surely provides ample incentive for different groups to pursue economic aims along with their sectoral interests. Accordingly, there may be a few noncontroversial areas of urban policy where residents can practice engaged local citizenship beyond voting. Unfortunately, some recent attempts by independent journalists to use the state's own legal mechanisms to expose controversial issues such as corruption in local government land policy have been stymied. This silent curriculum in the perpetuation of authoritarianism over local democracy no doubt discourages greater local activism and engagement beyond voting by a broad section of the population and civil society organizations – at least on the terms the reformists' optimistic ambitions for local democracy envisioned. I am aware of only a single NGO focused on urban issues in Tehran; it generally avoids controversial issues such as contesting restrictions on electoral participation of political parties or individuals the regime disapproves of or calling for greater transparency in local finances.

After 2004, the conservative-controlled city councils went a step further and dismantled many of the cultural centers and NGOs on the grounds that they provided gathering spaces for regime opponents. In their stead, the conservative local government promoted "mosque-based" (*masjid-mehvar*) and other more socially conservative neighborhood-based civic associations. These associations stressed religious and traditional family themes. Thus, the regime has successfully blocked the emergence of opposition parties, individuals with dissident views, and civil society associations from finding a foothold in local governance. As I argue in the next section, the regime has been equally successful in subordinating local government's legislative authority and thereby restricting its ability to advance a democratic agenda.

RESTRICTIONS ON LOCAL LEGISLATIVE AUTHORITY

Many proponents of greater decentralization – including, surprisingly, conservative local politicians – have argued that since the turn of the century the central government and parliament have consistently reduced local government authority both in the law and in practice.[34] My review of the changes in legislative oversight of local government decisions by central government bodies over the last five years concurs that the role of the municipal sector in provincial-level development planning has been diminished, empowering agencies of the central government (as well as the regime's security services). The overall result has been the weakening of what democratic potential political decentralization had.

The local legislative process is highly regulated. It unfolds as follows. A three-member Conformance Committee (*hayat tatbeeq*) representing the government, the judiciary, and the Provincial Council of Local Councils in each province reviews all the decisions of local councils. If within two weeks the committee does not identify violations of national laws and regulations or assertions outside the legal powers of local government, the council's decisions become law. If the council has objections, it must either revise or appeal to an arbitration committee (*hayat hal ekhtelaf*), which must render a final decision within twenty days.[35]

Without a comprehensive empirical review of the record of all council decisions, it is difficult to render a complete analysis of how this process affects local power and autonomy. The conservative former chairman of Tehran City Council, who is closely aligned with the *velayi* Islamists, has complained of a "governmental mentality" which he claims blocks local governments throughout the country from expanding their role. Another conservative on the Tehran council decried the parliament's anti-decentralization bias as short-sighted; giving greater responsibility to local councils, he insisted, would demonstrate that the government values collective and public wisdom (*kherad jami*), would fortify the bonds between society and state, and ultimately would contribute to national unity and social cohesion.[36]

Some recent changes appear to have allowed for a minor increase of local influence on local council decision-making processes. The Conformance Committee itself replaced the government-appointed county governor (*farmandar*) in the review

34 H. Bayadi, "[Governmental Mentality Opposes Local Councils]," *Fararu* (April 29, 2010).

35 The Central Arbitration Committee (responsible for cities above a population of 200,000) includes representatives from the offices of the president, minister of interior, and attorney general, the Court of Administrative Justice, the Parliament, and the Provincial Council of Local Councils.

36 Bayadi, "[Governmental Mentality Opposes Local Councils]."

role in 2016. Those in parliament who advocated for creating the committee argued that the county governor was ill-equipped to review local legislation and often acted arbitrarily.[37] The committee, they argued, would avert a high volume of complaints against the councils, alleviating the burden on the local judiciary and other decision-making bodies. The inclusion of a member of the Provincial Council of Local Councils on the review committee who could defend and justify the local council's legislation also explicitly empowered councils. In this one respect, the direction of change has been toward greater inclusiveness of the elected representative institutions, which strengthens (however marginally) the local legislative authority.

Whether this change really empowers the elected institutions is debatable; in practice, the weakening of the elected institutions in another more significant sphere of decision-making, namely the provincial-level planning committees, most likely outweighs whatever positive impact the Conformance Committee may have had. In each province a Provincial Planning and Development Council (*shuraye barname reezi va tosee ostan*) decides how, where, and on what the government's budget is spent; it is designed primarily to coordinate line ministry offices with each other. Since the inception of elected local government, this council has included a token nod to the people's elected representatives – including one member each from the parliament and from elected local councils, who sit as advisory members without a vote.

The marginal role of elected municipalities in provincial planning is in part a reflection of the smaller financial clout of the elected municipal sector relative to the central government's provincial bureaus. The provincial development budget includes assistance to municipalities to cover the latter's obligations for completing infrastructure projects designed by the central government. However, the volume of these transfers outweighs the own-source revenues of the municipal sector itself, reflecting the relative financial weakness of the municipal sector vis-à-vis the provincial government sector. For example, municipalities have marginal power to determine spending compared to central government agencies. Recent legislation revising the composition of the planning council has further weakened the already feeble influence of the elected institutions. This strengthening of centralized technocratic control over local planning does not bode well for the project of local democracy. While locally elected bodies have had marginally greater influence in the area of legislative oversight since 2016, this scarcely outweighs other changes.

As with the legal framework defining political participation, the available evidence in relation to legislative oversight shows that the intergovernmental design in Iran is highly regulated and effectively ensures a high degree of coherence and coordination between different parts of the governmental apparatus. While the top-heavy composition of the legislative oversight committees does not by itself imply any greater centralization of power than existed before, the picture that emerges

[37] Majlis Proceedings, "Majlis Proceedings (Conformance Committee) May 9, 2016," Majlis (May 9, 2016).

within the broader context of the relative influence in national planning (which, as we saw, tilts to the deconcentrated side) still depicts elected local democratic forces in a relatively marginal role within the intergovernmental system as a whole.

CONCLUSION: LOCAL GOVERNMENT IN THE CONTEXT OF IRANIAN NATION-STATE–BUILDING

In light of the foregoing analysis, three general conclusions emerge about the way political decentralization has shaped center–local relations and the prospects for local democracy. First, the evident robust institutionalization of the legal framework – covering the electoral, legislative, and administrative domains – demonstrates that the current Iranian regime is highly consolidated. In the case of local legislative authority, if less so in relation to political participation, the legal framework is, on the whole, well organized, clear, and transparent. By this I mean that state power in Iran is not arbitrary, even if it does not conform to standards of Western liberal democracy.

Second, administrative jurisprudence in Iran has consistently enforced the constitutional and legislative limits on local government, operating on the *ultra vires* principle that only authorized action is valid. As I have shown elsewhere through an analysis of the rulings of the Court of Administrative Justice, the Iranian legal system demonstrates almost no independence from the Majlis and other regime law-making bodies in the judicial determination of the scope of local government authority, even though exercising such discretion need not contradict the function of administrative law.[38] The legal system has thus far refused to explore alternative frameworks expanding local government law-making, such as the principles of subsidiarity. It is worth noting in this regard that there does not seem to be a conceptual barrier to incorporating notions such as subsidiarity in Iran; in fact, several international cases show that subsidiarity can be consistent with a constitutional commitment to a unitary, centralized design of the state.[39] Nothing in principle prevents the Iranian courts from exploring ways to elucidate, and perhaps even expand, the principles and justifications of decentralized authority even within the current Iranian constitutional framework.

Third, the expansion of the infrastructural power of the state can, under favorable circumstances, be a two-way street. That is, the institutions through which the state penetrates society and territory – such as political decentralization – can also empower society to express its demands back to the state. Elected local governments in Iran have on occasion used the institutional and legal capacity the central

38 K. Tajbakhsh, "Authoritarian State Building through Political Decentralization and Local Government Law: Evidence from the Islamic Republic of Iran," *Oñati Socio-Legal Series*, 10(5) (2020), 1040–74; K. M. Stack, "An Administrative Jurisprudence: The Rule of Law in the Administrative State," *Columbia Law Review* 115(7) (2015), 1985–2018.

39 A. Jackiewicz, "The Principles of Unitarism, Subsidiarity and Decentralization as a Constitutional Basis of Regional Self-government of the Republic of Poland," *Studies in Logic, Grammar and Rhetoric*, 31(44) (2012), 175–89.

government has given to them to test the limits of their autonomy (albeit in a very limited way). For example, some local councils have sought to permit candidates from a wider range of ideologies to compete in local elections, while others have actively supported independent civic organizations and NGOs as a way of expanding the social basis of local governance. In some cases, local government officials responding to constituent demands even in the context of strong central government oversight drive these actions. Local government dependence on central government may, in practice, be consistent with de facto amounts of local power, which can be used to advance local interests against the central government. That power can then be used to advocate for greater legal authority for local government, especially for officials in Iran's largest cities. At the same time, local government assertiveness may represent political capture, where local officials seek to expand their power and budgets by means of collusion with central government agencies or regime-aligned institutions (such as the security services) or by means of patronage to clients at the expense of a more inclusively defined general interest. Only empirical case analysis could determine the relative influence of these factors in any given city.

I have argued that local government in Iran, and the shape of intergovernmental institutions more broadly, is the outcome of the interaction between three societal projects: Islamization, technocratic modernization, and democratization. The *velayi* Islamists justified the formation of elected local councils by appealing to the Islamic notion of *shura* as a populist Islamic form of participation in the context of Islamic welfare paternalism. The technocrats reached for administrative and fiscal decentralization as a solution to local managerial failures and tolerated elections as a means of assuaging local grievances and gaining more accurate information on local conditions. That is, they solely sought to increase infrastructural power. The reformist Islamists championed the elected local councils as a means of mobilizing civil society, which they hoped would democratize the relation of state and society more generally, diminishing despotic power. However, once local governments were in operation, the (top-down) agenda of state-directed local government promoted by an alliance of *velayi* Islamists, state technocrats, and moderate Islamists defeated the reformists' (bottom-up) democratic agenda.

Two decades after their founding and five rounds of nationwide local elections later, the institutional vessels the reformists hoped would strengthen local democracy have remained but our political rivals have filled them. Instead of transforming the state and politics, the political decentralization reforms have consolidated the theocratic regime's institutional coherence while extending the reach of the administrative state throughout the entire national territory and into the smallest villages. The various laws defining the local government sector reveal that the evolution of local government has brought it in line with the institutional structure of the entire state, thereby contributing to the greater institutional coherence of the regime.

Elected local institutions in Iran are now fully integrated into the institutional structure and political culture of the ruling elites and public managerial class. As cities increase in size, wealth, and complexity of economic and social functions, it is likely that local government officials will play an increasing role in the administrative politics of the state. Local government functions today chiefly as a technocratic means of improving public sector services, which is of course critical for people's everyday livelihoods and welfare. At the same time, representative local bodies have yet to create a broad-based local constituency for effective accountable government, whether on Islamist or democratic terms. Moreover, the dominant Islamist model of participatory governance (*mardom salari deeni velayi*) – a participatory but illiberal alternative to the pluralistic and democratic civil society–based projects of local democracy the reformists sought to implement – has garnered support from a significant minority of the urban population. On the other hand, because representative local government simultaneously looks both down to society and up to the state, it offers local (civil) society a limited space for independent voices to influence local governance such as through public media. However, most of these voices currently have been effectively blocked from playing a meaningful role in influencing local governance.

Local government has been an integral part of the nation-state–building project in Iran since the early twentieth century. This conclusion is consistent with the literature on nation- and state-building, which holds that a critical ingredient necessary for successful nation-building is the supply of public goods – including security, infrastructure, and rule of law – to the population by a state effective throughout the entire territory of rule. When this is successful, populations are more willing to accept the power and rule of state elites and cooperate with them. Where local populations express their demands to the state through independent associations or political parties, they supplement the *intra*governmental dimension with state–society relations. Both processes can be either complementary or conflictual. For example, the higher the state's capacity to deliver public goods, the more states become attractive alliance partners and the greater their ability to incorporate populations into the nation-state–building project. This in turn contributes to greater national cohesion by permitting people to identify as members of a national community. This outcome need not depend on strong assumptions of ideologies of community or value consensus; influential studies of Western democratic welfare states have argued that the state's undertaking of a wide range of activities to assure citizens' welfare were *by-products* of rulers' efforts to secure revenues and compliance from the population; rulers supplied material benefits in exchange for the loyalty or acquiescence of most of the population; over time popular demands led to the civilianization of the state.[40] One unsettling version of this model contends that nation-building need not depend on democratization, with obvious relevance for the Iran case.[41]

40 C. Tilly, *Coercion, Capital, and European States, AD 990–1992* (Cambridge, MA: Blackwell, 1992); M. Mann, "The Infrastructural Powers of Authoritarian States in the 'Arab Spring'," unpublished draft (2014), 15.

41 A. Wimmer, *Nation Building: Why Some Countries Come Together while Others Fall Apart* (Princeton: Princeton University Press, 2018).

Viewing local government and decentralization as integral parts of the project of nation-state–building sheds light on some questions raised by the history reviewed in this chapter. What motivated the regime to decentralize the state system, integrating tens of thousands of individuals as candidates and millions more as voters into its institutional framework? An adequate answer must distinguish the state's impulse to expand its infrastructural power, its despotic power, or indeed both. An overly general and undifferentiated concept of centralization (or concentration of power) by itself cannot help provide a full account of state-building. As I have tried to show, it obscures some of the most salient features of the way state power has evolved in Iran over the last century through the expansion of both types of power; it also conceals how, precisely, contention over democratization has proceeded and the means whereby challenges to the Islamic state have been contained, through both exclusion and integration. A recent study that traces the failure of democratization in Iran to a "centralizing power relying … on repression … excluding a vast majority of the population from the polity" illustrates this analytical limitation.[42] However, interpreting centralization solely as an index of despotic power – the capacity of the state to undertake actions without routine, institutionalized negotiation with civil society groups – obscures the way in which the IRI has also consolidated its rule through integrating populations, including by means of political decentralization. As we have seen, this has involved integrating a large part of the population into the political system by allowing local popular electoral participation (albeit carefully managed). This expansion has been in response to popular dissatisfaction with the ways cities and towns have been managed even though those demanding increased local democracy did not explicitly express it.

Thus, we can say that the expansion of local government through political decentralization in the Islamic Republic has not led to the growth of local democracy – at least not in the ambitious terms articulated by the Islamist reformers, namely the dualistic model of state–civil society relations requiring a pluralistic social and political public sphere. Local government in Iran fits more closely the model of electoral authoritarianism, where the state exploits electoral mechanisms as an instrument of nondemocratic rule. A growing literature documents that elite actors have generally introduced political decentralization reforms, that these reforms typically do not further democratic purposes, and that independent social movements rarely demand them.[43] Further, they typically do not lead to democratic outcomes. The

[42] M. Parsa, *Democracy in Iran: Why It Failed and How It Might Succeed* (Cambridge, MA: Harvard University Press, 2016), 296.

[43] P. F. Landry, *Decentralized Authoritarianism in China: The Communist Party's Control of Local Elites in the Post-Mao Era* (Cambridge: Cambridge University Press, 2008); J. C. Teets, *Civil Society under Authoritarianism: The China Model* (Cambridge: Cambridge University Press, 2014); A. T. Bohlken, *Democratization from above: The Logic of Local Democracy in the Developing World* (Cambridge: Cambridge University Press, 2016); A. Cheema, A. I. Khwaja, and A. Qadir. "Decentralization in Pakistan: Context, Content and Causes," Working Paper No. RWP05-034, *Harvard Kennedy School Faculty Working Paper Series* (2005); A. Ü. Bâli, "From Subjects to Citizens? The Shifting Paradigm of Electoral Authoritarianism in Egypt," *Middle East Law and Governance* 1(1) (2009), 38–89.

Turkish Constitution, to take another example, defines decentralization simply as the deconcentration of central government offices to lower-tier jurisdictions and makes no claim that greater local democracy should be one of the goals of the intergovernmental system.[44] In fact, the design of local government in Turkey may have facilitated the central government's ability to manipulate local politics and administration as a means of consolidating its power while blocking the emergence of rival political forces from regions and localities.[45]

The Iranian case appears to be consistent with many, if not all, of these findings. The decentralization reforms of the first two decades of the twenty-first century have not enhanced an independent plural local democratic politics or civic sphere (although case studies of cities and towns may reveal some exceptions). Neither has it generated the kind of economic growth that undemocratic local government has achieved elsewhere, most notably in China.[46] Still, authoritarian control might be challenged in the future because the electoral integration of local populations provides the population a peaceful means of expressing preferences; this keeps the door open to future democratic possibilities even if these are tightly circumscribed at present. Whether the aspirations of the proponents of local democracy in Iran, Islamists and non-Islamists alike, are naive depends both on the unique conditions of contemporary Iran and also on the cogency of the assumptions underlying the theory of democracy that proponents of local democracy brought to the project. On both these counts there is cause for skepticism about the prospects for local democracy in the near term. Future economic crises and social unrest might create an opening to democratization at the local level, just as economic crisis spurred the decentralization reforms of the early 1990s. Yet the incentive structure built into the local government sectors' accountability relationships, the narrow array of political and social forces permitted to participate in local elections, and the weak levels of contestation suggest that the central government will continue to prioritize administrative decentralization over devolution of political authority to local areas. It may delegate greater responsibility to the government-controlled provincial planning agencies without ceding power. In sum, the administrative state – the intergovernmental system – has achieved more robust elaboration as a result of the decentralization reforms than the democratization of state–society relations reformists dreamed of. The decentralization that the reformists hoped would strengthen local democracy has only strengthened authoritarian government administration.

[44] Art. 123. "The organization and functions of the administration are based on the principles of centralization and local administration."

[45] See M. Cammet and D. Luca, "Local Winners and Losers in Erdoğan's Turkey," Belfer Center, Harvard Kennedy School of Government (June 19, 2018) (concluding that the "strong centralization of public finances offers Turkey's national governments a chance to manage and target public resources in an arbitrary way beyond principles of 'good governance'").

[46] C. Xu, "The Fundamental Institutions of China's Reforms and Development," *Journal of Economic Literature*, 49(4) (December 2011), 1076–151.

7

Salvaging State Legitimacy in Iraq through Decentralization

Ali Al-Mawlawi

Iraq's experiment with federalism and decentralization is a recent phenomenon. Prior to the fall of the Ba'ath regime in 2003, the country's modern nation-state experience was consistently characterized by highly centralized state structures that projected autocratic control over the territory. Explaining why Iraq took a different course after 2003 requires acknowledging the historical legacy of authoritarian rule, including the aftermath of the Gulf War, which led to de facto autonomy for the Kurdish provinces in 1991, and the imposition of crippling sanctions, which caused the deterioration of state institutions and public services. These events contributed to the breakdown in state–society relations and the country's standing with the international community.

At its core, federalism in Iraq may be understood as a means to legitimize and preserve the post-2003 order. The political elite that emerged after regime change, along with the foreign architects of the war, sought to utilize power-sharing mechanisms – political, administrative, and fiscal – to create a system that could be sustained in a highly pluralistic political environment that had never previously existed.

In 2005, Iraq ratified its new Constitution through a national referendum. It was at this moment that the country established federalism as the cornerstone of the new Iraq, declaring that Iraq was a "federal, democratic, pluralistic system."[1] Its authors conceived of federalism in two ways: firstly, as a means to reconcile the reality that had existed within the autonomous region of Iraqi Kurdistan since 1991. Following the end of the Gulf War, the no-fly zone imposed by Western allies led to the emergence of the Iraqi Kurdistan Region, comprising the provinces of Erbil, Sulaimaniya, and Duhok. Meanwhile, the rest of Iraq remained under the tight grip of the highly centralized regime of Saddam Hussein. The Constitution was designed to formally reconcile the reality of this region with the broader configuration of the state.

[1] Constitution of the Republic of Iraq, 2005.

Second, federalism was viewed by drafters of the new Constitution as a safety mechanism that could prevent the return of authoritarianism.[2] Iraq's modern history is plagued with military coups, mass rebellions, and violent conflict – all featuring a "strongman" at the center of power. By diffusing the authority of Baghdad, it was thought that an equilibrium could be created that would mitigate against the rise of another dictator and ensure that Iraq's diverse communities were all invested in the new order.

At every instance when Iraq's federal arrangement and the imperative of decentralization have been contested by political elites, a set of common issues has formed the backdrop to the debate. Article 109 of the Constitution summarizes the core issues at stake, affirming that "federal authorities shall preserve the unity, integrity, independence, and sovereignty of Iraq and its federal democratic system." These issues – a unified Iraq, its territorial integrity, and the democratic process – form the basis of the post-2003 order. For that reason, understanding the calculations of political actors sheds light on how the debate over federalism and decentralization has evolved over the past two decades. While the international and regional dimensions of Iraq's experience should not be discounted, it is no less important to understand how Iraqi agency ultimately shaped the decentralized state structures that exist today.

The literature on federalism describes two distinct motivations for territorial decentralization: "coming together" and "holding together."[3] In the case of the United Arab Emirates, seven emirates came together by pooling their sovereignty to establish a durable federation where the whole is greater than the sum of its parts. In contrast, Spain sought to pacify separatist movements in the Basque and Catalan regions through a power-sharing mechanism that would hold the country together. For political elites in Baghdad, federalism's primary utility was to address deep-seated societal divisions through a process of "coming back together." But they faced a difficult predicament: delegating too much power to subnational actors risked undermining the authority of a fragile national unity government; while conceding too little power would be insufficient to address grievances of disenfranchised communities and offer inadequate incentives to local actors whose political buy-in was essential to legitimizing democratization as a cornerstone of Iraq's new political system.

Beyond the issue of political legitimacy, a large gap exists between the formal implementation of decentralization and the practical realities on the ground, where delegation of powers to subnational entities has yielded few positive results and has exacerbated corruption and political infighting. While the federal government contends that it is close to completing the transfer of powers to the provinces in accordance

2 See P. Le Billon, "Oil, Secession and the Future of Iraqi Federalism," *Middle East Policy*, 22(1) (2015), 68–76.

3 A. Stepan, *Arguing Comparative Politics* (Oxford: Oxford University Press, 2001)

with laws regulating the process, much ambiguity remains regarding the authority and responsibilities of local governments, and power struggles in Iraq's state bureaucracies and courts of law are common features of a flawed decentralization process.

AN EVOLVING RATIONALE FOR DECENTRALIZATION

Understanding the motivations of both domestic and foreign actors that have supported and expedited the roll-out of decentralization in Iraq offers insights into how delegation of powers was instrumentalized to address key political objectives. These include the imperative to contain ethnosectarian conflict and to address the basic needs of an increasingly disaffected population. In both instances, the integrity of the country's political system was at stake, and decentralization was seen as a means to allay growing pressures on the central government.

The constitutional basis for decentralization can be found in Article 116, which states: "The federal system in the Republic of Iraq is made up of a decentralized capital, regions, and provinces, as well as local administrations." Decentralization in the Iraqi context refers to the transfer of authority to subnational entities at the level of provinces and below, while the federal arrangement recognizes regions as distinct administrative units that enjoy far more expansive and specific powers. Although the Constitution offers a procedure for the formation of new regions, the Kurdistan Region currently stands alone, rendering Iraqi federalism asymmetric. In this regard, the decision to formalize decentralization within the Constitution can be viewed as a means to partially remedy the asymmetry in Iraq's federal system.

Prior to 2005, Baghdad had almost no experience with empowering subnational entities. While Law 159 of 1969 established local administrations and gave provinces powers over security, public services, protection of freedoms, and control over borders, they were entirely run by Ba'ath Party officials who took orders from Baghdad, had no autonomy to determine provision of services or generate local revenue, and were entirely dependent on funding from the capital.[4]

Even after the 2005 Constitution was ratified, it took three years before Iraq's federal arrangement was codified through legislation. Known commonly as Law 21 of 2008, the Law of Governorates Not Incorporated into a Region lays out the administrative and legal framework for how longstanding powers at the center would be delegated to the provinces. Crucially, Law 21 overtly excludes the three provinces of the Kurdistan Region, thereby acknowledging the status of the region as a distinct administrative unit that enjoys a different level of autonomy consistent with provisions in the Constitution.[5] Law 21 has been amended three times; first in 2010,

4 A. Al-Mawlawi, "Exploring the Rationale for Decentralization in Iraq and Its Constraints," Arab Reform Initiative (July 31, 2019).

5 Section 5 of the Constitution outlines the powers of the regions. Article 117 formally recognizes the Kurdistan Region as a federal region and Article 120 determines that regions should adopt their own constitution to define their structure and powers.

then in 2013, and finally in early 2018, reflecting ongoing debate about the issue over the course of a decade.[6] At each milestone, greater powers were afforded to subnational entities, and ambiguities or inconsistencies in the law were addressed. Nevertheless, prior to 2015, there was little political will at the executive level to implement Law 21 because it did not reflect the priorities and concerns of the central government. At that time, Iraq was still recovering from a devastating civil conflict, and militant insurgents continued to pose a major threat to peace and stability. Baghdad's primary objective was to project and assert strength and authority across the country to pacify any lingering forces that sought to break up the country. Furthermore, even as late as 2013, Iraq was still bound by myriad sanctions imposed under Chapter VII of the United Nations Charter after Saddam's invasion of Kuwait in 1990, including the freezing of state assets abroad, restrictions on Iraq's ability to sell oil independently, and obligations to pay reparations to Kuwait. Coupled with the presence of tens of thousands of foreign troops, it meant that Iraq had still not fully reclaimed its sovereignty. In this climate, there was little inclination to cede powers to the provinces.

This position fundamentally changed in June 2014, when a pretext emerged for Baghdad to acknowledge the utility of Law 21. The capture of Mosul by the self-declared Islamic State (IS) and the consequent rampage that the terror organization unleashed across large swathes of Iraqi territory became a defining moment when the integrity of the state and the legitimacy of the political order faced an existential threat. The June 30 cover of *Time* declared "The End of Iraq,"[7] reflecting widespread international sentiment that Iraq's territorial losses to IS were irreversible and the country could not be put back together again. Indeed, throughout the first half of Iraq's war against IS, some observers and analysts not only predicted the breakup of Iraq but actively advocated for it as a solution to sectarian conflict in the country.[8]

For Iraq's leaders and their international backers, the question of power-sharing within a federal framework became central to salvaging the country's territorial integrity and offered a formula for bringing Iraq back from the brink of collapse. At the heart of this renewed interest in federalism was the imperative of understanding how IS had been able to achieve such rapid military gains. It took concerted and persistent efforts by militant insurgents over the course of several years to create an environment of fear, intimidation, and hopelessness that eventually paved the way for entire towns and cities to be captured. The IS organization played on the widespread disaffection of Sunni communities in the north and west of the country toward the central government to win local support and sympathy for its cause. Trust and confidence in federal and local security forces including the Iraqi army

6 Law 21 (2008) of the Provinces Not Incorporated into a Region.

7 M. Crowley, "The End of Iraq," *Time* (June 30, 2014).

8 A. H. Al-Musawi, "Unravelling the Coordinated Campaign to Break Up Iraq," *1001 Iraqi Thoughts* (October 27, 2016).

and police was almost entirely eroded, and Baghdad was viewed as an adversary by many Sunni Arab communities in the provinces of Mosul, Anbar, and Salahadin. Concurrently, the Kurds in northern Iraq saw a unique opportunity to pursue long-held aspirations for independence and positioned themselves in a way that could capitalize on Baghdad's difficult predicament. Masoud Barzani, the Kurdistan Region's president at the time, famously declared in 2015 that his region's new borders would be drawn in blood, meaning that whatever land the Kurdish Peshmerga reclaimed from IS would be incorporated into their territories. The issue held historical magnitude dating back to the founding of the modern state in 1921. While the Kurds have long claimed that land across northern Iraq was part of Kurdistan, these diverse areas became known as disputed territories, spanning from the Iranian border in the eastern province of Diyala to the Syrian border lands northeast of Mosul.[9]

Amid this context, a narrative emerged within the international community that the only way the country could be reunited to confront its common enemy was to pursue a power-sharing arrangement that could allow Baghdad to win back the support and cooperation of Sunni Arabs and Kurds.[10]

For that reason, the discourse over delegation of powers during the initial war period primarily focused on how to win the war and defeat IS. For many, it was inconceivable that Iraq's federal military and security forces could reclaim territory from IS – after being so easily routed – without radically reconfiguring the security apparatus. Here, the concept of empowering local armed actors to take on a pivotal role was conceived. It stemmed from the American experience with the Awakening Movement of 2007–08, where the tribes of Anbar were equipped and funded by US forces to fight back against Al-Qaeda in Iraq. The United States sought to emulate this model through the establishment of a US-style national guard that would reflect the country's ethnosectarian makeup at the local level, thereby enticing local communities to join the fight against IS.[11] Much like the broader rationale for decentralization, the reasoning was that local actors are more attuned to local needs and could more effectively navigate local terrain. Strengthening these armed actors was also seen as a way to offset the accumulated mistrust toward federal forces, which had precipitated their rapid withdrawal from northern and western Iraq. Deployed across the country (except for the Kurdistan Region),[12] these forces included the

9 For more information on Iraq's disputed territories, see "Reviving UN Mediation on Iraq's Disputed Internal Boundaries," International Crisis Group (December 14, 2018).

10 See, e.g., European Parliament Resolution 2014/2843 (September 18, 2014) (calling on the Iraqi government and parliament to "urgently review legislation and legal practice, reform the country's judicial system and security apparatus and implement inclusive policies towards all Iraqis"; UNSC Statement, SC/11571 (September 19, 2014) (emphasizing the need to advance an "inclusive political dialogue," and calling on the Iraqi government to adopt inclusive policies).

11 F. Wehrey and A. Ahram, "The National Guard in Iraq: A Risky Strategy to Combat the Islamic State," Carnegie Endowment for International Peace (September 23, 2014).

12 Although federal forces have de jure jurisdiction in the Kurdistan Region, Kurdish forces including the Peshmerga are in reality solely responsible for managing military and security matters.

Iraqi army under the control of the Ministry of Defense, Federal Police linked to the Ministry of Interior, and the elite Counterterrorism Service (CTS), which answers directly to the commander-in-chief.

In order to pressure the Iraqi government into adopting these measures, the United States sought to condition military assistance to Iraq on a series of security sector reform measures that were underpinned by the formation of a new government – viewed as essential to breaking the cycle of sectarian violence and limiting IS's ability to capitalize on political divisions.[13] This was encapsulated in what American officials coined "functioning federalism," which was essentially a multifaceted, long-term, political-military approach to tackling what were believed to be the root causes of IS. Functioning federalism focused on empowering locals by implementing five core principles: (1) allowing local citizens to take the lead in securing local areas; (2) affording local citizens with state benefits and resources; (3) withdrawing the Iraqi army from urban areas and assuming an "overwatch posture" that would primarily focus on protecting borders; (4) establishing close cooperation between local, regional, and national entities in order to "reduce operational space" for IS; and (5) ensuring that the federal government works on a reform package that addresses "legitimate grievances and [denies] a pretext for [IS] activities." The term "functioning federalism" implied that although a constitutional framework for federalism existed, it had not been implemented correctly, and the five principles aimed to offer a path for how federalism could become operational.[14]

Although thousands of local tribal fighters were trained and equipped through international assistance led by the United States,[15] and many more were incorporated into volunteer units within the Popular Mobilization Forces (PMF), the national guard bill faltered in parliament and was never passed. Among the biggest sticking points related to the chain of command. While some argued that these units should answer to provincial governors, many including the central government insisted that sole authority over them should reside with the prime minister in his capacity as commander-in-chief. This ties directly to an ongoing constitutional debate over the exclusive powers of the federal government. Article 110 lists nine exclusive authorities, among them, foreign policy, fiscal and customs policy, and national security policy, including "establishing and managing armed forces to secure the protection and guarantee the security of Iraq's borders." Given that the mandate of the national guard was to protect internal provincial boundaries, it

13 See statement by President Barack Obama on Iraq (August 9, 2014). Prominent voices in Washington also advised against an American military intervention before the formation of the new government. See, for example, R. Mardini, "U.S. Intervention in Iraq Will Only Worsen the Situation," *New York Times* (August 7, 2014).

14 Statement by Brett McGurk, US Senate Foreign Relations Committee Hearing: "Iraq at a Crossroads: Options for U.S. Policy, Testimony" (July 24, 2014).

15 For a detailed account of the US role in supporting so-called Tribal Mobilization Forces, see E. Gaston, "Sunni Tribal Forces," Global Public Policy Institute (August 30, 2017).

could be argued that granting governors authority over these units would not violate the Constitution. However, widespread resistance stemmed from fear of fragmentation and internal conflict, with the potential for armed actors to clash because of disparate chains of command.

Ultimately, delegation of security powers proved to be a red line,[16] arguably shaped by the central government's difficult experience managing relations with the Kurdistan Region and the Peshmerga forces throughout the war period. Two core issues emerged after the fall of Mosul that escalated tensions between Baghdad and Erbil. First, Peshmerga forces deployed outside the so-called Green Line, which sets the formal boundaries of the Kurdistan Region. When Iraqi federal forces withdrew from Kirkuk following IS's initial onslaught, the Kurdish leadership seized on the moment and swiftly moved to take the city. Kurdish nationalists consider the oil-rich province of Kirkuk central to their territorial aspirations, often describing its capital as the Jerusalem of Kurdistan. Baghdad has no chain of command over the Peshmerga, despite being responsible for paying the salaries of an estimated 120,000 personnel. Furthermore, internal divisions exist within the Peshmerga along party lines, with the Kurdistan Region's two main parties exerting control over their own units. Second, Kurdish authorities lobbied aggressively for the provision of heavy weapons and ammunition from the global coalition.[17] Baghdad was concerned that Barzani was seeking to stockpile weapons, so it tried to regulate military aid to the Peshmerga by insisting that all international deliveries should first pass through the capital. From the perspective of the federal government, empowering more local actors who do not answer directly to the commander-in-chief would recreate the same problematic dynamics that existed with the Peshmerga.[18]

What began as a debate over how federalism could address security priorities evolved into a comprehensive discussion about administrative, legal, and fiscal delegation of powers. The focus of decentralization shifted during the second half of 2017, when the threat of the so-called Caliphate subsided and Iraqi forces began planning for the final push to retake Mosul. By then, security across the country had vastly improved. Mass casualty attacks were significantly down, and federal forces including the CTS, Iraqi army, Federal Police, and the PMF were growing in confidence and had largely won the respect of local communities who viewed them as liberators.

By October 2017, after federal forces moved to retake disputed territories in response to the Kurdish independence referendum, the debate over empowering

[16] A draft National Guard bill was sent to parliament in early 2015 but it failed to reach agreement among the political blocs and ultimately failed to pass. For an overview of the contestation within parliament, see S. Al-Salhy, "Fighting for Iraq's National Guard," *Al-Jazeera* (February 2, 2015).

[17] "Kurds need more heavy weapons to face 'brutal' IS group," *France 24* (November 18, 2014).

[18] Based on conversations with senior officials in the Prime Minister's Office, August 2018. Also see diverging views among government officials and lawmakers in T. El-Ghobashy, "U.S.-backed Plan for Iraqi National Guard Falters," *Wall Street Journal* (October 16, 2014).

local security actors had effectively ended. From here on in, the policy on decentralization fell squarely on service delivery. Public attention shifted from the existential threat of IS, to concerns for their personal livelihoods. With the collapse of oil prices in 2014, the government had introduced austerity measures that included a partial hiring freeze in the public sector. Growing unemployment and years of neglect in basic services had led to growing disquiet over livelihoods, despite the fact that security had measurably improved for many communities across the country. Iraq has among the highest population growth rates in the region. Its population increases by almost one million every year, posing a huge burden on state resources.[19] Some 60 percent of the population are estimated to be under thirty-five, and while overall unemployment stands at around 16 percent, it could amount to nearly 40 percent among youth.[20]

The central government understood the political expediency of accelerating decentralization given two overriding challenges that it knew it could not address on its own: first, that it lacked the capacity to centrally administer basic services like education, healthcare, and public works for an ever-growing population; and second, that it needed to divert blame for failures in governance toward local authorities in order to create greater accountability at the subnational level.[21] In part, there were also national security considerations at stake. It was necessary to address the experience of the Sunni protest movement of 2013, which directed popular anger almost solely at Baghdad and was characterized as a Shi'i government. The only way was to change the public mindset that had become ingrained over generations of centralized rule – one that holds Baghdad exclusively responsible for the state of their affairs.

This realization developed alongside growing insistence from international donors including the World Bank about the need to decentralize service delivery to regain public trust in state institutions.[22] In recent years, a discourse has emerged about the growing gap between political elites and citizens. The experience of the 2018 parliamentary elections confirmed this trend. The low turnout, officially at 44 percent, reflected the electorate's lack of trust and confidence in their political representatives. To be sure, the binary framing of political elite versus citizens is overly simplistic, and fails to account for the interplay and exchange between the two groups in a country where patronage networks run deep and power is shared by multiple actors. But there is no denying the widespread sentiment of ordinary Iraqis that successive governments have failed to address their basic needs and meet

19 C. Cornish, "Iraq Baby Boom Exacerbates Bleak Prospects for Nation's Youth," *Financial Times* (March 4, 2019).

20 World Bank, *Jobs in Iraq: A Primer on Job Creation in the Short-Term* (Washington, DC: World Bank, 2018).

21 Based on conversations with senior officials in the Prime Minister's Office, August 2018.

22 See "Decentralization and Subnational Service Delivery: Status and Way Forward," World Bank (2016).

their aspirations following regime change in 2003. Polling in Iraq has consistently reflected public distrust toward both central and local government authorities.[23]

From 2015 onwards, Baghdad embraced Law 21 as an overarching framework for transferring crucial administrative, legal, and fiscal powers to the provinces.

UNPACKING LAW 21

Consisting of over fifty articles, Law 21 is split into four main sections, which outline, respectively: the nature of administrative units, the procedures for their formation, and their individual competencies; the powers and authorities pertaining to the heads of administrative units; issues related to financial resources, including the generation of local revenues; and details on the high commission responsible for overseeing the transfer of powers.

The three essential administrative units are defined as provinces (*muhafadha*), districts (*qadha'*), and subdistricts (*nahiya*). At each level, councils are established and the number of elected seats are allocated per capita, with council members enjoying four-year terms.[24] Article 2 gives provincial councils legislative and oversight authorities that are consistent with the Constitution. Additionally, the councils are responsible for electing the governor and two deputies, who can also be removed from office by a majority vote.

Law 21 asserts an oversight role for the Council of Representatives – Iraq's national parliament assembly – over provincial councils. Article 20 gives parliament the authority to object to decisions deemed in contradiction to the Constitution, but it also has the authority to dissolve provincial councils through an absolute majority and upon request from the governor or one-third of the provincial council itself. These measures are primarily reserved for acts of gross dereliction of duties or other significant violations of law. Likewise, the provincial council has similar powers to dissolve district and subdistrict councils that are under its jurisdiction.

The governor is the highest-ranking executive officer in the province and holds the rank of deputy minister. Powers include drafting the province's budget,[25] appointing civil servants on a permanent basis except for senior ranking positions, and exercising limited authority over the police force such as ordering investigations and establishing police stations. Federal authorities are also required to coordinate in advance with the governor before carrying out security operations within the province.

Among the most significant structural changes, Law 21 decentralizes the authority of eight federal ministries, namely the ministries of Education, Health,

[23] See polling data from the National Democratic Institute, including, "Iraqis Call on the New Government for Jobs, Services, and Reconstruction," NDI (November 2018).

[24] Note that the 2018 amendment to Law 21 annulled subdistrict councils.

[25] Although in effect this only includes operational spending, which mostly comprises salaries, while capital investment is largely determined by the federal government.

Municipalities and Public Works, Agriculture, Housing and Construction, Labor and Social Affairs, Youth and Sports, and Finance.[26] As per the law, the technical, legal, and administrative powers of existing local directorates linked to these ministries are to be transferred to the provincial government. Crucially, this means that local authorities are now directly responsible for a significant number of public employees that work in their respective provinces. This shift from a deconcentrated system to a decentralized one leaves the headquarters of these ministries with largely regulatory and policy-making roles. Article 45 notes that ministries should retain the function of "planning general policy," while the remaining functions, including budgetary allocations and staffing, should be "gradually" transferred to the subnational authorities.[27] A US-funded project analyzed 890 functions in 7 ministries and determined that only 200 should remain centralized in the ministries.[28] Additionally, Law 21 gives each administrative unit the authority to collect taxes, duties, and fees, as long as it is in accordance with federal laws. This is a point of major contention, made all the more poignant because of the Finance Ministry's resistance to decentralization, which is elaborated below.

Following amendments to Law 21, the legal authorities of local governments were expanded in line with constitutional provisions, namely Article 115, which states: "All powers not stipulated in the exclusive powers of the federal government belong to the authorities of the regions and provinces that are not organized in a region. With regard to other powers shared between the federal government and the regional government, priority shall be given to the law of the regions and provinces not organized in a region in case of dispute." The precedence of local laws over federal laws in areas where powers are shared is among the most important developments, but in practice provincial councils have spent very little time exercising their legislative functions.

The primary vehicle for implementing Law 21 is a cross-ministerial committee known as the High Commission for Coordinating among the Provinces (HCCP). Chaired by the prime minister, the HCCP includes ministers from the ministries slated for decentralization, in addition to governors and provincial council chairs. A minister of state for provincial affairs is responsible for heading the commission's secretariat and ensuring that decisions are followed up. Law 21 stipulates that the HCCP should accomplish its functions within two years, and in the event that these tasks are not completed, they shall be considered transferred by law.

26 Rising frustrations and dissatisfaction with the performance of hospitals and schools led to changes in the 2018 amendment to Law 21 that reasserted full federal authority over the ministries of Health and Education. Provincial governors objected and lodged legal challenges in the Supreme Court, which determined that there had been no constitutional infraction and upheld parliament's decision.

27 Law 21, Art. 45.

28 T. Diamond and C. Berkuti, "Improving Services and Strengthening Cohesion in Fragile States: The Case of Iraq," Chemonics (October 2017).

Finally, Law 21 abrogates older laws related to decentralization, including Law 159 of 1969, laws related to municipal councils from 1964, and Coalition Provisional Authority Order 71 of 2004 on local governmental powers.

LEGAL CHALLENGES TO DECENTRALIZATION AND PRACTICAL REALITIES

As disputes have played out over the extent to which powers should be delegated, both federal and local authorities have mounted legal challenges. These disputes are addressed by the Federal Supreme Court, which is the judicial authority responsible for interpreting the Constitution and resolving matters related to it. Two primary themes have emerged: first, issues related to the appointment and dismissal of senior officials at the provincial level within the decentralized ministries; and second, matters related to local revenue generation.

There are more than 5,000 senior public officials across the country who hold the rank of director-general and many of them are directly employed by local governments. These positions are highly lucrative and often politicized because they hold significant authority and control over state resources.

Law 21 gives provincial councils the authority to approve nominations for senior grades submitted by the governor (through an absolute majority vote). Once a nomination has been approved, the Council of Ministers is required to ratify the decision. The chair of Maysan provincial council appealed to the Supreme Court in June 2018, contending that the cabinet's authority to approve or reject nominations undermined the power of local governments to appoint senior officials. The court ruled against the claimant, noting that the Council of Ministers was the highest executive authority and should be consulted for senior appointments; that coordination between central and local governments was essential for such positions; and that it saw no contradiction with the principles of decentralization or the Constitution.[29]

There have been numerous instances where appointments and dismissals by local governments have been outright rejected and rebuffed by the line ministries. When the governor of Mosul issued a directive to replace the city's municipalities director in 2018, the minister of municipalities responded by asserting that the governor lacked the authority to do so.[30] This illustrates the unresolved nature of interpreting provisions within Law 21. Although the HCCP would in theory be responsible for mediating such disputes, in several instances they have been settled in administrative courts. Often this further strains the relationship between ministries and local authorities.

The appointment of senior security officials has also been a point of contention between central and local governments. Prior to the 2018 parliamentary elections,

[29] *Federal Supreme Court*, Court ruling on legal suit filed by head of Maysan Provincial Council against the Speaker of Parliament (June 27, 2018), www.iraqfsc.iq/krarat/1/2018/65_fed_2018.pdf.

[30] *Noor News*, "وزارة البلديات تجدد تأكيدها لمحافظ نينوى بعدم إمتلاكه صلاحية إعفاء مدير البلدية" (June 13, 2018).

Prime Minister Haider Al-Abadi appointed a new police chief in Basra, replacing Abdul Kareem Mayahi with Jasim al-Sa'di. The local government complained that they had not been consulted about the appointment, citing provisions within Law 21 as the basis for their objection. The governor of Basra insisted, as chair of the province's higher committee on security, that it was incumbent on Baghdad to coordinate such important decisions. Meanwhile, the deputy minister of interior insisted that such matters fell under the exclusive powers of the federal government, in accordance with the Constitution. While there is far greater scope for local governments to assert their role in the appointment of senior officials linked to the decentralized ministries, the federal government has shown great reluctance to cede control over appointments and dismissals within the other federal ministries.

Another related contention is the issue of oversight authority. In March 2019, the Supreme Court considered the constitutionality of two articles in a 2018 bill governing parliament's oversight authority over provincial governors. Law 13 of 2018 detailed mechanisms for how parliament could initiate impeachment proceedings against governors who were deemed negligent or had been accused of corruption. The governors of Anbar and Salahadin filed a joint appeal against the law, claiming that it violated the Constitution, and the Supreme Court ruled in their favor. The decision was based on Article 61 of the Constitution, which states that parliament can introduce impeachment proceedings against the prime minister and members of the cabinet, but makes no mention of governors. The ruling also cites Article 7 of Law 21, stating that authority to impeach lies with provincial councils.[31]

Officially, the federal government contends that the process of decentralization has almost reached its conclusion, based on the fact that powers have indeed been formally delegated to the provinces in accordance with Law 21. The chair of the HCCP secretariat, Torhan Mufti, claimed in February 2019 that most of the provinces had completed the process, and that 70 percent of decentralized powers had been delegated to the three liberated provinces.[32]

In reality, the frequent contestations within state institutions indicate that the process is by no means complete. The greatest resistance to decentralization has come from the Ministry of Finance.[33] As one of the eight ministries initially slated for decentralization, it has demonstrated the least progress in delegating powers. Although it has established local directorates,[34] they serve merely as an additional administrative layer. Here, decentralization is in reality just deconcentration, with no transfer of authority taking place. The point of contention is local revenue generation. There is much debate surrounding what qualifies as a toll or fee, or indeed what constitutes a tax, since the existing legal precedents seem to suggest that

31 *Al-Sumaria*, "الحكم بعدم دستورية مادتين تخوّلان مجلس النواب استجواب المحافظين" (March 6, 2019), https://bit.ly/3j4akqo.

32 *Sout Al-Iraq*, "نقل 70% من صلاحيات الحكومة الاتحادية إلى المحافظات المحرّرة" (February 26, 2019).

33 Diamond and Berkuti, "Improving Services," 3.

34 Known as the Administrative and Financial Affairs Directorate.

provinces do not have the authority to unilaterally impose new taxes, and the federal government has consistently rebuffed attempts to do so. Its reasoning is based on Article 28 of the Constitution, which states that no tax shall be imposed "except by law." To illustrate the point, one form of local tax that has been imposed without objection from the federal government is the pilgrims' tax in Najaf for religious tourists. This tax has been incorporated into law through successive federal budget bills, thereby pacifying objections from Baghdad.[35] Furthermore, revenues from holy shrines and other endowed properties (known as *waqf*) are not transferred to the federal treasury. In contrast, the Supreme Court ruled in 2013 that the imposition of a surcharge by Maysan province to issue passports (just over $4) was in violation of an existing federal law that determines a federal fee for issuance of passports.[36]

Notwithstanding a 2008 Supreme Court judgment affirming the right of provincial councils to collect taxes, very little has changed on the ground. Local authorities understand that if they fall out of favor with the Ministry of Finance, it could affect their share of the federal budget.[37]

Law 21 provides for what are commonly known as petrodollar payments to oil-producing provinces. In theory, these provinces are entitled to a share of revenues from oil and gas production or refined products. While the law states that the province should receive $5 from every barrel of crude oil produced from oilfields in its territory, petrodollar payments have often been frozen or delayed, particularly during fiscal crises, when oil prices have plummeted. The arrangement has been codified in successive federal budgets, although rather than allocating $5 per barrel, budget laws in the past have offered 5 percent of revenues, which has significantly reduced the petrodollar share. Nevertheless, the $500 million dispersed in petrodollar payments in 2019 falls far short of the amount due, given that Iraq generated nearly $80 billion in oil revenues that year.[38]

In February 2019, the Basra provincial council filed a legal complaint to the Supreme Court against the 2019 federal budget, claiming that its budgetary allocations fell far short of its rightful share, including allocations for petrodollar payments. The council claimed that 86 percent of government-generated revenues came from Basra, whereas the province was only allocated a 1.5 percent share of the budget.[39] Basra is not alone in its objections to budgetary allocations. Lawmakers from liberated provinces have also complained that their shares do not match the stabilization and reconstruction needs of their provinces. Iraq's Constitution requires the

35 "Law of Governorates Not Incorporated Into a Region: An Annotated Text," USAID (March 2011), 17.

36 *Federal Supreme Court*, Court ruling on legal suit filed by Governor of Maysan against the head of Maysan Provincial Council (July 8, 2014), www.iraqfsc.iq/krarat/1/2013/82_fed_2013.pdf.

37 "Despite court rulings that provinces are entitled to collect taxes and service fees, the Ministry of Finance is holding to its interpretation of Article 28 of the Constitution, which precludes local governments from generating their own revenue by limiting new local taxing fee collection until federal legislation is passed." Diamond and Berkuti, "Improving Services," 4.

38 *Ministry of Finance*, Open Budget Survey, mof.gov.iq/obs/en/pages/obsdocuments.aspx.

39 *Sout Al-Iraq*, "البصرة تطعن بقانون الموازنة وتُهدّد بالشروع في إجراءات تشكيل الإقليم" (February 27, 2019).

equitable distribution of financial resources to the provinces, based on the relative population of each province and their needs. But there is no clear formula to determine needs and allocations, and public-financing procedures within the ministries of Finance and Planning lack sufficient transparency.

The federal government's failure to honor petrodollar payments to oil-producing provinces has also emboldened local governments to resort to blaming Baghdad for failing services and poor infrastructure, citing lack of financial resources as the biggest obstacle to their work, thereby deflecting attention from mismanagement and corruption at the local level. This is despite the fact that local authorities typically do not manage to spend their entire annual budgets because of poor strategic planning and weak capacity. In 2018, overall budget execution nationwide for operational expenditures averaged under 85 percent, while capital spending was even lower at around 60 percent.[40]

This has also impacted the central government's economic reform agenda. One of the biggest ongoing challenges is addressing the electricity sector and fixing the shortage in power supply. Part of the strategy involved reducing demand on the national grid by enforcing electricity tariffs on consumers. As in other rentier states, citizens rarely pay for electricity, creating a heavy burden on a grid that continues to grow. The government proposed a win-win arrangement whereby residents in piloted neighborhoods would receive twenty-four hours of grid electricity in return for installing meters in every home and enforcing payment of tariffs through private collection companies. Not only would it cut wasteful usage, but it would generate nonoil revenues and cut out waste from private community generators, which were being subsidized by the government. The experiment was successfully implemented in several neighborhoods in Baghdad, so the government sought to roll out the scheme across the southern provinces but was met with heavy resistance from both local authorities and residents. Governors suggested that electricity bills should be covered by the debt owed to their provinces from outstanding petrodollar payments. Ultimately, Baghdad failed to get sufficient buy-in and the scheme was shelved.

This experience illustrates two important dynamics that are linked to decentralization. First, it demonstrates that vested interests continue to play a significant role in local governance. Many of the private generators that operate to fill the shortfall in electricity are owned by or linked to political actors. These actors were able to mobilize on the street to generate enough public opposition to derail the scheme. A second dynamic relates to a cultural mindset. The prevailing view among ordinary Iraqis is that delivery of services is the primary responsibility of the central government, and that paying for electricity would open the door for the imposition of other service tariffs and fees on the general public. The controversy over petrodollar

40 A. Al-Mawlawi, "Delays in the Iraq's 2019 Budget Reflect Growing Political Deadlock," LSE Blogs (January 14, 2019).

payments created a convenient pretext for many southern provinces to reject electricity reforms that would have, in the long run, enhanced public services.[41]

Nonetheless, some internationally supported decentralization efforts have yielded positive results. In Maysan, the sewage directorate was able to implement a plan to clean and maintain thousands of meters of sewage pipelines. Meanwhile in Najaf, garbage collection has vastly increased in breadth and scope, while also generating cost-saving mechanisms through enhanced efficiency and better maintenance systems.[42] The success of these initiatives can be attributed to project design. In these instances, international teams embedded themselves within state institutions and worked hand in hand with Iraqi officials until the desired outcomes were achieved. In contrast, other assistance programs have not committed to this integrated approach, resorting simply to organizing capacity-building workshops that involve little follow-up.

OBSTACLES AND CONSTRAINTS

Beyond the resistance from federal authorities to delegate powers, the key obstacles and constraints that have prevented decentralization from achieving its desired results include: the lack of competence and expertise by local administrative units to absorb greater authorities; corruption and vested interests; and political infighting leading to poor cohesion within local councils.

Paper-based financial and administrative systems are incapable of processing complex and expanded budgets and payroll systems. To illustrate the size of the expansion, in 2016, the total number of civil servants employed directly by provincial authorities across the country did not exceed 15,000. By 2019, Basra province alone had 70,000 public employees on its payroll, whereas even the smallest province in the country, Muthana, is now responsible for nearly 24,000 personnel.[43] Ostensibly, this suggests a significant amount of decentralization has taken place, but in reality Baghdad still retains a high degree of administrative control over these employees, and provincial budgets are entirely dependent on monthly disbursements from the federal government.

Budgetary allocations far exceed sums that local authorities have been accustomed to in the past. A mid-sized province like Dhi Qar received nearly $1 billion in 2019, including just under $175 million in capital spending for investment in its infrastructure. Managing these sums requires far greater sophistication in strategic planning, oversight, and financial management systems than what local bureaucrats at the governor's office can do. The lack of capacity is reflected in the relatively

41 H. Al-Rikabi, "An Assessment of Electricity Sector Reforms in Iraq," Al-Bayan Center (September 2017).

42 Diamond and Berkuti, "Improving Services," 7.

43 Based on author's analysis of successive federal budgets.

small funds allocated to the three provinces that were liberated from IS. In Mosul, for instance, direct budgetary allocations to the local government only amounted to some $230 million in 2019, despite being the second most populous province in the country. This can be explained by the low number of public employees under its payroll – standing at just over 1,400 – which accounts for the majority of operational spending. The low employment numbers reflect the fact that most public sector workers in the province are still tied to central ministries. For liberated provinces that have only recently emerged from IS occupation, local governments still lack sufficient capacity to manage expanded payrolls and capital spending.

Local authorities are also no more immune to endemic corruption than the central government. In fact, corruption is arguably more rampant at subnational levels because the broader interface with ordinary citizens creates more opportunities for corrupt practices such as bribery and extortion. Thus, expanding budgets without first addressing underlying structural flaws such as weak accountability only risks further exacerbating corruption and increasing the likelihood that budgetary spending will not lead to enhanced public services. Indeed, in a country like Iraq, where patronage networks are dominant and political actors have sought to manipulate authority over ministries for personal gain, transferring control to the provinces might simply replicate the dynamics that prevail in Baghdad.

Public financial management (PFM) reform is a key prerequisite to enhancing transparency, cash management, public investment, and procurement systems. The World Bank and the European Union established a multimillion-dollar program to offer technical assistance and capacity-building to Iraqi counterparts. It was aimed not only at improving Iraqi technical expertise, but also – and more importantly for the international community – at establishing trust and confidence in the allocation of financial assistance to reconstruction efforts.[44] However, significant flaws exist in the design of international assistance programs, evident in the fact that many of the same programs have been implemented in Iraq previously without producing desired results. The World Bank established a PFM program in 2009, but after its conclusion in 2013, an independent review assessed that its results had been "moderately unsatisfactory." Often the project goals are unrealistic, lack champions within the state bureaucracy, and lead only to short-term gains that are often undone because of inadequate follow-up and inconsistent support. Training sessions often lack a problem-driven approach where there is a process of iterative learning and adaptation that can be sustained beyond the training period.[45] In other words, capacity-building workshops often provide ready-made solutions that are not context-specific

44 A. Al-Mawlawi, "Designing a Successful Approach to Public Financial Management in Iraq," Al-Bayan Center (October 2018).

45 For more on "problem-driven iterative adaptation," see M. Andrews, L. Pritchett, S. Samji, and M. Woolcock, "Building Capability by Delivering Results: Putting Problem-Driven Iterative Adaptation (PDIA) Principles into Practice," in A. Whaites, E. Gonzalez, S. Fyson, and G. Teskey (eds.), *A Governance Practitioner's Notebook: Alternative Ideas and Approaches* (Paris: OECD, 2015), 123–33.

and lack sufficient incentives for stakeholders to embrace them. Here, a substantive political economy analysis needs to be undertaken prior to implementing a project in order to understand the motivations of public employees and the drivers at play.[46] One method of incentivizing staff is to do more to link public sector career progression with performance.

Often, the most effective remedy to corruption at the local level has been to bypass local decision-making by establishing ministerial-level committees that can unblock impediments. The Higher Committee for Investment is a case in point. Where there are unwarranted obstacles to issuing investment licenses and land allocation to projects of strategic importance, the higher committee intervenes to expedite the process, thereby circumventing bureaucratic procedures at the local level. Similar committees exist for the housing, agriculture, and education sectors. Infighting within provincial councils also represents a major obstacle to the functioning of local governments. In 2017, the governors of all three liberated provinces were impeached by their provincial councils. In Mosul, proceedings were initiated against Governor Nowfal al-Akoub after accusations of corruption were leveled against him. Akoub rejected the claims and remained in his position until 2019 when parliament removed him from office following the sinking of a river ferry in Mosul, in which over a hundred people died.[47] In Salahadin province, Governor Ahmed Al-Jubouri served prison time after he was found guilty of corruption but was released after being acquitted by an administrative court. In Anbar, Governor Suhaib al-Rawi was removed from his post and replaced by Mohammed al-Halbusi, who belonged to a rival party in the province. Subsequently, governors across the southern provinces and even in Baghdad have faced legal challenges to their authority. In some cases, incumbents have appealed to courts on the grounds of unfair dismissal, while in other cases, political rivals within the provincial councils have successfully removed and replaced sitting governors. Among the most notable examples is the case of Mohammed al-Mayahi, who was governor of Wasit province. In 2019, Mayahi was voted out of office by the provincial council in a motion led by his deputy, who belonged to a rival party. Mayahi appealed the decision in an administrative court on the basis that he had not been questioned before the vote of no confidence. The court suspended the decision pending an investigation before eventually ruling in favor of the provincial council.[48]

This degree of competition and incoherence was compounded by the fact that provincial councils exceeded their four-year term limit because 2017 elections could not be feasibly organized due to the ongoing war against IS. There was then little appetite to try in 2018 following the low turnout in parliamentary elections in May

46 "Decentralization and Subnational Service Delivery in Iraq: Status and Way Forward," World Bank (2016), 12.

47 *Al-Jazeera*, "Scores Dead as Ferry Sinks in Tigris River Near Iraq's Mosul," (March 21, 2019).

48 *Baghdad Today*, "بالوثائق. المحكمة الإدارية تصادق على إقالة محافظ واسط," (December 24, 2019).

and the ensuing debacle over the integrity of the results. This created a crisis of legitimacy at the local level, where political representation was out of sync with changes in the political landscape at the national and parliamentary levels. For that reason, rival political actors were spurred on to remove governors at their moment of weakness.

A major turning point came in late October 2019 when parliament moved to suspend provincial and district councils nationwide as a means of placating protesters demanding reforms and an end to corruption. Parliament framed the move as consistent with a commitment to curbing corruption, characterizing local councils as the primary offenders. In the words of Speaker of Parliament Mohammed al-Halbusi, the move was an attempt to "raise the standard of services and halt the real problems and violations in the provinces."[49] Although parliament's move was legally predicated on Article 20 of the decentralization law, which allows parliament to suspend local councils in the event of "gross dereliction of duties," suspending all local councils in one fell swoop was unprecedented and unorthodox. In a stark rebuke to local authorities but also as a means of fending off public anger, the central government openly supported parliament's decision. Though the decision to suspend provincial councils was made more palatable because they had exceeded their legal terms by more than two years, their absence is difficult to sustain without a constitutional amendment, since Article 122 explicitly states that provincial governors are to be elected by provincial councils. Nevertheless, parliament had sent a clear message to local authorities about who holds the reins of power and how the process of decentralization could be rolled back if it so desired.[50]

CONCLUSION

While the rationale for decentralization has evolved in response to the country's emerging threats and challenges, the overarching imperative for reconfiguring power-sharing arrangements in Iraq has been to preserve the legitimacy of the post-2003 order. From mitigating against the rise of another dictator to addressing the grievances of a disenfranchised electorate, political elites have pursued a self-interested top-down approach to decentralization as a means of ensuring their own survival.

But there is little interest in decentralization at the popular level. A 2017 National Democratic Institute (NDI) poll showed that only 14 percent of respondents believed that decentralization was a very effective means of achieving reconciliation.[51]

49 Remarks of Mohammed al-Halbusi, Council of Representatives (October 8, 2019), youtu.be/JKS_M6BaV8c?t=716.

50 A. Al-Mawlawi, "Is the Decentralisation Process in Iraq being Reversed?" LSE Blogs (December 2, 2019).

51 "Improved Security Provides Opening for Cooperation," Greenberg Quinlan Rosner Research (April 2018).

Another survey during the same period found that only 2.9 percent nationwide felt that resolving issues between Baghdad and the provinces should be a key priority for candidates competing in the 2018 parliamentary elections.[52]

The emergence of IS and the ensuing war posed an existential threat to the integrity of a unified Iraq. The architects of decentralization sought to reassert authority by winning back public trust and confidence at the federal and local levels. But polling data have consistently shown that citizens are dissatisfied with both national and local authorities. In September 2018, nearly 60 percent of respondents believed that access to basic services was getting worse. Moreover, only 27 percent expressed some degree of trust in provincial councils, and 24 percent in the central government.[53]

Delegation of powers focused on legal and administrative aspects, while fiscal decentralization – crucial to any province's ability to assert autonomy through generation of local revenues – fell short of its legally prescribed remit. That the commission responsible for rolling out decentralization measured success by the extent to which powers had been transferred to local governments *technically* rather than *functionally* suggests that their primary intention was to be able to claim that the decentralization process had been largely completed, regardless of whether the outcome had yielded any notable improvements in service delivery or good governance. By doing so, it was believed that they could plausibly shift blame for governance failures onto local authorities.

The first important test of decentralization's utility emerged during the summer of 2018 – four months after parliamentary elections were held – when violent protests erupted in Basra in response to a public health outbreak caused by contaminated drinking water. The protests coincided with a period of political flux, when parliamentary election results had just been announced but an agreement on the formation of the new government had yet to be resolved. For that reason, the protests had wide-ranging implications on the outcome of negotiations between political blocs to form the new government.

The water crisis exposed the local government's inability to address a basic service without significant support from the central government. In fact, both sides sought to blame each other for the crisis, culminating in an unprecedented showdown between the prime minister and the Basra governor during a parliamentary session that was supposed to discuss ways to address the crisis.[54] Instead, the two sides traded blows, accusing each other of failing to meet their responsibilities. The protests eventually subsided, but only after Baghdad sent a high-level task force to Basra to directly intervene and address the problem.

52 "Voter Attitudes towards the Next Rounds of Elections in Iraq," Al-Bayan Center for Planning and Studies (November 2017).

53 "NDI Poll: Iraqis Call on the New Government for Jobs, Services, and Reconstruction, August–October 2018," National Democratic Institute (November 20, 2018).

54 "Baghdad Lifts Basra Curfew as PM Pressed to Quit," *Deutsche Welle* (September 8, 2018).

Basra's woes effectively highlighted systemic problems that exceed what decentralization can address. Rampant corruption, widespread mismanagement, a culture of impunity, and deep political intransigence are among the country's biggest obstacles to reform. Decentralization can only yield its intended results if the right conditions exist. Crucially, though, identity politics has waned since the culmination of the war with IS, creating the potential for issues-based politics to emerge.[55] As sectarian and ethnic dividing lines recede, there is a growing appreciation among ordinary citizens across the country that shortfalls in basic needs are common to all Iraqis. How this might shape the course of decentralization is still unclear but federal and local authorities will find it increasingly difficult to mask their failures by appealing to ethnosectarian rhetoric.

A major issue that needs to be addressed is the dysfunction and incoherence within local governments caused by zero-sum politics. Here, electoral reform could offer a solution by breaking the cycle of intransigence that plagues provincial councils. Despite provisions within the Constitution and Law 21, elections at the district level have not been held since 2005. Generating electoral legitimacy for these administrative units would create greater accountability and empower them to exercise their functions. At the same time, it would diffuse the power of provincial councils and encourage members to become more attuned to the needs of their constituents and focus on their legislative functions. Furthermore, amendments to the electoral law could create an arrangement whereby governors are directly elected by the people through a first-past-the-post system rather than by provincial councils. This would give them a far stronger mandate to govern and enhance accountability mechanisms.[56]

But contestations over authority between national and subnational actors will persist in the near term as political elites continue to adapt to the realities of decentralization. So long as the underlying constraints and obstacles are not addressed, the entire decentralization process risks losing credibility and relevance to policymakers and the general public, especially if marked improvements to basic services do not materialize and local governments continue to defer to the central government to address their problems. More fundamentally, the imperative of salvaging state legitimacy by addressing systemic issues related to poor governance was brought into sharp focus during the 2019 demonstrations, which resulted in the resignation of the government. If decentralization reforms in Iraq set out to mend structural ties between Baghdad and the provinces, it is all the more pressing to think about how decentralization could be utilized to remedy the fragile relationship between the state and ordinary citizens.

55 F. Haddad, "The Waning Relevance of the Sunni–Shia Divide," The Century Foundation (April 10, 2019).

56 H. Al-Rikabi, "Reforming the Electoral System in Iraq," Al-Bayan Center (December 2017).

8

Decentralization Reforms in Post-Revolution Tunisia

The Struggle between Political and Bureaucratic Elites

Intissar Kherigi

Tunisia's post-uprising Constitution, adopted in January 2014, set in motion a decentralization process designed to end decades of highly centralized rule and deep regional inequalities. This process stems from two key concerns – the need to respond to the marginalization of interior regions, which played a prominent role in the 2010–11 uprising, and the desire by a new political class to draw a line under authoritarianism and prevent its return.

These twin objectives of development and democratization strongly shaped the drafting of Chapter Seven on Local Authority in the new Constitution. However, as the process turned to working out the details of decentralization in 2014–18, national bureaucratic elites were able to shape the content in a way that focused reforms narrowly on limited administrative changes and away from a deeper redistribution of decision-making powers and financial resources. The Local Authorities Code adopted in April 2018 thus establishes the administrative and legal autonomy of elected local authorities, while retaining decision-making powers and resources firmly at the center.

This chapter examines Tunisia's decentralization process from the start of the constitutional process in 2011 to adoption of the Local Authorities Code and holding of municipal elections in 2018. It begins with a brief historical overview of regional inequalities in order to reflect the temporal register through which these inequalities are debated and experienced.[1] The chapter adopts an actor-centered approach and analyzes how two key factors – institutional venue and party system coherence – shape the incentives and capacities of political and bureaucratic officials to shape decentralization. It draws on the literature on decentralization in other transitioning and developing countries and reveals the need for further research on the role of political parties in post-authoritarian and transitional contexts, the balance of power between political and administrative actors in such contexts, and how choices

[1] J. Schwedler, "Taking Time Seriously: Temporality and the Arab Uprisings," *POMEPS* (July 26, 2017).

regarding process design and policy venue at the outset of decentralization reforms shape subsequent outcomes.

THE HISTORICAL ROOTS OF REGIONAL INEQUALITIES

The 2010–11 Tunisian uprising brought to the fore questions of regional inequality and the failure of the country's developmental model in achieving an inclusive economy and access to basic services in the country's interior regions. Deep disparities exist between the northeastern and eastern coastal regions – the location of 85 percent of the country's gross domestic product and 80 percent of industry – and the western, central, and southern interior regions, which contain 50 percent of the country's oil, gas, and water resources and 70 percent of wheat production.[2]

The question of socioeconomic inequalities between regions intersects with a number of historical, cultural, ideological, and political divisions within Tunisian society. Regional disparities deepened significantly under French colonization.[3] After independence in 1956, regional inequalities were built into the structures of the state due to a political alliance that favored particular regions while marginalizing others.[4] The violent conflict between the two leaders of the independence movement, Bourguiba and Ben Youssef,[5] which took on regional undertones, lives on in local narratives today: "We have always been marginalized by the central authorities ... The region was considered to be Youssefist. The authorities were not happy with us ... It's been 62 years since independence ... till now, there has not been a single minister from Kebili ... We have been punished."[6] These regional inequalities have been exacerbated by economic liberalization since the 1970s, which saw huge investments in coastal regions and metropolitan centers while agriculture saw a decline, its share of public investment dropping from 20 percent in the 1970s to 10 percent in the 1980s.[7] On

2 H. Meddeb, "Tunisia's Geography of Anger: Regional Inequalities and the Rise of Populism," *Carnegie Middle East Center* (19 February 2020). For more on the rural origins of the uprising, see A. Gana, "The Rural and Agricultural Roots of the Tunisian Revolution: When Food Security Matters," *International Journal of Sociology of Agriculture and Food*, 19(2) (2012), 201–13.

3 G. White, *A Comparative Political Economy of Tunisia and Morocco: On the Outside of Europe Looking in* (New York: State University of New York Press, 2001); A. Larif-Beatrix, *Edification étatique et environnement culturel: Le personnel politico-administratif dans la Tunisie contemporaine* (Paris: O.P.U., 1988).

4 See B. Kchouk, "Recomposition de l'élite politique tunisienne (2011–2014) au prisme des révolutions est-européennes," *L'Année du Maghreb*, 16 (2017), 319–39; H. Bou Nassif, "A Military Besieged: The Armed Forces, the Police, and the Party in Bin Ali's Tunisia, 1987–2011," *Cambridge Journal of Middle Eastern Studies*, 47 (2015), 65–87.

5 M. Camau and V. Geisser, *Le Syndrome Autoritaire, Politique en Tunisie de Bourguiba à Ben Ali* (Paris: Presses de Sciences Po, 2003), 131–52.

6 Interview, trade unionist (Jemna, Tunisia, February 1, 2020).

7 Ibid.

the eve of the revolution,[8] interior regions were given only 18 percent of public investment compared with 82 percent to coastal regions, with privatization, the appropriation of agricultural lands by those in power, and land dispossession in rural areas further deepening disparities.[9]

The 2010–11 uprising, which began in interior regions, reignited old debates over these historical memories and regional inequalities, which were seen as the product of systematic marginalization of interior regions rather than mere neglect. The symbolic role of these regions in the revolution placed regional inequalities at the center of the political agenda and the constitution-drafting process that began in October 2011. While this process was marked by deep disagreement among political actors, there was a single point of consensus – the need to decentralize power and resources to elected regional and local authorities. The result is Chapter Seven, termed the Constitution's most "revolutionary" chapter.[10] It marks a radical rupture with Tunisia's tradition of highly centralized rule, granting elected municipal and regional councils financial and administrative autonomy, abolishing *a priori* control, and creating a Higher Council of Local Authorities with a role in national decision-making.

Despite its "revolutionary" nature, Chapter Seven was the most consensually adopted section of the Constitution. How can this be explained? This chapter traces the design of decentralization reforms between 2011 and 2018, from the initial drafting of constitutional provisions through to the new Local Authorities Code. While there is a vast literature on the emergence of decentralization following democratization, much of it focuses on the initial decision to decentralize and not on the subsequent process through which actors shape reforms.[11] As Falleti's work highlights, examining the balance of power between actors at the outset of decentralization reforms is key to understanding subsequent outcomes.[12]

The chapter adopts an actor-centered approach, analyzing the choices made between 2011 and 2018 through an examination of the actors involved, their interests, the interpretive frameworks that shape their views of decentralization, and the

[8] The term "revolution" is used here to reflect the language widely used by the actors themselves, whether politicians, bureaucrats, or activists, although a lively debate continues among Tunisians over whether the events constitute a revolution according to various definitions.

[9] See M. Elloumi, "Les terres domaniales en Tunisie," *Études rurales*, 192 (2013), 43–60; M. Fautras, "Land Injustices, Contestations and Community Protest in the Rural Areas of Sidi Bouzid (Tunisia): The Roots of the 'Revolution'?" Justice spatiale – Spatial Justice (2015), https://halshs.archives-ouvertes.fr/halshs-01512398/document.

[10] S. Turki and E. Verdeil, "L'état Actuel de la Décentralisation en Tunisie," in M. Harb and S. Atallah (eds.), *Local Governments and Public Goods: Assessing Decentralization in the Arab World* (Beirut: The Lebanese Center for Policy Studies, 2015), 14.

[11] L. Diamond, *Developing Democracy: Toward Consolidation* (Baltimore: Johns Hopkins University Press, 1999); M. Turner (ed.), *Central–Local Relations in Asia-Pacific: Convergence or Divergence?* (New York: St. Martin's Press, 1999).

[12] T. Falleti, "Of Presidents, Governors, and Mayors: The Politics of Decentralization in Latin America," paper presented at the Meeting of the Latin American Studies Association, Dallas, Texas, March 27–29, 2003.

resources they mobilize to shape the process. A dynamic, relational, actor-centered approach that analyzes the changing distribution of power among actors over a period of time is, it is argued, most appropriate for analyzing policy-making in a political transition marked by shifting relations between actors in the context of institutional changes that are "significantly transforming structures by constituting and giving power to new groups of actors, and by giving power to existing groups in different ways."[13]

The chapter draws on over one hundred interviews with actors involved in drafting Chapter Seven and/or the Local Authorities Code (politicians and bureaucrats, experts, and representatives of international organizations and civil society at national and subnational levels), and eight months of observation of parliamentary sessions and public events. It analyzes the roles of political and administrative actors in decentralization reforms across two phases – 2011–14 and 2014–18.[14] It argues that while the Constitution drafted in 2011–14 introduced a far-reaching vision of robust decentralization as a fundamental redistribution of political and economic power, the Local Authorities Code of 2018 restricts decentralization to a purely administrative and technical reform. This can be explained by two key factors – institutional venue and interparty and intraparty cohesion, as analyzed below.

PARTY SYSTEMS AND INCENTIVES AND CAPACITIES TO DECENTRALIZE

As Oxhorn argues, "[d]ecentralization should be viewed as part of a larger process of the social construction of citizenship, in which who participates and who does not matters."[15] Tunisia's decentralization process reveals deep political, ideological, cultural, regional, and economic divisions that underlie the struggle to define the role of the state and state–society relations.

Recent literature on decentralization has sought to understand the huge variation in decentralization outcomes and what factors shape these outcomes. In particular, the interests and preferences of national and subnational actors, and the balance of power between them, are identified as key explanatory factors. Much of this literature has focused on the electoral incentives of political actors.[16] While

[13] A. Allal. and M. Vannetzel, "Des lendemains qui déchantent? Pour une sociologie des moments de restauration," *Politique africaine*, 2(146) (2017), 5–28, at 5.

[14] Due to limited space, the roles of civil society actors and international organizations are not discussed.

[15] P. Oxhorn "Unraveling the Puzzle of Decentralization," in P. Oxhorn, A. D. Selee, and J. S. Tulchin (eds.), *Decentralization, Democratic Governance and Civil Society in Comparative Perspective: Africa, Asia, and Latin America* (Washington, DC: Woodrow Wilson Center Press, 2004), 3–30, at 9.

[16] D. J. Samuels, "The Political Logic of Decentralization in Brazil," in A. P. Montero and D. J. Samuel (eds.), *Decentralization and Democracy in Latin America* (Notre Dame, IN: University of Notre Dame Press, 2004); K. O'Neill, *Decentralizing the State: Elections, Parties, and Local Power in the Andes* (Cambridge: Cambridge University Press, 2005).

such incentives are important, Riedl and Dickovick provide a more comprehensive framework by examining how the coherence of the party system as a whole shapes not only the *incentives* of each political actor to decentralize but also their *capacity* to enact robust decentralization reforms.[17]

Riedl and Dickovick identify two key causal mechanisms that define the incentives of national political actors to decentralize – subnational footholds and patronage. The former refers to parties' ability to maintain and strengthen their power bases at the subnational level and prevent opponents from doing the same. Patronage refers to the opportunity to create new positions and resources at the subnational level to distribute to supporters. Thus, a national ruling party is likely to favor decentralization if it believes that it would enable it to expand its subnational footholds and sustain or expand patronage networks, even when out of power nationally. Meanwhile, opposition parties are likely to support decentralization where they view it as an opportunity to gain subnational footholds and patronage.

Furthermore, Riedl and Dickovick argue that hegemonic party systems may paradoxically create greater incentives to pursue decentralization than democratic regimes with fragmented party systems. Drawing on fourteen case studies of African countries, they argue that ruling parties in authoritarian, hegemonic systems are likely to decentralize if they detect an opportunity to consolidate their power by dominating local elections and strengthening local penetration. On the other hand, democratic but fragmented party systems that lack coherence may impede decentralization.[18]

In a fragmented party system where the ruling party does not possess strong party structures and national–local linkages, the central executive has little *incentive* to pursue robust decentralization, since this is unlikely to yield significant subnational footholds and patronage. In this case, the potential opportunity to gain subnational patronage through decentralizing power does not outweigh the costs of losing centralized control. In a fragmented political landscape in which vote shares are divided across a large number of parties, "each side has less incentive to push hard for reforms that will benefit their rivals equally."[19] Furthermore, highly fragmented party systems also tend to be characterized by instability, making electoral outcomes highly unpredictable. The inability of each party to form an assessment of the likely gains from decentralization weakens incentives to push for such reforms.

In addition to weakening incentives, lack of party system coherence also reduces the *capacity* of actors to push effectively for decentralization. In highly fragmented

[17] R. B. Riedl and J. T. Dickovick, "Party Systems and Decentralization in Africa," *Studies in Comparative International Development*, 49(1) (2014), 321–42. They define "robust decentralization" as taking place where the following elements are present: (1) subnational elections; (2) 10 percent or more of national revenues made available to subnational governments; (3) creation of a subnational civil service.

[18] Ibid., 322.

[19] Ibid., 328.

systems, Riedl and Dickovick argue, "the greater number of relevant players required to achieve a legislative majority creates coordination dilemmas to passing and implementing reforms that have general support but little coherent backing."[20] Even if parties have an incentive to decentralize, difficulties in forging cross-party agreement that overcomes entrenched resistance to reforms may "leave governance very top-down."[21] In contrast, a democratic, competitive, and coherent party system in which there is stable alternation between a small number of strong parties with significant subnational footholds does not face the same challenges. Such parties would have reasonable chances of winning subnational elections, need to maintain subnational support bases while out of power, and face fewer coordination problems.

The Role of the Central Bureaucracy: An Oversight?

Riedl and Dickovick's framework is useful in directing attention to how the overall party system shapes the incentives and capacities of political parties to promote decentralization reforms. However, an omission is the role of central bureaucrats in shaping decentralization. The central bureaucracy is a potentially powerful actor with a key role at every step of the decentralization process from policy design and drafting of legislation to implementation of reforms. As an institution with its own incentives and significant resources to influence reforms, its role must be considered.

The central administration is a central pillar of Tunisia's post-independence state.[22] Hibou identifies the "omnipotent bureaucracy" as one of "two main bodies in the service of [the] exercise of domination," alongside the ruling RCD (*Rassemblement Constitutionnel Démocratique*) party.[23] Bou Nassif's study of ministerial appointments under Ben Ali also shows extensive interpenetration between the administration and the RCD.[24] As Camau's work shows, this is an institutional feature of the post-independence state, which has been built on a systematic "fusion at the top between partisan and state bodies."[25] This system, which kept the bureaucracy under close political control, unraveled after the revolution when the ruling party was dissolved, providing opportunities for the bureaucracy to expand its influence.

20 Ibid., 328.

21 Ibid., 323.

22 Between 1956 and 1960, the number of state employees grew from 12,000 to 80,000 – from 5.7 percent to 18.8 percent of urban employment. "La question du travail (IV): l'etatisme triomphant des annees 1960," *La Presse* (June 7, 1991), 6. Today, the number stands at around 700,000.

23 B. Hibou, *The Force of Obedience: The Political Economy of Repression in Tunisia* (Cambridge: Polity Press, 2011), 110.

24 Bou Nassif, "A Military Besieged."

25 M. Camau, "Les institutions politiques des états maghrébins postcoloniaux," in M. Cherif, H. Mensching, and W. K. Ruff (eds.), *Introduction à l'Afrique du Nord contemporaine* (Aix-en-Provence: Institut de recherches et d'études sur les mondes arabes et musulmans, 1975), 10.

2011–14: UNDERSTANDING THE DECISION TO DECENTRALIZE

The first step in decentralization reforms began with the drafting of Chapter Seven of the new Constitution. The National Constituent Assembly (NCA) elected to draft a new constitution established a Committee on Local and Regional Authorities (CLRA) as one of six drafting committees. The CLRA began its work in February 2012, drafting twelve articles that sought to overturn the system of close tutelage over subnational authorities. These articles were discussed and adopted over the course of two years with remarkably little conflict, in marked contrast to other chapters of the Constitution. The final text was adopted with an average vote of 98.6 percent – the highest of any chapter in the Constitution.[26] What explains the quick pace and radical content of this first phase of the decentralization process?

A New Institutional Venue

The NCA, elected on October 23, 2011, was given a mandate to draft a new constitution after sustained social mobilization that demanded a new governance framework. The Kasbah 1 and 2 sit-ins in January and February 2011 saw protesters from various regions congregate outside the office of the Ben Ali–era prime minister to demand his resignation, dissolution of the ruling party, and election of a constituent assembly to draft a new constitution. Up until then, the regime had sought to diffuse protests by announcing early presidential elections and announcing an increase in the regional development budget and public employment programs. The regime's response demonstrates continuity in its policy paradigm – responding within the existing policy framework of addressing regional inequalities through expanding existing regional development programs and increasing public recruitment.

Underlying this policy paradigm was the regime's definition of regional inequalities as the product of spontaneous economic forces rather than of decision-making structures and policies that favor certain regions and marginalize others. This is clearly articulated in the White Book on Regional Development published by the 2011 interim government,[27] which analyzes regional inequalities as the product of interior regions having "relatively fewer [economic] activities able to stimulate a process of regional development."[28] The proposed solution is to "upgrade" these regions by increasing their "competitiveness" and encouraging convergence with more "dynamic" regions.[29]

[26] Calculated using figures on Al Bawsala, https://majles.marsad.tn/fr/votes/constitution.

[27] In place between Ghannouchi's resignation in February 2011 and the holding of NCA elections in October 2011.

[28] Livre Blanc – *Tunisie: Nouvelle Vision du Développement Régional* (Tunis: Tunisian Ministry of Regional Development, 2011), 32.

[29] Ibid., 12–13. This focus on "convergence" through investment in large-scale infrastructure reflects New Economic Geography, as adopted in the World Bank's 2009 World Development Report. World Bank, *Reshaping Economic Geography* (Washington, DC: World Bank, 2009).

Thus, while regional inequalities were placed squarely on the political agenda in 2011, the destabilization of the existing paradigm did not automatically lead to a new one. It was only with the establishment of the NCA that this occurred. As Baumgartner and Jones argue, the choice of institutional venue for the discussion of policy issues is significant as each venue carries its own set of "enduring rules for making decisions."[30] The NCA had significant decision-making authority, serving as a constitution-drafting assembly, legislature, and public arena, taking policy-making out of the closed circle of the presidency, government, and senior bureaucrats. In the NCA's debates, we see the problem construction or "policy image"[31] of regional inequalities shift away from being the result of lack of "dynamism" in interior regions to the product of an unjust distribution of political and economic power and the dominance of national elites who are "unwilling and unable to go beyond a centralized conception of development."[32]

A Cohesive Political Class of "Outsiders"

The shift in the framing of regional inequalities can be linked to the nature of the NCA's mandate and the profile of its members. The NCA contained a new class of decision-makers that was profoundly different to the traditional political elite in socioeconomic and territorial terms. Due to a ban on senior former ruling party members from running in the 2011 elections, the NCA's members were largely former outsiders to the established political elite. Nearly half represented parties banned or repressed under Ben Ali while nearly 20 percent had been imprisoned for political activities (31 percent and 27 percent from Ennahdha and Congress for the Republic respectively).[33] A coalition government was formed between former opposition parties representing 138 seats (63.5 percent) – Ennahdha (Islamist), Congress for the Republic (secular center-left Arab nationalist), and Ettakattol (secular social democrat). Despite their ideological differences, they had a history of cooperating in anti-regime activities and had already discussed the idea of forming a government before the elections.[34]

This shared experience of opposition created a degree of cohesion among these parties based on a common interest in reforming state institutions and preventing the return of authoritarianism. Opposition parties in the NCA, many of whom had also experienced state repression, shared these interests. This meant that even those

30 F. R. Baumgartner and B. D. Jones (eds.), *Policy Dynamics* (Chicago: University of Chicago Press, 2002), 24.

31 F. R. Baumgartner and B. D. Jones, *Agendas and Instability in American Politics* (Chicago: University of Chicago Press, 1993).

32 Interview, Faycal Jadlaoui Rapporteur, CLRA (Tunis, March 28, 2018).

33 D. Perez Faire, "La loi à l'Assemblée nationale constituante tunisienne: Recomposition et formation d'un nouveau personnel parlementaire tunisien," *L'Année du Maghreb*, 14 (2016), 187–204, at 193.

34 M. Zedermann and W. Limam, "Les leçons du Mouvement tunisien du 18 octobre, de l'unité contre la dictature à la lutte pour la sauvegarde de la démocratie," *Huffington Post* (March 30, 2016).

on opposing sides of the ideological spectrum had a shared interest in putting an end to centralized rule. As Mongi Rahoui, from the opposition communist Movement of Patriotic Democrats, explained:

> Our 2011 electoral program already contained a commitment to decentralization because we'd had enough of excessive centralization of power in Tunisia, like in the rest of the Arab world. We've suffered from dictatorship. We need to transfer power down to people and make radical, deep changes to the old regime. That's why our work in the Committee was consensual – unlike any other Committee in the NCA. Decentralization wasn't a polarizing issue for us.[35]

The preoccupation with decentralizing power as a safeguard against authoritarianism is omnipresent in the Committee's reports. These frequently refer to the need for "a complete rupture with the former system of excessive centralization,"[36] which is "characterized by monopolization of power, exclusion of the other and repression of every opposing view."[37]

In addition, many NCA members had shared territorial and socioeconomic interests. Unlike the traditional ruling elite, which largely hails from Tunis and coastal regions, Perez's study shows that NCA members came from a broad range of social and professional backgrounds, from the formerly unemployed and taxi drivers through to university doyens. This new political class largely lacked "the traditional economic, social and cultural resources of the former regime elite."[38] Furthermore, electoral rules gave large interior regions with lower population density extra representation.[39] The CLRA, in particular, contained almost a two-thirds majority from interior regions.[40]

As Dobry highlights, political crises can operate to change the *value* of particular resources in the political arena.[41] This can be seen in the Tunisian context where the new NCA members possessed a resource that enjoyed great value in the aftermath of a change of regime – lack of association with the former regime. In the post-revolution context, "a stint in prison or in exile becomes the foundations of a new legitimacy for these elected officials."[42] This symbolic capital was frequently mobilized in NCA members' discourse, which was saturated with references to personal, regional, and national histories of exclusion. As a member of the CLRA observed:

35 Interview, Mongi Rahoui, member, CLRA (Tunis, April 12, 2018).

36 CLRA report, October 2, 2012, 3.

37 Al Bawsala, *Report of the Committee on Local and Regional Public Authorities on the Draft Articles Relating to the Paper on Local Authority*, October 1, 2012.

38 Perez Faire, "La loi à l'Assemblée nationale constituante tunisienne," 194.

39 E. Gobe, "Système électoral et révolution: la voie tunisienne," *Pouvoirs*, 156(1) (2016), 71–82.

40 Fifteen of the Committee's twenty-four members came from interior regions, based on analysis of the members' biographies, https://majles.marsad.tn/fr/assemblee/commissions/4f3cf990b197de624e000004.

41 M. Dobry, *Sociologie des crises politiques* (Paris: Presses de Sciences Po, 1986).

42 Perez Faire, "La loi à l'Assemblée nationale constituante tunisienne," 200.

> Most of us came from marginalized regions – both in the Committee and in the Assembly as a whole. We were sons of the nation. Can you name one big businessman in the NCA? You wouldn't find any. We were mainly from modest backgrounds, elected to represent the people who've long been marginalized and excluded from power.[43]

The NCA members' discourse was also filled with a revolutionary repertoire that mobilized ubiquitous references to popular struggles against injustice and "the demands of the revolution" (*mataalib ath-thawra*) to legitimate their mandate to bring in a new governance framework:

> We were drafting the constitution just after a revolution, in a very special context. The revolution was a revolt against the entire model of governance. People felt completely excluded from power and they had had enough of discrimination against interior regions. We had a revolutionary mandate to rethink the entire model of governance, starting from the bottom up.[44]

This "special context" and the NCA members' own experiences of different forms of marginalization encouraged the search for structural solutions to socio-economic and regional inequalities, which continued to be a burning issue driving social mobilization after 2011. This and the strong presence of members from marginalized regions led not only to the adoption of Chapter Seven but the insertion of an additional article requiring the state to implement positive discrimination in favor of marginalized regions.[45] The far-reaching provisions on decentralization and marginalized regions adopted by the NCA thus supports conclusions from other contexts that the dominance of subnational interests at the outset of decentralization leads to more robust forms of decentralization being adopted.[46]

Muted Resistance: A Weakened Central Bureaucracy

Alongside a consensus among politicians on the need to decentralize, their efforts to introduce decentralization were facilitated by the fact that the central bureaucracy had little capacity to resist the proposed reforms. The post-revolution period witnessed a significant weakening in state authority and capacity at the national and subnational levels. Hundreds of protests, sit-ins, and strikes took place[47] and, as the closest physical manifestation of the state, local authorities were particular

43 Interview, Faycal Jadlaoui.

44 Interview, Sana Mersni, second rapporteur, CLRA (Tunis, April 12, 2018).

45 Article 12.

46 T. Falleti "A Sequential Theory of Decentralization: Latin American Cases in Comparative Perspective," *American Political Science Review*, 99(3) (2005), 327–46.

47 A. Bennasr et al. "Dilemmes de la réforme régionale tunisienne," *Revue d'Economie Régionale et Urbaine*, 5 (2015), 853–82.

targets of public anger.[48] Municipal financial resources fell by 50 percent[49] and the interim government was forced to take emergency measures such as requesting international assistance to pay municipal salaries and dissolving municipal councils, replacing them with temporary "*délégations spéciales*."[50]

The Ministry of Interior's Department of Local Government (DGCPL), which oversees local authorities, found itself facing a profound political and financial crisis and unable to manage local affairs, as many municipalities found difficulties delivering even basic services such as waste collection. Previously seen as a source of power, local authorities became a liability for the Ministry of Interior, which faced a broader crisis of legitimacy as a pillar of the "meticulous grid" of control, surveillance, and censorship imposed by the former regime.[51]

In light of the Ministry of Interior's weakened grip, the *délégations spéciales* experienced a degree of de facto decentralization. These local bodies were made up of a mixture of political and civil society representatives, and began to put forward new ideas and modes of local decision-making.[52] This de facto local autonomy and the crisis in state authority led officials to conclude that the only solution was to "lift the dominant hand of the central state from local government."[53] The DGCPL launched a reflection on these challenges in 2011, convening various workshops and conferences, largely funded by international donors, who encouraged it to consider decentralization as a solution to the local governance crisis.[54]

The changing incentives faced by the DGCPL encouraged it to work closely with the CLRA once the latter began its work in February 2012.[55] Public seminars and conferences during this period frequently featured CLRA members alongside DGCPL representatives.[56] However, while the DGCPL was present, its influence on Chapter Seven was limited. For instance, the CLRA rejected the ministry's attempts to insert an obligation that decentralization be implemented "in accordance with the principle of gradualism," viewing this as a strategy to obstruct reforms.[57] A

48 It was the action of a municipal agent that sparked the revolution, when Mohamed Bouazizi set himself on fire after a municipal police officer mistreated him. Municipal town halls and regional governors' offices have been the sites of many protests since 2011. Institut Tunisien des Etudes Stratégiques, *Quelle décentralisation dans une Tunisie reconfigurée?* (Tunis: ITES, 2014).

49 Interview, Mokhtar Hammami, former director-general, MLA (Tunis, May 18, 2016).

50 Interview, Mokhtar Hammami.

51 Hibou, *The Force of Obedience*, 81.

52 For example, Sayada Municipality's Open Gov initiative, K. Tarjem, "Tunisie: la ville de Sayada joue la carte de la transparence," *Le Monde* (June 8, 2015).

53 Interview, Mokhtar Hammami.

54 Ibid.

55 List of sessions available at http://majles.marsad.tn/uploads/documents/R_C_Collectivites_publiques.pdf.

56 See, for example, Association Internationale des Regions Francophones, "Séminaire sur la décentralisation et la gouvernance," Tunis, May 15–18, 2012; Seminar on Local Authority in the Constitution, Sfax, November 18, 2012.

57 Interviews, Faycal Jadaloui and Sana Mersni, 2019.

ministry official's proposal to establish constitutional protections for centrally appointed regional governors was also rejected, given that governors were closely associated with corruption by the former regime.[58] The only DGCPL proposal that was accepted was to insert a reference to adopting decentralization "within the framework of the unity of the state."[59] Other ministries were notably absent from the committee's sessions.[60] Despite having a clear interest in influencing Chapter Seven, it appears that the central bureaucracy lacked the resources needed to do so to any significant degree during this period.

Chapter Seven: A Radical Rupture with the Past

While decentralization is mentioned in only one article in the 1959 Constitution, the 2014 Constitution devotes thirteen articles to decentralization, which fundamentally reshape Tunisia's model of local governance. Local authorities are guaranteed financial and administrative autonomy, while subsidiarity requires that central government only exercise those competencies and responsibilities that cannot be performed at the level that is closest to citizens. Chapter Seven overturns the system of central *tutelle*, under which any decision by a subnational authority had to be approved by central authorities before it could be considered valid. Instead, only *a posteriori* central oversight is allowed over the legality of local or regional council decisions and only via judicial processes.

Chapter Seven also introduces political decentralization, firmly establishing the principle of representative democracy at local and regional levels, as well as participatory democracy and "open governance to ensure broader participation by citizens and civil society."[61] With regards to fiscal decentralization, the Constitution states that central authorities must provide additional financial resources to local and regional authorities, and accompany each transfer of powers with the requisite resources.[62]

2014: THE RESURGENCE OF THE CENTRAL BUREAUCRACY

While the Constitution establishes the broad principles of decentralization, the details were left to be worked out in a new legal framework. While members of the CLRA thought they would be drafting this legislation, the political crisis that

58 CLRA Minutes, April 17, 2012.

59 Article 14.

60 Interview, director-general, Ministry of Finance (Tunis, January 23, 2020).

61 Article 139.

62 Local government suffers from a chronic shortage of funding and represents less than 3 percent of the state's annual budget. See S. Turki and A. Gana "Les Territoires Ruraux en Tunisie a l'épreuve de la communalisation: Entre Complexité de le réforme et enjeux politiques," *Maghreb-Machrek*, 226 (2015), 53–71.

erupted in July 2013 shifted the NCA's attention to other more pressing priorities. The 2013–14 National Dialogue led to the adoption of the Constitution and appointment of a technocratic interim government in January 2014 until the holding of elections scheduled for October 2014. The NCA saw its authority diminished, while political parties had no presence in government and little influence over policy-making.

With the decline of the NCA as a venue for decision-making and political parties occupied with preparing for elections, control over decentralization shifted toward the DGCPL. The department began working on a new local government code and election law in March 2014, convening twenty experts to discuss how to implement Chapter Seven just two months after its adoption.[63] What explains the DGCPL's initiative, apparently without pressure from political actors, given that it stood to lose from the robust decentralization set out in the Constitution? The DGCPL's decision appears to have been shaped by a number of constraints that prevented it from obstructing decentralization altogether, first of which was the need to shape a process that appeared inevitable. As the former DGCPL director-general explained, "Chapter Seven of the constitution is here to stay. Decision-makers have to deal with it and develop a decentralization process that is realistic."[64]

Second, the DGCPL faced significant pressure from international donors to push decentralization forward, with technical and financial support tied to showing clear progress.[65] A vast array of international organizations and development agencies have been involved in this process, bringing an influx of funding.[66] The credibility of the DGCPL's senior officials has become closely associated with achieving progress on decentralization reforms, which have strengthened their position within government structures.[67] Formerly a minor department of the vast Ministry of Interior, the DGCPL was transformed into a new Ministry of Local Affairs and Environment (MLA) in February 2016 as a result of decentralization reforms. Subsequently, the senior bureaucrat leading the drafting of the Local Authorities Code, Mokhtar Hammami, was named minister of local affairs and environment in September 2018 due to the prominent role he had played in leading the reforms. Decentralization has thus become a means of significantly expanding bureaucratic resources.[68]

63 Interview, Hatem Mliki, expert (Tunis, May 20, 2016).

64 Interview, Mokhtar Hammami.

65 Interview, Riadh Mouakhar, minister for local affairs and environment (Tunis, February 9, 2018).

66 For example, the World Bank's Urban Planning and Local Governance program committed $560 million to support decentralization. A long list of decentralization support programs have been launched by multilateral and bilateral institutions, national municipal networks, political foundations, and international nongovernmental organizations.

67 The former DGCPL director-general, Mokhtar Hammami, was hailed as "the father of decentralization" in the Tunisian media and parliamentary debates for his role in drafting the code.

68 Bureaucrats have also been recruited as consultants by international organizations working on decentralization, becoming highly valued on the "expertise market" that has expanded with the influx of donor funding since 2011.

In December 2014, the DGCPL appointed a legal commission to draft the new Local Authorities Code, stating that it wanted it to be "a combination of the spirit of an external perspective of experts and academics on one hand, and the vision of the Tunisian administration characterized by realism and practical awareness of implementation on the ground."[69] The department selected the head of the commission (a law professor), set its terms of reference, and gave it three sets of documents to guide its work – the Constitution, a DGCPL guidance note, and Ministry of Interior studies on the structural difficulties facing local authorities.[70]

In the words of one of its members, the commission was seen to have worked "behind closed doors."[71] There was little consultation with political actors throughout the drafting process and the DGCPL did not consult the NCA's preparatory works or engage with its members,[72] although the NCA was still in place when the DGCPL began work on the new code. Instead, the DGCPL relied on a small circle of technical experts (largely law professors and consultants from the private sector) to work out the details of reforms.[73] These experts showed a clear preference for a highly technical, legalistic approach to designing the reforms, with little engagement with politicians or the public. As one of the main experts explained when asked about their interaction with political parties, "[w]here there's a visible, major political stake, they intervene and delay everything for you but for the rest – the model, the interactions – no … As parties, they had no input."[74]

This drafting process highlights an understudied area of Tunisia's transition – the relationship between politicians and bureaucrats. The dominance of the central bureaucracy in shaping decentralization reforms between 2014 and 2018 is part of a broader expansion of bureaucratic power after the revolution. The removal of the "disciplinary gaze" previously exercised by the ruling party has altered the relationship between politicians and bureaucrats, as one director-general explained:

> There was discipline before [2011] … Even as a Director and then as a Director-General, I wouldn't leave the administration without asking the Minister or my boss. I wouldn't meet anyone external without asking my boss … And especially not politicians! Now, people do whatever they want … Now, no one is accountable … The Minister is busy with his own affairs and there's no discipline … Unfortunately, people understand freedom as … the right to do whatever they want.[75]

69 Mokhtar Hammami, quoted in "Final Revised Version of Draft Local Authority Code Sent to Government to Examine in Ministerial Council to Be Held on 4 July," *Al Masdar* (June 28, 2016).

70 Interview, Afef Marrakchi, member, Drafting Commission (Tunis, May 18, 2016).

71 Ibid.

72 Ibid.

73 For example, see Centre pour la Formation et l'Appui a la Decentralisation, "Séminaire sur la Décentralisation et la Gouvernance," September 10–11, 2015; European Union in cooperation with Center for Support and Training for Decentralization and l'Ecole Nationale de l'Administration de Tunis, "Colloque sur la decentralisation et la cohesion sociale," June 11, 2015.

74 Interview, expert, MLA (Tunis, April 22, 2019).

75 Interview, director-general, Ministry of Finance (Tunis, January 23, 2020).

Information asymmetries between politicians and bureaucrats – a common feature of every state bureaucracy[76] – can be heightened during post-authoritarian transitions, which are often characterized by instability, high government turnover, and the entry of new political actors with little prior experience inside the state apparatus. Tunisia has seen ten governments between 2011 and 2019, which has reshaped the relationship with bureaucracy. As one senior bureaucrat noted, "[y]ou have ministers changing all the time. We [bureaucrats] relied on ourselves and developed solidarity among us. We understood they were just passers-by."[77] Politico–bureaucratic relations have been further strained by the announcement of reforms to "clean up the administration" and accusations, by politicians, of bureaucratic sabotage, creating mutual suspicion.

This has contributed to a decentralization design process that is strongly dominated by the central bureaucracy. Over the four-year period of drafting, senior bureaucrats produced seventeen versions of the draft code with little political input until submission of the final draft to parliament on May 5, 2017.[78] As one expert noted, "[d]ecentralization is a policy that isn't guided by politicians. It's a policy guided by a part of the administration, led by Mokhtar [Hammami]. He guides, he imposes on politicians their agenda … This is a singularity of what's happening in Tunisia."[79] This redistribution of resources in favor of bureaucrats has been compounded by a lack of cohesion among political actors regarding decentralization, as discussed below.

2014–18: CONFLICTING INCENTIVES AND COORDINATION CHALLENGES

Fragmented Party Systems and Weak Incentives for Reform

While the bureaucracy has experienced increased solidarity in the face of political uncertainty and instability since 2011, the political landscape has been increasingly fragmented and divided. The October 2014 elections brought about an elected government with deeply conflicting interests and a political landscape characterized by intraparty and interparty fragmentation.

Nidaa Tounes, a secular centrist party led by Beji Caid Essebsi, a former regime official, won the legislative and presidential elections. In the legislative elections, it won with 37.6 percent of votes while the next largest party, Ennahdha, gained 27.8 percent. The next largest party, Union Patriotique Libre (UPL), won 4 percent

76 M. Weber "Bureaucracy," in H. H. Gerth and C. Wright Mills (eds.), *From Max Weber: Essays in Sociology* (Oxford: Oxford University Press, 1946); G. Tullock, *The Politics of Bureaucracy* (Washington, DC: Public Affairs Press, 1965); A. Downs, *Inside Bureaucracy* (Boston, MA: Little, Brown and Co, 1967)

77 Interview, director-general, Ministry of Finance (Tunis, January 23, 2020).

78 For instance, members of the drafting commission expressed surprise that the government presented few comments on the draft code when it was submitted to the Ministerial Council in 2017.

79 Interview, expert, MLA (Tunis, April 22, 2019).

followed by a large number of small parties with a fraction of the vote. The election results reflected a shift in public priorities away from a strong pro-democracy agenda and toward security and economic concerns. This was encapsulated in Nidaa Tounes' successful campaign slogan, "*i'adat haybat ad-dawla*," meaning restoring the prestige and authority of the state and ending the perceived disorder of the post-revolution period.

The new legislature, the Assembly of People's Representatives (ARP) elected in October 2014, contained 217 representatives from 15 parties and 3 independent lists. The unity government formed with the support of 76 percent of the assembly was deeply divided over decentralization. These divisions can be explained by three key factors that are explored below, drawing on Riedl and Dickovick's framework.

A Deeply Divided Political Class

First, unlike 2011–14, there was no consensus on decentralization among governing parties. In fact, the parties had opposing historical experiences of the central state and conflicting socioeconomic and territorial interests. While the parties in the NCA and the 2011–14 coalition government had had shared experiences of state repression and lacked the economic and cultural capital of the established elite, the leading party in the post-2014 coalition, Nidaa Tounes, contained various former regime figures and received broad support from established elites.[80] While the 2011–14 government and assembly had been composed largely of outsiders to the state, who saw it as having failed to deliver development, national dignity, and freedom, the post-2014 assembly and government were led by individuals who had spent lengthy careers inside the state, including the president, prime minister, and parliamentary speaker.

Furthermore, parties in the post-2014 coalition government had divergent territorial bases. The 2014 legislative elections revealed a pronounced regional split between Nidaa (strong support in northern and coastal regions) and Ennahdha (strong base in the south and parts of the center).[81] This split was again evident in the 2014 presidential elections when the south largely voted for Moncef Marzouki, seen as the "pro-revolution" candidate promising to radically reform state institutions, while northern and coastal regions largely backed Beji Caid Essebsi, an establishment figure who promised to restore security and the economy.[82]

The 2011–14 consensus on decentralization gave way to conflicting readings of the historical legacies of central state rule. During ARP debates of the draft Local Authorities Code in 2017–18, a clear divide emerged between parties whose

80 V. Szakal, "Circumventing Political Exclusion: RCD after the Revolution and in the Coming Elections," *Nawaat* (September 14, 2014).

81 V. Szakal, "Strategic Vote, Non-vote, and the Relative Victor–Nidaa Tounes," *Nawaat* (November 2, 2014).

82 A. Kireev, "Tunisia: Presidential Election 2014," Electoral Geography 2.0 (2014), www.electoralgeography.com/new/en/countries/t/tunisia/tunisia-presidential-election-2014.html.

leadership was closely associated with the central state and those who have historically been outsiders to it. In the first plenary debate, representatives of Nidaa and its offshoots (Alhorra and the National Bloc) emphasized the dangers decentralization posed to the unity of the state and the inability of local authorities to govern effectively. "For decades, we have had centralized rule. And now we have corruption and chaos. Alhorra believes that implementing this code in one go will fragment the state, promote corruption and waste public resources. We need to respect the law and the unity of the Tunisian state."[83]

Meanwhile, representatives of the blocs whose leadership had a history of opposition to the central state – Ennahdha, Bloc Democrate, and Front Populaire – spoke strongly for decentralization, while portraying the central state as the primary threat.[84] For instance, the Front Populaire's representative[85] (who had been imprisoned several times for opposition to the Bourguiba and Ben Ali regimes) presented numerous amendments seeking to restrict the powers of the central state and declared, "[w]e should not be afraid of decentralization. The fear is of the central state's tendency to monopolize and of a return to the old system."[86]

The struggles over decentralization express a deeper conflict concerning the legacy of Tunisia's post-independence state and of Bourguibism. As Dakhlia notes, a fierce debate regarding this legacy has erupted since 2011, opening up "old questions that we thought, wrongly, had been left behind, even when we knew that the wounds of the past are still gaping."[87] The decentralization debate also divides the political landscape in ways that transcend the usual political and ideological lines. While Ennahdha, Bloc Democrate, and Front Populaire have been on opposing sides on nearly every issue between 2014 and 2019, the debate over the Local Authorities Code saw them adopt a common language (similar to the 2011–14 discussions of Chapter Seven) that expresses a shared *référentiel* or paradigm[88] for viewing the central state as a violently repressive and exclusionary structure that seeks to homogenize society and privileges a dominant "Sahel-based, *francisant* and bourgeois" identity.[89] This contrasts with the Bourguibist paradigm of a strong central

83 Alhorra representative, author's observation notes, ARP plenary, March 22, 2018.

84 Author's transcripts of ARP sessions and plenary debates, September 2017 to April 2018.

85 An alliance composed mainly of radical left-wing opposition parties that were outlawed before 2011.

86 Author's observation notes, ARP plenary session, March 22, 2018.

87 J. Dakhlia, "L'an I de la révolution tunisienne ou les résurgences d'un passé qui divise," *Jadaliyya* (December 5, 2012). This also links to the transitional justice process, which was designed so as to include victims of the crackdown on the Youssefists and has provoked a fierce debate. On this process, see M. Guetat, "Justice transitionnelle, justice rétributive et réconciliation: le cas de la Tunisie," in E. Gobe (ed.), *Justice et reconciliation dans le Maghreb post-révoltes arabes* (Tunis: IRMC, 2019).

88 B. Jobert and P. Muller, *L'État en action, politiques publiques et corporatisme* (Paris: PUF, 1987); P. Hall, "Policy Paradigms, Social Learning, and the State: The Case of Economic Policymaking in Britain," *Comparative Politics*, 25(3) (1993), 275–96.

89 L. Sadiki, "The Search for Citizenship in Bin Ali's Tunisia: Democracy versus Unity," *Political Studies*, 50 (2002), 497–513, at 511.

state that protects national unity, acting as an "agent of social transformation, to fashion the new man, a Tunisian citizen liberated from particularistic (tribal, ethnics, regional, class) allegiances and mentalities,"[90] as mobilized by Nidaa, Alhorra, and the National Bloc.

Fragmented Party Systems and Weak Incentives to Decentralize

The second factor that has obstructed decentralization is the highly fragmented and unstable nature of the political landscape. This has had the effect of both weakening incentives and capacities to decentralize. Few parties saw an incentive to push for decentralization in 2014–18, whether those in government or opposition.

Based on observation of parliamentary debates, corroborated by interviews with those who followed debates of the Local Authorities Code closely, only three parties strongly supported decentralization – Ennahdha, Bloc Democrate, and Front Populaire. In practice, only Ennahdha actively pushed for the code to be adopted and for municipal elections to be held.[91] The smaller Bloc Democrate and Front Populaire did not push for the reforms while most opposition parties, including the Front Populaire, demanded the postponement of municipal elections.[92] This lack of interest in decentralization can be explained by the degree of interparty and intraparty cohesion and the nature of each party's local presence, as analyzed below.

First, the fact that the party system is fragmented between many small parties means that parties have little incentive to support reforms that may benefit their rivals equally. Thus, even opposition parties like Front Populaire who supported decentralization in principle had little incentive to push hard for the reforms. Indeed, the last poll published before the May 2018 municipal elections showed that opposition parties stood to do poorly and were far behind Nidaa and Ennahdha, with these two winning 60 percent collectively and the rest of the vote divided across a large number of parties and independent lists.[93] As Riedl and Dickovick predict, the fragmentation of the vote between lots of small parties results in a large number of parties that are theoretically supportive of decentralization but have weak incentives to push for reforms.

Second, a political landscape characterized by high levels of volatility and frequent party switching make electoral outcomes extremely unpredictable. Since the 2014 elections, strong centrifugal competition has resulted in three of the four governing

90 L. Chouikha and E. Gobe, *La Tunisie de Bourguiba ou la modernisation autoritaire (1956–1987)* (Paris: La Decouverte, 2015), 16.

91 Interviews, bureaucratic officials, civil society activists, experts, international organization representatives, 2018 and 2019.

92 "Tunisie: Afek Tounes et sept autres partis politiques demandent le report des municipales," *Jeune Afrique* (September 5, 2017).

93 "Last Polls before Municipal Elections Shows North with Nidaa and South with Ennahdha," *Espace Manager* (February 13, 2018).

parties fragmenting. For instance, Nidaa saw thirty of its eighty-six parliamentarians defect in its first year in government.[94] As Riedl and Dickovick argue, parties experiencing high internal volatility face significant uncertainty regarding their electoral prospects, thus weakening incentives to go toward subnational elections.[95] Nearly all the parties interviewed indicated that they supported delaying decentralization because they were simply not prepared and were occupied by internal party struggles.[96]

Third, political fragmentation is compounded by weak local presence. Few parties have strong local structures, partly as a result of the very restricted political space prior to 2011.[97] The only party that is described as having strong local structures is Ennahdha, which is unsurprisingly the strongest supporter of decentralization.[98] Meanwhile, Nidaa Tounes, which had built a significant local presence prior to the 2014 elections, suffered a wave of local defections.[99] An absence of strong local structures means parties cannot capitalize on the benefits of competing for subnational footholds and thus have weak incentives to push for decentralization. In particular, most Tunisian parties display three structural problems that further weaken incentives to support decentralization – first, their weak local presence means they lack the capacity to present local candidates in a large number of localities. Second, in the event that a party obtains local seats, its local party structures lack the capacity to coordinate and follow up with its local councilors. Third, weak local–national linkages mean that central party structures lack the mechanisms and resources to supervise or guide the work of local councilors and to put in place mechanisms for coordination between local councilors and local party branches.[100]

Political Fragmentation and Weak Capacities for Reform

In addition to reducing incentives to decentralize, Riedl and Dickovick argue that fragmented party systems weaken the *capacity* of political actors to enact decentralization reforms. This is borne out in the Tunisian context in relation to both intraparty and interparty cohesion.

94 This has been blamed on lack of ideological coherence and absence of strong internal party structures. See Y. Cherif, "The Leadership Crisis of Nidaa Tounes," Carnegie Endowment for International Peace (December 8, 2015).

95 See also O'Neill, *Decentralizing the State*, 24.

96 Interviews, party officials, Afek Tounes, Alhorra, Front Populaire, Nidaa Tounes.

97 For instance, only Ennahdha and Nidaa were able to present candidates in all 350 municipalities in 2018. The next highest number was by the Front Populaire (forty-nine lists). Supreme Independent Election Authority (2018), www.isie.tn/elections/elections-municipales-2018/candidatures/.

98 This was raised by international organizations that trained parties for the municipal elections, who noted that most parties had weak or no local presence and that even local branches established in preparation for municipal elections closed soon after the elections.

99 See Cherif, "The Leadership Crisis of Nidaa Tounes."

100 Indeed, nearly all municipal councilors interviewed stated that they had little contact with or support from the local branch of the party that they represent. Furthermore, the nature of their relationship with the local branch (where one exists) remains unclear and conflicts are reportedly frequent.

At the intraparty level, the existence of a large number of very small political parties in the legislature and instability within most parties means that they lack the resources needed to effectively influence policy-making. Political officials – whether in government, parliament, or party structures – provided little input into the Code on Local Authorities until its submission to Parliament. Thus, between March 2014 and May 2017, political parties were largely absent from the drafting process.[101] Nearly all parties said that they had no party structure tasked with monitoring the decentralization process, despite this being a major reform. Some stated that they were aware of the drafting of a new decentralization code but lacked the time and expertise to contribute.

The pressures imposed by a tumultuous political transition – social, economic, and security crises, an unstable governing coalition, and party infighting – were frequently mentioned as constraints on parties' ability to influence not only decentralization but all policy processes. As one Afek Tounes leader explained, "[p]arties were busy with other things … we were going from fight to fight for *years*. Nidaa was imploding. Ennahdha was busy maintaining the balance. The others were miniscule and struggling to hold together. Political parties weren't busy with public affairs, they were busy with politico-political fights, between or within them." These internal challenges place parties and the legislature at a significant disadvantage to the bureaucracy, as one parliamentarian noted with frustration:

> Parties don't pay much attention to policy issues until they become immediately pressing. We [parliamentarians] don't get involved until a piece of draft legislation is submitted. The administration sees little reason to consult us … All the parties are busy with day-to-day management. They haven't developed any vision for decentralization … Ministries often give us proposals on the spot and we have to take a decision without proper analysis. The political actor comes right at the end of the policy process.[102]

Moreover, as Riedl and Dickovick predict, interparty fragmentation resulting from the large number of parties reduces parties' capacities to adopt reforms by creating significant coordination problems. This can be seen in the legislative process for the Local Authorities Code, which took nearly ten months to finalize at the committee stage.[103] After lengthy debate at committee stage, the committee was deluged with over 500 proposed amendments submitted by members in March 2018 – only two months before the scheduled date for municipal elections. As one parliamentary advisor noted, "[i]t's as if each member acts on their own, proposing

[101] Even parties within the coalition government provided little input. Members of the DGCPL drafting commission expressed surprise that the Ministerial Council presented few comments on the draft code when it was submitted to it in 2017.

[102] Interview, Executive Bureau member, ARP (Tunis, April 6, 2018).

[103] Interviews, Mohamed Naceur Jebira, chair, ARP Committee on Administrative Affairs and Armed Forces (Tunis, March 15, 2018), Besma Jebali, rapporteur (Tunis, March 15, 2018).

whatever amendment they come up with – they could've raised their comments with their representative on the committee at any time in the past year. But there is no coordination within each bloc, there's no party line. Some blocs aren't parties; they're groups of individuals – each states whatever position he happens to think of that day."[104]

To overcome these coordination problems, the assembly established a Consensus Committee – an exceptional measure that allows for negotiation between a small number of representatives to hammer out agreements and speed up the legislative process.[105] This mechanism (first used during the final discussions of the Constitution) illustrates the need to develop ways of addressing the significant coordination problems within the assembly.

Subnational Actors

While national political actors have had limited capacity to shape decentralization reforms in 2014–18, subnational political actors have had even less of a say. These can be divided into two categories – municipal council members (*délégations spéciales*) and local party branches.

Since 2011, the *délégations spéciales* have been appointed by the prime minister after consultation with governing parties. Their temporary status, conflicts over the appointment process, local power struggles, and high turnover have severely undermined their legitimacy and authority.[106] The limited research on these bodies has highlighted the intense and often paralyzing local power struggles they have faced, leaving many unable to fulfill the basic functions of local government and little time to influence national-level processes.[107]

The national representative body of municipalities, the National Federation of Tunisian Towns, has also played little role in shaping the new code. Despite having significant international funding and partnerships, it has been unable to act as a voice for municipalities. Its history as a "black box"[108] and instrument of central government control (previously under the Ministry of Interior and now the MLA) means it has little legitimacy in the eyes of its own members. When asked whether

[104] Interview, advisor to Nidaa Tounes bloc (Tunis, March 16, 2018).

[105] This drew criticism from some civil society organizations, who see the Consensus Committee as an arbitrary mechanism that undermines transparency. See Al Bawsala, *Rapport annuel d'observation des travaux de l'ARP (troisième session parlementaire)*, March 2018.

[106] See, for example, the dissolution of the Rades *délégation spéciale* for "the inability of the president to manage the situation and resolve conflicts," Decree no. 2016–823, *Journal Officiel de la Republique Tunisienne* (July 1, 2016).

[107] F. Volpi, F. Merone, and C. Loschi, "Local (r)evolutions in Tunisia, 2011–2014: Reconstructing Municipal Political Authority," *Middle East Journal*, 70(3) (2016), 365–81; J. A. Clark, E. Dalmasso, and E. Lust, "Not the Only Game in Towns: Explaining Changes in Municipal Councils in Post-revolutionary Tunisia," *Democratization*, 26(8) (2019), 1362–81.

[108] Interview, expert (Tunis, April 3, 2019).

it was seeking to advocate for the transfer of powers or resources to municipalities, its executive director (a Ministry of Interior civil servant) stated, "[w]e're not going to fight with ministries ... We can't today come to question political decisions. We need dialogue, and then to go with the right solutions ... We aren't divided. We are all actors of decentralization."[109] This language echoes former regime discourse, in which the role of representative structures is to serve the national project by neutralizing conflict in a system of "downward mobilization."[110]

Local political party branches have also been absent from the process. A section of the literature links decentralization to the degree to which political parties are themselves decentralized, arguing that where "party brokers" are located at the subnational level, there will be an incentive for parties to decentralize power.[111] While further empirical research is required in this area, it appears that Tunisian parties are highly centralized, with party brokers located at the national level. The deep conflicts and divisions in recent years have often involved local party structures breaking away in protest at being excluded from party decision-making.[112] The centralized nature of most parties leaves local branches with few resources or expertise with which to contribute to policy-making, particularly on complex reforms such as decentralization.[113]

Notably, the only subnational actors who mobilized to influence the drafting process are municipal general secretaries (the most senior members of the municipal administration). This can be explained by the fact that they had both strong incentives and the organizational capacities to do so. Municipal general secretaries have historically been appointed by the Ministry of Interior and are part of the national civil service. In May 2016, fearing that future elected councils would be given broad powers to hire and fire them and interfere in their work, they mobilized through their union, demanding that sections of the draft code be amended to reduce municipal council powers over general secretaries. Their mobilization resulted in a daylong private consultation with the minister for local affairs and the amendment

109 Interview (Tunis, April 21, 2016).

110 M. Camau, F. Amrani, and R. Ben Achour, *Controle politique et regulations electorales en Tunisie: les elections legislatives du 4 novembre 1979* (Aix-en-Provence: Edisud, 1981), 65.

111 W. Riker, *Federalism: Origin, Operation, Significance* (Boston: Little Brown, 1964); E. Willis, S. Haggard, and C. Garman, "The Politics of Decentralization in Latin America," *Latin American Research Review*, 34 (1999), 7–56; K. Eaton, "The Link between Political and Fiscal Decentralization in South America," in A. P. Montero and D. J. Samuels *Decentralization in South America* (Notre Dame, IN: University of Notre Dame Press, 2004), pp.122–54

112 Two of the governing parties in the 2015 coalition government, UPL and Afek, have imploded due to claims that party leaders take decisions without consulting their parties. For instance, several UPL parliamentarians and party leaders resigned from the party after the UPL's president decided to merge with the rival Nidaa Tounes party without any internal consultation process. Some parties have experienced such high levels of internal conflict that they have been unable to hold party congresses.

113 Interviews with local party representatives, 2016.

of some provisions.[114] This further illustrates the distribution of resources between political and administrative actors, with administrative actors able to mobilize representative structures characterized by stability, longevity, and a shared institutional identity, while political actors lack the internal cohesion, organizational structures, and expertise to effectively shape decentralization policy.[115]

Outcomes: Robust Constitutional Provisions, Weak Legislative Framework

The power balance between national and subnational actors, and between political and bureaucratic actors, is manifested in the contents of the new decentralization law. Chapter Seven of the Constitution mandates three forms of decentralization – political, administrative, and fiscal. While the Local Authorities Code provides for political decentralization (freely elected municipal and regional councils), it establishes very weak forms of administrative and fiscal decentralization. It remains vague on administrative decentralization, simply restating the principle of subsidiarity set out in the Constitution. Rather than specifying policy functions to be transferred to the subnational level, the MLA has stated that this process will be negotiated and implemented over a twenty-seven-year period, providing few details and declining to publish its national strategy despite repeated demands by political parties and civil society. Fiscal decentralization is equally weak. The code declines to give subnational authorities additional fiscal powers or resources. Even proposals to grant them a set share of value-added tax or other tax revenues were categorically rejected by the Ministry of Finance.[116]

However, once the draft code entered the ARP, political actors were able to shape some aspects. For instance, original proposals to allow regional governors to retain significant powers to intervene in the work of local councils were watered down. Similarly, broad central government powers to dissolve local councils and dismiss council members by decree were significantly amended and safeguards inserted. The changes imposed by political officials indicate a preoccupation with political aspects of decentralization while leaving the fiscal and administrative aspects largely as set by the bureaucracy.

This lack of focus on the redistribution of financial resources and decision-making powers leaves decentralization disconnected from broader questions of territorial development. As one expert noted:

> The decentralization process is unfortunately disconnected from regional development … The process [of regional development planning] is still very top down,

[114] Interview with Yosri Magdiche, head of training, Center for Support and Training for Decentralization (Tunis, April 20, 2016).

[115] For more on Tunisia's heritage of state corporatism, see E. Gobe, "Les syndicalismes arabes au prisme de l'autoritairisme et du corporatisme," in O. Dabene, V. Geisser, and G. Massardier (eds.), *Autoritarismes democratiques et democraties autoritaires au XXIe siècle: Convergences Nord-Sud* (Paris: La Decouverte, 2008), 267–84.

[116] Interviews, experts, and bureaucrats involved in the drafting process (Tunis, March–April 2019).

> sectorial. What involvement will there be of municipal councils and regional councils? … The central government doesn't have a vision of decentralization as it relates to regional development.[117]

This failure to connect decentralization to the territorial distribution of political and economic power reflects the legacies of the central state's sectorial approach to thinking about development and territory. Paradoxically, while the NCA's discussions of decentralization revolved around the need to reform decision-making structures so as to be more sensitive to questions of territory, decentralization design has reproduced the very same top-down decision-making processes, local–national balance of power, and sectorial logic that decentralization was initially designed to address. As one former senior official at the Ministry of Infrastructure explained:

> Our planning process today – one of the weaknesses is that it's sectorial. We think of planning in sectorial terms only – agriculture, health, roads, tourism, each separately. This might not correspond to a territorial logic … Development is really in the hands of the sectorial ministries in Tunisia. The Department for territorial planning produces the national land use plan and the regional plans. The Ministry of Infrastructure builds roads. The Ministry of Health builds hospitals. The Ministry of Education builds schools. There is no spatial or territorial reflection on what the region needs. This is what decentralization is supposed to achieve.[118]

CONCLUSION

Analyzing Tunisia's decentralization reforms reveals the existence of historical, cultural, socioeconomic, and territorial cleavages that are often obscured by the usual binaries highlighted in literature (particularly the secularist–Islamist binary). The struggle over decentralization reforms can be more broadly read as a struggle over the "official narrative on the Tunisian nation" between actors with divergent historical experiences of the state.[119]

Applying Riedl and Dickovick's framework to the Tunisian context sheds light on how actors' strategies are shaped not only by their own interests and ideas, but by the wider institutional arrangements that shape the incentives and capacities of individual and collective actors. The concept of institutional venue also helps to shed light on how resources and opportunities for policy change are shaped by institutional arrangements. While actors may have the desire to undertake reforms, their capacity to do so rests on a number of structural factors that determine their

117 Interview, expert, World Bank (Tunis, March 11, 2018).

118 Interview (Tunis, April 22, 2016).

119 S. Zemni, "The Tunisian Revolution: Neoliberalism, Urban Contentious Politics and the Right to the City," *International Journal of Urban and Regional Research*, 41(1) (2017), 70–83, at 79.

resources, opportunities, and constraints. Time itself emerges as a highly valuable resource in short supply during contexts of significant "political fluidity,"[120] highlighting how opportunities or "political windows" for policy innovation can be fleeting.

The shifting dynamics between political and bureaucratic actors in the post-revolution context has received little attention and is an area for further study. It is evident that the Tunisian administration has acted as "the locomotive behind the decentralization process" between 2014 and 2018,[121] framing the decentralization debate and controlling the content and pace of reforms. This has contributed to a highly legal-administrative vision of decentralization that has been accused of being "excessively technical and cautious."[122] The dominance of technical experts and the absence of a broader cross-government, political, or public debate on the details of decentralization have led to "a purely juridical reform … [rather than] a reform with social, political, economic even environmental implications."[123]

The absence of subnational voices during 2014–18 highlights how historical legacies continue to shape policy design and outcomes. Where subnational actors are weak before decentralization occurs, reforms are prone to be conceived and implemented in a highly centralized way that reflects the interests of national actors. The weaknesses of subnational authorities are then used to justify the continuation of that same system, based on subnational authorities' "lack of readiness" for decentralization.

With the election of over 7,200 elected municipal councilors in May 2018, it remains to be seen whether this balance of power will shift. Municipal councilors face a legal framework that gives them few powers and resources with which to meet high public expectations. As one international observer noted, "part of the reason they came up with the decentralization process was to address the needs of marginalized communities outside Tunis and the coast … but what has happened is that they've created these bodies but without actually empowering them to address those issues."[124]

However, it appears that municipal councils are increasingly challenging the existing distribution of powers and resources. The creation of a new mayors' union, the numerous legal challenges brought by municipal councils against regional governors for interference and obstruction, and the mobilization by municipal councils against central government decisions indicate that we may see a "policy ratchet effect"[125] whereby reforms generate their own set of supporters who push toward

[120] Dobry, *Sociologie des crises politiques*.
[121] Interview, Imed Hammami, chair, CLRA (Tunis, April 12, 2016).
[122] Interview, Ridha Louh, municipal advisor (Mannouba, April 18, 2016).
[123] Interview, activist, Al Bawsala (Tunis, April 3, 2019).
[124] Interview, expert, IRI (Tunis, March 7, 2019).
[125] E. Huber and J. D. Stephens, *Development and Crisis of the Welfare State: Parties and Policies in Global Markets* (Chicago and London: University of Chicago Press, 2001)

further reform and challenge the limited vision of decentralization imposed.[126] As one mayor noted:

> The central and regional authorities are not aware that the municipality has become an economic actor. They want to limit our role to providing basic services, collecting waste, lighting. They [governors] use the old methods against us – defamation, using security forces, blocking us with the law, lobbying … We have to be patient and keep working. We aren't here just to fix a few potholes. We are development actors now.[127]

[126] Numerous conflicts have already occurred between municipal councils and regional governors. See, for example, W. Samoud, "Le torchon brûle entre le maire de la Marsa et le gouverneur de Tunis," *Huffington Post Maghreb* (October 22, 2018).

[127] Interview, mayor (Kebili, February 3, 2020).

PART III

Decentralization and Self-determination

9

Autonomy beyond the State

Joost Jongerden

In the Kurdistan Region of Iraq (KRI) in 2017, voters could respond "yes" or "no" to the question posed in Kurdish, Turkmen, Arabic, and Assyrian: "Do you want the Kurdistan Region and the Kurdistani areas outside the administration of the Region to become an independent state?" In the same year, Kurds in Syria elected the co-chairs of the councils through which Kurds, Turkmen, Arabs, and Christians administered their communities. While the first vote was supposed to lead to the establishment of an independent state, yet ended in a series of political and military setbacks for the Kurdish political parties,[1] the second aimed to strengthen self-organization as a form of self-determination, yet faces an uncertain future due to the conditions in Syria and Turkish incursions.[2]

This chapter looks at these two different understandings of self-determination in Kurdistan. It does so against the context of processes of centralization and nationalization that occurred in the nineteenth and twentieth centuries and through which a new state order emerged that saw Kurds turned into a surplus population confronted with assimilation and erasure. This new situation was initially followed by the responses of Kurdish movements to either carve out a state of their own or else develop a far-reaching autonomy, until, at the beginning of the 2000s, a reformulation of the idea of self-determination emerged within one of the main social and political movements in Kurdistan, the Kurdistan Workers' Party (*Partiya Karkerên Kurdistan*, PKK).

1 B. Park, J. Jongerden, F. Owtram, and A. Yoshioka, "On the Independence Referendum in the Kurdistan Region of Iraq and Disputed Territories in 2017," *Kurdish Studies*, 5(2) (2017), 199–214; J. Jongerden, "Governing Kurdistan: Self-administration in the Kurdistan Regional Government in Iraq and the Democratic Federation of Northern Syria," *Ethnopolitics*, 18(1) (2019), 61–75; D. O'Driscoll and B. Baser, "Independence Referendums and Nationalist Rhetoric: The Kurdistan Region of Iraq," *Third World Quarterly*, 40(11) (2019), 2016–34

2 B. Küçük and C. Ozselcuk, "The Rojava Experience: Possibilities and Challenges of Building a Democratic Life," *South Atlantic Quarterly*, 115(1) (2016), 184–96.

THE PROBLEM OF CENTRALIZED-TERRITORIAL STATE FORMATION AND NATIONALISM

Kurdish concerns with self-determination emerged against a background of two intertwined processes: state formation and nationalism. The first process, a territorial centralization of political power, had taken place in the context of the disintegration of various forms of indirect rule within the Ottoman Empire from which the states of Turkey, Iraq, and Syria were carved out, among others. Following Tilly,[3] these territorial states can be defined as examples of "centralized, differentiated organizations the officials of which [...] claim control over the chief concentrated means of violence within a population inhabiting a large, contiguous territory."

The original citation from Tilly includes the notion that the officials "more or less successfully claim control over the chief concentrated means of violence," yet even as the main state actors to have emerged from the end of the Ottoman Empire after World War I, the regimes established in Turkey, Iraq, and Syria have had long periods in which they could not and still cannot successfully claim the monopoly of violence. Still, the centralization of the means of violence has substantially increased their ability to use force.

The second context for the process of Kurdish self-determination has been nationalism, a political concept holding that the borders of political units (state) and cultural units (nation) should coincide. This teaches that the power of a state depends on the degree to which its subjects respond to the ideal of the particular cultural identity thought to characterize the nation.[4] The aim of nationalism as a motivating ideal and structuring principle for the political is to territorialize a cultural identity-based political regime.[5] Only assimilation in the cultural identity affords access to political rights and full citizenship. The intertwining of centralized-territorial state formation and nationalism has proved to be a powerful and also lethal cocktail: the centralization of administration and means of violence in combination with the desire to suppress sociocultural differences in the name of the nation inscribes the possibility of ethnocide into the nature and functioning of the state and its body politic.[6]

Spread across Europe, North Africa, and Asia, the Ottoman Empire had been an assemblage of systems of direct and indirect rule. The rulers did not consider themselves the bearers of a national identity or representatives of a nation, and nor did they express the need to mold, shape, and create a population. The main areas

3 C. Tilly, "War Making and State Making as Organized Crime," in P. B. Evans, D. Rueschemeyer, and T. Skocpol (eds.), *Bringing the State Back in* (Cambridge: Cambridge University Press, 1985), 170–91, at 170.

4 R. L. Koehl, "The Politics of Resettlement," *The Western Political Quarterly*, 6(2) (1953), 231–42, at 231.

5 J. Jongerden, *The Settlement Issue in Turkey and the Kurds: An Analysis of Spatial Policies, Modernity and War* (Leiden and Boston: Brill, 2007), 2.

6 P. Clastres, *Archeology of Violence* (Los Angeles: Semiotext(e), 2010), 49.

that were effectively centralized were parts of the Balkans and Egypt along with key transportation routes, the remaining territories being mostly self-governed. Thus, the Kurdistan region within the Ottoman Empire was composed of emirates governed by Kurdish *mîrs*. This started to change in the first half of the nineteenth century, when the empire's rulers, facing disintegration and loss of territory to European powers (principally Britain, France, and Russia), started to enforce the authority of the Palace in Istanbul so as to strengthen the empire. As part of this push toward centralization, the Kurdish emirates were eliminated.[7]

As the central state became more assertive in (former) Ottoman territories, its marriage with an aggressive, nascent nationalism started to threaten Kurdish identity with extinction. Various uprisings, both short and protracted, occurred, motivated by the desire to claim and maintain some form of autonomy from the central administrations and in defense of a Kurdish identity. These rebellions, however, were geographically confined and in general politically limited to the followers of particular religious and tribal leaders.[8] Thus, the quest for self-determination and political decentralization around the question of Kurdistan emerged as a direct result of the processes of centralization and nationalization of politics and polity. As this process of state formation subjected the Kurds to a politics of assimilation and erasure, the ideas of self-determination and independent state formation started to become crucial political principles for resistance.

In the post-World War II period that saw the slow dismantling of the European colonial power, the ideal of self-determination operated as an organizing principle for national liberation movements and political parties claiming to speak on behalf of disenfranchised and colonized peoples around the world. This quest for liberation was primarily formulated within a Marxist-Leninist narrative: the dominant approach to resistance in decolonization struggles in the 1960s and 1970s. This was the case also for the Kurdish political movements and parties. Yet, for Kurds, the right to self-determination involved not only a separation – of the occupied territories from the post-imperial (Ottoman and Safavid), post-World War I "colonizing" states (Turkey and Iran, and the Anglo-French "mandates" that became Iraq and Syria) – but also a unification of these parts into one, namely, Kurdistan.[9]

7 M. V. Bruinessen, *Agha, Shaikh and State: On the Social and Political Organization of Kurdistan* (Utrecht: Proefschrift, 1978), 244; M. Eppel, "The Demise of the Kurdish Emirates: The Impact of Ottoman Reforms and International Relations on Kurdistan during the First Half of the Nineteenth Century," *Middle East Critique*, 44(2) (2008), 237–58.

8 See among others: Bruinessen, *Agha, Shaikh and State*; R. Olson, *The Emergence of Kurdish Nationalism and the Sheikh Said Rebellion, 1880–1925* (Austin: University of Texas Press, 1989); H. Bozarslan, "The Kurdish Nationalist Movement," in R. Olson (ed.), *The Kurdish Nationalist Movement in the 1990s: Its Impact on Turkey and the Middle East* (Lexington: University Press of Kentucky, 1996), 135–53; D. McDowall, *A Modern History of the Kurds* (London: I.B. Tauris, 2000); and W. Jwaideh, *The Kurdish National Movement: Its Origins and Development* (New York: Syracuse University Press, 2006).

9 A. R. Ghassemlou, *Kurdistan and the Kurds* (Prague: Czechoslovak Academy of Sciences, 1965).

Kurdish nationalists embraced the principle that a nation is entitled to a state, which exercises exclusive territorial control. It was in this context that Kurdish national liberation movements emerging after World War II mostly declared the establishment of an independent state in which to build a postcolonial society as their ultimate goal. It was this double legitimation of the struggle, in terms of both a right to national self-determination and as part of an international revolutionary struggle, that provided the framework in which Kurdish liberation movements and political parties in the 1970s linked their particular case to universalizing principles.[10]

Statist Responses: Failed Quests for Self-determination

Two main traditions that have shaped Kurdish politics and their quest for self-determination in its statist and nonstatist forms are to be distinguished, one marked by the push for autonomy and independence and the other by the development of self-constituting capacities and civil society.[11] The distinction, therefore, is between two fundamentally different models or radically divergent imaginations of the political. The first emerged from the Kurdistan Democratic Party (*Partiya Demokrata Kurdistanê*, KDP), the second from the PKK.

The KDP-led Push for Autonomy/Independence

The first tradition had its immediate historical roots in the Kurdistan Republic, a short-lived independent state with its center in Mahabad, a city in the east of Kurdistan, or what is today the northwest of Iran. The KDP, emerging from the Society for the Revival of Kurdistan (*Komeley Jiyanewey Kurdistan*), announced the Republic on January 22, 1946 – but the Iranian military (re)took control of the city within a year, on December 15, 1946, though skirmishes continued into the first months of 1947. In spite of its ephemeral real existence, the Kurdistan Republic became an important symbol for Kurdish state aspirations. In the years that followed, the tribal leader Mollah Mustafa Barzani, a commander of the army that had defended the Republic, became the dominant figure within the KDP, a position inherited by his sons.

During the 1960s and 1970s, the Barzani-led KDP not only dominated politics in southern Kurdistan (northern Iraq), but was also influential among Kurds in northern, northwest, and eastern Kurdistan (southeast Turkey, northern Syria, and northwest Iran, respectively). During this period, the Kurdish political parties

[10] H. Bozarslan, "Kurds and the Turkish State," in R. Kasaba (ed.), *Turkey in the Modern World* (Cambridge: Cambridge University Press, 2008), 333–56.

[11] J. Jongerden and A. H. Akkaya, "People beyond the State: Kurdish Movements and Self-determination in the 20th and 21st Centuries," in H. Bozarslan, C. Gunes, and V. Yadirgi (eds.), *The Cambridge History of the Kurds* (Cambridge: Cambridge University Press, 2021).

wholeheartedly embraced the principle of a nation's right to a state through which to exercise exclusive territorial control. Though dreams of an independent state continued to be nurtured, the immediate circumstances forced the KDP to make territorial autonomy its main political objective.

In Iraq, Barzani was able to negotiate territorial autonomy as part of a political settlement with the Ba'ath regime in 1970. However, hostilities continued and finally erupted again in 1974 with a full-fledged war between the army (Peshmerga) of the KDP and the Iraqi military.[12] The dissolution of the territorial autonomy agreement was followed by a lengthy program of Arabization and then the horrors of chemical attacks and mass deportations in 1987 and 1988.[13] In these events, we see the potential of genocidal actions unleashed at the intersection of a centralization of administration and means of violence in combination with the suppression of differences in the name of the nation.[14]

Opportunities for the Kurds in Iraq changed after the 1991 US-led First Gulf War, with Operation Desert Storm launched against Iraq's occupation of Kuwait. The de facto defeat of the Iraqi army on February 28, 1991 was followed by a Kurdish uprising and defeat again in 1991. The violent oppression and ensuing humanitarian disaster met with an outcry from international public opinion, which eventually resulted in the establishment of a no-fly zone and the creation of a "safe haven" in three Kurdish provinces in the north of Iraq. This enabled Kurdish party-militias to carve out territories, the western part dominated by the KDP and the eastern part by the Patriotic Union of Kurdistan (*Yekêtiy Niştîmaniy Kurdistan*, PUK), a breakaway faction of the KDP, led by Ibrahim Ahmad and Jalal Talabani. Together with the organization of parliamentary elections in 1992 and the establishment of the Kurdistan Regional Government (KRG) for the KRI, a process of state formation was initiated. This process was interrupted by infighting between the two main political parties between 1994 and 1998, which resulted in a sharp division of the region, split between the KDP in the west and PUK in the east.

When the USA invaded and occupied Iraq in 2003 (the Second Gulf War), the boundaries of the Kurdistan region were pushed southwards,[15] and then, in 2014, when the Iraqi army collapsed in Mosul under attack from the Islamic State of Iraq

[12] G. Stansfield, *Iraqi Kurdistan Political Development and Emergent Democracy* (London: Routledge, 2003); O. Bengio, "Autonomy in Kurdistan in Historical Perspective," in B. O'Leary, J. McGarry, and K. Salih (eds.), *The Future of Kurdistan in Iraq* (Philadelphia: University of Pennsylvania Press, 2006), 173–85.

[13] Human Rights Watch, *Genocide in Iraq: The Anfal Campaign against the Kurds* (1993); M. V. Bruinessen, "Genocide in Kurdistan? The Suppression of the Dersim Rebellion in Turkey (1937–38) and the Chemical War against the Iraqi Kurds (1988)," in G. J. Andreopoulos (ed.), *Conceptual and Historical Dimensions of Genocide* (Philadelphia: University of Pennsylvania Press, 1994), 16–21.

[14] Clastres, *Archaeology of Violence*, 49.

[15] A. Yoshioka, "The Shifting Balance of Power in Iraqi Kurdistan: The Struggle for Democracy with Uninstitutionalized Governance," *International Journal of Contemporary Iraqi Studies*, 9(1) (2015), 22–23.

and the Levant (ISIL) – now Islamic State (IS) – the Peshmerga moved further south in agreement with the central government in Baghdad, establishing control over the long-disputed city and oil-rich area of Kirkuk, among other places. However, the region remained divided between a northwestern part controlled by the Barzani-linked lineages dominant within the KDP and a southeastern part controlled by those of the PUK under Talabani.

In the relations between the Kurdistan region and Iraq, a half-hearted politics of recognition was preempted by processes of centralization and majoritarian rule. In 2005, when the dominant parties drafted a constitution, institutional solutions were sought to allow the different entities in Iraq to realize their aspirations for self-determination while simultaneously preserving the territorial integrity of the country.[16] A division of governing powers was agreed in which the government in Baghdad recognized the Kurdish authority based in Erbil, which now enjoyed some competences that were constitutionally separated (e.g., in the provisioning of internal security), while others were defined as responsibilities of both the central and regional authorities (e.g., as related to oil and gas extraction, power-plants, healthcare, education, and customs, among others).[17] This federal arrangement was undermined by a maximalist interpretation of the Constitution from the Kurdish side,[18] while on the Iraqi side the Sunni political leadership, generally Iraqi nationalists, had rejected the Constitution and the Shi'a political leadership came to favor simple majoritarian rule in a centralized unitary state, increasingly rejecting the constitution it had co-drafted.[19]

Reviewing the period 1991–2017, we can see a double process of failed state and regional autonomy construction. In Iraq, a deepening sectarian divide underpinned the ISIL insurgency, which thus became a civil war. In the KRI, initial steps toward the creation of a state were thwarted by infighting between the two blocs of kinship and tribal networks that had carved up the region into a west and east. Then, in September 2017, following the continued nonimplementation of agreements by the Iraqi administration, the KDP organized an independence referendum. This, however, badly backfired. Iraq forcibly rejected the move, replying to the political power

16 L. Anderson and G. Stansfield, "The Implications of Elections for Federalism in Iraq: Toward a Five-Region Model," *Publius*, 35(3) (2005), 359–82; G. Stansfield and L. Anderson, "Kurds in Iraq: The Struggle Between Baghdad and Erbil," *Middle East Policy*, 16(1) (2009), 134–45; S. Wolff, "Complex Power-Sharing and the Centrality of Territorial Self-governance in Contemporary Conflict Settlements," *Ethnopolitics*, 8(1) (2009), 27–45; A. Danilovich and F. Owtram, *Federalism as a Tool to Manage Conflicts and Associated Risks* (London: Routledge, 2014).

17 Iraq Constitution 2005; A. Danilovich, *Iraqi Federalism and the Kurds: Learning to Live Together* (London: Routledge, 2014), 58–59.

18 R. Alkadiri, "Federalism and Iraq's Constitutional Stalemate," *Chatham House Middle East and North Africa Programme* (2020).

19 M. Gunter, *The Kurds Ascending: The Evolving Solution to the Kurdish Issue in Iraq and Turkey* (New York: Palgrave, 2008); S. Kane, J. R. Hiltermann, and R. Alkadiri, "Iraq's Federalism Quandary," *The National Interest* (February 28, 2012).

play with one of its own and using its military to (re)occupy key areas, among these oil-rich Kirkuk, which in turn brought the KDP and PUK to the brink of war with one another. Overall, we can conclude that the party–kinship networks engaged in the making of the KRI are hardly able to maintain the appearance of a state, with the governance of affairs in the hands of two conglomerates of tribal lineages and their clientelistic networks. Iraq, meanwhile, though in name a federal system, based on the recognition of difference and diversity,[20] has seen its unitary state grafted onto sectarian divisions result in institutions run by "ethno-sectarian fiefdoms."[21]

PKK-Led Development of Self-constituting Capacities and Civil Society

The second current in the Kurdish movement emerged in the 1970s through the PKK and became hegemonic first in the Kurdish-dominated region of Turkey, and then in Syria. In the process of group formation in the 1970s, the organization identified with revolutionary struggles elsewhere, which they considered a common heritage of the oppressed, from the historic revolutions in Russia and China to the anti-colonial and national liberation struggles in Vietnam, Angola, Mozambique, Eritrea, and other places around the world.[22] In its 1978 founding manifesto, the PKK, like other anti-colonial and national liberation movements at the time, declared the establishment of an independent state to be its political goal.[23]

However, following a critique (and self-critique) on the character of national liberation struggles and the lived experiences of socialism, the PKK started to question whether independence really ought to be conceptualized and practiced as a state/nation-state construction. Although adhering to the idea of self-determination, the PKK did not continue to tie self-determination to the establishment of a state but rather to the development of peoples' capacities to govern themselves. This resulted in a redefinition of its political strategy.

The shift in thinking began with a critical inquiry into some of the basic tenets dominant in most liberation movements at the time, which included the idea that self-determination requires state formation. This process of political and ideological

20 M. Burgess, "Federalism and Federation: Putting the Record Straight," 50 Shades of Federalism Blog (2017).

21 R. Alaaldin, "Sectarianism, Governance, and Iraq's Future," Brookings Doha Center (November 2018).

22 J. Jongerden and A. H. Akkaya, "Born from the Left: The Making of the PKK," in J. Jongerden and M. Casier (eds.), *Nationalisms and Politics in Turkey: Political Islam, Kemalism and the Kurdish Issue* (Abingdon: Routledge, 2011), 123–42.

23 Most of the liberation movements that peaked in that period (1950–70) aimed at the establishment of a state and considered this to be the only model. To be a socialist and to give support for the establishment of a state by oppressed and colonized nations were considered one and the same. If you thought differently, you were not a socialist. A. Öcalan, *Demokratik Uygarlık Manifestosu/Kürt Sorunu ve Demokratik Ulus Çözümü: Kültürel Soykırım Kıskacında Kürtleri Savunmak*, book 5 (Neuss, Germany: Mezopotamya Yayınları, 2012), 271–72.

questioning began in the mid-1980s in the form of a state critique[24] and continued in the 1990s with a gender critique[25] and a critical reexamination of national liberation struggles and the conceptualization of national self-determination.[26] This reformulation of the framing of political struggle gained further traction after special forces abducted the PKK leader Abdullah Öcalan from Kenya and brought him to Turkey. Imprisoned on an island jail (İmralı) and facing court proceedings on multiple charges (primarily of treason against the state), Öcalan prepared a legal defense in which he developed a positive systematization of his critique of the way socialist and national liberation movements generally had tried to develop their alternatives.[27] The failure of these movements to redeem a promise of liberation brought the PKK to a position in which it started to question the very parameters of its national liberation struggle, and, importantly, the idea of state formation as the main objective of its struggle. Duran Kalkan, a senior leader of the PKK, formulated this as follows:

> [The PKK] examined all the national liberation struggles. They liberated, waged big battles, millions were martyred, and eventually they won, but the gains were minimal [...] We started a reexamination. When we were established, we took our inspiration more from struggles elsewhere than from the resistance movements in recent Kurdish history, which had all ended in a defeat, thus affecting PKK thinking. I mean, we took them [the national liberation movements] as an example, we were affected by these movements when we started our struggle, but these struggles did not bring what they should have brought. In fact, they went backwards and accepted what they had previously refused. You see, there had to be something wrong here. This demanded a reexamination. The emergence of a new paradigm [within the PKK] is very much influenced by this.[28]

Questioning the parameters of their struggle as well as a reconsideration of liberation struggles and post-liberation struggle (state) realities elsewhere, a paradigm shift followed.[29]

24 A. H. Akkaya, "The Kurdistan Workers' Party (PKK): National Liberation, Insurgency and Radical Democracy Beyond Borders," unpublished PhD thesis, Ghent University (2016); J. Jongerden, "Colonialism, Self-determination and Independence: The New PKK Paradigm," in M. Gunter (ed.), *Kurdish Issues: Essays in Honor of Robert W. Olson* (Costa Mesa, CA: Mazda Publishers, 2016), 106–21.

25 J. Jongerden, "Learning from Defeat: Development and Contestation of the 'New Paradigm' within the Kurdistan Workers' Party (PKK)," *Kurdish Studies*, 7(1) (2019), 72–92; I. Kaser, *"Mountain Life Is Difficult but Beautiful!": The Gendered Process of Becoming "Free" in the PKK Guerrilla* (London: Lexington Books, 2019), 11–30.

26 Akkaya, "The Kurdistan Workers' Party (PKK)"; and Jongerden, "Colonialism, Self-determination and Independence."

27 G. Yarkin, "The Ideological Transformation of the PKK Regarding the Political Economy of the Kurdish Region in Turkey," *Kurdish Studies*, 3(1) (2015), 26–46; Akkaya, "The Kurdistan Workers' Party (PKK)"; and Jongerden, "Learning from Defeat." Öcalan was able to gain access to literature, resulting in an extensive reading of political and social theory, philosophy, and history, after his lawyers had successfully claimed his right to prepare his own defense (as a member state of the European Court of Human Rights, Turkey was bound by the legal provisions of the related Convention).

28 Personal communication with Duran Kalkan, PKK official, November 28, 2014.

29 Akkaya, "The Kurdistan Workers' Party (PKK)."

RETHINKING SELF-DETERMINATION

On the basis of this questioning, Öcalan developed a new understanding of self-determination that developed in a post-Marxist framework of radical politics.[30] Revolving around the ideas of *democratic autonomy* and *democratic confederalism*, two concepts Öcalan borrowed from Murray Bookchin, he separated the idea of politics and the struggle for liberation and the aims of freedom and autonomy in civil society from the idea of the state as an institution of order that tends to become an instrument of oppression.

Democratic autonomy refers to the principle of self-constitution: practices in which people produce and reproduce the necessary and desired conditions for living through direct engagement and collaboration with one another. It seeks to create an institutional framework of "citizen assemblies" through which communities develop the capacities to govern their own affairs.[31] Though defined as a nonsecessionist understanding of self-determination,[32] it seeks to limit state power by developing self-governing bodies. Democratic autonomy implies a regrounding of the political status of people on the basis of self-government and relations of people with one another rather than peoples' relations with the state.[33]

Democratic confederalism, meanwhile, refers to the form that this takes: the strengthening of local administrative capacities through the organization of councils at the levels of village, neighborhood, district, city, and region. These self-governing bodies are part of "confederate structures"[34] – a multilayered network of councils. These "confederate structures" or layered networks of councils do not need to question the existing borders, yet neither do they need to accept these borders as a fact of life, Öcalan argues.[35] There is no need to demand abolition of the state, because the nation-state and borders lose their meaning in the context of the development of confederal structures. Mustafa Karasu, part of the PKK leadership, argues:

> Since democratic confederalism does not take the state as its main frame, it is also not about changing borders. On the contrary, it is a way of thinking and doing which is non-statist. The frame of reference in democratic confederalism is developing a system of people's democracy on the basis of self-organization. As such,

30 A. H. Akkaya and J. Jongerden, "Reassembling the Political: The PKK and the Project of Radical Democracy," *European Journal of Turkish Studies*, 12 (2012), 1–56.

31 C. Gunes, "Unpacking the 'Democratic Confederalism' and 'Democratic Autonomy': Proposals of Turkey's Kurdish Movement," in O. Akbulut and E. Aktoprak (eds.), *Minority Self-government in Europe and the Middle East* (Leiden: Brill Nijhoff, 2019), 246–67; and C. Gunes and R. Lowe, *The Impact of the Syrian War on Kurdish Politics across the Middle East* (London: Chatham House, 2015).

32 N. Bezwan, "Addressing the Kurdish Self-determination Conflict: Democratic Autonomy and Authoritarianism in Turkey," in E. Nimni and E. Aktoprak (eds.), *Democratic Representation in Plurinational States: The Kurds in Turkey* (London: Palgrave Macmillan, 2018), 59–82.

33 Duran Kalkan, personal communication, October 28, 2014.

34 A. Öcalan, *War and Peace in Kurdistan* (London: Transmedia Publishing, 2014), 33.

35 Ibid.

> people develop their own institutions, councils. If people organize themselves from the bottom-up and establish relations with each other, with other councils, democratic confederalism renders borders as insignificant.[36]

Revolving around the ideas of democratic autonomy and democratic confederalism, self-determination is now defined as a process of strengthening society against the state and developing capacity for self-government. In the different parts of Kurdistan, the twin ideas of democratic autonomy and democratic confederalism were translated into efforts to organize an active civil society as the means through which self-constitution, and as part of that self-administration, could be developed. In Turkey, in 2007, the movement established the Democratic Society Congress (*Kongre Civaka Demokratîk*), while the Movement for a Democratic Society (*Tevgera Civaka Demokratîk*) was established in Syria (in 2011), and the Free Kurdistan Society Movement (*Tevgera Azadi Komelgey Kurdistan*) and East Kurdistan Democratic and Free Society (*Komelgeha Demokratîk û Azad a Rojhilatê Kurdistanê*) were established in Iraq and Iran, respectively (in 2014).

These organizations all aim at the development of capacities for a form of self-administration. At the territorial level, councils and platforms have been established, where people meet, discuss their problems, and try to organize social life, from conflict mediation at the neighborhood level to the organization of pre- and after-school education. At the categorical level, women's centers were established to address problems, create solutions, and provide training for women's empowerment.

In Turkey, the development of these forms of self-organization was repressed after the remilitarization of the Kurdish issue that occurred as a result of the state's withdrawal from a so-called "peace process" and ensuing urban warfare in 2015–16 followed by an unprecedented political crackdown and the arrest and detention of thousands of Kurdish civil rights' activists and elected representatives.[37] Yet, in Syria, the implosion of the Ba'ath regime in the north of Syria (Rojava, West Kurdistan) created room for the development of this form of autonomy.[38]

In Rojava, the organization of democratic autonomy and democratic confederalism developed into a network administration. The smallest unit in the network is the commune (*komîn*). The commune sizes range from anywhere between a few

36 M. Karasu, *Radikal Demokrasi* (Neuss, Germany: Mezopotamya Yayınları, 2009), 219.

37 B. Baser, S. Akgönül, and A. E. Öztürk, "'Academics for Peace' in Turkey: A Case of Criminalising Dissent and Critical Thought via Counterterrorism Policy," *Critical Studies on Terrorism*, 10(2) (2017), 274–96; B. Esen and S. Gumuscu, "Turkey: How the Coup Failed," *Journal of Democracy*, 28(1) (2017), 59–73; J. Jongerden, "Conquering the State and Subordinating Society under AKP Rule: A Kurdish Perspective on the Development of a New Autocracy in Turkey," *Balkan and Near Eastern Studies*, 21(3) (2019), 260–73.

38 M. Knapp, A. Flach, and E. Ayboga, *Revolution in Rojava Democratic Autonomy and Women's Liberation in Syrian Kurdistan* (London: Pluto, 2016); M. Knapp, "The Roots of Democratic Autonomy in Northern Syria: Rojava," in M. Gunter (ed.), *Routledge Handbook on the Kurds* (London: Routledge, 2019), 382–95.

to 200-odd households, equivalent to a residential (urban) street or streets or to a village (rural). All residents of the commune are entitled to participate in the commune meetings. Each commune elects a council and its executive committee. This executive committee is headed by co-chairs – one woman and one man – with additional members held to a 40 percent gender quota. Beyond the commune, at the wider level, there are clusters of communes or neighborhood councils (*komîngeh*, also referred to as *tax*); then, depending on the size of the town or city, there are subdistricts (*belde*) and districts (*navçe*); and then there are cantons (*kanton*), later renamed provinces (*eyalet*) and regions (*herêm*). These councils all together form the autonomous administration.[39]

Parallel to this territorial administrative council system in Rojava, religious and cultural groups, like Arabs and Assyrians, and categorical groups, like women and youth, have their own organizations, which have the authority to make decisions over their own affairs. So the system of democratic autonomy, which grants rights to people to self-administer, and democratic confederalism, which provides the institutional arrangement for this, have resulted in more than just a form of self-organization marked by "territorial autonomy." To prevent majoritarian rule and stimulate the democratization of politics in multicultural entities, decision-making at a geographical level – from street and village to regional and confederal levels – sits alongside other decision-making vehicles for groups with different religious, ethnic, or cultural backgrounds than the majority group in a particular region. These minority communities have the right to organize themselves in a similar confederal structure and determine their own affairs, such as making decisions about how to organize and teach education in their language or practice their religion. This I refer to as "cultural autonomy." In a similar way, women have the right to organize themselves, deliberate, and decide about their agendas and priorities for political action, as a form of "categorical autonomy." Such categorical autonomy follows a decades-long struggle within and by the Kurdish movement for gender equality and women's rights.

This overall commitment to democratic pluralism has been explicitly expressed in the Social Contract, a foundational text agreed upon in 2014 that gave direction to the political system in Rojava: "Cultural, ethnic and religious groups and components shall have the right to name its self-administrations, preserve their cultures and form their democratic organizations. No one or component shall have the right to impose their own beliefs on others by force."[40] So, the principle of democratic autonomy and democratic confederalism as the organizational form in which this

39 M. Knapp, and J. Jongerden, "Peace Committees, Platforms and the Political Ordering of Society: Doing Justice in the Federation of Northern and Eastern Syria (NES)," *Kurdish Studies*, 8(2) (2020), 297–312.

40 Cited in C. Gunes, *The Kurds in a New Middle East: The Changing Geopolitics of a Regional Conflict* (London: Palgrave Macmillan, 2019), 71.

principle is expressed combine territorial and nonterritorial (cultural and categorical) forms autonomy.[41]

The community-based system of self-administration has been rather successful in its ideological objectives. One major accomplishment has been the development of equal gender participation in the administration. Another accomplishment, given the sectarian dimensions of the war in Syria, has been the integration of non-Kurdish groups and areas into the self-administration system. This integration, it is argued, is not because the non-Kurdish groups ascribe to the ideological principles of democratic confederalism per se, but for a variety of more practical reasons, among them the (proven) ability to provide a functioning administration with service delivery and security provision.[42]

Most of the opposition to the model of self-administration has come from KDP-aligned Kurdish political parties, which saw themselves marginalized.[43] Thus, when on September 22, 2017, elections were organized for the commune co-chairs in the Rojava region, they were boycotted by the pro-Barzani parties. The parties concerned claimed that the elections had been deliberately arranged to draw attention away from the independence referendum in Iraqi Kurdistan, which was planned for three days later, on September 25, 2017.[44] In spite of the boycott, however, local sources claimed a total of some 728,450 votes were cast, reportedly representing around 70 percent of all eligible voters in the region, which elected co-chairs for 3,938 communes from about 16,650 candidates.[45]

Given the participatory character of the self-administration model, it seems somewhat surprising that a review undertaken by Allsopp and Van Wilgenburg[46] showed only a few respondents – 16 out of the 180 – identifying Rojava with participation, while there are multiple mentions of the lack of qualified persons working in the administration as a source of dissatisfaction with self-administration. Yet the same survey also shows that the keywords participants identify most with Rojava are "security," "women's rights," "freedom," "language rights," and "democracy," all issues which make the region stand out as compared to the rest of Syria.

41 For a broader discussion, see also O. Akbulut and E. Aktoprak, *Minority Self-government in Europe and the Middle East* (Leiden: Brill, 2019).

42 H. Allsopp and W. Wilgenbrug, *The Kurds of Northern Syria: Governance, Diversity, Conflicts* (London: I.B. Tauris, 2019), 129–33.

43 This conflict has a long history. The popularity of the main Kurdish political parties in Syria had been falling since the 1990s, due among other reasons to their inability to gain concessions from the state. While support for these parties diminished, Kurdish national consciousness and youth activism increased. It was out of this contradiction between a crisis in traditional party politics and a rising political consciousness that the PYD became the strongest political force among the Kurds in Syria, at the expense of other Kurdish political parties. H. Allsopp, *The Kurds of Syria* (New York: Palgrave, 2014); and International Crisis Group, *Flight of Icarus? The PYD's Precarious Rise in Syria* (May 8, 2014).

44 W. Wilgenburg, "Barzani Affiliated Kurdish National Council Have Called for Boycott on Elections in Northern Syria," *The Region* (September 22, 2017).

45 Jongerden, "Governing Kurdistan," 61–75.

46 Allsopp and Wilgenbrug, *The Kurds of Northern Syria*, 157–59.

CONCLUSION

Two main traditions have shaped Kurdish politics and their quest for self-determination, one based on the state-idea, the other on the idea of peoples' self-constituting capacities.[47] The form of autonomy attempted in the Kurdistan region in Iraq was pushed for by the Kurdish political movement as part of a state-oriented politics of recognition. It had to provide institutional solutions allowing the Kurds to realize their aspirations for some form of self-administration within Iraq. This is a form of subsovereignty granted to institutions within a sovereign state and concerns the transfer of (limited) state functions and responsibilities to institutions that thus form a substate.[48] However, in the KRI, this quest has advanced two antagonistic political blocs, conglomerates of tribal lineages, and their clientelistic networks competing for resources. Moreover, the attempt to produce a system of federal decentralization of Iraq has been discarded because the main non-Kurdish political actors in Baghdad all prefer a unitary – not decentralized – state, which they compete to dominate based on rival sectarian claims.[49]

The balance of power has been shifting in favor of Baghdad over recent years, and the Kurdish parties have regressed from "kingmakers to more marginal players" in federal affairs.[50] The seemingly strong position of the KDP and PUK in the period following the US occupation of Iraq had to do with the weakness of the central state.[51] The KDP and PUK have failed to develop a coherent political system in Iraqi Kurdistan. They have been primarily concerned with sustaining themselves as distributive nodes in a patronage system. The resulting rivalry between the parties, and the clientelistic networks underlying these parties, created and sustained two separate administrations, with the KDP controlling the western part of the region and the PUK the eastern part.[52] The 2017 referendum and its aftermath, resulting in the loss of territories and resources, sharpened internal schisms and rivalries.[53]

This form of independence- and autonomy-seeking is to be distinguished from the autonomy strived for by the movement orienting itself to the doctrines of Abdullah Öcalan. When the PKK was established, independence was defined in terms of self-determination, which was envisaged and fought for through the establishment of an independent state. The construction of a state, however, was not regarded simply as an aim in itself, but also as a means by which to put an end to exploitative feudalistic,

47 Jongerden and Akkaya, "*People beyond the State*."

48 A. Reyes and M. Kaufman, "Sovereignty, Indigeneity, Territory: Zapatista Autonomy and the New Practices of Decolonization," *The South Atlantic Quarterly*, 110(2) (2011), 505–25.

49 Alaaldin, "Sectarianism, Governance, and Iraq's Future."

50 Alkadiri, "Federalism and Iraq's Constitutional Stalemate," 8.

51 D. Natali, "The Kurdish Quasi-State: Leveraging Political Limbo," *The Washington Quarterly* 38(2) (2015), 145–64.

52 F. H. Abdullah, "The Political System in Iraqi Kurdistan: Party Rivalries and Future Perspectives," *Asian Affairs*, 49(4) (2018), 606–24, at 606.

53 M. Eppel, "A Future for Kurdish Independence?" *Middle East Quarterly*, 25(2) (2018), 1–9.

land ownership-based relationships of Kurdish society. Öcalan started to question the capacity of the state to transform society, however, and came to consider it as the very seat of illiberalism, the structuring principle for and material enforcer of relations of domination and exploitation. Following Öcalan, this Kurdish movement started to conceptualize independence as the positive development of various forms of self-organization, not just as a way to empower society "against the state"[54] but also to develop a polity beyond the state. The principal aim, therefore, became the development of a *non*state public sphere.

In Rojava today, this involves the attempt at a radically new type of democracy based on the construction of and experimentation with forms of self-representative and extraparliamentary democracy organized around councils. In its project of democratic autonomy and democratic confederalism, the Kurdish movement has created its own alternatives while engaging with existing institutions, where necessary, striving for the development of forms of self-organization within, indifferent to, and outside or beyond, the state. This is not, strictly speaking, a project of decentralization, since that is defined by its relationship to a center, where (some) power is released outwards. The autonomy project of this Kurdish movement assumes power at the local level, which may then release (some) control upward to the wider network administration. This implies the development of a ground-up council system and the novel way in which self-determination has become defined in the Rojava case. This network administration is not like a decentralized administration since it is not based on the idea of a central state (in relation to which decentralization occurs, as referenced by its capital), but on the development of a new form of government. The councils established to this end are not envisaged as "lower" divisions of the central state, but a form of government based on the empowerment of people in their capacity as citizens.[55]

Finally, what is referred to as "the Kurdish issue" has been reconceived. The Kurdish issue was originally the product of a nationalization of territory under a central polity. In this new state order, the Kurds became a surplus population, the "state's other," which needed to be subjected, assimilated, and erased. The Kurdish quest for self-determination in the form of state formation as well as the quest for another form of polity, one not based upon but rather moving beyond the principle of nation-statehood, are both responses to this nation-statification of society.

54 P. Clastres, *Society against the State: Essays in Political Anthropology* (New York: Zone Books, 1989).
55 H. Arendt, *On Revolution* (London: Penguin Press, 1990), 253.

10

The Devil Is in the Details

Iraqi Kurdistan's Evolving Autonomy

Peter Bartu and Aidan MacEachern

Talk of decentralization in Iraq is usually dominated by attempts to define the extent and geographical reach of Kurdish autonomy in northern Iraq, including the question of natural resources. The primary challenge for the state has been how to accommodate a nationalistic ethnic group that has throughout its existence expressed a stalwart desire for self-rule if not independence.

This chapter examines Iraq's decentralization "moments" in 1970, between 1991 and 2003, and in the 2005 Constitution. It then explores the challenges of implementing Kurdish regional autonomy after 2005, focusing on governance and natural resources. It argues that despite a brief experience with independence,[1] self-rule or enhanced autonomy has been held hostage to several variables, namely: Kurdish disunity, the strength of the central government, and concerns in Turkey and Iran about the potential impact of Kurdish self-government in Iraq on their own Kurdish minority populations.[2]

IN LIEU OF INDEPENDENCE, MINORITY RIGHTS

A Kurdish nation-state was envisaged in the Treaty of Sevres, which provided for the partition of the Ottoman Empire immediately following World War I. It was, however, subsequently erased from the map when the borders of modern Turkey were renegotiated in the Treaty of Lausanne.[3] The vast majority of the Kurdish nation was divided between Turkey, Syria, Iran, and Iraq. Henceforth Kurdish ambitions for self-determination played out separately within each state.

1 Most notably, the Kurdish Republic of Mahabad established with Soviet-backing in Iran in 1945, which lasted less than a year. A. Roosevelt, "The Kurdish Republic of Mahabad," *The Middle East Journal*, 1(3) (1947), 247–69.

2 Since 2011, the Syrian revolution and civil war has animated long-suppressed Kurdish aspirations for self-rule in Syria and attracted a brutal military response from Turkey. However, it has also brought into stark relief an intense intra-Kurd competition across Syria, Turkey, and Iraq, the trajectory of which is unclear.

3 D. L. Logan, "Thoughts on Iraqi Kurdistan: Present Realities, Future Hope," *Iran and the Caucasus*, 13(1) (2009), 161–86, at 164.

This meant that for most of the twentieth century Kurds in Iraq were granted little more than token cultural autonomy, and even that was hard fought. That the Kurds required minority rights was acknowledged early. In 1926, the League of Nations was asked to determine the administrative fate of Mosul. Concluding that it should be part of Iraq rather than Turkey, the "Mosul Commission" noted that "regard must be paid to the desires expressed by the Kurds that officials of Kurdish race should be appointed for the administration of their country, the dispensation of justice, and teaching in the schools, and that Kurdish should be the official language of all these services."[4] In 1931, the Iraqi government enacted the "Local Languages Law," which allowed use of Kurdish as an official language in local courts in areas where Kurds were the majority.[5] In May 1932, the government of Iraq formally pledged before the League of Nations Council to uphold minority rights (freedom of religion and cultural autonomy) in advance of independence.[6]

These measures, however, failed to satisfy Kurdish national aspirations. Although many deemed Kurdish self-rule a chimera, nationalist sentiment had "created an emotional condition that must be reckoned with."[7] The first Kurdish insurrections, which occurred prior to Iraq's independence from British mandatory rule, were led by two brothers, Sheikh Ahmad (Khudan) Barzani and (Mullah) Mustafa Barzani.[8] In 1946, Mustafa Barzani founded the Kurdistan Democratic Party (KDP). Mobilizing Kurdish identity into a political movement, the Barzani family's influence on Kurdish political life cannot be overstated.

TOWARD RECOGNITION

The prospects for self-government in Iraqi Kurdistan changed after the July 15, 1958 coup against the monarchy and the introduction of the "Temporary Constitution"

4 League of Nations, "Question of the Frontier between Turkey and Iraq," report submitted to the Council by the Commission instituted by the Council Resolution of September 30, 1924, C.400.M.147.1925.VII, 89.

5 Law of Local Languages Law No. 74 1931, Art. 3, *Official Iraqi Gazette*, No. 989 (June 1, 1931). Kurdish and Turkmen were declared the official languages in courts where these communities were concentrated. This would not apply "to the technical departments and correspondence between the province … and districts, where these correspondences should be in Arabic." Law No. 74 1931, Art. 5.

6 S. Pedersen, "Getting Out of Iraq – in 1932: The League of Nations and the Road to Normative Statehood," *American Historical Review*, 115(4) (2010), 975–1000, at 997. The Iraqi Declaration of Guarantees to the Council of the League of Nations May 1932, League of Nations, Official Journal (1932), 1483. For a contemporaneous discussion of the declaration, see M.O. Hudson, "The Admission of Iraq to Membership in the League of Nations," *American Journal of International Law*, 27(1) (1933), 133–38. See also H. Muller-Sommerfeld, "The League of Nations, A-Mandates and Minority Rights during the Mandate Period in Iraq (1920–1932)," in S. R. Goldstein-Sabbah and H. L. Murre-van den Berg (eds.), *Modernity, Minority, and the Public Sphere: Jews and Christians in the Middle East* (Leiden: Brill, 2016), 276.

7 W. L. E., "Iraqi Kurdistan: A Little-Known Region," *The World Today*, 12(10) (1956), 417–32, at 431.

8 Logan, *Thoughts on Iraqi Kurdistan*, 165.

by General Abd al-Karim Qasim. This Constitution referred to the Kurds as "co-partners with the Arabs within the framework of Iraqi unity and to guarantee their communal rights."[9] General Qasim invited Mustafa Barzani to return from exile in the Soviet Union. It was thought that more administrative devolution, greater budgetary support, and an enhanced status for the Kurdish language might follow. However, when two years later the reforms had failed to materialize, the Kurds revolted, and fighting quickly spread. Qasim's government mounted two responses. First, armed revolt was put down with brute force. In addition, the government co-opted dissident Kurdish tribes to undermine popular support for the uprisings. This pattern continued on and off until June 1966, when the government broadcast a twelve-point program that was accepted by Mustafa Barzani as a starting point for negotiations. Known as the "1966 Declaration," it became a critical reference point for almost all subsequent efforts to reach a settlement, including the 2005 Constitution. In substance, it provided for the following:

> (1) the recognition of "Kurdish nationality" to be confirmed in the Permanent Constitution; (2) enactment of a Provincial Administration Law providing for decentralization and the transfer of wide powers to locally elected councils; (3) use of Kurdish for administration and public instruction; (4 and 5) parliamentary elections and representation of the Kurds in the National Assembly and all branches of the public service in proportion to their numbers in the total population; (6) generous grants for study abroad at all levels, establishment of a faculty of Kurdish studies in Baghdad University, and eventually, of branches of the university in "the north"; (7) appointment of Kurdish officials to Kurdish districts; (8) permission for political association and for literary and political publications; (9 and 10) a general amnesty "when violence ends" to include persons already convicted and deserters reporting with their arms, disbandment of the Cavaliers (Kurdish tribesman who sided with the government), and reappointment of absentee officials as far as possible to their previous posts; (11) formation of a special Ministry to supervise reconstruction and compensation for sufferers "in the north" and to coordinate administration in the various Kurdish districts; (12) resettlement of persons evicted from their homes, or compensation in lieu.[10]

A rapid turnover in government officials, including a second coup by military officers (the Revolutionary Command Council) in July 1968, ensured fitful progress in advancing this program. However, upon assuming office Ahmad Hasan al-Bakr began implementing aspects of it. A Kurdish Cultural Academy was initiated, a committee was formed to draft a law for a University of Suleimaniyeh, a general amnesty for deserters from the army and the police was proclaimed, and the restoration of

9 C. J. Edmonds, "The Kurdish War in Iraq: The Constitutional Background," *The World Today*, 24(12) (1968), 512–20, at 514.

10 An additional three articles covered in the local press stipulated: (1) release of all political prisoners; (2) specific permission for the KDP to function publicly; and (3) formation of all Kurdish districts of the Mosul *liwa* (district) into a new *liwa* of Duhok. Edmonds, "The Kurdish War in Iraq," 518.

dismissed civil servants to their previous posts began. More far-reaching reforms were undertaken when the government passed a Provincial Administration Law in 1969, which included the decentralization of local administration.

Following further negotiations, the Arab Socialist Ba'ath Party recognized the "legitimate presence of the Kurdish nationality" and the Kurdish issue as the key national challenge for Iraq in a 1970 proclamation known as the "March Manifesto."[11] Concretely, it approved opening a university in Suleimaniyeh, establishing a Kurdish science forum along with Kurdish-language newspapers, Kurdish writers' unions, an increase in Kurdish broadcasts on Kirkuk TV Channel, acknowledgment of *Newroz* day as a national holiday, reference to Kurdish nationality in the Constitution, and a general amnesty for all civilians and military personnel involved in the violence in the north. The March Manifesto also called for autonomy for the Kurdish areas in northern Iraq by March 11, 1974. Kurdish areas were to be determined by majority population, in accordance with a census that was ultimately never conducted.[12]

Mustafa Barzani sought regional control of the resources in the Kurdish areas and demanded a division of national revenues along ethnic lines. He also objected to the president of the Republic's power to dismiss the regional executive council. Moreover, a failed assassination attempt on Barzani by Baghdad dealt a blow to trust between the parties.[13] The Kurds sought external assistance from the United States, Israel, and the Shah of Iran, which came in the form of monetary support, weaponry, and training for the growing number of Peshmerga forces – or Kurdish military forces – under Barzani's resumed recruitment.[14]

Baghdad responded by refusing to allow Kurdish representatives in the national government and grew increasingly irritated with their refusal to close the Kurdish region's border with Iran. Further, the Ba'ath party and the Iraqi Communist Party (ICP) objected to decentralized control over petroleum resources, which they considered national in character, not regional.

In January 1974, delegations from the Ba'ath, the ICP, the KDP, and several independent Kurds met in Baghdad to finalize the government's proposed autonomy agreement. Some observers lauded the plan as a meaningful step forward, one contemporaneous report calling it a "real advance toward autonomy for the Kurdish people of Iraq" and "the most serious effort of its kind made by a present-day Middle Eastern government."[15] However, the KDP rejected it on the grounds that it gave Baghdad ultimate political and financial control over the Kurdish government, made no mention of resources and petroleum revenues, did not recognize the KDP

[11] March 11, 1970 Declaration by the Iraqi Revolutionary Command Council ("March Manifesto"). Copy on file with author.

[12] C. Paul, C. P. Clarke, B. Grill, and M. Dunigan, *Paths to Victory: Detailed Insurgency Case Studies* (Santa Monica, CA: RAND Corporation, 2013), 218.

[13] Ibid.

[14] Ibid., 218–19.

[15] "Iraq and Kurdish Autonomy," *MERIP Reports* (April 1974), 26–30, at 27.

as the sole representative of the Kurdish people, and failed to include the oil-rich province of Kirkuk. Veteran Iraqi Kurdish negotiator Mahmoud Othman explains that while the Kurds were offered positions in government, constitutional recognition, and development assistance, they were never treated as equals by the state.[16] In his view, the KDP also put too much faith in support from the USA, Israel, and Iran in their struggle against Baghdad.

In March 1974, the "Voice of Kurdistan" denounced the plan and issued a call to arms as fighting erupted in the north. Internal divisions among Kurdish representatives also began to consolidate. After Ba'athist forces defeated Barzani's insurrection in 1975, the Patriotic Union of Kurdistan (PUK) was established by Jalal Talabani, as a leftist alternative to the KDP.[17]

A Kurdish Autonomous Region comprising Duhok, Erbil, and Suleimaniyeh nevertheless operated from 1980 to 1991, pursuant to the government's 1974 plan. It had a twelve-member executive council that wielded both legislative and executive powers and a Legislative Assembly of fifty persons elected for three-year terms from among candidates approved by the central government. Both bodies were based in Erbil. The first legislative elections were held in September 1980 and the second elections took place in August 1986. Kurdish was used for all official communications at the local level. However, Baghdad made all decisions pertaining to justice, police, and internal security, its authority "most dramatically evident in the frontier areas, where government security units … forcibly evacuated Kurdish villagers to distant lowlands."[18]

More broadly, the Ba'ath government reorganized Iraq's provinces into eighteen governorates, often changing the names and altering their boundaries.[19] This included redrawing Kirkuk's boundaries in 1975 and 1976. Kurds interpreted these measures as Arabization because they stripped away districts whose populations were majority Kurdish and Turkmen. In 1976, the Kirkuk governorate was renamed Ta'mim, meaning "nationalization," a tribute to the state's newfound control of oil production.[20]

Throughout this period, Ba'ath-dominated Iraq underwent a steady transformation as the state consolidated control over natural resources and extended its apparatus of social control.[21] It was able to do so through the nationalization of its oil resources. Oil production soared and annual revenues increased to $8 billion in

16 Interview with Mahmoud Othman, Iraqi Kurdish politician, Erbil, Iraqi Kurdistan, in person, June 2019.

17 M. M. Gunter, "The KDP–PUK Conflict in Northern Iraq," *Middle East Journal*, 50(2) (1996), 224–41, at 229.

18 See "Kurdish Autonomy," in H. Chapin Metz (ed.), *Iraq: A Country Study* (Washington, DC: GPO US Library of Congress 1988), 187.

19 A. Bet-Shlimon, *City of Black Gold: Oil, Ethnicity, and the Making of Modern Kirkuk* (Stanford, CA: Stanford University Press, 2019), 174.

20 Ibid., 175.

21 Ibid., 188.

1975 – ten times the revenue Iraq received before nationalization.[22] From this position of strength, the Iraqi state sought to resolve not only the Kurdish question, but also its borders with Syria and Iran. This latter project would force semi-nomadic Yezidi communities on the border with Syria into collectives around Mt. Sinjar. Beginning in 1970, the state also cleared Fayli Kurd communities – Shi'a Muslims whose loyalty was perceived as suspect – away from the border with Iran. And, in the lead-up to the Iran–Iraq war in 1980, thousands of Fayli Kurds were deported en masse overnight to Iran from Baghdad and the border region. In 1983, when Iranian troops crossed into northern Iraq and took the town of Haj Omran, in cooperation with Masoud Barzani's KDP, the Iraqi government executed 8,000 men from the Barzan region.[23]

In 1988, additional operations known as *al-Anfal* (the spoils of war) in the hinterlands of Suleimaniyeh and Halabja saw thousands more Kurds killed in what Human Rights Watch described as genocide.[24] The campaign finished with the infamous March 16, 1988 chemical attack on Halabja in which 3,000–5,000 Kurdish civilians died, a majority of them women and children. This brutal campaign was a response to the KDP's and PUK's alignment with Iran from 1986 onwards and was seen as a ruthless settling of scores at the end of the Iran–Iraq war.[25] The preamble to the 2005 Iraq Constitution refers to the above crimes as the "racial oppression in the massacres of Halabja, Barzan, Anfal and the Fayli Kurds."[26]

Iraqi Kurdistan's First Genuine Autonomy, 1991–2003

In March 1991, toward the end of the First Gulf War, the Shi'a and Kurdish communities rose up against the Iraqi government, on the urging of US President George H. W. Bush, at one point threatening fifteen of Iraq's eighteen governorates. Government reprisals were swift, and 1.5 million Kurds fled into neighboring Iran, risking a treacherous journey through snowy winter mountains. Hundreds of thousands more were trapped at the border with Turkey, then in the grip of a counterinsurgency campaign against its own Kurdish community. The UN Security Council passed Resolution 688, describing Iraq's repression of the Kurds as a threat to international peace and security, which led to a massive emergency humanitarian operation (Provide Comfort I and II) and the establishment of a no-fly zone over northern Iraq. The combination of the no-fly zone and the economic devastation

22 "Iraq and Kurdish Autonomy," 26.

23 Q. Lawrence, *Invisible Nation: How the Kurds' Quest for Statehood Is Shaping Iraq and the Middle East* (New York: Walker & Co., 2008), 326.

24 Human Rights Watch, *Genocide in Iraq: The Anfal Campaign against the Kurds* (1993).

25 A tragically prescient US Congressional Report of the time noted, "[o]n the one hand, if the present government in Iraq survives the war … it is almost certain to punish those Kurds who collaborated with the Iranians." See "Kurds" in Metz, *Iraq: A Country Study*, 84–85.

26 Iraq Constitution 2005, Preamble.

of Iraq in the aftermath of the 1991 Gulf War effectively brought to an end direct central government control over Iraq's Kurdish region.

To enable displaced Kurds to return to their areas, the United States negotiated the withdrawal of the Iraqi government administration from the three recognized Kurdish provinces of Duhok, Erbil and Suleimaniyeh to a notional internal boundary known as the "Green Line." Never an official boundary, it nevertheless was controlled by Iraqi army checkpoints, which permitted minor business and trade. More importantly, it enabled the Iraqi Kurds to enjoy genuine autonomy for the first time.[27]

While this experience started well enough, with national elections and a new parliament in 1992, relations between the KDP and the PUK quickly deteriorated into a bloody civil war by May 1994.[28] Remarkably, the Iraqi army entered the conflict at the request of the KDP and expelled the PUK from Erbil in 1996, enabling the KDP to capture the capital city of the Kurdistan Region of Iraq's (KRI) once and for all.[29] In 1998, the conflict concluded with a power-sharing arrangement, which split the KRI into two separate administrative zones. The KDP took control of the northern governorates of Erbil and Duhok while the PUK retained its own power base in the governorate of Suleimaniyeh. The division resulted in two parallel and separate administrations that continue to this day. By the early 2000s, KDP–PUK relations had improved significantly. In 2003, both parties welcomed the US invasion, and took advantage of it, to take control of disputed areas south of the Green Line including Kirkuk, which they considered historically Kurdish.

The 2005 Constitution

After the 2003 invasion of Iraq, the Kurds were accorded an outsized role during the 2005 constitution-drafting process, consolidating their autonomous status. The Constitution was designed to constrain a strong central government. It put central and regional powers on an even footing. It allowed the Kurds to retain their own security forces. It also left open the possibility that the Kurds could exclusively exploit newfound natural resources in the Kurdish region. In addition, it empowered the Kurdistan region to write its own constitution to define its structures, powers, and authorities. Implementation of these provisions has been uneven, however, and the central government has been locked in interminable negotiations with the Kurdistan Regional Government (KRG) on each issue – to the mutual dissatisfaction of all. The devil has truly been in the details.

Although critics of the constitutional process observed that "it should have been clear … that Iraqi constitution-making would require a complex three-way

27 T. E. Ricks, "Operation Provide Comfort: a Forgotten Mission with Possible Lessons for Syria," *Foreign Policy* (February 6, 2017).

28 L. Khalil, "Worst Enemy: Kurdistan's History of Infighting," *The Interpreter* (October 24, 2017).

29 Bet-Shlimon, *City of Black Gold*, 189.

treaty-like negotiation,"[30] the Constitution was not endorsed by even one of the constitutional committee's fifteen Sunni representatives, and the country's Sunni Arab population voted overwhelmingly against it when it was put to a referendum in 2005.[31] And, "as it peremptorily confronted Sunni Arabs with a vision of Iraq they could not recognize, [the process] probably amplified the Sunni Arab insurgency and, in turn steepened the slide into civil war."[32] Others take the view, however, that the intent behind many of the constitutional provisions was to avoid "the institutional arrangements that made Iraq a prison for a significant share of its population and a threat in the region … that presided over genocide … and wars of expansion … and Saddam's past abuse of central authority" – in sum, it was "a principled bargain" that would enable regions to "block misbehavior by the federal government."[33]

In substantive terms the greatest point of contention has been the extension of Kurdish autonomy demands into the framework of governance throughout the country.[34] This was most evident in the division of responsibilities between the central government and its subnational units in constitutional articles 110–115, which provide for the potential territorial division of the country into regions and the management of natural resources, principally oil and gas.[35] According to Brendan O'Leary, the 2005 Constitution's provisions regarding natural resources were "part of a coherent and principled remaking of Iraq as a pluralist federation," providing for "a per capita allocation of oil revenues from currently exploited fields across Iraq," while allowing "agreement among regions to share wealth from new fields."[36]

These arrangements, moreover, are not exclusively a reflection of events set in motion after the American invasion. Rather, they are informed by the Iraqi government's 1966 twelve-point program and the 1974 Autonomy Plan. The 2005 Constitution's primary innovations were in the fields of natural resources (addressed further below) and security. In regard to the latter, Article 121 authorized the KRG to maintain police and "regional guards." This provision not only formalized arrangements in place since 1991, it also reflected constitutional recognition of the massacres of Kurds by central state forces during the 1980s.

Enabling legislation for implementing the Constitution's decentralization scheme was adopted on October 11, 2006 over another Sunni Arab boycott of parliament and Shi'i protests. As Bartu has documented, "the Law on the Operational Procedures

30 J. Morrow "Deconstructing Mesopotamia: Cutting a Deal on the Regionalization of Iraq," in L. E. Miller (ed.), *Framing the State in Times of Transition: Case Studies in Constitution Making* (Washington, DC: United States Institute of Peace Press, 2010), 563–98, at 587.

31 Ibid., 581.

32 Ibid., 564.

33 B. O'Leary, "Federalizing Natural Resources," in M. E. Bouillon, D. M. Malone, and B. Rowswell (eds.), *Iraq: Preventing a new Generation of Conflict* (Boulder, CO: Lynne Rienner, 2007), 191–93, at 191.

34 N. F. Haysom, "Forging an Inclusive and Enduring Social Contract," in M. E. Bouillon, D. M. Malone, and B. Rowswell (eds.), *Iraq: Preventing a New Generation of Conflict*, 143–51, at 145.

35 Haysom, "Social Contract," 146.

36 O'Leary, "Federalizing Natural Resources," 199.

for the Creation of Regions allowed for governorates to join regions through a request by one-third of the members of the governorate council together with the consent of one-third of the members of the legislative council of the region. Thus, one-third of the Kirkuk provincial council could elect to attach the governorate to the Kurdistan Region, as indeed could any of the provincial councils in the other adjoining governorates of Ninewa and Diyala."[37] After the January 2005 provincial council elections, the Kurdish Alliance dominated two of the three provincial councils, with twenty-six of forty-one seats in Kirkuk and thirty-one of forty-one seats in Ninewa, thereby providing a legal route to realize their claims to Kirkuk. Nonetheless, as there have been no provincial council elections in Kirkuk since passage of the law, Kirkuk remains a governorate under the central government as of this writing.

In 2011, when the American military officially exited Iraq, "regionalism" reached new heights with several governorates seeking to change their status due to perceived neglect from Baghdad and the desire to manage their own natural resources.[38] On October 27, the Salah al-Din provincial council voted to form a one-governorate region in response to arrests of former Ba'ath Party members.[39] On October 28, the governor of Ninewa told the government that the majority supported becoming a region. On November 30, the Anbar provincial council voted in favor of forming an autonomous region. Basra, Maysan, Dhi Qar, and Muthanna also considered the formation of regions, albeit with different degrees of resolve. In the end, though, none of these governorates was able to achieve the status of a constitutional region.

While these efforts spoke to a crisis in governance in Iraq broadly, there were two specific imperatives at play. Governorates, by becoming regions, could in theory enjoy greater powers and higher revenue allocations from the central government and could also establish and organize their own internal security forces. Second, the predominantly Sunni governorates were reacting to a perceived Shi'a supremacy in Nouri Al-Maliki's second government which quashed all attempts to form regions despite the formal provisions of the law. The government did, however, initiate a discussion of decentralization and some limited devolution of powers to the governorates. But by 2019, in the face of unprecedented protests in Baghdad and the southern provinces against corruption, power outages, contaminated water and poor quality public services, Iraqis were evidently losing faith in the ability of provincial governments to perform any better than the central state.[40] As explored below, being an autonomous region did not necessarily translate into good governance either.

37 P. Bartu, "Wrestling with the Integrity of a Nation: The Disputed Internal Boundaries in Iraq," *International Affairs*, 86(6) (2010), 1329–43, at 1334.

38 M. Ottaway, "Mission Impossible," *Foreign Policy* (March 4, 2014).

39 L. Hammoudi, "Saddam's Home Province Declares Regional Autonomy in Iraq," *McClatchy Newspapers* (October 27, 2011).

40 While this chapter focuses on the KRG it is important to flag the broader governance crisis in Iraq. See A. Al-Mawlawi, "Is the Decentralization Process in Iraq Being Reversed?" LSE Middle East Blog (December 2, 2019).

THE REGIONAL GOVERNMENT (KRG)

In 2005, the KRG consolidated its position in the new Iraq. International airports opened in Erbil and Suleimaniyeh. In 2006, the KRG launched a public relations campaign labeling itself "The Other Iraq," promoting its political stability, economic opportunities, and long history of friendly relations with the West.[41] External recognition quickly followed. Iraqi Kurdistan was ranked by the *New York Times* among the top thirty-four places to visit in the world. *National Geographic* listed it as number twenty.[42] Foreign direct investment increased. But these impressive infrastructure gains across the region obscured flaws in the muscle tissue of Kurdish governance.

In 2007, the KDP and PUK codified Kurdish governance through a formal Strategic Agreement that created a seemingly unified government while also acknowledging the division of roles within the KRG between the parties, including official endorsement for the PUK's Talabani as president of Iraq, and the KDP's Barzani as president of the KRG.[43] However, many within the PUK criticized the agreement as consolidating an asymmetrical power relationship, with the KDP as the senior partner. Moreover, the emergence in 2009 of a new Kurdish political party, Gorran (the Movement for Change), quickly challenged the KDP's and PUK's grip on Kurdish politics.

Led by Nawshirwan Mustafa, Gorran promised to decouple political partisanship from the state bureaucracy.[44] Gorran outpolled the PUK to become the second majority party in the KRG, winning twenty-five seats in the Kurdistan parliamentary elections of 2009.[45] In 2013, the eighth cabinet of the KRG was formed as a coalition government between the KDP and Gorran, thus marginalizing the PUK from its once dominant position in Kurdish politics.[46]

However, in 2015, when President Barzani refused to step down after reaching his term limits, his nephew Nechirvan Barzani, KDP vice-president and prime minister of the KRG, accused Gorran of organizing a series of protests in which KDP party offices were burned, three protesters were killed, and scores more were injured.[47] In response to the protests, Nechirvan banned the speaker of the Parliament, Gorran's Yousif Muhammad Sadiq, from entering Erbil and then dismissed him from his

41 Kurdistan Development Corporation, "Kurdistan: The Other Iraq," (January 11, 2005), www.theotheriraq.com/images/Advert2.pdf.

42 Ibid.

43 K. Hassan, "Kurdistan's Politicized Society Confronts a Sultanistic System," Carnegie Endowment for International Peace (August 2015).

44 Nashirwan Mustafa was a founding member of the PUK and served as the party's deputy secretary from 1976 to 2006. "Gorran Leader Nawshirwan Mustafa Dies at 73 after Long Battle with Illness," *Rudaw* (May 19, 2017).

45 K. Chomani, "Iraqi Kurdistan's Historic Election," *Foreign Policy* (September 28, 2013); 2009 was also the year that the Kurdistan National Assembly was renamed the Kurdistan Parliament.

46 C. Sagnic, "The Shifting Balance of Power in Iraqi Kurdistan: Division or Independence?" Moshe Dayan Center for Middle Eastern and African Studies (May 29, 2016).

47 I. Coles, "Three Killed in Violent Unrest in Iraq's Kurdistan Region," *Reuters* (October 10, 2015).

post as speaker, accusing him of "biased" rulings against the KDP.[48] Four Gorran members of the prime minister's cabinet were also dismissed.[49] The Kurdistan Parliament was then suspended for two years, undermining the entire institution.[50]

The KDP claimed Gorran was attempting a "coup d'état" against President Barzani and defended the extension of his presidential term as indispensable during the war against the Islamic State of Iraq and Syria (ISIS).[51] Although no agreement regarding the extension of Barzani's term limits was reached in parliament, he remained in power for another two years through a controversial court ruling,[52] resigning in 2017 after placing the majority of his remaining political capital behind an unsuccessful independence referendum (described further below).

The Draft Kurdish Constitution

Iraq's 2005 Constitution stipulates in Article 120 that each region should adopt a constitution defining the structure of its powers and mechanisms for exercising its authorities. Efforts to reach agreement on a Kurdish constitution have faltered, however, as a result of internal political divisions, particularly regarding the powers of the regional president.

A draft constitution completed in 2009 envisages a remarkable measure of autonomy from Baghdad. Article 3 affirms that the "laws of the Kurdistan Region are sovereign and supersede all laws issued by the Iraqi government." Additionally, it requires Kurdish courts to follow Kurdish law in the event of a contradiction with any federal law.[53] Furthermore, the draft constitution allows for the KRG to enter into agreements with foreign entities on all matters not exclusively assigned to the federal government in Article 110 of Iraq's 2005 Constitution and to sign deals with foreign entities if the federal government consents. This is especially important in the context of oil exploration and development contracts.[54] Article 7 establishes the Kurdish people's right to "determine their own destiny" and to opt out of their freely chosen association with Iraq's federal regions if the central administration departs from the federal model or abandons its constitutional principles.[55]

48 Z. Z. Wali, "Gorran Positions in KRG Cabinet Filled by New Ministers," *Rudaw* (October 27, 2015).
49 I. Coles, "Political Crisis Escalates in Iraq's Kurdistan Region," *Reuters* (October 12, 2015).
50 J. Stocker, "Kurdistan Parliament to Reconvene on September 14," *Globe Post* (September 13, 2017).
51 H. H. Hama, "Systemic Crisis in the Kurdistan Region of Iraq," Foreign Policy Research Institute (January 8, 2018).
52 "Iraqi Kurdistan's Court of Cassation to Decide Presidency in Case of Stalemate," *Kurdistan Independent Daily Newspaper* (August 1, 2015).
53 Kurdistan Parliament, "Draft Constitution of Kurdistan Region: Iraq" (2009), https://collections.lib.utah.edu/details?id=318869.
54 M. J. Kelly, "The Kurdish Regional Constitution within the Framework of the Iraqi Federal Constitution: A Struggle for Sovereignty, Oil, Ethnic Identity, and the Prospects for a Reverse Supremacy Clause," *Pennsylvania State Law Review*, 114(3) (2010), 707–808.
55 Kelly, "The Kurdish Regional Constitution," 735.

The draft constitution was put to a vote by the Kurdistan Parliament in June 2009, a month before fresh parliamentary and presidential elections. Barzani hoped that it would be approved by parliament and subsequently endorsed by a referendum within the same election cycle. At the time the Constitution was being considered, Barzani was also nearing the expiration of his two-term limit. The KDP argued that the ratification of the new constitution would allow him to reset his tenure and be reelected for another two terms.[56]

Although the Kurdistan Parliament did approve the draft constitution by ninety-six votes to one, with thirteen members absent, the referendum was postponed until after the elections, which saw an unexpected victory for Gorran, replacing the PUK as the second largest party within the parliament.[57] The PUK considered the Constitution an attempt to strengthen the KDP at their expense. This triggered an alliance between the PUK and Gorran resulting in the signing of a 2013 Memorandum of Understanding (MOU) between the two. The MOU called for a number of reforms and amendments to the draft constitution including establishing a parliamentary system, which would elect the president and limit key powers of the office. This tension reignited the decades-long political rivalry between the Barzani family and the political elites in Suleimaniyeh.[58] These developments led to a partisan stalemate, and Kurdistan has yet to convene a referendum on the draft constitution.

While the debate over the final structure of the government is unresolved, the KRG remains a semi-presidential system with a strong president who is commander-in-chief of the Peshmerga and head of the Regional Security Council.[59] In September 2018, parliamentary elections were held, and in March 2019, the parliament elected Nechirvan Barzani as president.

Divided Security Forces

According to the KRG's draft constitution, all security and Peshmerga forces are to be consolidated under a single ministry under the regional president.[60] But this also has not happened. Today, the Ministry of Peshmerga Affairs controls less than a third of nearly 150,000 Peshmerga soldiers in the region.[61] The remainder are split

56 "Q&A: Iraqi Kurdistan Region's Draft Constitution," *Kurdistan Independent Daily Newspaper* (June 11, 2013).

57 A. Allen, "Draft Kurdish Constitution: Updated," Global Justice Project: Iraq (June 24, 2009).

58 K. Sulaiman, "Saving Kurdistan from Its Political Drought," *The Washington Institute for Near East Policy* (December 20, 2016).

59 A. Yoshioka, "The Shifting Balance of Power in Iraqi Kurdistan: The Struggle for Democracy with Uninstitutionalized Governance," *International Journal of Contemporary Iraqi Studies*, 9(1) (2015), 21–35.

60 See Kelly, "The Kurdish Regional Constitution," 734.

61 The troops remain referred to as "mixed" because they are not truly unified. See P. Iddon, "The Importance of Unifying the *Peshmerga*," *Rudaw* (February 2, 2018).

evenly between the KDP's Unit 80 and the PUK's Unit 70.[62] Even the Ministry of Peshmerga Affairs remains structured according to party affiliation, with each supposedly "unified" brigade receiving a commander from one party and a deputy from the other. Thus, while these units are not technically controlled by political parties, the parties do control who represents them in these newly "unified" brigades.[63]

These divisions have hampered the Peshmerga's effectiveness. Lack of communication between the KDP's and PUK's respective intelligence services led to key defeats to Islamic State.[64] Furthermore, military operations were territorially divided into eight sectors, with the KDP and PUK each controlling four,[65] turning the Kurdish fight against ISIS into two distinct wars on separate fronts and exposing continuing factionalism within the Peshmerga forces.

Natural Resources

The allocation of authority over the exploration and production of oil and gas resources has been a continuing source of tension between Erbil and Baghdad. The dispute is rooted in conflicting visions of the federal bargain concluded in 2005. The Kurds interpret Article 112 of the Constitution to assign the federal government a narrow administrative role in the export and handling of petroleum resources and take the position that, in the absence of an agreement to the contrary, regional laws take precedence over federal laws under Article 115.[66]

Such an agreement has proved elusive. In 2008 and 2009, Iraq's oil ministry began offering contracts to foreign companies to operate existing oil fields or develop new assets for the first time since nationalization in 1972.[67] In May 2017,[68] the KRG had passed its own regional Hydrocarbon Law authorizing it to exercise independent control over its oil resources, directly negotiate production-sharing agreements and contracts with international investors, and begin exporting commercial quantities of crude.[69]

In June 2009, the two sides finally signed an accord that permitted the KRG to export 100,000 barrels per day from specific fields (excluding Kirkuk). Some 73

62 F. Fliervoet, *Fighting for Kurdistan? Assessing the Nature and Functions of the Peshmerga in Iraq* (The Hague: Clingendael's Conflict Research Unit, 2018), 16.

63 S. Helfont, "Getting *Peshmerga* Reform Right: Helping the Iraqi Kurds to Help Themselves in Post-ISIS Iraq," Foreign Policy Research Institute (May 16, 2017).

64 The International Crisis Group has attributed the 2014 defeat at Sinjar to the unwillingness of the KDP and PUK to share evidence that ISIS was planning an attack. See Fliervoet, *Fighting for Kurdistan*, 17.

65 Ibid., 17–18.

66 M. Gunter, *Out of Nowhere: The Kurds of Syria in Peace and War* (London: Hurst & Co., 2014), 48.

67 E. R. Wald, "Kirkuk's Oil Chessboard," *The Cairo Review*, 28 (2018).

68 Kelly, "The Kurdish Regional Constitution," 749.

69 Y. Voller, "Kurdish Oil Politics in Iraq: Contested Sovereignty and Unilateralism," *Middle East Policy*, 20 (2013), 68–82.

percent of the revenue would be designated to the Iraqi government, 15 percent to the KRG, and 12 percent to any foreign oil companies with which the KRG signed contracts.[70] However, the accord fell apart as a result of disputes about which of them should pay the foreign oil firms developing fields in the KRG region, an issue they were unable to resolve even after production and exports resumed in 2010. As a consequence, exports from newly developed fields have proceeded on a piecemeal basis.

At the same time, the KRG's relationship with Turkey underwent a strategic reset. In mid-May 2012 they announced a wide-ranging energy deal that would allow for up to two million barrels of oil per day to be exported from the KRG into Turkey,[71] even as budget disputes with Baghdad had led the KRG to halt oil exports through the federally controlled oil pipelines.[72] In 2013, the KRG built the Kirkuk–Ceyhan pipeline, which was designed to transport Kirkuk's oil out of Iraq solely through Kurdish territory.[73] The KRG then signed a contract with Turkey to cover the transportation and sale of its oil through the Ceyhan port. Turkey arranged for the KRG to receive payment from the sale directly, and not through the Iraqi government. This decisively brought Turkey into Iraq's politics, poisoning Ankara–Baghdad relations. It arguably also left the KRG, which had placed all its eggs in one basket, in a subordinate and vulnerable position.

A precipitous drop in global oil prices, with the price per barrel falling from $115 in June 2014 to $45 in 2017, left the KRG in an even more precarious position.[74] In retaliation for the KRG's dealings with third parties, Baghdad ceased agreed budgetary transfers to Erbil in January 2014.[75] Further, by September 2014, ISIS attacks had reduced oil output from Kirkuk to only 90,000 barrels per day, a 90 percent drop from earlier that year.[76]

The KRG's response to the loss of federal revenue has been improvisational and chaotic, resulting in political turmoil throughout the region.[77] Unable to pay the salaries of its massive civil sector, the KRG enacted severe austerity measures, reducing salaries by 30–75 percent.[78] This led to widespread and repeat demonstrations

70 Wald, "Kirkuk's Oil Chessboard," 47.

71 "A Tortuous Triangle," *The Economist* (December 22, 2012).

72 D. Dombey, "Turkey Agrees Energy Deal with Kurdish North Iraq," *Financial Times* (May 13, 2013).

73 The pipeline crosses into Turkey at the junction of Iraq, Syria, and Turkey and then turns west to Ceyhan, a small Turkish port city on the Mediterranean.

74 N. Barwari, "Understanding the Political Economy of the KRI: The Way forward toward Better Governance," LSE Middle East Blog (April 24, 2018).

75 D. Zhdannikov, "Exclusive: How Kurdistan Bypassed Baghdad and Sold Oil on Global Markets," *Reuters* (November 17, 2015).

76 Ibid.

77 For a full account of the KDP's fiscal improvisation see P. Osgood, "Selective Transparency: Things You Can't See about KRG Oil," LSE Middle East Blog (April 25, 2018).

78 M. L. Hansen et al., *Strategies for Private-Sector Development and Civil-Service Reform in the Kurdistan Region: Iraq* (Santa Monica, CA: RAND Corporation, 2014).

throughout Kurdistan but centered in Suleimaniyeh.[79] In some instances, protests turned violent. For example, in October 2015, security forces opened fire on demonstrators killing five and wounding dozens.[80] In December 2017, demonstrators called for the dissolution of the KRG and set fire to the offices of all five major political parties including Gorran.[81] In Koysinjaq, the mayor's office was set ablaze, while in Kifri hundreds of demonstrators stormed the offices of the KDP and pelted the building with stones.[82]

An added burden for the KRG was the influx of two million internally displaced persons (IDPs) from Mosul, Anbar, and Tikrit fleeing the war with ISIS. According to the KRG, IDPs now represent nearly 28 percent, or one in four, of the KRG's total population.[83] Not surprisingly, the KRG has struggled to provide housing, water and electricity services, schools, and health centers for everyone.[84]

THE REFERENDUM, ITS DISCONTENTS, AND THE TIES THAT BIND

In 2017, the Kurdistan Parliament reconvened following a two-year suspension and despite a boycott of the session by Gorran. Of the sixty-eight lawmakers who assembled, sixty-five voted in favor of holding a referendum on independence.[85] In doing so they rebuffed pressure from Baghdad, Turkey, Iran, the United States, and the United Nations Security Council. Only Israel and Russia openly supported the referendum.

The referendum push was seen by critics as a political maneuver by Barzani to deflect attention from the internal crises in the KRG, with time running out on the latest and most controversial extension of his presidential term limit.[86] It is possible the KRG was seeking to leverage the results in order to bolster its position in negotiations with Baghdad.[87] But this reading fails to acknowledge just how well attuned Baghdad, Tehran, and Ankara are to Kurdish fragilities at any given moment, a reality that Barzani clearly appreciated. In this light, the referendum is best understood as an attempt by Barzani to shore up his legacy domestically.

79 A. Mohtadi, "What's Required for Kurdistan to Overcome Its Economic Crisis?" *Jerusalem Post* (January 23, 2018).

80 I. Coles, "Political Crisis Escalates."

81 "Kurdish Protesters Set Fire to Party Offices in Northern Iraq," *Reuters* (December 8, 2017).

82 A. F. Presse, "Iraqi Kurdistan Protests Turn Deadly," *Dawn* (December 20, 2017).

83 "Kurds and the Refugee Crisis," *The Kurdish Project* (2015).

84 "Kurdistan Region Still Hosts about 1.5 Million IDPs and Refugees," Kurdistan Regional Government Representation in Spain (February 14, 2019).

85 R. Jalabi, "Iraq's Kurdish Parliament Backs Sept 25 Independence Referendum," *Reuters* (September 15, 2017).

86 Barzani's second term extension expired in 2015. N. Watts, "Most Kurds in Iraq Support Independence. So Why Did Some Voters Stay Home during Last Week's Referendum?" *Washington Post* (October 6, 2017).

87 "Oil and Borders: How to Fix Iraq's Kurdish Crisis," International Crisis Group (October 17, 2017).

On September 25, 2017, 92.7 percent of voters answered "yes" to the question: "Do you want the Kurdistan Region (KR) and the Kurdistani areas outside the Region's jurisdiction to become an independent state?"[88] The decision to include the controversial disputed territories, including oil-rich Kirkuk, resulted in a severe backlash. Immediately after the vote, Iran closed its borders with the KRG at the request of Baghdad, and both Iran and Turkey closed their airspace to the region.[89] (Turkey neither closed its land border with the KDP nor applied any sanctions against the KDP, despite condemning the referendum. They were business partners after all.)

In October 2017, PUK-controlled Peshmerga units withdrew from Kirkuk against the orders of the KRG. This allowed the Iraqi government to take control of Kirkuk and its airport, military base, and multiple oil facilities. With the loss of Kirkuk's oil the KRG lost even more oil revenues, further exacerbating the region's already acute economic vulnerability.[90] In addition, the Central Bank of Iraq imposed financial sanctions, cutting off the region's access to foreign currency. The sanctions hit hard as the Kurdish banks carry little liquidity, and the KRG's access to foreign currency from oil exported through Turkey had been severely diminished by the loss of Kirkuk oil production to Baghdad.[91]

On October 25, the KRG officially suspended the referendum results. While the referendum was a discouraging episode, it should be seen in the broader historical context. The circumstances confronting the Kurds are in some ways analogous to 1975, when their national cause suffered a substantial setback.

In the first week of November the KRG was still able to make its full monthly revenue share payments of around $100 million to the foreign companies involved in oil production. If these payments were to stop then oil production and exports could be suspended. Along with the renewed hard-currency restrictions this left the KRG little option but to abandon independence plans and control of its own borders in return for the lifting of financial sanctions and a resumption in the delivery of its share of central fiscal transfers.[92] In December 2017, the Iraqi government renegotiated the revenue-sharing agreement with the KRG from 17 percent to 12.6 percent, in line with both the budget transfer quotas of the pre-2003 period and the KRG's estimated population.[93] On January 29, 2018, having effectively imposed federal

88 Turnout for the independence vote was over 72 percent. M. Charountaki, "The Kurdish Referendum: The Referendum's Aftermath and Its Historic Connotations," *Harvard International Review* (December 10, 2018).

89 B. McKernan, "Kurdish Referendum: Iran Closes Border with Iraqi Kurdistan over Independence Vote Fears," *The Independent* (September 25, 2017).

90 Over four years, private sector jobs in the region decreased by 90 percent, from 730,000 in 2013 to about 73,000 in 2017. M. Hussein, "The Collateral Damage of the KRI's Economic Policy," LSE Middle East Blog (April 17, 2018).

91 "Central Bank Ramps Up Financial Sanctions on the Kurds," The Economist Intelligence Unit (November 17, 2017).

92 "Iraq Policy Trends," The Economist Intelligence Unit (June 1, 2015).

93 Hussein, "Collateral Damage."

control over the KRI's banking sector, the Iraqi parliament voted to lift sanctions on its banks. The experience with sanctions may, however, discourage companies from investing in the KRG, as similar measures could be reimposed at short notice.[94]

Although in 2018 the KRG made fresh commitments to transparency in the oil and gas sector, they have been described as "casual," and the KRG remains one of the "world's most opaque natural-resource reliant governments."[95] Indeed, its "buccaneering improvisation" has left the KRG with a "deinstitutionalized financial system" that calls into question the very "viability of the region."[96]

Today, the KRG's oil exports are simply insufficient to cover its expenditures. The KRG is willing to hand over the oil sector to Baghdad if it will pay its debts of almost $25 billion.[97] Baghdad, on the other hand, wants the oil but not the debt. At least one PUK leader has called for turning Kurdistan's entire oil production over to Baghdad to secure the region's share of the budget and prevent it from being exploited under the "economic independence" banner adopted by the current regional government.[98] While some Kurds advocated bypassing the KRG altogether and linking each governorate directly to the central government, it is not clear whether this is constitutional.

The Kurds are down but they are not out. They want to be independent, notwithstanding the 2017 debacle and disputes between Kurdish factions, their dependence on oil and gas, and their vulnerability to their neighbors. Baghdad, Ankara, and Tehran have learned to live with Iraqi Kurdistan's enhanced autonomy, but not more. This could change relatively quickly. For example, one analysis of the KRG in February 2019 captures its governance challenges well, noting the need for a new social contract between the Kurds and their leadership.[99] However, another, from *The Economist* in June 2019, leads with the headline "Comeback Kurds," noting especially the continuing expansion in oil and gas investments and "like its gas, Kurdistan is rising."[100] A 2016 Oxford study of the KRI's oil and gas prospects describes its production outlook to 2025 as staggering.[101]

This is a new environment, which affects the confidence of both the KRG and the federal government and their assessments of each other's strength. How to deal with this windfall, if fully realized, is also animating divisions among the Kurds and their policy choices vis-à-vis Baghdad, Tehran, and Ankara. It might even split the KRG.

94 "Parliament Lifts Sanctions on Banks in Kurdistan," The Economist Intelligence Unit (February 13, 2018).

95 Osgood, "Selective Transparency."

96 Ibid.

97 Hussein, "Collateral Damage."

98 Ibid.

99 C. Salih and M. Fantappie, "Kurdish Nationalism at an Impasse," The Century Foundation (February 4, 2019).

100 "Comeback Kurds: Two Years after a Disastrous Referendum, Iraq's Kurds Are Prospering," *The Economist* (June 15, 2019).

101 R. Mills, "Under the Mountains: Kurdish Oil and Regional Politics," Oxford Institute for Energy Studies (January 2016), 1.

In negotiations over the 2019 national budget the KRG committed to transfer 250,000 barrels per day from its own fields to the State Oil and Marketing Organization in exchange for Baghdad covering KRG employee salaries and a budget allocation of 12.67 percent. The budget does not address the KRG's excess export revenues above this figure.

The KRG is believed to owe around $25–30 billion to international oil companies in deals never agreed to by Baghdad, and KRG President Nechirvan Barzani has asked the central government to "allow the KRG to export oil until oil companies are completely compensated and then commit to hand over the 250,000 barrels [to the state oil company]."[102] Nechirvan also allegedly pressed the federal government to drop its 2015 arbitration with Turkey at the International Chamber of Commerce in which Baghdad is seeking $26 billion compensation for importing Kurdish oil without Baghdad's consent. And there is a pending federal lawsuit in Baghdad against the KRG for its exploitation of the Khurmala dome field in Kirkuk from 2008, initially filed in 2012.[103]

While some politicians are inclined to give the KRG time to adjust its debt, others are hostile to compromises seen as "conceding the rights of the rest of the Iraqi components" and outside the law.[104] Members of the Finance Committee in the Council of Representatives accused the KRG of "behaving like a state" and threatened to withdraw support in the 2020 federal budget. These issues risk becoming an annual exercise. Whether they will settle into a more institutionalized framework, constitutional or otherwise, is difficult to predict.

In 2019, Baghdad and Iraq's southern governorates experienced unprecedented protests against government failure in almost every sector. Some 500 demonstrators were killed and thousands more were injured by various government militias, forcing the resignation of Prime Minister Adel Abdul Mahdi. The protesters called for constitutional change and an end to the post-2005 political system, which has been dominated by unaccountable communally based political parties. Iraqis across the board sought to reclaim a secular nationalism and identity from before it had been so coercively misapplied by the Ba'ath Party under Saddam Hussein.[105] Iraqis were also fed up with chronic insecurity, sectarian civil war, ISIS, and the proxy conflict in their country between the USA and Iran, as well as Turkey for that matter.

The twin shocks of Covid-19 and the collapse of oil prices, on which the federal government and the KRG are so dependent, occurred in 2020. Collectively, these have laid bare an unsustainable political and social compact. In all of this it seems

102 O. Sattar, "Nechirvan Barzani in Baghdad to Discuss Oil," *Al-Monitor* (June 27, 2019).

103 S. Kullab and staff writers, "Federal Lawsuit Targeting Kurdistan Oil Exports Delayed Again," *Iraq Oil Report* (June 17, 2019).

104 The quoted MP is Faleh Ziadi, although others are similarly inclined. See O. Sattar, "Nechirvan Barzani in Baghdad."

105 For an excellent discussion of Iraqi identity, see T. Dodge "Beyond Structure and Agency: Rethinking Political Identities in Iraq after 2003," *Nations and Nationalism*, 26(1) (2019), 108–22.

unlikely that the 2005 Constitution will be amended. This is because it theoretically offers so much protection to the KRG, and its design reflects the Kurds' bitter experience in Iraq. Conversely, as we have seen, Kurdistan is also unable to exit Iraq by declaring independence, primarily on account of their economic vulnerability and the structure of Iraq's financial sector. How Iraq's many challenges will be resolved is an open question. But the Kurds will need to participate in these policy discussions, and this, more than ever, means being formally engaged with government and politics in Baghdad.

CONCLUSION

The Kurdish struggle for autonomy in Iraq has been long and arduous but not linear. Initial concessions on Kurdish language and culture were driven by Iraq's obligations for entry into the League of Nations in the 1930s. Greater acceptance and formal recognition of the Kurds came after the 1958 overthrow of the Iraq monarchy. "Decentralization" was seen as an appropriate policy response by the government in 1963 to the Kurdish question in Iraq, in contrast to Turkey, Syria, or Iran where such concessions were never entertained. Essentially, it took a decade of conflict for the Kurdish project to consolidate in Iraq. This happened within a revolutionary developmental state framework present not just in Iraq but across the Middle East and North Africa region.

When the Revolutionary Command Council stated in its March 11, 1970 Declaration that "the issue of the national aspirations of the Kurds in Iraq is at the top of the problems that the Arab Revolution Movement is facing," it was serious. Solving the Kurdish question, it was believed, would provide the basis for Iraq to at once resolve "domestic backwardness" and address the "wider struggle of imperialism and Zionism."[106]

The "final deal" in 1974 elicited mixed reactions among Kurds, and it led to the creation of the PUK. Some commentators saw it as a genuine historical achievement and a regional conceptual leap in what the Arab world and decentralization could offer. Here, the question of natural resources and the external role of neighbors and others was central. The Ba'ath party and the ICP believed oil and gas to be a national, not regional, responsibility. The KDP wanted regional control. In pressing for more concessions from Baghdad, the KDP sought external assistance from the USA, Iran, and Israel. When that dried up, autonomy was imposed on the Kurds on central government terms, and after a fashion, there was a notional Kurdish autonomy throughout the 1980s. But the period is chiefly remembered for the mass atrocities against the Faylis, the Barzanis, and the victims of the *Al-Anfal* and Halabja massacres, described by some as genocide.

[106] March Manifesto (March 11, 1970).

After the 1991 Gulf War the Kurds enjoyed their first genuine experience with self-rule. This was overseen by external security providers, chiefly the USA and the UK, who policed the no-fly zone. In the period 1995–2003 the Kurds received per capita budgetary support from Baghdad calculated at 12.6 percent of the national budget. And the contours of present-day Kurdish governance were established through the KDP–PUK power-sharing deal after their civil war.

The 2003 invasion of Iraq and the 2005 constitution-making process provided an opportunity for a historical reset of center–periphery relations on Kurdish terms and consolidated the gains of the 1990s. The Kurds were also well represented in the federal government in Baghdad and the development of the region proceeded apace, buoyed by a decade of sustained high oil prices and investment in the Kurdish region. When Erbil and Baghdad could not agree the terms by which the Kurds would exploit their oil and gas resources, the KRG went heavily into debt to international oil companies that built and reticulated new extraction infrastructure through Kurdistan and Turkey. This saw a strategic reset in the KDP's relations with Turkey but caused Baghdad to cease budgetary transfers to the KRG, just as oil prices crashed and ISIS emerged. Overnight bankruptcy revealed just how poorly the KRG was being run.

The 2017 independence referendum was partly introduced to obscure this fact. The reaction from Baghdad and Iran was swift, and the status quo ante in terms of Kurdish control over northern Iraq was restored to 2003, made clearest in the Kurds' loss of Kirkuk. The involvement of the late Qassem Soleimani, the Islamic Revolutionary Guard Corps (IRGC) *Al Quds* commander, in negotiating the withdrawal of the PUK Peshmerga from Kirkuk provided colorful detail in the Kurds' reversal of fortunes. But it was the abrupt severance of the KRG from Iraq's banking sector through financial sanctions that caused immediate Kurdish submission.

The twin challenges of Covid-19 and the collapse in the global energy sector in 2020 will require cooperation and some nimble reforms by the federal government and the KRG as well as Kurdish policymakers in leadership roles in Baghdad. The ties that bind may prove more resilient than the centrifugal forces in the relationship. Regardless, none of this takes away the obligation by the KRG to find an adequate governance framework. This would require, at a minimum, unifying the Peshmerga, agreeing to a clear and constitutional apportionment of powers, diversifying its economy, and getting its own finances in order. Additionally, the KRI needs to generate a consensus on its energy infrastructure and revenues. Otherwise, it will continue to develop in an ad hoc and extra-legal fashion. And its autonomy will be defined by Baghdad, Ankara, and Tehran. Decentralization has afforded the Kurds considerable autonomy in Iraq; the question remains how they might translate that autonomy into structures of governance that address internal demands and enable them to withstand external pressures.

11

Turkish Kurdistan

Decentralization Reimagined

Aslı Ü. Bâli

The Kurdish political movement in Turkey made decentralizing reforms a central plank of talks with the government to address the longstanding "Kurdish question" over the last decade. The Kurdish "peace process," as these talks were known, came to a crashing halt in 2015 when Turkish President Recep Tayyip Erdoğan entered an electoral coalition with an ultranationalist party to counter the rising appeal of the pro-Kurdish political party – the Peoples' Democratic Party (HDP). Erdoğan unceremoniously abandoned peace talks and resumed the state's conventional, militarized approach to managing Kurdish political demands for cynical reasons tied to electoral calculations, but also due to anxieties about increasing Kurdish autonomy across the border in Syria. In the years that have passed since 2015, the ongoing coalition between Erdoğan's Justice and Development Party (AKP) and ultranationalists has sustained its coercive approach to Kurdish political demands, undermining any possibility of a return to negotiations.[1]

Despite the suspension of peace talks, the six years of on-again, off-again reconciliation efforts from 2009 to 2015 yielded important insights about the contours of a political solution. More importantly, with or without a Turkish interlocutor, the Kurdish political leadership in Turkey has undertaken a long-term process of reformulating the movement's goals. The trajectory of that leadership – from pursuing secession to developing new theories of decentralization as a model for self-determination (without shifting territorial borders) – has produced novel experiments in governance reform and self-determination as well as a concrete roadmap for conflict resolution. This chapter examines Kurdish proposals on confederalism as a means of achieving identity-based autonomy and governance reform without territorial change.

The chapter begins by offering background on Turkish Kurdistan,[2] followed by a brief description of centralized authority in Turkey and the evolution of Kurdish

1 "Turkey: No New 'Resolution Process' Planned," *Anadolu Agency* (May 18, 2018); D. Butler, "Move to Ban Kurdish Party Shows Erdogan's March to Nationalism," *Reuters* (March 19, 2021).

2 While the chapter focuses on the Turkish context, the Kurdish political movement is transnational and deeply affected by cross-border developments. The fate of devolutionary proposals in Turkey is directly impacted by developments in Syria and Iraq, while the Kurdish communities in both of

political thinking in this context. The next section examines the reconciliation process in Turkey between 2009 and 2015 and Kurdish leaders' views on decentralization in those negotiations. The final section considers the Kurdish political project of democratic confederalism in light of debates on the benefits and limitations of decentralization in the comparative law literature.

KURDISTAN, DIVIDED

The emergence of the state system in the modern Middle East witnessed the division of contiguous Kurdish lands among four contemporary states: Turkey, Syria, Iraq, and Iran. In each country, the Kurdish community is the largest ethnic minority with a distinct language, history, and in many cases syncretic religious practices. The Kurdish community shares a common history across these borders, with ancestry in the mountainous region of Mesopotamia spanning eastern Turkey, northern and eastern regions of Syria and Iraq, and the northeast of Iran for thousands of years.[3]

Some historians date the emergence of Kurdish nationalism as far back as the sixteenth century,[4] while others treat it as a more recent phenomenon that is contemporaneous with the emergence of other minority nationalisms in the Ottoman Empire beginning in the nineteenth century.[5] The shared common heritage across the contiguous, landlocked territory of the thirty-five million Kurds of the Middle East – including their tradition of centuries of semi-autonomous self-government under different imperial orders – forms the basis for the community's demands for collective self-determination, first given clear political expression at the international level following the end of World War I.[6]

The Kurdish population resisted forced inclusion in the new states of the region through a series of failed revolts. In Turkey, the government's initial approach was to deny the existence of a separate Kurdish identity and enforce mandatory assimilation.[7] The Kurdish community responded with armed resistance in the Sheikh Said rebellion (1925) and the Dersim revolt (1937), among others, resulting in massacres at the hands of

those countries live under the long shadow cast by Turkish intervention in their politics. The following chapters in this volume address other Kurdish communities in the region: Joost Jongerden, "Autonomy beyond the State," Chapter 9; Peter Bartu and Aidan MacEachern, "The Devil Is in the Details: Iraqi Kurdistan's Evolving Autonomy," Chapter 10; and Samer Araabi and Leila Hilal, "Decentralization in State Disintegration: An Examination of Governance Experiments in Syria," Chapter 17.

3 M. M. Gunter, *The Kurds: A Modern History* (Princeton: Markus Wiener Publishers, 2016).

4 See, e.g., A. Hassanpour, *Nationalism and Language in Kurdistan* (San Francisco: Mellen Research University Press, 1992), 53–55.

5 See, e.g., D. McDowall, *Modern History of the Kurds* (London: I.B. Tauris: 2004); see also H. Özoğlu, *Kurdish Notables and Ottoman State: Evolving Identities, Competing Loyalties and Shifting Boundaries* (Albany: SUNY Press, 2004).

6 McDowall, *Modern History*, 121–37.

7 Gunter, *The Kurds*, 27–32.

the Turkish military and the execution of rebel leaders.[8] During this period, countless Kurdish villages were destroyed followed by massive deportations, with the state seeking to alter the ethnic composition of the region by encouraging Balkan and Assyrian communities to resettle in Kurdish lands.[9] In 1937, the Turkish state imposed martial law on the southeastern provinces of the country and the repression of the Kurdish community escalated dramatically.[10] The region remained a military zone until 1965.[11]

Following a turbulent decade of political polarization and violence during the 1970s, a military coup in 1980 decimated the left-leaning parties and movements in Turkey, disproportionately affecting Kurdish activists.[12] With the demobilization of the Turkish left, Kurdish activists regrouped around an explicitly nationalist, Marxist-influenced platform.[13] In 1984, the Kurdistan Workers' Party (PKK) launched an armed insurgency against the Turkish state with the declared goal of secession to create an independent Kurdistan. The PKK insurgency was met with Turkish military incursions by ground and air from 1984 to 1999, resulting in as many as 40,000 deaths, largely of Kurdish civilians.[14] In addition, Turkish policies emptied hundreds of Kurdish villages in a new round of ethnic transformation.[15] This period of violence ended with the declaration of a long-term ceasefire in 1999 following the capture of PKK leader, Abdullah Öcalan. A decade later, under the leadership of the AKP, the Turkish state entered into a fitful peace process with Kurdish political leaders.

Between 1965 and 2022, the position of the Turkish state evolved from denialism and assimilation to a degree of cultural recognition of Kurdish identity and, more recently, acknowledgment that the "Kurdish question" in Turkey requires political resolution.[16] The Kurdish community today comprises between fifteen and eighteen million of Turkey's eighty million people and is divided territorially between the Kurdish provinces of the southeast and the urban centers in the west of the

8 R. Olson, "The Kurdish Rebellions of Sheikh Said (1925), Mt. Ararat (1930), and Dersim (1937–8)," *Die Welt des Islams*, 40(1) (2000), 67–94; and M. van Bruinessen, "Genocide in Kurdistan? The Suppression of the Dersim Rebellion in Turkey (1937–8)," in G. J. Andreopoulos (ed.), *Conceptual and Historical Dimensions of Genocide* (Philadelphia: University of Pennsylvania Press, 1994), 141–70. Historians view both revolts as centered as much on religious as ethnic demands to maintain traditions of semi-autonomy and preserve religious brotherhoods that were being abolished as part of the state's secularization project.

9 R. H. Öztan, "Settlement Law of 1934: Turkish Nationalism in the Age of Revisionism," *Journal of Migration History*, 6(1) (2020), 82–103.

10 McDowall, *Modern History*, 196–210.

11 Gunter, *The Kurds*, 27–31.

12 J. Jongerden and A. H. Akkaya, "The Kurdistan Workers Party and a New Left in Turkey," *European Journal of Turkish Studies*, 14 (2012), 1–20.

13 J. Jongerden and M. Casier, "Understanding Today's Kurdish Movement: Leftist Heritage, Martyrdom, Democracy and Gender," *European Journal of Turkish Studies*, 14 (2012).

14 A. K. Özcan, *Turkey's Kurds: A Theoretical Analysis of the PKK and Abdullah Ocalan* (London: Routledge, 2010).

15 J. Jongerden, "Village Evacuation and Reconstruction in Kurdistan (1993–2002)," *Etudes Rurales*, 186 (2010), 1–22.

16 Güneş Murat Tezcur, "Prospects for Resolution of the Kurdish Question," *Insight Turkey*, 15(2) (2013), 69–84.

country. Kurdish political organizing has also evolved dramatically. For the first three decades of the multiparty era, ethnically Kurdish but largely assimilated politicians served significant roles in major Turkish political parties. As an example, one of Turkey's most influential prime ministers and later presidents, Turgut Özal, came from a family in Malatya with Kurdish roots on his maternal side.[17] While such biographical details were often widely acknowledged, Kurdish citizens' ability to compete in electoral politics depended on their embrace of an assimilated identity.

Pro-Kurdish political parties have formed in Turkey since 1990 marking a new phase of Kurdish political participation. But from the moment that such parties began to form, the Turkish Constitutional Court (TCC) distinguished itself as one of the most activist courts in the world with respect to party closures. Beginning with the People's Labor Party formed in 1990 and banned in 1993, there have been six pro-Kurdish parties subjected to constitutional closure by the TCC on allegations of threatening the territorial integrity of the Turkish state.[18] There are currently two major Kurdish political parties that work in tandem at the national and local levels. The first is the Democratic Regions Party (DBP), which defines itself as a social democratic Kurdish political party and restricts its activities to local and regional government in the Kurdish provinces. The Peoples' Democratic Party (HDP) serves as a fraternal party to the DBP, contesting local and regional elections outside of the Kurdish provinces (where the DBP does not run candidates) and competing in national elections. The HDP became the first pro-Kurdish party in the history of the Turkish republic to successfully compete in national elections in 2015 when it surpassed the electoral threshold (the highest in the world at 10 percent), seating eighty pro-Kurdish parliamentarians.[19] The leader of the HDP, Selahattin Demirtaş, also ran as a presidential candidate in 2014, earning a surprising 10 percent of the vote, and again in 2018 – this time from detention – again garnering a surprisingly high proportion of the vote.[20] Yet the party and Demirtaş face the real possibility

[17] "The Life and Times of Revolutionary Turkish Leader Turgut Ozal," *TRT World* (April 17, 2020).

[18] These parties were the Freedom and Democracy Party (OZDEP, 1993); the Democracy Party (DEP, 1993–94); the People's Democracy Party (HADEP, 1994–2003); the Democratic People's Party (DEHAP, 2002–07); and the Democratic Society Party (DTP, which merged with DEHAP, 2007–09). Each was subjected to closure by the TCC, often after successfully contesting local and even parliamentary elections, with their elected members stripped of parliamentary immunity and founding members banned from political activities. The HDP is the most recent party facing a constitutional closure case. "Turkey's Constitutional Court Accepts HDP Closure Indictment," *Daily Sabah* (June 21, 2021).

[19] Subsequent snap elections in November 2015 resulted in a loss of twenty-one seats for the HDP, though it still garnered 10.75 percent of the national vote, enough to surpass the electoral threshold again, seating fifty-nine MPs. Prior to the HDP's success, pro-Kurdish parties had run candidates as independents to avoid the high electoral threshold for parties.

[20] Despite campaigning from detention in 2018, Demirtaş secured 8.4 percent of the vote (coming in ahead of the nationalist candidate Meral Akşener, as the third highest vote getter), in a presidential election that was held under a state of emergency with rampant censorship and campaign restrictions that tilted the electoral landscape dramatically in favor of the AKP. K. Shaheen, "Just Election in Turkey Not Possible, Says Imprisoned Kurdish Candidate," *The Guardian* (June 23, 2018).

of repression, with a closure case against the HDP ongoing in 2021 and Demirtaş behind bars since 2016 on various allegations of support for terrorism.

Between them the DBP and the HDP garner over 50 percent of the Kurdish vote in the country, with much of the remainder going to the AKP (which has appeal among religiously conservative Kurdish communities) and a smaller proportion to minor Kurdish parties.[21] Both parties align themselves politically with the basic orientation of Abdullah Öcalan, though the HDP maintains more of a distance from the PKK. Importantly, the PKK itself has also evolved dramatically since it declared an armed insurgency in 1984. Today the PKK, together with the recognized political parties that represent a pro-Kurdish platform in Turkey, demands greater autonomy from the state through decentralization and expanded cultural and political rights rather than secession. The transformation of the PKK's position, the formation of the BPD/DBP/HDP and the emergence of civic space in Turkey for debating questions of identity and cultural rights all reflect significant changes. Some of this evolution is a consequence of the demographic changes resulting from Kurdish forced migration to Turkish cities and some of it is a result of shifting ideological orientations on the Kurdish and Turkish sides.

TURKEY, KURDISTAN, AND DECENTRALIZATION

The Centralized Turkish State

The shift in Kurdish demands from secession to a form of decentralization that affords a degree of territorial autonomy within the existing borders of Turkey is both innovative and daunting. Why daunting? The highly centralized institutions of the Turkish republic mean that proposals for decentralization require a dramatic transformation of the state's relationship to society. Turkey is a unitary state with two tiers of administration – central and local – in which "a strong central authority … presides over local administration through a tutelage relationship."[22] The country is divided into provinces, which are divided into districts, which in turn are divided into four types of municipal administration: special provincial, village, municipal, and metropolitan municipal.[23] Only these four types of local government are

[21] These smaller parties span the spectrum from religiously conservative Kurdish constituencies (like the far-right Sunni Islamist Free Cause Party, Hüda-Par) to far-left parties that continue to favor secessionism (like the Communist Party of Kurdistan (KKP)). There are also two parties that strongly support federalism: the Rights and Freedoms Party (HAK-PAR) and the Freedom and Socialism Party (ÖSP). None of these parties garner more than a few percentage points in the Kurdish provinces (though they do sometimes elect candidates to municipal office) nor do they enjoy support beyond the Kurdish provinces.

[22] E. Tan, *Decentralization and Governance Capacity: The Case of Turkey* (London: Palgrave, 2019), 79–80.

[23] Turkey currently has eighty-one provinces, each of which is governed by a centrally appointed civil servant as governor (*Vali*). Districts are also governed by civil servant appointees (*kaymakam*).

governed by elected officials – provinces and districts have appointed leaders. The thirty metropolitan municipalities in Turkey are the largest cities, accounting for over three-quarters of the country's population.[24] Overall there are 1,396 municipalities in the country, 60 percent of which have a population of 5,000 or fewer (and represent a mere 11 percent of Turkey's population).[25] Municipalities enjoy a measure of financial and administrative autonomy and are tasked with providing a wide range of services.[26]

The Turkish political system is characterized by a degree of financial and administrative decentralization but very limited political decentralization. The absence of political decentralization is partly a consequence of distrust in the Kurdish movement and concern that delegating policy authority in the southeast would encourage secessionism.[27] In Turkey, decentralization is designed to achieve "a more efficient regulatory state, rather than the empowerment of local government."[28] The principle of deconcentration is enshrined constitutionally, with the central government directed to delegate authority to provincial-level appointed officials where possible, within a broader framework that permits "the devolution of powers and responsibilities to local government through specific legislation but upholds the superior position of central government to ensure public services are carried out uniformly and appropriately."[29] The constitutional status of administrative tutelage sets clear constraints on decentralization, ensuring that decision-making authority remains with the central government.

Over the last three years, even this limited decentralization has been abrogated in the majority Kurdish southeastern provinces. Following a failed coup attempt in 2016, the government declared an emergency enabling the Ministry of Interior to replace elected mayors with centrally appointed trustees. Elected officials from one hundred municipalities, of which ninety-four were governed by elected representatives from the pro-Kurdish HDP, were removed.[30] Subsequently, new legislation permanently empowered the Ministry of Interior to suspend elected mayors and dissolve municipal councils on grounds of corruption or alleged support for terrorism.[31] In the six months following local elections in 2019, another fourteen elected HDP

[24] Metropolitan municipality is defined as a city with a population over 750,000.

[25] M. S. Tosun and S. Yilmaz, "Decentralization, Economic Development and Growth in Turkish Provinces," World Bank Policy Research Working Paper No. 4725 (2008),

[26] These services include management of geographic and urban information systems, management of utilities infrastructure (including water and sewage), urban planning, environment, parks, culture, tourism, youth and sports, social services, vocational and skills training, and management of economic and commercial development, and in the case of some of the largest cities, control over municipally managed state-owned enterprises.

[27] Tan, *Decentralization and Governance Capacity*, 6.

[28] Ibid., 98–99.

[29] Turkish Constitution, Article 127.

[30] Tan, *Decentralization and Governance Capacity*, 80.

[31] Ibid., 107.

officials were replaced by appointed trustees under the new legislation.[32] The combined effect of emergency decrees, presidential decrees, and anti-terrorism laws has been to suspend elected local government in a majority of the Kurdish-populated regions of the country, imposing instead rule by central government trustees drawn from the governing AKP party.

Öcalan's Decentralized Vision

The Turkish government's actions in the last five years suggest that the state continues to view decentralization as empowering Kurdish separatism. Ironically, Kurdish leaders have moved from secession toward decentralization precisely to facilitate a political solution to their status within Turkey's existing borders. Having concluded that armed insurgency would not succeed, the movement's ideological leader – Öcalan – publicly shifted direction, seeking a model for internal self-determination that guarantees some autonomy for the Kurdish community without territorial change. Over the course of two decades, he has written extensively about what such a model would entail, refining his proposals into a theory that he describes as "democratic confederalism."

The transformation in Öcalan's thinking has been the subject of countless studies on the dozens of volumes about decentralization, self-determination, and democracy that he has published since 2002.[33] Some aspects of his political evolution have been particularly well documented, including the influence of Benedict Anderson's work, which persuaded Öcalan to view nations as social constructions rather than primordial identities.[34] In the place of nationalism, Öcalan argues that the Kurdish community should pursue greater autonomy, cultural rights, and the decentralization of political power to make meaningful citizenship and participation possible.

32 "Turkey: Kurdish Mayors' Removal Violates Voters' Rights," Human Rights Watch (February 7, 2020).

33 Much of this writing has been produced as submissions to Turkish courts as well as the European Court of Human Rights in lieu of legal defenses to the indictments he faced. Öcalan's prison writings lay out a political program to end the conflict between the Kurdish movement and the Turkish state. Examples of the volumes published from his "defense" texts include: A. Öcalan, *Savunma: Kürt Sorununda Demokratik Çözüm Bildirgesi* (Istanbul: Mem Yayınları, 1999); A. Öcalan, *AIHM Savunmalari: Sumer Rahip Devletinden Demokratik Cumhuriyete* (Diyarbakır, Turkey: Mezopotamya Yayınları, 2001); and A. Öcalan, *Demokratik Uygarlık Çözümü* (Istanbul: Amara Yayıncılık, 2015) (a five-volume set originally published between 2009 and 2012, republished together in 2015). Among the best scholars of Öcalan's political thought are Cengiz Güneş, Ahmet Hamdi Akkaya, and Joost Jongerden. See, e.g., C. Güneş, "Unpacking the 'Democratic Confederalism' and 'Democratic Autonomy': Proposals of Turkey's Kurdish Movement," in O. Akbulut and E. Aktoprak (eds.), *Minority Self-government in Europe and the Middle East: From Theory to Practice* (Leiden: Brill, 2019), 246–67; and A. H. Akkaya and J. Jongerden, "Reassembling the Political: The PKK and the project of Radical Democracy," *European Journal of Turkish Studies*, 14 (2012), 1–19. See also, D. Gerber and S. Brincat, "*When Öcalan Met Bookchin: The Kurdish Freedom Movement and the Political Theory of Democratic Confederalism*," *Geopolitics* (October 2018), 1–25.

34 N. Danforth, "An Imprisoned Nationalist Reads Benedict Anderson," *Dissent* (March 7, 2013).

He emphasizes a transformation in the conception of citizenship from an ethnic to a civic model. Indeed, Öcalan once gave an interview in the Turkish newspaper *Radikal* describing aspirations for a Kurdish nation-state as an expression of a kind of capitalist distortion in his thinking that he now rejects.[35]

If Anderson can be credited for the shift away from secessionist nationalism, it is an obscure American leftist who may have been the more important influence on the subject of decentralization. Murray Bookchin, an ecological activist and sometime anarchist who spent a half-century career in Vermont arguing for a form of libertarian socialism, is an unlikely inspiration for Kurdish forces in Turkey and Syria.[36] But the influence of his writing on Öcalan was sufficiently profound that his books – largely forgotten in the USA – are taught in Kurdish classrooms in the autonomous Kurdish region in northeastern Syria and circulate among progressive Kurds in Turkey.[37] Öcalan has argued that "Bookchin's proposed system of confederal participatory democracies provides the base of a new model of democratic modernity beyond the nation-state: not just for the Kurds but for the region in general."[38] Without romanticizing the influence of Bookchin, his feminist, ecological, and participatory democratic ideas are echoed in the forms of political experimentation practiced by Kurdish communities in Turkey and Syria in the last decade.[39]

In concrete terms, what have these ideas meant for the Kurdish political movement in Turkey? In 2001, Öcalan publicly stated that an independent Kurdish state was not a feasible objective. He also noted that territorial autonomy within Turkey through a federation would be an insufficient solution to the Kurdish question due to the dispersal of the Kurdish population throughout the country following forced relocation. Thus, territorial autonomy within Turkey for the southeastern provinces alone would not solve the dilemma of Kurdish political participation and cultural rights. Instead, he articulated a model of a democratic union that would maintain Turkish territorial integrity, but allow formal Kurdish political representation, drop all constraints on Kurdish language, and abandon military approaches to managing the Kurdish question.[40] The initial focus on democratization and a pluralist

35 Y. Sunca, "The Bifurcated Trajectory of Nation Formation in Kurdistan: Democratic Confederalism, Nationalism and the Crisis of Capitalist Modernity," *Nations and Nationalism*, 26(4) (2020), 979–93, at 981.

36 W. Enzinna, "A Dream of Secular Utopia in ISIS' Backyard," *New York Times* (November 27, 2015).

37 S. Kajjo, "Writings of Obscure American Leftist Drive Kurdish Forces in Syria," *Voice of America* (January 16, 2017).

38 D. White, "Murray Bookchin's New Life," *Jacobin* (July 2016).

39 M. Knapp, "Communal Democracy: The Social Contract and Confederalism in Rojava," *Comparative Islamic Studies*, 10(1) (2016), 87–109.

40 These ideas are laid out in his European Court of Human Rights defense: *AIHM Savunmalari: Sumer Rahip Devletinden Demokratik Cumhuriyete* (Diyarbakır, Turkey: Mezopotamya Yayinlari, 2001), portions of which appear in English in: A. Öcalan, *Prison Writings: The PKK and the Kurdish Question in the 21st Century* (London: Transmedia Publishing, 2011).

conception of citizenship was later accompanied by an emphasis on decentralization. By 2004, Öcalan's writings began to describe a model of delegative democracy with an emphasis on extending democratic processes and rule from the most local, grassroots level of village and city communes upward through delegates to city councils, municipalities, and ultimately a people's congress. These institutions would coexist with a far more limited central state that would retain authority over national security, foreign affairs, and some fiscal appropriations. As his thinking continued to evolve, proposals on democratization and decentralization merged into the framework of "democratic confederalism," a complex model combining self-rule within Turkey's borders with a broader democratic confederation uniting Kurdish communities across borders.[41]

Öcalan's writings and the detailed instructions that he conveyed to the Kurdish political movement through his lawyers during the last two decades have been deeply influential, in part because he remains a revered political leader and in part because his thinking resonates with a long tradition of left political organizing in Turkey's Kurdish community. This influence can be seen in the reorganization of the PKK), deemphasizing armed struggle in favor of democratization as the solution not only in Turkey but in all the states where Kurdish communities are present in the Middle East (with particular significance for Syria where the PKK is also heavily represented). The result within the PKK and among its supporters has been a reconceptualization of Kurdish national unity through the aspiration for a "Democratic Middle Eastern Union," enabling closer ties between Kurdish communities in Iraq, Iran, Turkey, and Syria without establishing a separate state.[42]

By 2003, the political movement of the Kurdish community in Turkey was renamed the Kurdistan People's Congress (or Kongra-Gel) in line with Öcalan's vision for internal Kurdish democratization. Later, the political structure was reformed again into the Union of Kurdistan Communities (KCK), which is now a vehicle for internal democratization that expresses pan-Kurdish commitments to a confederal union across borders. The KCK structure enables a double move: first, each Kurdish community seeks decentralized self-rule that allows them to realize cultural and political rights within the existing states in the Middle East. Equally, under the KCK, each of these self-governing communities is also related to a political and social organization that includes all of Kurdistan in a confederate nonstate democracy. In the words of one scholar, "as an entity [the KCK expresses the aspiration for a confederate union that] will exist and operate across the states that have a Kurdish population but crucially without attempting to change the established and internationally recognized borders."[43]

41 The fullest articulation of this theory is the five-volume set *The Democratic Civilizational Solution*.

42 Güneş, "Unpacking the Democratic Confederalism," 254–55.

43 Ibid., 258.

For Öcalan and his followers the evolution in his thinking has resulted in a transformation of both means and ends. The Kurdish national movement was born in the spirit of the decolonization movements of the 1960s in pursuit of secession through armed struggle. But both the goal of secession and the means of armed struggle have given way more recently to advocacy for forms of democracy and decentralization designed to realize rights through direct representation at the grassroots level with a model of local self-government that would coexist with the central government. In Öcalan's conception of democratic confederalism, legislative bodies allow each member of the municipality to vote on local matters while higher levels of government – comprising elected delegates from the various local governments – serve to coordinate between municipalities and implement their decisions. The central government attends to national security and foreign affairs, but broad authority on matters of social services, education, cultural institutions, environmental policy, and economic organization resides with the decentralized institutions of the democratic confederation.

In short, Öcalan has replaced the goal of secession from Turkey with the objective of a thoroughgoing transformation of the Turkish constitutional order (and the constitutional orders of the three neighboring states that host large Kurdish communities). In line with this vision, the HDP's political platform advocates the accommodation of Kurdish rights within a framework of democratic autonomy, proposes a decentralized political system and the empowering of local administrations to ensure citizens' direct participation in decision-making at the local, regional, and national levels, and views democratization and decentralization as means to address the demands of the Kurdish minority for autonomy.[44] While the Turkish state has limited appetite for decentralization, the formal shift of pro-Kurdish political parties' goals toward confederalism produced an opening for talks between Turkish officials and the Kurdish leadership beginning in 2009.

PEACE PROCESSES AND THE DECENTRALIZATION DEBATE

Peace Talks: 2009–2015

Turkey is a divided country along multiple different lines including ethnicity, religion, and sect. When the AKP was first elected in 2002, the party represented the

44 Earlier pro-Kurdish political parties went even further in aligning their political platforms with "democratic confederalism." In 2007, the DTP advocated for twenty to twenty-five self-governing regions in Turkey that would bring together two to three existing provinces into a self-governing region. Each would have a regional parliament and administration deciding on matters like education, culture, and social services, with policing and legal services authorities shared jointly by regional and central government, while foreign affairs and national security would remain under the exclusive authority of the central institutions. These proposals contributed to the closure of the party in 2009, because the idea of self-ruling regions was deemed a threat to territorial integrity by the TCC.

promise of overcoming the first two of these cleavages with a platform that sought to incorporate religiously observant constituencies (though still hostile to heterodox versions of Islam) and embraced ethnic pluralism in the name of religious brotherhood. The party won the support of some proportion of the Kurdish community and sought to expand that support by adopting liberal policies on cultural recognition. The possibility of a moderate Islamist party successfully initiating a reconciliation process with the Kurds was greeted with cautious optimism. By the second term of the AKP's rule, cultural identity issues were being openly debated in Turkey and the relaxation of restrictions on the use of the Kurdish language was widely welcomed.

The first significant step toward direct talks between Turkish state officials and Kurdish representatives was under the broader rubric of the "democratic opening" of 2009 (which began with secret negotiations between the two sides in Oslo in 2008). The talks were embedded in a set of broader initiatives to address democratic shortfalls of the constitutional order and improve human rights protections generally. Public debates in this period included a range of topics, from the outsize role of the military in civilian politics to the high electoral threshold that long excluded Kurdish political parties from being seated in parliament. In 2009, Öcalan prepared a 160-page roadmap for solving the Kurdish problem. The document itself was confiscated by Turkish authorities and never formally submitted to the government, but its basic contents are known.[45] Öcalan proposed the decentralization and democratization of the Turkish state along the lines of "democratic confederalism."[46] His proposal also echoed aspects of the European Charter of Local Self-Government (adopted in 1985 and ratified by Turkey), enabling Turkey to adopt a strategy of devolution consistent with EU guidelines and in line with EU accession, which was a formal goal of the government at the time.[47]

Recalling the Ottoman millet system as a kind of proto-federalism, Öcalan's model would have involved significant local autonomy at the provincial level either across the country or, at a minimum, in Kurdish-majority provinces, creating a federacy of sorts.[48] While the AKP was willing, in principle, to consider models of decentralization (particularly those framed in Ottoman terms), the details of Kurdish proposals exceeded the kinds of symbolic and largely cultural autonomy the state was willing to countenance. For instance, suggestions that Kurdish be recognized as a second official language, that local self-defense units be permitted at the provincial level, and that the Kurdish provinces adopt a socialist economic model involved greater

45 A. Öcalan, *The Road Map to Democratization of Turkey and Solution to the Kurdish Question* (Cologne: International Initiative "Freedom for Abdullah Öcalan – Peace in Kurdistan," 2011).

46 Ibid.

47 European Charter of Local Self-Government, Strasbourg (October 15, 1985).

48 Öcalan, *The Road Map*.

autonomy than the AKP was prepared to discuss. Moreover, the deeply centralized character of the Turkish state remained a significant obstacle for imagining a political future along Öcalan's lines in 2009.

The AKP formally described their democratic initiative as the "National Unity and Fraternity Project" (*Milli Birlik ve Kardeşlik Projesi*) and also engaged in outreach to the Armenian, Greek Orthodox, Roma, and Alevi communities as part of the same initiative.[49] Several roundtable meetings were conducted in 2010 with civil society representatives to discuss human rights and democratization measures. With respect to the "Kurdish opening" (*Kürt Açılımı*), these included: devoting one television and radio channel of the Turkish public broadcaster to twenty-four-hour Kurdish broadcasts, and allowing privately owned television and radio stations to broadcast in other languages than Turkish; allowing Kurdish languages to be taught at the university level; renaming residential areas in accordance with local preferences; a national mechanism to prevent torture; the establishment of an independent human rights institution; prohibiting the prosecution of children under terrorism laws; and the creation of a commission for complaints against Turkish security forces.[50] The exclusion of the electoral threshold and indeed electoral considerations from the measures being contemplated made clear the constraints of the "opening" envisioned by the AKP.

A PKK effort to repatriate thirty-four members from Iraq to Turkey as part of the Kurdish opening backfired as crowds welcoming returning members were perceived as a victory parade for the PKK. At the end of 2009, the TCC delivered a closure judgment against the pro-Kurdish Democratic Society Party (DTP) party whose members had been involved in the Kurdish opening discussions. Massive security operations were carried out throughout the southeastern provinces, with over 1,000 Kurdish political activists, many of whom were members of the KCK, arrested on allegations of supporting the PKK. Despite ongoing roundtables about the democratic initiative in 2010 and the passage of constitutional amendments that went some distance in limiting the military's jurisdiction over civilian politics, the specifically Kurdish elements of the project were suspended for much of the year. With parliamentary elections scheduled for June 2011, the AKP would risk no further outreach to the Kurdish community beyond electoral patronage strategies at the provincial level to garner votes.

The 2011 elections witnessed the AKP winning nearly 50 percent of the popular vote – its strongest performance – while the newly formed pro-Kurdish Peace and

49 A. Bölükbaşı, "'Demokratik Açılım' ile 'Milli Birlik ve Kardeşlik Projesi' Arasında AK Parti Dönemi Kimlik Politikaları," *Uluslararası Sosyal Araştırmalar Dergisi*, 9(47) (2016), 454–65 ("Identity Policies during the AKP Period: Between 'Democratic Opening' and 'National Unity and Fraternity' Project," *Journal of International Social Research*).

50 "Interior Minister Atalay Outlines Democratic Initiative," *Hürriyet Daily News* (November 13, 2009).

Democracy Party (BDP) ran a slate of independents who won thirty-six seats, an impressively large contingent of pro-Kurdish parliamentarians. In the aftermath of the elections, the AKP initiated a new round of talks – this time with senior PKK leaders meeting with Turkish officials from the National Intelligence Organization in Oslo. The most promising element of the talks was that the AKP was engaging directly with the PKK leadership.[51] However, as those talks were unfolding, actions by the state on the ground endangered any possibility of reconciliation with renewed crackdowns against Kurdish civil society activists resulting in hundreds of pretrial detentions.

Despite the mixed signals from the Turkish government – engaging in talks while also undertaking large-scale detentions – January 2013 saw the beginning of a publicly declared "peace process with the PKK." In March 2013, Öcalan published letters (sent to PKK leaders in Iraq, Iran, and Europe) calling for a ceasefire, the withdrawal of fighters from Turkey, the release of prisoners, disarmament and reintegration of PKK fighters into Turkish society, and constitutional reforms. Öcalan also referenced planned elements of a transitional justice process, such as a truth commission.[52] Eventually, six clear demands were set forth by Kurdish leaders in the context of the peace process: release of prisoners connected to the detention of KCK representatives; improvement of the conditions of Öcalan's detention; introduction of mother-tongue Kurdish education; reduction of the 10 percent electoral threshold; expanded civil liberties; and delisting of the PKK as a terrorist organization.[53] The AKP's proposed democratic package of rights in response to these demands was far more limited: allowing private schools for Kurdish-language education; restoring Kurdish village names; permitting the use of the Kurdish alphabet on official signage; freedom of political campaigning in Kurdish; and abolition of the daily pledge of allegiance to Turkish identity required of all students. This package fell far short of Kurdish demands but talks continued. By February 2015, Turkey's deputy prime minister and other government officials sat in a meeting alongside elected Kurdish deputies for the public reading of a letter from Öcalan calling on PKK fighters to disarm and laying out broad principles to guide the peace process.[54]

Öcalan's declaration centered on ten points that were pitched at a very high level of abstraction, calling for debates about the definition and content of democratic politics, democratic assurances of free citizenship, a new security structure,

51 The meetings were held in secret but were soon made public by opponents of direct talks with the PKK. Prosecutors, allegedly affiliated with the Gülen movement, initiated an investigation of the head of the National Intelligence Organization (MIT), Hakan Fidan, for imperiling national security by engaging with the PKK leadership. News of Fidan's interrogation made the talks with the PKK public in 2012.

52 A. J. Yackley, "Kurd Rebel Leader Orders Fighters to Halt Hostilities," *Reuters* (March 21, 2013).

53 Gunter, *The Kurds*, 53–54.

54 G. Dalay, "The Kurdish Peace Process: From Dialogue to Negotiation," *Al Jazeera Studies* (April 22, 2015).

embrace of a pluralist conception of identity, and a new constitution built on decentralization and socioeconomic justice.[55] In short, the proposed ten points sought to translate his political proposals for "democratic confederalism" into a concrete action plan in the context of peace talks.[56] To the negotiators seeking to iron out details of prisoner exchanges and modest language reforms, this came across as not so much a roadmap for peace as a manifesto for a progressive political movement. Still, what was contained in the declaration was a reflection of the evolution of the one-time Marxist revolutionary's thinking about devolution and democracy as the principal vehicles for the expression of the Kurdish community's self-determining aspirations.

The meeting between pro-Kurdish deputies and AKP officials in the spring of 2015 proved to be the high-water mark of the "peace process." As with earlier openings, impending elections brought with them instrumental vote-getting strategies inimical to a process of social reconciliation. Erdoğan, who was now president and bent on concentrating power in the executive rather than allow decentralization, made public his displeasure over the joint meeting between pro-Kurdish and AKP delegates.[57] Soon thereafter he would publicly grumble that pro-Kurdish parties were garnering the electoral dividends of the peace process. In April 2015, Öcalan was returned to solitary confinement and denied communication with his lawyers or other representatives, and talks were suspended. Following parliamentary elections in which the pro-Kurdish HDP party succeeded in surpassing the electoral threshold (rather than running candidates as independents) resulting in the AKP's loss of an outright majority in parliament for the first time in twelve years, the peace process came to a crashing end.[58] Erdoğan ended the ceasefire with the PKK using a pretext in July 2015 to initiate a brutal military campaign in the southeast provinces.[59] The remilitarization of the Kurdish question facilitated an electoral alliance

55 Ibid.

56 The proposal was the basis for the Dolmabahçe Agreement, which was quickly repudiated by the Erdoğan government in what became the prelude to the remilitarization of the Kurdish question. "Erdoğan's Denial of 'Dolmabahçe Agreement' Sparks Row," *Hurriyet Daily News* (July 20, 2015); see also C. Çiçek and V. Coşkun, *The Peace Process from Dolmabahçe to Present-Day* (Ankara: Peace Foundation, 2016).

57 "Turkey's President Erdogan Told to 'Stop Interfering' in Government Business," *Guardian* (March 22, 2015).

58 HDP leader Demirtaş had declared in advance of the election that his party would block Erdoğan's ambitions for amending the constitution to replace Turkey's parliamentary form of government with an executive presidency. By denying the AKP a majority of seats in parliament, the HDP did indeed constitute a formidable obstacle and Erdoğan responded by dropping his efforts to gain support among Kurdish constituencies, turning instead to a coalition with the ultranationalist MHP to stem electoral losses.

59 The government's onslaught was also motivated by two non-electoral factors. First, developments in northern Syria and the emergence of an autonomous Kurdish enclave with significant international military support (as part of the anti-ISIS campaign) were interpreted as a national security threat by the Turkish military. Fears that the Kurdish community on the Turkish side would become better armed and organized through participation in the Syrian Kurdish military campaign may have been

with the ultranationalist National Movement Party (MHP), which, in turn, allowed the AKP to reverse its electoral losses in snap elections in November 2015, laying waste to the peace process along the way.[60]

Lessons of the Peace Process

The lessons of the attempts at reconciliation between 2009 and 2015 are numerous. First, the talks reflected the influence of Öcalan's thinking on questions of nationalism, self-determination, and decentralization among Kurdish leaders. Key demands were framed in ways that resonated with Öcalan's writings about "democratic confederalism." A second important point is that Turkish society met the possibility of reconciliation with the Kurdish community with far greater enthusiasm than was evident in early periods. Third, the popularity of Selahattin Demirtaş, co-leader of the pro-Kurdish HDP party, across a broad spectrum of progressive voters, including ethnic Turks (as evidenced by his presidential run in 2014), suggests that ethnic divisions may become less salient for the opposition as resistance to the AKP is consolidated in an increasingly polarized Turkey. Finally, the HDP's ability to craft a political platform – one inclusive of Armenian and Alevi interests (and minority interests more broadly) – advocating for women's issues, children's and LGBT rights, environmental protection, socioeconomic justice, and civil rights has meant that pro-Kurdish political organizing has become the principal vehicle for the progressive movement in Turkey.

In this context, Öcalan's reconceptualization of self-determination around democratization and decentralization may have broader appeal to Turkish electorates tired of repression by the central state. The HDP candidate lists submitted for the June 2018 parliamentary elections included few ethnically Kurdish candidates in major metropolitan centers (Istanbul and Ankara) and the list as a whole featured Yezidis, Armenians, Greek Orthodox, prominent critical journalists, purged academics, and others alongside well-known Kurdish candidates in other provinces. HDP lists are also well known for their gender parity and now serve as a big tent for all manner of left civil society organizations in Turkish political life. As a result, the appeal of calls for decentralization and democratization, though grounded in pro-Kurdish politics, have the potential to draw on much wider constituencies in Turkey.

Evidence that the HDP has been deeply influenced by Öcalan's ideological transformation is not limited to the peace talks. In an essay in 2015, the party's leader, Demirtaş, wrote that the homeland of the Kurds is also claimed by many other

exacerbated when several major urban centers in the southeast issued declarations of "democratic autonomy" and organized "self-defense units." These declarations were inspired by Öcalan's arguments but were viewed by the state as a form of armed secessionism.

60 S. Ekim and K. Kirişci, "Turkey's 'Re-run' Elections, Explained," Brookings (October 30, 2015); "Turkey Election: Ruling AKP Regains Majority," *BBC* (November 2, 2015).

(overlapping) groups with equally legitimate claims on the territory (including Armenians, Yezidis, Assyrians, Alevis, and Turks, among others). He denounced the government's approach of pitting groups against each other and advocated, instead, a form of democratic confederalism in which parliament would be "supervised by democratic, local, civic assemblies" and powerful local government would provide small communities with democratic autonomy as well as hold national-level authorities accountable.[61] The KCK, which has representation from Kurdish groups affiliated with the PKK across Syria, Iraq, and Turkey, also reflects a version of confederalism, with urban assemblies that send delegates to provincial-regional assemblies, which in turn send delegates to the Peoples' Assemblies that then select representatives to the 300-person Peoples' Congress of Kurdistan.[62] In short, both the principal political party representing the Kurdish movement in Turkey and the primary pan-Kurdish political organization have currently adopted internal structures that reflect commitment to democratic confederalism.

While the 2009–15 period demonstrated that Öcalan's ideas have been mainstreamed in the Kurdish political movement, the same period witnessed little movement on the side of the Turkish state toward a more pluralist conception of citizenship or a more decentralized model of governance. Even at the height of reconciliation efforts during the "peace process" between the PKK and the AKP, there remained significant legal obstacles to expressions of Kurdish identity, and draconian anti-terror laws and criminal code provisions were routinely used to prosecute Kurdish politicians and civil society activists. Moreover, the option of militarizing the Kurdish question remained ever-present and the AKP repeatedly demonstrated its willingness to resort to repression when politically expedient. Today, not only Demirtaş as party leader but also twelve other MPs from the HDP have been stripped of their parliamentary immunity and manage the party from detention based on charges of supporting the PKK.[63] Dozens more HDP mayors and provincial officials have been removed from their positions and replaced by "trustees" appointed by the AKP since 2016.[64] Far from decentralization, the only level at

[61] S. Demirtaş, "The Middle East, the Kurdish Process in Turkey and Radical Democracy," *Kurdish Policy Quarterly*, 13 (2015), 27–33.

[62] A. Sandıklı, "The Structure and Activities of the KCK Terrorist Organization," Wise Men Center for Strategic Studies (October 11, 2011). (Wise Men Center for Strategic Studies is named for the group created by the Turkish government to present elements of the peace process to the Turkish public.)

[63] "Turkey: Crackdown on Kurdish Opposition," Human Rights Watch (March 20, 2017).

[64] The attempted coup was undertaken by elements of the Turkish military who sought to oust Erdoğan and the AKP. Once the coup attempt was put down, Erdoğan declared a state of emergency that continued for two years. Under emergency rule, Erdoğan was able to pass a package of constitutional amendments that transformed the republic's political institutions from a parliamentary to a presidential system, concentrating power in the executive. Since his reelection as president in 2018, in a vote held under state of emergency, Erdoğan wields unprecedented powers. Despite the end of the state of emergency, these powers include the ability to remove elected municipal and provincial officials and replace them with trustees selected from his own party. Following municipal elections

which local government is directly elected in Turkey is rapidly being transformed into a government of unelected trustees of the central state.

Despite the bleak outlook, the progress made between 2009 and 2015 in clarifying Kurdish political demands suggests that decentralization will be a crucial component of a resolution to the Turkish–Kurdish conflict in the long run. Moreover, public support for the Kurdish "peace process" – measured at over 80 percent by one poll in April 2013[65] – demonstrates the viability of models of shared citizenship when polarizing government tactics are suspended. Beyond that, Öcalan's vision of democratic confederalism offers progressive Turks a vehicle for correcting the democratic deficits of the Turkish political order – including excessive concentration of power in the executive – and advancing better governance and increased local accountability for all citizens. The possibility of a political alliance between ethnically Kurdish and Turkish citizens in support of improved governance through decentralization may be one of the most promising avenues to explore upon resumption of a peace process down the line. The 2019 municipal elections demonstrated the potential of such an alliance, with the Kurdish communities in Turkey's largest municipalities tacitly acting in coalition with the principal opposition Republic People's Party (CHP) and voting strategically to elect opposition candidates that would displace AKP mayors in Istanbul and Ankara.[66]

KURDISH DECENTRALIZATION IN COMPARATIVE CONTEXT

The Kurdish community in Turkey offers a fascinating example of a call for devolutionary federalism as an alternative to secessionism in the wake of violent conflict. In such cases, the literature raises important questions about how to tailor the particular pattern of decentralization to satisfy the desires of substate minorities without entrenching ethno-regional divisions or exacerbating secessionist demands. In line with the approach taken by John McGarry[67]

in spring 2019 – with pro-Kurdish parties seating over ninety mayors and other municipal officials in the southeastern provinces – Erdoğan resumed the replacement of elected officials with trustees. See, e.g., K. Fahim, "Turkey Suspends Three Mayors, Alleging Links to Kurdish Militants," *Washington Post* (August 19, 2019).

65 A. Albayrak, "Parsing Peace Polls," *Wall Street Journal* (April 19, 2013) (noting that 88.1 percent of ethnic Turks – and 97 percent of Kurds – favored the government's effort to resolve the Kurdish "problem" "peacefully, with non-military means and through negotiation" in a poll conducted by the independent Turkish research company, GENAR).

66 M. Ibrahimoğlu, "Kurdish Voters Look to Imamoğlu to Fulfil Broken Promises of AKP," *Ahval* (June 14, 2019); Fazıl Hüsnü Erdem has argued that the new presidential system in Turkey has made possible a form of coalition politics that might make formal coordination with pro-Kurdish parties more likely going forward. F. H. Erdem, "Changes in a New Era of Turkey's Politics," Democratic Progress Institute (July 2019).

67 J. McGarry and B. O'Leary, "Federation as a Method of Ethnic Conflict Regulation," in S. Noël (ed.), *From Power Sharing to Democracy: Post-conflict Institutions in Ethnically Divided Societies* (Montreal: McGill-Queens University Press, 2005), 263–96.

and Liam Anderson[68] in their work, the central question posed by the case of Turkish Kurdistan is whether federalism can serve as a method of ethnic conflict regulation.

The classic understanding of decentralization involves the transfer of responsibility and authority from the central government to the provincial or local level of government (or, in some instances, to both). There are traditionally thought to be three dimensions to such decentralization: political (transfer of authority), administrative (transfer of responsibility for public service delivery), and fiscal (assignment of revenues locally to manage responsibilities for certain services). Decentralization can vary in degree across these three dimensions and administrative and political decentralization need not be linked (e.g., local and provincial governments may remain accountable to the center politically, despite greater fiscal and administrative responsibilities). Federalism, in turn, is one form of decentralization in which the regional or provincial government is granted a particularly high level of political autonomy, creating effectively two levels of government, each of which enjoys a degree of autonomy in its separate sphere.[69]

When considered in light of the literature, Kurdish demands correspond to a form of devolutionary federalism designed to resolve secessionist pressures in a previously unitary state. Choudhry and Hume describe "post-conflict federalism" as an undertaking "not to make a new state but to reconstitute the existing one along federal lines in order to prevent it from coming apart."[70] In a gloss on this model, the Kurdish approach clearly defines the constituent units, too, in pluralist terms (whereas Choudhry and Hume remain agnostic as to their internal constitution), enabling multiple identities to be represented within each confederal entity.[71] Unfortunately, however, the Turkish state currently views Kurdish demands as an existential threat best addressed militarily rather than through a post-conflict political solution. Kurdish leaders are thus left to persuade their own population that a democratic confederal solution is possible while trying to convince the Turkish state that a military solution is infeasible.

68 L. Anderson, "Ethnofederalism and the Management of Ethnic Conflict: Assessing the Alternatives," *Journal of Federalism*, 46(1) (2016), 1–24.

69 See, e.g., W. Riker, *Federalism: Origin, Operation, Significance* (Boston: Little, Brown & Co., 1964); see also, Kr. M. Bakke, *Decentralization and Intrastate Struggles: Chechnya, Punjab and Quebec* (New York: Cambridge University Press, 2015).

70 S. Choudhry and N. Hume, "Federalism, Secession and Devolution: From Classical to Post-Conflict Federalism," in T. Ginsburg and R. Dixon (eds.), *Research Handbook on Comparative Constitutional Law* (Northampton, MA: Edward Elgar, 2011), at 23.

71 Öcalan's thinking might also be usefully situated in Liam Anderson's typology. L. D. Anderson, *Federal Solutions to Ethnic Problems* (London and New York: Routledge, 2013), 6–7. Anderson's definition of ethnoterritorial federation is one in which one or more territorially concentrated ethnic groups are accommodated with a subunit homeland, while the territories of the ethnic majority are also divided into subunits (as with Canada or India). This model might be compared to Öcalan's vision, which would reorganize the Turkish state in ways that split regions with an ethnic Turkish majority as well as majority Kurdish areas into multiple units.

Assessing Öcalan's theories through the lens of institutional design, the Kurdish project might best be described as one of symmetrical federalism in which the constituent political units (regions composed of two to three provinces) would be formally equal in their rights, powers, and duties. There would be several majority Kurdish regions within this scheme – though they would also have internal diversity, including Arab, Alevi, and other minorities – but also several majority ethnically Turkish regions with substantial Kurdish minorities (given the territorial dispersion of the Kurdish community). In this sense, federalism as proposed by Kurdish leaders in Turkey would have both ethnic and anti-ethnic dimensions, to borrow Anderson's terms.[72] Earlier framings of Kurdish demands were premised on asymmetric federalism with special autonomy rights for Kurdish provinces.[73] Öcalan's reconceptualization embraces a more homogenous or symmetrical model of federalism in part to account for the dispersal of the Kurdish population across the country and in part because he rejects privileging ethnic conceptions of citizenship.[74] Rather, Öcalan has developed a theory of the legitimate claims of a national community like the Kurds that is tied to a pluralist definition of citizenship, embracing communal representation of multiple identities through grassroots democratic participation and confederal associations among nonnationally defined territorial units.[75]

Öcalan's writings on the benefits of confederalism and devolution also echo the advantages typically cited in the literature on governance. These include improved service delivery through local governments, promotion of democratic citizenship through greater accountability, and broader citizen participation. Much of the literature suggests, however, that multiethnic federal states tend to

72 Anderson, *Federal Solutions to Ethnic Problems*, ch. 3.

73 Interestingly, while asymmetric federalism has traditionally been viewed as an unstable arrangement, recent scholarship suggests that there may be more potential to models of constitutional asymmetry (in which constituent units in a federal system have different characteristics). See, e.g., M. Sahadzic, "Constitutional Asymmetry as a Tool to Manage Diversity," Fifty Shades of Federalism (2018).

74 I thank Will Kymlicka for an enlightening exchange that clarified the relationship between Öcalan's repudiation of the nation-state and his continued commitment to the national rights of the Kurdish community. Those rights are to be realized in Öcalan's theory at two levels: first, through the systematic internal democratization of the Kurdish community itself through practices of local self-rule and, second, through representation of Kurdish interests at higher levels of government in a multinational confederation. This confederation, in turn, would adopt a non-national pluralist definition of citizenship accommodating all of the underlying national identities located within the territory. Öcalan conceives of a non-national state (states within the existing borders of the Middle East that do not privilege a particular nationality) as well as a non-state democracy (a democratic confederation among the Kurdish communities across the borders of the four Middle Eastern states that serves as a pan-state political union).

75 Öcalan also has important reflections on the need to represent other identity-based claims, including those of women and youth in particular that are important features of his theory – together with ecological stewardship and socialist economic organization – that lie beyond the scope of this chapter.

fail. Does the Kurdish model face the same pitfalls? As an initial observation, against the backdrop of nearly a century of episodic violence the choice is not necessarily between ethnoterritorial federalism and other stable political arrangements but rather between devolutionary alternatives and continued violence. Moreover, the fact that the Kurdish community is no longer located in one or even several subnational territories suggests that any division of the two communities at this stage would require extreme violence (and involve mass dislocation and ethnic cleansing). Against this backdrop, experimenting with new constitutional design arrangements that provide for devolutionary models of autonomy has much to recommend it.

Of course, the critical question is to understand why some federal arrangements have failed and others succeeded. The literature points to a number of explanations. One turns on the strength of regionally defined parties, which gravitate toward secessionist preferences over time.[76] In the Kurdish case, both the HDP and the smaller splinter pro-Kurdish parties do not primarily define themselves as regional parties (indeed, the HDP is the national platform and the DBP continues to coordinate with the national party to run candidates for local elections) and other national parties (including the AKP) attempt to cut across regional and ethnic divisions with religious or ideological platforms. The HDP has been careful to build an inclusive platform that appeals to many non-Kurdish communities across the country, advocating for women's issues, unions, environmentalism, and LGBT rights among others, thus providing a progressive, nonnationalist platform. Decentralization could cause parties to become more regionally defined over time, but the HDP represents a promising political configuration of nonregionalism at this point.

Another explanation in the literature for the success or failure of ethnofederal arrangements relates to the motivations of the territorially concentrated group.[77] Kurdish motivations are, of course, related to both ethnicity and the inequality between the Kurdish provinces and the rest of the country. Kurds have been subjected to institutional obstacles to the expression of their identity, targeted for persecution, and starved of resources, while the Turkish state has repeatedly leveraged ethnic tensions for political gain. So the community has both ideational and material motivations for mobilization. But there is also good evidence that the current strategy of the HDP has channeled collective Kurdish mobilization into coalition-building rather than secessionism. Kurdish strategic voting for CHP candidates in the 2019 local elections demonstrates the potential of this strategy, successfully displacing AKP rule from the country's principal cities. The dispersion of the Kurdish community across the country and into the main western urban

76 D. Brancati, *Peace by Design: Managing Intrastate Conflict through Decentralization* (Oxford: Oxford University Press, 2009).

77 Bakke, *Decentralization and Intrastate Struggles.*

centers has both enabled this strategy of coalitional organizing and undercut the degree to which interregional inequalities between the traditionally Kurdish southeastern provinces and the rest of the country are the central defining feature of the Kurdish politics.[78]

While there is nothing about the Kurdish model that can definitively rebut worries about the instability of ethnofederal arrangements, the pluralist commitments of Kurdish leaders and the geographic dispersion of the community suggests some potential for overcoming concerns that democratic confederalism would serve as a slippery slope toward secession.

CONCLUSION

The Kurdish community's conception of decentralization might best be characterized as a kind of "holding together" of ethnoterritorial federalism in the Turkish context, embracing a model of a democratic union between Turks and Kurds within Turkey and loose confederal ambitions across Turkey's borders with Iraqi and Syrian Kurdish communities. In the words of the HDP's representative to the USA, the "most widespread political program among [the Kurdish movement] today is based on secularism, women's rights, a vision of the state that does not exclude based on ethnicity or religion, but accommodates the region's rich diversity through decentralization."[79] But in the Kurdish case, the worry that holding together federalism simply lowers the costs of eventual secession is offset by both the geographical dispersion of the Kurdish community and the political commitments of its leadership.

Indeed, the impetus for secession is less likely to come from democratic confederalism than from the continued insistence on repressive assimilation by the Turkish state. Having once recognized that the Kurdish community's demands require political resolution, the Turkish government has now opted to remilitarize the Kurdish question, which may fracture internal Kurdish community support for a decentralized political arrangement. If the escalating repression of Kurdish political leaders does not crush their resolve to pursue a political resolution, however, the innovative proposals for decentralization and conflict resolution they have developed hold great promise. Indeed, Öcalan's vision of democratic confederalism may even prove appealing to a broader spectrum of Turkish citizens seeking an alternative to the overweening central state. In a post-Erdoğan scenario, support for decentralizing power in Turkey may prevail even if it does not result in full-blown democratic

78 Bakke argues that interaction effects between decentralization and interregional inequality may impact the peace-preserving potential of decentralization – ironically the Turkish state's earlier campaigns to displace Kurds from the southeast may cut against this concern in the Kurdish context.

79 G. Ozcan, "To Win in Syria, America Must Rethink Its Kurdish Policy," *National Interest* (September 8, 2019).

confederalism. Moreover, a loose confederal arrangement across Turkey's borders with Iraq and Syria need not be treated as a utopian fantasy. As recently as 2010, it was the Turkish government that encouraged an open border with Syria for trade purposes, with the collateral effect of enabling Kurdish communities on either side to develop closer economic and social ties. Similarly, the Turkish state has maintained fifteen years of mutually beneficial trade relations with the Kurdistan Region of Iraq, nurturing far closer ties with Erbil than Baghdad. Öcalan's political vision is particularly interesting for seeking to reconcile existing borders with a political model that acknowledges the transnational character of the Kurdish community and the need for cross-border representative institutions.[80]

Öcalan's "democratic confederalism" is a model for disaggregating nation and state in order to accommodate multiple national identities within existing territorial borders. The proposal also emphasizes grassroots democratization that actively involves the citizenry in participatory decision-making over the issues that most directly affect them. The features of Öcalan's model tie together responsive local government services and recognition of group rights – that is, governance and self-determination – as two facets of democratic decentralization. Ultimately, Öcalan believes that all of the states in the Middle East will have to democratize and decentralize for Kurdish unity to be nested within a broader democratic unity that preserves existing borders. While Öcalan's prolific writing provides no blueprint for how the region might move toward such greater democratization at a time of intense and destabilizing violence, the mere fact that a former leader of an armed secessionist insurgency has become an influential oracle of decentralization and democratization within his own community serves as a source of optimism for a region sorely in need of a new trajectory away from centralized authoritarian rule and ethnosectarian conflict.

[80] For instance, the Palestine Liberation Organization at one time constituted such a representative institution for the transnational Palestinian community, but this was explicitly in the context of a traditional self-determination movement. The KCK provides an alternative model that builds similarly representative transnational institutions without aspiring to statehood.

12

Control, Responsibility, and the Israeli-Palestinian Decentralization Debacle

Sari Bashi

This chapter examines governance within the framework of the Israeli occupation of the Palestinian territory – the Gaza Strip and the West Bank, including east Jerusalem. I explain how delegation of authority over service provision, civilian affairs, and the daily running of the territory devolved into a decentralization debacle. The result is that 4.5 million Palestinians are controlled by an authority that disavows responsibility for governance and are governed by authorities that lack the control needed to create decent living conditions.

The chapter will analyze how delegation of responsibility to local authorities, in the context of a belligerent military occupation, was perceived by some as part of a transition to national liberation. I will suggest that a central flaw in that process was the willingness to temporarily bend a cardinal principle of international humanitarian law (IHL), which governs situations of occupation: aligning responsibility with control. The transfer of responsibility from Israel to Palestinian authorities, without ceding the control needed to exercise that responsibility, created a crisis of accountability, in which both the Israeli and Palestinian authorities abdicate responsibility for Palestinians in Gaza and the West Bank.

I will also suggest that the delegation of responsibility to the Palestinian authorities, especially beyond what was supposed to be a five-year interim period, contributes to the perpetuation of Israel's occupation of the Palestinian territory. When Israel and the Palestine Liberation Organization (PLO) signed and began implementing the Oslo Accords in the 1990s, some believed in good faith that delegation of responsibility to the Palestinian Authority, a domestic governing body established by the PLO, would be part of a transition to end the occupation. More than twenty-five years later, it is clear that, far from hastening an end to the occupation, such delegation has made it cheaper and easier for Israel to maintain it. The Israeli military is freed from the burden and expense of administering most services to Palestinian residents, and while the two largest Palestinian factions still purport to work for liberation and resistance, they have shifted their energies from ending the occupation to running the daily lives of occupied persons. Under these circumstances, we should evaluate not just the quality of the governance that decentralization has created, but also whether attempts to improve that governance would be desirable or whether they would help perpetuate a status quo of foreign occupation.

Scholars of the Middle East rarely analyze the Oslo process and the relationship between the Israeli and Palestinian authorities through the lens of decentralization, perhaps reflecting the dominance of the partition or two-state framework as a lens for viewing Israel-Palestine. An alternative framework, suggested here, challenges whether passing authority over local service provision to Palestinian hands is actually a step toward partition and the creation or liberation of a Palestinian state. Instead, such delegation could be seen as the devolution of power from the central (Israeli) government exercising (de facto) sovereignty to the local (Palestinian) government whose de jure sovereignty comes no closer to being realized in fact by the responsibility for local affairs. This use of decentralization in the context of aspirations of state-building is not unique to Israel-Palestine, and analyzing it raises hard and as-yet-unanswered questions about decentralization under military occupation and, more broadly, what happens when responsibility is delegated without ceding the control necessary to actually succeed at service provision.

The focus of the chapter is on governance – service delivery and accountability to Palestinian residents of the occupied Palestinian territory (OPT), who enjoy a special status as "protected persons" under the international rules on belligerent occupation. So in evaluating the effects of decentralization, I focus on the service provision and daily life that the delegation of power to was supposed to address: the IHL responsibility of the occupying power to restore normal life in the territory, meaning the proper functioning of civilian institutions such as infrastructure, economy, education, health services, and more.

INTERNATIONAL HUMANITARIAN LAW

The international law of belligerent occupation contains an inherent tension between the violence that an occupying power uses to obtain control over a territory and the duty of care that it owes to the foreign civilians who find themselves under its control. The law of occupation takes the fact of control by a foreign power as given and seeks to regulate the exercise of that control, increasingly in order to protect residents of the occupied territory. Article 43 of the Hague Regulations[1] requires an occupying power to restore, as much as possible, public order or normal civilian life, and at the very least basic humanitarian services, and the Fourth Geneva Convention enumerates humanitarian obligations that the occupier owes.[2]

[1] Hague Regulations concerning the Laws and Customs of War on Land (entered into force October 1, 1907), Art. 43.

[2] Fourth Geneva Convention Relative to the Protection of Civilian Persons in Time of War (adopted August 12, 1949, entered into force October 12, 1950). See also Protocol Additional to the Geneva

The occupying power may delegate such responsibilities to local authorities, but such delegation does not exempt it from overall responsibility for service provision.[3] Because occupation is a temporary state of affairs and does not confer lawful sovereignty upon the occupier, and because of the right of the occupied people to self-determination,[4] delegating authority to local actors could be a step toward the occupying power fulfilling its obligation to prepare the territory for self-rule at the conclusion of the occupation.

Transferring an occupying power's civilian population into the occupied territory is a war crime under the Rome Statute establishing the International Criminal Court; establishing civilian settlements in the occupied territory is strictly forbidden.[5] Doing so raises the specter of annexation and/or colonialism, as it negates the temporary nature of the occupation and undermines the protections that the local population enjoys.

SERVICE PROVISION IN THE OPT

For the first twenty-five years of the Israeli occupation of the OPT, Israel assumed direct responsibility for the welfare of Palestinian civilians through parallel military governments established in Gaza and the West Bank and eventually a "Civil Administration" run by the military. Some authority was delegated to local officials, especially in the first decade, as part of a policy of "government but not administration," predicated on keeping local authorities intact. Local officials strained that policy by resisting Israeli rule.[6] The international community, especially the United Nations Refugee Works Agency, filled in gaps by providing funding, services, and infrastructure.[7]

Nominally, the Israeli authorities accepted the responsibility of the occupying power to provide services and ensure the proper functioning of the economy, infrastructure, and governmental services, including as part of a strategy of "enlightened occupation," in which Israel sought to improve the living conditions of Palestinians in the West Bank and Gaza, to discourage them from resisting the occupation.[8] However, the indefinite nature of the occupation and the colonial

Conventions of August 12, 1949, and relating to the Protection of Victims of International Armed Conflicts (Protocol I) (adopted June 8, 1977, entered into force December 7, 1978).

3 Fourth Geneva Convention, Art. 47. See also arts. 7, 8, 29.

4 International Covenant on Civil and Political Rights (adopted December 16, 1966, entered into force March 23, 1976), art 1.

5 Fourth Geneva Convention, Art. 49; Rome Statute of the International Criminal (adopted July 17, 1998, entered into force July 1, 2002), Art. 8(2)(b)(viii).

6 I. Feldman, *Governing Gaza: Bureaucracy, Authority and the Work of Rule, 1917–1967* (Durham, NC: Duke University Press, 2008), 226–27.

7 S. Gazit, *Trapped Fools: Thirty Years of Israeli Policy in the Territories* (London: Frank Cass, 2003), 36.

8 Ibid., 17.

project of establishing civilian, Israeli-only settlements in the territory undermined the integrity of the government services and economic planning provided by the Israeli authorities.[9] Palestinian laborers were encouraged to work in Israel and Israeli settlements, employment that provided an influx of cash, but there was little investment in Palestinian industries.[10] The Israeli military seized resources – including land, water, and rocks – and allocated them to Jewish settlers unlawfully transferred to the West Bank and Gaza. The occupation de-developed the Palestinian economy[11] and created two systems of governance – civilian government for Israeli settlers, now numbering more than a half million people, and military government for Palestinians.

At various points, the Israeli authorities sought to stem resistance to the occupation by offering to delegate some competences to local authorities, often as part of an attempt to sideline the PLO, whose leadership was mostly outside the occupied territory.[12] Indeed, since the 1970s, in US-brokered peace negotiations, successive Israeli prime ministers offered local autonomy – increased control over local governance – as an alternative to self-rule and sovereignty, an offer which was not accepted.[13]

In 1987, the First Intifada, the uprising against the occupation, broke out. It began as a popular uprising, famously depicted as young Palestinian demonstrators hurling stones at Israeli troops, who violently cracked down on them. However, participants in the uprising also engaged in economic resistance, trying to disrupt dependence on Israeli products and workplaces as a way of disengaging Palestinians from the Israeli economy. Palestinian local committees organized strikes, boycotted Israeli products, and set up cooperatives and mutual assistance groups to grow food and create local alternatives to services provided by Israel.[14] Levels of trust were high among and within the so-called popular committees: grassroots activists who operated under the framework of a unified leadership but with autonomy at the local

9 L. Farsakh, "The Political Economy of Israeli Occupation: What is Colonial about It?" *Electronic Journal of Middle Eastern Studies*, 8 (2008), at 5.

10 S. Gazit, "The Carrot and the Stick," *The Palestinian Yearbook of International Law Online*, 9(1) (1996), 459–62; Gazit, *Trapped Fools*, 122.

11 S. Roy, *The Gaza Strip: The Political Economy of De-development* (Washington, DC: Institute for Palestine Studies, 1995). The following comment by then Defense Minister Yitzhak Rabin, reported in the *Jerusalem Post* on February 15, 1985, is instructive: "[T]here will be no development in the occupied territories initiated by the Israeli Government, and no permits will be given for expanding agriculture or industry, which may compete with the State of Israel." See M. K. Shadid, "Israeli Policy towards Economic Development in the West Bank and Gaza," in G. Abed (ed.), *The Palestinian Economy: Studies in Development under Prolonged Occupation* (London: Routledge, 1988), 121–38, at 134.

12 A. Bregman, *Cursed Victory: A History of Israel and the Occupied Territories* (London: Allen Lane, 2014), 109.

13 Ibid., 108–9, 162; See also Y. Sayigh, *Armed Struggle and the Search for State: The Palestinian National Movement 1949–1993* (Oxford: Clarendon Press, 1997), 643.

14 See Sayigh, *Armed Struggle and the Search for State*, 615, 619.

level. The PLO, however, quickly co-opted the grassroots efforts, asserting control over the unified leadership structure from its base in Tunis.[15]

International pressure and the inability of the Israeli military to quell the uprising pushed Israel to negotiate with the Palestinian leadership. In 1993, Israel and the PLO signed the Oslo Accords, ushering in an era of provisional transfer of authority to the newly created Palestinian Authority (PA). In essence, the Oslo Accords created the autonomy that Israel had offered in previous peace initiatives but this time as a transitional measure, although the end game – called the "final status" – was not specified. Israeli troops withdrew to the perimeter of Palestinian cities and eventually transferred civilian control over 40 percent of the West Bank and most of the Gaza Strip to the PA. The Israeli military maintained overall control over the territory, including exclusive security control over external borders, 82 percent of the West Bank, and parts of Gaza, and Israeli troops continued to conduct periodic incursions into the cities from which they had withdrawn.

Under the Oslo Accords, the PA assumed responsibility for services such as health, education, welfare, infrastructure, and other civilian affairs, setting up a special ministry for coordinating with Israeli authorities, especially for movement of people and goods. Israel continued to control borders, the population registry, and the majority of the land and resources, limiting the ability of Palestinian ministries to plan and execute. Palestinian local authorities were given a limited amount of power, expanded or contracted at will by the Israeli authorities. Economic arrangements maintained Israeli control over the customs regime and required newly created Palestinian public authorities to purchase goods such as water, electricity and fuel.[16] Good governance under those circumstances would have been difficult for the most efficient, most virtuous of leaders, and PLO leaders returning from exile displayed little efficiency or virtue in governance. Monopolies sprouted, PLO leaders amassed wealth, and (credible) allegations of corruption helped the Israeli government undermine the legitimacy of the PA, even as Israel depended on it to provide services to the civilian population – services which, under IHL, remained the responsibility of the occupying power.[17]

A critical point in the transition from the intifada to quasi-Palestinian autonomy was the shift from grassroots leadership, under the umbrella of the PLO leadership in Tunisia, to direct rule by newly returned PLO exiles. The high levels of trust and solidarity, characteristic of the early stages of the intifada, eroded. The returning exiles had negotiated the Oslo Accords in secret, against the will of many local leaders of the intifada, who had hoped for more concessions in exchange for ending the

15 Ibid., 632, 636–37.

16 The Israeli-Palestinian Interim Agreement on the West Bank and the Gaza Strip, Annex V Protocol on Economic Relations (Israel-PLO) (adopted September 25, 1995).

17 See, e.g., N. Parsons, *The Politics of the Palestinian Authority: From Oslo to al-Aqsa* (New York: Routledge, 2005), 103–4.

uprising.[18] Declining economic conditions in the West Bank and Gaza – in large part due to Israeli crackdowns on the intifada and subsequent restrictions on the movement of people and goods – increased the financial dependence of Palestinian residents on the newly created PA, which received an influx of funding from donor countries eager to support the peace process. The PA also offered public sector jobs to a growing number of unemployed people.[19]

The arrangement for partial Palestinian autonomy was supposed to last from 1994 to 1999 pending the resolution of so-called "final status" issues, which were to be negotiated separately.[20] Yet the PA continued to play the role outlined by the Oslo Accords even after the expiration of the interim period and the outbreak of the Second Intifada in 2000. Two decades later, it continues to accept responsibility for civilian affairs, despite having made no progress in extending its control over the territory in the West Bank and having achieved only a pyrrhic victory in gaining more control in the Gaza Strip.

Control without Responsibility: Israel

With the transfer of some competencies to the PA in the 1990s, the Israeli authorities took the position that they were no longer responsible for civilian life in the West Bank and Gaza. They acknowledged the continued state of belligerent occupation[21] but drew a distinction between control over land and responsibility for the people living in that land. Israel claimed that responsibility for civilian affairs had passed to the PA, and all claims by individuals should be directed to the PA.[22] This was the Israeli response even when addressing decisions within Israel's sole discretion, for example whether to allow Palestinian patients or students to enter Israel for purposes of receiving health services or accessing higher education.

The contrast between Israel claiming control but abdicating responsibility became especially stark during the early phase of the coronavirus pandemic in March 2020. Newly elected Israeli public officials were finalizing a plan to formally annex parts of the West Bank, claiming the land belonged to the Jewish people.[23]

[18] Sayigh, *Armed Struggle and the Search for State*, 658.

[19] Parsons, *The Politics of the Palestinian Authority*, 131.

[20] Declaration of Principles on Interim Self-Government Arrangements (Israel-PLO) (adopted September 13, 1993), art I.

[21] While many Israeli politicians call some or all of the OPT "disputed" territory or territory belonging to the Jewish people, the government's legal position before domestic courts was, at least until 2005, that the West Bank and Gaza, except for east Jerusalem, are "territories held belligerently" and that the laws of occupation apply. See for example HCJ 7015/02 *Ajuri* v. *IDF Commander in the West Bank*, 56(6) PD 352 (2002), para. 13.

[22] See, e.g., State's Response, October 17, 2006 in H.C.J. 8242/06 *Salameh* v. *IDF Commander in the West Bank* (Supreme Court of Israel) (unpublished, decided May 25, 2009), para. 20, www.gisha.org/UserFiles/File/LegalDocuments/SawsanSalame/StateResponse18_10_2006.pdf.

[23] C. Levinson and J. Lis, "Netanyahu, Gantz Agree on West Bank Annexation Proposal as Unity Deal Nears," *Haaretz* (April 6, 2020).

Yet Israeli officials informed Western diplomats that it was the responsibility of the Palestinian authorities "to manage the virus in their territories."[24]

In 2005, the Israeli government declared it recognized even less accountability for Gaza, after it implemented the "disengagement" plan from the Gaza Strip. Israel withdrew its troops to the perimeter of Gaza, with sporadic reentrances and remote control over an area of land inside Gaza, near the border, where access is prohibited.[25] Israel maintained control over the territorial waters and airspace of Gaza, the tax system, and the population registry, including the question of who is a resident of Gaza and therefore allowed to enter and leave.[26] Incursions into Gaza – including large-scale invasions in 2006, 2008–09, 2012, and 2014, and also frequent incursions on a much smaller scale[27] – continue to the present time.

Once the redeployment around Gaza was complete, the Israeli authorities claimed that the Israeli occupation of Gaza had ended, and that the laws of belligerent occupation no longer applied to Israel's relationship to residents of Gaza, now numbering two million people. This was the case, even when claims were made relating to matters under Israeli control, such as the transfer of goods into and out of Gaza, movement of people between Gaza and the West Bank or Gaza and the outside world, or access to agricultural land and fishing waters controlled by the Israeli military.

Between 2007 and 2010, the Israeli government even pursued a policy of deliberately reducing the standard of living in Gaza as part of what it called "economic warfare," blocking the passage of people and goods into and out of the Gaza Strip and restricting the quantity and type of food allowed to enter. When challenged about the humanitarian effects of its policy, the Israeli government argued that its responsibility was limited to allowing the quantities of fuel, food, and other goods into Gaza that would meet the humanitarian needs of Gaza residents, as calculated using mathematical formulas that took into account the number, age, and gender of Palestinians in Gaza.[28] In defending its policy before the Israeli Supreme Court, the Israeli government said it had determined the kinds and quantities of food necessary to meet the humanitarian needs of Palestinians in

24 Israeli Ministry of Foreign Affairs, "Briefing for Foreign Ambassadors on Coronavirus Management and Cooperation with the Palestinians" (March 31, 2020).

25 United Nations Office for the Coordination of Humanitarian Affairs-Occupied Palestinian Territory, "The Humanitarian Impact of Restrictions on Access to Land Near the Perimeter Fence in the Gaza Strip" (August 3, 2018). Israel has provided contradictory information about what the zone includes, but the area where access is banned or creates physical risks has comprised up to 17 percent of the Gaza Strip, depending on the time period in question.

26 *Gisha*, "Disengaged Occupiers: The Legal Status of Gaza" (January 2007).

27 In 2018, for example, Israeli soldiers made incursions into Gaza an average of 1.8 times per week. United Nations Office for the Coordination of Humanitarian Affairs-Occupied Palestinian Territory, "Protection of Civilians Report" (January 1–14, 2019).

28 *Gisha*, "A Guide to the Gaza Closure: In Israel's Own Words" (September 2011).

Gaza, but that "supplying Gaza with food items which are not of a humanitarian nature or products in quantities exceeding those necessary for humanitarian needs is not made possible."[29]

In other words, the delegation of responsibility for some aspects of governance led Israel not only to abdicate responsibility for governance but also to take steps to disrupt service supply inside Gaza, with the explanation that disrupting the economy and infrastructure in Gaza was a means of waging warfare against Hamas. If people in Gaza suffered as a result, the Israeli government said, it was the fault of Hamas.

The current Israeli policy toward civilian life in Gaza is ambivalent. The Israeli authorities have removed some restrictions on economic development as a "humanitarian" gesture but continue to impose other restrictions that de-develop the Palestinian economy. Transfer of goods outside Gaza, for example, is limited by quotas and categories of goods, such that outgoing goods in 2019 were less than a quarter of the level recorded in the first half of 2007.[30] Many inputs, notably construction materials, are restricted as "dual use" goods.[31] While there are warnings within Israel's security establishment that the economic and humanitarian collapse inside Gaza endangers Israeli security, the proposed solution is for greater international investment in Gaza,[32] reflecting the position that Gaza is someone else's responsibility. At various points in time, the Israeli government continued to pursue an expressly punitive policy, closing commercial and passenger crossings to civilian use in response to rocket fire by armed groups or demonstrators hurling rocks and flying incendiary kites toward Israel and conditioning an improvement in conditions in Gaza on regime change or on Hamas preventing attacks by armed groups.[33]

Israeli policy toward service provision by the PA is ambivalent as well. Israel periodically subverts service provision to exact concessions or to punish political moves by the PA to challenge Israeli control, undermining but not eliminating the PA's ability to provide services. For example, Israel withheld tax monies it collects on behalf of the PA – disrupting salary payments and government services – in response to the victory of the Hamas party in 2006 parliamentary elections,[34] after the Fatah-run PA

[29] HCJ 4250/08 *Afaneh Brothers LTD. v. Ministry of Agriculture*, State Response, September 18, 2008, paras. 12–13 (Hebrew); *Gisha*, "Reader: Food Consumption in the Gaza Strip – Red Lines" (October 2012).

[30] *Gisha*, "Fact Sheet: Kerem Shalom Crossing" (March 2020).

[31] *Gisha*, "Info Sheet: Dark-Gray Lists" (January 21, 2015).

[32] For example, the former Israeli coordinator for government activities in the territories called for a "Marshall Plan" for Gaza: Y. Mordechai, M. Milstein, and Y. Amitai, "The Next Gaza: The Gaza Strip Between a Dead End and a Glimmer of Hope," *Strategic Assessment*, 20(3) (2017), 9–19. See also Y. Kubovich, "Israeli Security Officials Oppose Defense Chief's Decision to Cut Gaza Fuel Transfers," *Haaretz* (October 14, 2018).

[33] See for example *Gisha*, "Erez Crossing Still Closed" (August 26, 2018); *Gisha*, "Israel Is Still Blocking Virtually all Movement to and from Gaza Via the Crossings It Controls," (October 18, 2018); M. Bachner, "Bennett, Liberman, Condition Humanitarian Steps on Hamas Freeing Israelis," *Times of Israel* (June 10, 2018).

[34] Gisha, *Disengaged Occupiers*, 56.

signed a reconciliation agreement with its rival faction, Hamas, and in response to a request by the Palestinian leadership to join the International Criminal Court. It has also withheld tax moneys in response to the United Nations recognizing Palestine as a nonmember state and UNESCO accepting it as a member[35] and to protest the PA paying compensation to the families of Palestinians injured, killed, or imprisoned by Israel in the context of political violence.[36] In 2014, the Israeli military refused to grant Palestinians in Gaza entry permits into Israel for purposes of medical treatment, because the referral, submitted by the Palestinian Health Ministry, was written on the letterhead of the "State of Palestine" rather than the PA.[37] In 2002, when Israel invaded West Bank cities during the Second Intifada (uprising), it ransacked government ministries, taking payroll information and school records in what a *New York Times* report called "a systematic effort by the Israeli Army to strip institutions of the PA of as much data as possible."[38] These are just a few examples of actions that the Israeli authorities have taken against the Palestinian authorities that infringe on their ability to provide civilian services.

Responsibility without Control: The PA

The PA is the mirror image of Israel: responsibility without (sufficient) control. The PA collects small amounts of direct taxes and fees but receives half its operating budget from value-added and import taxes that Israel imposes and collects on its behalf, and the remainder from foreign donors. Although the PA is tasked with providing services and fulfilling governmental functions, its police force is barred from operating in 82 percent of the West Bank. It lacks planning, licensing, and zoning control over 60 percent of the West Bank. It does not control movement of people and goods into and out of the Palestinian territory or within its different parts. Access to natural resources such as water, rock, fishing waters, and agricultural lands remains highly restricted by Israel.[39]

The PA is responsible for economic development but cannot end restrictions on the movement of people and goods that choke the economy. It cannot grant entry to foreign investors, provide assurances against impediments to their projects, or even prevent the physical destruction of those projects by Israel. It cannot stop the Israeli authorities from demolishing homes and shutting down businesses.

35 "Israel Freezes Palestinian Tax Funds," *Al Jazeera* (January 4, 2015).

36 Law Freezing Funds Paid by the Palestinian Authority Related to Terrorism from the Funds Transferred to It by the Israeli Government (Israel) 5778-2018, S.H. 2730, at 732 (July 8, 2018).

37 J. Rudoren and F. Akram, "Even a Stationery Logo Pits Palestinians against Israel," *New York Times* (February 12, 2014).

38 S. Schmemman, "Palestinians Say Israeli Aim Was to Destroy Framework, from Archives to Hard Drives," *New York Times* (April 16, 2002).

39 World Bank, Report No. AUS2922, "West Bank and Gaza, Area C and the Future of the Palestinian Economy" (October 2, 2013).

The Palestinian leadership accepted a dual role – governing the territory while simultaneously conducting a struggle for national liberation. Initiatives to achieve one goal impeded the success of the other and forced zero-sum trade-offs. When Palestinian militants initiated combat activities against Israeli security forces, Israel shut down travel and closed the crossings needed to transfer goods for sale. When Palestinian leaders were asked to forward a report alleging war crimes in Gaza by Israeli forces to the UN General Assembly, Israeli and American officials successfully deterred them from doing so.[40] At the time, the PA was awaiting Israeli approval for a number of initiatives that the Palestinian private sector badly needed, including approval for the frequency needed to have 3G cellular phone technology and infrastructure for the planned middle-class city of Rawabi in the West Bank. The United States Congress, acting on behalf of Israel, passed legislation authorizing cutting funds to the PA if, against the wishes of Israel, the Palestinian leadership obtained full membership at the United Nations or succeeded in initiating an International Criminal Court investigation against Israeli suspects, among other things.[41]

In August 2009, the Palestinian leadership launched a campaign for recognition of Palestine as a state.[42] It culminated in the November 29, 2012 United Nations General Assembly resolution[43] upgrading Palestine's status to nonmember observer state and its recognition by nearly 200 countries. The PA, especially under the leadership of Prime Minister Salam Fayyad (2007–13), engaged in an economic reform and development program aimed in part at persuading donor countries of its readiness for statehood.

Some have argued that the program ultimately weakened resistance to the occupation. For example, rather than engage in economic boycotts, a tool that had been used by Palestinians during the First Intifada, the PA invested in economic development projects that could succeed despite Israeli restrictions on licensing, construction, freedom of movement, and access to land. Designed to persuade donors of Palestine's readiness for statehood, the initiative advanced a model of economic development that could succeed in a state of perpetual occupation – perhaps at the expense of resisting or challenging Israeli displacement of Palestinian sovereignty.[44] The result has been what some have called "fragnation" – an increasingly fragmented Palestine, suffering from economic and political stagnation and firmly entrenched in an indefinite occupation.[45]

40 J. Malsin, "Whither Goldstone? Did the PA Kill the UN's Gaza Report?" *Foreign Policy* (October 27, 2010).

41 Consolidated and Further Continuing Appropriations Act, 2015, 83 HR (US), sec. 7041(i)(2)(A)(i), 510.

42 Salam Fayyad, Palestine National Authority, "Ending the Occupation, Establishing the State, Program of the Thirteenth Government" (August 2009).

43 UNGA Resolution 67/19 (2012).

44 I. Shikaki and J. Springer, "Building a Failed State: Palestine's Economy and Governance Delinked," Al Shabaka (2015).

45 O. Dajani and H. Husseini, "The Emerging Reality in Palestine: Entrenched Occupation and 'Fragnation'," NOREF (October 2014).

Partial Control, Ambivalent Responsibility: Hamas

In 2006, the Palestinian faction Hamas assumed control of most organs of the Palestinian government after winning parliamentary elections held throughout the Gaza and the West Bank, including east Jerusalem. A series of uneasy power-sharing arrangements between Hamas and its rival faction, Fatah, ended in bloody fighting in 2007 that left Hamas governing Gaza and Fatah governing the West Bank, the latter under the auspices of the PA. Unlike the Fatah-controlled PA, Hamas did not see itself as bound by agreements with Israel and did not directly coordinate with Israel, but it allowed the PA to continue to do so to facilitate movement of people and goods into and out of Gaza, including for maintaining infrastructure services such as electricity and water. Hamas retained its identity as a movement resisting the Israeli occupation but also became consumed by daily governance activities. It remained heavily dependent on its rival faction, the Fatah movement controlled by Mahmoud Abbas, for purchase of basic services such as electricity, water, and fuel from Israel, coordination with the Israeli authorities for the movement of people and goods, purchase of medical supplies, and more.

Hamas, too, was forced to make trade-offs between its aspirations to function as a resistance movement and its practical desire to avoid retaliation that would worsen Gaza's economic and humanitarian situation. Hamas leaders struggled to govern Gaza under the crippling restrictions of Israel's "economic warfare." One year into their rule, they negotiated a reduction in military operations from June to November 2008 in exchange for a 25 percent increase in the volume of goods entering Gaza via the crossings with Israel and some otherwise banned construction materials.[46] As Israel conditioned movement of people and goods on Hamas preventing attacks from armed groups in Gaza on Israel – as it had done to the PA when the latter controlled the interior of Gaza – Hamas began indirectly negotiating the ability to provide better services in exchange for more strictly policing its border with Israel. Like the PA, Hamas agreed to quell acts of resistance in exchange for the flow of people, goods, and funding it needed to govern. Indeed, after the 2010 formal repudiation of an overtly punitive policy against Gaza, the Israeli military began to argue against Israeli government decisions that undermined service provision in Gaza, arguing that better services would encourage the Hamas regime to suppress anti-Israeli violence.[47]

Case Study: Electricity in Gaza

The electricity shortage in Gaza is an example of the effects of decentralization on service provision. When Israel captured Gaza in 1967, 5,000 households in

[46] *Gisha*, "Gaza Closure Defined: Collective Punishment" (December 2008), 3.

[47] See, e.g., Y. Kubovich and J. Khoury, "The Security Establishment Criticizes the Call to Freeze Transfer of Qatari Money to the Strip," *Haaretz* (January 8, 2019).

Gaza were connected to a rudimentary electricity grid. In December 1969, Israel began connecting Gaza to its own electricity grid. While providing electricity was part of Israel's obligations as the occupying power to develop the infrastructure, the decision to do so by connecting Gaza to the Israeli grid reflected the colonial aspect of Israel's occupation. The decision increased Palestinian dependence on Israel and linked Israeli settlements in Gaza to the grid, an indicator of the indefinite nature of the occupation. Israel agreed to allow the PA to build a power plant in Gaza only in the 1990s, and it began operating in 2002, providing less than half of Gaza's electricity needs. Israel continued to supply the majority of Gaza's electricity, but now the PA established the Gaza Electricity Distribution Company and purchased electricity from the quasi-public Israel Electric Company.[48] The Gaza power plant used industrial diesel purchased from an Israeli petrol company contracted by the Israeli government. Israel continued to control the commercial crossings and the supply of fuel via a transfer point on the Gaza–Israel border. So dependence on Israel for electricity continued, but now in the form of commercial contracts.

The transfer of responsibility for electricity provision in Gaza from Israeli to Palestinian hands – without changing the nature of control over the electricity infrastructure – facilitated abdication of responsibility for electricity provision, first by Israel and then by Fatah and Hamas.

In June 2006, following the capture of an Israeli soldier by members of Hamas and other Palestinian armed groups in Gaza, Israel bombed Gaza's power plant, plunging the Strip into darkness. The damage was repaired gradually, and by December 2006 the plant was back to a production capacity of 80 megawatts, below its maximum production capacity but similar to the amount generated prior to the bombing.[49] However, in October 2007 Israel began limiting the amount of industrial diesel it allowed to be transferred to Gaza, thus limiting the production capacity of the plant.

The justification for restricting the fuel and electricity supply was explicitly punitive, as part of its "economic warfare" against the Hamas regime in Gaza.[50] The Israeli government made detailed calculations of how much fuel and electricity were required, it said, for humanitarian services such as hospitals, public transportation, and sewage treatment, claiming the right to deliberately reduce supplies so that no "extra" electricity or fuel would be available for the economy in Gaza or for use by the Hamas regime. Should shortages arise despite these calculated quantities being permitted to enter, the Israeli government argued, that was the responsibility of the Hamas government:

48 *Gisha*, "Electricity Shortage in Gaza: Who Turned Out the Lights?" (May 2010).

49 Ibid., 3–4.

50 HCJ 9132/07 *AlBassiouni* v. *Prime Minister*, State Response, November 2, 2007.

> "Prioritization" in the distribution of fuel within the Gaza Strip is not within Israel's control. If the terrorist organization controlling the Strip chooses to distribute the fuel and diesel transferred to the Strip by putting a priority on uses such as launching Qassam [rockets] against Israel, transporting launching vehicles and other such things, over humanitarian uses, then Israel has no control over that.[51]

The results were predictable: Gaza's electricity shortage intensified dramatically, disrupting the functioning of hospitals, sewage treatment plants, water distribution, factories, households, and other institutions that, after Israel connected Gaza to a centralized grid, are dependent on electricity.[52]

In 2010, Israel canceled the restrictions on the entrance of industrial diesel to Gaza and said it was canceling its policy of economic warfare. By that time, Hamas had begun bringing diesel from Egypt through a system of underground tunnels underneath the Gaza–Egypt border. The electricity crisis, however, got worse as the years went by. First, there was little investment in the badly degraded electricity infrastructure, which was inadequate for Gaza's rapidly growing population. Second, Israeli bombing, especially during the 2008–09, 2012, and 2014 wars, further damaged the electricity grid and power plant. Third, Israeli restrictions on the movement of people and goods into and out of Gaza made it difficult to obtain spare parts, enhance local expertise, or bring in foreign experts and, perhaps most importantly, conduct the kind of economic activity needed for people to have money to pay electricity bills. Fourth, as the restrictions on the movement of people and goods deepened, financial disputes between the Fatah-controlled PA and the Hamas-controlled de facto government in Gaza further reduced supply. Fifth, Egypt closed most of the tunnels that had brought diesel into the Gaza Strip.

Collection rates for electricity bills in Gaza plummeted from 83 percent in 1998–2000 to 39 percent in 2010, amid rising unemployment, faltering economic activity, and frequent power outages.[53] Factional tensions escalated. Beginning in 2009, the PA began intermittently reducing the amount of electricity it purchased for Gaza, both indirectly, through the purchase of industrial diesel for the power plant, and directly, from the Israel Electric Company. The European Union, which had directly purchased industrial diesel for the power plant from the Israeli fuel

51 *AlBassiouni* v. *Prime Minister* (n. 50) Supplementary State Affidavit, November 19, 2007 para. 5.

52 Affidavit from Rafiq Maliha, manager of Gaza's power plant, May 12, 2008, submitted to Israeli Supreme Court in HCJ 4258/08 (Israel) *Gisha* v. *Defense Minister*, unpublished, given June 5, 2008; United Nations Office for the Coordination of Humanitarian Affairs – Occupied Palestinian Territory, Gaza Strip Fuel Situation Report, April 23, 2008; United Nations Office for the Coordination of Humanitarian Affairs – Occupied Palestinian Territory, "Impact of Fuel Shortages on Gaza Sanitation – Polluting the Sea" (April 29, 2008).

53 *Gisha*, "Who Turned Out the Lights?"

company Dor Alon since 2006, converted its contribution in 2009 to direct budgetary support for the PA. The move was done in the name of strengthening Palestinian autonomy over budget and services, giving the PA discretion to decide how to spend the money. Unable to agree with Hamas over contributions to the cost of the fuel, the PA reduced the amount it bought, forcing the power plant to cut production.[54] Hamas blamed the PA for reducing supplies, while the PA blamed Hamas for not collecting electricity fees from consumers and institutional customers and for not paying more for the diesel.

The funding dispute over the industrial diesel continued intermittently over the years, disrupting supply. On a number of occasions, the government of Qatar donated fuel and money to stem the crisis.[55] In April 2017, the Palestinian factions expanded the dispute to the electricity purchased directly from the Israel Electric Company, which still constitutes the majority of Gaza's electrical supply. The PA asked Israel to reduce the amount of electricity it sold to Gaza by 30 percent, saying it was no longer willing to pay for the full amount and citing lack of progress in negotiations over reconciliation with Hamas. Israeli military officials expressed concern that the power cuts would further destabilize Gaza, threatening Israeli security.[56] The Israeli government could have chosen to continue supplying the full amount of electricity without full payment or could have continued to deduct the full payment from the tax moneys it transferred to the PA, in line with similar unilateral decisions to withhold payment of tax moneys owed to the PA. Instead, the Israeli authorities implemented the cuts in June 2017, calling the decision an "internal Palestinian dispute."[57] The cuts lengthened Gaza's power outages to eighteen hours per day, until the PA announced in January 2018 that it was willing to resume full payment, and supply improved somewhat.[58]

Yet later that year, the Israeli government appeared to resume an explicitly punitive policy toward electricity services, refusing to allow Qatari donations of fuel for the power plant to reach Gaza.[59] "To improve the reality in the Gaza Strip, the Hamas regime must be toppled. Anyone who wants more than four hours of electricity a day must topple the Hamas regime," then Israeli Defense Minister Avigdor Lieberman said in June 2018.[60] These power shortages in Gaza continue to interfere with humanitarian services like medical care, water distribution, and sewage

54 Ibid.

55 *Gisha*, "Hand on the Switch: Who's Responsible for Gaza's Infrastructure Crisis?" (January 2017).

56 A. Issacharoff, "Israel's Dilemma: Electricity to Hamas Leaders or Danger of War in South," *Walla* (May 5, 2017).

57 E. Levy, "Electricity Supply to Gaza Not Yet Reduced, Hamas Doesn't Want Confrontation," *Ynet* (June 14, 2017).

58 N. al-Mughrabi, "Palestinian Authority Says Resuming Payment for Gaza's Israeli Electricity," *Reuters* (January 3, 2018).

59 Kubovich, "Israeli Security Officials Oppose Defense Chief's Decision to Cut Gaza Fuel Transfers."

60 Bachner, "Bennett, Liberman Condition Humanitarian Steps."

treatment, and they burden Gaza's already crippled economy by forcing businesses to purchase expensive generators or limit operations.

The electricity crisis in Gaza is a microcosm of the disastrous effects of decentralization on service provision throughout the Palestinian territory. For the first three decades of the occupation, Israel made some investments in electricity provision, but inadequately and through a colonialist model that cultivated Palestinian dependence on Israeli services and infrastructure, physically and economically. Despite transferring responsibility for electricity provision to Palestinian hands, Israel retained control over elements on which the system's success depended: the ability to bring supplies, spare parts, and experts into and out of Gaza; the movement of people and goods needed for Gaza's economy to generate funds to pay electricity bills; and the physical safety of the electricity grid and power plant. The PA arrangements for an "independent" power plant, on the other hand, born out of the Oslo Accords, were of questionable integrity. Two-thirds of the shares of the Palestine Electric Company, which runs the plant, are in private hands, and the company receives the industrial diesel needed to run the plant free of charge from the PA, together with a guaranteed monthly payment of $2.5 million, ostensibly for additional operating costs. The company continues to receive full payment, even though it produces no more than 90 of the 140 MW promised – and often much less.[61] In 2017, the Palestine Electric Company reported $8.6 million in profits.[62]

Ineffective Governance, Ineffective Resistance

The implications of decentralization for the 4.5 million Palestinian residents of the Palestinian territory, excluding east Jerusalem, have been dire, with Gaza residents paying the heaviest price. All three authorities disavow responsibility and interfere with the governing initiatives of the other. At the same time, the demands of everyday governance interfere with resistance to the occupation – political, diplomatic, and military – in ways that arguably help to perpetuate the indefinite centralization of power in the hands of the occupier. In the meantime, the occupier continues to pursue a colonial agenda of settlement and land seizure that make good governance by anyone impossible.

More difficult to quantify is the breakdown of trust within Palestinian society. Palestinian institutions, billed as "state-building" initiatives, lack the power to deliver adequately, and factional fighting has exacerbated the physical fragmentation caused by Israeli-imposed travel restrictions. Disappointment with the Oslo Accords, which failed to end the occupation and resolve the Palestinian refugee problem, contributed to Palestinians' mistrust toward the PLO and PA,[63] which

[61] *Gisha*, "Hand on the Switch."
[62] Palestine Electric Company, "2017 Annual Report," 19.
[63] R. Khalidi, *The Iron Cage: The Story of the Palestinian Struggle for Statehood* (Boston: Beacon Press, 2006), 158–59.

mirrored many of the PLO's corrupt practices.[64] PLO leaders returning from exile to lead the PA were seen as fulfilling their own "right of return," at the expense of Palestinian refugees in the diaspora.[65] Arafat's system of patronage – and the relatively better economic position of those returning from exile, compared with Palestinians who had stayed in the West Bank and Gaza throughout the Israeli occupation – further eroded trust.[66] His successor, Mahmoud Abbas, whose lawful term as president expired in 2009, has failed to rehabilitate the reputation of the PA.[67]

The utter failure of governance in the Palestinian territory has many causes. Indeed, good governance would be surprising in any territory subject to more than fifty years of occupation. Yet the decentralization project that began in the 1990s has a number of flaws that sabotage governance and help perpetuate indefinite military occupation.

First, while the Oslo Accords did not purport to end the occupation, they did have the effect of weakening attempts to hold Israel accountable for its continued control over Palestinians in the occupied territory. Perhaps the Accords' strategy, to build trust by enhancing Palestinian autonomy over local matters as a prelude to negotiations over ending the occupation, could have worked with better luck and more responsible behavior by leaders. But while peace deals should certainly reflect optimism, their success should not be dependent on exaggerated assumptions of good faith among the parties. The Accords' structure had been rejected for years by Palestinian negotiators but was ultimately accepted by the PLO leadership-in-exile at a time when the organization was in financial and political crisis.[68] The Accords helped reestablish the authority of the Tunis-based nationalist leaders but failed to realize their nationalist goals. Twenty-five years later, the transition has become indefinite. Had the godparents of the Accords – primarily the United States and Europe, but also US-allied Arab regimes such as Egypt, Jordan, and Saudi Arabia – held Israel accountable for its obligations as an occupying power, the trap of Oslo might have been avoided. Another way it could have been avoided would have been for the PLO to dismantle the PA once final status talks broke down. That option is still available to the Palestinian leadership, as will be discussed in the conclusion of this chapter.

Second, at least since the assassination of Israeli Prime Minister Yitzhak Rabin, who entered into the Oslo Accords, the Israeli authorities have deepened their control of the parts of the Palestinian territory which they claim for Israeli Jews. The

[64] Tariq Dana, "Corruption in Palestine: A Self-enforcing System," *Al Shabaka* (August 19, 2015), 2–3.

[65] Khalidi, *The Iron Cage*, 181.

[66] See, e.g., Parsons, *The Politics of the Palestinian Authority*, 130–32.

[67] See, e.g., Palestinian Center for Policy and Survey Research, "Public Opinion Poll No. 69" (September 20, 2018), pcpsr.org/en/node/736.

[68] See, e.g., Parsons, *The Politics of the Palestinian Authority*, 55–57.

Israeli settler population more than doubled from about 295,000 in 1997 to 622,670 in 2017.[69] While the nature of Israeli control has fluctuated since the 1990s,[70] the overall trend has been for Israeli forces to withdraw to the perimeter of densely populated Palestinian areas,[71] close them off into enclaves,[72] disavow responsibility for what happens inside them, and consolidate control over large swaths of land, primarily east Jerusalem and Area C, for Israeli civilian use. In other words, delegation of authority to the Palestinian authorities is used as cover for deepening control over the parts of the land Israel claims for itself while abdicating responsibility for the people living in the rest of the Palestinian territory.

Third, poor performance and corruption by Palestinian leaders fueled the governance and resistance crisis. The late respected Palestinian psychologist Eyad Sarraj put it well when he said that "Israel wrote the script, and the two actors – Hamas and Fatah – are playing their roles superbly."[73] The PA was created under the shadow of Israeli control, following decades of exile and failed attempts at ending the occupation, and under circumstances in which it was given very partial control over the reins of governance. Yet the outcome might have been different had the PLO leaders who created the PA not performed so poorly. The PLO had operated for decades as an underground movement, weakened by dispersal and assassinations[74] and acting as a quasi-state in exile.[75] But the skills that helped the PLO survive as a clandestine, nimble, quasi-guerrilla organization did not help it set up an authority based on rule of law, transparency, balance of powers, and other foundations of statehood and governance. When PLO leaders returned to the OPT from their exile in Tunis, they brought with them the practices of securing loyalty by offering access to resources, especially by using the large public sector to create dependence and discourage criticism.[76] Hamas had initially been viewed as untainted by corruption,[77] but once it gained power after winning a

69 B'Tselem, "Statistics on Settlements and Settler Population" (January 1, 2019).

70 *Gisha*, "Scale of Control," 38–40.

71 With some exceptions, Israeli troops tend not to enter Area A of the West Bank, where most Palestinian urban centers with the exception of Jerusalem are located. In 2005, Israel withdrew to the perimeter of Gaza and dismantled its civilian settlements there.

72 In 1995, Israel built a fence around Gaza; beginning in 2000, Israel set up numerous internal checkpoints within the West Bank and Gaza that bisected the areas and eventually built, beginning in 2003, the separation barrier inside the West Bank.

73 Amira Hass, "Even as Gaza Reels from Floods, Hamas and Fatah Remain Divided," *Haaretz* (December 20, 2013).

74 Khalidi, *Iron Cage*, 158–59.

75 Ibid., 174–76.

76 Dana, "Corruption in Palestine." See also U4 Anti-Corruption Resource Center, "Overview of Corruption and Anti-corruption in Palestine," (January 19, 2012).

77 A March 2006 public opinion poll found high levels of optimism about Hamas governance and the perception among a third of respondents that it had won elections because voters wanted clean government. "Public Opinion Poll No. 19," Palestinian Center for Policy and Survey Research (March 16–18, 2006).

plurality in 2006 elections, it too was seen as rewarding loyalty, rather than merit, in allocating resources.[78]

The fourth set of factors contributing to this entanglement is the conduct of donors to the PA and, to a lesser extent, Hamas, who make the status quo sustainable by funding the services that otherwise would be the responsibility of the occupying power, thus allowing Israel to perpetuate the occupation without bearing the financial cost.[79] Thus far, European donors have been reluctant to take serious measures against actions by Israel that interfere with service provision funded by European governments, such as the demolition of schools and homes in Area C of the West Bank, destruction of infrastructure in Gaza, and restrictions on movement that thwart economic development plans. European donors have even been reluctant to insist on allowing travel for their own scholarship holders from Gaza, agreeing to onerous bureaucratic demands from the Israeli authorities and even escorting the students through Israeli territory en route to travel abroad, as if it were the responsibility of European diplomats to address any security concerns arising from the transit.[80] The flow of funding, while declining, still constituted 22 percent of Palestinian gross national income in 2012.[81] It enables the status quo. Under the current circumstances and without the political will to challenge Israeli policies that thwart growth, the aid cannot provide a horizon for development.

IS GOOD LOCAL GOVERNANCE – GOOD?

The experiment in autonomy in Palestine is context specific, of course, but it does serve as a warning against violating a fundamental principle of successful decentralization, namely the need not just to delegate responsibility but also to cede the power needed to fulfill that responsibility. In the context of a military occupation, the dilemma is particularly acute. On the one hand, we want more power in the hands of representatives of the local population, out of skepticism about the beneficence of foreign military rule and in order to prepare the people for the exercise of self-determination. On the other hand, we should also be skeptical of the willingness of an occupying power to cede the control necessary for local governments to succeed and the temptation to abdicate responsibility under the guise of strengthening local autonomy.

78 It is difficult to find accurate data regarding corruption or perceptions of corruption within Gaza, because the Hamas authorities crack down on those who accuse it of corruption and run their affairs in a nontransparent way. See Human Rights Watch, "Two Authorities, One Way, Zero Dissent: Arbitrary Arrest and Torture under the Palestinian Authority and Hamas" (October 23, 2018).

79 O. Dajani and H. Lovatt, "Rethinking Oslo: How Europe Can Promote Peace in Israel-Palestine," European Council on Foreign Relations (July 2017).

80 *Gisha*, "Obstacle Course: Students Denied Exit from Gaza" (July 2009).

81 J. Wildeman and A. Tartir, "Unwilling to Change, Determined to Fail: Donor Aid in Occupied Palestine in the Aftermath of the Arab Uprisings," *Mediterranean Politics*, 19 (2014), 433–34.

Foreign donors supporting the PA have encouraged and funded measures to strengthen municipal and village governance, providing recommendations firmly rooted in the Oslo paradigm. They provide actionable suggestions for improvements that can be made within the context of Israeli restrictions.[82] But during a military occupation that has become indefinite and colonial – characterized by settlements and de facto annexation – perhaps we should question the desirability of good local governance, where such governance relieves the occupying power of the burden of administering the territory and thus perpetuates the occupation. Where decentralization takes place in the context of negating the right to genuinely representative government – whether because of military occupation or another nondemocratic regime – we might evaluate it not just based on service provision but also on the extent to which it furthers or undermines a broader project of democratic transformation.

Here we might recall the strategy of the African National Congress (ANC) to render South Africa ungovernable so long as apartheid continued. There are of course important differences between the challenges and agendas of the ANC and the PLO, but both nationalist movements in exile aspired to topple an unrepresentative and oppressive regime. The ANC governed only once the white minority had ceded power. Prior to that, its policy was to subvert attempts at governance by "puppet local government authorities," in the words of ANC leader Oliver Tambo, until democratic transformation took place:

> To bring about the kind of society that is visualised in the Freedom Charter, we have to break down and destroy the old order. We have to make apartheid unworkable and our country ungovernable. The accomplishment of these tasks will create the situation for us to overthrow the apartheid regime and for power to pass into the hands of the people as a whole.[83]

Current attempts to strengthen local Palestinian authorities have, according to the World Bank, contributed to improvements in access to basic services such as piped water and solid waste collection, absolute goods that contribute to the physical health of Palestinians in the West Bank and Gaza Strip.[84] There are also suggestions that more responsive municipal and village authorities can build confidence among residents, a critical aspect not just of good governance but also of rehabilitating the trust and solidarity needed for resistance to the occupation. And while the factional split between Hamas and Fatah has, since 2007, negated the possibility of holding national elections, Palestinians in the West Bank were able to choose local representatives in municipal elections held in 2012 and 2017. As donor countries support

82 World Bank, "The Performance of Palestinian Local Governments: An Assessment of Service Delivery Outcomes and Performance Drivers in the West Bank and Gaza" (June 15, 2017).

83 Address by Oliver Tambo to the Nation on Radio Freedom, July 22, 1985.

84 World Bank, "Performance of Palestinian Local Governments."

attempts to strengthen local governance, however, they would do well to consider not just their immediate impact on service delivery, important as that is, but also the extent to which better local governance supports or undermines what should be a broader project of ending the occupation and achieving genuine self-rule. The Palestinian leadership is of course also considering that question. In recent years, the PLO has issued decisions to dismantle the PA or end its economic and security cooperation.[85] Most of those decisions have not been implemented, but in mid-2020 some security and other forms of coordination were temporarily suspended, in the wake of an Israeli plan to formally annex an additional section of the West Bank.[86]

Without an end to the occupation, even with continued donor support, significant improvements in service delivery and governance are unlikely, and realizing freedom and independence is impossible. Better sanitation, the infrastructure needed for health and economic growth, and relationships of trust between local officials and their constituents are building blocks for a healthy, cohesive society. But Palestinian leaders – and those they claim to represent – will have to make hard choices about how those services fit into the broader project of national liberation.

85 J. Khoury, "PLO Votes to Suspend Recognition of Israel until It Recognizes a Palestinian State," *Haaretz* (October 29, 2018).

86 "Palestine Cuts off All Ties with Israel and US: Is It a Bluff?" *Guardian* (May 25, 2020).

13

"Stuck Together"

Can a Two-State Confederation End the Israeli-Palestinian Conflict?

Omar M. Dajani and Dahlia Scheindlin

The conflict in Israel-Palestine[1] is seen through a variety of frames: as a competition between rival national movements, each asserting a right to self-determination in the territory both claim as their patrimony; as a religious war for dominion over a land holy to the three Abrahamic faiths; as a fight for liberation from a settler-colonial regime; and as a struggle for individual rights to enfranchisement, equality, refugee return, and restitution. None of these framings on its own fully captures the history of the conflict or the reality on the ground, and each frame implies a different vision of a just solution.

The solution embraced by the international community for the last twenty to thirty years[2] has privileged resolving the national conflict by dividing Israel-Palestine into two states, reprising an idea endorsed by the UN General Assembly in 1947.[3] The broad contours of the contemporary two-state solution (2SS) took form over the course of two intensive efforts by Israel and the Palestine Liberation Organization (PLO) to negotiate what they called a "permanent status agreement" – in 1999–2001 and 2007–08. Underlying much of this framework was a logic, advanced by Israeli leaders, that peace was best achieved by maximizing physical separation between the two peoples.[4] An effectively demilitarized Palestinian state would be established on the West Bank and Gaza Strip, with its

1 Throughout this chapter we use the label "Israel-Palestine" to refer to the territory that comprised Mandatory Palestine (1922–48) and includes the State of Israel and the occupied Palestinian territory (i.e., the Gaza Strip and the West Bank, including East Jerusalem).

2 Although a substantial segment of the international community expressed support for a 2SS as early as 1989, UNGA Resolution 44/42 (December 6, 1992), the European Union and the United States did not formally endorse it until 1999 and 2000, respectively.

3 For a critical analysis of the UN General Assembly's partition plan, see A. Imseis, "The United Nations Plan of Partition Revisited: On the Origins of Palestine's International Legal Subalternity," *Stanford Journal of International Law*, 57(1) (2021), 1–54.

4 For a discussion of the politics of separation, see O. Dajani, "Divorce without Separation? Reimagining the Two-State Solution," *Ethnopolitics*, 15(4) (2016), 366–79, at 367–69.

capital in east Jerusalem, and west Jerusalem would be recognized as the capital of Israel. The border between the two states would be based on the armistice line in place between 1949 and 1967 (the "Green Line"). Israel would annex some settlements (offering some territory on its side of the Green Line in exchange), while the residents of other settlements would be obliged to relocate to Israel. A small, symbolic number of Palestinian refugees would be permitted to return to Israel, the vast majority to make their home instead in the Palestinian state or in third countries.

Over the last two decades, prospects for the realization of this vision dimmed. During a third effort to conclude a permanent status agreement, mediated by the Obama administration in 2013–14, Israeli Prime Minister Benjamin Netanyahu abandoned key elements of the compromise, declaring his unwillingness to evacuate any settlements[5] and rejecting the return of any Palestinian refugees to Israel.[6] In 2015 he also declared his opposition to the creation of a Palestinian state.[7] Four years later, the United States embraced Netanyahu's positions, proposing a status for Palestine so territorially and functionally circumscribed it could hardly be called statehood.[8] During the same period, popular support for a 2SS steadily declined among both Israelis and Palestinians, with doubts intensifying about its merits and continuing feasibility.[9] In recent years, politicians, policy analysts, activists, and scholars have accordingly directed increasing attention to alternative solutions

One such alternative is the establishment of an Israeli-Palestinian confederation. Proponents of confederation present it as a middle ground between a 2SS and a one-state solution. As Yossi Beilin explained in the *New York Times*, "[t]oo many Israelis fear that a one-state marriage would destroy either our identity as a Jewish state or our claim to democracy. And a two-state divorce is unlikely to produce a prosperous and stable Palestine."[10] Confederation, he argued, offers a "practical and realistic" framework for resolving issues that have divided the parties in the past.

Our aim in this chapter is to describe, and offer a critical assessment of, confederal approaches to resolving the conflict in Israel-Palestine. In the first section, we review why prospects for the conventional 2SS have declined and what other models have been advanced as alternatives. In the second section, we place confederation in

5 R. Ahren, "Netanyahu: I Won't Forcibly Evacuate Settlements," *Times of Israel* (March 9, 2014).

6 H. Keinon and K. Abu Toameh, "Netanyahu on Palestinian 'Right of Return': There Is No Room for Maneuver," *Jerusalem Post* (January 16, 2014).

7 J. Rudoren, "Netanyahu's History on Palestinian Statehood," *New York Times* (March 20, 2015).

8 "Peace to Prosperity: A Vision to Improve the Lives of the Palestinian and Israeli People," Trump White House Archives (January 2020). For a searing critique of the plan, see D. Levy, "Don't Call It a Peace Plan," *American Prospect* (January 30, 2020).

9 Public opinion trends and critiques of the 2SS among Israelis and Palestinians are discussed later in this chapter.

10 Y. Beilin, "Confederation Is the Key to Mideast Peace," *New York Times* (May 14, 2015).

historical and theoretical context. In the third section, we describe a range of confederal proposals for Israel-Palestine. We conclude, in the fourth section, by exploring process and institutional design considerations presented by confederation as a framework for resolving the Israeli-Palestinian conflict.

QUESTIONING THE TWO-STATE SOLUTION

In 2002, the UN Security Council unanimously endorsed “a vision of a region, where two States, Israel and Palestine, live side by side within secure and recognized borders.”[11] Although the international community continues ritually to affirm its support for that vision,[12] the council acknowledged in 2016 that it was already “imperiled.”[13] In this section, we outline reasons for declining enthusiasm for the 2SS and review alternatives.

A Closing Window of Support among Israelis and Palestinians

Over the history of the conflict, elite legitimization of the 2SS has been matched by public support among both Israelis and Palestinians for only a limited window. During the Palestine Mandate, the idea of partition elicited intense debates among Jews and fierce opposition among Palestinians. After 1948, it was moribund for several decades. Israel’s Labor Party began in the 1980s to express concerns about the demographic and moral threat posed by “permanent domination of the Arab Palestinian inhabitants of Judea, Samaria, and Gaza Strip.”[14] But it was only during the first Palestinian intifada that public opinion surveys began to register significant Israeli support for a Palestinian state, that support rising after the Oslo Accords and reaching a majority by the end of the 1990s.[15] While Palestinian leaders signaled interest in a 2SS as early as the 1970s, the PLO formally accepted partition (implicitly recognizing Israel) only in 1988,[16] recognizing Israel formally in 1993 as part of the Oslo Accords. The Accords elicited the support of 60–75 percent of Palestinians through the 1990s.[17] In 2010, 71 percent of Israelis supported a 2SS, along with 57

[11] UNSC Resolution 1397 (2002).

[12] See, e.g., UNGA Resolution 75/172 (December 28, 2020) (stressing the urgency of realizing Palestinian self-determination through a two-state solution).

[13] UNSC Resolution 2334 (2016).

[14] T. Magal, D. Bar-Tal, N. Oren, and E. Halperin, “Psychological Legitimization – Views of the Israeli Occupation by Jews in Israel: Data and Implications,” in D. Bar-Tal and I. Schnell (eds.), *The Impact of Lasting Occupation* (Oxford: Oxford University Press, 2013), 122–86.

[15] Y. Ben Meir and O. Bagno-Moldavsky, *Vox Populi: Trends in Israeli Public Opinion on National Security 2004–2009* (Tel Aviv: Institute for National Security Studies, 2010), 76.

[16] Declaration of the State of Palestine (1988).

[17] “Public Opinion Poll #1: Palestinian Israeli Agreement: ‘Gaza-Jericho First’,” Palestinian Center for Policy and Survey Research (PCPSR) (September 10–11, 1993); “CPRS Public Opinion Poll #20,” PCPSR (October 1995).

percent of Palestinians.[18] Since that time, however, support among both Palestinians and Israeli Jews has declined. According to a joint Israeli and Palestinian survey from September 2020, only 43 percent of Palestinians and 42 percent of Israeli Jews supported the idea.[19]

Perhaps the leading driver of declining opposition to a 2SS is diminishing confidence that it can be achieved in light of large-scale settlement expansion, mutual distrust, and a (correct) reading of the political map. Polling indicates that perceived feasibility is clearly correlated with opposition or support for a 2SS.[20] Surveys conducted from 2010 to 2018 show that a minority among Israelis believed that negotiations would lead to an agreement – generally between one-fifth and one-third.[21] When Israelis and Palestinians were asked whether the solution remained feasible given the extensive spread of settlements, a majority of Palestinians said in 2017 that it was no longer feasible, and one year later a plurality (nearly half) of Jewish Israelis reached the same conclusion.[22] Both groups continued to express that view in 2020.[23]

That said, the substantive terms of a 2SS have never commanded enthusiastic support from either Israelis or Palestinians. Compromises on individual elements generally elicited less support than the overall package.[24] Indeed, since 2010, support for some elements – particularly the symbolic return of Palestinian refugees (for Israelis), demilitarization of the Palestinian state (for Palestinians), and the division of Jerusalem (for both) – has barely exceeded 20 percent.[25] Moreover, respondents from both groups consistently expressed less enthusiasm for a 2SS after hearing in detail about the compromises it would require.[26]

The conventional 2SS's waning potential is a consequence not only of falling public support, but also of political obstruction on one side and fraying political authority on the other – factors that both reflect and contribute to public skepticism. As Israel's leader from 2009 to 2021, Netanyahu implemented numerous policies to entrench Israel's control over the West Bank, including explicitly rejecting the creation of a

18 "Joint Israeli-Palestinian Poll #35," PCPSR (March 2010).

19 N. Rosler, K. Shikaki, and D. Scheindlin, "Palestinian Israeli Pulse: A Joint Survey," PSR and Evens Program, Tel Aviv University, PCPSR (October 2020).

20 K. Shikaki and D. Scheindlin, "Role of Public Opinion in the Resilience/Resolution of the Palestinian-Israeli Conflict," PCPSR (December 2018), 4.

21 The finding is consistent in all monthly surveys throughout the last decade, within this general range. See Israel Democracy Institute Guttman Center for Public Opinion and Policy Research and Tel Aviv University's Evens Program in Mediation and Conflict Resolution, Peace Index (2010–18), Israel Democracy Institute.

22 K. Shikaki, D. Scheindlin, and N. Rosler, "Palestinian Israeli Pulse: A Joint Survey," PCPSR (October 26, 2020).

23 Ibid.

24 J. Shamir, "Public Opinion in the Israeli Palestinian Conflict: From Geneva to Disengagement to Kadima to Hamas," United States Institute of Peace (2007).

25 K. Shikaki and D. Scheindlin, "Role of Public Opinion in the Resilience/Resolution of the Palestinian-Israeli Conflict," PCPSR (December 2018).

26 Ibid.

Palestinian state.[27] During this same phase, the fragmentation of Palestinian political authority, as a result of Israeli movement restrictions and the Fatah–Hamas conflict, contributed to the erosion of Palestinian President Mahmoud Abbas' popular legitimacy and constrained his ability to advance a 2SS had there been an opportunity.[28] Finally, the physical reality of creeping annexation[29] has steadily increased the costs of Israeli withdrawal while leaving little territory for Palestinian statehood. The physical implementation of a full Israeli withdrawal, even from the dwindling remaining Palestinian territory, becomes more complex and problematic as time goes by.

Alternatives to a Two-State Solution

A range of approaches to managing or resolving the conflict have been urged as alternatives to the conventional 2SS. These alternatives fall into four main categories. The first is maintenance of the status quo – a "one-state reality" and apartheid system in which the Israeli government controls all of Israel-Palestine, allowing Palestinians in the Gaza Strip and in West Bank cities and towns limited self-government while restricting their access to Israel – and simultaneously imposing obstacles even within the fully Israeli-controlled parts of the West Bank (Area C) that encourage Palestinians to concentrate themselves in Area A.[30] The second is Israel's annexation of some or all of the West Bank. Proponents of this approach offer varying ideas about the status of West Bank Palestinians, from continuing to afford them limited autonomy within a shrinking territorial space to offering them Israeli citizenship, Israeli residency combined with Jordanian citizenship, or "incentives" to emigrate to Jordan.[31] All would sever the Gaza Strip and its Palestinian population from the rest of Israel-Palestine. The third approach is the creation of one democratic state across all of Israel-Palestine. What distinguishes this approach from annexation is that it envisages equal citizenship for all persons in the country. Proponents of this approach differ about whether the state should be unitary and liberal, binational (in which Israeli Jews and Palestinians would enjoy not only individual rights but also collective rights as peoples), and/or federal.[32] The fourth category of alternatives

27 "Netanyahu: No Palestinian State on My Watch," *Times of Israel* (March 16, 2015).

28 For example, in a 2015 survey, approximately two-thirds of Palestinians demanded that Mahmoud Abbas resign. "Palestinian Public Opinion Poll #58," PCPSR (December 10–12, 2015). This figure varied just slightly over the years, and in 2020 remained at precisely two-thirds who demanded his resignation. "Palestinian Public Opinion Poll #78," PCPSR (December 27, 2020).

29 See O. M. Dajani, "Israel's Creeping Annexation," *AJIL Unbound*, 11 (May 10, 2017).

30 D. Egel, et al., "Alternatives in the Israeli-Palestinian conflict," Rand Corporation (February 21, 2021). For Israeli planning in Area C, see N. Kadmon, "Acting the Landlord: Israel's Policy in Area C, West Bank," B'Tselem (June 2013).

31 See Y. Fleisher, "A Settler's View of Israel's Future," *New York Times* (February 14, 2017).

32 For a critical overview of these approaches, see B. Bashir, "The Strengths and Weaknesses of Integrative Solutions for the Israeli-Palestinian Conflict," *Middle East Journal*, 70(4) (Autumn 2016), 560–78, at 573.

reimagines the 2SS. One example is the plan propounded by Avigdor Lieberman, which would maximize ethnic segregation by redrawing Israel's border to "exchange" Palestinian Arab population centers just inside Israel for Israeli settlements outside it. Another example, which instead challenges the logic of separation, is the creation of an Israeli-Palestinian confederation. We now turn to exploring that idea.

CONTEXTUALIZING CONFEDERALISM

In many divided societies, efforts have been made to design public institutions in ways that strike a balance between the accommodation of identity groups' self-determination/national representation claims and the territorial integrity of states. What is novel about the proposals described in this chapter is their choice of confederation as that middle ground. In this section, we describe the distinguishing features of confederations and consider why they have been somewhat neglected as an institutional framework for resolving or managing self-determination conflicts.

What Distinguishes Confederations?

A confederation is "a governmental entity created by independent sovereign States that join together to perform some governmental functions under common authority."[33] Sovereignty of the member states distinguishes confederations from other systems of decentralized governance explored in this volume. Confederations' member states usually possess separate international personalities.[34] Decisions by confederal institutions tend to be taken on the basis of member states' mutual consent[35] and to occur following policy-making processes at the member state level.[36] In addition, member states typically are permitted to opt out of decisions taken by the confederal government and even to withdraw from the confederation, which functions as a "contractual union of states."[37]

Other characteristic features include a weak confederal government – or, alternately, a set of joint institutions whose powers are limited to specific issues (like economy and defense) and whose authority may be further constrained by constituent, devolved entities.[38] In addition, joint institutions in a confederal government

[33] F. L. Morrison, "Confederations of States," in Anne Peters (ed.), *Max Planck Encyclopedia of International Law* (Oxford: Oxford University Press, 2007).

[34] Ibid.

[35] J. McGarry and B. O'Leary, "Territorial Pluralism: Its Forms, Flaws and Virtues," in F. Requejo and M. Caminal (eds.), *Federalism, Plurinationality and Democratic Constitutionalism* (New York: Routledge, 2012), 17–50, at 23.

[36] C. B. Blankart. "The European Union: Confederation, Federation or Association of Compound States?" *Constitutional Political Economy*, 18 (2007), 99–106, at 99–100.

[37] A. Warleigh, "History Repeating? Framework Theory and Europe's Multi-level Confederation," *Journal of European Integration*, 22(2) (2007), 173–200, at 184.

[38] McGarry and O'Leary, "Territorial Pluralism," 23.

typically interact with citizens through the governments of each member state, rather than directly.[39] But some confederations establish common citizenship, in addition to citizenship in their constituent states.

It would be helpful to name examples of confederations. But the task is complicated by evolving and inconsistent use of the term. For instance, though Switzerland calls itself a confederation, it has been a federation since the middle of the nineteenth century. Additionally, where there is a lack of consensus regarding a political system's present status or future trajectory, political actors may avoid labeling it entirely. For example, the Constitution of Bosnia and Herzegovina nowhere defines the overarching political system linking together its two constituent entities (the Federation of Bosnia and Herzegovina and the Republika Srpska), and its future is hotly contested. Some Bosnian Serb leaders seeking greater autonomy have called for it to become a confederation while certain Bosniak leaders have called for its transformation into a unitary state.[40] Similar debates persist regarding the future of the European Union, which itself has both federal and confederal features.[41]

Perhaps the clearest recent example of a confederation is the State Union of Serbia and Montenegro, which existed between 2003 and 2006 and provided a framework for coordinating the foreign, defense, and economic policy of its member states. Comprised of the units remaining in the rump Federal Republic of Yugoslavia following its breakup a decade earlier, its creation was a compromise between the Montenegrin independence movement, which sought to advance integration into Europe, and EU officials, who feared that Montenegro's secession would amplify tensions regarding the future status of nearby Kosovo and Republika Srpska.[42] Indeed, the Montenegrins agreed to the arrangement mainly as a way station toward partition, insisting that the Constitutional Charter include an opt-out clause that allowed either republic to hold a referendum on independence by 2006.[43] This historical context also helps explain why Serbia and Montenegro did not establish separate international personalities until after their confederation was dissolved.[44]

In this chapter, we treat confederation as a union between sovereign states with agreed-upon shared powers managed by joint institutions. Yet we recognize that political institutions can be hybrid and dynamic, moving along a decentralizing (or centralizing) trajectory over time. Our aim in this chapter is not to defend an ideal type but, instead, to tease out the implications of various hybrid institutional design choices.

39 Ibid.

40 A. Zdeb, "A Federation Like No Other: The Case of Bosnia and Herzegovina," 50 *Shades of Federalism* (2018).

41 See N. Aroney, "Types of Federalism," in Anne Peters (ed.), *Max Planck Encyclopedia of Comparative Constitutional Law* (Oxford: Oxford University Press, 2016).

42 "Montenegro's Referendum," Europe Briefing No. 42, International Crisis Group (May 30, 2006), 2.

43 N. Caspersen, "Elite Interests and the Serbian-Montenegrin Conflict," *Southeast European Politics*, 4(2–3) (2003), 104–12, at 114.

44 See Constitutional Charter of the State Union of Serbia and Montenegro, Art. 14.

Post-conflict Confederalism?

Although confederal models have recently been urged (or mentioned) as solutions to identity conflicts in a number of other contexts – Catalonia, Cyprus, Kurdistan, and Yemen – there is little experience with confederation as a framework for managing identity conflict in divided societies. Its merits as an institutional choice are also undertheorized, particularly in contrast to the vast literature on federations. One thing we seek to understand is whether confederations are underappreciated as a means of containing conflict, or whether there is less literature because confederations raise problems that make them unsuitable to the context task of resolving or containing conflict.

Over the last half century, government institutions in countries around the globe have been designed with a view toward reconciling demands by identity groups for self-determination with a set of geopolitical imperatives – in particular, the preservation of the international territorial order and the avoidance of violent conflict. In many contexts this balance is achieved through some combination of power-sharing at the center (e.g., through consociational arrangements) and devolution of power from the center. Federalism in particular has become a routine, if rarely uncontroversial, option for deeply divided societies,[45] offering a formula not only for the "coming together" of self-governing polities into a union (as in the United States and Australia), but also for the "holding together" of multiethnic states (as in India and Spain).[46]

That confederations have not often been used to hold states together may be explained by two features. On the one hand, their character as contractual unions from which members can withdraw of their own volition can make them unstable configurations. Of the few confederations in existence during the last century, only two have held to this day, and both – the European Union and Bosnia and Herzegovina – are better understood as hybrids between confederation and federation. Accordingly, if one of the aims in a given post-conflict situation is to design institutions that will preserve a state's territorial integrity, establishing a confederation from which constituent units can withdraw at will is not an obvious choice. At the same time, some unions that started as confederations, such as Canada, Germany, Switzerland, and the United States, later evolved into federations. Thus, even if confederations are not robust enough to hold together a polity, they may provide a framework for cooperative governance that enables the polity to grow together.

On the other hand, one of the leading arguments for partition is that elites from conflicting identity groups no longer need to continue bargaining with each other,

[45] See S. Choudhry and N. Hume, "Federalism, Devolution and Secession: From Classical to Post-conflict Federalism," in T. Ginsburg and R. Dixon (eds.), *Research Handbook on Comparative Constitutional Law* (Northampton, MA: Elgar 2010).

[46] A. Stepan, *Arguing Comparative Politics* (Oxford: Oxford University Press, 2001).

reducing violence in the medium and long term.[47] Because the member states of a confederation must coordinate policy with respect to a defined range of issues, confederations present some of the potential for conflict that one encounters in unitary or federal states.

In view of these attributes, why are confederal solutions for Israel-Palestine attracting interest? As we turn to that question, it bears remembering that the aim in this context is not to hold together a fractious polity in the face of secessionist pressures but, instead, to achieve mutual self-determination for two peoples who are stuck together on a territory both claim. What has prevented that from happening is not international opposition to partition but the parties' inability to reach agreement on the terms of their separation. They have been able neither to separate completely, due to geography, nor to live completely together, due to nationality.

THE APPEAL OF AN ISRAELI-PALESTINIAN CONFEDERATION

A growing array of activists, academics, journalists, political analysts, and politicians – from Israel, Palestine, and elsewhere, and with diverse political commitments and affiliations – have advocated confederal schemes for Israel-Palestine (though not all use the term confederation).[48] In this section, we consider key components and variations of these proposals, which vary in content and level of detail.

Key Elements

Proposals for an Israeli-Palestinian confederation are predicated on the formalized association or union of two states. Beyond this bare concept, most share several common elements.

47 See T. Chapman and P. G. Roeder, "Partition as a Solution to Wars of Nationalism: The Importance of Institutions," *American Political Science Review*, 101 (2007), 677–91.

48 Proposals and studies exploring confederal solutions for Israel-Palestine include the following (in chronological order): D. J. Elazar, "Federal/Confederal Solutions to the Israeli-Palestinian-Jordanian Conflict: Concepts and Feasibility," Jerusalem Center for Public Affairs (1998); Russell Nieli, "Finally, a New Idea: The Marriage of a One-State and a Two-State Solution," *Tikkun*, 24(4) (2009), 33–78; Israel Palestine Creative Regional Initiatives (IPCRI), *Two States in One Space: A New Proposed Framework for Resolving the Palestinian-Israeli Conflict* (Jerusalem: IPCRI, 2014); E. Etzion and Y. Hirschfeld, *An Israeli-palestinian Confederation: A Viable Alternative for the "Two States Solution"* (Netanya: S. Daniel Abraham Center for Strategic Dialogue, 2015); D. Scheindlin and D. Waxman, "Confederalism: A Third Way for Israel-Palestine," *The Washington Quarterly*, 39(1) (2016), 83–94; B. Avishai, "Confederation: The One Possible Israel-Palestine Solution," *New York Review of Books* (February 2, 2018); O. H. Rahman, "The 'State-Plus' Framework: A Confederal Solution for Israel-Palestine," Brookings Doha Center Analysis Paper Number 29, Brookings (December 2020). In addition, Israeli journalist Meron Rapoport and Palestinian political activist Awni Al-Mashni founded a popular movement, called "A Land for All" or "Two States, One Homeland," that advocates a confederal solution to the conflict. Its website is www.alandforall.org/english/?d=ltr.

First, the constituent states are envisioned as *sovereign, independent entities* – each possessing a distinct constitutional order and the legal attributes of statehood. The proposals vary somewhat about whether the two states' powers and responsibilities would be formally symmetrical. A number suggest, for example, that Israel would maintain broader powers and responsibilities in the realm of security, while Palestine would be effectively demilitarized.[49] In addition, a few proposals consider broadening the confederation to include Jordan.[50]

Second, confederation proposals depart from the logic of separation in various ways. Perhaps the most important of these is the reenvisioning of the border and citizenship regime between the two states. While the proposals vary regarding where the border would be, they agree that it would be relatively open: following a transitional period, all Israelis and Palestinians would have the right to move freely across all of Israel-Palestine (e.g., for work, study, travel, religious observance), as in Europe's Schengen Area. The border therefore demarcates the two states' territories but does not shut them off hermetically from each another.

Another way these proposals depart from the separation paradigm is by offering a measure of *freedom of residence* within the two states. Most confederation proposals allow each state's citizens to become permanent residents of the other state.[51] This mechanism would give Israeli settlers residing in the West Bank a choice of remaining in their homes as residents of a Palestinian state, as an alternative to relocating to Israel (with exceptions, e.g., in circumstances where settlements were built on stolen private land or where individuals have a record of violence). The same mechanism would allow Palestinian refugees from Israel (again excepting those whose records suggest they present serious security risks) to achieve a form of return by (re)establishing homes in Israel. Under the terms of permanent residence, citizens would vote in the national elections of their state of citizenship rather than of residence (as in the EU), preserving the political/voting majority of each national group.

Similarly, confederation proposals agree that the city of Jerusalem would host the capital of both states and would be open to all their citizens, abandoning the idea advanced during permanent status negotiations of a hard international border dividing the city. Most proposals provide that Jerusalem would be managed jointly, perhaps with international involvement in the Old City and holy places.[52]

49 See, e.g., Nieli, "Finally, a New Idea," 38; IPCRI, *Two States in One Space*, 229; Rahman, "The State-Plus Framework," 27.

50 See, e.g., Elazar, "Federal/Confederal Solutions"; O. Eran, "The Idea of a Jordanian-Palestinian Confederation, Revisited," INSS Insight No. 1092, INSS (September 6, 2018).

51 While freedom of residence for all Israelis and Palestinians is central to some proposals, such as "A Land for All," others would restrict this right to settlers remaining in Palestinian territory and to Palestinian refugees returning to Israel. See, e.g., Beilin, "Confederation is the Key"; Rahman, "The State-Plus Framework," 23.

52 For two of the more detailed discussions of joint sovereignty in Jerusalem, see Rahman, "The State-Plus Framework," 24–25, and IPCRI, *Two States in One Space*, 118–19.

Third, the Israeli-Palestinian confederal union would establish *joint institutions* to address matters of common concern. Proposals differ about the character and scale of these institutions, as well as the spheres they would govern. Most imagine a thin layer of joint institutions – at least initially. All recognize that substantial cooperation in addressing security threats, regulating economic activity, and managing the natural environment and natural resources will be necessary. Some go further, however, calling for binding mechanisms for resolving disputes and protecting human rights[53] (some even arguing for a human rights court).[54] Some proposals envisage joint political institutions, as well.[55]

The Debate about Confederation

Proponents of an Israeli-Palestinian confederation argue that it avoids pitfalls presented by other two-state and one-state solutions. In contrast to a separation paradigm, it is attentive to both peoples' attachment to all of the land of Israel-Palestine. By creating a relatively open border, a confederation model lowers the stakes of determining where the border is. In addition, by delinking citizenship and residency, it defuses some of the core political obstacles to a 2SS, such as Jerusalem, borders, settlements, and refugees. It also provides a framework for cooperation, which is critical in view of the small space the states cohabit. Indeed, this approach may help to legitimate such cooperation – particularly to the extent that rights and obligations are to become symmetrical. In contrast to one-state solutions, confederation offers both peoples national self-determination, giving each the opportunity to express its identity and pursue its interests through the apparatus of the state while avoiding the ethnic competition for numerical supremacy likely to afflict a single democratic state. In these respects, its advocates submit, confederation is more feasible and more desirable than the alternatives.

Critics of confederal schemes raise a range of concerns. Those advocating a conventional 2SS assert that a free movement regime would pose a threat to security, or at least be perceived as such and rejected politically.[56] This security concern overlaps with resistance to turning some of Israel's most vociferous opponents of Palestinian statehood (i.e., settlers) into residents of a Palestinian state, subject to Palestinian sovereign authority that they are unlikely to respect. Critics also submit that freedom of residency would pose a particular burden due to major economic gaps and political disparities. They also see the two

53 See, e.g., Nieli, "Finally, a New Idea," 37; IPCRI, *Two States in One Space*, 45–46.

54 See "Shared and Agreed Principles," A Land for All, para. 7.

55 See J. Avesar, "The Israeli-Palestinian Confederation Proposal," *Palestine-Israel Journal of Politics, Economics, and Culture*, 14(2) (2007).

56 S. Efron and E. Gottesman, "Is Israeli-Palestinian Confederation All that It Is Hyped Up to Be?" +972 *Magazine* (May 3, 2021).

sides' lack of trust and uneven history of cooperation as a poor basis for forging successful joint institutions. Other critics argue that confederation provides Israel's settlement project with a veneer of legitimacy, inappropriately equating Israeli settlers, whose presence in the West Bank violates international law, with Palestinian refugees, whose right to return to their homes in Israel was recognized in UN General Assembly Resolution 194.[57] Advocates of one-state solutions contend that a confederation would entrench asymmetries[58] and impede genuine decolonization.[59]

So far, however, the confederal approach remains largely unfamiliar among Israelis and Palestinians. As a result, while there has been initial public opinion research, there is little by way of robust public debate, and support and critiques come mainly from policy-oriented thinkers.

INSTITUTIONAL AND PROCESS DESIGN CONSIDERATIONS

In this final section, our aim is to advance the discussion about confederal models by identifying some of the distinct institutional and process design issues they raise. At the outset, we emphasize that we do not believe that confederation presents more – or more difficult – problems than those posed by any of the alternatives. After all, the last half century has proven that there is nothing straightforward about attempting to achieve a 2SS premised on ethnic separation. Rather, our intention in this section is to highlight these issues in order to facilitate further exploration of confederal policy options.

Ethnicization and Minority Protection

Confederation, like the conventional 2SS, offers both Palestinians and Israelis the gold standard of self-determination – national independence. But the idea of "two states for two peoples" underlying both versions raises questions: how should each of the two "peoples" be defined? What does it mean to establish a state "for" each of them? And to what extent will supranational instruments and institutions safeguard the rights of minorities in each state, whether they are citizens or merely permanent residents? These questions have particularly far-reaching implications for confederal proposals, which contemplate a greater degree of Israeli-Palestinian cohabitation in both states than other models.

Self-determination theory has long struggled to reconcile two distinct conceptions of the nation – a romantic vision rooted in "an authentic communal feeling,

57 Bashir, "Integrative Solutions," 573.

58 Halper, *Decolonizing*, 236–37.

59 H. Chacar, "Confederation Can't Answer the Most Important Issue in Israel-Palestine," +972 *Magazine* (July 2, 2019).

a togetherness, a sense of being 'us' among the relevant group"[60] and a liberal vision of a community instead linked together by a set of decision-making processes that allow its members "to participate in the conduct of their common affairs within the State."[61] The tension between these visions is already prominent in Israeli discourse pitting a "Jewish state" (the prevailing national ethos) against a "state of all its citizens," including its Arab/Palestinian citizens.[62] The Knesset presumed to resolve the question in a 2018 Basic Law, declaring Israel "the nation state of the Jewish people, in which it realizes its natural, cultural, religious and historical right to self-determination," and emphasizing that the right is "unique to the Jewish People."[63] But Palestinian and some left-wing Jewish Israelis continue to press for a more expansive conception of an "Israeli" nation that embraces non-Jews.[64] For their part, Palestinians, denied a state of their own, have not had the opportunity to determine who is entitled to Palestinian citizenship, but when they have undertaken to define their national community in formal instruments, they have tended toward a more liberal conception.[65] In a confederal system marked by significant Israeli-Palestinian cohabitation, some effort to reimagine the "stories of peoplehood"[66] on both sides of the border may be valuable.

A related question is how "dyed by a nation's color"[67] each state would be. Degrees of ethnicization may be imagined along a continuum. At one end, "two states for two peoples" can simply mean that at the time of the agreement, a majority in each state identifies as "Jewish" (or "Israeli") and "Palestinian," respectively, and accordingly each national group has an advantage in determining its policy preferences through participation in the democratic process, but no formal national identity is decreed. Toward the other end of the continuum, each state may align itself with an ethnonational identity, regardless of population demographics. This may involve

60 M. Koskenniemi, "National Self-determination Today: Problems of Legal Theory and Practice," *The International and Comparative Law Quarterly*, 43(2) (1994), 241–69, at 246.

61 Ibid., 249.

62 See A. Patten, "The Idea of Israel as a Jewish State," *Theoretical Inquiries in Law*, 21(2) (2020), 531–59.

63 Basic Law: Israel – The Nation-State of the Jewish People (2018) [Israel].

64 See The National Committee for the Heads of the Arab Local Authorities in Israel, "The Future Vision of the Palestinian Arabs in Israel," Adalah (2006), 10–11; R. Fish, "Bi-nationalist Visions for the Construction and Dissolution of the State of Israel," *Israel Studies*, 19(2) (2014), 15–34, 26.

65 See, e.g., the 1988 Palestinian Declaration of Independence, which embraces "non-discrimination in civil rights on grounds of race, religion or colour or as between men and women, under a Constitution ensuring the rule of law and an independent judiciary and on the basis of true fidelity to the age-old spiritual and cultural heritage of Palestine with respect to mutual tolerance, coexistence and magnanimity among religions."

66 The term comes from R. Smith, *Stories of Peoplehood: The Politics and Morals of Political Membership* (Cambridge: Cambridge University Press, 2003). Its implications are explored in W. Kymlicka, "Devolution and the Promotion (or Evasion) of Minority Rights," Chapter 3 in this volume.

67 A. Wimmer, *Nationalist Exclusion and Ethnic Conflict: Shadows of Modernity* (Cambridge: Cambridge University Press, 2002), Kindle locations 1132–33.

symbols such as the national flag and anthem as well as more concrete policies – such as the state's official language, immigration and naturalization preferences, and even access to voting rights, governmental services, benefits, and/or positions. As a state moves toward greater ethnicization, its policies are more likely to exclude minorities and conflict with anti-discrimination norms. Such policies may also empower "ethnic entrepreneurs" who sow division.[68]

In light of this experience, a crucial question is whether an Israeli-Palestinian confederation would define norms and establish institutions that safeguard the rights of minorities in each member state. Commitments to minority rights – entrenched in constitutional provisions and/or in international commitments – have come to be seen as critical to the stability of new political configurations in divided societies.[69] But their uneven success suggests the need for mechanisms of adjudication and enforcement beyond just a stated commitment – especially in a context where Israeli Jewish settlers make their home in a Palestinian state and Palestinian refugees make theirs in an Israeli state. The potential for discrimination is strong, and giving national judiciaries full responsibility for minority protection could subject courts to political pressures that challenge their legitimacy no matter how they rule.

As suggested by several proposals, a supranational court could both safeguard minority rights and help to keep the peace.[70] The design of such an institution might draw inspiration from models such as the European Court of Human Rights and the Constitutional Court of Bosnia and Herzegovina. A range of questions requires thorough consideration: who would have standing to bring claims? What other limits would be placed on the court's jurisdiction? Would the court be comprised only of Israeli and Palestinian jurists or also include judges from elsewhere? What incentives for compliance with its rulings could be fashioned?

Scale and Authority of Confederal Institutions

More broadly, which matters would be assigned to confederal institutions and how will they take decisions? Options range from assigning limited authority to a narrow set of joint institutions to establishing joint political institutions with far-reaching powers, such as a shared legislature (like the European Parliament) or shared

68 L. D. Anderson, *Federal Solutions to Ethnic Problems: Accommodating Diversity* (New York: Routledge, 2013), 70.

69 See N. Berman, "But the Alternative is Despair: European Nationalism and the Modernist Revival of International Law," *Harvard Law Review*, 106(8) (June 1993), 1792–1903 (exploring interwar minority protection treaty regime); United Nations Partition Plan for Palestine (1947), ch. 2 (recommending constitutional commitments to minority protection); Laeken Declaration on the Future of the European Union (December 15, 2001) (declaring EU membership open only to states that respect minorities).

70 See IPCRI, *Two States in One Space*, 45–46; A Land for All, "From Conflict to Reconciliation: A New Vision for Palestinian-Israeli Peace, Draft for Discussion," 17.

presidency (as in Bosnia-Herzegovina). Many variations are possible, as reflected by Bosnia's hybrid model, which combines shared political institutions, functionally constrained joint institutions, and extensive devolution to constituent entities.[71] Decision-making may be on the basis of equality (as in the Oslo framework), population size, or some combination. One study suggests incorporating consociational aspects (such as fixed representation of each community and rotating leadership or veto powers not bound exclusively to population size).[72]

In light of the longstanding asymmetry between the parties and the conflict between them, it may be prudent to minimize thick shared institutions initially. A necessary starting point would be specific bodies for joint security (including external security, such as borders and immigration), environmental and epidemiological challenges, and economic policies, alongside mechanisms or institutions capable of guaranteeing minority rights. However, a shared legislature or presidency may be too complex and conflictual an undertaking at this stage.

That said, one lesson of the Dayton Accords in Bosnia is the need for adjustability to adapt the model over time.[73] In this spirit, a confederation arrangement may stipulate, for example, that a shared legislature can become a possibility in the future, pursuant to a defined decision-making procedure emerging from representatives of joint institutions, or ratification by mutual referendums.

Allocation of Security Authority

One of the most challenging dimensions of establishing an Israeli-Palestinian confederation will be building a credible and effective cooperative framework for security that is capable of responding to both external and internal threats. Advocates of confederal models for Israel-Palestine agree that effective security arrangements are critical, but they differ about whether a confederation's two member states would possess symmetrical rights and obligations in that realm. The "A Land for All" movement envisages cooperation on the basis of equality in responding to security threats.[74] Other proposals have urged the approach advocated by Israel in past peace talks, under which Palestine would consent to demilitarization, and Israel would possess exclusive authority to respond to external threats, also retaining some latitude to deploy military forces within Palestinian territory under certain

71 For explanation and critique of this structure, see N. Tzifakis, "The Bosnian Peace Process: The Power-Sharing Approach Revisited," *Perspectives* (January 2017).

72 IPCRI, *Two States in One Space*, ch. 1.

73 See, e.g., D. S. Hamilton, "Fixing Dayton: A New Deal for Bosnia and Herzegovina," NextEurope No. 1, Wilson Center (November 1, 2020) (observing that Dayton's architects, anticipating the need for change, incorporated means of reform into its terms).

74 A Land for All, "From Conflict to Reconciliation," 10–11. The movement embraces "mutuality, partnership, and equality" as general principles, ibid., 2, even if there are fields (such as economy) in which equality remains aspirational at present.

circumstances.[75] The divergence between these approaches is substantial, but any two-state approach would have to resolve the same debates. Indeed, during all three rounds of negotiations toward a conventional 2SS, Israel insisted on maintaining a presence on the Jordan Valley, along with control over airspace. This incursion on Palestinian sovereignty was among the reasons negotiations failed. While the concept of equal partnership on security would face stiff political resistance among Israel's security establishment, marked asymmetry as part of the final status may prevent any agreement – confederal or otherwise – from being reached at all.

Confederation raises a set of distinct security issues in relation to freedom of movement and extraterritorial protection of citizens. Freedom of movement need not involve the elimination of border crossings between the states. But economic, political, and aesthetic considerations would eventually militate against the maintenance of obtrusive barriers to cross-border movement. At the same time, the more porous the internal borders become, the more control each side will seek over determining who is permitted to enter the common space through external crossings. In other contexts where states have consented to free movement across borders, such as the Schengen Area in Europe and the UK-Ireland Common Travel Area, they have relied on common standards for visa issuance and information-sharing, including through the maintenance of common databases to track entries and exits.[76] Instituting such a system in Israel-Palestine, which is less than 1/100th the size of the Schengen Area and would involve only two states, is in many respects a more manageable task. But it is a far cry from the current regime, in which Israel enjoys ultimate authority over the entry and exit of all persons into the common space. Moreover, while the European system developed incrementally, the centrality of freedom of movement to the idea of an Israeli-Palestinian confederation (and the resolution of issues like settlements, refugees, and Jerusalem) would make it politically costly to defer its implementation until some later juncture when greater trust is established.

A second feature of confederal models that presents distinct security challenges is the presence of potentially large communities of Israeli or Palestinian noncitizens in each of the states. We anticipate three kinds of issues. First, these communities are likely to be seen by their host state as presenting security risks, necessitating deep security cooperation between the two states. Second, members of these communities would themselves be vulnerable to security threats, as well as to official harassment and discrimination. Both groups' home states would have an interest in ensuring their citizens are protected and have effective redress for

75 See, e.g., IPCRI, *Two States in One Space*, ch. 6; Nieli, "Finally, a New Idea," 37. The chapter in the IPCRI initiative was written in part by researchers at the Institute for National Security Studies, including former senior IDF figures.

76 See N. Morag, "Border Management in Europe: Is the Paradigm Evolving?" *Homeland Security Affairs*, 16(1) (2020).

mistreatment. It would not be surprising if Israel sought the right to exercise jurisdiction over its citizens even in Palestinian territory – as it insisted when negotiating the Oslo Accords – but such a step would undermine Palestinian sovereignty. Even were Israel to relinquish jurisdiction over Israeli enclaves in the West Bank, however, it would likely assert a unilateral right to intervene to protect Israelis in the event of acute security risks, as advocated by Israeli-Palestinian Creative Regional Initiatives' (IPCRI) working group on security.[77] This possibility raises difficult questions: would Israel accept Palestine reserving the same right? And to what extent could third-party forces or guarantees play a role in reducing unilateralism by either party? Third, the prospect of some Israeli settlements becoming enclaves under the sovereignty of a Palestinian state – and of substantial numbers of Palestinian refugees "returning" to live as residents in Israel (where a large Palestinian minority already possesses citizenship) – raises the question of whether these communities would be afforded a measure of local autonomy, including the right to police themselves.

It is worth adding that while addressing any of these challenges will require deep coordination and cooperation between security and intelligence forces of each side, there is already some infrastructure and decades of real-world practice in place, since Oslo established joint security institutions and mechanisms. This "security coordination" has come to be vilified by Palestinians based on its association with Oslo and its attendant asymmetries. But, if implemented in a situation grounded in equality and advancing a resolution of the conflict, it might gain some legitimacy.

Addressing Economic and Political Asymmetries

Implementing freedom of movement in an Israeli-Palestinian confederation would require giving urgent attention to two kinds of asymmetries. The first of these is the enormous economic asymmetry that already exists between Israelis and Palestinians. In 2018, Israel's gross domestic product per capita rose to $41,720, while among Palestinians in the West Bank and Gaza Strip it stood at only $3,562.[78] While freedom of movement across the common space may help ameliorate inequality, the gap will not quickly be bridged.[79] Moreover, income inequality within Israel is also stark, Palestinian citizens of Israel experiencing poverty rates four times higher than those among other Israelis (other than Haredi Jews).[80] In light of these realities,

77 IPCRI, *Two States in One Space*, 239.

78 "GDP Per Capita (Current US$) – Israel," The World Bank (updated 2020).

79 Compare, for example, Germany's experience, where a "stark and persistent" wage gap persists between East and West, thirty years after unification – and despite a common language. S. Heise and T. Porzio, "Why East Germans Are Not Taking Advantage of the Large Wage Gap between East and West Germany," VoxEU (February 29, 2020).

80 *OECD Economic Surveys: Israel 2018* (Paris: OECD Publishing, 2018), 15.

any free movement regime must anticipate – and attempt to manage – the effects of income disparities on the movement of labor (and other persons) within the common space, as people move from areas where the economy is weaker to those where it is stronger.[81] That said, one factor that may mitigate this effect in Israel-Palestine is the country's small size, which allows individuals to work on the "other" side while continuing to live in their national state. Indeed, it bears recalling that, until the Second Intifada, hundreds of thousands of Palestinian residents of the West Bank and the Gaza Strip traveled daily to Israel for work, while Israelis routinely visited Palestinian cities in the West Bank and Gaza, for shopping and touring.

A second asymmetry could arise from the creation of a confederation: to the extent that each state hosts large communities who are permanent residents but not citizens, there would be gaps in political rights – and, potentially, also in entitlement to public benefits and services. These gaps could undermine permanent residents' ability to secure fair treatment and also exacerbate existing economic inequalities. This problem is already evident in Jerusalem, whose Palestinian residents for the most part lack Israeli citizenship and who suffer discrimination in education, law enforcement, urban planning and construction.[82] At the same time, continuing discrimination against Palestinian citizens of Israel makes clear that citizenship does not guarantee access to the political system.

Although most confederal proposals give only passing attention to these asymmetries, the authors of the IPCRI study propose addressing them through a combination of two devices. First, while permanent residents lack citizenship in their state of residence, they might "enjoy a rich type of *social citizenship* that grants a safety net of social and economic rights, access to services, freedom from discrimination based on nationality and possibilities for social mobility."[83] Second, the negative implications of lacking representation in national-level politics might be contained through far-reaching *political decentralization*: both citizens and permanent residents would be entitled to participate in local and regional governments, which would in turn be empowered to take most decisions affecting the day-to-day lives of the communities they serve. According to the authors, "[t]his construction mitigates the formal legal gaps of political rights between citizens and residents. Conversely, the stability of the union relies on the ability to create a socioeconomic safety net for all persons residing between the Jordan River and the Mediterranean Sea."[84]

In attempting to address these asymmetries, the IPCRI proposal raises difficult questions. First, because Israel is one of the most centralized states in the

81 See J. Arango, "Explaining Migration: A Critical View," *International Social Science*, 52(165) (September 2000), 283–96, at 285.

82 "East Jerusalem Facts and Figures 2021," Association for Civil Rights in Israel (May 10, 2021).

83 IPCRI, *Two States in One Space*, 73 (emphasis added). Extending this kind of social citizenship to permanent residents is not uncommon in developed economies.

84 Ibid.

developed world,[85] and local government in the Palestinian Authority is unevenly developed,[86] it is necessary to determine how each state would ensure a constitutional shift of this scale is implemented. After all, decentralization is a lengthy and complex process, even when pursued by only one central government and in less challenging circumstances than these.[87] Second, it is uncertain whether decentralizing government would actually help to redress inequalities and protect minority rights. The literature suggests that, depending on macroeconomic factors and institutional design, decentralization is just as likely to exacerbate income inequality as to ameliorate it.[88] In addition, as Will Kymlicka describes in this volume, depending on design choices, decentralized government may even prove disempowering to minorities.[89] Third, since the IPCRI study's vision of social citizenship can only be implemented if both states have the capacity to offer citizens and residents alike a safety net, the economic asymmetry between the two governments must also be addressed, which itself may bolster separatist sentiment in Israel.[90] These challenges, to be sure, may be overcome, but doing so will require careful and deliberate institutional design.

Exit

If Israel and/or Palestine find that confederal arrangements have ceased to serve their interests, would they have the right to exit the union? Such a right is a characteristic, even defining, feature of confederations.[91] As discussed above, it helps explain why confederation has tended not to be an institutional framework chosen for resolving ethnoterritorial disputes. In fact, one study concludes that the primary reason federal arrangements are chosen in lieu of confederal arrangements is to impose costs for defection in circumstances where states have much to lose if

85 Israel's rate of subnational government expenditure constitutes around half the average among unitary states in the Organisation for Economic Co-operation and Development (OECD) – and only a little more than a third of the average among all OECD members. "Israel: Unitary Country," OECD (October 2016).

86 "The Performance of Palestinian Local Governments: An Assessment of Service Delivery Outcomes and Performance Drivers in the West Bank and Gaza Strip," World Bank (June 2017).

87 See generally P. Smoke, "Rethinking Decentralization: Assessing Challenges to a Popular Public Sector Reform," *Public Administration and Development*, 35 (2015), 97–112.

88 For a helpful review of this literature, see C. Goerl and M. Seiferling, "Income Inequality, Fiscal Decentralization, and Transfer Dependency," IMF Working Paper 14/64, International Monetary Fund (2014), 5–7.

89 See W. Kymlicka, "Devolution and the Promotion (or Evasion) of Minority Rights."

90 See K. M. Bakke and E. Wibbels, "Diversity, Disparity and Civil Conflict in Federal States," *World Politics*, 59 (2006), 1–51, at 12 (describing destabilizing consequences when wealthier regions regard transfers to poorer ones as burdensome).

91 Exit was agreed to be permissible in the treaties establishing two of the contemporary confederations we discuss above – the State Union of Serbia and Montenegro (under Article 60 of the Union's Constitutional Charter) and the EU (under Article 50 of the Treaty on European Union).

cooperation breaks down.[92] Where federal arrangements are chosen, the question of whether to allow secession has been fraught.[93]

In an Israeli-Palestinian confederation, allowing exit – and dismantling the aspects of joint governance and freedom of movement and residence – would raise all the inherent, well-known obstacles to full separation. The same obstacles that ultimately undermined the ability to reach a conventional 2SS would be on the table once again.

But whether or not exit from an Israeli-Palestinian confederation is permitted, experience suggests that clarity is preferable in such circumstances.[94] If exit is allowed, it seems critical to agree in advance on a range of substantive and procedural questions – both to disincentivize a breakup and to ensure that, if it occurs, it unfolds as smoothly as possible. These questions might include the necessary constitutional hurdles (such as a decision by referendum and/or supermajority) and pacing (incorporating safeguards to ensure such a decision is not taken precipitously). Substantive questions might include external border security, Jerusalem arrangements, and the fate of the communities who took up residency options on the "other" side pursuant to confederal arrangements. Such principles could be designed in a way that discourages voluntary exit. For example, if the agreed confederal border is on or close to the Green Line, this is a disincentive for Israel to move toward hard partition since it would mean losing access to territory it has long sought to annex. Conversely, if Israel were to retain control over external security in the event the confederation is dismantled, as it is likely to demand, that would discourage Palestinian exit. Of course, while defining these principles in advance – at least as defaults that apply absent agreement to the contrary – would be beneficial to both sides, helping to prevent opponents of the union from painting an unrealistically rosy picture of exit, reaching agreement on such principles would be a complicated undertaking.

Process Challenges: Implementation

A holistic view of conflict resolution must take into account three stages: negotiations, agreement on a solution, and implementation. This chapter has mainly addressed the form of a confederal solution, while observing ways in which this approach could offer options that break through longstanding obstacles to reaching agreement. In the following section, we devote a brief discussion to the issues

92 See C. Rector, *Federations: The Political Dynamics of Cooperation* (Ithaca, NY: Cornell University Press, 2009), 15.

93 See T. Ginsburg and M. Versteeg, "From Catalonia to California: Secession in Constitutional Law," *Alabama Law Review*, 70 (2019), 923–85, at 924.

94 See S. Mancini, "Secession and Self-Determination," in M. Rosenfeld and A. Sajó (eds.), *The Oxford Handbook of Comparative Constitutional Law* (Oxford: Oxford University Press, 2012), at 3.

surrounding implementation, recognizing that a full examination could easily constitute a study of its own.

Implementing confederal arrangements will necessitate overcoming another kind of asymmetry. Transforming the current one-state reality into a two-state confederation would require sweeping changes to the status quo. Many, perhaps most, of these changes would benefit Palestinians without offering tangible short-term rewards to Israelis. This kind of asymmetry makes gradual implementation tricky. One lesson from the failure of the Oslo Accords is that momentum toward implementation tends to slow or stop when powerful *reciprocal* incentives are not in place.[95] While these problems are not unique to confederal models, they are particularly consequential insofar as such models attempt to resolve the issues of settlements and refugees through a free movement regime: if implementation of free movement slows, it would not adversely affect Israeli settlers (who already reside in what would become a Palestinian state), but might cause deferral of Palestinian refugee return to Israel, unraveling the basis of the agreement. Following the Oslo experience, it would be surprising if Palestinian leaders agreed to such a framework without credible guarantees of implementation.

The provision of guarantees by regional and/or international actors may take a variety of forms, ranging from the symbolic act of co-signing a peace agreement to assuming more concrete and specific roles in mechanisms for the resolution of disputes between the parties.[96] According to one recent study, such mechanisms are more likely to produce the confidence necessary for far-reaching concessions if they are binding.[97] But, while international actors have at times played constructive roles in helping to resolve disputes about past Israeli-Palestinian agreements (e.g., through fact-finding),[98] Israel has been reluctant to accept binding third-party dispute resolution since losing its arbitration with Egypt in Taba in 1988.[99]

CONCLUSION

An Israeli-Palestinian confederation, like other two-state solutions, offers a means of reconciling the Zionist and Palestinian national movements by affording both

95 O. Dajani, "Understanding Barriers to Peace: A Palestinian response," *Negotiation Journal*, 20 (2004), 401–8.

96 For a survey of options, see A. Varga, "Witnesses and Guarantors," in M. Weller, M. Retter, and A. Varga (eds.), *International Law and Peace Agreements* (Cambridge: Cambridge University Press, 2021), 211–36.

97 See K. Beardsley and N. Lo, "Third-Party Conflict Management and the Willingness to Make Concessions," *Journal of Conflict Resolution*, 58(2) (2014), 363–92 (finding that binding third-party conflict resolution mechanisms encourage parties to make asymmetric concessions).

98 For example, the Central Intelligence Agency facilitated Israeli-Palestinian security cooperation by helping to resolve disputes about the arrest, imprisonment, or release of terrorism suspects. V. Loeb, "CIA Emerges to Resolve Mideast Disputes," *Washington Post* (September 30, 1998).

99 Dajani, "Understanding Barriers to Peace," 404–5.

peoples national self-determination. But, unlike separation-based paradigms, it is also responsive to other dimensions of the conflict. By establishing a regime of free movement and residence across the territory, it takes seriously both peoples' cultural, historical, and religious attachment to all of the land of Israel-Palestine. It also offers a framework through which individual rights – to nondiscrimination, restitution, return, and equality – may be advanced. A confederal approach therefore has the potential to break through obstacles that have impeded a negotiated resolution of the conflict, including the issues of borders, Jerusalem, refugees, and settlements.

Confederation is not free from challenges. It lacks a substantial track record as an institutional framework for managing identity conflict. Indeed, it has been implemented in only a few cases in recent history, and in most of these the system created was neither labeled a confederation nor endured as one – evolving toward greater separation or greater integration. Moreover, the very features that makes confederation attractive to two peoples "stuck together" in a century-long identity conflict – that both can achieve a measure of independent governance in the same land, that decision-making is to be consensual, and that either can exit in prescribed circumstances – make confederation prone to paralysis and instability. These features could also perpetuate power asymmetries, impeding Palestinians' ability to transform a status quo deeply prejudiced against them.

Further, while the separation of citizenship from residency may provide fresh solutions for Jewish settlers in the West Bank and Palestinian refugees returning to Israel, implementation raises difficult questions – particularly about minority protection and security. While the protection of each noncitizen minority's rights would require institutions for adjudication of claims that are accepted and authoritative on both sides, such institutions in turn would require a measure of agreed-upon common norms. This might require moving from the thin confederation that some envisage to a more robust – and more integrated – normative and institutional system.

That said, our intention in this chapter has not been to urge a particular form of confederation as a means of resolving the Israeli-Palestinian conflict. We have sought instead to consider what confederation has to offer as an alternative to other options and to highlight the key design questions it raises. Where relevant, we have identified a toolbox of approaches to addressing these questions, drawing upon various confederation proposals and experience elsewhere. While confederation presents challenges, we believe there are means of meeting them. Specific solutions require further study, but policies that have been developed in other hybrid systems – from peaceful federations to confederation-like models implemented following major conflicts of the twentieth century – can be reference points for future adaptation.

In Israel-Palestine, it seems likely that a hybrid system, incorporating some features of confederation and some more common in federal states, will be necessary to strike the right balance between self-determination, individual rights, accountability, cooperation, and stability. As in other contexts, it also seems likely that such a system will need to develop over time, through adjustment and negotiation long after the ink has dried on a peace agreement. While such an enterprise would be complicated, no ostensibly simple solution to this conflict has so far proven successful.

14

"Dans ses Frontières Authentiques"?

Morocco's Advanced Regionalization and the Question of Western Sahara

Omar Yousef Shehabi[*]

Postcolonial Morocco has been defined by the battle for power between its conservative monarchy and its nationalist movement. This struggle has colored the state's efforts at regionalization and its conquest of the former Spanish colony of Western Sahara, which are highly intertwined.[1]

The monarchy, which has historically drawn support from the country's rural and tribal areas, has maintained the French colonial practice of co-opting local elites. The 1971 royal decree which first established regions helped the monarchy mobilize this base of support during a period of profound regime instability, including repeated coup attempts.

Regime instability also drove King Hassan II to enforce Morocco's claim of sovereignty over Western Sahara. The nationalists' irredentist concept of *le grand Maroc*

[*] I wish to thank Sara Husseini and Daniel Zisenwine for their comments on an earlier draft of this chapter.

[1] The question of Western Sahara involves a morass of overlapping concepts and terminology. One must distinguish Western Sahara – the former colonial territory of Spanish Sahara – from Moroccan constructs such as the Saharan or Southern Provinces (the boundaries of which have shifted repeatedly) or the more amorphous "Moroccan Sahara." Western Sahara is divided by a sand berm which Morocco built in the 1980s at varying distances west of its borders with Mauritania and Algeria. The Berm consolidated Moroccan control over roughly 80 percent of the territory, including all its economically productive areas (the so-called *zone utile*).

With credit to Isaías Barreñada, "Western Saharan and Southern Moroccan Sahrawis: National Identity and Mobilization," in R. Ojeda-García, I. Fernández-Molina, and V. Veguilla (eds.) *Global, Regional and Local Dimensions of Western Sahara's Protracted Decolonization: When a Conflict Gets Old* (New York: Palgrave Macmillan, 2017), 277–94, at 291 n. 1, this chapter uses the following terminology: "Western Sahara" refers to the territory of the former Spanish colony. Where distinctions between the Moroccan-controlled and Polisario-controlled areas are required, the UN terminology is used. "Sahrawi" refers to indigenous Hassaniya Arabic-speaking tribal groups, regardless of their geographic location. Where distinctions amongst Sahrawis are required, principally in distinguishing Western Sahara Sahrawis from southern Moroccan Sahrawis, their location or origin are specified. "Western Saharan" refers to the current inhabitants of Western Sahara under Moroccan rule, including both Sahrawis and *dakhilis,* noting that both groups hold Moroccan citizenship as a result of Morocco's 1976 annexation of the territory. "Saharan" is used only with respect to Moroccan policy in its self-described Saharan or Southern Provinces, which include the whole of Western Sahara and parts of southern Morocco.

envisaged Moroccan rule over Mauritania, Western Sahara, and parts of Algeria and Mali. Under pressure from the nationalist movement and other players in Morocco's political system,[2] Hassan in 1975 staged the Green March, a theatrical military exercise and civilian march into Western Sahara which successfully pressured Spain into negotiating the territory's "return" to Moroccan control.[3] Ironically, Morocco's success in imposing and entrenching its rule over Western Sahara in the years that followed – the only part of the *le grand Maroc* vision to be fulfilled – shifted the balance of power decisively in the monarchy's favor. Retaining the territory remains dogma across the Moroccan political spectrum and an existential imperative for the king, whose role as guarantor of the state's territorial integrity, "*dans ses frontières authentiques*," is constitutionally enshrined.[4] Morocco's overarching goal in integrating the territory and thereby settling the Western Sahara question on its terms is to unfreeze Maghreb regional and global integration, which is central to its development strategy.

On February 20, 2011, weeks after the Tunisian revolution and days after the Egyptian revolution, demonstrators took to the streets in all major Moroccan cities, protesting corruption and a lack of housing, work, and educational opportunities, and demanding constitutional reforms toward greater democracy. Although the protests were relatively small in scale, they spawned the February 20 movement (M20). The M20 was a broad coalition of established activists, opposition forces, and new participants, held together by emphasizing local concerns and deemphasizing ideology.[5] The monarchy ultimately outflanked the M20 using its traditional strategy of repression and co-optation; the latter involved initiating a constitutional drafting process and mobilizing high voter turnout in the July 2011 referendum which approved the new constitution.

While the 2011 Constitution enshrined "advanced regionalization" (*régionalisation avancée*) as the basis for the kingdom's territorial organization, it doubled down on the post-independence mythology that Morocco lacks "regional tradition let alone political regionalism."[6] Concerted promotion of national unity over historical or cultural identities, which the state casts as the common provenance of all Moroccans, dictates that the regions are administrative divisions rather than expressions of autonomy.

While advanced regionalization was conceived before the M20 protests, its design and implementation dovetails with the new constitutional order. In practice, however,

2 For the history of the nationalist movement in Morocco and its relationship with the monarchy, see D. Zisenwine, *The Emergence of Nationalist Politics in Morocco: The Rise of the Independence Party and the Struggle against Colonialism after World War II* (London: I.B. Tauris, 2010).

3 See J. Weiner, "The Green March in Historical Perspective," *Middle East Journal*, 33 (1979), 20–33.

4 Constitution of Morocco (2011) Art. 42(2).

5 M. Bennani-Chraïbi and M. Jeghllaly "The Protest Dynamics of Casablanca's February 20th Movement," *Revue française de science politique* (English), 62 (2012), 103–30, at 112–15.

6 R. Ojeda-García and Á. Suárez-Collado, "Western Sahara in the Framework of the New Moroccan Advanced Regionalization Reform," in Ojeda-García, Fernández-Molina and Veguilla, *Global, Regional and Local Dimensions of Western Sahara's Protracted Decolonization*, 189–212, at 203.

greater regional competences and executive authority have been blunted by central government oversight, now coupled with judicial review of council decisions. Morocco retains its colonial-era dual administrative structure, wherein representatives of the monarchy, drawn from the country's governing elite (the *makhzen*), shadow elected officials and civil servants at all subnational levels. This structure survived the constitutional reform and compromises the state's capacity for meaningful devolution.

The literature has approached advanced regionalization from a governance perspective. This chapter examines it principally through a conflict management lens, with particular focus on its implications for the fate of Western Sahara. The first section of this chapter traces the history of devolved governance in Morocco from the precolonial Sherifian state to fitful post-independence deconcentration and regionalization efforts. The second section reviews developments in the Western Sahara political process since Mohammed VI ascended the throne in 1999. The third section surveys the key principles of advanced regionalization, including the delimitation, governance, powers, funding, and central government oversight of the regions. The fourth section compares advanced regionalization with the Autonomy Plan and illustrates how Morocco has subsumed Saharan autonomy into the advanced regionalization project. The fifth section argues that advanced regionalization underpins Morocco's two-pronged strategy of a firmer external position on Western Sahara coupled with internal efforts to minoritize and folklorize Sahrawi identity. The goal of this strategy is to disassociate the question of Western Sahara from the decolonization/self-determination paradigm and reframe it as a matter of Sahrawi minority rights and cultural preservation. However, this strategy has the potential to shift the dynamics of the Sahrawi nationalist movement and inaugurate a new chapter in the struggle for Western Sahara.

MOROCCAN DECONCENTRATION, DECENTRALIZATION, AND REGIONALIZATION IN HISTORICAL CONTEXT

The enduring role of the *makhzen* and the dual administrative structure it sustains are defining features of the Moroccan political order. The monarchy's success in co-opting officials at all levels of the state structure and conquering Western Sahara strengthened its hand in the royalist–nationalist struggle. That struggle and the attendant regime instability have informed the monarchy's fitful pursuit of deconcentration and decentralization.

Morocco inherited from French bureaucratic practice the distinction between local representatives of the central government, *déconcentrées*, and local elected officials, *décentralisées*.[7] As used herein, deconcentration therefore refers to the

7 M. Catusse, R. Cattedra, and M. I. Janati, "Decentralization and Its Paradoxes in Morocco," in B. Drieskens, F. Mermier, and H. Wimmen (eds.), *Cities of the South: Citizenship and Exclusion in the Twenty-First Century* (London: Saqi Books, 2007) 113–35, at 114.

administrative process of transferring competences within the central government from its national to its local apparatuses and bureaucrats.[8] Decentralization refers to the political process of transferring competences and resources to local elected authority.[9] As discussed below, regionalization in Morocco has generally been an exercise in deconcentration, while *advanced* regionalization promises decentralization by reducing central government dominance of regional elected officials.

Precolonial Moroccan Rule over the Bled Siba *as Proto-regionalization*

In the Moroccan narrative, Western Sahara formed part of the *Bled Siba* ("land of dissidence") of the precolonial Sherifian state: areas predominantly inhabited by Berber tribes who were beyond the administrative control (i.e., taxing authority) of the *makhzen*[10] and repeatedly fought the sultan's army to preserve their political independence, while accepting the sultan's spiritual authority. The *Bled Siba*, which encompassed much of contemporary Morocco's central and southern regions, was contrasted from the *Bled Makhzen*: mainly Arab areas whose tribes paid taxes to the sultan and served in his army.[11] In unsuccessfully prosecuting its sovereignty claim[12] over Western Sahara before the International Court of Justice (ICJ) in 1975, Morocco framed its relationship with the *Bled Siba* as a form of decentralized rule: "the difference between the *Bled Makhzen* and the *Bled Siba*, Morocco maintains, did not reflect a wish to challenge the existence of the central power so much as the conditions for the exercise of that power; and the *Bled Siba* was, in practice, a way of [e]ffecting an administrative decentralization of authority."[13] In particular, Morocco contended that the *unanimité* between the *makhzen* and *siba* lands was most fully expressed during periods of external threat.[14] Thus the *Bled Siba* has been

8 World Bank, *Decentralization and Deconcentration in Morocco: Cross-sectoral Status Review* (2009), 7.

9 Ibid.

10 *Makhzen* ("storehouse") referred initially to the treasury established in the sixteenth century, which held taxes paid to the Moroccan sultan by loyal tribes. M. Daadaoui, *Moroccan Monarchy and the Islamist Challenge: Maintaining Makhzen Power* (New York: Palgrave MacMillan, 2011), 42. The term came to stand more broadly for the centralized political system under the sultan (and, later, king). The modern *makhzen* has been defined as "a network of official authorities subordinate to the king, comprising privileged individuals and extended families close to him" and spanning the public and private sectors." A. Houdret and A. Harnisch, "Decentralization in Morocco: The Current Reform and Its Possible Contribution to Political Liberalisation," German Development Institute (2017), 16 n. 4.

11 Daadaoui, *Moroccan Monarchy and the Islamist Challenge*, 54.

12 *Western Sahara*, Advisory Opinion [1975] ICJ Rep 12, 47 [103].

13 *Western Sahara* [1975] ICJ Rep 12, 45 [96].

14 ICJ Pleadings, *Western Sahara*, vol. 3, 180. The ICJ found that the sultan's limited administrative control over the *Bled Siba* did not extend to Western Sahara. *Western Sahara* [1975] ICJ Rep 12, 48 [105–6]. While acknowledging "the position of the Sultan of Morocco as a religious leader" to the tribes of Western Sahara, the court concluded that spiritual authority alone did not establish sovereignty. Ibid., 47 [103].

characterized, using the international law concepts of that era, as a vassalage under Moroccan suzerainty, wherein ties between the Crown and the *Bled Siba* were, in the first instance, political and religious rather than administrative and territorial.[15]

Morocco came under the Franco-Spanish protectorate in 1912. The French protectorate, which covered roughly 95 percent of Moroccan territory, extended its writ to the country's hinterlands. In contrast, while Spain fought a bloody war to pacify its protectorate's northern enclave in Morocco's Rif region, it exercised no greater authority in its strip of southern Morocco, bordering its Western Sahara colony, than the sultan had.[16] Spain did not even establish a colonial administration in Western Sahara for nearly half a century after its conquest.[17] This history at least partly explains why the monarchy has felt compelled to retain tighter control of areas formerly under Spanish control, namely the Rif and, since its "reintegration," Western Sahara.[18] It may also explain why developing and co-opting local elites in the country's hinterlands continues to play a central role in the regionalization strategy. Viewed through this lens, the stultifying effect of the dual administrative structure on decentralization efforts might be regarded as a feature rather than a flaw.[19]

Regionalization in Post-independence Morocco

Moroccan deconcentration and decentralization initiatives have been grouped into three phases, with advanced regionalization representing the third and current phase.[20]

Decentralization in postcolonial Morocco began with a 1959 law regarding communal elections. Laws adopted in 1960 delimited the boundaries of municipalities and rural communes.[21] The first local elections were held later in 1960. Prefectures and provinces, corresponding to urban and rural areas, respectively, were established in 1963. Provincial and prefectural assemblies participated in the first parliamentary elections that year. A 1973 decentralization law and a 1976 revised communal charter expanded the competences of elected communal officials.[22]

[15] J. Castellino and E. Dominguez-Redondo, "The Identity Question: Who Are the Sahrawis and What Is Their 'Home'?" in A. Boukhars and J. Rousselier (eds.) *Perspectives on the Western Sahara: Myths, Nationalisms and Geopolitics* (Plymouth: Rowman & Littlefield, 2014) 29–53, at 32–33.

[16] P. Curtin, *The World and the West: The European Challenge and the Overseas Response in the Age of Empire* (Cambridge: Cambridge University Press, 2002), 203–04.

[17] Spain's initial interest in Western Sahara was principally protecting the nearby Canaries. Barreñada, "Western Saharan and Southern Moroccan Sahrawis," 278.

[18] S. Zunes, "East Timor and Western Sahara: A Comparative Analysis on Prospects for Self-determination," in K. Arts and P. Pinto Leite (eds.) *International Law and the Question of Western Sahara* (Leiden: International Platform of Jurists for East Timor, 2007), 109–32, at 125.

[19] Houdret and Harnisch, "Decentralization in Morocco," 17–18.

[20] Ojeda-García and Suárez-Collado, "Western Sahara in the Framework of the New Moroccan Advanced Regionalization Reform," 192.

[21] World Bank, *Decentralization and Deconcentration in Morocco*, 9.

[22] Ibid., 9–10.

The "first phase" of Moroccan regional policy began with a 1971 royal decree dividing the country into seven regions. This phase corresponded to a period of acute regime instability, including a state of emergency, a regressive 1970 Constitution that abolished the Parliament's upper house (which, in practice, never convened) and expanded the king's powers, and failed coups in July 1971 and March 1972. Amid this volatility, the regions gave form to the monarchy's patronage network in the country's hinterlands.[23] Maintaining control of the periphery, in turn, gave credibility to the monarchy's claim that, unlike the nationalist parties whose support was concentrated in cities, the king had nationwide support.[24] Each region had a council comprising provincial and prefectural councilors as well as representatives of professional associations and trade unions.[25] The regional councils lacked legal status and formal competences. They played a "consultative and publicity role," spreading news of the central government's land reform and development initiatives.[26] A 1977 royal decree directed the *walis* (governors) representing the Crown at the regional and provincial/prefectural levels to coordinate and monitor the delivery of deconcentrated government services.[27]

Regionalization remained dormant for the next two decades. Meanwhile, the monarchy's fears of competing power bases at the communal and provincial/prefectural levels led it to "establish overlapping and competing institutions whose jurisdiction was based on vague and shifting laws."[28] This weakened and created competition among local elected officials, who turned to the Crown to affirm their authority.[29] Fragmentation thus enabled the monarchy to reassert greater control over urban policy.

Conquering the Western Sahara in 1975 gave the monarchy a new source of legitimacy as guardian of the state's territorial integrity, and with it greater control of the political system.[30] The influx of Moroccan settlers following the 1991 ceasefire with the Sahrawi national liberation movement, the Frente Polisario, was a pivotal expression of sovereignty over Western Sahara and tactical victory in the conflict with the Polisario.

"Second phase" regionalization served to consolidate those gains by establishing the framework for a "full administrative apparatus" in Western Sahara.[31] A 1992 constitutional amendment which modestly expanded parliamentary powers also gave

23 Á. Suárez-Collado and R. Ojeda-García, "The Effects of the Moroccan Advanced Regionalization Process in Western Sahara," *Transmodernity*, 5(3) (2015), 75–98, at 78.

24 See N. Mouline, "Reconsidering the Rif Revolt (1958–59)," *Jadaliyya* (January 28, 2015).

25 A. Boum and T. Park, *Historical Dictionary of Morocco*, 3rd ed. (Lanham: Rowman & Littlefield, 2016), 419.

26 Ibid.

27 World Bank, *Decentralization and Deconcentration in Morocco*, 10.

28 Catusse, Cattedra, and Janati, "Decentralization and Its Paradoxes in Morocco," 119.

29 Ibid., 117.

30 A. Tourabi, "Reform in Times of Revolution," Arab Reform Initiative (2011), 3.

31 Boum and Park, *Historical Dictionary of Morocco*, 420–21.

the regions legal status as territorial collectivities.[32] A new 1996 Constitution made Parliament's lower house fully directly elected and reconstituted the upper house. Restoring bicameralism also restored the function of regional councils as electoral colleges in elections to Parliament's upper house.[33]

A 1997 law redistricted the country into sixteen regions and gave form to the regional councils.[34] The new regions were "explicitly delimited with the idea of breaking the country's old cultural, historical, linguistic and tribal identities."[35] Each regional council was tasked with developing economic, social, and spatial development plans in line with national plans,[36] as well as investment promotion, environmental protection, and water resource management. In practice, however, the requirement of central government supervision (*tutelle*) for all expenditures and other budgetary matters left the regions without "capacity for legislative initiative."[37]

In sum, regionalization in its first and second phases was conceived and implemented not as decentralization, but as an additional level of deconcentration, premised on "the necessity of a centralized state to ensure the maintenance of political control and the country's territorial integrity, cohesion and homogeneity."[38]

THE WESTERN SAHARA QUESTION, 1999–2008

Mohammed VI ascended the throne upon Hassan II's death in July 1999.[39] Five months into his reign, the UN mission charged with implementing the self-determination referendum in Western Sahara, MINURSO, completed its provisional voter list for the referendum.[40] The voter identification process launched in 1994 had grown progressively more contentious and partisan, particularly concerning applicants presented by Morocco with dubious ties to Western Sahara.[41]

32 I. Lakrini, "Incremental Constitutional Reform in Morocco: An Approach to the 2011 Constitution," in S. Florensa (ed.), *The Arab Transitions in a Changing World: Building Democracies in Light of International Experiences* (Barcelona: Institut Europeu de la Mediterrània, 2016), 130–43, at 136.

33 Ibid., 136. Since 1996 the regional councils have elected 72 of the upper house's 120 seats.

34 Dahir No. 1-97-84 of April 2, 1997, Promulgating Law No. 47–96 regarding the Organization of Regions, Official Bulletin No. 4470 (1997).

35 Suárez-Collado and Ojeda-García, "The Effects of the Moroccan Advanced Regionalization Process in Western Sahara," 78.

36 World Bank, *Decentralization and Deconcentration in Morocco*, 11–12.

37 Ibid., 12.

38 Suárez-Collado and Ojeda-García, "The Effects of the Moroccan Advanced Regionalization Process in Western Sahara," 78.

39 J. Liddell and M. Monjib "Morocco's King Mohammed VI: 10 Years and Counting," Brookings Institution (August 5, 2009).

40 Report of the Secretary-General on the Situation Concerning Western Sahara (December 6, 1999), UN Doc No S/1999/1219, 9.

41 C. Dunbar, "Saharan Stasis: Status and Future Prospects of the Western Sahara Conflict," *Middle East Journal*, 54(4) (2000), 522–45, at 529.

Confronted with Morocco's determination to appeal every case in which its applicants were ruled ineligible to vote, the UN began backing away from its commitment to the referendum.[42] Secretary-General Kofi Annan instructed his personal envoy for Western Sahara, James Baker III, to "explore ways and means to achieve an early, durable and agreed resolution."[43]

Baker began by enquiring "if Morocco, as the administrative power of Western Sahara, was prepared to offer or support some *devolution of authority* for all inhabitants and former inhabitants of the Territory."[44] Baker's first proposal, the "draft framework agreement," envisaged limited autonomy and a status referendum within five years, in which anyone resident in the territory for one year could vote.[45] It did not guarantee that the referendum would include independence as an option. Baker achieved his principal objective of securing Moroccan acceptance of the plan, which the Polisario rejected and Algeria opposed.[46]

Baker introduced his more detailed "peace plan for self-determination of the people of Western Sahara" in 2003. It called for a five-year self-rule period under a Western Sahara Authority elected by voters listed on the UN's identification list (i.e., only Sahrawis native to the territory) followed by a status referendum that would include independence as an option.[47] All persons continuously resident in Western Sahara since December 30, 1999, meaning most settlers (*dakhilis*[48]), could vote in the referendum. With Algerian encouragement, the Polisario ultimately accepted the plan. Morocco, however, declared a referendum with an independence option contrary to what it considered the basic premise of a political solution: "devolution by the Kingdom of Morocco of strictly enumerated legal powers to a decentralised authority."[49]

The Security Council declared Baker's second plan "an optimum political solution" but underscored that any solution must be consensual, in essence acquiescing to Morocco's rejection.[50] Morocco formally rejected Baker's second plan in 2004 and

42 Report of the Secretary-General on the Situation Concerning Western Sahara (February 17, 2000), UN Doc No S/2000/131, 5. In total, Morocco appealed over 130,000 cases. Ibid., 34.

43 Ibid., 37.

44 Report of the Secretary-General on the Situation Concerning Western Sahara (June 20, 2001), UN Doc No S/2001/613, 2 (emphasis added).

45 Framework Agreement on the Status of Western Sahara ("Baker I Plan") (2001) UN Doc No S/2001/613, Annex I.

46 Reports of the Secretary-General on the Situation Concerning Western Sahara (2002) UN Doc No S/2002/41, 2 (Moroccan acceptance) and UN Doc No S/2002/178, 2 (Polisario and Algerian rejection).

47 Peace Plan for Self-determination of the People of Western Sahara ("Baker II Plan") (2003) UN Doc No S/2003/565, Annex II.

48 "Insiders," meaning those from inside Morocco proper.

49 "Observations of the Kingdom of Morocco on the New Proposal of James Baker Entitled 'Peace Plan for Self-determination of the People of Western Sahara'" (March 10, 2003) UN Doc No S/2003/565 Annex III, 23.

50 UNSC Resolution 1495 (2003) [1].

declared its refusal to entertain any proposal involving a referendum with an independence option, an interim administration, or a transition period.[51] The Security Council's next resolution on Western Sahara made no mention of the plan, prompting Baker to resign.

In April 2007, Morocco presented its own Autonomy Plan for Western Sahara, which claims to fulfill self-determination insofar as it anticipates a negotiated autonomy statute that would be submitted to a referendum.[52] The Security Council welcomed Morocco's "serious and credible" plan while "also taking note" of the Polisario's contemporaneous proposal.[53] Since then, annual Security Council resolutions renewing MINURSO's mandate have repeated this formulation and called for negotiations "toward a realistic, practicable and enduring political solution … based on compromise."[54] The secretary-general was at pains to argue "the fact that the Council had ruled out a nonconsensual solution to the question of Western Sahara did not imply diminished respect for international legality."[55]

At the Security Council's direction, Morocco and the Polisario, along with Algerian and Mauritanian representatives, held four rounds of direct negotiations in 2007–2008 at Manhasset, New York. Morocco insisted that its Autonomy Plan must be the "starting point and final objective of the negotiation process."[56] The Manhasset talks yielded no substantive progress and the parties have not held direct negotiations since. "Roundtable meetings" between them were convened by the secretary-general's personal envoy, Horst Köhler, in December 2018 and March 2019.[57]

In November 2020, the Polisario declared an end to the 1991 ceasefire after the Moroccan army took control of the Guerguerat crossing on the Western Sahara–Mauritania border.[58] As of March 2021, the Polisario continues to claim regular attacks on Moroccan positions. However, the resumption of low-level hostilities has not created a particular sense of urgency. Neither has the December 2020 US presidential proclamation which recognized Moroccan sovereignty over Western Sahara and declared: "an independent Sahrawi State is not a realistic option for resolving the conflict and … genuine autonomy under Moroccan sovereignty is

51 "Reply of the Kingdom of Morocco to Mr. Baker's Proposal Entitled 'Peace Plan for the Self-determination of Western Sahara'" (April 9, 2004) UN Doc No S/2004/325 Annex I.

52 "Moroccan Initiative for Negotiating an Autonomy Statute for the Sahara Region" ("Autonomy Plan") (2007) UN Doc No S/2007/206, Annex I, 8.

53 UNSC Resolution 1754 (2007) preamble.

54 UNSC Resolution 2548 (2020), 2.

55 Report of the Secretary-General on the Situation Concerning Western Sahara (October 16, 2006) UN Doc No S/2016/817, 15.

56 A. Theofilopoulou, "Western Sahara after Three Negotiating Rounds: What Is to Be Done?" Center for Strategic & International Studies (2008).

57 UNSC Resolution 2494 (2019) preamble.

58 Letter dated February 18, 2021 from the Permanent Representative of South Africa to the United Nations addressed to the President of the Security Council (February 19, 2021) UN Doc No S/2021/162.

the only feasible solution."[59] This persistent inattention has given Morocco the chance to "resolve" the Western Sahara question *sub rosa* through its regionalization strategy.

ADVANCED REGIONALIZATION

Like his father, Mohammed VI announces Saharan policy in yearly royal addresses commemorating the anniversary of the Green March in November 1975. The king's announcement in his 2008 Green March address of "a gradual, sophisticated process of regionalization which will cover all parts of the Kingdom, especially the Moroccan Sahara region" made explicit the link between Morocco's regionalization efforts and its Western Sahara strategy.[60]

The Mandate and Process of Advanced Regionalization

In his January 2010 speech establishing a Consultative Committee on Regionalization (CCR), the king laid out four fundamental principles for advanced regionalization: (1) respect for the unity of the state, nation, and territory; (2) solidarity and "interregional complementarity" between regions; (3) harmonization and balance so as to prevent conflicts between the regions and other subnational institutions; and (4) broad deconcentration.[61] This and other royal addresses comprised the CCR's mandate.[62]

The CCR defined the goals of regionalization to be increasing citizen participation in social, cultural, and economic development, modernizing state institutions, and improving territorial governance.[63] Its work did engender a degree of civic participation: the CCR received 124 submissions from political and social actors across Moroccan society.[64] The majority of these submissions focused on delimiting new regional boundaries, reorganizing regional political institutions, and redefining the regions' relationship with central state authority.[65] However, the monarchy's control of the process also caused certain political parties and civil society actors to boycott the CCR's consultative sessions.[66] More significantly, popular interest in

59 Recognizing the Sovereignty of the Kingdom of Morocco over the Western Sahara, Proclamation No. 10126, 85 Fed. Reg. 241 (December 15, 2020).

60 Commission Consultative de la Régionalisation, "Extraits du discours de SM le Roi à l'occasion du 33ème anniversaire de la Marche Verte" (November 6, 2008).

61 Commission Consultative de la Régionalisation, "Discours Royal du 3 janvier 2010 à l'occasion de l'installation de la Commission Consultative de la Régionalisation."

62 Commission Consultative de la Régionalisation, "Mission."

63 Ibid.

64 Ojeda-García and Suárez-Collado, "The Project of Advanced Regionalisation in Morocco," 52.

65 Ibid.

66 Ibid.

regionalization waned once the M20 protests erupted in early 2011, demanding a democratic constitution drafted by an elected constitutional assembly and broadly challenging state corruption as well as the lack of housing, work, and educational opportunities.[67] By the time the CCR published its report in March 2011, public attention had shifted to the constitutional reform process through which the king sought to defuse the protests.

The contours of advanced regionalization as sketched by the CCR are incorporated in the 2011 Constitution, adopted by referendum four months after the CCR's report.[68] The Constitution divides power between the regions' inherent competences, competences shared with the state, and competences transferred by the state according to the principle of subsidiarity.[69] It provides that regions shall dispose of their own financial resources and those allocated by the state, and that any delegation of competences must be accompanied by a transfer of corresponding resources.[70] It creates a social improvement fund for human development and infrastructure, as well as an interregional solidarity fund to ensure an equitable division of resources and reduce financial disparities between regions.[71] Additionally, it guarantees direct universal suffrage in regional council elections and the right of natural and legal persons to petition the councils.[72] It establishes the regional council president as the executive of council decisions.[73] It charges *walis* with assisting regional council presidents in carrying out decentralized competences and coordinating deconcentrated national competences.[74] The Constitution also specifies the contents of an organic law on regionalization, including the distribution of competences, rules governing regional council elections, membership, and governance, and regional funding mechanisms.[75]

A draft Organic Law on Regions was introduced in parliament in March 2015. Among the objections which the main opposition parties raised to the draft was its regional *découpage* (delimitation of boundaries), in particular that of the Saharan regions.[76] The Organic Law was adopted in July 2015 after extensive parliamentary debate. Regional, prefectural/provincial, and communal elections were held on September 4, 2015.

67 Given the diversity of the M20 coalition, the movement's demands were kept purposely "vague and non-prioritised." B. Chraïbi and Jeghllaly, "The Protest Dynamics of Casablanca's February 20th Movement," 115.
68 Constitution, Arts. 135–46.
69 Ibid., Art. 140; Organic Law 111–14, Arts. 6, 94.
70 Constitution, Art. 141.
71 Ibid., Art. 142.
72 Ibid., Arts. 135, 139.
73 Ibid., Art. 138.
74 Ibid., Art. 145; Organic Law 111–14, Arts. 83, 88.
75 Ibid., Art. 146.
76 Ibid., 196.

Regional Découpage

While the king directed that regionalization should advance a common national identity, the CCR received numerous proposals urging it to promote the country's cultural diversity and pluralism.[77] The CCR seems to have ignored these proposals in formulating its criteria for delimiting the boundaries of the new regions. Still, opposition to its regional boundary delimitations was largely confined to leftist parties and the Rif autonomy movements, who variously pushed for a "great Rif" region across northern Morocco or a smaller region grouping speakers of the Riffian Amazigh dialect, Tarifit.[78] In the Organic Law on Regions, Parliament made some changes to the CCR's proposed boundaries of the northern regions, including the Rif, but rejected either of these options.[79]

A few political parties encouraged the CCR to embrace asymmetrical autonomy and a special status for Western Sahara in line with the Autonomy Plan. In his January 2010 speech inaugurating the CCR, the king himself tied advanced regionalization to developing the Sahara and defending the state's "territorial integrity".[80] The CCR therefore set out to redraw the Saharan regions so as to facilitate the Autonomy Plan and reinforce Morocco's political and strategic position.[81] Parliament adopted unchanged the CCR's delineation of the Saharan regions.

Democratic Governance of Regional Institutions

Advanced regionalization significantly enhances the democratic governance of the regional councils. Previously, regional councils were elected by and from members of prefectural/provincial and communal councils. The 2011 Constitution enshrines direct elections to the regional council, while the Organic Law establishes a system of proportionate representation.[82]

Proportionate representation, coupled with the constitutional ban on regional parties, fulfills the national unity mandate by preventing "autonomy blocs" from forming within the regional councils. Consistent with its strategy of melding Sahrawis into the national body politic, the Moroccan state ensures that Sahrawis are deliberately overrepresented in parliamentary and subnational elections by

77 Ojeda-García and Suárez-Collado, "The Project of Advanced Regionalisation in Morocco," 52 n. 33.

78 Ibid., 56 n. 57.

79 Ojeda-García and Suárez-Collado, "Western Sahara in the Framework of the New Moroccan Advanced Regionalization Reform," 203.

80 "Discours Royal du 3 janvier 2010 à l'occasion de l'installation de la Commission Consultative de la Régionalisation," January 3, 2010.

81 Commission Consultative de la Régionalisation, "Rapport sur la régionalisation avancée/Livre II: Découpage regional" (2011), 137.

82 Constitution, Art. 135; Organic Law 111–14, Arts. 8–9.

limiting the number of *dakhili* candidates. Sahrawi voting historically proceeds along tribal lines, with relatively greater fluidity in allegiance to specific political parties.[83] Owing to this phenomenon and resulting candidate recruitment strategies, the parties represented among parliamentary constituencies in Western Sahara span the ideological spectrum.[84] However, a point of consensus among them is their embrace of the state's official discourse on the territory, centered on the Autonomy Plan as supplemented by advanced regionalization, greater democratization, and progress on human rights.[85]

Regional Powers, Funding, and State Oversight

Advanced regionalization modestly increases the powers and resources of the regional councils. The regions are given a preeminent role relative to other territorial collectivities in regional development and planning initiatives.[86] Through control of the social improvement fund established in the 2011 Constitution, the regions are expected to play a greater role in upgrading infrastructure.[87] To fund these additional responsibilities, the Organic Law establishes corporate and income tax transfers to the regions.[88] It envisages that the regions will supplement their budgets with income from property and investments as well as taxes, fees, and fines levied by regional councils.[89]

Building on the 2011 Constitution, the Organic Law on Regions also enhances the executive role of the regional president. The law vests the regional president with the authority to take "all necessary measures" to execute council decisions, including the regional development program, planning scheme, and budget.[90] The president exercises the region's regulatory power and directs the provision of decentralized administrative services.[91]

83 V. Veguilla, "Changes in Moroccan Public Policies in the Western Sahara and International Law: Adjustments to a New Social Context in Dakhla," in Ojeda-García, Fernández-Molina, and Veguilla, *Global, Regional and Local Dimensions of Western Sahara's Protracted Decolonization*, 235–56, at 240–42.

84 I. Szmolka, "Western Sahara and the Arab Spring," in Ojeda-García, Fernández-Molina, and Veguilla, *Global, Regional and Local Dimensions of Western Sahara's Protracted Decolonization*, 101–20, at 111–12.

85 L. Feliu and M. Parejo, "Western Saharan Members of the Moroccan Parliament," in Ojeda-García, Fernández-Molina, and Veguilla, *Global, Regional and Local Dimensions of Western Sahara's Protracted Decolonization*, 213–34, at 220.

86 Constitution, Art. 143; Organic Law 111–14, Art. 5.

87 Constitution, Art. 142; Organic Law 111–14, Art. 229.

88 Specially, the law provides that state transfers to the regions shall consist of 5 percent of corporate and income tax revenues and 20 percent of revenue from taxes on insurance contracts, plus credits from the general budget, with a view to reach a 10 billion Moroccan dirham ($1.05 billion) ceiling by 2021. Organic Law 111–14, Art. 188.

89 Ibid., Art. 189.

90 Ibid., Art. 101.

91 Ibid., Arts. 102–3.

Tutelle/Contrôle Administratif

Having inherited the French system of *tutelle* during the protectorate, it seemed logical for the CCR to follow France's lead in scaling back, if not eliminating, the central government's *a priori* review of regional council action. Accordingly, the CCR's plan envisaged that "*renforcement des contrôles a posteriori*," including greater judicial review of council decisions, would allow for substantial "*limitation des contrôles a priori et d'opportunité*."[92] Indeed, the Organic Law formally abolished *tutelle* (in Arabic, *wissayah*) in favor of *contrôle administratif* (Arabic, *raqqabah*) to be exercised by the *wali*, although *tutelle* remains in practice.[93]

The key area in which the Organic Law scales back central government control is regional finances. The Law denominates the regional president *ordonnateur du budget*, responsible for the region's revenues and expenditures.[94] The *wali* retains the right to voice objections in regional council proceedings and gains the right to seek judicial review, but his *a priori* approval is no longer required. Overall, however, the *wali*'s *contrôle administratif* over the regional council preserves the dual administrative structure.[95] That *contrôle* extends to the budget, all decisions impacting expenditures and revenues, administrative organization and delegations of authority, regional and spatial planning, the establishment of regional development companies, the delegation of regional public services and works, the disposition of property, and twinning projects with foreign entities.[96]

While it remains early days, the regions continue to suffer from weak administrative capacity due to inadequate resources and underdeveloped institutions. The Regional Agencies for the Execution of Projects, which the law established in each region, have yet to become fully operationalized.[97]

SUBSUMING SAHARAN AUTONOMY INTO ADVANCED REGIONALIZATION

The Western Sahara Question in the Era of Advanced Regionalization

Morocco's efforts to subsume the question of Western Sahara's final status into advanced regionalization are reflected in the yearly royal addresses commemorating the Green March. In his 2012 speech, the king stated that Morocco "will not,

92 Commission Consultative de la Régionalisation, "Rapport sur la régionalisation avancée/Livre I: Conception générale" 23 [20–21].
93 Organic Law 111–14, ch. III, Arts. 112–15.
94 Organic Law 111–14, Art. 209.
95 Ojeda-García and Suárez-Collado, "Western Sahara in the Framework of the New Moroccan Advanced Regionalization Reform," 202.
96 Organic Law 111–14, Art. 115.
97 Ibid., ch II, Arts. 128–44; Houdret and Harnisch, "Decentralization in Morocco," 947–48.

under any circumstances, allow the fate of the Sahara to be determined by the other parties' schemes and failed maneuvers … In this respect, I wish to reiterate our commitment to implement advanced regionalization, making sure our southern provinces are given priority in this process."[98] A year later, Morocco defeated a US proposal to give MINURSO a human rights monitoring and reporting mandate in Western Sahara and the Tindouf camps.[99] In his 2014 speech, the king called the Autonomy Plan "the most that Morocco can offer" and stated that "by starting to implement advanced regionalization and adopting a development model, Morocco wishes to increase the chances of finding a lasting solution to the artificial dispute over our territorial integrity."[100]

In 2017, the king conditioned Morocco's international engagement on the Western Sahara question on the UN and relevant actors, recognizing as "obsolete" and rejecting "any solution other than the full sovereignty of Morocco over Western Sahara and its autonomy proposal," and acknowledging "the Security Council as the only international body tasked with overseeing the settlement process."[101] The Security Council has never declared the situation in Western Sahara a threat to international peace and security, nor would doing so deprive the General Assembly and its subsidiaries of their competences related to the territory, which remains listed as a non-self-governing territory to which Chapter XI of the Charter applies.[102] Declaring these UN organs to have no role in the process signals a return to Morocco's pre-Autonomy Plan posture of denying that Western Sahara is, or even involves, a question of self-determination.

The Autonomy Plan and Advanced Regionalization Compared

There is an obvious incongruence in comparing the Autonomy Plan, consisting of thirty-five articles, which by its terms "aims to set the stage for dialogue and a negotiation process that would lead to a mutually acceptable political solution," with

98 Morocco Ministry of Culture and Communication, Full Text of the Royal Speech to the Nation on 37th Anniversary of Green March (November 12, 2012).

99 C. Lynch "Susan Rice Gets the Morocco Block," *Foreign Policy* (April 24, 2013).

100 Morocco Ministry of Culture and Communication, Full text of Royal Speech to Nation on 40th Anniversary of Green March (November. 6, 2015).

101 As summarized by the secretary-general in Report on the Situation Concerning Western Sahara (March 29, 2018) UN Doc No S/2018/277, 3 [11]. For full speech, see Morocco Ministry of Culture and Communication, HM the King Delivers Speech to Nation on 42nd Anniversary of Green March (November 6, 2017).

102 As a colonial territory, Western Sahara remains within the responsibility of the General Assembly's Fourth Committee and the Special Committee on Decolonization (the "Committee of 24"). Regarding the role of the General Assembly and the Committee of 24 on Western Sahara, see S. Koury, "Legal Strategies at the United Nations: A Comparative Look at Namibia, Western Sahara, and Palestine," in S. Akram, M. Dumper, M. Lynk, and I. Scobbie (eds.), *International Law and the Israeli-Palestinian Conflict: A Rights-Based Approach to Middle East Peace* (Abingdon: Routledge, 2010) 147–83.

the comprehensive Organic Law on Regions, which consists of 256 articles and fulfills the advanced regionalization process.[103] Nevertheless, the Organic Law clearly abandons several basic principles of the Autonomy Plan and cannot be reconciled with it. The most significant retrenchments relate to funding from exploitation of the region's natural resources (chiefly phosphates and fisheries) and guarantees for Sahrawi representation in the regional assembly.

Under the Autonomy Plan, the Sahara autonomous region would be funded *inter alia* by proceeds from its own natural resources *and* natural resources exploited elsewhere in the country, in amounts or percentages to be negotiated.[104] In contrast, the Organic Law does not include the proceeds of natural resources, whether originating inside or outside its territory, among a region's financial resources.[105] Instead, the region's funding comes from state allocations of national corporate, income, and insurance tax revenues, plus the region's own taxing, borrowing, and property holdings. Admittedly, the Autonomy Plan references self-determination only as a procedural requirement, satisfied through negotiations and a referendum; it does not suggest that its funding provisions are intended to satisfy the corollary right to permanent sovereignty over natural resources.[106] Nevertheless, advanced regionalization, which is premised on a unified national identity and the king's instruction to promote "interregional solidarity," retreats from even the barest notion that a region has a particularized interest in exploiting its own natural resources.

Regarding representation in the region's institutions, the Autonomy Plan broke from the official Moroccan discourse on Sahrawi identity by identifying Sahrawis among the region's "populations." The plan guarantees that Sahrawis, including returning refugees, will "hold a privileged position and play a leading role in the bodies and institutions of the region."[107] Recognizing that *dakhilis* will outnumber Sahrawis even with the full repatriation of refugees, the plan divides seats in the regional parliament between those elected by the various Sahrawi tribes and those elected by universal suffrage of the region's population, effectively double-counting the Sahrawi electorate.[108] In contrast, the 2011 Constitution and Organic Law provide for strict universal suffrage to the regional councils.

103 Autonomy Plan, UN Doc No S/2007/206, Annex I [7].

104 Funding under the Autonomy Plan would also come from regional taxes, duties and levies, proceeds from the Region's assets, and central government funds "allocated in keeping with the principle of national solidarity." Autonomy Plan, UN Doc No S/2007/206, Annex I [13].

105 Organic Law 111–14, Art. 186, identifying as region's financial resources its "own resources" as defined in Article 189, financial resources allocated from the state (consisting of tax revenue transfers), and the proceeds of borrowing (*du produit des emprunts*).

106 The UN Human Rights Committee understands permanent sovereignty over natural resources as the "economic content" of right to self-determination as set forth in Article 1(2) ICCPR and ICESCR. United Nations Human Rights Committee, "CCPR General Comment No 12: Article 1 (Right to Self-determination) the Right to Self-determination of Peoples" (1984) [5].

107 Autonomy Plan [4].

108 Ibid. [19].

However, the extent of state interference in regional council elections remains to be seen. Owing to the monarchy's tight control of Saharan policy, Western Saharan constituencies have largely been excepted from increasing transparency in the electoral process. Historically, candidate lists and even election results were negotiated between the monarchy and the political parties.[109] This system relaxed during the 2000s as wealthy elites, representing pro-monarchy parties, began competing for seats in their home constituencies, thereby "displacing other candidates such as the 'militants' in the opposition or ex-opposition parties."[110] One would expect the same trend in Western Sahara as Morocco reconciles its traditional "minority management" policy toward the Sahrawis (which involves selecting tribal elites as candidates) with the growing political force of the *dakhilis*, particularly its second generation.[111] Yet, as Victoria Veguilla has illustrated, Saharan *walis* discourage *dakhilis* fitting the profile of this new breed of parliamentarian from standing for election. This approach is coupled with the *makhzen*'s longstanding strategy of co-opting local elites by facilitating their election as regional, provincial, or communal presidents, appointing them as senior civil servants, or providing them with business opportunities. Further, Sahrawis are overrepresented in parliament because Moroccan parliamentary districts are not apportioned according to population and grossly overrepresent rural areas, particularly the Saharan regions.[112] The objective is to prevent "a radical transformation in the local power structure" which might cause Sahrawi unrest and renew international attention to Western Sahara.[113]

Sahrawi Identity and Nationalism under Moroccan Rule

Morocco's recent diplomatic maneuvers, such as defeating MINURSO human rights monitoring and rejoining the African Union (AU),[114] have reinforced its domestic narrative that Sahrawi nationalists are "lackeys for the former colonial power and/or of a new imperialism."[115] The king's role as guardian of Morocco's

[109] Sater, "Parliamentary Elections and Authoritarian Rule in Morocco," 394; Carnegie Endowment for International Peace, "Arab Political Systems: Baseline Information and Reforms – Morocco" (2007), 18, https://carnegieendowment.org/files/Morocco_APS.doc.

[110] Veguilla, "Changes in Moroccan Public Policies in the Western Sahara," 238.

[111] Ibid., 237–38.

[112] In the 2016 parliamentary elections, the resident-to-MP ratio for the three Saharan regions ranged from 35,516 to 54,176, compared with 128,000 to 147,000 residents-per-MP in the prefectures of Casablanca, Fez, Marrakesh, and Salé. B. López García and M. H. de Larramendi, *The 2016 Parliamentary Elections in Morocco: Context and Interpretations* (Madrid: Real Instituto Elcano, 2017), 7–8.

[113] Veguilla, "Changes in Moroccan Public Policies in the Western Sahara," 240–43.

[114] Morocco quit the AU in protest of the AU's 1984 recognition of the Polisario-led Sahrawi Arab Democratic Republic, which administers the sparsely inhabited territory east of the Berm as well as the Tindouf camps. Morocco rejoined in 2007 after a campaign of pursuing trade and investment agreements throughout sub-Saharan Africa.

[115] Zunes, "East Timor and Western Sahara," 128.

"territorial integrity" is thereby colored as not merely a nationalist cause but an anti-colonial one (with nationalism and anti-colonialism historically synonymous in Morocco, which was split between colonial empires). That narrative defies the fact that the Polisario has no patron equivalent to France or the USA nor, after a thirty-year ceasefire and with dramatically reduced military support, poses any meaningful military threat.[116] Morocco has long portrayed Sahrawi refugees in the Tindouf camps as Moroccan citizens held as captives (*séquestrés*) by the Polisario, an unsubstantiated charge.[117] Today, it also regards the Polisario as having taken hostage the loyalties of Sahrawis living under Moroccan rule. In response, the state continues its efforts to co-opt new Sahrawi elites and to prioritize the Saharan provinces in the state's economic and development agenda. The monarchy has linked its initiatives in these areas to the advanced regionalization strategy. Yet these initiatives compete with a state apparatus that suppresses all manifestations of a Sahrawi political program and views both southern Moroccan and Western Saharan Sahrawis with suspicion. As such, the initiatives have not had their intended effect of normalizing Moroccan rule in the Sahara, a necessary precondition for a symmetrical devolution scheme such as advanced regionalization.[118]

The official Moroccan narrative reduces Sahrawi identity to a geographic one: cultural traits which all Moroccans, regardless of ethnic background, may adopt by residence in the Saharan provinces.[119] Native Sahrawis are referred to as "Hassani," in reference to their Hassaniya Arabic dialect. As Hassaniya is also spoken in Mauritania and Mali, use of the term "Hassani" dilutes the notion of the Sahrawi as a national community and native minority. The 2011 Constitution, which contains two references to "Hassani" language and culture but nowhere acknowledges a Sahrawi ethnic or national identity, formalizes the Moroccan narrative. Its preamble declares that Morocco's "one and indivisible national identity" is a "convergence of its Arab-Islamist, Amazigh and Saharan-Hassanic components."[120] Article 5 proclaims Amazigh "the common provenance of all Moroccans, without exception," and elevates it to an official language, on par with Arabic.[121] In contrast, the same article commits the state to protect *speakers* of Hassaniya Arabic and the *cultural expressions* deriving from the language, to the extent legitimately practiced within the framework and discourse of national unity.[122]

116 Ibid., 120.

117 See Human Rights Watch, "Off the Radar: Human Rights in the Tindouf Refugee Camps (2014)," 24.

118 See T. Ginsburg, "Constitutional Design Options for Territorial Cleavages in the Middle East," Chapter 4 in this volume.

119 J. Mundy and S. Zunes, "Moroccan Settlers in Western Sahara: Colonists or Fifth Column?" in O. Haklai and N. Loizides (eds.) *Settlers in Contested Lands: Territorial Disputes and Ethnic Conflicts* (Stanford: Stanford University Press, 2015), 57.

120 Constitution, preamble.

121 Ibid., Art. 5(3).

122 Ibid., Art. 5(5).

Morocco's rigid construction of national identity and its tenuous hold on Western Sahara drive its policy toward Sahrawi identity, which Isaías Barreñada has described as acculturation followed by folklorization.[123] State policies historically discouraged or prohibited manifestations of Sahrawi national identity, language, culture, and history.[124] Pro-self-determination Sahrawi artists, including poets and pastoral storytellers, have been jailed, censored, blocked from participating in publicly funded cultural events, and have had their works destroyed.[125] Today, state-led initiatives ostensibly promoting "Hassaniya" culture "exploi[t] a simplified, 'folklorized' and decontextualized version of Sahrawi culture in order to better control it and reduce it to an asset of Morocco's tourism industry."[126] Whether by design, neglect, or lack of state capacity, government schools in Western Sahara do not teach Hassaniya Arabic despite the constitutional guarantee of its preservation.[127] The Moroccan historical narrative, centered as it is on the monarchy, independence, and the Green March, leaves no space for teaching Sahrawi history. Sahrawis are generally portrayed as being uncivilized prior to Morocco's "reintegration" of the Saharan provinces.

In sum, the Moroccan constitutional order preserves a national discourse which aggressively promotes themes of national unity and territorial integrity. The state denies a Sahrawi national identity (as opposed to Hassani cultural identity) and moves forcefully against its manifestations (often with the support of *dakhilis*, who are comprised heavily of veterans of the armed forces). This discourse was baked into the CCR's mandate for the Saharan regions and undermines the potential of advanced regionalization as an effective conflict resolution strategy.

Moroccan Co-optation and Development in the Sahara

Morocco's Saharan strategy involves co-opting and retaining the loyalties of Sahrawi elites. These loyalists ratify and mediate Moroccan policies within Western Sahara and, as state-proclaimed representatives of the Sahrawi community, champion them abroad. If normalizing Moroccan rule in the Sahara is a principal driver of advanced regionalization, then co-optation is part and parcel of the regionalization strategy.

The Royal Advisory Council on Saharan Affairs (CORCAS), which King Hassan established in 1982, had fallen into desuetude by his death in 1999. Mohammed's ascension and its promise of political reform encouraged Sahrawi student activists

[123] Barreñada, "Western Saharan and Southern Moroccan Sahrawis," 289.

[124] Morocco's relative neglect of the Sahrawis in southern Morocco, many of Western Saharan origin, during the period 1958–75 meant that they largely avoided the state's acculturation project. For this reason, among others, the Sahrawi national movement has never seriously questioned the "Sahrawiness" of their compatriots in southern Morocco. Barreñada, "Western Saharan and Southern Moroccan Sahrawis," 288.

[125] R. F. Kennedy Human Rights, Collective of Sahrawi Human Rights Defenders et al., "Report on the Kingdom of Morocco's Violations of the ICESCR in the Western Sahara" (2015), 22–23.

[126] Ibid., 22.

[127] Ibid., 18.

to establish protest camps in Laayoune later that year, which Moroccan forces violently dispersed. Demonstrations across Western Sahara in May 2005 and periodically throughout the year led Mohammed to reconstitute CORCAS in 2006. Its 141 members include Sahrawis from both southern Morocco and Western Sahara.[128] By royal decree, CORCAS has five committees, responsible for social affairs, human development, and the environment; external affairs and cooperation; human rights, public freedoms, and the populations of the Tindouf camps; economic affairs, education, and training; and promoting Hassanic (Sahrawi) culture, information, and communication.[129] CORCAS meets with foreign officials of states lacking diplomatic relations with the Polisario and heralds their reaffirmed commitment to Morocco's "territorial integrity." Its members are part of the Moroccan delegation to UN bodies involved in Western Sahara.[130] Although CORCAS is a consultative body, certain development projects in the Saharan provinces have reportedly been subject to its approval.[131] However, there is little evidence that CORCAS has been effective in winning the loyalty of new Sahrawi elites. It is composed of establishment figures who have served since 2006, although the four-year mandate of the current membership expired in 2010.[132]

From Morocco's perspective, reestablishing CORCAS may have backfired in that it helped remake Sahrawi identity according to a "traditionalist discourse" grounded in "cultural resistance against the occupier."[133] This has long been the approach of the Polisario, which since the 1975 displacement of Sahrawi refugees from Western Sahara (in Arabic, the *intilaqa*) has "introduced novel democratic institutions derived from indigenous cultural values" in the Tindouf refugee camps.[134] Disaffection with Moroccan rule – and with loyalist Sahrawis – may have pushed Sahrawis in the occupied territory further toward the Polisario.[135] Despite exile and limited international support, the Polisario has maintained support west of the Berm. It has also attracted Sahrawis from southern Morocco to its nationalist program, although its territorial ambitions remain steadfastly confined to Western Sahara. As a result of Morocco's full-fledged annexation of Western Sahara, coupled with its policies (e.g., regional and provincial delimitation) and institutions (e.g.,

128 Barreñada, "Western Saharan and Southern Moroccan Sahrawis," 289.

129 Conseil royal consultatif pour les affaires sahariennes, "Committees."

130 Including the Human Rights Council, the General Assembly Fourth Committee, and the Committee of 24. See Conseil royal consultatif pour les affaires sahariennes, "Domestic Activities" and "Foreign Activities."

131 Veguilla, "Changes in Moroccan Public Policies in the Western Sahara," 244.

132 Conseil royal consultatif pour les affaires sahariennes, "Royal Decree" and "Members."

133 C. Barona and J. Dickens-Gavito, "Memory and Resistance: A Historical Account of the First 'Intifadas' and Civil Organizations in the Territory of Western Sahara," in Ojeda-García, Fernández-Molina, and Veguilla, *Global, Regional and Local Dimensions of Western Sahara's Protracted Decolonization*, 259–76, at 260.

134 Zunes, "East Timor and Western Sahara," 130.

135 Barreñada, "Western Saharan and Southern Moroccan Sahrawis," 280–81.

CORCAS) which intermix Sahrawis from southern Morocco and Western Sahara, southern Morocco Sahrawis "have not structured their own differentiated discourse within the national movement."[136]

The result is that Moroccan rule over all Sahrawi areas is entrenched but not normalized:

> Policies of positive discrimination have generated suspicion in Morocco, tensions with the indigenous population persist, settlers who have not received the promised benefits are discontented, police control is systematic and the political liberalization enjoyed in the public arena in Morocco in recent years has been very limited in the Sahrawi areas, both in southern Morocco and in the occupied territory.[137]

This restive situation has caused the king to retain control over Saharan policy although he delegated key details of advanced regionalization to the government. Since advanced regionalization is largely about normalizing Moroccan rule in Western Sahara, this incongruence is as telling as it is problematic. Mundy and Zunes posit that Morocco rejects any referendum with the option of independence because it has doubts over the loyalty of the settlers, many of whom are southern Morocco Sahrawis and some of whom were forcibly relocated to Western Sahara following the 1991 ceasefire.[138] Could Morocco fear that further "hard integration" might backfire and foster Sahrawi separatism? Given the continued salience of "greater Morocco" in the national narrative, Moroccan claims of *Sahrawi* irredentism are pure gaslighting. Although the Sahrawis span Morocco, Algeria, and Mauritania, the Polisario has steadfastly confined its territorial claim to Western Sahara, as it must given its position that Western Sahara remains a case of decolonization. But as demonstrated by the dubious record of autonomy arrangements in undemocratic societies, the crucible of political repression reshapes national identity and objectives.

CONCLUSION

Writing in 2007, Catriona Drew called Western Sahara "a case of decolonization in an otherwise predominantly secessionist era."[139] Given sparse international support for the secessionist movements behind the 2017 independence referenda in Iraqi Kurdistan[140] and Catalonia, Western Sahara may now be a case of decolonization in a post-secessionist world.

[136] Ibid., 288. Nor have they espoused an irredentist vision of a greater Sahrawi homeland, meaning that "they are opting to support a Sahrawi national state project that initially excludes them." Ibid.

[137] Ibid., 280.

[138] Mundy and Zunes, "Moroccan Settlers in Western Sahara."

[139] Drew, "The Meaning of Self-Determination: 'The Stealing of the Sahara' Redux," in Arts and Pinto Leite, *International Law and the Question of Western Sahara*, 87–105, at 93.

[140] See P. Bartu and A. MacEachern, "The Devil Is in the Details: Iraqi Kurdistan's Evolving Autonomy," Chapter 10 in this volume.

Of course, decolonization in Western Sahara lost its racialized dimension when Spain ceded the territory to Morocco and Mauritania in 1975. The Sahrawis have thus suffered from what Adom Getachew has identified as the failure of anti-colonial nationalists to "recognize dispossession as a separate and autonomous form of imperial injustice," distinct from imperial domination and exploitation.[141] Moreover, as decolonization gave way to an era of "new humanitarianism" in which the postcolonial state was more an agent of privation and insecurity than of liberation, a culturally laden security discourse has captured the question of self-determination in Western Sahara.[142] Franco-American support for the Moroccan position forebodes a failed micro-state, overrun by terrorism, in an already-volatile Sahara-Sahel region.[143] It also plays on distrust of the Polisario's "indigenous socialism" and support among "revolutionary states" such as Cuba, South Africa, and its host in exile, Algeria.[144] The Polisario and its campaign for an independent Western Sahara are presented as hopelessly anachronistic at best and a threat to international security at worst. Such enquiries into the Polisario's ideology and governance capabilities, which are relevant in the current era with its concepts of "conditional self-determination" and "earned independence," would have been anathema in the decolonization era. The Polisario's commitment to a devalorized paradigm of decolonization is thus a liability to its nationalist program.

Meanwhile, renewed international interest in minority rights protections has given Morocco, through its constitutional reforms and advanced regionalization initiative, the opening to define the Sahrawis as a linguistic-cultural minority. Including Sahrawis from southern Morocco and Western Sahara in this program without distinction aims to strip Sahrawi identity of its national aspirations in any territorial space.

If advanced regionalization had introduced genuine subsidiarity, it might have complemented the state's efforts to render the Sahrawis a docile minority. Thomas Franck described subsidiarity as the modern expression of countervailing tendencies between association with the "nation" and its central authorities, on the one

[141] A. Getachew, *Worldmaking after Empire: The Rise and Fall of Self-determination* (Princeton: Princeton University Press, 2019), 86.

[142] Ibid., 104. This narrative runs parallel to, and complements, the prospect that the pro-Western Moroccan monarchy would collapse if it lost Western Sahara and be replaced by a regime less cooperative in regional counter-terrorism efforts.

[143] A prominent American proponent of this view, J. Peter Pham, was appointed US special envoy for the Great Lakes Region of Africa in November 2018. See Middle East Institute, "The Western Sahara Crisis" (March 11, 2010).

[144] S. Zunes, "Nationalism and Non-alignment: The Non-ideology of the Polisario," *Africa Today*, 34(3) (1987), 33–46, 38. As an example of hostility to the Polisario's quasi-socialist ideology, Pham objects, in nakedly neoliberal terms, to a constitutional article which provides that "[a]fter the complete recovery of national sovereignty, market economy and private initiative shall be recognized," claiming that it contradicts the constitutional right to private property and "virtually assures economic insecurity and underdevelopment." J. P. Pham, "Not another Failed State: Toward a Realistic Solution in the Western Sahara," *Journal of the Middle East & Africa*, 1(1) (2010), 1–24, at 15.

hand, and subnational units or identifications which transcend governance, on the other. The effect of subsidiarity is, in Franck's words, to "diversify the objects of personal loyalty."[145]

But Morocco's advanced regionalization will assuredly not have that effect because it is conceptually incongruent with the state's broader Saharan strategy. Morocco's postcolonial sovereignty claim was based on the loyalty of Sahrawi tribes to the sultan, which whether framed as "religious" or "traditional" ties, describes a relationship of fealty – a vertical loyalty. Its post-conquest strategy of cultivating royalist Sahrawi elites while denying a Sahrawi national identity sought to restore such a relationship. The 2011 Constitution held out the promise of a change in strategy. Its recognition of the Hasaniyya Arabic language and "Saharo-Hassanic" culture as part of the Moroccan national fabric,[146] although words not backed by deeds and a form of cultural appropriation, at least extends a claim of horizontal loyalty. Yet advanced regionalization seeks to reinforce traditional, vertical forms of authority. Alongside the monarchy's co-optation strategy, advanced regionalization represents the state engaging the Western Sahara and the wider Sahrawi population under its rule principally in geostrategic and security terms. The effect is further alienation, tighter security control, and Moroccan rule that grows more entrenched without ever becoming normalized, domestically or internationally.

It is doubtful US recognition of Moroccan sovereignty over Western Sahara, even if affirmed by the Biden administration, will change that equation. That the US traded its recognition for Morocco upgrading relations with Israel is a double-edged sword. The Israeli connection reduces the chance that the Biden administration reverses its decision. However, US recognition is tainted not only by its rankly transactional nature, but by association with the counterparties to the transaction: Donald Trump and Binyamin Netanyahu. Although the resonance of the Palestinian issue has diminished, the circumstances by which Morocco won US backing for its territorial claim nevertheless entrench its standing as a Western-reliant reactionary monarchy, further antagonize Algeria, and complicate its foreign relations, including its burgeoning relationship with China.[147]

Thus it has been said that "Moroccan policy toward the Western Sahara is a success in the sense that it has not been a failure."[148] With the Autonomy Plan as evidence of its good faith, Morocco's international patrons can shield it from the consequences of denying self-determination in Western Sahara. But they cannot steer the aforementioned internal dynamics nor unlock the regional integration that

[145] T. Franck, "Clan and Superclan: Loyalty, Identity and Community in Law and Practice," *American Journal of International Law*, 90 (1996), 359–83, at 369.

[146] Constitution, preamble and Art. 5(5).

[147] Y. Zoubir, "Expanding Sino–Maghreb Relations: Morocco and Tunisia," Chatham House (2020), 12.

[148] I. W. Zartman, "Morocco's Saharan Policy," in Boukhars and Roussellier, *Perspectives on Western Sahara*, 55–70, at 68.

the Saharan question keeps on ice. Morocco's readmission to the African Union and flurry of intra-African trade and investment suggests a belief that it can resolve the regional problem directly, or at least neutralize the Polisario on the latter's "own territory." To date, a detached international community has taken at face value the monarchy's claim that advanced regionalization facilitates implementation of the Autonomy Plan, when and if negotiated and ratified. The US proclamation of recognition declared the Autonomy Plan "the only basis for a just and lasting solution to the dispute over the Western Sahara territory." In reality, advanced regionalization withdraws the Autonomy Plan's promise of a unified Saharan region that would profit directly from its abundant but nonrenewable natural resources and guarantee adequate Sahrawi representation in the regional assembly. A more explicit retraction of the Autonomy Plan or, more likely, renewed unrest borne of the vicious cycle of disaffection and repression may force the international community, however reluctantly, to take the question of Western Sahara seriously.

PART IV

Decentralization, Conflict, and State Fragmentation

Decentralization, Conflict, and Sub-nationalism

15

Devolution and Federalism in Collapsed States

Constitutional Process and Design

George R. M. Anderson and Sujit Choudhry

This chapter examines four cases of collapsed states from the Middle East and North Africa region – Lebanon, Libya, Somalia,[1] and Yemen. In each case, state collapse was marked by the breakdown of national institutions and the effective loss of a functioning central government, at least for a period. Different governance arrangements appeared across the territory of the country, with various actors asserting authority over different areas, often through violent conflict. This is an extreme version of "decentralized" governance, the subject of this volume. State collapse leads to an inherently unstable situation that can evolve through different phases, including civil war and military intervention by outside powers.

This chapter discusses the nature of state collapse and its bearing on constitution-making processes and constitutional design. The examination of our four cases sets the stage for a synthetic and analytical conclusion that draws out our major findings, including lessons for constitution-making processes and constitutional design in collapsed states.

WHAT IS A COLLAPSED STATE AND DOES THIS CONTEXT AFFECT CONSTITUTION-MAKING PROCESSES AND CONSTITUTIONAL DESIGN?

The term "collapsed state" differs from "fragile state" and "failed state." The last two terms have been applied to wildly diverse situations – as is reflected by the development of numerous indices, such as the Fragile States Index, the Index of State Weakness in the Developing World, and the Bertelsmann Transformation Index – so much so that it has been argued that the "concept of failed state is so flawed that it ought to be abandoned."[2] State collapse, by contrast, is a narrower and more

[1] While not in the Middle East and North Africa region, Somalia neighbors the region, is a predominantly Muslim country and member of the League of Arab States, and is perhaps the archetype of a collapsed state. Moreover, Arab states have been deeply engaged in its politics.

[2] A. Tailor, *State Failure* (London: Palgrave, 2013), 224. Also see Z. Iqbal and H. Starr, *State Failure in the Modern World* (Stanford: Stanford University Press, 2016), 14–22.

tractable concept, because, as Iqbal and Starr put it, it is premised on "an explicit view of failure in its extreme form" and "captures the idea of a state without a functioning government, incapable of providing order and carrying out the responsibilities that international law has always expected of states claiming sovereignty."[3]

Because the threshold for a collapsed state is relatively high, very few states – even fragile ones – pass the threshold. For example, Lembach et al. operationalized a definition of state collapse occurring along three dimensions of state function in parallel – making and enforcing rules, wielding a monopoly over coercive power, and collecting public revenues – for at least six months, yielding a list of seventeen cases of collapsed states between 1960 and 2007, including Lebanon and Somalia. Our examination of the underlying indicators as of 2017 would retain Somalia and add Libya and Yemen. Iqbal and Starr – relying exclusively on the Polity IV database, which classifies some states as "interregnum" – identified twenty-six such states between 1946 and 2010. We reviewed the 2017 Polity IV database on the basis of this criterion, which led to the identification of thirty-one collapsed states between 1946 and 2017, including Lebanon, Libya, Somalia, and Yemen.

In a collapsed state there may cease to be even the pretension of a nominal government, or the nominal government's writ may be reduced to a small area and limited functions. In Yemen and Somalia, the nominal governments had periods in exile. Remnants of state institutions may be controlled by a central authority or armed rivals, depending on territorial location. Nonstate institutions may emerge in localities and regions that fill the vacuum left by the state. Actors operating at the local level may include traditional leaders, heads of militias, and criminal gangs. The territorial extent of their authority, their functions, their ties to supportive external governments, and their standing with the local population, will vary. They can be in conflict with one another as well as with any central government forces. State control may have been voluntarily or involuntarily ceded to or shared with actors other than legally recognized sovereign authorities.[4] Finally, there may be "ungoverned spaces" in which neither state nor nonstate institutions operate, which are truly anarchic and lacking in any semblance of governance.

In our cases, state collapse was a product of civil war (or at least the military takeover of the capital by the Houthis in Yemen). Civil wars do not necessarily lead to state collapse, because a government may lose control of some parts of the country but remain functional, with an army and central bureaucracy.[5] The civil war in Syria has not seen state collapse, in that the Assad government has never ceased

3 Iqbal and Starr, *State Failure*, 24.

4 A. L. Clunan and H. A. Trinkunas, "Alternative Governance and Security," in A. Clunan and H. Trunkunas (eds.), *Ungoverned Spaces: Alternatives to State Authority in an Era of Softened Sovereignty* (Stanford: Stanford University Press, 2010), 275–93.

5 Of course, governments that have remained fairly functional can lose civil wars, but their defeat may be followed by the victorious rebels quickly assuming power, in which case the state has not collapsed.

to function. The success of the Islamic State in taking over much of northern Iraq did not threaten the central institutions of Iraq. While collapse is normally associated with a failure of security and civil war, the extent and nature of violence after collapse varies greatly. There may be relatively little violence, or violence confined to particular areas or groups. The extent and character of violence can change over time, especially in countries going through long periods of collapse.

The proliferation of competing centers of power of very different kinds can greatly complicate state rebuilding. Constitution-making may have to be preceded by or integrated with a peace process.[6] Peace processes focus on ending violence (at least among the parties to the peace) and institutional design is often neglected, or a secondary consideration; they often produce interim governance arrangements, with longer-term constitution-making to follow. Absent a military victor, in a collapsed state the main players must negotiate if peace is to be achieved because none is able to impose an outcome. Foreign intervenors are often active in collapsed states and in associated peace processes, where they may also be partisans in the internal dispute. Because of collapse, there are no established procedures, so many process issues arise, including: the relationship between political issues (including constitution-making) and security issues (such as the demobilization, disarmament, and reintegration of nonstate forces into a single set of security sector institutions under civilian authority[7]); the participants in the negotiations (which may change from the peace process to a constitution-making process); the choice and role of mediators; and the key milestones on a political roadmap, such as interim power-sharing, elections, and the creation of constitutional assemblies.

Because a collapsed state has been territorially fragmented, one constitutional design option could be to build a new state on the basis of federalism or devolution,[8] perhaps basing the new regime on the territorial fragments in existence on the ground. But equally, a centralized model may be preferred given concern that federalism may risk the disintegration of the state. Moreover, elites will have their own interests, which may include power-sharing arrangements at the center. Designing and agreeing on a detailed constitution can be extremely time-consuming and fraught. Interim arrangements potentially offer a path forward from fragmentation and civil war to peaceful constitutional politics, while possibly deferring a conclusive answer on these fraught questions of constitutional design.

6 C. Bell and K. Zulueta-Fülscher, *Sequencing Peace Agreements and Constitutions in the Political Settlement Process* (Stockholm: International IDEA, 2016); G. Anderson and S. Choudhry, "Territorial Cleavages and Constitutional Transitions: Political Mobilization, Constitution-Making Processes, and Constitutional Design," in G. Anderson and S. Choudhry (eds.), *Territory and Power in Constitutional Transitions* (Oxford: Oxford University Press, 2019), 374–428.

7 Z. Barany, S. Choudhry, and K. Roach, "Security Sector Reform and Constitutional Transitions: Challenging the Consensus," in Z. Barany, S. Bisarya, S. Choudhry, and R. Stacey (eds.), *Security Sector Reform and Constitutional Transitions* (Oxford: Oxford University Press, 2019), 247–81.

8 Anderson and Choudhry, "Territorial Cleavages and Constitutional Transitions."

FOUR CASES OF COLLAPSE

Lebanon

Shortly after Lebanon's independence in 1941, sectarian leaders negotiated the National Pact, which provided for politics to be based on an elite power-sharing arrangement, with the effect that "both the parliamentary system and the executive ... were not only a mirror of confessionalism, but also enhanced it." Lebanon was effectively run by a small number of key families, with political loyalties primarily to clan and sect.[9] Given the weak consensus among the ruling sects, the state was relatively weak but highly centralized. The National Pact gave the greatest influence to the Christian, mainly Maronite, community, which also enjoyed the highest standard of living.

By the 1970s this power-sharing system was under strain. There was increasing civil unrest associated with poverty and underdevelopment, especially in the Sunni and Shia populations, which now outnumbered the Christians.[10] The sectarian communities were divided over the military activities of the Palestine Liberation Organization (PLO) and the presence of Palestinian refugee communities in southern Lebanon. Fighting between Maronite and Palestinian forces broke out in 1975, leading to the civil war, which lasted until 1990. The war drew in military interventions by Syria and Israel, as well as a short-lived multinational force of American, French, Italian, and British troops. The fighting was not only between the different sectarian groups and outside forces but also, especially in the later years, within the sectarian groups, with bewildering shifts of alliances between groups and outside powers.

While in the early years of the war, the Lebanese state survived in a reduced form, largely under the control of the Christians, in 1982 the president, a Christian, suspended the Constitution and the government's reach became limited to a Maronite-controlled mini-state. Israel, allied with Maronite forces, then invaded southern Lebanon and surrounded the PLO, which negotiated its withdrawal from the country. The sectarian character of the conflict among Lebanese intensified, with confessional segregation and militia rule becoming the norm.[11] The Lebanese state, always weak, effectively collapsed. The government of Lebanon consisted of little more than one militia among others, controlling a small area, though the Central Bank, Foreign Ministry and presidency remained quasi-functional. The cabinet was often paralyzed, and the Parliament was ineffective. The army split along confessional lines.[12]

[9] Nurit Kliot, "The Collapse of the Lebanese State," *Middle Eastern Studies*, 23 (1987), 54–74 at 67.

[10] For an analysis of demographic shifts see Kliot, "The Collapse of the Lebanese State," 61–65.

[11] F. Traboulsi, *A History of Modern Lebanon* (London: Pluto Press, 2007), 228.

[12] M. Zahar, "Peace by Unconventional Means: Evaluating Lebanon's Ta'if Accord," in D. Rothchild, S. Stedman, and E. Cousens (eds.), *Ending Civil Wars* (Boulder, CO: Lynne Rienner, 2001), 567–97, at 570.

From 1985 to 1990 the various militias largely renounced fighting one another, respected mutual borders, and "entertained close ties between themselves for a better spoliation and control of everything Lebanese."[13] These militia cantons approximated the elements of a Weberian state in that they offered security, held territory, gathered taxes, ran bureaucracies, and delivered services.[14]

In the summer of 1988, the country entered its ultimate political deadlock, with a failure to agree on a candidate for president and the emergence of competing claimants to be prime minister. In January 1989, the Arab League appointed a committee to mediate the crisis. Mediation failed initially, after which serious military escalation broke out, and Arab League mediators formulated a truce plan which called for a ceasefire and for the surviving members of Lebanon's Parliament elected in 1972 to meet in Taif, Saudi Arabia to negotiate peace. These representatives had largely been spectators during the conflict, and most had limited power bases, but they "were left to their own devices to hammer out the details of the agreement", with foreign mediators backing off after preparing the ground.[15]

The Taif Agreement addressed both the internal and external aspects of Lebanon's crisis.[16] It resulted in a significant readjustment of the National Pact and in practice ended Maronite hegemony and created more equal power-sharing among Christians, Sunnis, and Shias. Executive power was transferred from the Christian-held president to the Council of Ministers, where important decisions required two-thirds approval, giving each community an effective veto. Militarily, it called for all Lebanese and non-Lebanese militias to disband within six months and provided for the Syrian forces (about 40,000 troops) to assist the Lebanese government in spreading its authority over a period of two years. Most factions in Lebanon welcomed the agreement, but the Maronite leader Michel Aoun, after indicating his support, came out against it; he refused to step down as (the contested) president and moved to dissolve Parliament. A major conflict then broke out between the Lebanese Army, headed by Aoun, and the Lebanese Forces, a Christian-based militia. In late 1990, when Syria joined the US coalition expelling Iraq from Kuwait, it got US approval to move against Aoun, whom it defeated and sent into exile. Thus, "Syria effectively became the external implementer of Ta'if," which it did reflecting its priorities.[17]

The Taif Agreement paved the way for the reconstruction of Lebanon in the 1990s. Syria's role as political guarantor contributed to stability but it came under severe strain after Hafez Assad passed responsibility for Lebanon to his son Bashar

[13] Traboulsi, *History of Modern Lebanon*, 231.

[14] P. Kingston and M.-J. Zahar, "Rebuilding a House of Many Mansions: The Rise and Fall of Militia Cantons in Lebanon," in P. Kingston and I. Spears (eds.), *States-within-States: Incipient Political Entities in the Post-Cold War Era* (New York: Palgrave, 2004), 81–98.

[15] Zahar, "Peace by Unconventional Means," 570–1.

[16] Taif Agreement (November 4, 1989).

[17] Zahar, "Peace by Unconventional Means," 575.

in 1998. Bashar increasingly favored Hezbollah and opposed Sunni Prime Minister Hariri, who was close to Saudi Arabia. Bashar's anti-Hariri sentiment peaked when the UN Security Council passed Resolution 1559, calling on Syria to leave Lebanon and Hezbollah to disarm.[18] Hariri's assassination in 2005 sparked huge anti-Syrian protests by Sunnis and Christians in Lebanon, and forced Syria to withdraw. Bahout says this marked the "clinical death of Taif" and led to open hostility between the Sunnis and Shias.[19] In Syria's absence the country's politics became even more chaotic and dysfunctional.

By mid-2020, Lebanon was "at a breaking point. Its economy was imploding, and with it social stability."[20] The crisis was the "result of decades of colossal political and economic mismanagement and corruption enabled by sectarian power-sharing."[21] The government had resigned in 2019 in favor of a more technocratic regime, but the old sectarian, elite politics still dominated. After the massive explosion of a fertilizer plant in Beirut in August 2020, huge demonstrations by civil society brought the resignation of the government. There was a "complete collapse of trust in all institutions" and, for many, a rejection of the sectarian style of politics in favor of a national identity and shared interests as citizens.[22] In October 2020, the president designated Saad Hariri as prime minister and charged him with forming a government of technocrats, breaking with sectarian office-sharing. But by March 2021 the old system still blocked this from happening.

Municipalities have played an increasing role, as they did in addressing the Syrian refugee crisis after 2011.[23] Although some Christians advocated federalism as part of the civil war settlement, the more widely shared objective was to restore national institutions in a centralized regime and end localized militia rule. Section III of the Taif Agreement called for administrative decentralization, including enhanced prerogatives for governors and the election of district (*caza*) councils. It took until 1998 to agree on holding municipal elections, which have happened every six years since, but the *National Development Report 2008–2009* found that political elites viewed decentralization as threatening their leadership and clientelist relations.[24] The Sleiman–Baroud draft law of 2014, which would establish elected district councils and executives with enhanced fiscal resources, has not been enacted.[25]

18 S/RES/1559 (2004).

19 J. Bahout, *The Unraveling of Lebanon's Taif Agreement* (Washington, DC: Carnegie Endowment for International Peace, 2016), 14.

20 M. Yahya, "At a Breaking Point," Diwan, Carnegie Middle East Center (April 20, 2020).

21 Ibid.

22 Ibid.

23 M. Yahya, comments in M. Young (ed.), "*How Will the Coronavirus Crisis Affect Your Middle Eastern Focus Area in the Coming Months?*" Diwan, Carnegie Middle East Center (April 2, 2020).

24 N. El-Mikaway and C. Melim-McLeod, *Lebanon: Local Government in Complex Environments* (Cairo: United Nations Development Program, 2010).

25 M. Akl, *Administrative Decentralization in Lebanon* (Beirut: Democratic Renewal Movement and Konrad Adenauer Stiftung, 2017).

Hezbollah has emerged as a uniquely powerful actor: it maintains its militia (ostensibly to continue the combat with Israel) and controls a section of southern Lebanon. Indeed, it is the country's largest nonstate provider of health care, social services, and schools.[26]

Libya

Muammar Qaddafi ruled Libya from 1969 to 2011, after coming to power in a coup.[27] Qaddafi initially consolidated power by abolishing the parliament and opposition parties, establishing state control over religious institutions, and nationalizing banks and oil companies. He fashioned a regime around a set of institutions, including a prime minister (the General People's Secretary) and cabinet (General People's Committee) with ministers (secretaries) and a parliament (General People's Congress).[28] The regime was highly personalized, with power being wielded by Qaddafi along with members of his tribe and regime loyalists (and later his family). Qaddafi funded patronage networks with oil revenues. Qaddafi's foreign policy – especially his support for terrorist groups – led to international sanctions, which combined with lower oil prices, urbanization, population growth, youth unemployment, and poor economic management put stress on the regime. Qaddafi's son, Saif al-Islam, led half-hearted economic and political reforms, which ultimately foundered.

In 2011, inspired by events in Tunisia, protests in Benghazi escalated into armed rebellion and plunged Libya into civil war.[29] Aided by North Atlantic Treaty Organization airstrikes, armed rebels took Tripoli in late August, while Qaddafi fled to Sirte. After his fall, a self-appointed interim authority – the National Transitional Council (NTC) – asserted control over the Libyan state, but from the outset its control was limited. Hundreds of local militias had arisen as part of the uprising. There was never a single, integrated armed force after Qaddafi. The security landscape is fragmented. Militias forced weak ministers and authorities to hire their men and they effectively controlled some ministries (or carved up control among themselves).[30]

26 B. R. Early, "'Larger than a Party, yet Smaller than a State': Locating Hezbollah's Place within Lebanon's State and Society," *World Affairs*, 168 (2006), 115–28.

27 For overviews, we have relied on R. B. St. John, *Libya: From Colony to Independence* (Oxford: Oneworld, 2008); D. Vandeville, *A History of Modern Libya*, 2nd ed. (New York: Cambridge University Press, 2012); and F. Wehrey, *The Burning Shores: Inside the Battle for the New Libya* (New York: Farrar, Straus and Giroux, 2018).

28 "Holding Libya Together: Security Challenges after Qadhafi," International Crisis Group (December 15, 2011).

29 M. P. Boduszyński and D. Pickard, "Libya Starts from Scratch," *Journal of Democracy*, 24 (2013), 86–96.

30 U. Laessing, *Understanding Libya since Gaddafi* (London: Hurst, 2020), ch. 2.

This fragmentation posed a major challenge to the consolidation of a national political process,[31] intersecting with other cleavages – for example, the strong regional identity in the east in Cyrenaica (with Benghazi as its capital), which had longstanding grievances of discrimination by Qaddafi for favoring the western region of Tripolitania. Libya's third historical region is Fezzan in the south, largely populated by non-Arabs. Despite fragmentation and regionalism, the NTC issued a Constitutional Declaration in August 2011 that created an interim government charged with drafting an electoral law for elections to a new parliament, the General National Congress (GNC). The GNC would replace the NTC, oversee the drafting of a new constitution and then itself expire. The elections to the GNC in July 2012 saw roughly half of eligible Libyans (and 60 percent of registered voters) participate. The vote yielded a deeply divided body with a substantial Islamist component. The GNC proved unable to establish shared security sector agencies under civilian authority, or to launch the constitutional process.

In response to political paralysis, the GNC unilaterally extended its mandate from February to late December 2014. This move led General Khalifa Haftar, the head of the self-styled Libyan National Army based in Cyrenaica, to call for the dissolution of the GNC. This resulted in a compromise, in March 2014, whereby the Constitutional Declaration was amended to allow for the election of a new parliament, the House of Representatives (HoR). These elections took place in June 2014. The elections, in which 40 percent of registered voters participated, marked a sharp defeat for the Islamists, who in turn refused to accept the legitimacy of the HoR and reconvened the GNC. The Libyan Supreme Court – arguably under coercion from the Islamists – declared the election of the HoR unconstitutional in November 2014, which the HoR and Haftar refused to accept. This constitutional crisis precipitated the return to civil war with competing parliaments and governments – the GNC in Tripoli, and the HoR in Benghazi under the control of Haftar.

Since 2014, there have been several attempts to end the civil war through international mediation. The United Nations sponsored a process that resulted in the Libyan Political Agreement (LPA) of December 17, 2015, which provided for the merger of the HoR and the GNC.[32] It would reconstitute the HoR as a bicameral legislature with the HoR as the lower chamber and the GNC as an upper chamber (renamed the Shura Council). The LPA also established a new power-sharing executive, the Presidential Council (nine members), as well as a cabinet and the Government of National Accord (GNA) with seventeen members headed by the prime minister.

The LPA failed. The GNC did not sign it and it remains a separate body. Although seven members of the LPA's new Presidential Council arrived in Tripoli in March

[31] "Divided We Stand: Libya's Enduring Conflicts," International Crisis Group (September 14, 2012).

[32] Libyan Political Agreement (December 17, 2015), https://unsmil.unmissions.org/sites/default/files/Libyan%20Political%20Agreement%20-%20ENG%20.pdf.

2016, the remaining two members boycotted it, thereby depriving the council of legitimacy and rendering it unable to assert effective authority. The expanded HoR never convened. The GNA remains the internationally recognized government, but has not been recognized by the HoR, and has been ruled unconstitutional by courts in the HoR-controlled east – fueling competing claims of constitutional legitimacy.

The LPA lacked an overarching strategy on security issues to be integrated with its political arrangements. Haftar opposed the LPA because it designated the Presidency Council as the commander-in-chief, thereby removing his power. The LPA did not address disarmament, demobilization and reintegration, and security sector reform at all, though these were integral to reestablishing the Libyan state's monopoly on coercive power and would allow militias to envision their role in a future Libyan state. As well, the LPA did not acknowledge the facts on the ground and failed to institutionalize a role for local administrations, which were under the control of militias.

The Libyan Constitution Drafting Assembly (CDA) began its work in April 2014, prior to the LPA. It was elected with very low turnout, but with equal representation from each of Libya's three regions – Cyrenaica, Fezzan, and Tripolitania – reflecting the importance of regional identities and setting the stage for decentralization. Amid conflict between the HoR and the GNC, the drafting assembly continued its work and its role and independence were recognized by the LPA. In 2017, it produced a draft that provided for a strong president and very limited decentralization, replicating the constitutional patterns of the past to respond to the reality of the collapse of the Libyan state.[33]

Armed conflict continued. In 2019, Haftar marched on and laid siege to Tripoli, but faced fierce resistance.[34] Outside powers have played increasingly direct roles in this phase of the conflict, with the United Arab Emirates (UAE) and Russia providing military aid to Haftar, and Turkey (joined by Qatar) intervening militarily to support the GNA.[35] Turkey's intervention in the spring of 2020 turned the tide against Haftar, while Russia, in response, increased its support to him with fighter jets.[36]

In January 2020, Germany hosted a conference attended by eleven countries, the UN, the African Union, the Arab League, and the European Union. The Berlin Process supported the LPA, including the establishment of the Presidency Council and a roadmap through to parliamentary and presidential elections, but made no

33 Draft Libyan Constitution (July 29, 2017), www.temehu.com/CDA/final-draft-libya-constitution-29-july-2017-english-translation.pdf. For an analysis, see Z. Al-Ali, "Libya's Final Draft Constitution – a Contextual Analysis," International IDEA (October 4, 2017).

34 F. Wehrey and W. Lacher, "Libya's New Civil War and What the United States Can Do about It," *Foreign Affairs* (May 30, 2019).

35 J. Harchaoui, "The Libyan Civil War Is about to Get Worse," *Foreign Policy* (March 14, 2020); E. Badi, "Russia Isn't the Only One Getting Its Hands Dirty in Libya," *Foreign Policy* (April 21, 2020).

36 "Turkey Wades into Libya's Troubled Waters," International Crisis Group (April 30, 2020).

reference to the work of the CDA.[37] It called for unified security sector institutions under civilian leadership.

Haftar rebuffed the Berlin Process in April 2020, claiming a mandate from the Libyan people to lead Libya.[38] Haftar's external allies distanced themselves from this attempt at national leadership and his position was weakened by his failed assault on Tripoli and subsequent retreat. A tentative ceasefire in August 2020 was formally approved that October, and this gave momentum to UN-led talks through a forum of seventy-five representatives of the two competing legislatures. By February 2021, delegates had agreed on a voting system, which they used to elect an interim president and prime minister, who would serve until elections late in 2021. Although the process was tainted by evidence of lavish bribes having influenced the vote, the interim prime minister won a vote of confidence for his cabinet from the HoR in March 2021.

Somalia

The collapse of the Somali state was effectively complete by the mid-1990s. The oppressive regime of Siad Barre fought a bloody civil war through the 1980s, and in 1990 the combined opposition forces converged on Mogadishu and Barre fled. However, the largest opposition force, the United Somali Congress, split into competing factions, leading to looting, disruption, and famine. Interclan fighting in the early 1990s "when Somali civilians … conducted clan cleansing against other largely unsuspecting Somali civilians … marked the shift to the dominance of a new logic … and ripped Somalis apart in new ways," undermining the prospects for reconstruction.[39] Somaliland broke off and declared independence in 1991. With the collapse of the state, there was no pretense of national government during the 1990s, and largely a "patchwork quilt" of local political orders, often run by warlords, in neighborhoods, towns, and villages, though a regional government was established in Puntland in 1998.

In 2000, at the initiative of the president of Djibouti, the Somalia National Peace Conference met and established the Transitional National Government (TNG). This was essentially a deal among leading Mogadishu-based businessmen, powerful Djiboutian interests, and Islamists, but it was opposed by an important paramilitary group in the south, the state of Puntland, and Ethiopia. The TNG failed to establish security or effective institutions. Major Saudi funding to the TNG was quickly dispersed among key players and "reinforced in the minds of the political elite that

[37] The conference conclusions are annexed to Letter Dated January 22, 2020 from the Permanent Representative of Germany to the United Nations Addressed to the President of the Security Council, S/2020/63.

[38] "Interpreting Haftar's Gambit in Libya," International Crisis Group (May 4, 2020).

[39] L. Kapteijns, *Clan Cleansing in Somalia: The Ruinous Legacy of 1991* (Philadelphia: University of Pennsylvania Press, 2013), 12–13.

state-building pacts, even if stillborn, attracted easy money from external actors" so additional actors found it in their interest to come to the table.[40]

A breakthrough political settlement emerged from the intensive Intergovernmental Authority on Development (IGAD)-led process in Mbagathi (Kenya) from 2002 to 2004. As Ken Menkhaus has written:[41]

> [This c]ritical elite bargain … has been challenged, renegotiated, or reshaped several times since 2004, but … has remained the basic framework for the country's tenuous political settlement … It produced an accord on which a nominal government, known as the Transitional Federal Government (TFG) existed from 2003 to 2012. The post-transitional successor government … formed in 2012, the Federal Government of Somalia (FGS), has also been based largely on the elite bargain first struck in 2004.

A key feature was the "4.5 formula," a power-sharing arrangement at the center which apportioned political spoils equally to the four largest clans, with the small clans sharing a half portion. The bargain also recognized facts on the ground, notably the existing government in Puntland and the domains of various warlords.

This elite bargain was far from creating an effective system of government. The TFG and Parliament were in exile, gaining a toehold presence in the country only in 2005. However, an alternative group, the Islamic Courts Union (ICU), allied with the business community and civil society, expelled the warlords in 2006 and brought order to Mogadishu and much of the south. The ICU was unacceptable to the international community and many regions of Somalia, and Ethiopia intervened militarily in 2006 and, with Somali allies, pushed the ICU out of its areas of power. Some elements of the ICU broke off to form al-Shabab. Ethiopia withdrew in 2009, to be replaced by the 20,000-person peacekeeping African Union Mission in Somalia (AMISON), which permitted the TFG and Parliament to establish a presence in Mogadishu.

The Parliament had been formed using the 4.5 formula, whereby elders of each clan select their parliamentary representatives, who in turn elected the president. The Parliament initially had 275 members but was doubled to 550 to accommodate 200 former partisans of the Islamic Courts and seventy-five civil society members. The enlarged Parliament elected the former ICU chairman as president in 2009. The period from 2009 to 2012 was marked by paralysis. External aid fed a culture of extreme corruption, while the TFG was a "government" with almost no real presence or functions. In 2012, the international community sponsored a new process whereby 14,000 clan representatives were selected to elect a new parliament charged with drafting a constitution for the Federal Republic of Somalia.

[40] K. Menkhaus, *Elite Bargains and Political Deals Project: Somalia Case Study* (London: Stabilization Unit, Government of the United Kingdom, February 2018), 15.

[41] Menkhaus, *Elite Bargains and Political Deals*, 15.

The intent was to achieve a complete constitution, but the Constitution that emerged in 2012 failed to resolve both the allocation of powers between the federal and state governments and the number and boundaries of the states (though it set criteria for state creation). A key focus since 2012 has been putting in place the new regional states. Puntland had existed since 1998. Galmudug had existed informally since 2006 and sought official recognition in 2013, which was agreed in 2014. In 2013, the Ethiopian government mediated the Addis Agreement between the federal government and a self-declared Jubaland administration, giving recognition to the state and agreeing on certain transfers of powers. In the same year, the federal government and local representatives held a conference on creating a southwest state: this proved contentious because local groups split over whether it should be a three- or six-region state. The federal government insisted on a three-region state, which would have been consistent with the Addis Agreement. This view prevailed at the price of merging the two competing administrations into an oversized ministry.

Mohamed Abdullahi Mohamed was elected president in 2017 and strongly favored centralization. Under his leadership, Parliament approved laws regarding elections, petroleum, mining, taxation, civil aviation, and fisheries, which the president of Puntland rejected as illegal. The federal government became increasingly antagonistic toward the member states, which formed a common front, so that politics became "two increasingly distrustful forces entangled in political tug of war of unprecedented gamesmanship."[42] The regional state leaders suspended ties with the federal government in 2018. Subsequently, President Mohamed interfered in state elections, successfully seeing his supporters elected as heads of two states.

By 2020, the elite bargain was largely broken. The federal government had tense relations with most regional states and with powerful warlords sitting in Parliament. Events were challenging Menkhaus' argument that "[s]uch a path towards state-building is messy, fluid, conflictual, and not at all amenable to most state-building aid programs. But it is a much more realistic model of how weak states seek to claim, and gradually build, authority over their territories."[43]

In 2017, the federal government set out a roadmap for completing the constitutional review and holding elections by 2020. Given the security situation, there would be indirect elections, with a few thousand delegates electing the Parliament that would elect the president. But by February 2021, leaders still had not resolved key mechanics or the date for the election, and opposition leaders hostile to the president claimed his term had expired so they were ceasing to recognize him as president. International mediators called for a cooling of the tense environment, which had seen violent clashes between opposition supporters and security forces.

42 Heritage Institute for Policy Studies, *Options to End Somalia's Current Political Stalemate* (October 2018), 1–2.

43 K. Menkhaus, "State Collapse and Local Response in Somalia," in I. Trauschweizer and S. M. Miner (eds.), *Failed States and Fragile Societies: A New World Disorder?* (Athens: Ohio University Press, 2014), 142–50, at 149.

The international community has played a mixed role in Somalia's long transition. The Intergovernmental Authority on Development (IGAD) and the UN, largely supported by Western donors, have sponsored endless meetings and tried to respect the principle of a process led by local actors. But geopolitics has been at play as well. "Somalia has become a chessboard in the power game between Qatar and Turkey on one side and Saudi Arabia, the United Arab Emirates and their allies on the other."[44] The UAE is building a massive base in Somaliland and is also bypassing the federal government to strike deals with regional states. Mogadishu, the only real redoubt of the federal government, has a vast Turkish base and its port is run by a Turkish company. Ethiopia, which had favored the regional states, has shifted to supporting Mogadishu, notably in Jubaland where there has been intense jockeying over local control, which sparked a serious military clash between federal and state forces. Kenya, for its part, supports Jubaland. These tensions divert efforts to defeat al-Shabab's insurgency. Long-time observer Alex de Waal suggests Somalia's international backers might outlast al-Shabab – if slowly and haltingly – given some positive economic developments. But this "war must be won politically as well as militarily … [so] the Somali government must cultivate an Islamist constituency of its own, winning over most of the political and financial backers of the ICU."[45] And defeating al-Shabab would still not resolve the deep divisions over the form of the Somali state.

Yemen

When the Arab Spring sparked a popular uprising in 2011 that forced the resignation of Yemen's long-time strongman Ali Abdullah Saleh, the country was already politically stressed and Saleh faced "a bewildering array of political conflicts."[46] Saleh had proved a master of patronage politics, playing sheikhs and tribal chiefs off one another.[47] Discontent was boiling in the South, which had been exploited following unification with the North in 1990 and then brutally repressed after a revolt in 1994. In the northern border area, the armed movement rooted in the Zaidi-Shia tradition led by Hussein Badreddin al-Houthi had fought five short wars against Saleh and was openly hostile. The economy was extremely weak, with high unemployment, which gave city dwellers ample grievances.

The transition to a new regime was remarkably quick. Abdrabbuh Mansur Hadi, Saleh's weak vice-president, became president and a national unity government was

44 "How the Crisis in the Gulf Could Spread to East Africa," *BBC* (April 8, 2018).

45 A. de Waal, "Can Somalia Ever Win against Al-Shebab?" *Foreign Policy* (October 19, 2017).

46 T. Juneau, "Elite Struggles, State Collapse and Regional Security: Yemen and the Arab Awakening," *Orbis*, 57(3) (2013), 408–23; S. Phillips, *Yemen and the Politics of Permanent Crisis* (New York: Routledge, 2011).

47 I. Blumi, *Chaos in Yemen: Societal Collapse and the New Authoritarianism* (New York: Routledge, 2011), 155–56. Blumi argues that this represented a break from Yemen's earlier, more deliberative and accommodative politics.

formed by Saleh's party and the established opposition parties, but it had no representatives of dissidents from the South, the Houthis, and civil society. The government proved dysfunctional, while the economy and security deteriorated. The United Nations and neighboring Arab countries promoted an ambitious National Dialogue to set national goals and the basics of a new constitution. However, the National Dialogue suffered from having 565 delegates required to achieve consensus, and from the absence of key powerful players, including Saleh, who acted as spoilers from the outside. The National Dialogue reached a weak consensus in favor of federalism, with an unwieldy model of six regions on top of the existing twenty-two governorates, and with many important issues, such as the division of powers, very unclear. On the critical issue of state delineation, Hadi pushed through a six-region model that was totally unacceptable to the Houthis, who would be a minority in a state with no access to the sea and no important resources. The proposed state structure was also detested by some leading southerners, who wanted the South to be one region. While the National Dialogue was meeting, the Houthis had advanced militarily down from the North. When rioting over the end of fuel subsidies broke out in August 2014, the Houthis entered an alliance with their old enemy Saleh and took over control of Sana'a. Hadi's position was hopeless and he resigned. Within days, he revoked his resignation and established himself in Aden, supported by international recognition as the legitimate president.

The Houthis and Saleh's forces then launched an offensive on the South. Meanwhile, Saudi Arabia formed an international coalition of ten Arab states (backed by the United States, the United Kingdom, and France) supporting Hadi. The Saudis undertook a campaign of heavy air bombardments in aid of government troops and brought in several thousand Sudanese mercenaries. Their allies, the UAE, deployed 3,500 land troops, with some 5,000 air and offshore troops in support. The war quickly became internationalized, though the various members of the coalition had quite different objectives.

By the spring of 2016, Peter Salisbury wrote that Yemen was a deeply fragmented "chaos state."[48] This was something of an exaggeration in that the Houthis had effective control of much of the North, including Sana'a – though their regime was characterized by oppressive taxation, a lack of services, and a singular focus on warfare. The situation was still very fluid in other areas, but by 2020 the division of the country fell into roughly five areas controlled respectively by the Houthis, the Hadi government, southern separatists, the Joint Resistance forces (along the Red Sea), and local authorities in Hadramawt.[49]

Early in the combat, the Saudis pushed for United Nations Security Council Resolution 2216, which called on the Houthis to withdraw from Sana'a, hand over seized weapons, and cease actions within the authority of the government of

48 P. Salisbury, "Yemen: Stemming the Rise of the Chaos State," Chatham House (May 2016).

49 "Rethinking Peace in Yemen," International Crisis Group (July 2, 2020).

Yemen.[50] This resolution provided no real basis for negotiations because it called for the Houthis to give up all their gains before entering talks and increasingly became an obstacle to diplomatic progress.

A first serious engagement was in 2016 when the Houthis and Saleh met Hadi in Kuwait, though the real negotiations were backroom talks between the Saudis and the Houthis. It was rumored that a deal might see the Houthis agree to secure the Saudi–Yemen border, and to distance themselves from Iran and become allies with Saudi Arabia (which they once had been); in return, the Saudis would agree to the Houthis being dominant in a national unity government. The deal failed, apparently because Saleh insisted the sanctions on him be lifted and there be a role for his son.

The Saudis were being heavily criticized for their bombing campaign and the worsening humanitarian situation, when the exiled, Washington-based Saudi journalist, Jamal Khashoggi, was murdered in October 2018. The negative international reaction put Saudi Arabia under even greater pressure, which led it to agree to UN-mediated talks in Stockholm between the Hadi government and the Houthis. Under US pressure, the Saudis agreed to a package including a ceasefire in Hodeidah and other ports and their opening for humanitarian aid, a swap of 15,000 prisoners and detainees, and discussions toward creating a humanitarian corridor to the Taiz governorate.[51] The deal led the UAE, which had wanted to push into Hodeidah, to start withdrawing its ground troops from Yemen.

The Stockholm Accord may have prevented a bloodbath, but it did not stop the war. The Saudis were shocked in the fall of 2019 by a missile attack on the Aramco refineries (perhaps by the Iranians), which led to direct, secret talks between the Saudis and Houthis, though with little progress. Earlier in August, the Southern Transitional Council (STC) had seized Aden from the Hadi government. In December, the Saudis brokered the Riyadh Agreement to create a new government equally made up of Hadi and STC ministers, but this collapsed within weeks and the STC declared self-governance for at least part of the South.

In the absence of diplomatic progress, the Houthis moved forward militarily, taking Al-Jawt in early 2020 and then threatening Mahrib, the last government allied bastion in the North, into 2021. With the Houthis in a strong position militarily, there were still no serious negotiations in early 2021. The new Biden administration marked an American shift toward trying to end the war, while the UN warned of potentially the worst famine in seventy-five years. Any peace would require buy-in from the Saudis and perhaps the UAE[52] but the Saudis have trouble defining a face-saving exit. The Houthis indicated after the STC took Aden that they would support

[50] S/RES/2216 (2015).

[51] Stockholm Agreement (December 13, 2018), https://dppa.un.org/en/full-text-of-stockholm-agreement.

[52] P. Salisbury, "Yemen: National Chaos, Local Order," Chatham House (December 20, 2017).

a federal regime but offered no specifics and they would expect a leading role in the national government. The short-lived Riyadh Agreement would have brought the STC to the negotiating table, but they are now on the outside as are the Joint Resistance forces and authorities in Hadramawt. Given the difficulties in multilateralizing the negotiations, the Saudis may try to impose a settlement if they can reach an understanding with the Houthis, but any agreement made without buy-in from key domestic groups may prove untenable.

ANALYSIS

Challenges of Constitution-Making Processes in Collapsed States

The most fundamental reason why constitution-making is so difficult in collapsed states is the depth of the divisions among the factions. In our four cases, there are advocates of strong centralization and of federalism or devolution – even secession, as in Yemen and Somalia. These different preferences can be ideological, but they also reflect what groups or leaders see as being in their self-interest. Progress in a constitutional process requires the key parties to conclude that continuing their combat is no longer in their interests, which may happen only after both are exhausted by fighting. Even then, finding common ground may prove elusive.

Any process to design a political settlement and a future constitution faces difficult questions. *When* should the major issues of constitutional design be addressed – during or after peace negotiations? *Who* should participate in drafting the new constitution? *What* issues should be addressed in *which* order? A peace process focuses on ending violence through a ceasefire and peace agreement, but may not address institutions. Peace negotiations are usually confidential and limited to active combatants – who may include foreign intervenors. Peace agreements often establish interim governance arrangements, notably power-sharing, as well as basic principles of process and substance for the future constitution. Constitution-making is often a longer-term process that allows for engagement with a broader cross section of political actors, such as opposition parties and civil society. The process of amending or writing a constitution might include elections or a referendum.

In Lebanon, the peace and constitutional processes were tightly integrated. The Taif Agreement emerged from peace negotiations among parliamentarians, who later constitutionalized relevant provisions. This worked because the constitutional revisions were relatively limited, with consensus on retaining a centralized regime (thus avoiding the complications of negotiating a federal arrangement). However, in Libya, Somalia, and Yemen, constitution-drafting has followed, or been separate from, peace negotiations.

A constitutional process would normally be led by a parliament or constituent assembly. Electing such a body in situations of state collapse or deep insecurity may be impossible. Alternative approaches to create a constitutional forum may be necessary, and were attempted in Somalia, Libya, and Yemen. In Somalia, the Mbagathi process from 2002 to 2004 struck the fundamental power-sharing bargain among clan elites that permitted the creation of the TFG. It took the fifteen-member Federal Constitutional Commission several years before delivering an incomplete draft constitution to the National Constituent Assembly of 825 delegates. The assembly had been "selected", not elected, proved dysfunctional, and was able to approve only a provisional and incomplete constitution. Critical issues of federal design were left unresolved, and their resolution requires the agreement of the heads of all the regional states and the federal government – a distant prospect given current divisions.

The legitimacy of Libya's CDA of sixty members was weakened by its small electorate and very low turnout. The larger, more representative HoR easily challenged its legitimacy, and its draft constitution died in a context of civil war and political infighting. In Yemen, effective parliamentary elections could not be organized, so 565 delegates were named to the National Dialogue, which was to decide the country's future constitutional form. This was unwieldy and undermined by key players on the outside who played the role of spoilers. The eventual draft constitution was unclear on key issues of federal design and the proposed six-region structure was widely rejected. Even so, the results of the National Dialogue have remained a reference point for some combatants in the civil war.

Role of International Actors in Constitution-Making

The Busan Partnership for Effective Development Co-Operation, now endorsed by over 150 countries, aims to shift donor-led interventions in fragile countries to equal partnerships, with "country-led and country-owned transitions out of fragility."[53] In our cases, while the United Nations has tried to mediate following these principles, some sovereign countries have intervened militarily and tried to influence political developments in a highly directive and brutal manner as partisans to the conflict.

Sean Kane has written that "[t]here is broad consensus that (external military) intervention results in longer and deadlier civil wars and reduces the likelihood of a negotiated settlement."[54] He argues that mediators should design processes to include both international and domestic actors and sequence the external and internal dimensions of the conflicts, with the withdrawal of foreign troops as a primary objective. In all our cases, there has been significant military intervention by outside states drawn in by the vacuum created by state collapse.

53 "A New Deal for Engagement in Fragile States," International Dialogue on Peacebuilding and Statebuilding (November 30, 2011).

54 S. W. Kane, "Making Peace when the Whole World Had Come to Fight: The Mediation of Internationalized Civil Wars," *International Peacekeeping*, 29(2) (2020), 117–203.

Syria had 40,000 troops in Lebanon prior to the Taif Agreement, and kept them there until 2005, far beyond the two years stipulated for their withdrawal. It finally withdrew only because of Lebanese reaction to the assassination of former Lebanese prime minister, Rafik Hariri. Ethiopia invaded Somalia in 2000 to defeat the ICU and withdrew after two more years, having no interest in siding with competing clans on the shape of the federation. Around 20,000 AMISON troops were brought in to combat al-Shabab, but they have played no political role and al-Shabab itself remains outside the political process. Saudi Arabia was engaged from the outset in Yemen's civil war, and the Hadi government has become a virtual agent of the Saudi government. The UAE's intervention in Yemen resulted in the STC becoming an effective military force that took on Hadi's forces and claimed independence. Finally, the conflict in Libya has become a virtual proxy war, with Haftar supported by Russia, the UAE, and Saudi Arabia, while the GNA has received military support from Turkey and financial aid from Qatar.[55] These interventions reflect geopolitical and ideological rivalries with Saudi Arabia, the UAE, Egypt, and allies opposing Iran, Turkey, Qatar, and Syria; Western powers largely support the former group and Russia the latter.

Kane sees mediators as neutral and distinct from the partisan actors. However, in Yemen, the United Nations' neutrality was undercut initially by Security Council Resolution 2216, which was pushed through by the Saudis and their allies; it asserted the legitimacy of the Hadi government and basically called on the Houthi to surrender prior to talks. Subsequently, the Saudis negotiated in secret with the Houthis, in the absence of a mediator or Hadi, while under the Biden administration the UN Special Envoy had an early meeting with a Houthi leader. In Lebanon, the Arab League, along with Saudi Arabia and Syria, set the stage for the Taif negotiations and had the leverage to produce an agreement – which a neutral international mediator might not have. Moreover, Syria assumed a central role in Lebanese politics as the "implementer" of the Taif Agreement for fifteen years.

Involving external intervenors in peace negotiations – whether through mediated talks or otherwise – is clearly important, but is limited in what it can achieve. External intervenors typically play a more substantive role in initial peace negotiations than in any subsequent process of constitution-making. Thus, while IGAD and the UN have played the major role in shaping Somalia's constitution-making process, with funding from supportive governments, their role has been more as facilitators than mediators, and they have not taken positions on the substantive issues. However, Somalia's "country-led and country-owned" processes have proven incapable of resolving the deep differences among the internal factions, and the UN and other external actors have lacked the leverage to push them to conclude

55 R. Aliahoum, "Libya's War: Who Is Supporting Whom?" *Al Jazeera* (January 9, 2020).

an agreement. The National Dialogue process in Yemen, which preceded collapse, was similar in that the UN and the Gulf Cooperation Council played a largely neutral role on substance and lacked the leverage to force the relevant parties to the table and a resolution of core issues. In Libya, the UN-sponsored CDA approved a draft constitution, but the assembly had limited legitimacy and its draft failed to win support from the warring factions.

In sum, external intervenors may necessarily be engaged in peace negotiations in which certain terms, such as troop withdrawal, will apply directly to them. Moreover, they may be able to lean on their internal partisans to agree to peace. On occasion, that peace agreement may also be a constitutional settlement, as happened in Lebanon (and similarly in Bosnia). However, externally imposed constitutional settlements may lack consensus in the society and prove hard to sustain. If a peace settlement is followed by a constitution-making process, external actors would normally have less stake in the outcome and so may promote a domestically owned process, which may be mediated or facilitated by an international body. But given deep divisions, domestically owned processes may prove incapable of reaching a substantive conclusion about the future constitutional order, and the society may continue for years with an uneasy peace, a frozen conflict, and the confusion of a partial constitutional transition – as in Somalia, where De Waal suggests the political order may never revert to a Weberian model of statehood.[56]

Interim vs. Longer-Term Options for Devolution

A particular challenge for constitution-making after state collapse can arise when a federal or devolved structure is an option. While territorial fragmentation in a situation of state collapse may suggest federalism or devolution as a natural response, negotiating federalism can be an order of magnitude more difficult than negotiating a unitary regime, given the need to decide the number and boundaries of constituent units, the allocation of powers, and the institutional arrangements at the center. Realities on the ground may create a status quo ante and path dependencies for the ultimate design of the state, giving parties whose goal is regional autonomy greater leverage than they would have had under the previous regime. Thus in Somalia, Puntland has been able to maintain a veto on any transfer of its powers to the federal government. But even in these cases, as Somalia illustrates, it may be necessary to proceed by steps, perhaps with interim power-sharing arrangements at the center or step-by-step building of the central and regional governments. Of course, there is no guarantee that collapse sets the stage for a new federal or devolved regime. Lebanon opted for centralization with

[56] A. de Waal, *The Real Politics of the Horn of Africa: Money, War and the Business of Power* (Cambridge: Polity, 2013).

only the most modest and tardy gestures of decentralization. The draft Libyan constitution of 2017 was centralizing, but given the subsequent evolution of the conflict this might change.

The debates in Yemen illustrate some of the dynamics of negotiating a federal arrangement. The Yemeni Constitution is unitary, and its twenty-two governorates were essentially administrative with final authority reserved to the central government. While there has been a measure of consensus on federalism, Hadi's proposed six-region map was unacceptable to the Houthis and most southerners, and the allocation of powers in the draft constitution was far from settled. With the civil war, both the Houthis and Hadi's forces claim to support federalism, but neither has advanced a real vision of federalism, and the STC's first preference is secession. Even if there were some agreement on federalism in principle, it would take time and hard negotiations to resolve its form and to implement it – but no such result can be assured. The priority for the Houthis has always been power-sharing at the center (and given their strength, likely with Houthi predominance). The STC will likely demand substantial political devolution from the outset. The lack of consensus on a new regional state structure might encourage recourse to a regime devolved to the existing governorates, which have some legitimacy as political units.

A contrast with Lebanon is instructive. During the civil war, it was divided into militia cantons which each provided security and public services. Reconstitution as a federal state was never a goal for most parties because populations were so intermixed and elites favored central power-sharing. The focus of constitutional politics was not on territorial autonomy, but legislative and executive power-sharing, representation in the bureaucracy and military, and sharing fiscal resources. In Libya, the negative experience of state collapse led the CDA to prepare a draft constitution with a strong president and very limited decentralization and no hint of federalism or devolution, though that approach may be questioned once peace negotiations begin, given the strength of autonomous sentiment in the east.

Paralysis arising from competing longer-term constitutional visions, as in Yemen, can be addressed in three ways: deferral, interim arrangements, and incrementalism. Somalia combines deferral with incrementalism. Its 2012 constitutional framework was incomplete, notably in not resolving the allocation of powers between the federal and state governments and the number and boundaries of regional states. It effectively deferred these issues. The number and general definition of regional states has been largely resolved incrementally with the exception of the status of Mogadishu. However, despite having a constitutional review process, the allocation of powers remains unresolved, leaving a constitutional gap in which the federal and regional state governments engage in raw power politics.

At an early stage in peace negotiations, a key challenge may be how to frame interim arrangements between parties that may deeply disagree on the future structure of the state. Renad Mansour and Peter Salisbury have argued that in collapsed states such as Yemen, the first step in reconstituting public authority should consist in developing institutional links between remnants of state bureaucracies and de facto authorities, to restore some semblance of coherence and coordination in providing basic public services and maintaining public order.[57] On their argument, focusing on this "middle" layer should come before addressing larger questions of the constitution-making process and constitutional design. They appear to suggest an interim measure moving from fragmentation to some sort of devolution short of federalism, but they do not describe the legal mechanisms for pursuing their "middle-out" approach. One option proposed in Libya and Yemen is to adopt and adapt existing laws on devolution, which provide a ready-made set of institutional tools that are familiar. Whether such a modest first step would be acceptable to all the parties – especially in Yemen – could depend on other elements of agreement, including interim power-sharing at the center.

Integrating Security and Political Issues in Constitution-Making

An issue that is too often overlooked is the integration of security and political issues in constitution-making,[58] notably over security sector governance. Constitutions frequently set out the institutions, procedures, and norms for common security sector agencies. A peace agreement provides a pathway for separate armed factions to come under a single command structure, through a process of disarmament, demobilization, and reintegration. How a peace agreement addresses interim security sector governance arrangements is key for the success of a constitutional process. The question is whether such arrangements enable armed groups to see a future for themselves in new security institutions or, at least, adequate protections for them after disarmament and demobilization. If they do not, the political process may be stillborn.

Lebanon was the one partial success story from among our cases. The Taif Agreement addressed both political and security issues in the same document, which were viewed as part of an integrated package to reconstitute the Lebanese state. In exchange for the reconfiguration of central power-sharing, the parties agreed to engage in a process of demobilization, disarmament, and reintegration, coupled with the deployment of state security personnel across Lebanon and the recruitment across sectarian lines. The Syrians undertook to assist Lebanese state security forces, over a period of two years, "to spread the authority of the State of Lebanon" across its entire territory. The exception was Hezbollah, which was permitted to remain armed on the grounds that it operated in an area then under Israeli control. However, now, twenty years after Israeli withdrawal, Hezbollah has built up a large independent

57 R. Mansour and P. Salisbury, "Between Order and Chaos: A New Approach to Stalled State Transformations in Iraq and Yemen," Chatham House (September 9, 2019). For a similar argument in the context of Libya, see J. R. Allen et al., "Empowered Decentralization: A City-Based Strategy for Rebuilding Libya," Brookings Institution (February 11, 2019).

58 Barany, Bisarya, Choudhry, and Stacey, *Security Sector Reform and Constitutional Transitions*.

force that regularly clashes with the Israelis and controls much of southern Lebanon. At this point, with Lebanon in deep distress, the success of Taif looks like a temporizing fix that failed to address the fundamental problems of governance.

A vivid example of the failure to properly integrate security and political issues in constitution-making is Libya. One reason the NTC was unsuccessful was that the constitutional process continued to move forward without concrete progress on the integration of armed militias into a single command structure that in turn was accountable to political institutions. The LPA's failure was different – it did address security governance, by designating the Presidential Council as the commander-in-chief of the armed forces, but impliedly denied that role to Haftar, who then opposed the LPA. In both cases, the constitutional process would have had more success if security sector governance had provided better incentives to armed groups to participate by providing them with an institutionalized role.

In Somalia, security issues also remain an obstacle to moving further in the constitutional process. The federal army is small and relatively ineffective. Most regional leaders have their own militias, some of which have clashed with federal forces, and the issue of integrating all these groups into the national army received little attention in the process that produced the 2012 Constitution. AMISON tries to bring enough security to permit the governments to function more effectively. Despite this lack of a coherent, shared security framework (and of an ability to hold elections), Somalia has created the federal parliament and government and regional legislatures and governments, but these will remain fragile and partial in the absence of progress on security issues.

Finally, the multilateral framework for the Yemen peace process, found in Security Council Resolution 2216, fails to integrate the political and security tracks. It recognizes the legitimacy of the Hadi government and demands that the Houthi unilaterally cease military operations, disarm, and discontinue exercising governmental functions, prior to the commencement of a political process (including any constitutional change). It provides no guarantees to the Houthi with respect to security sector governance or the future shape of a constitutional settlement. Insistence that the Houthi comply with Resolution 2216 would create an enormous obstacle to reaching a political solution to the Yemeni conflict and is unrealistic given their military successes in the field (and in absorbing parts of the Yemeni army). Any credible peace proposal must address the Houthis' concerns. The experience of conflict in the South illustrates how difficult this could be. In response to armed clashes between the STC and the internationally recognized government – which led to the STC seizing control of Aden – Saudi Arabia brokered the Riyadh Agreement, which was signed by the parties in November 2019. The agreement provided the STC with executive power-sharing in the Hadi government in exchange for bringing its armed forces under the command of the Ministry of Defense and the Ministry of Interior. The deep lack of trust among the parties led to the failure of the agreement within days of its signature.

CONCLUSION

State collapse and the absence of a functioning government is characterized by the territorial fragmentation of a country, with different areas under different claimants to authority and some ungoverned spaces. There may be extensive fighting over control of various areas and significant fluidity in alliances on the ground. International actors may be drawn in as partisans of different factions or as potential mediators and facilitators of conflict resolution and state reconstruction. Peacemaking in such a context requires the main factions – and their sponsors – to accept that the costs of fighting outweigh any benefits and to agree on structured negotiations with one another, which may be a phased arrangement; this may take years. Sustainable peace requires agreements on governance arrangements, including potentially interim power-sharing, a constitution-making process, transitional security arrangements, and some guiding principles for a reconstructed state. While a federal or devolved governance arrangement may seem a logical response to such territorial fragmentation, the factional elites may prefer power-sharing at the center. And if they do opt for a federal or devolved structure, they face vexing issues in defining the constituent units, the allocation of powers, and the nature of central institutions, which may result in an extended period of muddled governance and power politics with no constitutional clarity. In the end, it may not be possible to recreate a state on the Weberian model after state collapse, but various forms of de facto or de jure decentralized governance may offer an alternative trajectory.

16

The Promise – and Limits – of Stabilization through Local Governance in Libya

Karim Mezran and Elissa Miller

Good governance and stability in Libya remain elusive targets at the national level, despite continued efforts by numerous Libyan actors, the United Nations, and the international community. The United Nations Support Mission in Libya (UNSMIL) has made little progress since 2014 in resolving Libya's ongoing political crisis. Prospects for future elections remain in doubt, while the parliament – officially known as the House of Representatives (HoR) – continues to lack the necessary quorum to deliberate and advance important national legislation.[1] The internationally recognized, UN-backed Presidency Council and Government of National Accord (PC/GNA), meanwhile, struggle to exert influence throughout much of the country. The decision by the leader of the self-declared "Libyan National Army" (LNA), Khalifa Haftar, to launch a military campaign to seize the capital of Tripoli in April 2019 ignited a new phase of the conflict and quashed hopes for a national reconciliation effort.[2] Simultaneously, the interference of foreign actors, at times acting as spoilers supporting competing proxies and at others appearing to marshal peace talks, has contributed to the widening of existing national rifts.[3] This is especially evident in Emirati, Egyptian, and Russian support for Haftar's forces, and in the PC/GNA's success in June 2020 in pushing back Haftar's forces from the west with support from Turkey.

Amid national political paralysis, however, Libya has witnessed some progress at the local level. In the absence of capable or unified national institutions, local governance authorities, primarily municipal councils, have sought to develop the capacity to deliver on the needs of Libyan citizens, prompting both internal and external stakeholders to consider a formal process of decentralization. A sustainable model of decentralization in Libya would not be synonymous with federalism. Rather, it

[1] T. Megerisi, "Elite Jockeying in Libya's Transition," Carnegie Endowment for International Peace (February 22, 2018).

[2] P. Wintour, "UN Postpones Libya National Conference Amid Fighting in Tripoli," *The Guardian* (April 9, 2019).

[3] K. Mezran and E. Miller, "Libya: From Intervention to Proxy War," Atlantic Council (July 11, 2017).

would involve establishing a clear legal framework for local governance that would ultimately be dependent on the existence of a strong, national state.

However, the debate surrounding decentralization in Libya has largely been a superficial one; decentralization exists de facto rather than de jure.[4] Prior to 2011, Muammar Qaddafi's *Jamahiriyya* created a facade of local governance subordinate to an informal patronage system that centralized authority in Qaddafi's hands. Local government had little power to make decisions that would affect citizens' lives.[5] The weakness of Qaddafi-era governance is reflected by Libya's intense post-2011 fragmentation at both the institutional and community levels. Meanwhile, the political will for a clear plan of action surrounding decentralization remains elusive. The current debate surrounding local governance invokes the idea of "decentralization without decentralizers," echoing a 1994 book by former special representative of the UN secretary-general to Libya, Ghassan Salame, on "democratization without democrats" in the Arab world.[6] Nowhere is this more obvious than with Libya's Law 59. The 2012 law was adopted to establish legal parameters for an existing de facto local governance system, rather than to set out a plan that would strengthen local bodies and provide clarity surrounding the relationship and division of labor between the national government and municipalities.

National political deadlock suggests that the establishment of an agreed legal framework for decentralization is a long way off. Libya's Constitution Drafting Assembly (CDA) included a nod to decentralization in its 2017 constitutional draft, but there is little substantive debate about what formalized decentralization would look like in practice. Part of the reason for the broadly two-faced approach toward decentralization – local governance is often talked about but its implementation is not seriously discussed – is the reluctance of various stakeholders to hand over authority to local actors. In an intensely competitive internal conflict in which various armed groups, militias, and political rivals are vying for authority, little incentive exists to commit to a political agreement, let alone a framework to devolve power to local government structures.

This chapter begins with an overview of the development of a Libyan identity in the twentieth century and the failure of the federalist movement after the 2011 revolution. We then shift to examining Law 59 and the existing legal framework for decentralization, as well as efforts since the law's issuance to further codify decentralization and allocate authority to local structures. This section also discusses best practices for decentralization – such as a clear legislative framework – and the chief obstacles to those practices in Libya. The chapter then turns to an analysis of local de

4 "Decentralisation in Libya," Democracy Reporting International (September 12, 2013).

5 Y. M. Sawani, "Public Administration in Libya: Continuity and Change," *International Journal of Public Administration*, 41(10) (2017), 807–19.

6 G. Salame, *Democracy without Democrats? Renewal of Politics in the Muslim World* (London: I.B. Tauris, 1994).

facto decentralization experiences in Libya and their results. Finally, we discuss the major challenges facing decentralization in Libya, chiefly violence and economic collapse, and how they manifest at both the local and national levels. We conclude that investment in the development of local authority in Libya is critical, including engagement in the long-term process of reconstructing state–society relations. In principle, the devolution of authority from the national to the local has the potential to dramatically improve governance. Yet in practice, it remains unclear whether Libya possesses the necessary political will and national cohesion to allow such a process as the basis for stabilization.

THE LIBYAN IDENTITY: A FAILED PROJECT?

Libya has a peculiar history regarding the process of national identity formation. Beginning in the early 1500s, the Ottomans occupied the coast of Libya and administered the territory as two separate governorates (*wilayet*) – Tripolitania and Cyrenaica. Neither the various successive powers that controlled the territory nor the local population undertook substantial efforts to foster a sense of unity between the two provinces, much less a shared national identity. Ottoman control of the territory, which was superficial and mostly limited to the villages along the Mediterranean Sea, was temporarily ended by a coup staged by local military leader Ahmed Caramanli in the eighteenth century. In order to expand his power, Caramanli staged a number of expeditions to subjugate the nomadic tribes that dominated the interior of the country. While he saw only marginal success, this was significant because it marked the first time a local ruler established a direct relationship between Libya's interior and the coast.

The second Ottoman administration, which began with the reoccupation of Tripolitania and Cyrenaica in the 1830s, reestablished the old interior–coastal division in two separate administrative units. In Tripolitania, the Turks established authority over a large number of tribes from the interior, most of whom pledged allegiance to the sultan in Istanbul. In Cyrenaica, however, the Turks found a stronger and more cohesive enemy in the form of the Sufi *tariqa* of the Sanussiya. This Sunni Muslim sect established a quasi-state entity in the interior and negotiated a compromise with the Ottoman authorities in which it maintained self-rule in exchange for allegiance to the sultan and the payment of minimal taxes.[7]

In 1911, the Italians invaded both Tripolitania and Cyrenaica and colonized the territory. The Italians divided the administration of Libya into three provinces, adding the mostly desert territories of the south, the Fezzan, to Tripolitania and Cyrenaica. This changed in 1934 when the governorship of Italo Balbo united the colony as a

7 R. B. St. John, *Libya: From Colony to Independence* (London: Oneworld Publications, 2008).

single administrative entity from 1934 to 1940. This was the first time the country was ruled as a single entity. World War II saw the rapid defeat of the Axis forces in North Africa and the establishment of British control over Tripolitania and Cyrenaica and French control over the Fezzan.[8]

Divisions among the population came clearly to the fore during the postwar period. The population of Cyrenaica in the east aligned behind Idris, the leader of the Sanussiya, and wanted him to rule as king over all of Libya. The British authorities, allied with Idris and, seeking to maintain control over the territory, supported demands for a united monarchy. In Tripolitania, meanwhile, Libya's nationalist movement was fragmented among political parties that were broadly in favor of the establishment of an independent sovereign Libyan republic.[9]

The international community mediated a formula to allow Libya to gain its independence.[10] In order to accommodate the tribal and personal rivalries and divisions among the population, a federal monarchy under Idris I was established in December 1951 and organized into the three provinces of Tripolitania, Cyrenaica, and the Fezzan. The first task of the new government should have been to bridge societal divisions and to foster a sense of national identity. Unfortunately, the monarchy did not rise to the task. King Idris proved a reluctant monarch who was more interested in religious issues and in governing his Sufi sect than in the day-to-day administration of the country.[11] He relied on the eastern tribes and elites to administer Libya and contributed to fostering rather than bridging existing divisions within the country. Federalism ultimately became a stumbling block for national identity formation.

In 1963, a modification to the Constitution abolished the federal system and transformed the political system into a unitary monarchy. The pro-Western position of the regime as well as its conservatism alienated Libyan youth, who found significantly more appeal in the Arab nationalism propagandized by Egyptian leader Gamal Abdel Nasser. Thus, when Muammar Qaddafi and his fellow officers staged their coup to overthrow the monarchy in 1969, they found much support among the population, particularly the youth. These new leaders emphasized pan-Arabism over a Libyan identity, and Qaddafi, whose objective was to unite Libya with other Arab states, exercised all his efforts to impede the creation of strong state institutions that could rally Libyans around a national vision. When the Arab nationalist idea fell from grace, Qaddafi embraced another transnational

8 C. G. Segre, *Quarta Sponda: The Italian Demographic Colonization of Libya* (Berkeley: University of California, 1970).

9 M. Khadduri, *Modern Libya: A Study in Political Development* (Baltimore, MD: Johns Hopkins University Press, 1963).

10 A. Pelt, *Libyan Independence and the United Nations: A Case of Planned Decolonization* (New Haven: Yale University Press, 1970).

11 H. Serrano Villard, *Libya: The New Arab Kingdom of North Africa* (Ithaca, NY: Cornell University Press, 1956).

vision, pan-Africanism.[12] In reality, however, Qaddafi's system was characterized by the intense centralization of power. The host of tiered assemblies and committees established by his Popular Revolution obscured the fact that Qaddafi and his close circle were "the top political elite, ruling on the basis of their initial coercive seizure of power and their charismatic legitimacy."[13] Qaddafi's rule systematically prevented the emergence of capable institutional structures during his more than four decades in power.

Despite the failure of Libya's post-independence regimes to actively forge a national identity, continuous interactions between the populations of the various parts of the country, coupled with a strong urbanization process that uprooted many tribal enclaves, contributed to a tangible sense of "Libyan-ness" by the beginning of the new millennium. However, weak state institutions remained an impediment to national identity formation, which became evident in 2011 when revolts provoked the fall of the Qaddafi regime. The victorious rebel forces, which from the outset of the revolution were divided and fragmented, proved incapable of harnessing the necessary consensus to begin the process of building strong state institutions. Their failure resulted in the entrenchment of localism and tribalism; in the absence of a state, the population increasingly relied on nonstate, local, and traditional authorities.

Meanwhile, the immediate post-Qaddafi environment witnessed support among some constituencies for a federal system. In the aftermath of the revolution, some eastern groups in particular feared the marginalization they experienced under Qaddafi's rule would continue.[14] They argued for a federal system that would represent each of the country's three regions equally, regardless of population size. In March 2012, Abu Bakr Buera and eastern tribal and military leaders established the Council of Cyrenaica in Libya (CCL) – originally the Cyrenaica Transition Council – in the east with the main demand of establishing a federal Libyan state with a semi-autonomous eastern region. The CCL's demand was rejected by the National Transitional Council (NTC), Libya's transitional governing body after Qaddafi's ouster (notably, the NTC was at the time headed by Mustafa Abdel Jalil, who himself was from the east). However, the CCL had sufficient political influence to convince the NTC to amend the constitution-drafting process – only days before the 2012 parliamentary elections to elect a 200-member General National Congress (GNC). The GNC was meant to appoint a constitutional committee to draft Libya's constitution. Instead, the amendment pushed by the CCL stipulated that the sixty-member committee would be directly elected by the Libyan people

[12] D. Vandewalle, *Libya since Independence: Oil and State-Building* (Ithaca, NY: Cornell University Press, 1998).

[13] R. A. Hinnebusch, "Charisma, Revolution, and State Formation: Qaddafi and Libya," *Third World Quarterly*, 6(1) (1984), 59–73.

[14] W. Pusztai, "Does Federalism Have a Future in Libya?" Atlantic Council (August 22, 2016).

and modeled on Libya's 1951 constitutional committee, which included twenty members from each region.[15]

Other actors made attempts to institute federalism during this period. The commander of the Petroleum Facilities Guard, Ibrahim Jadhran, under the impression that the federalist movement was failing and seeking to roll back Tripoli's influence and return to eastern Libya its fair share of oil wealth, used his military command to try to impose a federalist system by force. For ten months in 2013, Jadhran effectively cut off the west from the oil-rich eastern Gulf of Sidra and attempted to sell Libya's oil illegally from the east before reaching a partial agreement with the country's western authorities. Notably, head of the CCL Buera condemned Jadhran's use of force.

The federalists eventually won thirty seats in the 2014 parliamentary elections for the House of Representatives and, led by Buera as president of the federalist National Union Party, became a powerful bloc in the new legislative body. Ultimately, however, the national fight over federalism and rifts among the federalist bloc – primarily based in the east – led to the movement's failure. Libyans in the west largely rejected federalism, viewing it as an attempt by eastern elites to monopolize the country's oil wealth – the majority of which is located in the east. Violent actions in support of federalism, such as those by Jadhran, as well as clashes between pro- and anti-federalists in Benghazi, prevented any serious consideration of implementing federalism. In addition, support for federalism failed to flourish in post-2011 Libya because the federalists were split and disagreed on many issues – including the extent of devolved powers and the geographic boundaries of regions over which local governments would have jurisdiction – and never reached a consensus.[16] A 2011 survey by the International Republican Institute found that only 7 percent of respondents in the east indicated a preference for a federalist system.[17] As post-2011 instability dragged on, the populations of Libya's regions became too fractured along lines of tribal and communal rivalries for federalism to serve as a potential solution to the country's divisions. A 2017 survey underscored this reality, with a minority of respondents indicating that federalism was a priority issue for ongoing constitutional reform in Libya.[18]

THE STATUS OF DECENTRALIZATION IN LIBYA

The post-2014 power struggle in Libya produced an environment characterized by localism and fragmented authority, which led to greater reliance on local authorities.

15 W. Pusztai, "The End of a Country: The Break-up of Libya?" Italian Institute for International Political Studies (September 2016).

16 K. Mezran and M. Eljarh, "The Case for a New Federalism in Libya," Atlantic Council (December 23, 2014).

17 D. Murphy, "Eastern Libya Poll Indicates Political Islam Will Closely Follow Democracy," *Christian Science Monitor*, December 26, 2011.

18 "Public Opinion in Libya 2017," International Foundation for Electoral Systems (February 28, 2018).

Libya's existing system for transferring selected powers and responsibilities from the center to the periphery, however, remains ad hoc and underdeveloped. This limits the capacity of local authorities to expand efforts or projects that may contribute to stability at the broader national level.

Libya's Law 59

Libya's existing legal framework for decentralization consists mainly of Law 59, which in late 2012 established over a hundred municipalities made up of elected municipal councils spread across Tripolitania, Cyrenaica, and the Fezzan.[19] The municipalities were further divided into wards, which lacked any sort of formal governance structure. The legal framework of Law 59 is weak and does not specifically delegate duties or rights to municipalities. Under the law, most basic services – including education, finance, housing, water, sewage, and electricity – fall under the purview of central state agencies. The duties of municipalities include managing civil registration, dealing with municipal guards, overseeing local infrastructure, issuing local licenses, monitoring environmental and health related issues, and special projects.[20] Moreover, municipalities are not mandated to collect taxes. Their sole source of income is transfers from the central government that are only meant to cover operating costs. Essentially, local services are meant to be supported by centralized financial flows about which municipal councils have little knowledge and even less control.[21]

The limited duties afforded to municipal councils ensured that Law 59 fell short of instituting an actual, substantial system of decentralization. The lack of financial resources to municipal councils and the subsequent deterioration in public services have had a tangible impact on the population. For example, at least 22 percent of primary healthcare facilities in Libya are closed.[22] A number of decisions issued by the minister of local governance in 2014 aimed to give municipalities greater authority to charge service fees to generate revenue, but the ministry subsequently froze the implementation of those decisions, making the only financial resources available to municipal councils those provided by the central government.[23]

In practice, little interaction exists between the national government in Tripoli and the municipal councils. The PC/GNA is weak and lacks the authority to

19 Law No. 59 2012, Libya Interim National Transitional Council.

20 B. Mikaïl and S. Engelkes, "Peace by Piece: Solving the Libyan Puzzle through Municipalities," Konrad Adenauer Stiftung (December 27, 2019).

21 "Rapid Diagnostic on the Situation of Local Governance and Local Development in Libya," United Nations Development Program (November 2015).

22 "Humanitarian Needs Overview: Libya," United Nations Office for the Coordination of Humanitarian Affairs (January 19, 2020).

23 "Municipal Revenue Generation: A Short Guidebook for Libyan Municipalities," United States Agency for International Development (January 2016).

regulate the relationship between the state and local authorities. Some municipalities efficiently administer primary services and control of their territory even within the existing opaque legal framework, while others remain inept or paralyzed by underfunding. A lack of financial resources impedes the delivery of local services, and a majority of municipalities do not collect taxes or revenues.[24] Municipal councils also lack expertise and technical competence following years of institutional insignificance under the Qaddafi regime. In 2017, almost half of Libyans said they were not at all satisfied with the quality of services that municipalities provide.[25]

Meanwhile, in areas in the east under the control of rogue commander Khalifa Haftar and his Libyan National Army (LNA), which is essentially a loose coalition of tribes and militias, local development is effectively dependent on the LNA. In 2016, the LNA established the Military Investment and Public Works Committee, which marginalized local civilian authorities by taking over administrative functions and lucrative contracts, such as waste management and recycling services in the cities of Benghazi and Ajdabiya.[26] The LNA has also expanded its influence into public and political life by replacing democratically elected local officials with military governors.[27]

At the same time, although they are challenged in delivering needed services to their constituents, many municipal councils enjoy a considerable level of legitimacy. In a 2019 survey of fifteen municipalities across Libya, a majority of respondents said they viewed their council as a legitimate body.[28] This was up from a 2016 survey that found a third of Libyans viewed their municipal councils as the most legitimate actor representing the population.[29] In comparison, the PC/GNA and HoR have received significantly lower approval ratings, demonstrating that "Libya's municipal councils will continue to serve as the face of governance in their communities, no matter how events unfold at the national level."[30] Empowering municipalities through the consistent funding of budgets, as well as developing a revised decentralization law that affords municipalities key powers, is critical to formalizing the powers of local authorities. This would go a long way toward assisting local authorities to professionalize their staff, improve the delivery of critical services, and create municipal development plans.

24 "New Poll of 15 Libyan Municipalities Shows Support for Councils, Concerns over Service Delivery," International Republication Institute (May 15, 2019).

25 "Public Opinion in Libya 2017."

26 T. Eaton, A. Alageli, E. Badi, M. Eljarh, and V. Stocker, "The Development of Libyan Armed Groups since 2014: Community Dynamics and Economic Interests," Chatham House (March 17, 2020).

27 F. El Kamouni-Janssen, H. Shadeedi, and N. Ezzeddine, "Local Security Governance in Libya," Clingendael Institute (October 2018).

28 "New Poll of 15 Libyan Municipalities."

29 "Libya Poll: High Confidence in Legitimacy of Local Councils, Despite Poor Outreach by Local Governments," International Republican Institute (November 9, 2016).

30 "New Poll of 15 Libyan Municipalities."

Municipal councils, however, face a missed opportunity due to a lack of engagement with constituents at the local level, often due to resource constraints that limit service delivery and outreach. Awareness of municipal council activities remains low. Over two-thirds of Libyans say they know nothing at all or very little about their municipal councils, and a majority say they have never interacted with any municipal council staff in their area. This has negative implications for future local elections, for example. A handful of municipal councils in western and southern Libya held local elections in March and April 2019, but turnout was low at 38 percent.[31] Prior to the voting, Libya's Central Committee for Municipal Councils Elections was uncertain whether voting would even proceed due to a lack of funding from the PC/GNA.[32] Meanwhile, only about a third of eligible voters say they are likely to vote in future municipal elections.[33] Given the widespread perception of legitimacy that municipal councils enjoy, they are well placed to engage with citizens and respond to their needs, but the current structural framework continues to present a major impediment.

The Decentralization Debate and the Constitution

A major challenge in addressing Libya's political crisis is the drafting of and voting on a new constitution that might clarify the roles, responsibilities, and resources available to municipal councils. Chapter 6 of the draft constitution released by Libya's Constitution Drafting Assembly in 2017 addresses the issue of decentralization. However, the draft is vague regarding how to empower local bodies, and instead prioritizes peace and stability as broad concepts.[34] It envisions a three-tiered system of government comprising the central government in Tripoli, governorates, and municipalities but does not address the number of governorates, the responsibilities and authorities of local municipalities, and how new legislation regarding decentralization will be implemented. Notably, although the draft states that "local government units shall enjoy autonomous, transferrable, and shared powers from and with the central authority," it does not specify what those shared powers are and how the central government will delegate responsibilities to the local level. Clarity regarding the empowerment of local and municipal governance structures is paramount, as local political stability can play a key role in establishing a foundation for national accountability and participation.

The draft also falls short in terms of addressing the current challenges faced by local municipalities in securing revenue. Chapter 6 grants local government

[31] A. Elumami, "Libya Holds Municipal Elections in First Vote for Five Years," *Reuters* (March 30, 2019).

[32] "Lack of Funding May Prevent over Half of Libya's Local Elections," *Reuters* (February 5, 2019).

[33] "New Survey on Libyan Voters' Attitudes toward Political Situation and Future Elections," International Foundation for Electoral Systems (December 8, 2018).

[34] Z. Al-Ali, "Libya's Final Draft Constitution: A Contextual Analysis," International Institute for Democracy and Electoral Assistance (2017).

bodies financial and administrative independence and provides that "governorates and municipalities shall have … self-generated resources including duties, remedies, and taxes of local nature."[35] Presumably, the devolution of powers to local bodies, therefore, would also include generating and managing revenue streams. Regarding levying taxes, effective governance would involve ensuring the efficient and accountable delivery of services at the local level, but these two issues are not tied together. For example, one option to boost revenue collection could be to privatize select services through a fee-for-service model for a sector like waste management. Taxes would still cover the basic operational costs of the service, performed by municipal workers, but additional fees would allow for the variable costs from user to user.[36]

It also remains likely that some local governing bodies will require additional support, especially in the country's poorest municipalities. Some form of revenue assistance for local services and administration from the central government or governorate levels would be necessary to guard against glaring inequalities. A clear, constitutionally established revenue distribution system could help prop up particularly disadvantaged municipalities, as well as establish a clear relationship between these various levels of government.

Any intragovernmental revenue-sharing scheme would likely come under criticism from various stakeholders. A revenue distribution system perceived as unequal – whether by the most impoverished municipalities requiring more assistance or wealthier municipalities in oil-rich areas disputing the redistribution of revenue sourced from their territories – could generate resentments and corrupt activity. A clear distributive structure that generates consensus through transparency is necessary to promote local development.[37] The draft constitution begins to address this issue in Chapter 8, calling for the "distribution of national revenues fairly and equitably" between local and national governance structures based on population density, the distribution of the population, and levels of available services and infrastructure.[38] Yet the lack of specific mechanisms for accountability and transparency in the CDA draft is problematic.

In failing to present a detailed vision for decentralization, the CDA draft effectively postpones decisions regarding concrete legal provisions for a decentralized governance structure for future lawmakers to tackle. There are a number of problems with this approach. Admittedly, the development of such a legal structure is challenging absent a resolution to the ongoing political crisis in Libya. Yet a vague draft constitution in the current environment may serve to entrench existing political deadlock. In the case of Tunisia, for example, the 2014 Constitution's failure to

35 Al-Ali, "Libya's Final Draft Constitution."

36 E. Miller and A. Taylor, "A Way Forward for Devolving Local Power in Libya," Atlantic Council (October 4, 2017).

37 "Decentralisation in Libya."

38 Al-Ali, "Libya's Final Draft Constitution."

establish a clear legal framework and implementation plan for a new municipal system contributed to the repeated postponement by national authorities of local elections.[39] The failure of the CDA in 2017 to offer approaches for dealing with operational-level challenges that a decentralization process will undoubtedly face was a lost opportunity.

It is worth noting that the constitution-drafting process was plagued with challenges from the start, which impeded the legitimacy of the CDA. Less than 50 percent of registered voters, who themselves comprised only one-sixth of the Libyan population, turned out to elect the CDA in 2014.[40] The committee's mandate was for eighteen months, but it took three years to agree on and put forward a draft constitution. Members from the south, in particular Tebu and Tuareg representatives, claimed that the draft was not inclusive and did not give sufficient protection to Libya's minority groups due to insufficient representation on the committee. Several members from the east and the south boycotted the July 2017 vote. As such, the draft was approved with just over the required two-thirds majority, which some viewed as an indication of a lack of consensus among members of the CDA, and which in turn raised questions about the legitimacy of the draft.[41]

Disagreements continued to plague the CDA after the vote. In August 2017, an administrative appeals court invalidated the CDA's vote to approve the draft in a move pushed by its opponents. In February 2018, the Tripoli Supreme Court blocked the legal challenges to the draft, in effect clearing the way for a referendum and subsequent elections.[42] However, days later, the eastern-based HoR, which since the presentation of the draft has argued against its validity, refused to issue a referendum, effectively throwing the entire constitutional process into limbo.[43] In mid-2018, the head of the CDA resigned, declaring his "unwillingness and inability" to continue to work with or lead the body.[44] A constitutional amendment passed by the HoR in November 2018 further politicized the constitutional question by dividing the country into three voting districts – the three historical provinces – and stating the draft would only be ratified in a future referendum if more than two-thirds voted in favor nationwide, including a minimum of 51 percent in each of the three regions.[45] An intensification of the conflict in April 2019, resulting from what would

39 Ibid.

40 "The 2014 Constitutional Drafting Assembly Elections in Libya," The Carter Center (June 11, 2014).

41 G. El-Gamaty, "Libya's Road to Peace: Constitution First, then Elections," *Middle East Eye* (April 16, 2018).

42 "Libya's Supreme Court Blocks Legal Challenges to Draft Constitution," *Reuters* (February 14, 2018).

43 "Libya: MPs Refuse to Recognize the Constitution Drafting Assembly," *Asharq Al-Awsat* (February 21, 2018).

44 A. Assad, "Libyan Constitution Drafting Assembly's Chairman Resign," *Libya Observer* (July 29, 2018).

45 S. Zaptia, "HoR Passes Referendum Constitutional Amendment and Approves PC Restructuring," *Libya Herald* (November 26, 2018).

be a failed push by Haftar to militarily seize control of Tripoli, further put the constitutional debate on hold.

With little other option, municipal bodies in Libya will continue to operate in an uncertain climate. A clear, constitutionally based vision for accountable and effective decentralization remains necessary for the empowerment of local governance. UNSMIL has consulted with Libyan authorities on a timeline for adopting a new constitution, while other initiatives have proposed the selection of an entirely new committee, under UN supervision, to draft a new text.[46] Progress would require buy-in from competing national authorities in both the east and west to confront the legal and practical debates surrounding decentralization.

Redefining Decentralization

As noted above, Libyans have been living with an incomplete system of decentralization since the passage of Law 59. It is clear that a future constitution – whether a version of the 2017 CDA draft or an entirely new text – must substantively address the decentralization issue. That process should look to the 2018 Libya National Conference Report.[47] In 2017, UNSMIL's Ghassan Salame announced an Action Plan for Libya that would begin with a national conference held through consultative meetings with citizens and municipal councils across the country. The results of this dialogue process, held from April to July 2018, offer valuable insights into what Libyans want from a system of empowered local governance.

The National Conference results made clear that Libyans value national unity but seek a more decentralized form of government that gives municipalities and cities a more significant role in day-to-day management and administration. The majority of participants agreed that executive powers for local bodies should include service provision, public service management, social mediation, raising local revenue – including through investment and partnerships – and local security. This is far more expansive than the powers currently afforded to municipal councils under Law 59.

It is clear that one of the key concerns for Libyans is the issue of fair central revenue distribution. Indeed, the lack of a clear distributive system and perceptions of inequality are key drivers of discontent and, in some cases, conflict. Participants in the National Conference suggested that the central government afford municipalities greater allocations for local development, reconstruction, and infrastructure. Proposed criteria for the equitable distribution of resources included distribution based on geographic areas, distribution according to contributions to the national

46 M. Alaa El-Din, "Egypt's Sisi Announces Cairo Declaration to End Crisis in Libya," *Ahram Online* (June 6, 2020).

47 "The Libyan National Conference Process Final Report," Centre for Humanitarian Dialogue (November 2018).

income, distribution according to need, and distribution based on population size. Participants also suggested the establishment of a special fund to reinvest oil profits in local development. A key underlying concern related to equitable distribution was the potential consolidation of political, economic, and service institutions in Tripoli that could leave citizens in peripheral areas without access to administrative resources. Although the conference discussions did not result in a consensus on how to implement distributive practices, there was broad agreement that municipal council budgets and responsibilities should be increased.

Despite the National Conference's success in bringing together thousands of Libyans to consult on their visions for a way forward, the absence of a central authority remains the chief challenge – whether for decentralization or any of the other many national reforms necessary for long-term stability. Still, the conference suggested interim steps to lay the groundwork for a more clearly decentralized system of government. For example, some participants suggested that municipal budgets be independent from the state and directly disbursed by the Central Bank of Libya (CBL). While municipalities would still be required to present budget proposals to relevant central government authorities, direct distribution from the CBL could help ensure that municipalities are somewhat protected from national-level political disputes. Although the CBL has certainly not been immune from Libya's conflict – as evidenced by the establishment of a parallel central bank in the east aligned with Haftar's allies – the head of the CBL, Sadiq al-Kabir, has demonstrated pragmatism in balancing between the GNA and pro-Haftar camps in order to avoid complete economic collapse.[48] The CBL could, through a pilot program, work directly with municipal leaders to provide modest funds, drawn from oil revenue managed by the bank, for local development projects. Kabir's track record of supporting financial reforms, including austerity measures to reduce bloated public expenditures, could make the CBL the ideal institution to lead a transparent, locally focused effort.[49] Direct partnership with the CBL would also address Libyans' concerns of widespread corruption at the national political level.

Local leaders also have an opportunity to influence a future process of national consolidation. Participants in the National Conference suggested that the current Ministry of Local Governance be replaced with a Supreme Council for Local Administration, made up of municipal representatives, who could bridge the gap between the local and national levels. Such local leaders could exercise a collective voice drawing on community support in a post-conflict reconstructive phase. Finally, any new constitutional drafting or amendment process should consider the lessons learned from the National Conference and what Libyans want from their local government bodies. While much of the National Conference results

48 J. Harchaoui, "Libya's Looming Contest for the Central Bank," *War on the Rocks* (April 1, 2019).

49 A. Lewis, "Interview-Libya Central Bank Head Says Conflict Upset Reform Steps," *Reuters* (July 25, 2019).

focused on the relationship Libyans want between local bodies and central government, they also offer potential bottom-up, grassroots approaches to improve local governance.

Recent positive steps indicate the feasibility of allocating greater responsibilities to municipal councils in the absence of a resolution to Libya's political crisis. In February 2019, the GNA decided to transfer the management of some local services to municipal councils to facilitate service provision. In September of that year, the Ministry of Local Governance transferred a number of economic responsibilities to municipal councils, including consumer protection, the management of commodity pricing, and oversight of markets and commercial stores. The decision also gave municipal councils greater authority over local investment and projects.[50] In March 2020, the Ministry of Local Governance adopted a resolution to allow municipalities to raise financial revenues through fees and public property rents and royalties.[51] Such decisions provide far more sustainable solutions than the ad hoc allocation of funds to municipal councils to meet the needs of citizens amid ongoing conflict.[52] Although comprehensive reform and the establishment of a formal decentralized structure remain necessary, taken together, these steps demonstrate an understanding by authorities in Tripoli of municipal demands for a greater role in local administration.

LOCAL APPROACHES TO DECENTRALIZATION

The debate surrounding decentralization broadly recognizes that the success or failure of a decentralization strategy differs from country to country, at both the national and local levels, and is context dependent. In the case of Libya, the question is not whether decentralization can contribute to stabilization, but under what conditions it can do so and whether the current political, security, and economic dynamics meet those conditions.

The advantages of decentralization are generally recognized as twofold. First, decentralization bolsters the accountability of local officials by bringing the government closer to the people. While Libyans cited frustration with economic mismanagement and corruption at the national level, many noted that corruption was less of a concern at the municipal level because local communities could engage in public oversight and more easily advocate for accountable public spending.[53] Second, decentralization may help improve the efficiency of service provision and delivery.

50 "نقل 7 اختصاصات من وزارة الاقتصاد إلى وحدات الإدارة المحلية بالبلديات" ("Transferring 7 Specializations from the Ministry of Economy to Municipal Administrations"), Alwasat (September 20, 2019).

51 "اعتماد قرار يتيح للبلديات الحصول على موارد مالية" ("Adoption of a Resolution that Allows Municipalities to Obtain Financial Resources"), *Libya Akhbar* (March 31, 2020).

52 S. Alharathy, "PC to Allocate 100 Million LYD to War-Affected Municipalities," *Libya Observer* (May 1, 2019).

53 "The Libyan National Conference Process Final Report."

Municipal officials are assumed to have better information about local conditions, making local spending more reflective of local preferences and priorities.[54] This is a central issue in Libya, where the country's more than a hundred municipalities face very different challenges.

Decentralization also has the potential to spur greater innovation in developing solutions to local problems, particularly through cooperation between local officials and civil society. For example, Misrata's Municipal Council and Civil Society Commission regularly communicate with the public to share information and partner on community development. One joint effort led to the establishment of the Fund for the Support of Voluntary Works, which supports civil society organizations engaged in city beautification projects.[55] In addition, a number of municipalities use online communication and social media – particularly Facebook – to boost engagement, communication, and transparency with their constituencies. At least an estimated one-half to two-thirds of the Libyan population is active on Facebook, making it the most popular social media platform.[56] Several municipal councils have thousands or tens of thousands of followers and regularly post about local services.[57] It is therefore unsurprising that social media messaging from municipal councils and other local institutions was one of the key modes of outreach for the UN-sponsored National Conference process.[58]

Skeptics of decentralization caution that such a process can have serious negative repercussions if the conditions on the ground do not exist for success. First, decentralization can exacerbate existing inequalities, particularly between wealthier and poorer municipalities. This is a concern because Libyan municipalities are distributed between the oil-rich and coastal parts of the country and the more remote municipalities of the interior that have far fewer resources. Supplementary fiscal transfers from the central government – or directly from the CBL, as discussed above – may be necessary to assist poorer municipalities. Caution is necessary to ensure that fiscal decentralization would not complicate regional disparities by generating resentment among them depending on the chosen distribution scheme.[59]

Meanwhile, fiscal inequalities can also reveal disparities between the divergent capacities of municipalities to deliver needed services. This relates to the danger of

54 K. M. Bakke and E. Wibbels, "Diversity, Disparity, and Civil Conflict in Federal States," *World Politics*, 59(1) (2006), 1–50.

55 "Libyan Local Governance Case Studies," Delegation of the European Union to Libya (September 2017).

56 "Libya: Presidential and Parliamentary Elections Scene Setter," Stanford Internet Observatory (October 2, 2019).

57 F. Talbot, "Local Government and Community Engagement: Assessment of Facebook Use by Municipal Councils in Tripoli," The Libya Reverb Project (April 2016).

58 "Libyan Local Governance Case Studies."

59 Bakke and Wibbels, "Diversity, Disparity, and Civil Conflict in Federal States."

decentralizing before establishing sufficient local capacity. Local institutions do not operate in isolation from the larger governing environment, and poor implementation of decentralization could lead to increased inefficiency and waste in service delivery.[60] Inefficiency risks damaging the accountability of local governance. Some argue that a certain capacity threshold must be met in order for local officials to take on greater responsibility. This may not be possible in Libya, however, where national reform and capacity-building will inevitably be a slow, long-term process. As is already taking place, local governing bodies are more likely to be forced to "work with what they've got" in practice as they seek greater de jure powers.

The desire for stronger local governance clearly exists in Libya – and is driven by local officials and their constituents. In 2018, a study of civil society organizations in Libya funded by the British government found that despite the limitations of local councils' formal authority, respondents expressed confidence in local councils and viewed them as integral partners in community development.[61] Indeed, local initiatives in Libya at the municipal level have taken many forms since the 2011 revolution. Three broad categories are examined here: service improvement initiatives, efforts to build networks of municipal leaders, and local security provision. Each of these categories offers evidence of how, in the absence of a capable national authority, municipal councils have taken steps to fill the gap and meet citizens' needs.

Service Provision

Municipal councils have pursued revenue generation through various schemes based on local contexts, essentially ignoring restrictions on their ability to directly collect fees to fund services. The Zliten municipal council levied a tax on the purchase of cement from one of Libya's largest cement factories, which is located in the city. Crucially, the council worked with the company to study the effects of the tax mechanism and shared a strategy with Zliten's residents.[62] In Zuwara, the municipal council raised revenues by taxing the nearby border crossing with Tunisia, which it used to provide local services.[63] Other municipalities have turned to public–private partnerships to fund local projects and services. The municipal council in Janzur, for example, partnered with civil society and the private sector to open an account for donations to fund the opening of a hospital.[64] In the Fezzan, some municipal authorities have unofficially taxed businesses through local police forces or armed

60 "Decentralization in Client Countries: An Evaluation of World Bank Support, 1990–2007," World Bank Group (2008).

61 Institute for War and Peace Reporting, "The Post-revolution Pioneers: Emerging Opportunities and Implications for Libyan Women and Civil Society," Binda Consulting (2018).

62 "Municipal Revenue Generation: A Short Guidebook for Libyan Municipalities."

63 "Libyan Local Governance Case Studies."

64 "Municipal Revenue Generation: A Short Guidebook for Libyan Municipalities."

groups, including in Kufra, by collecting fees from road tolls.[65] Such practices, however, may raise questions about the relationship between municipal authorities and local armed groups, which is discussed further below.

Municipal responses to the outbreak of Covid-19 and subsequent global health crisis are especially illustrative of the benefits of devolving authority to the local level. Municipal leaders quickly organized to raise awareness about the virus – such as in Adjabiya in early March 2020 – and expedite testing – such as in Abu Salim, where rapid response teams were trained and deployed to collect samples from local health staff.[66] A comprehensive study of municipal council responses to the outbreak from March 12–26, 2020 found that municipalities quickly formed emergency committees to coordinate and report on cases, launched awareness campaigns, identified isolation sites for the infected, and began inspections of public areas.[67] Municipal council members also organized to demand assistance from the PC/GNA in combating the virus, citing understaffed health facilities and a lack of necessary supplies and equipment.[68] Municipal leaders criticized the PC/GNA for not delivering promised funding to combat the virus, with some circulating a petition on social media calling for the resignation of the health minister. Other municipal leaders announced that they would not accept funding from the PC/GNA because it had not come soon enough, and instead launched local fundraising campaigns to pay for the virus response. It is telling that, amid the crisis and facing criticism, the PC/GNA in April 2020 publicly announced it would cede its authorities for the provision of health services to municipalities to counter Covid-19.[69] The quick reaction of local leaders to this crisis, juxtaposed with the PC/GNA's slow response, speaks to emerging capacities at the local level to meet citizens' needs.

Local efforts have in many cases been augmented by international development programs and assistance. The UN Development Program's (UNDP) work in Libya emphasizes strengthening local government authorities' capacity to provide services to local communities. The US Agency for International Development (USAID) has developed training on revenue management and governance capacity for officials in the Ministry of Local Government, elected mayors, and municipal council members in Libya. Several USAID and US State Department projects have sought to enhance the technical skills of local officials through computer training and

65 Eaton et al., "The Development of Libyan Armed Groups since 2014."

66 "حملات للتوعية بفيروس كورونا بالبلديات الليبية ونقابة الصحة العامة تطمئن المواطنين" ("Coronavirus Awareness Campaigns in Libyan Municipalities and the Public Health Syndicate Reassure Citizens"), Alwasat (March 7, 2020).

67 "Rapid Assessment Municipality COVID-19 Preparedness Libya," Deutsche Gesellschaft für Internationale Zusammenarbeit (April 30, 2020).

68 "عمداء 29 بلدية يطالبون الرئاسي بإعادة النظر في مخصصاتهم" ("Mayors of 29 Municipalities Call on the President to Reconsider their Allocations"), *Libya Alahrar* (April 4, 2020).

69 S. Zaptia, "40 Western Libya Municipalities Welcome Tripoli Anti-coronavirus Government Allocations; Two Reject Allocations, Government Cedes Health Powers to Municipalities – NCDC Refutes Recovery of Libya's First Patient," *Libya Herald* (April 1, 2020).

program management. Additionally, US-funded projects have focused on building partnerships between citizens and their local government representatives.[70] The EU, meanwhile, launched an initiative in 2016 that partners European and Libyan cities in an effort to support Libyan mayors and offer training on management and administrative skills.[71] In partnership with UNDP, the EU is continuing to expand its program to train municipal leaders on civil works and service delivery and support local economic development and community building.[72] The provision of technical skills in particular is an entry point for boosting local governance capacity amid the current conflict environment.

Local Networks

Collective calls by municipal leaders for central government assistance to combat the Covid-19 crisis were built on previous efforts to boost the shared voice of Libya's municipalities, push for a stronger legal foundation for decentralization, and work toward a locally led solution to Libya's conflict. In July 2017, Sabratha hosted a meeting of forty-seven municipal leaders who agreed to establish an Association of Libyan Municipalities to facilitate communication with the central government.[73] In December 2017, more than ninety mayors from across Libya met in Tunisia.[74] Among the key issues discussed was the need to fully implement Law 59 to place the provision of basic municipal services under their control. The eastern town of Shahat in 2018 hosted a forum of Libyan mayors who called for an end to the country's political deadlock through elections and the formation of a unity government.[75] Most notably, 107 local leaders met in Tripoli in March 2019, just weeks before Khalifa Haftar launched his April 2019 offensive on the capital, and called for the country's High Judicial Council to take control of the country in the absence of a resolution between Libya's major two warring sides. Local leaders from both the west and the east attended the Shahat and Tripoli meetings.

These collective efforts demonstrate not only the active role that municipal leaders have taken in the absence of a strong central government, but also their willingness to join together to propose shared solutions to national crises. These initiatives boost the capacity of local actors to "build, maintain, and activate networks of

70 J. Slutzker, "In New Democratic Libya, Local Governments Build Leadership and Citizen Trust," Creative Associates (October 26, 2016).

71 T. Rutter, "The EU Cities Helping Libya's Local Authorities Provide Vital Public Services," *The Guardian* (March 28, 2017).

72 "The European Union Increases Funds to EUR 18 Million for UNDP Resilience Programme in Libya Targeting 20 New Municipalities," Delegation of the European Union to Morocco (May 6, 2020).

73 "Municipalities Seek to Give Themselves a Loud and Unified Voice," *Libya Herald* (July 30, 2017).

74 "In Historic Meeting, Mayors Agree to Work Together for Libya," *Libya Herald* (December 9, 2017).

75 "ملتقى شحات ينتهي بالإجماع على إجراء انتخابات برلمانية ورئاسية عاجلة" ("Shahat Forum Ends with Unanimous Agreement to Hold Parliamentary and Presidential Elections"), Alwasat (January 23, 2018).

stakeholders across sectors and levels of government."[76] Such cross-municipal networks are crucial to supporting meaningful change across communities.

Decentralized Security

Decentralization in Libya is not limited to service provision. After 2011, Libya's security sector witnessed intense fragmentation due to failed efforts at security sector reform by authorities in Tripoli and a proliferation of informal armed groups. As a result, many communities turned to local informal armed groups as a security solution. While a number of armed groups became enmeshed in corruption schemes, violent state capture, and illicit activities, other local forces emerged that contributed to greater security for citizens in the midst of wider national violence and instability.[77]

There is significant evidence that Libyans place greater trust in local rather than national forces to provide day-to-day security. A 2018 survey found that a majority of households looked to local structures – security directorates, municipal councils, or tribal forces – to provide security. Only in Tripoli was the PC/GNA described as the dominant security provider; responses from other municipalities indicated a much wider range of local security solutions.[78] Zuwara offers an example of local security provision. In 2013, a group of volunteers founded a Counter Crime Unit to address instability. The unit was endorsed by the municipal council, and it cooperated with local authorities in a 2015 campaign to arrest migrant smugglers.[79] The Counter Crime Unit, along with the Zuwara municipal council, Military Operations Room, council of elders, and a local crisis committee, formed a joint committee to hold trials for smugglers. The decision to hold local trials was made precisely because Libya's national judicial system was barely functioning. This effort, combined with social campaigns organized by the municipal council and civil society organizations, drastically reduced the scale of migrant smuggling in the city. Such inclusive models strongly impact local perceptions of armed group involvement in security.

Social legitimacy is an important component of whether an armed group provides effective local security. An armed group that draws its members from and maintains close links with the community, which allows for oversight, operates from a strong position vis-à-vis the local context. This is the case in several neighborhoods in Tripoli. In the Abu Slim neighborhood, the Central Security Unit introduced a tax to raise revenues that are reinvested into public works in areas under the armed

[76] A. J. Harkness, B. Katz, C. Conroy, and R. Tilchin, "Leading Beyond Limits: Mayoral Powers in the Age of New Localism," Brookings Institution (October 24, 2017).

[77] W. Lacher, "Tripoli's Militia Cartel: How Ill-Conceived Stabilisation Blocks Political Progress, and Risks Renewed War," German Institute for International and Security Affairs (April 2018).

[78] El Kamouni-Janssen, et al., "Local Security Governance in Libya."

[79] "Leaving Libya: Rapid Assessment of Municipalities of Departures of Migrants in Libya," Altai Consulting (June 2017).

group's control.[80] The self-identification of such groups as security units – language that conveys a level of formality – is meant to communicate legitimacy to the local community. In the Fezzan, the social links between armed group members and their communities make it difficult to distinguish between community members and informal security providers. Tribal armed groups have organized security centers, referred to as security rooms, at the city and neighborhood levels to provide policing.[81] These groups often perform security functions in consultation with social leaders and more formal local bodies.

In some cases, municipal councils may be able to address insecurity through conflict resolution initiatives. Local leaders are uniquely placed to support mediation efforts.[82] The Municipal Council of Zliten created the Conflict and Dispute Resolution Committee, which is composed of fifteen respected local sheikhs and is tasked with resolving property disputes within the municipality.[83] Local leaders also helped broker agreements between the Tebu and Tuareg in 2016, the Tebu and Zway in the south in 2018, and Misrata and Zintan in 2018, among others.[84]

The 2018 National Conference offers insights into how to conceive of decentralized security. The conference results reflect widespread concern over weak and ineffective state structures that fail to provide security. They also reflect agreement on the importance of cooperation between national institutions and local forces for public safety. Participants in the conference argued that municipal councils should coordinate and manage security affairs at the local level through security directorates or municipal guards that could also cooperate with national security institutions.[85] To be sure, rebuilding security in Libya will require long-term security sector reform and disarmament, demobilization, and reintegration processes that are tailored to Libya's unique context. Yet, if empowered with the necessary authorities, local governance structures like municipal councils are best placed to lead such demobilization efforts on the ground.

CHALLENGES TO DECENTRALIZATION IN LIBYA

Despite progress made in developing local governance capacity from the bottom up in Libya, local councils and municipalities continue to face significant challenges across the board. Fundamentally, the absence of a functioning central state – which exacerbates national political fractures and invites external interference in Libyan

80 Eaton et al., "The Development of Libyan Armed Groups since 2014."
81 Ibid.
82 J. S. Vericat and M. Hobrara, "From the Ground Up: UN Support to Local Mediation in Libya," International Peace Institute (June 2018).
83 "Libyan Local Governance Case Studies."
84 A. Decina, "Cohesion through Decentralization," *The Cairo Review of Global Affairs* (Summer 2019), 93–104.
85 "The Libyan National Conference Process Final Report."

affairs that contributes to the perpetuation of violence – is the primary challenge. The success or failure of local stabilization initiatives are inextricably tied to the broader environment of violent destabilization. Although some cities have been less impacted by the conflict and enjoy marginal stability – chiefly cities such as Ghadames and Beyda that are controlled by a single entity and not subject to contests for authority – there are effectively no sectors in which service delivery has not been detrimentally impacted. Critical resources, including oil and water, are leveraged by armed groups as tools of warfare. Additionally, the lack of financial resources and limitations on generating revenue, combined with the rise of parallel economic structures and a burgeoning war economy, severely endanger the already weak capacity of local institutions. Finally, the failure to implement constitutional standards, responsibilities, and authorities for national and subnational institutions perpetuates the lack of clarity currently surrounding local governance legislation in Libya.

It is unlikely that a formal decentralization process is possible absent a national ceasefire, political settlement, and national reconciliation effort. There is a risk in the interim that de facto decentralization may foster separatist tendencies as well as dangerous rivalries among loosely connected entities. This risk is uniquely strong in Libya for two reasons. First, many citizens already identify more strongly with their cities, regions, tribes, and families than with an overarching Libyan national identity. The marginalization that some cities and regions experienced under Qaddafi engendered a mentality of suspicion or exclusion among some municipalities, which fuels competition and mistrust. The atomization of security is problematic in this context when rivalries between tribes or competing armed groups erupt into violence, limiting freedom of movement between neighborhoods or cities and endangering access to services. Local reliance on armed groups for security, or in some cases service provision, risks further entrenching their positions and sparking violent confrontation over control of contested resources. Competition over resources is a key driver of conflict in Libya, and many municipal councils lack both the authority and the resources to rein in armed group activity.

Second, national-level competition threatens to co-opt certain local actors or groups as proxies. Khalifa Haftar, for example, displays a strategy of capitalizing on local grievances to expand his support beyond the east where his LNA is dominant. Haftar's April 2019 offensive on Tripoli accentuated this divide. Pressure to essentially pick a side led some municipal councils to align with either the PC/GNA or the LNA, although such moves gave them little agency or authority. Subsequent divergences within communities weakened municipalities and offered armed groups an opportunity to take charge.[86] In the Fezzan, for example, Haftar's co-optation of local Arab tribes in early 2019 facilitated his capture of the major

[86] Mikaïl and Engelkes, "Peace by Piece."

city of Sebha, and his forces' subsequent advance into the south precipitated major clashes between the Arab tribes and the Tebu population. This "divide-and-rule" proxy strategy essentially grafts national-level narratives that are driving Libya's civil conflict onto local communities, which derails locally brokered ceasefires or peace deals.[87] A similar dynamic is evident at the international level, with external states supporting local allies in service of self-interested agendas, often inflaming local tensions. For instance, PC/GNA-aligned forces, with Turkey's support, pushed back the LNA's yearlong assault on Tripoli in June 2020, producing additional insecurity at the local level such as "revenge crimes" in areas previously under Haftar's control and now reclaimed by the PC/GNA.[88]

The broader political divide between the east and west in Libya has also impacted the legitimacy of local governance structures. Municipal councils are meant to run for four-year terms, but the divided political environment and security challenges are impediments to regular electoral practices. The 2019 municipal elections saw voting in twenty municipalities for the first time in five years, but legal obstacles or conflict prevented forty-eight other municipalities from going ahead with the polls.[89] The managing body for local elections, the Central Committee for Municipal Council Elections, was made a casualty of intensified violence in May 2020 when indiscriminate shelling attributed to the LNA destroyed three warehouses containing ballot boxes and other election materials.[90] The work of the committee has been severely hampered by national-level disagreements and violence on the ground.

Meanwhile, Haftar's campaign to seize power in Libya, backed by the eastern HoR, impeded the independence of local governing bodies in the east. As the LNA seized territory in the east, it became an increasingly prominent actor at the local level. LNA Chief of Staff Abdulrazaq al-Nadhouri, who the HoR appointed as a military governor in the east in 2016, abolished ten democratically elected municipal councils and replaced them with military governors. Some local mayors attempted to push back; a group of seven democratically elected mayors in 2017 issued a joint statement demanding their reinstatement.[91] The HoR also held municipal elections separately from national institutions in Tripoli and established "steering committees" to run local affairs, including in municipalities that already had elected councils, in an effort to consolidate control. A formal national political agreement is necessary to bring these municipal councils back under civilian control. These moves exacerbated local conflict, fragmented local structures, and demonstrated

87 R. Murray, "Libya: Haftar's 'Divide and Rule' Plans on the Edge of the Sahel," Italian Institute for International Political Studies (September 9, 2019).

88 "U.N. Examines Reports of Looting in Retaken Libyan Towns," *Reuters* (June 7, 2020).

89 J. Fischer, "Libya: A Strategy for Stabilization and Governance," Creative Associates (March 24, 2020).

90 S. Williams, "Acting SRSG Stephanie Williams Briefing to the Security Council," United Nations Support Mission in Libya (May 19, 2020).

91 Eaton et al., "The Development of Libyan Armed Groups since 2014."

the ways in which local governing bodies have become casualties in Libya's civil conflict.

Another thorny issue for potential decentralization is that of devising a new plan for the fair distribution of oil and government revenues. As noted above, one way to empower municipal councils in the absence of a central government that can distribute resources is to facilitate a direct relationship with the CBL. Oil, however, has become a tool leveraged by various parties in the conflict in an effort to improve their relative positions. The LNA, for example, imposed a blockade on eastern oil ports in early 2020 that starved the country of oil revenues. Dwindling resources at the national level result in further economic hardships at the local level. Physical control by armed groups over institutions like the CBL or the National Oil Corporation in Tripoli acts as a proxy for influence. The centralization of oil revenues in Tripoli without trusted oversight by a national authority viewed by a majority of Libyans as legitimate, only fuels competition for control. Moving toward a system of taxation and revenue generation at the local level will require a significant cultural shift – a daunting task even during peacetime. A national resolution that addresses not only Libya's political divide but also the economic drivers of the conflict is necessary before any new national system of distribution can be established. Such a resolution would need to address grievances in the east about the control of oil resources in Tripoli and the politicization of key national economic institutions.

CONCLUSION: IS DECENTRALIZATION A REAL SOLUTION TO LIBYA'S CRISIS?

Evidence and experiences on the ground suggest that the devolution of powers from the central to the local could greatly contribute to addressing Libya's governance challenges. Decentralization is necessarily a delicate process that balances national-level state-building with the development of capacity and efficacy of the political class at the local level. The central government requires clear authorities and capabilities that it can devolve, through a transparent legal process, to the local level. In turn, local governments must develop the capacity to effectively administer and oversee these governance functions and manage, in an accountable manner, the accompanying responsibilities devolved by the central state. In the context of Libya, this traditional manner of decentralization is likely not feasible in the short or even medium term.

Nevertheless, in fragile states where formal power is limited, such as Libya, the local soft power produced by webs of small, community-based actors can effect positive change in state–society relations. While state-building and reconciliation efforts at the national level remain immensely important in healing the country's wounds, harmonizing these efforts with those produced by networks of local actors – municipal councils, civil society, and other trusted, informal local authorities – can foster a synergy that helps to sow the roots of stability.

Decentralization in Libya must walk a careful line between empowering local communities and exacerbating the existing local fragmentation. Support from a unified international community for the development and nurturing of such networks of stakeholders, aimed at cutting through competing national-level conflict narratives, could contribute to tangible, on-the-ground progress.

Despite the many outlined challenges, the case of Libya demonstrates that local governance can respond to citizens' needs in the midst of deep national political fractures. The principal lesson is that the empowerment of local governance institutions has the potential to serve as a critical piece of the puzzle in moving toward a future scenario of national reconciliation and stabilization.

17

Decentralization in State Disintegration

An Examination of Governance Experiments in Syria

Samer Araabi and Leila Hilal

The highly centralized character of governance in Syria obscures the state's long history of experimentation with decentralization. The principle of administrative decentralization has been consistently embraced in successive Syrian constitutions and various attempts at legislative reform by the government of Bashar al-Assad. Syria's de jure adherence to administrative decentralization was in fact a hallmark of its state formation and modern history. Its governance landscape, however, has been largely shaped by the government's prioritization of security and loyalty to party and president under successive regimes. This has rendered subnational governance entities, including local administrative councils, largely devoid of independence from the center, despite the longstanding constitutional commitment to decentralization. Instead, decentralization has primarily been advanced as a vehicle for political control by the state, and as such has consistently failed to systemically take root as a means of inclusive or efficient governance.

This chapter traces the origins of administrative decentralization and governance in Syria, based on research conducted in Lebanon, Jordan, Turkey, and Syria. It covers the situation prior to the uprising of 2011, and continues through 2017, a period of fragmentation of authority between the Bashar al-Assad government, the Arab opposition, and Kurdish parties. The experimentation with decentralization across different territories led to markedly different modalities of governance with important implications for the future of the Syrian state.

In government-controlled regions, decentralization emerged as a defining benchmark of liberal reforms under Bashar al-Assad's rule. This led the way to limited political openings for civil society and growing assertions of independence in planning and implementation among some municipalities. The changes culminated in a draft decentralization law, published in 2009. Following the onset of the uprising, the government enacted Law 107, which significantly altered the draft, rendering it internally contradictory and gutting the majority of its progressive provisions. To the extent that the government applied any of Law 107's aspects during the conflict, it was mostly as a cynical exercise to retain control by proxy and to divert authority and resources to loyalist areas.

For the Syrian Opposition,[1] political interest in decentralization dovetailed with their stated goals of democratization. In practice, the Opposition was saddled with conflict, aid distortions, and rising jihadist control, which prevented it from implementing a functional system of governance with organized and effective delegation of power from the center to local levels. Instead, Opposition-held areas faced a fragmented situation of ad hoc governance in pockets of territory deserted by government forces. The situation has been further compromised in recent years by three compounding factors: the loss of territory in the face of a government counteroffensive, a widespread takeover of remaining areas by religious hardliners, and the presence of Turkish forces (and Turkish national security priorities) in much of the Opposition-held northwest.

In the predominantly Kurdish areas in the country's northeast, specific conflict dynamics enabled the Democratic Union Party (PYD), the leading Kurdish party, to embrace a new system of decentralization. Kurdish forces declared autonomy within a new political entity called "Rojava" based on a platform of robust political and administrative devolution modeled on Kurdish leader Abdullah Öcalan's theories of "democratic confederalism." The system represents a radical departure from existing governance frameworks in other areas of Syria. The experiment in Rojava is a more successful case given the political philosophy and agenda underpinning the movement as well as engagement by the Syrian state and external actors. It is, however, not without its problems and contradictions.

This chapter examines how these three systems have adapted and responded to one another, creating a set of complex dynamics that will likely echo into Syria's political future. Even as Opposition areas face collapse, and the future of Rojava is increasingly uncertain, local governance modalities developed in these areas continue to operate in regions retaken by the government. The continued experimentation and local decision-making taking place within these local bodies may well have implications for Syria, and the broader Middle East, for decades to come.

The analysis in this chapter is based on approximately six months of research focusing on actors involved in local governance across the Syrian political spectrum. Research primarily took the form of a series of structured and semi-structured interviews conducted with government officials, activists, policymakers, and civil society organizations. Most interviews took place in the Turkish cities of Gaziantep, Antakya, and Istanbul, though additional interviews took place in Beirut, Lebanon and Amman, Jordan. Additional conversations with actors in Syria took place over Skype. The authors also observed several meetings and workshops for Syrian local opposition bodies held in Gaziantep. Several interviewees provided copies of primary source material, including government decrees and minutes of meetings, some of which are cited in the text below. Additional context and detail, particularly

[1] Throughout this chapter, we use the term "Opposition" to refer to the bodies operating within and around the National Coalition for Syrian Revolution and Opposition Forces (SOC).

about Opposition governance structures, were the result of an ethnographic study conducted during three years the authors spent advising governance modalities and coordinating humanitarian and stabilization assistance from the Turkish border city of Gaziantep, from 2014 to 2017.

BACKGROUND: DECENTRALIZATION IN SYRIA'S MODERN HISTORY

Decentralized government is not a new development in Syria, having been a feature of governance during Ottoman and French rule, in the country's first post-independence constitution, and in the Ba'athist legal order that emerged in the 1960s and 1970s. Both before and after independence, however, it has more often been used to extend and consolidate central authority than as a means of promoting accountability and distributing power. By the early 2000s, Syria appeared poised to move toward meaningful administrative decentralization as part of a package of neoliberal governance reforms, but the transformation advocated by reformers was not realized prior to the outbreak of conflict in 2011.

Decentralized Governance in Pre-independence Syria

Under Ottoman rule, local communities in Syria enjoyed a measure of self-government, particularly prior to the centralizing *Tanzimat* reforms of the late nineteenth century. The central government in Istanbul appointed provincial governors, who were charged primarily with raising tax revenues, and *kâdis*, who exercised judicial and notarial roles. But it otherwise permitted – and over time came to rely on – self-government by local notables and religious leaders. On one account, the empire had devolved by 1800 into "a loose confederation of regional rulers throughout the realm who paid lip service to the sultan-caliph in Istanbul and sometimes even cash tribute."[2] In response to internal and external pressures, the empire undertook measures to reassert central authority during the nineteenth century. In an attempt to mollify European states, it also established a special autonomy regime for Mount Lebanon following episodes of intense sectarian violence across Syria. Both moves engendered resistance from some local elites and later influenced the pan-Arab movement to promote local administration in Syria and Egypt.[3]

French imperial machinations also contributed to an elite embrace of administrative decentralization in Syria.[4] France assumed control over much of the country following the Ottoman Empire's defeat in World War I and was formally granted

[2] I. M. Kunt, "Devolution from the Centre to the Periphery: An Overview of Ottoman Provincial Administration," in J. Duindam and S. Dabringhaus (eds.), *The Dynastic Centre and the Provinces* (Leiden: Brill, 2014), 30–48, at 47–48.

[3] A. Abdelaziz, *Ottoman Administration in Syria (1864–1918)* (Cairo: Dar al-Ma'arif, 1969), 60.

[4] For a discussion of the genesis of borders in the Levant, see A. Ü. Bâli, "Artificial States and the Remapping of the Middle East," *Vanderbilt Journal of Transnational Law*, 53 (2020), 396–445.

the mandate for Syria in 1923 by the League of Nations. After severing Lebanon from Syria in 1920, French authorities further divided Syria into five administrative units organized roughly along communal lines – a divide-and-conquer strategy intended to counter Arab and Syrian nationalism and foster loyalty to French rule, particularly among religious minorities.[5] France pursued this strategy through a range of institutional arrangements, including a short-lived "Syrian Federation" and subsequently a "Syrian Union" from which newly formed Druze and Alawite administrative units were separated.[6] Although most of these units were later reincorporated into Syria, France ceded one of them – the Sanjak of Alexandretta – to Turkey, and encouraged Lebanon to follow a separate path to independence. Thus, one of Syrians' formative experiences with decentralization involved the foreign imposition of an ethnofederal scheme that was calculated to divide the Syrian polity and which resulted in the dismemberment of Syrian territory. These ethnic divisions have persisted, precipitating conflict in today's Syria; however, the ethnofederal scheme was abandoned after independence in favor of a unitary Arab republic with administrative decentralization.[7]

Decentralization in Syria's Early Constitutional Order

During the two decades following Syria's independence in 1946, the new state took halting steps toward the establishment of democratic – and decentralized – government.[8] In 1950, an elected constitutional commission issued Syria's first constitution establishing democratic parliamentary rule[9] and providing for administrative decentralization to be implemented by majority-elected provincial councils.[10] Consistent with the pan-Arab agenda of Arab revitalization, provincial councils were granted competencies such as fighting disease, protecting women and children, strengthening educational opportunities for communities, ensuring potable water delivery, and developing infrastructure.[11] Although the constitution was suspended following a military coup in 1951,[12] its provisions (including those on administrative decentralization) continue to hold sway. Even the Opposition has pushed for it to serve as the basis for a political transition in UN-sponsored negotiations to end the civil war.[13]

5 P. S. Khoury, *Syria and the French Mandate: The Politics of Arab Nationalism* (Princeton: Princeton University Press, 1987), 58.
6 Ibid., 138.
7 Syria Constitution 1950, Arts. 1, 126–29.
8 A. Alawak et al., *Centralization and Decentralization in Syria: Concepts and Practices* (Istanbul: Omran, 2018), 69–70.
9 Syria Constitution 1950, Art. 1.
10 Syria Constitution 1950, Arts. 126–29.
11 Syria Constitution 1950, Art. 129; Abdelaziz, *Ottoman Administration*, 60.
12 Alawak et al., *Centralization and Decentralization*, 70.
13 The Carter Center, "Syria: Options for a Political Transition" (2015), 15–16.

In the ensuing years, even as a series of military coups and civilian successions for the presidency unfolded in Damascus, Syria's modern administrative decentralization structure began to solidify. Between 1950 and the early 1960s the parliament adopted an administrative structure, dividing the country into provincial-, district-, and village-level administrative units with the purposes of delegating governance powers to subnational levels.[14] Syria's brief unification with Egypt as the United Arab Republic from 1958 to 1961 had the opposite effect, however, leaving power concentrated in the center.[15]

Centralization under Ba'ath Rule

The Ba'ath Party's seizure of power in 1963 marked a clearer shift toward the centralization of governance in Syria.[16] In an attempt to both maximize political control across Syria and meet popular expectations about economic development, the Ba'athist government amended Syria's administrative scaffolding. Under Law No. 15, Syria was divided into fourteen provinces with further municipal and district subdivisions within each province.[17] All administrative units, including the fourteen provinces, were legally and practically subordinate to the newly established Ministry of Local Administration.[18] In addition, the 1973 Constitution elevated the Ba'ath Party to be the "leading" party of the "state and society".[19] It provided that administrative units would be led by "People's Councils," but left their responsibilities unclear.[20] Membership in the councils was allocated to certain groups, including farmers and party syndicates of workers, artisans, and low-income workers,[21] with a smaller percentage to be elected.[22]

Ultimately, little independent decision-making authority was vested in the local administrative councils, which largely served as instruments of control by the centralized Ba'ath Party.[23] With provincial units dominating the administrative hierarchy, executive heads of the provincial councils – governors – were appointed by the president, serving as direct proxies of the central government.[24] Along with appointed council members, these governors exercised governance and intelligence oversight.[25]

[14] Municipalities Act No. 72 1956; Administrative Organization Act No. 496 1957.

[15] Alawak et al., *Centralization and Decentralization*, 69–70.

[16] O. A. Hallaj, "Geographies of Absence: Radicalization and the Shaping of the New Syrian Territoriality," *New England Journal of Public Policy*, 29(1) (2017), 1–32, at 7.

[17] Local Administrative Law No. 15 1971.

[18] Legislative Decree No. 27.

[19] 1973 Constitution Art. 8.

[20] 1973 Constitution, Art. 9.

[21] Law No. 15, Art. 76.

[22] The member to elected ratio was 60:40, Law No. 15 1971, Art 10.

[23] Alawak et al., *Centralization and Decentralization*, 158–64.

[24] Law No. 15 1971, Art. 10.

[25] Ibid., Art. 10(10).

Together, these measures formed "a multilayered governance system that create[d] vertical systems of control supported by horizontal systems of patronage across the whole Syrian terrain."[26] Decentralization thus was utilized as a tool through which the center was able to maintain absolute control over the population while building a political economy that ensured the state's stability. Elections for some local council seats took place; however, they did little to counterbalance state control. Through a variety of means, the Ba'ath Party and security agencies interfered to ensure only loyalist independent candidates were fielded for elections.[27] The councils had minimal staff, with top-level managers typically assigned to their roles by central proxies.[28]

Ideologically homogenizing the administrative state helped the Ba'ath Party to bolster control, but left it unable to meet changing needs. For instance, state budgets were assigned to provinces in equal amounts, irrespective of population numbers or actual local requirements.[29] Burgeoning informal settlements around provincial municipal centers were underserved.[30] Yet, the culture of patronage, elite hierarchies, and rampant security violations bred impunity and intolerance. Administrative decentralization as practiced by the Syrian Ba'athist state guaranteed the presidency absolute control but represented a missed opportunity to knit Syria's diverse communities together and transform society and state into a unified nation.

Decentralization as the Centerpiece of Neoliberal Reforms

Following the death of Hafez al-Assad in 2000 and his son Bashar's succession to the presidency, administrative decentralization once again arose as a core strategy for enhancing governance in Syria. Western educated and English speaking, Bashar was greeted as a reformist by some Western governments, which provided support to the program of economic liberalization he initiated and encouraged the political opening it seemed to portend. This shift was also initially welcomed by a new generation of businesspeople, professionals, and civil society activists, who gravitated to opportunities to open Syria's economy, improve governance systems, and expand public participation. At the same time, Assad's embrace of economic liberalization gradually weakened his capacity to manage the network of patronage relationships that his father had cultivated across the country, supplanting

26 Hallaj, "Geographies of Absence," 7. The system extracted loyalty at the national level through similar networks. See Bassam Haddad, *Business Networks in Syria* (Stanford: Stanford University Press, 2012), vi.
27 Hallaj, "Geographies of Absence," 8.
28 Interview with City Assessment Specialist, UN Human Settlements Programme, Beirut, April 2017.
29 Hallaj, "Geographies of Absence," 9.
30 Ibid.

traditional intermediaries with bottom-line-oriented business elites in Damascus and other large cities.[31]

The prospect of increased EU trade and investment in Syria under the EU-Med Neighborhood Policy (ENP) appears to have been an important driver of decentralizing reforms during this period.[32] Although stymied by regional security concerns, the ENP negotiations led the EU to call for a reform program based on administrative, fiscal, and political decentralization at the city or municipal level.[33] Per EU strategy, decentralization was viewed as a way to strengthen institutions, reduce the central state's authoritarian grip, and promote political pluralism, including through civil society and local governance engagement, and increased transparency and accountability.[34] The ambitious agenda coincided with Syria's Action Plan for 2006–13, authored by Prime Minister Abdallah Dardari.[35] A complementary EU-funded Municipal Administrative Modernization Programme (MAM) included several technical assistance projects to help municipalities build local public administration capacities and effectiveness.[36] The second phase (MAM2) aimed specifically to improve the quality of life in urban centers and to create more independent and citizen-oriented Syrian municipalities.[37]

The efforts culminated in the drafting of a new decentralization law in 2008.[38] Although it did not breach the bounds of administrative decentralization, it provided for substantial devolution of administrative competencies to the provincial and municipal levels.[39] The draft law further struck at the heart of the Ba'ath's top-heavy systems of control by eliminating the powerful role of an appointed provincial governor. Drafters understood that in order to restore genuine independence and functionality to elected local councils, interference by central government proxies would need to be eliminated.[40] As described in the next section, this draft served as an impetus for a new law on administrative decentralization, which the Assad regime issued as part of its effort to respond to the mass unrest that began in March 2011. However, the new law's geographic reach would be constrained by civil war

31 K. Khaddour, "Local Wars and the Chance for Decentralized Peace in Syria," Carnegie Middle East Center (2017), 5–7.

32 V. Delattre, "Syria on the Edge of a New Cooperation Era? Prospects for the EU–Syrian Association Agreement," Friedrich Ebert Stiftung (April 2010).

33 European Neighborhood and Partnership Instrument: Syrian Arab Republic, Strategy Paper 2007–13 and National Indicative Programme 2007–10, eeas.europa.eu/archives/docs/enp/pdf/pdf/country/enpi_csp_nip_syria_en.pdf.

34 Ibid.; Alawak et al., *Centralization and Decentralization in Syria*, 164.

35 Tenth Five-Year Plan (2006–10), Law No. 25 (May 8, 2006).

36 One such project included work with the Damascus municipality to improve administrative procedures and beautify a park for residents in the Old City.

37 Interview with Mahmoud Ramadan, former co-director, Common Space Initiative, Beirut, January 2017.

38 Interview with SIG minister, Gaziantep, Turkey, May 2017.

39 Local Administration Law No. 107 2011.

40 Interview with SIG minister, Gaziantep, Turkey, May 2017.

and the fragmentation of authority it produced, effecting a complex and dynamic reality of de facto decentralization across substantial parts of the country.

CIVIL WAR AND COMPETING MODELS OF DECENTRALIZATION (2011–2019)

In March 2011, following the uprisings toppling decades of authoritarian rule in places such as Egypt and Tunisia, Syria's streets erupted with mass protests after the arrest, torture, and killing of an eleven-year-old child who was caught writing graffiti calling for an end to the Assad regime. The significant proxy interests in Syria, led primarily by Iran and Saudi Arabia, quickly transformed a citizen-led pro-democracy protest movement into an armed and brutal civil war. Gulf-backed opposition forces quickly took up arms to fight the regime as it rounded up and tortured hundreds of activists to quell the uprising. The fighting left large swathes of the country under Opposition control in areas from which the government retreated. These areas included the Damascus countryside and much of the southern, northwestern, and eastern parts of the country. In eastern areas, Kurdish parties emerged as a powerful force, leaving the country roughly divided along Opposition, Kurdish, and government lines of control. Within each geographic space, multiple nonstate and paramilitary actors assumed control over different cities, towns, and neighborhoods, particularly in Opposition-held areas, contributing to deep fragmentation that manifested in numerous ways, including systems of governance.

Government-Controlled Territory: Decentralization as a Mechanism of Control

Facing Western censure for its violent response to the protests, the Assad government issued a new administrative decentralization law in October 2011. The law, entitled Law 107, was intended to signal democratic reforms under the guise of devolution of powers to municipalities.[41] The law failed to go far enough in undoing the government's authoritarianism, retaining key elements of control on which the Ba'ath Party had come to depend. Moreover, the majority of its reforms, such as the delegation of planning powers to municipalities, were never implemented. Ultimately, the state maintained party and security control over local councils and failed to adequately empower municipal councils to exercise local authority. An unwillingness to relinquish any measure of control and allow meaningful citizen participation continues to animate the state and its approach to decentralization up to the present.

Law 107 included some, but not all, elements of the EU MAM draft.[42] This new legislation vested enhanced power at the municipal level, delegating planning,

[41] "'Decentralization' from Ba'ath Party's Viewpoint," *Enab Baladi* (May 9, 2018).

[42] Local Administration Law No. 107 (2011).

budgeting, and implementation competencies to the municipal councils while tasking the provincial councils with greater regional coordination responsibilities.[43] However, Law 107 retained presidentially appointed governors at the provincial level.[44] Law 107 led to the demarcation of new administrative lines, consolidating thousands of rural villages into legally recognized townships. According to Omar Abdel Aziz Hallaj, the former CEO of the Syria Trust for Development, this move was intended to enable the state to further extend its patronage reach into the countryside through state budget transfers to the newly created townships.[45] The decision to grant localities a larger planning role and to retain the role of governors, who were symbols and agents of the highly centralized regime of the past, highlighted the government's ambivalence about greater decentralization and likely also reflected disputes within presidential circles about how far to take reforms.

In 2012, the government also passed a new Constitution in response to calls for a political transition. The 2012 Constitution pays quick homage to the virtues of decentralization, referencing "the principle of decentralization of authorities and responsibilities" as it applies to the organization of local administration units.[46] However, it fails to elaborate on the delegation of power, stating simply that the "authority, mandate, and revenues" of local administrative units are determined by national law, effectively leaving Law 107 as the legislative bedrock for decentralization in areas controlled by the government. Instead, the 2012 Constitution's signal innovation was to eliminate the Ba'ath Party's status as "the leading party in the society and the state,"[47] providing for the political system instead to be "based on the principle of political pluralism."[48]

According to close observers and scholars of governance in Syria, the government has not implemented key provisions of Law 107.[49] Indeed, in government-controlled areas, the conflict has had the practical effect of further reinforcing centralized control at the provincial level. Provincial governors appointed by the central state in government-controlled areas have absorbed much of the power that Law 107 assigned to municipal/township councils and relevant ministry units. Foreign humanitarian organizations in Syria explained that before implementing public service projects such as utility rehabilitation projects in Syrian towns under government control, agencies required the approval of the Ministries of Administrative Law and Environment and/or Social Affairs.[50] Secondary clearances from localized security militias were also a condition for approval, creating a two-tiered system of approval for any such activity.[51]

43 Hallaj, "Geographies of Absence," 16.
44 Law No. 107 (2011), Art. 20.
45 Hallaj, "Geographies of Absence," 16.
46 Syria Constitution (2012), Art. 130.
47 Ibid., Art. 8.
48 Ibid., Art. 8.
49 Hallaj, "Geographies of Absence," 16.
50 Interview with UN Human Settlements Programme, city assessment specialist, Beirut, April 2017.
51 Ibid.

Similarly little progress has been made in realizing the 2012 Constitution's commitment to political pluralism. Elections for local administrative councils in areas under government control were held in December 2011 and 2018. Reports indicated that some 70 percent of candidates for the elected seats were aligned with the National Progressive Front, the Ba'ath-dominated political coalition that operates alongside and within all levels of Syrian government.[52] The central government's failure to delegate authority despite legal requirements in legislation and constitutional text devised by the government itself underscores the cynical use of decentralization as a method of control of greater territory and population through the deployment of party and security affiliates. It is likely that in the absence of a political transition or new social contract between citizens and government, decentralization will continue to serve authoritarian patterns. This is further evidenced by the Opposition's own failed experiment with decentralization.

Opposition-Controlled Territory (2011–2017): Decentralization as a Matter of Political and Practical Necessity

As the internal conflict in Syria escalated into full-scale civil war in 2012, opposition groups took control of substantial territory, particularly in northwestern Syria. Though these groups largely operated independently of one another, political actors and militia representatives developed a centralized leadership under the banner of the National Coalition for Syrian Revolution and Opposition Forces (SOC). Though other opposition alliances and coalitions existed, the bodies operating within and around the SOC are the focus of this chapter, referred to as "the Opposition" to differentiate from opposition groups writ large. In Syria's "liberated" areas, the Opposition created its own governance modalities, largely modeled on the government's local administration systems.[53] Opposition actors initially formed local councils to assume local governance functions. As Opposition-controlled areas expanded, more complex systems of local governance emerged at various levels, including sublocal councils within large cities such as Aleppo and governorate-level provincial councils, as well as, eventually, a pseudo "national-level" executive branch commonly referred to as the Syrian Interim Government (SIG).[54] Since December 2016, however, the majority of these areas have been retaken by government forces, assisted by Russian air power and Iran-backed militias. As of summer 2022, the only areas still under Opposition control are parts of Idlib province, and these too are under assault. Accordingly, while this section

[52] Interview with UN Human Settlements Programme, city assessment specialist, Beirut, April 2017; see also "Decentralization from Ba'ath Party's Viewpoint."

[53] Interview with SIG minister, Gaziantep, Turkey, May 2017.

[54] The SIG was established in March 2013 at an SOC conference in Istanbul to administrate Opposition-held territories. It was headquartered in the Turkish border town of Gaziantep, with nearly a dozen ministries covering education, infrastructure, local administration, energy, and others.

offers a glimpse of how decentralized governance functioned in Opposition areas at the height of the conflict, the arrangements we describe for the most part were no longer in place by 2020.

The Opposition's foray into decentralization was shaped by four interacting factors: an attempt to retain the infrastructure (and legitimacy) of the Syrian state, an anarchic and uncoordinated donor environment, and an acute lack of capacity for the Turkey-based leadership to direct events on the ground, all within the context and constraints of near constant warfare and bombardment. The governance structures in these areas largely mirrored the framework laid out by Law 107, but local authorities proved to be the bodies with real agency. Meanwhile, the Opposition relied on piecemeal support from donors for both funding and expertise, leading to widely asymmetrical implementation of governance modalities. While particular bodies – at national, regional, and local levels – implemented their own agendas, the central leadership proved largely incapable of imposing standardized systems of governance and coordination across such a diffuse governance landscape. This system proved to be unsustainable in the long term, but it gave birth to bold and remarkable experiments in democracy, representation, and governance.

Shortly after its establishment in 2013, one of the first acts of the SIG was drafting and adopting its own version of Law 107, the Rules of Procedure for Local Administration (RPLA), which was meant to serve as the primary source of "legislation" governing the decentralized political framework of all Opposition-controlled areas.[55] The Opposition took the strategic decision to broadly mirror the text of Law 107 to ensure continuity between Opposition and government areas.

The Opposition's political leadership also embraced administrative decentralization out of concern that the establishment of a federal system would bolster centrifugal dynamics in Syria. Proclaiming that "preserving Syria's territorial integrity" was among its fundamental principles,[56] the SOC sharply (if obliquely) criticized Kurdish efforts to establish an autonomous system of governance on the ground, emphasizing that decisions about the structure of the state could not be taken unilaterally by any segment or faction in the country.[57] Some opposition leaders held the view that even discussing federalism could pave the way toward Kurdish separatism.[58]

Unlike Law 107, however, the RPLA was not officially promulgated through any formal ratification mechanism, and as such has been subject to frequent revision by SIG officials, members of local and provincial councils, activists, and a

55 Rules of Procedure for Local Administration, 2016. Copy on file with authors.

56 "Coalition Principles," National Coalition of Syrian Revolution and Opposition Forces (October 6, 2012).

57 See, e.g., "No Place for Projects Against the Will of the Syrian People," press release, National Coalition of Syrian Revolution and Opposition Forces (March 17, 2016).

58 Interview with SOC members, Gaziantep, Turkey, May 2017.

number of other involved actors. On at least two occasions, these groups met or corresponded online to update and refine policies laid out in the RPLA – as a means of responding to realities on the ground and, thereby, of bolstering the SIG's legitimacy among local actors in Syria. In this respect the RPLA is better understood as a fluid set of guidelines for governance structures affiliated with the Opposition than as a formal set of legal rules. "It's not a Qur'an," stated one interviewee involved in the drafting process; "it's open to changes and updates as needed."[59] Though this approach may have compromised broader adherence to and familiarity with details of the RPLA among local governance actors in Opposition-controlled areas, it allowed the document to evolve constantly to better suit changing local conditions.

In the absence of a central executive authority and as a way to distinguish Opposition behavior from the government's, the SIG devolved several governance competencies from executive-appointed officials down to the council structures themselves.[60] The sweeping authority of the centrally appointed governor in Law 107, including the ability to approve or veto all projects, and control over security functions, were distributed to the provincial council's chair and secretary-general instead.[61] Dismantling the role of the governor as a proxy for the central government and security control was a key demand of pro-democracy activists in the uprising.[62] Its removal from the RPLA was thus interpreted as a move to edit out authoritarianism. However, the decision was due largely to the practical limitations of fractured territorial control, namely, the absence of anyone who could effectively act in the capacity of a governor.[63] In addition, the Opposition leaders sought to recentralize power within the SIG in other ways, attempting to control local entities by dictating projects and controlling their financial flows.[64]

Other changes to the RPLA reflected tangible logistical hurdles faced by the Opposition in establishing broader representative structures. For example, Law 107's Supreme Council for Local Administration, which was charged with coordinating between provincial councils, was originally omitted from the RPLA altogether, but later reinserted when attempts to establish such a body became more realistic.[65] These attempts collapsed in 2014, however, and few interviewees expressed confidence that the Supreme Council would be revived.

While the RPLA provides a general set of procedures outlining overall responsibilities and realms of authority, the thirty-nine-page document leaves the scope of particular delegations of responsibility largely open for interpretation. More

59 Ibid.
60 Interview with Aleppo City Council member, Gaziantep, Turkey, June 2017.
61 Rules of Procedure for Local Administration, 2016. Copy on file with authors.
62 Interview with SIG Ministry of Local Administration, Gaziantep, Turkey, May 2017.
63 Ibid.
64 Ibid.
65 Ibid.

precise detail on the practical implementation of local administration, including particular responsibilities, revenue streams, authorities, and oversight capabilities, is provided by the internal rules and bylaws of each of the constitutive bodies themselves.[66]

However, due to the proliferation of documentation across all affiliated bodies (the Interim Government, Provincial Councils, Local Councils, Sub-Local Councils, etc.), the extent of contradiction and variation between the bylaws of different bodies was quite high. The distribution of authority across local, regional, and national entities was unclear with respect to educational curricula, infrastructure project management, and monitoring and evaluation exercises. Although the SIG in Gaziantep might claim authority over a particular matter, its lack of funding rendered it unable to exercise that authority. Instead, each council assumed the responsibilities necessitated by their specific circumstances, regardless of whether a "higher-level" entity should – or could – execute those functions more appropriately.

Furthermore, bylaws were frequently reviewed and updated as councils changed, resulting in even further variation over time. Though the Ministry of Local Administration, Relief, and Refugees collected the bylaws of all cooperating local councils, it had little power of compulsion in enforcing standardization or in asserting the oversight responsibilities of higher-level bodies like the provincial councils or the ministry itself. The problem was compounded by the absence of clear delineations of authority in practical matters of project implementation.

As one example, in 2014 the Opposition's Ministry of Education produced a "national" education plan for Syria, including curriculum requirements, exam schedules, and teacher salary scales, mostly in line with Damascus' existing standards.[67] Though provincial councils were tasked with implementing and monitoring these policies, they often found themselves stuck between competing directives from above and below. Local actors had their own educational initiatives and priorities, often secured through funding from international donors, including nongovernmental organizations such as Save the Children and the International Rescue Committee, which funded specific schools in northern Aleppo and Idlib province.[68] Many of these donor-funded projects deviated significantly from "central" dictates emanating from the SIG in Gaziantep. Provincial councils, with no control over funding and staffing of educational institutions at the local level, could not effectively steer local educational initiatives in a direction more in line with national priorities.

66 See council descriptions in "Local Governance Inside Syria: Challenges, Opportunities, and Recommendations," Institute of War and Peace Reporting (March 2014).

67 United Nations Economic and Social Commission for Western Asia, "Education Sector Policy Paper" (July 2019), 8–10.

68 See, for example, education programming referenced in Save the Children, "Syria Fighting Forces Hundreds of Schools to Close" (October 6, 2017).

Similar issues pervade other sectors. A particularly dangerous example concerns access to water, which is historically dependent on a large reservoir directly underneath much of Idlib and Aleppo provinces. To ensure the sustainability of the reservoir, the SIG issued guidelines delineating how a limited number of wells could produce sufficient water to be shared across broader communities. Nevertheless, at least a dozen local councils directly lobbied international donors for well-digging projects, and many organizations and governments (including the USA, the UK, and France) were happy to oblige. SIG officials and outside experts have expressed concern that this overextraction may permanently reduce water levels.[69]

Despite these issues, local councils were wary of receiving "orders from above" by higher-level authorities such as provincial councils or the interim government. Council members repeatedly stated that the role of provincial councils was confined to the supportive functions of coordination and monitoring, and not management or oversight. They argued, not without reason, that local councils were the only qualified actors to understand and respond to the ever-changing dynamics on the ground of a country at war, where decisions need to be made quickly and where idiosyncrasies born of the conflict are complex and manyfold.[70]

Provincial councils, on the other hand, generally claimed the authority to manage and structure all projects implemented within their governorates. Several provincial councils attempted, with middling success, to require local councils to seek approval for all project financing and implementation.[71] Without any mechanisms for compulsion, however, and in the absence of any significant financial support, higher-level governance institutions had little to offer local councils other than bureaucratic delays, political infighting, and shaved budgets. Councils that recognized the importance of supervisory regional structures even bemoaned the failure of the Opposition to solidify proper administrative hierarchies, but they continued to operate largely autonomously.[72]

This reluctance to accept control from above turned prominent local councils into the strongest advocates for administrative and political decentralization, though largely as a product of exigent circumstances rather than as a manifestation of their political ideology. In fact, many prominent council members clung to the hope that in the future, political power could be recentralized into a more capable executive body, in essence expressing willingness to surrender the very power they themselves were wielding. More than one interviewee described an ideal future where a strong and capable central government would be making decisions that better benefited the people as a whole.[73]

69 United Nations Office for the Coordination of Humanitarian Affairs, "2019 Humanitarian Needs Overview" (March 2019), 81.

70 Interviews with Aleppo City Council and Idleb City Council, Gaziantep, Turkey, in person, June 15, 2017.

71 Interview with Aleppo Provincial Council, Gaziantep, Turkey, in person, June 16, 2017.

72 Interview with Aleppo City Council, Gaziantep, Turkey, in person, June 15, 2017.

73 Observation notes from Deutsche Gesellschaft für Internationale Zusammenarbeit (GIZ)-sponsored workshop for local council administration, Gaziantep, Turkey, on file with author (September 2014)

Meanwhile, higher-level bodies at the national or governorate level tried to consolidate stronger centralized authority. Official Opposition governance documents devised a central structure to oversee the implementation of projects and programs by more local bodies, with additional oversight by relevant ministries.[74] The SIG Ministry of Education, for example, was to oversee provincial council coordination of its centralized workplan, while the provincial councils themselves were to oversee implementation within their jurisdiction. The provincial councils were also officially tasked with the monitoring and evaluation of local projects, as an additional accountability mechanism between the local and national levels. In reality, however, higher bodies struggled to establish any systems of administrative oversight in Opposition territories. For provincial councils, oversight in practice mainly took the form of elaborate monitoring and evaluation exercises executed by "enumerators" working on behalf of donor agencies involved in stabilization programming. In addition, governorate and national bodies often directly undertook the implementation of projects, replicating the type of work being conducted locally rather than assuming a more supervisory character.

This dynamic can be seen clearly in the financial flows of the various governance bodies operating within Opposition-controlled Syria. Officially, funds should have flowed downward from the national level through the governorates down to local bodies, while local councils retained some revenue-generation authorities of their own.[75] Local council budgets, as elaborated by Opposition governance bodies, were to be largely financed by central government disbursements. In reality, each council operated with relative financial independence as a consequence of donors' disregard for hierarchy or administrative structure. Most local and provincial councils received the vast majority of their budgets directly from international project financing, which further reduced incentives for structural coordination or the establishment of oversight authorities. USAID's Office of Transition Initiatives, along with the UK Department for International Development, were the primary Western donors to local and provincial councils, with additional financing from France and other European Union donors. Additional untold millions were provided by donors from Saudi Arabia, Qatar, and the United Arab Emirates, most of which was disbursed directly in cash and is therefore untraceable.

For the ever-shrinking areas still under Opposition control, two additional sources of local power have further undermined attempts at effective decentralization: hardline Islamist groups and the Turkish government. Hay'at Tahrir al-Sham (HTS), the coalition of opposition military groups headed by the notoriously hardline Islamist group Jabhat Al-Nusra (since renamed Jabhat Fateh Al-Sham), has historically coexisted uneasily with ostensibly secular, nationalist local administration systems. Some councils collapsed after direct attacks or kidnappings by HTS groups, while

74 Interview with SIG minister of finance, Gaziantep, Turkey, in person (May 27, 2017).

75 Rules of Procedure for Local Administration, 2016. Copy on file with author.

many others became dominated by representatives of HTS, rendering formerly democratic systems less accountable to local populations and concerns.[76]

Meanwhile, in the areas of northern Syria occupied directly by Turkish forces and their auxiliaries, local councils continue to operate, but have been officially severed from provincial or "national" opposition structures at the insistence of Turkish authorities, who do not recognize the legitimacy of the provincial councils. City councils have "officially" disavowed connections with their respective provincial councils, but have found ways to work around these restrictions by creating new "consultation committees" to advise the councils, often consisting of provincial council members.[77] The future of these systems remains shrouded in uncertainty.

The salience of the Syrian Opposition may be at its end, but it remains noteworthy for its experimentation with novel forms of representation and governance. With the retreat of the state, and the absence of a new effective centralizing authority, communities in Opposition areas were left to define – and defend – their own notions of financing, service delivery, elections, and popular legitimacy. Unlike the slow and reactive approach of government-controlled areas, where decentralization was little more than a facade to maintain political control, decentralization was thrust on local bodies of the Opposition as a matter of practical necessity, and invested them with real power and authority. With that freedom came a flourishing of potentialities. But without a center around which these bodies could cohere, and in the face of a constant onslaught from both the government and more hardline Islamist rebels, the long-term viability of this system was constantly imperiled. The model in Kurdish-controlled regions, meanwhile, synthesized both a coherent central strategy and capable local bodies.

Kurdish-Controlled Territory: Decentralization by Design

Kurdish regions of Syria, along with other areas dominated by Kurdish military groups, have followed a markedly different course than those under government or Opposition control. Alone among the major parties to the conflict, their system of governance was decentralized by choice – part of a radical new governance framework designed by the imprisoned Kurdish leader Abdullah Öcalan. Representing a significant shift from his previous embrace of a nationalist model of self-determination that emphasized Kurdish liberation, Öcalan's vision of "democratic confederalism" was designed with ethnic and religious heterogeneity in mind. It has remained deeply rooted in core political principles of regional autonomy and active, engaged citizenship even as it has adapted to changing realities on the ground and an increasing non-Kurdish constituency. But though it has proved to be a more successful experiment with decentralization than the systems described above, Rojava,

76 Interview with prominent Opposition activist, Gaziantep, Turkey, in person (June 13, 2017).

77 Ibid.

as the Kurdish-controlled region became known, has still struggled with the incorporation of non-Kurdish areas under its control, and with the contradictions of a top-down, centrally planned approach to decentralization.

Historically, Kurdish political movements in Syria have aligned with those in Iraq and Turkey. Kurdish movements connected to Iraq, led by the Kurdish National Council (KNC), have historically been dominant and once played a nominal role within the Opposition bodies described above. Their political orientation can loosely be categorized as liberal, federalist, and nationalist. The other current, borne of the Kurdistan Workers' Party (PKK) in Turkey, is primarily represented by the Democratic Union Party (PYD), and is ideologically more left-wing, socialist, and communitarian.

While the KNC attempted to pursue Kurdish recognition through existing channels of dialogue and process, the PYD seized the opportunity to build a new type of social order. In the wake of the government's retreat in 2011, the PYD's military wing was quick to take over the state functions of service delivery and security, assuming near-total control over large swathes of Kurdish-majority regions in Syria's north. A series of military victories against the Islamic State of Iraq and Syria (ISIS), tactical alliances with international forces, and an entente with the government, led to further territorial gains across historically Arab areas, including Deir-ez-Zor, Manbij, and Raqqa. The PYD's political project pivoted away from nationalist rhetoric, denouncing the concept of the nation-state itself in the Charter of the Social Contract adopted in 2014 as a governing framework for the region,[78] and Kurdish references were systematically removed from the PYD and the governance systems it was developing.[79] A nonsectarian umbrella organization containing the PYD and allied parties – including Arab and Syriac groups – was formed to spearhead the transition to democratic confederalism: the Movement for a Democratic Society (TEV-DEM).

The system built by the PYD – by some accounts begun as early as 2006 – was based on the writings of PKK founder Abdullah Öcalan.[80] The contours, functions, and indeed the very name of this system has changed over the years. Although it is widely known as Rojava, the Autonomous Administration of North and East Syria omits all explicit Kurdish identifiers. During the period of this research, Rojava was divided into three cantons – Jazira, Kobane, and Afrin – though continued expansion and reorganization has led to a current subdivision into seven "regions." Each of the three cantons, styled Democratic Autonomous Administrations (DAAs), has significant decision-making power, but issues of defense remain firmly centralized

78 Charter of the Social Contract, Autonomous Administration of North and East Syria (January 29, 2014).

79 Ibid.

80 H. Allsopp and W. van Wilgenburg, *The Kurds of Northern Syria: Governance, Diversity and Conflicts* (London: I.B. Tauris, 2019), Kindle location 2394.

under the authority of the Syrian Democratic Forces, a military coalition heavily dominated by the PYD's military wing. In 2016, the TEV-DEM delineated a non-sectarian federal entity above the DAAs with its own, sometimes overlapping, governance responsibilities.

Unlike Opposition and government areas, regions under Kurdish control have not been governed pursuant to Law 107 or any direct iteration thereof. Instead, foundational governance principles for the Kurdish region found expression in the Social Contract. The Social Contract lays out the legal framework for the DAAs, as well as the roles, responsibilities, and authorities of governance bodies that operate at the local, regional, and Rojava-wide levels. Though the Social Contract makes no mention of the Local Administration Law operating in other regions, it contains numerous provisions for decentralized governance.

Pursuant to the PKK's concept of democratic confederalism, the administrative system works from the bottom up. Neighborhood-level communes collectively form community-level people's councils, which themselves aggregate into people's councils for the district level, and so on – ending ultimately with the People's Council of West Kurdistan, which has jurisdiction over all of Rojava. These bodies operate at similar levels to those laid out in Law 107, which defines subdistricts, districts, governorates, and "national"-level structures, but the style, naming, and function of the bodies in Rojava is rather different. Across Rojava, authority is generally considered to reside at the level of the "commune," which enjoys autonomy over local affairs, and emanates upward.

Oversight operates bi-directionally, with legislative bodies overseeing the executive and administrative bodies within their jurisdiction, and local bodies overseeing the work and efficacy of broader representative structures. Interviewees familiar with Kurdish governing systems stated that commune representatives, for example, may report directly to canton-level bodies about the behavior or efficacy of district-level councils. Governance structures also contain strict guidelines for gender, ethnic, and religious inclusion at all levels of authority, such that each people's council contains Kurdish, Arab, and Assyrian representatives, with balance between Muslims and Christians and a double chairship to ensure both male and female representation.

Though the Social Contract lays out general guidelines, each constituent body maintains its own internal rules and bylaws that delineate its authorities and capabilities.[81] The various bylaws and internal rules of procedure appear to be largely consistent across the board, but the implementation of particular legislation can vary widely between the regions. Significant differences in press freedoms, reconstruction funds, and military conscription have been reported across each of the cantons.[82] Further complicating the picture, this legal and political framework has

81 Ibid., Kindle location 2528.

82 Ibid., Kindle location 2530.

passed through numerous iterations, with the Social Contract superseded by a 2016 version establishing a "Democratic Federal" system across Kurdish-controlled regions.[83]

Legislative functions are carried out by legislative assemblies that exist at both the canton/DAA and Rojava-wide levels. The assemblies pass laws, draft budgets, appoint members of the Supreme Constitutional Court, and importantly, retain the authority to oversee all administrative and executive bodies within their jurisdiction.

Executive functions in Rojava are undertaken by executive councils, which, unlike the bodies operating under the government or within the Opposition, exist largely at the canton/DAA level, rather than the "national" level, meaning that each of the three Kurdish cantons contains different ministerial and executive structures, rather than governorate-level offices that report back to central ministries. Despite the delineation of each executive council's ministerial functions in the Social Contract, the ministries present in each of the cantons differ markedly. For example, the more developed Jazira canton contains broader governance functions, administrative capabilities, and even press freedoms than those of the Kobane canton.[84]

The independence of the judiciary is enshrined in the Social Contract.[85] It also defines the powers and jurisdiction of independent Judicial Councils, which operate at the canton/DAA level, and of the Supreme Constitutional Court, which operates across Rojava and has the authority to interpret and review the constitutionality of all laws passed and decisions taken by legislative assemblies and executive councils.

Outside of this system, a few Opposition-style local councils continue to operate in Kurdish-held areas. As Kurdish-aligned forces moved into predominantly Arab areas, TEV-DEM supported these councils as a way to ensure Arab participation and representation, but the power and influence of these bodies is highly circumscribed.[86] One of their primary functions is managing referenda to determine their area's future relationship with the Kurdish Autonomous Region. Where a referendum produces a positive result, the council is dissolved and local administrative authority is transferred to the corresponding DAA counterpart.[87] These councils consequently seem unlikely to be a permanent feature of governance in Rojava.

Although authority in Rojava is formally vested at the commune level, there appears to be some degree of unofficial political oversight by TEV-DEM members who operate within or parallel to these structures, ensuring a certain adherence to broader political expectations and alignment with the strategic interests

[83] Social Contract of the Democratic Federation of Northern Syria (December 29, 2016).
[84] Allsopp and van Wilgenburg, *The Kurds of Northern Syria*, Kindle location 2528.
[85] Charter of the Social Contract, Art. 63.
[86] Allsopp and van Wilgenburg, *The Kurds of Northern Syria*, Kindle location 3030.
[87] Interview with prominent Kurdish activist, Istanbul, Turkey, in person, April 1, 2014.

of the region as a whole. The main conflict over authority and mandate appears to take place between the structures of the DAA and those of TEV-DEM, the PYD-dominated political coalition with party organs operating "in parallel to the state and to the local administration."[88] In this sense, Rojava's governance structure broadly mirrors that of government-held areas, where the Ba'ath-dominated National Progressive Front often functions as the real locus of political and administrative decision-making.[89]

The commissions operating at various administrative levels of the DAA, concerning gender, economics, justice, defense, etc., often have parallel equivalents within TEV-DEM.[90] This has led to accusations that party leaders control political decision-making, leaving local administrations to simply validate predetermined outcomes. Though each level of the Kurdish administrative structure should be elected by their constituents, the selection process is reportedly heavily dominated by influential locals and TEV-DEM actors.[91] When the foreign relations head of the PKK was asked about their coordination with the DAA, he acknowledged that the party does "offer suggestions, without giving specific instructions," but denied that party officials "directly interfere."[92]

As a consequence of the nonsectarian and explicitly inclusivist framework of the DAA, many non-Kurdish residents of Rojava report higher levels of satisfaction with the DAA than they did under the TEV-DEM administration, though the "de-ethnicization" of the governance discourse may have undermined the support of nationalistic Kurds.[93] The DAA's inclusion of local leadership representing most relevant constituencies in northeast Syria – Kurdish, Arab, Assyrian groups chief among them – may have bolstered its legitimacy across ethnic groups, at the cost of "retaining pre-existing power relations, rather than replacing them."[94] These ethnic considerations also extend to security services, as separate local policing forces generally manage issues related to each of their respective constituencies.[95]

On the external front, the withdrawal of US support for the anti-ISIS coalition in Syria, along with Turkey's offensive along Syria's northern border, have raised new questions about the long-term sustainability of the democratic confederalist system and its uneasy detente with the Syrian state. Significant reductions in international support for the PYD may not only adversely affect its ability to hold and defend Rojavan territory, but also likely redirect resources away from internal governance priorities to those related to regional defense. How this will impact the fragile ethnic and sectarian equilibrium in these areas remains an open question.

88 Allsopp and van Wilgenburg, *The Kurds of Northern Syria*, Kindle location 3220.
89 Ibid., Kindle location 2510.
90 Ibid., Kindle location 2510.
91 Ibid., Kindle location 927.
92 "PKK Foreign Relations Head Speaks out," *Al-Monitor* (July 29, 2016).
93 Allsopp and van Wilgenburg, *The Kurds of Northern Syria*, Kindle location 4179.
94 Ibid., Kindle location 4292.
95 Ibid., Kindle location 2844.

CONCLUSIONS AND FUTURE TRAJECTORIES

Syria's experiment with decentralization is far from concluded. The Syrian war continues, with shifting frontlines and controlling authorities across Opposition and Kurdish areas. Government-held areas are plagued by deep fragility due to the lack of a political resolution to the conflict, with the citizen grievances that gave rise to the 2011 uprising continuing to fester. Severe sanctions imposed on the government by Western countries also preclude reconstruction from proceeding.[96] Ultimately, it remains unclear whether the government will attempt to take back all territories lost during the war, including Idlib province in the northwest and Rojava. At the time of writing, government negotiations with Kurdish PYD representatives around security and other issues suggest the likelihood of asymmetrical governance between Rojava and the rest of Syria protracting into the future; however, numerous geopolitical factors in the region will determine the viability of these arrangements. The experiences across the three geographies examined here nevertheless provide useful insights for understanding governance and decentralization in Syria and beyond. Particularly notable are the differing degrees of coherence, democratic adherence, pluralism, and service effectiveness between the three areas.

Successive constitutional and legislative mandates for administrative decentralization upheld by the government ensured a clear structure of administrative units for decades. With the adoption of Law 107, attempts toward expanding municipal power were unrealized even though it was understood that devolution would bolster the government's legitimacy. The state was unable or unwilling to relinquish its systems of control or delegate real power to the local level from the center. The tight control maintained by the central government produced coherence at the expense of reforms that may have served to quiet dissent and stave off the civil war that devastated the country. In the aftermath of the war, the failure to grant municipalities adequate resources has likely undermined opportunities for stabilization and service delivery, which the government has centrally controlled to benefit loyalists and largely exclude neighborhoods and areas associated with the Opposition. Democracy and pluralism have suffered an even greater blow: the elections held since the war began have been rife with misconduct,[97] not to mention the widespread disenfranchisement of Syrians who reside in Opposition areas and can no longer participate.

On the other hand, the Opposition's inability to create a strong central authority resulted in significant decision-making power and participation at the local level but left the governance landscape ad hoc, contested, and heavily susceptible to external

[96] A. McDowall, "Long Reach of U.S. Sanctions Hits Syria Reconstruction," *Reuters* (September 2, 2018).

[97] A. Lund, "Syria's Phony Election: False Numbers and Real Victory," Carnegie Endowment for International Peace (June 8, 2014).

interests – from Western donor aid to Gulf proxy military manipulation. De facto decentralization in Opposition areas did enable a greater degree of pluralism, in terms of the participation of women and technocrats, and a greater degree of local democratic experimentation – such as mechanisms for voting for local council membership and public feedback on the performance of local councils. Some, though not all, local councils made meaningful attempts at improving the representation and agency of their constituents in their governance functions. On the other hand, in the absence of a centralized body with enforcement power, Opposition areas failed to achieve the coherence and capacity needed to institute the true administrative decentralization system sought by the public and Opposition political representatives. Effective service delivery softened the blow, but its uneven distribution likely caused as many problems as it solved, and ultimately left the Opposition weak in terms of reclaiming central authority from these functioning bodies, as it advocated for a transition of power at the national level.

In Rojava, the push for decentralization came from the top down, organized around a fully formed ideology put forward by a respected Kurdish national leader, Abdullah Öcalan. The system of "democratic confederalism" gave birth to a new, much more coherent governance regime. Drawing on their constitutive founding document – the Social Contract – the administrative levels of government and their roles and duties were more clearly delineated than those of their Arab counterparts, with a greater balance of power between the different levels. The inclusion of a court system and mechanisms of oversight and accountability, along with highly empowered local-level communes within regionally specific cantons, has also made Rojava a more democratic system – at least on paper. The communes formed the nexus of widespread community engagement and representation, though it remains unclear whether this has been driven by the system's intrinsic legitimacy or as a by-product of the needs arising from war.[98] In practice the domination of the PYD has led to inter-Kurdish disputes and authoritarian accusations.[99]

Looking across the three geographies, the Syrian state will likely have to grapple with the question of whether to pursue a path of administrative decentralization or federalism. While federalism does not enjoy strong support among Arab Syrian nationals, governance coherence and codetermination within Kurdish-controlled areas will likely either force Syrians to contend with the possibility of a federalized system or live with an unresolved asymmetric state for the indefinite future. Meanwhile, the experience of empowered local governance in Opposition areas will continue to influence Syrian civil society and support public advocates in their calls for greater devolution of power from the center to the municipal level. The changes happening at the local level, however, risk being drowned out by the geopolitical battles raging within Syria and across the region. In a region that has been

98 Allsopp and van Wilgenburg, *The Kurds of Northern Syria*, Kindle location 4209.
99 Ibid., Kindle location 4202.

dominated by authoritarians since independence, "new" approaches too often fall prey to established systems of power, as occurred in the government's attempt at decentralizing reform. Radical experimentation of the type seen in Opposition and Kurdish areas required both an absence of authority and an influx of resources – neither of which could viably last indefinitely. Even the bold new path staked out in Rojava, backed by a powerful military and capable civil servants, struggles to overcome both its own contradictions and the sheer weight of the forces of the status quo pressing against them. But these struggles are not lost to history. They continue on, in local community dynamics, political accommodations, and the memories of participants. Perhaps these will be sufficient seeds for new growth; only time will tell.

18

Decentralization in Yemen

The Case of the Federalist Draft Constitution of 2015

Benoît Challand[*]

This chapter explores a paradox – the apparent impossibility of decentralization in a country where orography, a long history of political fragmentation, and a "weak" central state authority appear naturally to favor decentralized authority. A historical exploration of governance in different parts of Yemen since 1960 reveals longstanding demands for decentralized governance, as well as the existence of a strong society capable of formulating and pressuring the central authority to implement reforms. The difficulty has been turning these aspirations into legal change in the face of an array of obstacles, including limited resources.[1] After reviewing that history, this chapter analyzes efforts from 2013 to 2015 to produce a new constitutional order built on federal principles – first through a broad-based national dialogue and then through a far less inclusive constitutional drafting process. This quite revolutionary project, presented in 2014 as "a broad national consensus,"[2] was made possible by the country's 2011 protests. But it was eventually buried under Gulf Cooperation Council (GCC) coalition bombs, which started falling on Yemen in March 2015 and indirectly paved the way for a secessionist project in southern Yemen beginning in 2017. The chapter concludes by exploring the circumstances that led to the rejection of a federalist solution and the eruption of civil war in Yemen.

* I am grateful to Zaid Bin Ali Alwazir, Rafat al-Akhali, Dr. Nadia al-Sakkaf, Baligh al-Mekhlafi, and Mohammed al-Khalifa, for sharing thoughts about federalism and decentralization in Yemen with me. The views of Abdullah Al-Saidi, Dr. Abdul-Ghani Al-Iriany, Aysha Jamal, Abdulsalam Mused, and Ahmad Muthana have provided new substance to the research, in particular the last two for the question of possible secession in the South. Additionally, Sheila Carapico, who read a longer draft of this text and identified gaps in my arguments; Joshua S. Rogers, for his vast historical knowledge on Yemeni political economy; Celine Morgan, for her contacts in Yemen; and George Anderson, in his capacity as a member of the UN Standby Team of Mediators in Yemen in 2014 and 2015: all four deserve my gratitude. The remaining approximations remain my sole responsibility. An Arabic-language version of this chapter, in a shorter format, was published by the Yemeni journal *Al-Masar*, 65 (2021), al-masar.org/.

1 On the political economy of civic activism and local governance, see S. Carapico, *Civil Society in Yemen: The Political Economy of Activism in Modern Arabia* (Cambridge: Cambridge University Press, 1998), and J. Rogers and B. Challand, "The Political Economy of Local Governance in Yemen. Past and Present," *Contemporary Arab Affairs*, 13(4) (2020), 45–69.

2 This formulation, *ijma'watani wasi*, is taken from the synthesis document of the NDC. See "Thirteen Questions," NDC, 6, www.ndc.ye/ndcdoc/Thirteen_Questions.pdf.

The chapter draws substantially from ten interviews conducted with Yemeni activists, intellectuals, and politicians involved in the political process since 2011, as well as material generated by the National Dialogue Conference (NDC) in 2013 and 2014. The interviews were conducted in multiple locations (though never in Yemen itself) in 2012 and again between June 2018 and January 2020.

THE DECENTRALIZATION PENDULUM IN YEMENI REPUBLICAN HISTORY BEFORE 2011

Since the 1960s, repeated demands for decentralization emerged from below as a way to ground the idea of republican politics. Promises to anchor local structures of governance recur at critical junctures throughout Yemeni history, yet Yemen never functioned as a federal or formally decentralized state. Even if Yemen's administrative map has been redrawn many times to recognize forms of local government, and even if federalism would be a natural, congenial way to protect territorial or sectarian minorities and to redistribute natural resources, which are spread unevenly across the country, power has been retained by the capital and central government institutions.

What are the sources of fragmentation that have propelled decentralization in twentieth- and twenty-first-century Yemen? We can identify two clusters: political divisions and social fragmentation. A key political division is the North–South divide, which dates back to the colonial era. The North emerged from the Ottoman yoke in the early twentieth century, while the South remained under British control until 1967. Both had parallel, yet distinct revolutionary movements that established republics: the socialist People's Democratic Republic of Yemen (PDRY), established in the South in November 1967; and the Yemen Arab Republic (YAR), which ousted a Zaydi monarchy in the North, following a civil war from 1962 to 1970. Yemen was "reunified" under northern leadership in 1990, but southern resentment has remained a source of disharmony, particularly following a failed campaign in 1994 to regain independence. Another centrifugal force is the so-called Huthi movement in the North, which grew after President Ali Abdallah Salih's military campaigns against Sa'ada, the northern stronghold of the pro-Zaydi revivalist group in the 2000s.[3] Compounding these political divisions are geographical ones, with enclaves only loosely connected to one another.

In terms of social fragmentation, two factors are significant: stratification and sectarianism. For centuries, Yemen's social system has been highly stratified according to tribe and caste/class. The idiom of tribalism was reinforced by President Salih, who bolstered his power by making an alliance with the main tribe, the Hashid,

[3] For a detailed account of regionalisms, see S. W. Day, *Regionalism and Rebellion in Yemen: A Troubled National Union* (Cambridge: Cambridge University Press, 2012).

and promoting his kin and tribal connections.[4] In terms of sectarian divisions, Yemen's religious communities have coexisted peacefully for centuries, including a Shafei (Sunni) majority, a Zaydi (so-called Fiver Shia) community that strived to reestablish an imamate in northern Yemen after 1911, and a small Isma'ili (Sevener Shia) community scattered across the North. The "majority denomination in the coastal and southern midland provinces are the Shafeis, who are Sunni (in the same way that Lutherans or Methodists are Protestant), but rarely identify themselves as such" – even if historically they distinguished themselves from the Zaydi regimes in Sanaa and in Upper Yemen.[5] The population of the South is predominantly Shafei. But it would be a mistake to believe that these religious categories fully explain divisions among Yemenis.[6] While a strong sense of local identification exists, this is generally expressed not in religious or caste/class terms but rather in regional terms, with identity corresponding roughly to governorate borders.[7]

These divisions fueled dissatisfaction with centralized rule even before Yemen's unification in 1990. In the North, although tribes and peripheral actors were promised decentralization during the civil war, the YAR's December 1970 Constitution paid only lip service to local governance.[8] Remittances, sent by Yemenis working in the Gulf region and accruing directly to communities, allowed local development associations (LDAs) and cooperative movements to boom during the 1970s and 1980s.[9] Where the state was unable to build essential institutions at the village level – a school, dispensary, or bridge – local civil society organizations from the *ta'awun* (cooperative) movement stepped up.[10] In 1978, municipal councils were established, some of which were elected.[11] When the central state was weak due to infighting at the top or inadequate financial resources, the popular components of local activism and governance were strong.[12] This changed when Ali Abdallah Salih took power in July 1978, ending a rapid succession of three presidents in two years.

4 The tribal-military alliance around Salih and his kin resisted requests for decentralization from 1978 until 2011. See ibid., 16, 137. See also J. Rogers, "Violence and the (Trans)formation of the State in the Yemen Arab Republic 1962–1970," unpublished PhD thesis, University of London, SOAS (2018) (illustrating how tribal segments rose to prominence in the republican era because of their role as "war specialists" during the civil war of 1962–68).

5 S. Carapico and S. P. Yadav, "The Breakdown of the GCC Initiative," *MERIP*, 273 (2014).

6 Messick notes the fluidity and porosity between Shafei and Zaydi legal interpretations over time. B. Messick, *The Calligraphic State: Textual Domination and History in a Muslim Society* (Berkeley: University of California Press, 1993).

7 Interview with Rafat Al-Akhali, Executive Bureau member in charge of local authority, Government of National Unity (2012–14) and minister of youth and sports (2014–15), Oxford (September 9, 2019).

8 P. Dresch, *Modern History of Yemen* (Cambridge: Cambridge University Press, 2000), 124.

9 Ibid., 131. See also Rogers and Challand, "Political Economy," and M.-L. Clausen, "Decentralization as a Strategy of Regime Maintenance: The Case of Yemen," *Public Administration and Development*, 40(2) (2020), 119–218, at 122.

10 Carapico, *Civil Society in Yemen*, chs. 5–6.

11 N. Toye, "Les autorités locales au Yémen (1963–2002)," *Arabian Humanities*, 10 (2002).

12 Carapico, *Civil Society in Yemen*, 111.

He created his own movement, the General People's Congress (GPC), to solidify his authority.[13] From 1984 onwards, with new oil revenues falling into the hands of the central government, the GPC became an increasingly top-down organization that merged with the LDAs to form a de facto ruling party. Local initiatives and room to maneuver were stifled, putting an end to de facto decentralization in the North. This pattern only deepened after unification.[14]

In southern Yemen, the idea of decentralization was intimately linked to British manipulations. In 1963, London established a Federation of Arab Emirates of the South to placate growing southern Yemeni discontent with colonial rule. Under pressure from Nasser's project of a United Arab Republic, the British offered to create a federation comprising both Aden and the eastern protectorates, but it was tainted by imperial designs, and thus rejected by local actors.[15] Between 1963 and 1967, southern Yemenis fought the British presence, and on November 30, 1967, a unitary state of a unique kind was born in the Arab world: a Marxist-leaning republic. The ruling party, renamed the Yemeni Socialist Party (YSP) in 1978, feared regionalism, which it associated with "backward" tribal identities. Thus, the PDRY's governorates were not given names until 1980 – they were simply numbered 1 to 6.[16] Regional fragmentation nevertheless remained ingrained in the ruling party's internal cleavages, one group coalescing around Ali Nasir Mohammed and ministers from the Abyan and Shabwa regions, and the other around Ali Salem Al-Bidh and the Hadrami followers.[17] So deep was this schism that in 1986, a bloodbath put an end to a YSP political meeting– leaving dozens dead, and soon thousands in the rest of the country.[18] Although Al-Bidh ultimately emerged victorious from the internal war of 1986, he remained isolated and weakened. With the Soviet Union's collapse in 1989, his party had no choice but to accept unification with YAR. But relying on informal transitional agreements to secure co-participation in decision-making, the South missed the opportunity to enshrine mechanisms of power-sharing in the new constitution.[19]

The Republic of Yemen was established in May 1990 as a unitary republic with some genuflection toward decentralization.[20] Parity between North and South was

13 Dresch, *Modern History of Yemen*, 154–56.

14 Day, *Regionalism and Rebellion in Yemen*.

15 S. W. Day. "The Federal Plan in Yemen: History of an Idea and Its Current Development," in N. Brehony and S. Al-Sahran (eds.), *Rebuilding Yemen: Political, Economic and Social Challenges* (Gottingen: Gerlach Press, 2015), 24–41, at 29.

16 H. Lackner, *PDR Yemen: Outpost of Socialist Development in Arabia* (London: Ithaca Press, 1985), 54.

17 Dresch, *Modern History of Yemen*, 169–70.

18 Day, "The Federal Plan in Yemen," 34.

19 For a discussion of the political economy that sustained these episodes, see Rogers and Challand, "Political Economy."

20 See R. Detalle, "Pacte d'Amman: L'espoir déçu des Yéménites," *Monde Arabe Maghreb-Machrek*, 145 (1994), 113.

guaranteed in the body tasked with writing a new constitution (ratified in 1991) and in the transitional government, with the YSP and GPC on equal footing as members of a ruling coalition. The process of unification resulted, however, in a concentration of power in the hands of the northern governing cliques.[21] Salih remained president and Al-Bidh became vice-president. In 1993, Al-Bidh lamented that, while the political system born of unification had federalist trappings, it did not have enough institutional mechanisms to protect it from a gradual "take over" by the northern elites.[22] In February 1994, YSP and GPC signed the so-called "Amman Accord" under Jordanian auspices.[23] It proposed a new legislative body, the Consultative Assembly (*majlis al-shura*), a kind of senate in which the different regions of the country were represented, alongside the 301-member Chamber of Deputies (*majlis al-nuwwab*) representing the population.[24] The accord also granted more administrative and fiscal autonomy to local authorities, with the vice-president given a role as "protector of decentralization."[25] Al-Bidh wanted a formal federalist solution, but many in the North accused the YSP of using the term "federalism" to mean secession and therefore to bring *fitna* (the Islamic term for sedition) into the country.[26] The compact was never implemented because war broke out, the North crushing the secessionist southern movement during a short but grueling civil war between May 5 and July 7.

The postwar 1994 Constitution ignored all of the compromises of the Amman Accord. The promise to revive local authority was stalled until the 2000 Local Authority Law, which was applied inconsistently.[27] Furthermore, these new local authorities had very limited financial means and reported directly to the governor, himself a political appointee of the president.[28] Although the 1994 Constitution preserved the upper chamber, *majlis al-shura*, it ceased to be the quasi-federal institution envisaged in the Amman Accords. It is a consultative body with very limited power, in particular that of confirming candidates to the presidential elections.[29]

Thus, prior to 2011, Yemeni society repeatedly made demands for more direct involvement in political matters, in particular with initiatives to protect local

21 Day, *Regionalism and Rebellion in Yemen*.

22 Ibid.

23 Toye, "Les autorités locales," para. 21.

24 Carapico notes that the proposal for two chambers was made during popular consultations in 1992 to ensure "equal representation from all governorates and enhance the power of local government." Carapico, *Civil Society in Yemen*, 165, 174.

25 Toye, "Les autorités locales," para. 21.

26 Day, *Regionalism and Rebellion in Yemen*, 115.

27 R. Al-Akhali, "The Challenge of Federalism in Yemen," Atlantic Council (May 2014).

28 Toye, "Les autorités locales."

29 The Upper Chamber is also tasked with reviewing drafts of basic laws and electing Supreme Court judges. Established by presidential decree in 1997, its first fifty-nine "senators" were appointed by the president, thus strengthening "the hand of the executive." Carapico, *Civil Society in Yemen*, 194–95. It was eventually suspended by Salih.

governance. There was a pattern of willingness by the central authority, in moments of weakness or vulnerability, to discuss decentralization as a way to co-opt possible contention. But incumbent authority always managed to prevent the implementation of decentralization reforms.

This pattern contradicts the clichés that depict Yemen as a "failed state." Yemen has multiple sites of popular political involvement that do not exist in other Arab countries. There is a cat-and-mouse game between center and periphery forces, as well as various state–society cleavages that can be deliberately used by the executive to impose its mediation. Yemen is a country with a strong tradition of local self-help and popular or civil society participation that manages to push each incumbent central authority to offer compromises. But because of shifting political economy factors (remittances dropped drastically after 1990 when hundreds of thousands of Yemenis working in Saudi Arabia were expelled), the frail republican legal culture, and weak representational institutions (parliaments, in particular), these promises of decentralization never transformed Yemen substantially. Instead, Salih and the GPC, clustered around elites from the tribal northern highlands, managed to derail all these local initiatives and demands.

But with the 2011 uprisings, federalism reached an unprecedented level of popular legitimacy and acceptance. The problem, with this new swing of the pendulum, was that it would be accompanied by cumbersome foreign sponsors, bringing heavy baggage and vitiating the principle of decentralization.

THE GCC INTERVENES IN THE 2011 REVOLUTION

Protests erupted in Yemen in 2011, soon after Tunisia's. They mixed specific regional grievances with general calls for dignity and social justice. As in Egypt and Tunisia, cross-sectional, multigenerational, and cross-class alliances were present in *Maydan at-Taghayyir* ("Change Square"), the name given to the rebellious encampments in the north of Sanaa and in other large cities in Yemen.[30] At first, youth activists from the South were eager to make connections with their northern brothers and sisters trying to unseat President Salih; they converged at sit-ins in the city of Ta'iz.[31] Three fronts of opposition that had emerged in the ten years before the 2011 "revolution" were also instrumental in toppling Salih. Two were articulated through territorial contentions: the Huthi rebellions in the North after 2004 and *Hirak* in the South. The third, a coalition of parties called the Joint Meeting Parties (JMP), emerged in 2005.

[30] For an overview of the 2011–13 protests, see H. Lackner, *Yemen in Crisis. The Road to War* (London: Verso Books, 2019); and L. Bonnefoy. *Yemen in the World* (Oxford: Oxford University Press, 2018), 36–39, 58–61.

[31] S. Dahlgren, "A Poor People's Revolution: the Southern Movement Heads toward Independence from Yemen," *MERIP*, 273 (2014).

The Huthis' bone of contention has multiple components. Too often reduced to its sectarian component (Zaydi as Shia vs. Sunni),[32] it also has regional and sociological dimensions. Since the 1934 Ta'ef treaty with Saudi Arabia, Yemen's northern border has remained in dispute. In the early 2000s, President Salih implemented various policies that alienated the Zaydi heartland around Sa'ada, to the point where arms were taken from 2004 onward, with six rounds of wars against the leaders of a Zaydi revival, from the Huthi family.[33] The sociological component pertains to Huthi leaders' attempt to resuscitate the ideal of the imamate and of a stratified social structure. Although not all Zaydi Yemenis adhere to this societal vision, the movement grew in strength in response to Salih's highly personalized rule and the persecution of the Huthis (whose initial leader, Hussein Badreddin al-Huthi, was killed in 2004). It later formed a political party, called Ansar Allah.

The second territorial resentment is also rooted in Salih's cynical maneuvers: turning a blind eye when al-Qaeda fighters settled in southern Yemen after the Afghan war, Salih used resulting instability as a pretext for heavy-handed intervention. In southerners' view, the South was "colonized" as Salih and his allies took over formerly nationalized land, companies, and other assets of southern individuals and institutions.[34] *Hirak* (the Southern Peaceful Movement) is the name given to a loose coalition of southern protesters – associations of soldiers and civilians forced into retirement in 1994, various public forums, and lay citizens who felt that Salih's grip on power was becoming tenuous from 2007 onwards.[35] *Hirak* was split on the desired end point (a federal state or secession), but its catalogue of grievances resonated with the spirit of the 2011 protests.

The third opposition front, the Joint Meeting Parties (JMP), was established in 2005 when a cluster of parties realized that without an anti-GPC block, nothing would change in Yemen. At the heart of the coalition stood Islah, the Yemeni Muslim Brotherhood party. It also included the YSP – still somewhat popular in the South – and three other minor parties: Al-Haqq, the Unionist Party, and the Popular Forces Union Party.[36] In a document published in September 2009 and titled the Preparatory Committee for National Dialogue,[37] the JMP listed federalism among its key demands as a way to generate a more equitable power distribution in the

32 The sectarian component emerged only a few years before the 2011 protests. I. Fraihat, *Unfinished Revolutions: Yemen, Libya, and Tunisia after the Arab Spring* (New Haven: Yale University Press, 2016), 40; Carapico and Yadav, "The Breakdown of the GCC Initiative."

33 These measures include a redrawing of the Saudi border in 2000 and the support, by Salih, for creating a Salafi institute in Dammaj, near the Zaydi capital. See Bonnefoy, *Yemen and the World*, 27, 55.

34 Day, *Regionalism and Rebellion in Yemen*, 138, 142–43.

35 Ibid., 227; Dahlgren, "A Poor People's Revolution,"

36 M. Browers, "Origins and Architects of Yemen's Joint Meeting Parties," *International Journal of Middle East Studies*, 39(4) (2007), 565–86.

37 See "Yemen's Vision for National Salvation," Yemenvision (March 21, 2010).

whole country.[38] The expression "National Dialogue," which reemerged in 2012, had its origin in this document.

The JMP was the most vocal of the three in endorsing, leading, and instrumentalizing the popular protests. Unwilling to give up power, Salih used intimidation to break them up, soon deploying live ammunition. After the killing of more than 150 protesters in the first six months and mass defections from military units, Salih was forced to step down. Yet, ever agile in the face of danger, he snatched a golden exit during negotiations for a GCC-brokered transition. Signed in Riyadh on November 23, 2011, the GCC Initiative called on the Yemeni Parliament to adopt laws granting Salih immunity from legal and judicial prosecution.[39] The latter handed power to the deputy he had himself chosen years ago, a meek figure from the ruling GPC party, Abdrabbuh Mansur Hadi. In February 2012, Hadi secured 99.8 percent of the vote, becoming the new president and charged with leading a constitutional reform.

THE NDC AND THE TRANSPARENT PATH TO CONSTITUTIONAL RECOMMENDATIONS

In light of the flaring violence, the United Nations appointed Jamal Benomar as special advisor to Yemen. His office worked during the summer of 2011 with the GCC to discuss transition scenarios. "Transition," in this dynamic, became a matter of top-down control defined by the GCC in the manner it deemed most secure for its stability. As an external sponsor of the initiative, it had obtained de facto veto power in domestic Yemeni affairs. This sidelined the Parliament, since its hands were tied to the calendar of the GCC transition.[40] The GCC Initiative ushered in the formation of a Government of National Unity (GNU) – half drawn from the ruling GPC party, and half from the opposition, namely Islah[41] – which explored resurrecting the 2008 National Strategy to revive local authorities.[42] But with popular protests throughout 2012 pushing for more democratic change, and with UN assistance, a more inclusive transition process was undertaken.

Building on a 2011 transition plan devised by UN Special Advisor Benomar,[43] President Hadi appointed a Liaison Committee comprising eight members (representing the five leading parties, as well as youth, women, and civil society) early

38 S. A. Zyck, "Mediating Transition in Yemen: Achievements and Lessons," International Peace Institute (2014), 3.

39 Fraihat, *Unfinished Revolutions*, Appendix I.

40 Personal email communication with Abdul-Ghani Al-Iriany, Senior Researcher at the Sanaa Center, April 17, 2018.

41 See Fraihat, *Unfinished Revolutions*, 233.

42 Interview with R. al-Akhali (September 20, 2019). Al-Akhali was involved with these discussions until his appointment as minister in December 2014.

43 Whereas the GCC Implementation Mechanism lists only the GPC and the JMP as the recognized parties, UN Security Council Resolution 2051, of June 2012, speaks of an "all-inclusive National Dialogue Conference."

in 2012. Efforts were also made to bring the Huthi and *Hirak* on board.[44] This preliminary step of connecting to the various constituents and parts of the "revolution" was very important in generating an inclusive body that was clearly much more representative than the Parliament and the GNU. The Liaison Committee in turn served as the core of a larger Preparation or Technical Committee,[45] which established a list of twenty confidence-building measures that the president of the republic committed to addressing. Among these demands were apologies to the populations of Sa'ada and southern Yemen for the brutal campaigns against them, the reinstatement of personnel forcibly retired after the 1994 war, the return of confiscated land in the South, and the release of all those imprisoned since the start of the revolution. President Hadi signed on to these demands, but most remained empty promises.

The "Inclusive National Dialogue Conference" (NDC) was established on March 18, 2013. It was tasked with leading an open discussion about the future form of the country, though southern secession was off the table. According to the presidential decrees that defined its parameters, its recommendations would be nonbinding.[46] The new constitution would be drafted by a "constitutional committee" meant to "implement the decisions of the NDC ... ahead of a popular referendum." By agreement between the UN Special Advisor, the Technical Committee, and the presidency, the NDC would have 565 participants – half from the South, where the most pressing political issues and the more articulated demands for reforms were made.

The logic of representation followed that of party lines: the ruling party (and its allies)[47] secured the largest quota of 131 members, followed by ten other parties with quotas ranging from four seats for four small coalition members, to seven seats for a newly formed Salafi party, al-Rashad,[48] and fifty seats for Islah. Fixed quotas of forty each were allocated to bolster the presence of women, youth (defined as persons under forty years), and civil society organizations, the three "revolutionary" constituencies represented in all the preparatory and "kitchen cabinet" meetings held by Benomar as facilitator.[49] Finally, President Hadi could appoint an additional sixty-six members. A massive undertaking, the NDC employed nearly a hundred staff.[50]

44 Interview with Dr. Nadia Al-Sakkaf, Liaison and Technical Committee member, NDC Presidency member, minister of communication (2014–15), Swindon, via WhatsApp (September 9, 2019). She met, for example, with Abdelmalik al-Huthi, the Huthis' hardline ideologue.

45 Ibid.

46 See Presidential Decree Nos. 30 (July 14, 2012) and 46 (September 17, 2012).

47 The presence of small political formations mirrors what Dresch calls the tendency by the GPC of "cloning" (*intinsakh*) any institutions that it deemed as a possible challenger in the 1990s. See Dresch *Modern History of Yemen*, 211.

48 L. Bonnefoy, *Salafism in Yemen: Transnationalism and Religious Identity* (New York: Columbia University Press, 2012), 249–90.

49 Interview with Dr. Al-Sakkaf (September 21, 2019).

50 The NDC operated with a $24 million budget provided by international governmental donors and held its work in Sanaa's five-star Mövenpick Hotel. See Dahlgren, "A Poor People's Revolution."

There was widespread interest and support for the work of the NDC, with live TV coverage and visits in eighteen of the twenty-one governorates outside of Sanaa. But it also had opponents. Ansar Allah was partly in, partly out, depending on the current of the Huthi movement, which ranged between a pragmatic republican wing and a hardline Zaydi monarchist position. Along with the *Hirak* bloc, it was the party with the lowest rate of attendance in the NDC plenary sessions,[51] but some members did subscribe to the overall discussions.

Among southern Yemenis, the NDC was largely seen as a barrier to their aspiration for secession. According to a long-term observer, "it was difficult to find anyone in Aden who believed in the National Dialogue. The conference's recommendation [actually, one of the twenty Demands] that Qatari money be used to compensate southerners who were illegally fired or whose land was confiscated, was too modest to turn the tide of skepticism."[52] Most southerners sitting in the NDC, whether as YSP members or as representatives of *Hirak*, were appointed by President Hadi, and agreed with the premise of preserving Yemeni unity. This was not what people in Aden and in the Hadramawt aspired to. In 2014, a *Hirak* leader in Aden estimated that 90 percent of the former South opposed the NDC.[53] The leader of the NDC's *Hirak* bloc did propose a federalist solution envisaging a federal Yemen comprising two regions only, the former North and the former South, with a referendum allowing for self-determination in the South after five years. Nicknamed the Sudanese Model, this option was unacceptable to the GCC and President Hadi.[54] The *Hirak* leader stepped down and was replaced by other southerners close to Hadi, whom the population in the South did not recognize as their representatives.[55]

Despite this skepticism, the NDC finished its work on January 26, 2014, which, by coincidence, was the day Tunisia adopted its new post-Ben Ali Constitution. The NDC passed a final document, listing 1,578 recommendations taken with a simple-majority vote in one of its working groups. In order to realize a "full emancipation from the past by ending the centralization and abuse of power," the

51 *Hirak* filled 69.2 percent of its seats during a sample of plenary and working groups sessions, while Ansar Allah had a rate of 72.7 percent. The members directly appointed by President Hadi had the lowest participation, with 65.7 percent presence, while all other parties and informal groups (youth, women, and civil society) sent delegates to occupy 80–95 percent of their allocated seats. The most assiduous parties were the Nasserite Popular Unionist Party and YSP, each with 89.7 percent rate of participation, Islah with 87 percent, and GPC at 82.2 percent. These statistics are based on analysis of attendance lists found on the NDC website, focusing on a sample of eleven out of the total eighty-seven attendance lists, roughly a list every three weeks, from April 2013 to January 2014.

52 Dahlgren, "A Poor People's Revolution"; G. Anderson, "Yemen's Failed Constitutional Transition," in M. Anderson and S. Choudhry (eds.), *Territory and Power in Constitutional Transition* (Cambridge: Cambridge University Press, 2019), 312–29, at 317.

53 A. L. Amira-Augustin, "'Aden wird siegen'; Der Südwiderstand" *INAMO, Informationsprojekt Naher undr Mittlerer Osten*, 83 (2015), 11–16.

54 N. Brehony, H. Lackner, and S. Al-Sahran, "Introduction," in Brehony and Sarhan, *Rebuilding Yemen*, 1–23, at 22 n. 24.

55 Anderson, "Yemen's Failed Constitutional Transition," 319.

NDC recommended founding a federal state, with new institutions, including a Constitutional Court, and mechanisms to ensure a "broad national partnership, representation of the regions and enable citizens to exercise their political rights and participation in governance."[56]

The sense of achievement was substantial.[57] Despite some shortcomings – a lack of full representativeness in *Hirak* and silence regarding the number and borders of federal regions – the NDC had three broader positive impacts. Any revolutionary context witnesses a battle between political leaders who invoke legality as the basis for moving forward (and thus argue for continuity of existing institutions) and those who think that the legitimacy generated by mass mobilization should provide the basis for reforms. Yemen was no exception. The NDC offered a vehicle for the preservation of the revolutionary groupings' legitimacy. The debates of 2013 eclipsed a weak GNU and a locked parliament, both of which represented the legality component of the GCC Initiative. Second, the NDC's numerous outcomes were invoked by many actors after January 2014, showing that the dialogue identified key common goals. A third by-product of the NDC was the UN Security Council's invitation to adopt a law on transitional justice,[58] something expressly forbidden by the 2011 GCC Initiative.

FINALIZING THE DRAFT CONSTITUTION BEHIND CLOSED DOORS: THE REGION COMMITTEE AND THE CDC

The NDC Consensus Committee had suggested that the Constitution Drafting Committee (CDC) be composed of thirty members, with extensive experience in law and proven expertise in constitutional issues, and that it limit its work to six months to maintain momentum. But Hadi appointed only seventeen members – mostly Islah and GPC members – with only four women, one YSP member, and a professor close to the Huthis.[59] He also decided that twelve months would be necessary to prepare a new charter.[60] Indeed, if the NDC was inclusive, local (with visits in most governorates), and transparent in its functioning, the CDC was politically biased toward factions docile to the president, influenced by outside actors, and opaque. Decisions were made during closed-door meetings, with the president or

56 NDC, "Thirteen Questions."

57 In a poll taken in April 2014, 25 percent of the population were opposed to the outcomes of the NDC and feared that federalism would yield partition; 75 percent percent were thus not opposed to the main recommendations of the NDC. Al-Akhali, "The Challenge of Federalism," 4. Anderson, who was involved as part of the UN Standby Team of Mediators, is less positive, pointing to only a "paper-thin consensus on federalism" when the CDC concluded its work. Anderson, "Yemen's Failed Constitutional Transition," 319.

58 UNSC Resolution 2140 (February 26, 2014), Art. 8.

59 "Jadal fil-Yemen Hawla Tashkil Lajnat Siyaghat al-Dustur," *Erem News* (March 10, 2014).

60 A. Falahi, "Yemen's Fraught Constitution Drafting Committee," Carnegie Endowment for International Peace (2014), 2.

the GCC sponsors setting the parameters.[61] Some saw the decision to hold certain CDC meetings in Gulf countries outside of Yemen[62] as a reminder that the real drivers in the "transition" process were outside actors, not Yemenis.

Despite the enormous difficulties in the country from the summer and fall 2014 described below, Hadi and the CDC were able to present a completed draft of the Constitution in mid-January 2015.[63] The massive text is made of 446 articles, grouped into ten different overall sections. Hadi boasted that twelve of the main fourteen "grand visions" penned by the NDC were included in the final draft. The theme of federalism figured prominently throughout the text. Article 1 states that: "The Federal Republic of Yemen is a federal State, civil, democratic, Arab Islamic, independent and a sovereign country; based on the will of the people, equal citizenship and the rule of law."

The proposed federal architecture is a classical bicameral system, as a way to ensure differentiated representation for the population and for territorial entities. Article 138 describes the lower chamber, the Chamber of Deputies, with 260 members. Rather than first-past-the-post elections, its members are "elected through a general, free, secret, direct and equal vote under the closed proportional list system." Article 139 offers protection for the southern regions (Aden and Hadramawt), which are guaranteed 40 percent of the seats. The higher chamber, called the "Federal Council" (*majlis al-ittihad*), consists of eighty-four members, including twelve from each region, six representing the city of Sanaa and six representing the city of Aden. They too "are to be elected through general, free, secret, direct and equal vote" but using a proportional list system within each region. Symbolically, special representation is accorded not only the capital city, Sanaa, but also Aden, the "capital" of the South, offering a thin element of asymmetric federalism to assuage fears of a northern takeover of the South. Both chambers have legislative power, but the Federal Council has additional tasks, such as approving the size and representativeness of the armed forces (Art. 142). Decisions in that body are to be taken by majority, unless two-thirds of the representatives of the South (the regions of Aden and Hadramawt) oppose decisions concerning the vital interests of the South (Art. 143). Article 144 stipulates that a National Assembly (*jamaʿyya waṭaniyya*) is composed of a joint session of the House of Representatives and the Federal Council.

Notable progress is made in this "federalist" section: bicameralism; over-representation of the South, which comprises 20 to 25 percent of the population but receives 35 percent of the seats in the upper chamber; proportional representation

61 Decision-making inside the CDC had to be unanimous, and in cases when this was not possible, three-quarters of the votes were necessary to pass with a quorum of two-thirds of its members. See Zyck, "Mediating Transition in Yemen," 9, 11; C. Schmitz, "Yemen's National Dialogue," *MEI Policy Paper* (2014), 5.

62 "The First Substantive Revision of the Draft Constitution Continues," *Saba Net* (September 13, 2014).

63 The full draft of the Constitution can be found at www.ndc.ye/constitution_draft.pdf.

in both chambers; subsidiarity; and a clear attribution of powers in the legislature over the armed forces.

But what are the limitations of the draft constitution? The flow of sections and articles is not always clear, and it is at times overcrowded with provisions that eclipse the main points of a new power-sharing agreement. For example, Articles 43 to 71, which deal with broad social issues – including access to healthcare and phasing out of *qat* consumption – come before the chapter describing the parliamentary and federal system, the basic elements of this "post-revolution" state. Anderson also notes that the federalist openings are very detailed for legislative arrangements but very vague regarding the composition and decision-making procedures of the executive.[64] Neither the NDC nor the CDC had clear, systematic, and manageable solutions for the reallocation of financial resources (oil, municipal, and real estate taxes) or for appointments to the future Constitutional Court. Ambiguities also remain concerning the staffing and training of regional authorities and the organization of relations between municipalities and regions.[65]

Before turning to the multiple reasons that saw Yemen enter a civil war, let us engage with the argument that it was the direct result of the project of a federalist constitution.[66]

THE CONTESTED MEANING OF FEDERALISM

In the debates over "federalism" between 2011 and 2015, the term was the source of some confusion and ambiguity, but not animosity.

In the NDC's early debates, two terms were used interchangeably to speak of a federal order: *fidiraliyya* and *ittihadiyya*. The first rendering is an Arabization of the term used in Romance languages, while the second is derived from the Arabic word for "union" (*ittihad*). Federal order and federal state are mostly rendered as *nizam ittihadi* and *dawla ittihadiyya*. In one of the NDC's final documents, these expressions are used ten times, while *al-fidirali* appears only once, although it is, strictly speaking, a closer rendering of federalism.[67] Abdul Kareem Al-Eryani, co-chair of the NDC and a historical figure in Yemen, acknowledged that the term *fidiraliyya* remained largely misunderstood among the Yemeni public. The indirect rendering through the periphrasis *nizam ittihadi* might have had the advantage of underlining the *unity* component (as many have feared decentralization would be the first step

64 Anderson, "Yemen's Failed Constitutional Transition," 325.

65 Ibid., 321. Al-Akhali, "The Challenge of Federalism," 2–3, poses similar questions: how do you divide and share power across three levels? Which one legislates on the regional/federal level? How are natural resources allocated? The NDC had a rather clumsy formulation that these natural resources should belong to states and then be distributed in participation with regional and federal authorities.

66 M. Shuja al-Deen, "Federalism in Yemen: A Catalyst for War," Sanaa Center (February 2019). See also Anderson, "Yemen's Failed Constitutional Transition."

67 NDC, "Thirteen Questions," 4.

in breaking apart the unity of the country). Interestingly, Dr. Al-Eryani also indicated that a highly decentralized state could count, in his view, as a federal state.[68]

It is tempting to see the host of external sponsors, many of them "Western," as a liability for Yemeni acceptance of federalism (as confirmed by Dr. Al-Eryani's observation that federalism could be seen as another cultural import). But a close look at internal Yemeni debates shows that arguments of cultural incommensurability between "Yemeni values" and federalism are unfounded. Indeed, the only powerful institution reluctant to support the move to federalism was international, not Yemeni – namely the International Monetary Fund (IMF).[69] A towering Yemeni intellectual, Zaid Bin Ali al-Wazir, wrote a book in 1990 fully centered on the idea of federalism in Yemen.[70] The book, expanded in 1993, 1998, and 2011, included a historical account of de facto decentralization in Yemen, from the time of the Prophet to the time of unification and a theoretical discussion of why federalism is an integral part of democratic life. The book, which met with considerable controversy at the time of its original publication,[71] argues that decentralization is one of the three pillars on which Yemenis should build a new political order: republic, democracy, and decentralization ("*al-jumhuriyya, al-dimuqratia, al-lamarkaziyya*").[72] Other groups have also proposed a federalist solution for Yemen. In May 2009, associations in the Shabwa governorate called for a federal division of powers.[73] This came four months before the JMP made its own pitch for federalism, as described above. A five-region federal Yemen was also discussed in fall 1993.[74] Thus, numerous discussions of federal reforms occurred before the 2011 "revolution," and these came from a variety of actors – intellectuals, politicians, and local associations.

During the drafting of the Constitution, Yemeni intellectuals descended into the public arena. Some defended federalism's pedigree in Yemen. The first defense of federalism overlapped with the argument that democracy, once rendered as *shura* (deliberation), rather than *dimoqratiyya*, was not invented in the West, but is an Islamic

68 The interview, carried out in December 2012, is available at www.youtube.com/watch?v=7mo69TxjH8U. The reference to federalism is at 5:10.

69 For the IMF, federalism would send the state budget through the roof. See al-Akhali, "The Challenge of Federalism," 4 n. 10. Anderson, "Yemen's Failed Constitutional Transition," 326, also believes that the three-tiered federal arrangements favored by the NDC would have been "beyond the human and financial capacity of the country."

70 Dresch, *Modern History of Yemen*, 143, describes his work as "a sophisticated structural account of the country's political and intellectual life."

71 Interview with Zaid Alwazir, a republican intellectual from a prominent *sada* family from North Yemen who was marginalized for his family connection to the Imamate period, Fairfax, Virginia, USA (June 26, 2019).

72 Z. A. Alwazir, *Nahwa wahda yamaniyya ittihadiyya la-markaziyya* [Toward a Federal and Decentralized Yemeni Unity], 3rd ed. (Sanaa: Yemen Heritage Center, 1998), 6.

73 A campaign related in the pages of *The Yemen Times*. See Day, *Regionalism and Rebellion in Yemen*, 267.

74 Day, "The Federal Plan in Yemen," 32.

principle initiated by the Prophet himself during his time in Medina.[75] Nor does a cursory look at the position of Islamist factions reveal any declared animosity toward the proposed federalist solution: Islah, which had been a driving force behind Salih's replacement, supported President Hadi's federalist path. Similarly, Rashad, a Salafi party established after the revolution, fully endorsed the NDC process, supported the plan for a democratic and federal Yemen based on consultation of the various political factions, and condemned the Huthi coup in February 2015 described below.[76]

Federalism in general is accepted by a vast majority of Yemenis because it permits the articulation of regionalism and other sources of internal fragmentation. But many were dubious that the proposed six regions were the right choice. Some proposed embracing the so-called federalism of the provinces, or governorates (*fidiraliyyat al-wilayat*), a loose decentralization plan based on the existing twenty-two provinces (*wilayat*, or *muhafazat*) that existed in Yemen before the revolution. I was told by a former minister that UN Special Advisor Benomar had floated this idea to the eight members of the State-Building Committee at the end of 2013. A secret vote indicated a small majority (five to three) preferred this solution over the fewer regions advocated by Hadi.[77]

THE PATH TO CIVIL WAR AND END OF FEDERAL YEMEN: BURYING A FEDERALIST CONSTITUTION

The crisis in 2014 was amplified for much larger reasons than the constitution-drafting process. Three sets of nongovernmental actors (the Huthis, *Hirak*, and Ali Abdallah Salih), along with Hadi and the GNU, are responsible for the end of the political process. Chief among them are the Huthis, who objected to the borders of the six regions, but not to federalism,[78] and Salih, who believed a political comeback was possible. The two groups used their numbers and combined firepower to challenge Hadi's authority at the end of 2014. The real *Hirak* in the South (as opposed to

75 M. A. Al Saidi, "Mohammad the Prophet Was the Founder of Regional Federalism," *Dunya al-Watan* (February 21, 2014). The parallel is made to the so-called Medina Constitution because the Prophet granted some degree of freedom to the different communities. Other plans in 2014 to call governorates *makhalif*, an ancient Yemeni term used to describe provinces during the early Islamic times, wanted to generate positive religious connections to the theme of federalism.

76 J. Kuschnitzki, "A Party for Salafis? The Building of al-Rashad in Yemen's Transition Period," in M.-C. Heinze (ed.), *Yemen and the Search for Stability* (London: I.B. Tauris, 2018), 204–27, at 209, 219. Point 6 of the party's platform, available at alrshad.net, declares support for "the principle of separation of powers, [...] so as to achieve the participation of members of the Yemeni society all away from regionalism, racism, and sectarianism."

77 Interview with Al-Akhali (September 9, 2019). Al-Akhali thinks that this would be a natural arrangement to accommodate the prevailing regional identities, which more or less "fit" within the administrative borders of governorates, and therefore could provide a solution to the number of federal entities to create.

78 Brehony, Lackner, and Al-Sarhan, "Introduction," 9; T. Thiel, "Yemen's Imposed Federal Boundaries," *MERIP Online* (July 20, 2015).

the NDC *Hirak*) felt that the more the crisis escalated in Sanaa, the more legitimate its silent preparation for secession would be. The other parties involved in the GNU had neutralized each other, so no solution could come out of the regular legislative and political process. All the ingredients for a perfect storm were assembling during the year 2014. The straw that broke the back of a more or less peaceful political process was the dire economic situation, which was exacerbated by pressure from the IMF to cut fuel subsidies at the end of July 2014.[79]

It was at this moment that the Huthis, led by the demagogy of their leader Abdel-Makil Huthi, launched massive protests in the North. Surfing on the wave of popular protests against subsidy cuts, they felt they could march over Sanaa.[80] Taking the city on September 21, 2014, they obliged Hadi to sign the Peace and National Partnership Agreement (PNPA) the next day. It called for a new government representing all factions, the appointment of presidential advisors from the ranks of Ansar Allah and *Hirak*, and the application of the NDC's recommendations, in particular those of its working group on Sa'ada.[81] In the six-page document, the NDC was mentioned fifteen times, the term "consultation" six, and the GCC Initiative none.

Despite the appointment of a new prime minister, Khaled Bahah, in November, along with fresh figures who joined as ministers, because of their revolutionary and NDC involvement, the tension between the Huthis and Hadi exploded on January 17, 2015. When the first complete draft of the Constitution circulated on January 4, 2015, the Huthis pressured President Hadi to redraw the border of the landlocked Azal region, the northern province where most of the Huthi supporters are based. The way the map was drawn did not grant them access to the Red Sea or the part of the Jawf and Ma'rib provinces where petroleum resources abound.[82] Hadi refused to change the map, releasing the official draft on January 17, 2015 (see Figure 18.1).

Kidnappings and personal attacks occurred on that day, with Hadi and the prime minister soon placed under house arrest. On January 22, 2015, they both resigned, leading to a constitutional crisis. The Huthis then performed what amounts to a coup on February 6, 2015, issuing their unilateral Constitutional Declaration establishing a five-member Presidential Council and a new government in the form of a "Supreme Revolutionary Council" with branches throughout the country, and replacing the Parliament with a Transitional National Council made of 551 members.[83] The international community objected, with United Nations Security Council Resolution 2201, dated February 15, 2015, condemning the illegality of the Huthis' move. Saudi Arabia pushed Hadi and Bahah to retract their resignations, since a power vacuum was too risky for the future of the country. On February 21,

79 Anderson, "Yemen's Failed Constitutional Transition," 322.
80 Brehony, Lackner, and Al-Sarhan, "Introduction," 10.
81 The text of the PNPA can be found at peacemaker.un.org/yemen-national-partnership-2014. The preamble explicitly endorses federalism and the outcomes of the NDC.
82 Day, "The Federal Plan in Yemen," 25; Thiel, "Yemen's Imposed Federal Boundaries."
83 Lackner, *Yemen in Crisis*, 162.

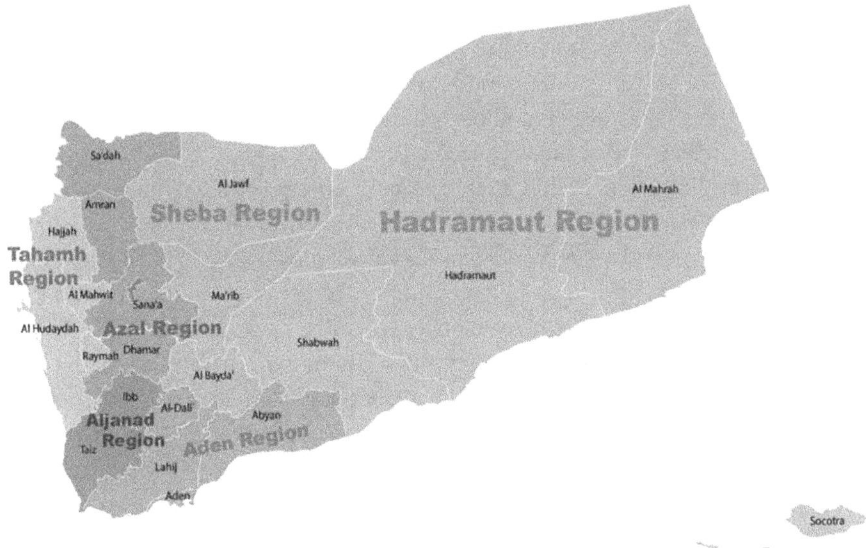

FIGURE 18.1 A federal Yemen: regions proposed in 2015 draft constitution. Source: https://blogs.lse.ac.uk/mec/files/2014/03/YemenMap.jpg.

2015, Hadi escaped house arrest and fled to Aden, leading to a Huthi military campaign toward Aden to seize full power.[84] Facing the risk of a total military takeover of the country by the Huthis, the GCC launched a bombing campaign on March 25, 2015. Since then, no progress toward restoring peaceful negotiation has been made, and millions of Yemenis have been impacted by the shifting military campaigns of the Huthis and their allies – supporters of former President Salih – first against Aden, and later toward Ta'iz and Hodayda.

The last development for our analysis of federalism occurred in the South. In 2015, the bulk of *Hirak* turned into an armed group, the so-called Southern Resistance (*al-muqawama al-junubiyya*).[85] It successfully broke the four-month siege of Aden by the Huthis and Salih in July 2015. One of the southern military leaders, Aydarous Al-Zubaydi, who had been forced to retire after the 1994 war, rose to prominence. He was appointed governor of Aden by Hadi in the first months of 2017 but sacked at the end of April.[86] On May 4, 2017, massive protests expressed support for al-Zubaydi. On the same day, the "Aden Declaration" was promulgated, charting the path toward the South's full independence.[87] A week later, on May 11, 2017,

84 Day, "The Federal Plan in Yemen," 25.

85 Made of young men of the popular committees, various local civilian militias, and former soldiers. See Amira-Augustin, "Aden wird siegen," 13.

86 Author's interview with Abdulsalam Mused (chairman) and Ahmad Muthana (vice-chairman), Directorate for Foreign Affairs, Southern Transitional Council, Washington DC (January 14, 2020).

87 STC, *Political Vision* (2019), 25–29 (document on file with author).

a Southern Transitional Council (STC), *al-majlis al-intiqali al-janubi*, with Aydarus al-Zubaydi as the chairman, was called into existence and waged a small war to oust the weak presence of Hadi's troops and loyal ministers. The STC also established a National Assembly made of 303 members, and declared self-rule in November 2017, but never crossed the line of full secession.

It is striking that "Yemen" has ceased to be a name worth mentioning in the South. The state that the STC hopes to create is called "Arabian South" (*al-junub al-ʿarabi*). The STC embraces federalism only insofar as it aspires for its new state to be federal.[88] It is far from clear that all southern Yemenis recognize the authority of the STC. Some members of *Hirak* do not appreciate the style of the STC leadership,[89] and many in the Hadramawt and in the distant governorates of Mahra and Soqotra refuse its authority.[90] Yet, following the Riyadh Agreement of November 2019, the STC has been recognized as an integral part of the political process in Yemen and is here to stay. Until December 2020, Hadi continued to govern from Riyadh, and the STC has extended its grip, with the support of the United Arab Emirates (UAE), over the South.

The last significant development for the Huthis was the death of Salih in December 2017. Salih, who had regained partial control over Sanaa, felt he could achieve a full return to power. Aware that the Huthis were personae non gratae for the international community because of their ideological alliances with Iran and organizational support from Hezbollah in Lebanon, Salih accepted an opening made by the UAE, expressing willingness to turn his back on the Huthis in November of that year.[91] Considered a traitor, he was killed by the Huthis a couple of days later, on December 4, 2017. The Huthis since then have been the masters of most of northern Yemen, with Islah and Ali Mohsen controlling the region around Ma'rib, jealously protecting its oil resources ahead of a final showdown with the Huthis.

CONCLUSIONS

Demands for decentralization have a long history in Yemen, provoking rich internal debates. Federalism is not a foreign concept in that part of the Arabian Peninsula. Political economy factors (the presence of remittances for decentralization and fluctuating rents for the central state, e.g., from oil revenues)[92] and "facts on the ground" (typically, who has military control) matter greatly in determining whether quests for decentralization can actually turn into effective political change.

88 See STC, *Political Vision*; or STC, المجلس الانتقالي الجنوبي يصدر بيانا سياسيا هاما, (August 15, 2019).

89 S. Dahlgren, "The Battle for South Yemen," *MERIP*, 292 (2019).

90 Interview with Mohammed Ahmad al-Khalifa, president of the Yemeni Foundation for Renaissance and Development, Socotra, founder of the Yemen Popular Uprising Committee, Hadibo, via WhatsApp (January 2, 2020 and June 15, 2020).

91 See F. Edroos, "How Did Yemen's Houthi-Saleh Alliance Collapse?" *Al Jazeera* (December 4, 2017).

92 Rogers and Challand, "Political Economy."

Accordingly, the 2015 draft constitution was not *the* cause for the current civil war, nor should one expect it to be *the* solution for the future Yemen. The project of a federalist Yemen, as envisioned between 2013 and early 2015, was only a revealing prism of the complex political process that was initiated by the 2011 uprising. I approached this federal project as a dependent variable shaped by historical and contradicting social (marginalization), economic (remittances, foreign aid), and political (ideological, subnationalisms) forces, and by regional factors (the GCC Initiative and recent Saudi and UAE military campaigns since 2015). Others prefer to see it as an independent variable, leading to questions of success or failure.

Questions such as whether the NDC adopted the right recommendations, whether an alternative map of the six regions could have prevented a civil war, or whether a truly asymmetric federalism, or a federalism of the provinces (*fidiraliyyat al-wilayat*), could provide a new path for future negotiations are widely debated. There is no doubt that the timing of the Huthi takeover of Sanaa and of preparations by southerners for secession are connected to the passing of the draft constitution. Ultimately, it will be Yemeni actors who decide what pieces of old puzzles to use, and which realities on the ground (a Huthi-governed northern Yemen? A Riyadh-based Hadi government? An STC-ruled Arabian South?) they prefer to support.

More generally, constitutional change is a long-term endeavor. Even Tunisia, an Arab country that is considered stable and rather successful in altering its constitutional order, still struggles with new laws and administrative measures to accompany its 2014 decentralizing reforms. It is easy to get lost in the legal or administrative details and to interpret politics in a uniquely top-down manner. I chose in this chapter to foreground legitimacy over legality, and to evaluate the strength of societal and intellectual demands rather than the robustness or weakness of the state. It is clear that popular legitimacy flowed, even if in an imperfect manner, from the 2011 encampment to the process of a National Dialogue. But this legitimacy has been confiscated by a variety of actors, many non-Yemeni.

PART V

Conclusions

19

Federalism and Decentralization in the MENA Region

Types and Trajectories

Aslı Ü. Bâli and Omar M. Dajani

The preceding chapters have surveyed insights from the theoretical literature on decentralization and provided detailed case studies from across the MENA region. Our cases are organized around three categories: first, relatively conventional decentralization initiatives in which reforms were adopted to improve governance; second, contexts in which decentralization has been contemplated as a framework for self-determination for the region's stateless communities; and, finally, decentralization initiatives undertaken in the shadow of conflict and state fragmentation. In this final chapter, we develop theoretical insights drawn from the rich terrain for qualitative comparison across these three contexts. We offer reflections on key characteristics of the shared regional context and a typology of factors driving decentralization in the Middle East and North Africa (MENA) region. We argue that an important contribution of the volume lies in identifying a broader array of motivations for, and actors driving, decentralization than currently reflected in the scholarly literature and in parsing the implications for the institutional design of decentralized government. We conclude the chapter by distilling patterns from the cases to identify distinct trajectories of decentralization that are evidenced in the MENA region and their entailments.

SHARED CONTEXT

Debates about the merits of federalism and decentralization in the MENA region have been shaped by a set of historical experiences and geopolitical dynamics common to many of our cases. This shared context helps to explain why efforts to decentralize government have elicited both enthusiasm and suspicion – and also why they have proved so susceptible to obstruction and diversion.

The Elixir and the Allergen

A paradox runs through the case studies in this volume: while "decentralization," broadly imagined, is a leading item on reform agendas across the region and championed as a cure-all by actors both inside and outside government, "federalism" tends to be so politically inflammatory that its mere mention disables reasoned public discourse, limiting opportunities to explore its potential contours and benefits. The reasons for this disjuncture, as explained below, have as much to do with the region's history as with differences between these two models of devolved governance, federalism triggering anxieties about territorial fragmentation that linger on from the region's traumatic colonial experience and early state formation processes. In different ways, moreover, both the open-armed embrace of decentralization and the abiding suspicion of federalism operate as impediments to constructive change.

In view of the global trend toward decentralization over the last forty years, it is unsurprising that it has figured prominently in discourse about how to improve public sector performance in the MENA region. What is striking is the breadth of the political coalitions that have supported it – a phenomenon we see both before and after the so-called Arab Spring. In Iran, for example, decentralization emerged in the 1990s as a rare point of consensus among technocrats who saw it as a prerequisite for modernization of the country's economy, Islamist reformists who hoped it would advance democratization and help shift power away from the clerical elites in the central government, and those selfsame ruling elites, who saw in decentralization a populist vehicle for mobilizing support for the regime.[1] Decentralization also elicited broad support prior to the uprising and civil war in Syria: a natural complement to the privatization spree undertaken by Bashar al-Assad early in his reign, it not only found its way into the regime's five-year action plan in 2006, but was also identified as a priority area in the EU strategic framework for Syria, which called for more far-reaching reforms.[2] Similarly, in Tunisia, decentralization commanded the support of virtually all of the blocs engaged in the constitution-drafting process following the 2011 revolution, proving to be one of the few common agenda items among liberals and Islamists, both of whom saw it as a way to rein in the overbearing central state and redress inequalities between the country's prosperous coastal regions and its marginalized interior.[3]

The breadth of the coalitions supporting decentralization in these countries may be attributed, at least in part, to the elasticity of the concept itself. Decentralization encompasses an extraordinary diversity of arrangements, which helps to explain its appeal for parties on both the right and the left of the political spectrum.[4] It can

[1] See K. Tajbakhsh, "Decentralization, Ideology, and Law in the Islamic Republic of Iran," Chapter 6 in this volume.

[2] See S. Araabi and L. Hilal, "Decentralization in State Disintegration: An Examination of Governance Experiments in Syria," Chapter 17 in this volume.

[3] See I. Kherigi, "Decentralization Reforms in Post-revolution Tunisia: The Struggle between Political and Bureaucratic Elites," Chapter 8 in this volume.

[4] See C. Pollitt, "Decentralization: A Central Concept in Contemporary Public Management," in E. Ferlie, L. E. Lynn, and C. Polllitt (eds.), *The Oxford Handbook of Public Management* (Oxford: Oxford University Press, 2007).

be the lynchpin of an ambitious democratizing agenda that involves meaningful devolution of authority to subnational government units and institutes robust mechanisms of downward accountability. Alternatively, it can stand for a far narrower set of reforms that aims at bolstering administrative efficiency without significantly diluting the central government's power or giving citizens the ability to hold it to account. This elasticity in the meaning of decentralization makes it an easy slogan to embrace. Governments eager to claim the mantle of reformism can impress domestic or international audiences by championing decentralization while leaving themselves substantial latitude to determine the scope and pace of concrete measures. Conversely, it offers would-be democrats a framework and vocabulary for promoting change without obliging them to reveal the character and scale of the political transformation they aspire to achieve. These dynamics make reaching a consensus about the need for decentralizing reforms easier at the outset, but they may later make it more difficult to formulate and implement specific structural reforms. As discussed further below, decentralization's conceptual elasticity also enables regimes intent on capturing the reformist agenda to instrumentalize it defensively by deconcentrating authority in ways that actually serve to consolidate and even extend central government power.

While decentralization tends to be seen as an elixir, federalism produces something closer to a severe allergic response. To be sure, federal government has been a recurring demand among self-determination movements in the region, from Kurdish groups in Iraq, Syria, and Turkey, to Cyrenaicans in Libya to southern Yemenis. In most of these contexts, however, it has provoked fierce controversy, triggering associations with longstanding, and at times existential, challenges to territorial integrity. Thus, the decision to establish a federal system in Iraq's 2005 Constitution elicited strident opposition from both Sunni and Shi'i Arabs in the country,[5] and a decade later it was similarly rejected by Arab opposition groups in Syria, which sharply criticized Kurdish parties for implementing federal arrangements de facto during the civil war.[6] Federalism also provoked furious debate during the early stages of Libya's transition, before being abandoned in favor of a more modest decentralization initiative.[7] Only in Yemen has federalism won the support of a substantial majority of the population, but even there considerable effort was expended during the national dialogue process to address widespread popular misperceptions about its meaning and implications and to highlight its endogenous roots.[8]

5 J. Morrow, "Iraq's Constitutional Process II: An Opportunity Lost," Special Report 155, United States Institute of Peace (November 2005), 8.

6 See S. Araabi and L. Hilal, "Decentralization in State Disintegration: An Examination of Governance Experiments in Syria," Chapter 17 in this volume.

7 See K. Mezran and E. Miller, "The Promise – and Limits – of Stabilization through Local Governance in Libya," Chapter 16 in this volume.

8 B. Challand, "Decentralization in Yemen: The Case of the Federalist Draft Constitution of 2015," Chapter 18 in this volume.

To be sure, the tendency in the MENA region to see federalism as a prelude to partition or secession is neither unique nor wholly unjustified. In other regions, the postcolonial experience has produced similar anxieties and suspicions.[9] Moreover, we live in an age in which elites across the globe pay lip service to pluralism while routinely treating minority claims for autonomy as illegitimate.[10] Although the scholarly literature is sharply divided about whether federal states are more vulnerable to secession and civil conflict than those with unitary systems,[11] federalism's track record on both fronts provides ample basis for concern.

Still, there remains something distinctive in the remarkable power of the MENA region's memories of, and apprehensions about, territorial fragmentation. Rather than treating this as a peculiarity of political culture, our cases suggest it may be explained by the convergence of three factors. First, postcolonial state formation across the region occurred in the wake of Western strategies of territorial disaggregation – including the Ottoman Empire's dismemberment and the fragmentation of Arab territories into multiple states. The fact that these strategies were advanced in some cases through foreign imposition of federal systems and other minority protection regimes lingers on in the popular imagination. Second, the state-building processes in the region were understood in homogenizing terms premised on the equation of the nation with an ethnonational majority.[12] Together, these two factors have produced a region of weak states in terms of governance capacity and defensive ethnonational commitments, with nations' frontiers routinely presented in ethnomajoritarian terms (as in "Arab Syria" or Turkey as the nation of the "Turks").[13] The third factor is the centrality of the Middle East to geopolitical competition among great powers, resulting in frequent destabilizing conflicts. Contemporary experiences including the wars of foreign intervention in Iraq and Libya and the significant foreign participation in the proxy wars in Yemen and Syria reinforce ongoing anxieties about intervention and partition. As a consequence, demands for the accommodation of ethnic and/or religious differences through any form of territorial pluralism elicit a ferocious response, with federalism in particular being associated with the breaking of nations and states.

9 See, e.g., Asnake Kefale, "Federalism and Regional Politics in Africa," *Oxford Research Encyclopedia: Politics* (July 2019) (describing African leaders' hostility to federal proposals as a result of experience of colonial partition).

10 W. Kymlicka, "Devolution and the Promotion (or Evasion) of Minority Rights," Chapter 3 in this volume.

11 For a survey of competing views, see L. D. Anderson, *Federal Solutions to Ethnic Problems: Accommodating Diversity* (Abingdon: Routledge 2013), chs. 2–4.

12 See, e.g., B. White, *The Emergence of Minorities in the Middle East: The Politics of Community in French Mandate Syria* (Edinburgh: Edinburgh University Press, 2011).

13 Here the MENA region's experience resonates with Partha Chatterjee's classic account of the ways in which anti-colonial nationalism in India remained bound to the very ideas it struggled against, particularly in the conceptions of nation and nationalism. Partha Chatterjee, *Nationalist Thought and the Colonial World: A Derivative Discourse* (Minneapolis: University of Minnesota Press, 1993).

This allergic reaction has been both instrumentalized and exacerbated by regimes attempting to shore up domestic political support. Rather than entertaining greater autonomy within the state's territorial borders, regimes have often attempted to consolidate control in the hands of the central government by deploying fears of internal threats while pursuing policies of coercive assimilation. In extreme cases, this strategy has contributed to state collapse, the central state's rejection of autonomy demands tipping a precarious political balance into armed conflict. In Yemen, the country was moving toward the adoption of a federal scheme in its National Dialogue Conference only to have a presidentially appointed constitutional committee structure the terms of its implementation in ways that disempowered key groups.[14] The result was the withdrawal of the Houthi movement from the process and, ultimately, civil war. Similarly, fears of marginalization in the eastern region of Libya following the fall of Qaddafi produced demands for federalism.[15] The rejection of a semi-autonomous region in the east by the National Transitional Council was among the causes of the continuing conflict.

While resistance to a political transition that includes robust decentralization goes some way toward explaining the circumstances of conflict and state collapse in places as diverse as Rojava, Benghazi, and Aden, the course of those conflicts also suggests that some scheme of decentralized government may represent the best-case scenario for a post-collapse trajectory in these cases. By preserving nominal territorial integrity while accommodating the devolution of power away from the center, such arrangements may serve as an intermediate post-conflict position poised between secession and full reintegration of autonomous regions in a unitary state. Such an intermediate position may also emerge as the de facto, rather than de jure negotiated, outcome of conflict, as in Somalia.[16] The fact that such an option can only be envisioned following armed conflict is a testament to the depth of the resistance by central states: only when their bargaining position is dramatically weakened by conflict, and self-determination movements have demonstrated their capacity to impose de facto decentralized arrangements through armed struggle, does a political settlement involving more robust autonomy arrangements become imaginable.

If the region's extreme sensitivity to perceived threats to the territorial integrity of states has a silver lining, it is that it has encouraged innovative thinking about the structure of the state on the part of self-determination movements in the region. One clear example is the turn toward "democratic confederalism" by the Kurdish leaderships in Turkey and Syria.[17] Reconceptualizing the idea of internal

14 Challand, "Decentralization in Yemen," Chapter 18.

15 Mezran and Miller, "The Promise – and Limits – of Stabilization through Local Governance in Libya," Chapter 16.

16 See G. R. M. Anderson and S. Choudhry, "Devolution and Federalism in Collapsed States: Constitutional Process and Design," Chapter 15 in this volume.

17 See J. Jongerden, "Autonomy beyond the State," Chapter 9 in this volume; A. Ü. Bâli, "Turkish Kurdistan: Decentralization Reimagined," Chapter 11 in this volume; Araabi and Hilal, "Decentralization in State Disintegration," Chapter 17.

self-determination, they have shifted from advocating asymmetrical autonomy for the Kurds to embracing a radical but symmetrical form of devolved governance applicable across the states where they live. This new approach is meant not only to assuage apprehensions about secession, but also to establish common cause with other reform movements committed to mitigating the concentration of power in the executive branch and promoting democratization.

To be clear, our aim here is not to suggest that federalism or other less robust forms of decentralization are appropriate for every country in the region – or likely to be free from challenges in any of them. We hope instead that by drawing attention to the ways in which historical experience and political opportunism have influenced discourse about this set of institutional design options, it becomes easier to disentangle concerns about their merits from reflexive reactions to the baggage they carry with them.

Sweeping Promises, Weak Commitments

Debates over federalism and decentralization in the MENA region are also framed by an international legal and geopolitical order that is nominally supportive of decentralizing initiatives but has often operated to undermine the very principles it proclaims.

The international law framework governing self-determination is a case in point. Riddled with ambiguities and internal tensions, it promises far more than it has proved capable of delivering. International law affirms the right of "all peoples" to self-determination, pursuant to which they are entitled to "freely determine their political status and freely pursue their economic, social and cultural development."[18] It distinguishes, however, between two distinct paths toward self-determination. On the one hand, as the International Court of Justice reaffirmed in its advisory opinion on Kosovo, the law of self-determination has "developed in such a way as to create a right to independence for the peoples of non-self-governing territories and peoples subject to alien subjugation, domination and exploitation."[19] This right to "external" self-determination entitles a people in such circumstances to opt either for independence or for association with or integration into another state, pursuant to a set of procedural mechanisms intended to ensure their choice is freely made. On the other hand, a people claiming self-determination outside of such circumstances is expected instead to exercise the right "internally" – that is, through "pursuit of its political, economic, social and cultural development within the framework of an existing state."[20]

18 International Covenant on Civil and Political Rights, Art. 1; International Covenant on Economic, Social, and Cultural Rights, Art. 1.

19 *Accordance with International Law of the Unilateral Declaration of Independence in Respect of Kosovo*, Advisory Opinion [2010] ICJ Rep. 403, 436.

20 *Reference re. Secession of Quebec* [1998] 2 SCR 217 [Canada], para. 126.

International law is, however, largely indifferent about both the form internal self-determination should take and the process through which it should unfold. Although international human rights law affords some protection to the rights of ethnic and religious minorities, it does so primarily through equality and anti-discrimination norms that vest in individuals, rather than "peoples" or groups.[21] Conceiving of self-determination in this way is ironic: "Breaking down the group into its composite elements, into a mere aggregate of individuals therewith, undermines the very thing it aims to advocate."[22] Efforts to develop instruments recognizing the collective rights of minorities have, however, produced only nonbinding commitments.[23] Indeed, in contrast to both the minority rights regimes that were imposed on newly independent states a century ago[24] and the procedural mechanisms and institutions created to monitor the realization of external self-determination in the context of decolonization, the international system does little to guide – much less to direct – internal self-determination within existing states.[25]

The indeterminacy of this normative framework is compounded by uncertainty about when a people prevented from exercising its right to internal self-determination is legally justified in pursuing unilateral secession from a sovereign state. This uncertainty is rarely resolved in favor of the people seeking self-determination unless it has the capacity – in its own right or with the assistance of a powerful patron – to press its claim by force. As Marc Weller observes, self-determination movements operating outside of recognized colonial contexts face an international system "structured in such a way as to help the central state ensure their defeat" – one that characterizes them as "secessionist rebels" or "terrorists" and imposes few legal constraints on how they are engaged, leaving them subject to "the very legal order of the state from which they seek to escape."[26]

The weakness of international commitments to both external and internal self-determination is vividly illustrated by our cases. First, even where the international

21 See O. M. Dajani, "Responding to Ethnic and Religious Conflict in the Emerging Arab Order: The Promise and Limits of Rights," *U.C.L.A. Journal of International Law and Foreign Affairs*, 17 (2013), 29–74, at 59–60.

22 J. Klabbers, "The Right to Be Taken Seriously: Self-determination in International Law," *Human Rights Quarterly*, 28 (2006), 186–206, at 205.

23 Examples include the United Nations General Assembly's Declaration on the Rights of Persons Belonging to National or Ethnic, Religious and Linguistic Minorities, G.A. Resolution 47/135, Annex, U.N. Doc. A/Res/47/135/Annex (December 18, 1992), and the Council of Europe's Framework Convention for the Protection of National Minorities, February 1, 1995, E.T.S. No. 157.

24 On the minority regimes, see N. Berman, "'But the Alternative Is Despair': European Nationalism and the Modernist Renewal of International Law," *Harvard Law Review*, 106(8) (1993), 1792–1903.

25 A narrow exception was the scrutiny attached to minority protection regimes within newly established European states following the dissolution of the Soviet Union and Yugoslavia. See S. Mancini, "Secession and Self-determination," in M. Rosenfeld and A. Sajó (eds.), *The Oxford Handbook of Comparative Constitutional Law* (Oxford: Oxford University Press, 2012), 12.

26 M. Weller, "Settling Self-determination Conflicts: Recent Developments," *European Journal of International Law*, 20 (2009), 111–66, at 113.

community has recognized a people's right to external self-determination – and, accordingly, where the international bias in favor of the territorial integrity of states should not pertain – powerful states have been successful at diverting self-determination claims into frameworks involving extremely limited self-government. Thus, despite a virtually unanimous international consensus that the Sahrawi and Palestinian peoples are entitled to opt for independence, the international community has acquiesced in the imposition of arrangements that fall far short of it. Second, outside of the colonial context, states have interpreted internal self-determination very narrowly, and they have faced modest international pressure to embrace a more expansive conception of how to accommodate pluralism within their territory. The experiences of the Kurdish communities in Turkey and Syria reflect the brutal consequences of the latitude afforded states and the strictures imposed on minority identity groups seeking to preserve cultural rights and political autonomy within a shared territory governed by an ethnic majority. Even the one counterexample of the Iraqi Kurds, who managed to attain meaningful autonomy when international pressure produced a new federal structure for Iraq following the 2003 war, sounds a cautionary note. When the government of Iraqi Kurdistan arranged a referendum on self-determination, the decision to pursue the plebiscite together with its results were roundly condemned by the international community. And when the Iraqi central state deployed its military to seize the city of Kirkuk and other territories by force, international support for Baghdad's position obliged the Kurds to accept their loss of territory. In short, then, the international context in the case of our self-determination cases has provided existing states with cover for pursuing assimilationist or denialist policies, and continued rights deprivations, while doing little to incentivize creative thinking about decentralized design solutions that might accommodate pluralism. Self-determination movements consequently face a Hobson's choice: either accept arrangements that deny them meaningful autonomy or take up arms in order to alter their bargaining position.

Efforts to advance federalism and decentralization in the MENA region also face a fraught geopolitical context. At once the object of great power competition and unrelenting pressure to address issues ranging from transnational terrorism to migration flows, the regimes in the region maneuver in a complex political space defined not only by internal constraints but also by regional and global rivalries.

The challenges presented by these dynamics are particularly pronounced in our cases involving internal conflict. In these cases, interventions by external actors have served more often to prolong conflict than to facilitate a post-conflict transition that might resolve competing territorial claims through a framework of decentralized shared governance. In all four cases – Iraq, Libya, Syria, and Yemen – conflict has produced forms of de facto decentralization, in which local coordination committees, armed groups, and/or national liberation movements provide municipal services and security and establish local governing arrangements, as conflict excludes the central state from control over significant swaths of territory. The ability to impose facts on the ground by dint of arms shifts bargaining power in favor of local actors in ways that might incentivize the central state to concede de jure to a decentralized arrangement that preserves territorial integrity. Yet the fact that many of these actors – including the central state itself – benefit from external patrons that supply arms and material support means that the pursuit of further advantage or the prospect of regaining territory forestalls the initiation of a post-conflict settlement.

In sum, then, the MENA region's contemporary experience with federalism and decentralization is not being written on a blank slate. It is unfolding in a historical, legal, and political context that shapes its development in contradictory ways – at once generating expectations and constraining (or distorting) their realization.

DRIVERS OF DECENTRALIZATION

Against the backdrop of the shared context described above, recent decentralizing initiatives in the MENA region are animated by a striking diversity of motivations. We see decentralization deployed as both a bulwark against authoritarianism and as a strategy for consolidating it; as a vehicle for the emancipation of long-oppressed identity groups and as a dangerous diversion from meaningful self-determination; as a platform for managing governance in circumstances of state collapse and as a framework for reconstituting the state following conflict. In this section, we examine each of these drivers, situating them in relation both to the literature's long-prevalent typology and to one another.

Scholarship exploring the drivers of decentralization continues to be influenced by the typology introduced by Alfred Stepan in the early 2000s.[27] Stepan observed that a system of decentralized government may be created not only to unite political communities facing common external challenges, but also to accommodate – or subvert – demands for self-determination from groups within the state. Focusing on federal systems, he identified three ideal types: "coming together," "holding together," and "putting together."[28] In the first, modeled on the United States, a federation emerges from a compact between previously sovereign polities that allows them to retain some of their powers while delegating others to a central government for the purpose of enhancing collective security or achieving other goals. As Stepan observed, however, "[s]ince the emergence of nation-states on the world stage in the aftermath of the French Revolution, *no* sovereign democratic nation-states have

27 A. Stepan, *Arguing Comparative Politics* (Oxford: Oxford University Press, 2001); R. Dixon, R. Levy, and M. Tushnet, "Theories and Practices of Federalism in Deeply Divided Societies," *Federal Law Review*, 46(4) (2018), 481–90; K. T. Muluye, "Holding Together, Coming Together or Putting Together? A (Re)examination on the Formation of Ethiopia's Federation," *RUDN Journal of Public Administration*, 7(1) (2020), 70–82.

28 Stepan's typology echoes the distinction between "integrative" and "devolutionary" federalism earlier propounded by Lenaerts. K. Lenaerts, "Constitutionalism and the Many Faces of Federalism," *American Journal of Comparative Law*, 38 (1990), 205–64.

ever 'come together' in an enduring federation."[29] More commonly, he explained, federal governments are the products of a different logic, in which the leaders of unitary states facing self-determination disputes – such as India, Belgium, and Spain – decide that devolving authority is the only way to hold their countries together in a democratic order.[30] The third type, the "putting together" federation, is "a heavily coercive effort by a nondemocratizing centralizing power to put together in a multinational state, some of the components of which had previously been independent states."[31] Patterned after the Soviet Union, its purpose is also to hold a state together in the face of demands for self-determination. What differentiates it from a "holding together" federation is its nonvoluntary and nondemocratic character.

Distinguishing between the drivers of decentralization helps make sense of differences in institutional design. Units negotiating aggregation into a federal union come to the table with a greater measure of sovereignty – and, typically, greater bargaining power – than those seeking devolution of authority from a state of which they are already part. Accordingly, the units in "coming together" federations tend to be better able than those in "holding together" federations to secure the constitutional entrenchment of privileges such as overrepresentation of less populous states in the upper chamber of the central government legislature and the allocation of robust powers to the units themselves.[32] For the same reason, policing powers tend to be more centralized in "holding together" and "putting together" federations than in "coming together" systems.[33] Thus, the bargaining power of the actors negotiating the parameters of a decentralized system of government help to explain its features.

While that insight guides our analysis, our own typology apprehends a broader array of motivations for decentralization and is constructed differently in three respects. First, whereas Stepan's typology addressed only federal systems, ours juxtaposes a

[29] A. Stepan, "Federalism and Democracy: Beyond the U.S. Model," in D. Karmis and W. Norman (eds.), *Theories of Federalism: A Reader* (New York: Palgrave Macmillan, 2005), 255–68, at 267 (emphasis in original). Stepan may have overlooked the MENA region's one "coming together" federation: the United Arab Emirates (UAE), whose seven sheikhdoms joined together to establish a political union and federal constitutional order following independence from Great Britain in 1971. The UAE, however, is not, and has never pretended to be, a democracy. Its federal structure was conceived less as a check on central authority than as a means of preserving the prestige of leading tribal families. F. Heard-Bey, *Abu Dhabi, the United Arab Emirates and the Gulf Region: Fifty Years of Transition* (Berlin: Gerlach Press, 2017), 256–70. The literature's inattention to authoritarian variations of decentralized government is one gap we hope this volume can help to fill.

[30] A variation on this second category is what has been called "post-conflict federalism." See S. Choudhry and N. Hume, "Federalism, Devolution and Secession: From Classical to Post-conflict Federalism," in T. Ginsburg and R. Dixon (eds.), *Research Handbook on Comparative Constitutional Law* (Northampton, MA: Edward Elgar, 2010).

[31] Stepan, "Federalism and Democracy," 258. A variation on this third category is "forced-together federalism," where a federal system is imposed by an outside actor such as a colonial power. See N. Bermeo, "The Import of Institutions," *Journal of Democracy*, 13 (2002), 96–110.

[32] A. Stepan, "Federalism and Democracy," 258.

[33] B. T. Taylor, "Force and Federalism: Controlling Coercion in Federal Hybrid Regimes," *Comparative Politics*, 39 (2007), 421–40, at 430.

broader array of forms of decentralized governance, even as we give due attention to the salient differences between them. We made this choice not only because federations remain relatively rare in the MENA region,[34] but also because, over years of bargaining, governments and popular movements pivot between advocating different degrees and forms of decentralization. Analyzing them together helps us to ascertain what is gained (and lost) when a decision is made to move from one to another. Second, our typology is attentive to *which kinds of actors are driving decentralization* – to whether the process is directed from within or outside government and whether decision-makers are undertaking to devolve or consolidate authority. Third, our typology reflects the reality that the motivations behind advocating a decentralized system are often *hybrid and dynamic*. A system will usually bear the marks of compromises between different sets of interests and values, rather than embodying a singular vision. In addition, its evolution over time may reflect shifts in the bargaining position of different political actors. Accordingly, the six types that we set out below are neither mutually exclusive nor static.

Anti-authoritarian Decentralization

Federalism was conceived in part to serve as a bulwark against tyranny,[35] and political decentralization continues to be promoted as a means of checking the authority of "overzealous national governments."[36] There is some debate, however, about which institutional features are most effective at preventing reversion to authoritarianism.[37] One recent study suggests that what matters most is the distribution of authority over functions critical to the consolidation of power (such as policing, judging, and administering elections), concluding that for this reason federal systems tend to be better able to impede authoritarian capture of the central government than unitary systems.[38] As other studies have shown, however, the autonomy accorded units within a federal system may make them susceptible to anti-democratic and even authoritarian practices at the local level.[39]

The desire to prevent reversion to authoritarian rule was a primary motivation behind the embrace of decentralization in Tunisia's 2014 Constitution, which was crafted by a constituent assembly comprised almost entirely of members of

34 See P. G. Roeder, "Decentralization to Manage Identity Conflicts," Chapter 2 in this volume.

35 Federalist 51 (1787).

36 *Democratic Decentralization Programming Handbook* (Washington, DC: USAID, 2009), 23.

37 See A. Huq and T. Ginsburg, "How to Lose a Constitutional Democracy," *UCLA Law Review*, 65 (2018), 80–169.

38 D. Landau, H. J. Wiseman, and S. R. Wiseman, "Federalism for the Worst Case," *Iowa Law Review*, 105 (2020), 1187–255, at 1252–54. For a more skeptical view, see E. L. Rubin and M. Feeley, "Federalism: Some Notes on a National Neurosis," *UCLA Law Review*, 41 (1994), 903–52, at 927–35.

39 For an exploration of the mechanics of subnational authoritarianism, see Edward L. Gibson, "Boundary Control: Subnational Authoritarianism in Democratic Countries," *World Politics*, 58 (2005), 101–32.

opposition parties that had been banned or repressed by the previous regime.[40] It was also among the primary reasons a federal system was adopted in Iraq's 2005 Constitution[41] and recommended by Yemen's National Dialogue Conference in 2014,[42] though in both countries support for federalism was also driven by the desire of substate ethnic/regional groups (i.e., Iraqi Kurds and southern Yemenis) to secure a greater measure of autonomy from the central government.

Although anti-authoritarian sentiment was a leading driver of these moves toward decentralizing government in all three countries, each highlights in different ways the challenges of designing a constitutional order capable of serving as an effective constraint on executive power. Tunisia's Constitution declares unambiguously that "[l]ocal government is based on decentralization,"[43] and provides that the principle of subsidiarity should guide the allocation of powers between local authorities and the central government,[44] but it does little itself to delineate which powers will be exercised by each, leaving the question to be resolved later through the legislative process. This gap has been exploited by a resurgent central government bureaucracy, which has slowed the pace of decentralization, sapping the process of political momentum.[45] It has also limited the effectiveness of decentralization as a constraint on "democratic backsliding."[46]

In contrast to Tunisia's Constitution, Iraq's defines with greater specificity which functions will be exercised by the central government, regions, and governorates, respectively.[47] Nevertheless, this more thoroughly elaborated institutional architecture proved insufficient to prevent Iraq's backslide into authoritarianism a decade ago, in part because key features of the federal scheme were never implemented[48] and in part because the constraints it did establish were circumvented through the creation of extra-constitutional bodies.[49] It also bears noting that while Iraq's federal system helped insulate the Kurdistan region from resurgent authoritarianism in Baghdad, it may make it harder to check anti-democratic practices by Kurdish leaders in Erbil.

While both Tunisia's and Iraq's experiences highlight the risks of deferring the making or implementation of important decisions regarding the structure of decentralized government to legislative or administrative processes down the road,

40 Kherigi, "Decentralization Reforms in Post-revolution Tunisia," Chapter 8.
41 Bartu and MacEachern, "The Devil Is in the Details," Chapter 10.
42 Challand, "Decentralization in Yemen," Chapter 18.
43 Tunisia Constitution (2014), Art. 131.
44 Ibid., Art. 134.
45 Kherigi, "Decentralization Reforms in Post-revolution Tunisia," Chapter 8.
46 Dokhi Fassihian, "Democratic Backsliding in Tunisia: The Case for Renewed International Attention," Freedom House (2018).
47 Iraq Constitution (2005), arts. 110–23.
48 D. Romano, "Iraq's Descent into Civil War: A Constitutional Explanation," *Middle East Journal*, 68 (Autumn 2014), 547–66, at 553–54.
49 M. Sullivan, "Maliki's Authoritarian Regime," Institute for the Study of War (2013).

Yemen's offers a reminder that protracted constitutional transitions present dangers of their own. Its national dialogue process did facilitate broad-based popular engagement with the idea of federalism; however, inattention during that long process to worsening economic circumstances on the ground coupled with a shallow commitment to democracy at the top created an opening for challenges to the federal scheme that was ultimately proposed, contributing to the country's descent into civil war.[50]

Ultimately, none of these experiences points to either an ideal "anti-authoritarian constitution" or an ideal process for developing one. But together they illuminate a dilemma facing societies charting a path away from authoritarian rule: constitutional entrenchment of an institutional scheme that clearly places certain governmental powers outside the reach of the executive may help to forestall a return to authoritarianism at the center, but it is a difficult bargain to achieve, and its success or failure may be as much a function of the political and strategic context as of its design.

Authoritarian Decentralization

Although decentralization is often urged as a democratizing measure, a growing body of research suggests that certain forms not only are compatible with authoritarianism, but actually can enhance the resilience of authoritarian regimes. Thus, even as China has presided over one of the world's most far-reaching programs of administrative and fiscal decentralization, Beijing has succeeded in preserving political authority at the local level – in large part through Communist Party control over the appointment and promotion of cadres.[51] In Africa, too, decentralization is often driven by national parties intent on creating a subnational foothold by creating patronage networks and participating in local elections.[52] Autocratic regimes in Africa have also employed other strategies to prevent subnational governments from becoming sites of meaningful political participation and contestation, such as creating "institutional gaps" by establishing elected local structures but denying them decision-making authority.[53]

In Iran, Iraq, Jordan, Morocco, and Syria, regimes have adopted decentralizing reforms with considerable fanfare – in some cases, explicitly framing them as democratizing measures – but they have deployed a combination of strategies to preserve and even enhance authoritarian rule. First, where elected subnational

50 P. Salisbury, "Federalism, Conflict and Fragmentation in Yemen," Saferworld (October 2015).

51 P. F. Landry, *Decentralized Authoritarianism in China: The Communist Party's Control of Local Elites in the Post-Mao Era* (New York: Cambridge University Press, 2008).

52 R. B. Riedl and J. T. Dickovick, "Party Systems and Decentralization in Africa," *Studies in Comparative International Development*, 49(1) (2014), 321–42.

53 L. Aalen and R. L. Muriaas, *Manipulating Political Decentralization: Africa's Inclusive Autocrats* (New York: Routledge, 2018), 47–51.

government bodies have been established, their capacity to serve as accountability mechanisms and to influence policy is constrained by institutional gaps. In Iran, elected city councils are allowed only a marginal role in development planning, which is dominated by appointed provincial-level agencies with greater budget authority.[54] In Jordan, governorate-level elected councils have merely advisory roles and lack the authority to raise revenues or to initiate legislation.[55] And Morocco's "advanced regionalization" initiative has only modestly increased the resources and powers of elected regional councils, subjecting many of their decisions to supervision by appointed governors.[56]

Second, some regimes have devolved responsibilities from the central state to the local and regional levels in order to deflect demands for governance improvement addressed to the national government. In Iraq, the central government viewed the acceleration of decentralizing reforms as a politically expedient means of diverting responsibility for poor service delivery in the areas of education, healthcare, and public infrastructure to local authorities while meeting the demands of international donors.[57] This not only undermined efficiency by producing confusion over authority and policy implementation, it compromised accountability by rendering the authority structures themselves more opaque to local constituents.

Lastly, regimes have continued to favor deconcentration over reforms that give more robust roles to subnational governments. In Syria, the government has vested additional powers in presidentially appointed governors and has consolidated thousands of villages into recognized townships dependent upon the central government for funding, thereby expanding the state's patronage network further into Syria's rural periphery.[58] In Iran, the central government continues to assign fiscal and administrative responsibility for local development to centrally appointed and funded provincial planning agencies.[59] Morocco has largely preserved the system of deconcentrated governance the regime erected in the 1990s, despite its establishment of elected regional councils.[60] And even in Iraq, whose 2015 decentralization law provides for the substantial reallocation of authority from line ministries

[54] See K. Tajbakhsh, "Decentralization, Ideology, and Law in the Islamic Republic of Iran," Chapter 6 in this volume.

[55] A. Ranko, M. Lotz, H. Abu Ghazaleh, and I. Haase, "The Municipal and Governorate Council Elections of August 2017: Decentralization Efforts in Jordan," *Konrad Adenauer Stiftung Country Report Jordan* (August 2017), 1, 4.

[56] See O. Y. Shehabi, "'*Dans ses Frontiers Authentiques*'? Morocco's Advanced Regionalization and the Question of Western Sahara," Chapter 14 in this volume.

[57] A. Al-Mawlawi, "Salvaging State Legitimacy in Iraq through Decentralization," Chapter 7 in this volume. This phenomenon has also been observed elsewhere. See Q. H. Beazer and O. J. Reuter, "Who Is to Blame? Political Centralization and Electoral Punishment under Authoritarianism," *The Journal of Politics*, 81 (2019), 648–62.

[58] Araabi and Hilal, "Decentralization in State Disintegration," Chapter 17.

[59] Tajbakhsh, "Decentralization, Ideology and Law in the Islamic Republic of Iran," Chapter 6.

[60] Shehabi, "'*Dans ses Frontiers Authentiques*'?," Chapter 14.

to provincial governments, local directorates of the powerful Ministry of Finance continue to exercise effective control over provincial budgets.[61]

Because deconcentration remains so prevalent in the region, it bears emphasizing the important ways in which it differs from other forms of decentralization. Although deconcentration may increase the responsiveness and efficiency of service delivery by bringing government closer to the people it serves, it is not a democratizing measure. Nor does it act as a constraint on central government authority. To the contrary, deconcentration represents an extension of the central government's reach into the lives of its constituents. Seen in this light, tentative steps toward political decentralization through the establishment of elected municipal, provincial, or regional councils look like little more than a fig leaf when coupled with the maintenance, and in some cases expansion, of central government power through deconcentrated institutions. In fact, by coupling the two approaches we describe – symbolic political decentralization and far-reaching deconcentration – regimes are able to exploit rather than resist reforms, all the while consolidating their control.[62]

Emancipatory Decentralization

Decentralized government has long been urged as a means of accommodating demands for self-determination without disrupting the international territorial order.[63] Its merits as an alternative to partition or secession are, however, a point of sustained debate,[64] as is the optimal design of decentralized government institutions.[65] In relation to both questions, the literature tends to focus on the capacity of decentralized institutions to forestall secession and/or civil war. What this preoccupation with the "holding together" of states obscures is decentralization's emancipatory potential. Our cases suggest that decentralization can offer a framework for an expansive vision of internal self-determination – one conceived to deliver not only

61 See Al-Mawlawi, "Salvaging State Legitimacy in Iraq through Decentralization," Chapter 7.

62 In other contexts, this phenomenon has been aptly labeled "authoritarian upgrading." S. Heydemann, "Upgrading Authoritarianism in the Arab World," Saban Center for Middle East Policy, Brookings Institution Analysis Paper No. 13 (October 2007).

63 Aaland Islands Case, Advisory Opinion of the International Committee of Jurists of the League of Nations, *L.N.O.J. Spec. Supp. No.* 3 (October 1920).

64 For competing views, see T. Chapman and P. G. Roeder, "Partition as a Solution to Wars of Nationalism: The Importance of Institutions," *American Political Science Review*, 101 (2007), 677–91, and N. Sambanis and J. Schulhofer-Wohl, "What's in a Line? Is Partition a Solution to Civil War?" *International Security*, 34 (2009), 82–118.

65 An important strand of this debate focuses on whether political institutions should be structured to provide for power-sharing between identity groups after elections (consociationalism) or to incentivize the development of intergroup coalitions before elections (centripetalism). For a discussion of challenges facing both approaches, see D. L. Horowitz, "Ethnic Power Sharing: Three Big Problems," *Journal of Democracy*, 25 (2014), 5–20.

enhanced self-government to long-disenfranchised groups, but also a fundamental restructuring – even reimagining – of the state.

The Kurdish experiment with decentralization offers a compelling trajectory. Under the label of "democratic confederalism," Abdullah Öcalan, the long-imprisoned leader of the Kurdish national liberation movement in Turkey, has crafted a blueprint for the political future of the region straddling the four states where the majority of Kurds reside.[66] Combining a transborder confederation with a highly devolutionary distribution of power within existing borders, democratic confederalism has been broadly embraced at the grassroots level by Kurdish communities in both Turkey and Syria.

Two features of this experience are distinctive. First, in contrast to the top-down deconcentration initiatives undertaken by the central governments in Ankara and Damascus, this model of decentralized governance has been conceptualized and implemented by nonstate actors with strong grassroots networks. In Turkey, the pro-Kurdish HDP/BDP party energized municipal elections with political platforms emphasizing local empowerment. In each municipality where the party has won local elections, a gender-balanced ticket of co-mayors has taken office, supported by a party structure that includes unofficial but democratically elected village and neighborhood councils, which have input into municipal policy. This model was built upon by Öcalan's followers in Syria, where a window of opportunity arose from the central government's loss of control over Kurdish areas. Here, again, grassroots participation in village councils served as the foundation of a pyramid-shaped political structure, in which local representatives were elected to each successive level of regional and provincial government. To be sure the pro-Öcalan PYD exercises considerable influence over these structures. But in direct contrast to the top-down centralized model of rule in Iraqi Kurdistan – which benefited from de jure recognition in the Constitution of federal Iraq – de facto decentralization in northern Syria has emerged as an exemplar of bottom-up democratic governance.

The second distinctive characteristic of the Kurdish movement's approach to decentralization has been the degree to which it has blended self-determination demands with measures designed explicitly to address governance deficits. While Öcalan's organization, the PKK, originally fought for an independent Kurdish state, its goals have since shifted. The project is now understood to be unifying the Kurdish communities across Syria, Turkey, and eventually Iraq and Iran in a new form of direct democracy without a central state. The movement is committed to the principle that emancipation requires multiethnic social democracy in which every community is entitled to cultural rights and political inclusion within an overarching but thin political framework designed to facilitate shared governance without concentrating or centralizing power. This vision has come closest to realization

[66] See Bâli, "Turkish Kurdistan," Chapter 11.

in the predominantly Kurdish region of northern Syria where three cantons with de facto autonomy established a federation, known as the Democratic Federation of Northern Syria (more commonly known as Rojava). The federation's constitutive instrument – the Charter of the Social Contract – declares the objective of building "a society free from authoritarianism, militarism, centralism and the intervention of religious authority in public affairs." Thus, rather than viewing decentralized government as a step toward an independent Kurdish state – or as a consolation prize in the absence of one – democratic confederalism conceives of it as the cornerstone of a new political order.

In practice, Rojava has been governed in the midst of a raging civil war, the advent of the exterminationist military challenge posed by the Islamic State between 2014 and 2018, and constant incursions by the Turkish military to prevent the emergence of an independent Kurdistan on that country's southwestern border. Further, internally the movement faces the potential limitation of being tied to the views of its charismatic leader in ways that may produce ideological rigidity. Complaints that the party wields excessive central control and that the war has produced atrocities on all sides are important correctives to an overly naive view of the political experiment in Rojava. Still, in the context of an entire society mobilized for a war effort, the fact that the Kurdish movement has prioritized forms of democratic participation and has produced a sufficiently attractive political model to attract Arab and other non-Kurdish Syrians to join the Kurdish-led Syrian Democratic Forces against the Assad regime and take up residence in Rojava is a testament to a conception of self-determination that emphasizes governance and embraces pluralism even as it advances national cultural rights.

Confederalism has also attracted the attention of Israeli and Palestinian intellectuals and activists, who see in it a potential solution to the national conflict dividing their country.[67] The movement for an Israeli-Palestinian confederation is less intellectually coherent and less revolutionary than its Kurdish counterpart: it is advocated by an array of thinkers with varying ideological commitments and political goals, and it seeks not to jettison the idea of "two states for two peoples," but to embed it within a supranational governance framework. In addition, though it has won a measure of grassroots support among both Israelis and Palestinians, the ideas underpinning it have yet to be implemented anywhere in Israel-Palestine. Even so, it articulates an emancipatory vision of decentralized government that both privileges the principle of self-determination and undertakes to give it new meaning. It would offer Palestinians in the occupied territory liberation from the prevailing one-state reality in which they lack both a state of their own and a voice in the election of the government that controls their lives. At the same time, it is attentive to the desire

67 See O. M. Dajani and D. Scheindlin, "'Stuck Together': Can a Two-State Confederation End the Israeli-Palestinian Conflict?" Chapter 13 in this volume.

of Israeli Jews for self-determination, affording an alternative to the emergence of a single democratic state in Israel-Palestine in which Jews are a minority.

In two ways, moreover, Israeli-Palestinian confederal proposals move beyond conventional nationalist self-determination paradigms, reimagining the relationship between territory, nation, and state. By linking a two-state solution to a set of shared confederal institutions and a regime of freedom of movement, they challenge the logic of partition, accepting the reality that the lands of Israel and Palestine occupy the same space – and that both peoples have an attachment to all of the territory. Second, rather than achieving mutual self-determination by dividing the territory into ethnic enclaves through gerrymandering (or, worse, ethnic cleansing), they are built on the assumption that both states within the confederal union will be ethnically heterogeneous. In addition, one set of proposals advocates radical decentralization of governance *within* each state in the union as a means of reducing the stakes of national citizenship by making local government the site where most consequential decisions are taken. Thus, decentralized government in this context is conceived not as a framework for holding a state together in the face of secessionist challenges, but as a way of reordering government to enable two peoples who are "stuck together" to achieve meaningful self-determination without full territorial partition. To be sure, the realization of this vision faces significant challenges, particularly in the absence of the territorial base, broad popular support, and party infrastructure that the Kurdish movement for democratic confederalism has successfully leveraged. But it does offer a compelling alternative to the binary choice between one-state and two-state solutions.

Imperial Decentralization

Decentralized government may serve not only as a path toward self-determination but also as a means of channeling the demands of identity groups for autonomy or independence into frameworks that preserve, and even strengthen, "imperial formations."[68] The appropriation of decentralized governance for this purpose was a principal motivation behind the establishment of the Soviet federal system, which inspired Stepan's "putting together" type. Contrived as a vehicle for containing self-determination movements from regions where non-Russian ethnic groups

[68] This phrase, borrowed from Ann Laura Stoler, "Imperial Debris: Reflections on Ruins and Ruination," *Cultural Anthropology*, 23(2) (2008), 191–219, strikes us as especially apt as applied to these cases. Stoler suggests that "[i]n working with the concept of imperial formation rather than empire, the emphasis shifts from fixed forms of sovereignty and its denials to gradated forms of sovereignty and what has long marked the technologies of imperial rule – sliding and contested scales of differential rights," adding that "such formations are *states of deferral* that mete out promissory notes that are not exceptions to their operation but constitutive of them: imperial guardianship, trusteeships, delayed autonomy, temporary intervention, conditional tutelage, military takeover in the name of humanitarian works, violent intervention in the name of human rights and security measures in the name of peace." Ibid., 193 (emphasis in original).

were concentrated, it deployed a coercive apparatus to channel and constrain expressions of ethnic difference, controlling ethnic politics "by prohibiting all but sanctioned political entrepreneurs from pursuing any but the regime's instrumental strategies of plan fulfillment and social transformation."[69] In addition, the actual authority of units within the Soviet federal system was more illusory than real: even as an increasing number were granted formal autonomy, the process was attended by "marked and steady centralization of economic and political power in Moscow."[70]

Decentralization is instrumentalized in similar – but more extreme – ways in two of our cases. The people of Western Sahara and the Palestinian people are both recognized to possess the right to self-determination. In both contexts, however, long-running, internationally mediated peace processes have been steered into a cul-de-sac of limited self-government, preventing Sahrawis and Palestinians alike from achieving national self-determination and allowing Morocco and Israel to tighten their grip over occupied territory. What distinguishes these cases from Soviet federalism is the far more limited power devolved to authorities in the Palestinian territory and Western Sahara, as well as Israel's and Morocco's overt annexationist agendas. Under the cover of ostensibly decentralizing initiatives, the central governments in Rabat and Jerusalem have taken a range of steps to fortify their control over – and claims to – these regions while disempowering the groups seeking self-determination.[71]

To be sure, there are important differences between the governance regimes in Western Sahara under Morocco's Advanced Regionalization initiative and in the West Bank and Gaza Strip under the Israeli-Palestinian Oslo Accords. First, Advanced Regionalization is a package of decentralizing reforms initiated by Morocco's monarchy and applied symmetrically throughout Morocco, while the current asymmetric governance regime in the West Bank and Gaza Strip is an outgrowth of the bilateral agreements concluded between Israel and the Palestine Liberation Organization during the 1990s.[72] Second, unlike Israel, Morocco is undertaking to absorb the population of the territory it is occupying: it has not only annexed Western Sahara, but has also extended citizenship to its residents. Indeed,

69 P. G. Roeder, "Soviet Federalism and Ethnic Mobilization," *World Politics*, 43 (1991), 196–232, at 199.

70 See V. Aspaturian, "The Theory and Practice of Soviet Federalism," *Journal of Politics*, 12 (1950), 20–51.

71 These steps include: transferring civilians from within their own territory to alter the regions' demographic composition; commandeering land and resources for their own use; erecting legal and physical barriers that undermine their territorial integrity; and violently repressing resistance.

72 While the governance regime in the West Bank and Gaza Strip emerged from an international agreement between Israel and the Palestine Liberation Organization, the five-year transitional period for which the arrangements were explicitly conceived has long since elapsed. In the absence of a new agreement on "permanent status," Israel's military enforces the status quo, blocking even symbolic Palestinian moves toward independence.

the differences in these policies reflect a fundamental difference in the way each state conceives of national identity. On the one hand, Morocco conceptualizes the Moroccan nation in a manner that encompasses the county's considerable cultural, linguistic, and religious diversity but is hostile to the notion of national minorities.[73] It has enacted a range of centripetal policies to counteract Sahrawi separatism, redrawing internal administrative boundaries to split the population across regions and giving Sahrawis overrepresentation in regional and national political institutions. In contrast, Israel's Basic Law defines the country as "the nation State of the Jewish people," providing that only the Jewish people are entitled to exercise self-determination within its territory,[74] and the Arab minority within Israel is rarely included in the political coalitions that govern the country.

While these differences are significant, what these regimes have in common is their use of decentralized governance as a framework for subverting self-determination and normalizing the occupation and even annexation of territory. Advanced Regionalization has effectively sidelined not only the United Nations–supervised process for facilitating Western Sahara's self-determination, but also Morocco's own Autonomy Plan for the region.[75] And the Oslo Accords have proven to be a similarly effective diversion.[76] Negotiated in secret as a means of bypassing the UN-sanctioned multilateral peace process commenced in Madrid in 1991, they were patterned to a substantial extent on the Israel-Egypt Framework for Peace, which was agreed by Egypt and Israel more than a decade earlier and was devised "to be a vehicle for perpetuating Israel's control of the [West Bank and Gaza Strip]."[77]

De Facto Decentralization

Decentralized governance may arise not only as a state is coming together, but also as it is coming apart. During periods of partial or total state collapse,[78] substate governments sometimes assume increased authority without formal authorization through constitutional, legislative, or administrative processes. This phenomenon, which we call de facto decentralization, has received little scholarly attention, though some of the issues it raises are addressed in the policy literature on

[73] See Shehabi, "'*Dans ses Frontiers Authentiques*'?" Chapter 14.
[74] Basic Law: Israel – The Nation-State of the Jewish People (2018) [Israel].
[75] See Shehabi, "'*Dans ses Frontiers Authentiques*'?" Chapter 14.
[76] See S. Bashi, "Control, Responsibility, and the Israeli-Palestinian Decentralization Debacle," Chapter 12 in this volume.
[77] J. Singer, "Developing the Concept of Palestinian Autonomy," *The Cairo Review of Global Affairs* (Winter 2019), 146.
[78] For a definition of state collapse, see Chapter 15 in this volume. The concept of "partial state collapse" to which we refer here involves circumstances where a central government has ceased to be able to assert control in significant portions of the state's territory, but otherwise remains fully functional.

governance in fragile and conflict-affected states.[79] It warrants consideration as a type of its own not only because it is an empirical reality in several countries in the MENA region – presently in Libya, Yemen, and parts of Syria (and, in the relatively recent past, in Iraq and Lebanon too) – but also because experience suggests it can be durable. This appears to be particularly true in states where effective centralized rule has been ephemeral – as in Somalia and Yemen.[80] But it may also be the case where the convergence of deep internal divisions within a polity and external support for the parties to a conflict produces enduring stalemate.[81] Its durability suggests, moreover, that it may have features that make it an attractive alternative to the prospect of a recentralizing effort imposed by hostile and/or authoritarian political actors.

Our cases offer a basis for a few preliminary observations regarding features of de facto decentralization. First, what is striking is how much governance takes place even during periods and in regions where the central government has ceased to operate. As internal conflicts have stretched on in Libya and Syria, local governments have been crucial sources of security and a range of other public services, also offering forums for dispute resolution. Second, these governments are often perceived by their constituents as possessing greater legitimacy than central government institutions. Karim Mezran and Elissa Miller's study of Libya attributes this legitimacy to the thick social links between local government officials and their constituents,[82] but Jongerden's account of governance in Rojava suggests that relative quality and reliability of service provision are significant as well.[83] Third, while de facto decentralization presents obvious challenges in relation to harmonizing policy and ensuring equitable distribution of resources across localities, our cases point to factors that exacerbate or mitigate these dynamics. On the one hand, external assistance from foreign donor governments and nongovernmental organizations to local governments has hindered efforts to achieve policy coordination across Opposition-held areas in Syria.[84] On the other hand, the experience in Rojava suggests that where local governments are held together by a coherent ideological framework and a robust party structure, decentralized governance need not come at the expense of policy coherence.[85]

79 One example in this genre is United Nations Development Programme, *Local Governance in Fragile and Conflict-Affected Settings: Building a Resilient Foundation for Peace and Development* (New York: UNDP 2016).

80 See Alex de Waal, *The Real Politics of the Horn of Africa: Money, War, and the Business of Power* (Cambridge: Polity, 2017), 110; see also Chapter 18 in this volume.

81 These circumstances are sometimes characterized as "frozen conflicts." T. G. Grant, "Frozen Conflicts and International Law," *Cornell International Law Journal*, 50 (2017), 361–413.

82 Mezran and Miller, "The Promise – and Limits – of Stabilization through Local Governance in Libya," Chapter 16.

83 Jongerden, "Autonomy beyond the State," Chapter 9.

84 See Araabi and Hilal, "Decentralization in State Disintegration," Chapter 17.

85 Ibid.

Reconstitutive Decentralization

When the reconstitution of a state is being negotiated following a period of partial or total collapse, substate actors may demand decentralized government as a condition for reentering the union. This process of "coming back together" is distinct from the "holding together" and "coming together" scenarios long recognized in the literature. As discussed above, the power that a constitution accords the units in a decentralized government depends in part on the bargaining position of central and substate actors at the time a state is constituted. Accordingly, a central government emerging from a period of collapse may find it difficult to impose arrangements on substate actors in territory still outside its control. A modest grant of autonomy that might have sufficed to hold the state together may be deemed inadequate after the state has come apart – particularly if substate actors are seeking constitutional ratification of arrangements that are already de facto in place. In contrast to classical "coming together" situations, however, the bargaining power of such actors may be constrained by their inability to obtain recognition as an independent state due to the international political context.

Iraq, during its 2005 constitutional process, exemplifies this type. Following more than a decade of de facto self-government outside the reach of Baghdad's authority and the dismantling of the central state after the American invasion in 2003, Iraqi Kurds were well positioned to demand significant autonomy in negotiations over a new constitution. But despite polling that indicated a clear preference among Iraqi Kurds for independence over integration,[86] secession was ruled out by transnational political pressures – particularly anxiety among neighboring governments about Kurdish irredentism and the United States' commitment, as the occupying power, to preserving Iraq's territorial integrity. The result was a constitutional bargain that allowed Iraqi Kurds to retain a far greater measure of self-government in Iraq's new federal system than they had been able to secure during previous rounds of negotiations with Baghdad in the 1970s but that also denied them independence.

To be sure, a constitutional pact establishing a decentralized political order is not the only pathway from collapse. We see two other strikingly different post-collapse governance models in the region and its immediate vicinity. One is full recentralization, which may occur either through the consolidation of authority by the central government (or some competing actor) across the national territory – as has occurred through much of Syria since 2018 – or through the implementation of a national compact among warring factions that provides for power-sharing within the central government – as occurred in Lebanon under the Taif Agreement.[87] The

[86] Morrow, "Iraq's Constitutional Process," 13.

[87] See Anderson and Choudhry, "Devolution and Federalism in Collapsed States," Chapter 15. Lebanon's experience suggests, however, that even where state collapse does not lead to a constitutional framework built on decentralized governance, power-sharing within the central government itself is likely to be restructured in ways that reflect the balance of power on the ground at the time the deal is struck.

other model for post-collapse governance is sustained de facto decentralization, as exemplified by Somalia's experience. There, extended political and military stalemate has produced few mechanisms for coordination between units, though the legal fiction of a shared polity perseveres as a result of external pressure and a thin political compact.[88]

Which of these paths will be taken in other countries where conflict has created islands of de facto decentralized government will depend on several factors. The role of external actors clearly looms large. Powerful global and regional actors played a significant role in shaping the processes through which the Lebanese and Iraqi states were reconstituted and in enabling the Assad regime to reconsolidate authority over formerly Opposition-held areas in eastern Syria; and external involvement in the continuing conflicts in Libya, northwestern Syria, and southern Yemen has already prolonged conflict, sustaining de facto decentralization. Lebanon's experience also points to other potentially significant factors, such as whether a preexisting constitutional structure channeled substate communities toward power-sharing at the center and the size and contiguity of the decentralized units.

We anticipate, however, that substate actors accustomed to a substantial measure of de facto autonomy will be reluctant to "come back" into a preexisting union absent a commitment to robust decentralization that is constitutionally entrenched and guaranteed either by their own military capacity or by external actors.[89] Arrangements involving a more modest devolution of authority, which may have sufficed to hold a state together at a stage when the central government retained control over the national territory, seem less likely to pass muster following an extended period of de facto self-government – particularly where there is a past history of broken central government commitments to decentralization.

TRAJECTORIES

Although decentralized government is neither foreign nor unfamiliar to the MENA region, the contemporary experience examined in this volume relates mostly to initiatives of relatively recent vintage. In this final section, as we undertake to distill lessons from these cases and to prognosticate about what the future holds, we are mindful of the hazards of generalizing from such a short track record. We also recognize that, despite the sweeping global embrace of decentralization, and the voluminous literature the subject has attracted, data regarding its merits remain strikingly inconclusive.[90] Our aim, accordingly, is to engage in empirically grounded

88 Ibid.

89 This is borne out by experience in frozen conflicts on the former Soviet Union's periphery. See D. Dascalu, "Frozen Conflicts and Federalization: Russian Policy in Transnistria and Donbass," *Columbia/SIPA Journal of International Affairs* (May 22, 2019).

90 For a survey and critical analysis of this data, see generally D. Treisman, *The Architecture of Government: Rethinking Political Decentralization* (Cambridge: Cambridge University Press, 2008).

theory-building that avoids the "facile institutional recommendations" that have shaped so much policy in this field.[91] With that said, we close with two observations about the trajectories of MENA countries' diverse experiences with decentralization and a concluding comment on how best to frame the relevance of decentralizing initiatives to the challenges confronting the region at present.

Decentralization as a Perennial Bargaining Process

The region's experience reveals that decentralization is best understood not as a bargain concluded between national and substate actors during a constitutional moment, but as a continuous bargaining process that is influenced by changing power relations among diverse actors with evolving goals. This observation builds upon Falletti's characterization of decentralization as a "*process* of public policy reforms and not as a description of the state of being of the political or fiscal systems at a point in time."[92] But the experience in the MENA region brings three important dimensions of this process to the foreground. The first is that not all of the actors participating in this bargaining process conform to a national centralizer vs. substate decentralizer binary. In a number of our cases – Iran, Iraq, Libya, Morocco, Syria, Tunisia, and Yemen – decentralization is driven not only by local actors who are seeking more authority, but also by political reformers in the capital who see decentralization as a means of restraining authoritarian rule or, conversely, by central government elites who see it as a mechanism for extending the reach and legitimacy of the central state. This complex reality may significantly influence the design and implementation of decentralization. For example, where it is advocated from the center as an anti-authoritarian measure (as in Tunisia and Iraq), insufficient attention may be given to nurturing engagement (and/or building capacity) at the local level, causing the implementation of even far-reaching reforms to falter.

A second dimension of the bargaining process highlighted by our cases is its perennial quality. It does not end when a constitution is adopted, a statute is passed, or a peace agreement is signed. To be sure, the terms set out in such instruments may define the path subsequently taken and generate policy feedback. Our cases show, however, that even after a commitment to decentralization is formalized, the necessity of elaborating upon and ultimately implementing it renders it subject to indefinite bargaining on a trajectory typically marked by both advances and reversals. In many of our cases, the bargaining extends across decades, and even approaches that are initially abandoned – Syria's 1950 Constitution, Iraq's 1966 Declaration, the 1978

[91] J. Erk, "Federalism and Decentralization in Sub-Saharan Africa: Five Patterns of Evolution," *Regional and Federal Studies*, 24(5) (2014), 535–52, at 539.

[92] T. Falleti, "A Sequential Theory of Decentralization: Latin American Cases in Comparative Perspective," *American Political Science Review*, 99(3) (2005), 327–46, at 328 (emphasis added).

Framework for Peace agreed by Israel and Egypt at Camp David – continue (for better or worse) to serve as reference points in subsequent rounds of negotiations. The perennial character of the bargaining process also means that the actors engaged in it – and the interests and concerns they bring to the table – may shift over time. Thus, the implementation of a decentralization program may come to be captured by a central government bureaucracy reluctant to cede power (as in Tunisia and Iraq) or by military officials more intolerant of risk than the politicians who inked an initial peace agreement (as in Israel-Palestine). These shifts not only may alter the implementation of an agreed program, they also may undermine the credibility of commitments made in subsequent rounds, making compromise more difficult to achieve.

A third salient dimension of the bargaining process is the dynamic character of parties' interests and power relations. There is nothing arm's length about a deal structuring the distribution of authority in a country: every round of bargaining influences, and is influenced by, the relative power of the actors involved. Recognition of this reality shapes our expectations about how conflict is likely to affect the trajectory of bargaining in our cases. Control over territory, in particular, appears to play an outsized role in determining which terms parties negotiating post-conflict arrangements will be prepared to countenance. Thus, we anticipate that it will be far more difficult to persuade Kurds in Syria to accept watered-down administrative decentralization (in lieu of more substantial autonomy) or to persuade southern Yemenis to accept a federal system (in lieu of confederation or independence) than it was when the central governments in those states maintained full control over their territory. Failure to appreciate the implications of such shifts in power dynamics may produce long-term stalemate.

Entrenching Decentralization

Our case studies demonstrate that the scale and durability of decentralizing reforms depend less on their constitutional entrenchment than on the institutions leading each stage of the design and implementation processes and the inclusivity and pacing of those processes. Across our cases, decisions about decentralization have been made and implemented through diverse processes and instruments. In a number, they have been given constitutional footing, albeit with substantial variation in the scope of the commitment to decentralization, the prominence it is given, and the issues left to be resolved by the legislature and central bureaucracy. Their paths into constitutions have also varied substantially – in some cases emerging from broadly inclusive processes like Yemen's national dialogue; in others, as a product of executive initiative, like the 2011 Moroccan Constitution. Elsewhere, decentralization has been initiated through legislation, regulation, or decree. And in a few cases, it has emerged from, or is expected to be a central feature of, peace agreements.

There is a tendency in the comparative law literature to view constitutional entrenchment of political commitments as optimal, because it produces reflexive noncontroversial compliance and constrains elites' ability to reverse changes they have instituted,[93] thereby enhancing the credibility of their commitments.[94] One important lesson offered by our cases is that such entrenchment does not necessarily translate into effective long-term implementation. First of all, the constitutional status of decentralization may reveal little about the central state's actual commitment to meaningful devolution of power. In Morocco, for example, it remains largely a paper commitment. Moreover, even where constitutionalization reflects a genuine desire to distribute authority away from the central government, as in Iraq and Tunisia, the devil is in the details. Constitutions that provide broad commitments but little concrete direction as to implementation may give way to protracted processes that are easily neglected or reversed.

The variation in the instruments by which decentralization may be implemented presents an opportunity to consider the relationship between process and outcome. Several important variables emerge from our cases. The first is *which institutions are leading* the process at each stage. Across all of our authoritarian decentralization cases, a recurring dynamic is the instrumentalization of ostensibly decentralizing reforms by the executive to consolidate authority rather than distribute it. The case of Tunisia suggests, moreover, that even where decentralization is initiated by a reformist and broadly representative constituent assembly, over time a recalcitrant central government bureaucracy can greatly influence the pace and scale of implementation.[95]

A second important variable is the *degree of inclusiveness* of the process through which decentralizing reforms are designed. The strength of Tunisia's constitutional commitment to decentralization arises in part from the fact that the uprising that initiated political transition was led by organized parties – including long-standing opposition movements supported by trade unions with large grassroots support – that took the reins of the transitional process. By contrast, in Yemen the ouster of the authoritarian regime was externally brokered in a "managed transition" that brought to power, on an interim basis, officials associated with the prior regime. That the former dictator Ali Abdallah Saleh's deputy became interim president exemplifies this problem. While the National Dialogue Conference was an elected body that was both inclusive and participatory, it remained vulnerable

93 See generally D. C. North and B. R. Weingast, "Constitutions and Commitment: The Evolution of Institutions Governing Public Choice in Seventeenth-Century England," *Journal of Economic History*, 49(4) (1989), 803–32.

94 See generally D. J. Levinson, "Parchment and Politics: The Positive Puzzle of Constitutional Commitment," *Harvard Law Review*, 124(3) (2011), 659–746; T. Ginsburg, "Locking in Democracy: Constitutions, Commitment and International Law," *NYU Journal of International Law and Politics*, 38 (2006), 707–59.

95 See Kherigi, "Decentralization Reforms in Post-revolution Tunisia," Chapter 8.

to predation by a central government in the hands of remnants from the authoritarian system.

One dimension of inclusiveness likely to be especially consequential is the extent to which reforms are driven from the center or from the periphery. In Morocco, though decentralizing reforms were conceived in part to address underdevelopment and self-determination demands at the periphery, the reform process has been run entirely from the center, and limited popular participation and transparency have left the decentralization enterprise without a clear constituency. In Iran, decentralization has been advocated by a complex mix of actors, but central government institutions initiated the process and have carefully controlled its implementation. Perhaps unsurprisingly, a vision focused on service delivery has prevailed over one focused on democratization. The elaboration and implementation of decentralization in Tunisia has also been hampered by the fact that it has been driven largely by actors at the national level. In contrast, one of the features that has contributed to the vibrancy of Kurdish democratic confederalism is its marriage of a coherent ideological vision with bottom-up mechanisms for implementation that encourage iterative and locally tailored governance initiatives.

A third important variable is the *pacing* of decentralizing reforms. Decentralization, as we have emphasized, is appropriately understood not as a singular decision taken at one moment in time, but instead as a long-term process that involves numerous decision points and whose trajectory may shift as political winds change. Again, the Tunisian case here is instructive: the gradualism and incrementalism of the Tunisian approach runs the clear risk of producing opportunities for subversion. But the attention paid to the duration, sequencing, and pacing of decentralizing reforms in the Tunisian context may yet prove to be the enduring strength of that country's experiment with devolving authority to its regions. The appeal of Tunisia's slow-burning decentralization process is the possibility that reforms may build support as they are implemented over time without engendering the resistance that may be occasioned when sudden transfers of power result in a loss of authority for key actors at the center. In addition, as a practical matter decentralization will require capacity-building at regional, provincial, municipal, and local levels for the relevant actors to be equipped to exercise new authorities competently.[96]

Indeed, while the question of capacity-building is paid a great deal of lip service in both the academic and policy literatures, its far-reaching significance is easy to overlook precisely because the requirements of developing local capacity are so varied and context specific, and ultimately unfold in the mundane domains of everyday

96 On the need for capacity-building, see A. Houdret and A. Harnisch, "Decentralisation in Morocco: The Current Reform and Its Possible Contribution to Political Liberalisation," Discussion Paper, German Development Institute (2017), 7.

bureaucratic practices. That being said, a failure to attend to capacity-building is certain to doom decentralizing reform. Local government incapable of delivering services due to lack of resources and human capital is a sure-fire recipe for enabling national governments to present themselves as the sole competent authority in the country and reconsolidate power at the center. Indeed, this is one of the ways that central states instrumentalize decentralization to shore up their own legitimacy, as evidenced in the cases of Jordan and Iraq.

Against this backdrop, the appeal of a slow-burning decentralization process must be understood in tandem with its profound risks. The Yemeni case exemplifies an inclusive and slow-moving negotiation process for the design of decentralizing reforms. Through careful, calibrated, and participatory processes the NDC produced the first example of a plausible roadmap for a post-authoritarian Yemen in that country's history.[97] The fact that the process was ultimately derailed is due to a number of factors, not least bad faith by a central government propped up by external sponsors rather than local constituencies. But the dénouement in Yemen is also partly attributable to the fact that too little was implemented for parties to maintain faith that the process would yield meaningful devolution of powers.

CONCLUSION

In the MENA region, decentralization has not been the cure-all some hoped it would be, but it may yet prove to be a necessary element of efforts to accommodate demands for self-determination and to reconstitute states in the wake of internal conflict.

Our cases suggest that, as a vehicle for democratization, decentralization presents as many risks as opportunities. Perhaps the most profound risk is authoritarian capture of the reform agenda. Regimes in Iran, Jordan, Morocco, and Syria have effectively used decentralizing reforms to contain democratization by implementing measures that preserve and even extend the reach of central governments, while simultaneously creating weak forms of political decentralization that spread responsibility for governance failures to local governments without meaningfully sharing authority with them. Even where decentralization has been championed specifically as a means of preventing reversion to authoritarian rule – in Iraq, Tunisia, and Yemen – progress has been fitful, and serious backsliding has occurred. Reformers also face the challenge of devising strategies for maintaining political momentum even as decentralization necessarily becomes a more technical – and bureaucratic – enterprise. This track record does not foreclose the possibility that the varying degrees of local empowerment and citizen engagement these

97 See Challand, "Decentralization in Yemen," Chapter 18.

openings have allowed will help blaze a trail toward enhanced accountability and democratic decision-making in the future. At present, however, that path remains largely theoretical.

Although decentralization also presents risks as a framework for self-determination, it is difficult to conceive of a plausible alternative to it in the MENA states where identity groups demand a measure of self-government. To be sure, the experience of Palestinians and Sahrawis demonstrates that forms of decentralized governance can be appropriated by powerful states to advance imperial designs. Those cases support the argument that weak forms of decentralization have the potential to be disempowering of minority groups, even where they are sold as incremental steps toward more robust self-government. However, the reality of Kurdish self-government in Iraq and Syria confirms that meaningful self-determination through decentralized government is possible in the MENA region and, where secured through a constitutional commitment to far-reaching devolution and/or independent self-defense capacity, can afford minorities protection as well as agency. Of course, the models presented by the Kurdistan Regional Government in Iraq and by Rojava are premised on markedly different visions of both governance and self-determination. Only time will tell which will prove more durable and whether either offers a viable model for Palestinians, Sahrawis, southern Yemenis, Cyrenaicans, and other identity groups seeking self-determination.

Moreover, where demands for self-determination intersect with an experience of de facto decentralization due to partial or total state collapse, as is the case in all of these contexts, an agreement providing for robust political decentralization (along with power-sharing within the central government) is likely to be a crucial element of state reconstitution. In this context, decentralization may not be sufficient to enable some measure of conflict resolution, but it will very likely be necessary.

***

Our study draws on cases from a region seldom regarded as a propitious site for decentralization. In examining the potential of decentralizing initiatives to address persistent challenges of governance failure, identity conflict, and self-determination in the MENA region, we have not sought to offer a unifying theory of the conditions that result in "successful" decentralization. Instead, the volume serves to cast much needed light on the many experiments with decentralization currently underway in the MENA region, contributing new research on understudied cases to the empirical literature. That survey, in turn, enables us to offer a theoretical discussion in this chapter that expands the toolkit for thinking about the diverse circumstances and purposes for which actors may embrace or promote decentralization. While decentralizing initiatives are no panacea, their relevance to the MENA region should not be underestimated. Indeed, the lessons we draw from our cases provide insights not only concerning obstacles to decentralization but also about the circumstances in which the complex historical, institutional, and geopolitical sources of resistance to decentralization in the MENA region might counterintuitively provide the terrain for innovative framings that realize a stabilizing, or even emancipatory, role for decentralizing initiatives. Moreover, some of these insights may be generalizable to other parts of the postcolonial world. We hope that the strategies to implement or deflect decentralizing reforms that our cases reveal, and our discussion of the attendant lessons, will yield a research agenda for further comparative analysis.

Index

www.ingramcontent.com/pod-product-compliance
Lightning Source LLC
LaVergne TN
LVHW011659200926
848484LV00004B/996
* 9 7 8 1 1 0 8 8 3 1 2 3 9 *